Andalucía

THE ROUGH GUIDE

W9-AVC-076

Rough Guide to Andalucía Credits

Text editors:	Jo Mead and Samantha Cook
Editorial:	Martin Dunford, John Fisher, Jonathan Buckley, Greg Ward, Jules Brown, Graham Parker and Alison Cowan
Series editor:	Mark Ellingham
Production:	Susanne Hillen, Andy Hilliard, Gail Jammy, Vivien Antwi, Alan Spicer
Cartography:	Melissa Flack
Publicity:	Richard Trillo
US Publicity:	Jean-Marie Kelly
Finance:	Celia Crowley, Simon Carloss
Administration:	Tania Hummel

Acknowledgments

Thanks from Geoff to Josep Vergés and Angela García for help, hospitality and advice in Almería, and to Claire Hunt in Málaga and Pau Sandham in Sevilla. Valuable assistance on the ground in Andalucía was also given by Vicente Serra, Enrique Díaz, Pedro Lorenzo Gomez, María Jesús Meca, Juan Mejias, José María Fernandez, Josefina and Andreas del Castillo, Manuel Sanchez, Cristina Alvárez, José María García Rincon and Juan Carlos Jimenez Barrientos. Thanks also to Tony Wailey for Civil War background and to Huw Morgan for information on birdspotting. Lastly thanks to my long-suffering *compañera* Jane Devane for unflagging help and inspiration; Mark would like to add special thanks to Natania Jansz, Esteban Pujals, Pilar Vazquez, and Chris, Annie and Chlöe. Both authors would also like to say a big thankyou to their editors, Jo Mead and Samantha Cook, for eagle-eyed attention to the text – and some memorable marginalia.

This first edition published 1994 by Rough Guides Ltd, 1 Mercer Street, London WC2H 9QJ.
Distributed by The Penguin Group:

Penguin Books Ltd, 27 Wrights Lane, London W8 5TZ
Penguin Books USA Inc., 375 Hudson Street, New York 10014, USA
Penguin Books Australia Ltd, 487 Maroondah Highway, PO Box 257, Ringwood, Victoria 3134, Australia
Penguin Books Canada Ltd, 10 Alcorn Avenue, Toronto, Ontario, Canada M4V 1E4
Penguin Books (NZ) Ltd, 182–190 Wairau Road, Auckland 10, New Zealand

Rough Guides were formerly published as Real Guides in the United States and Canada.

Illustrations in Part One and Part Three by Ed Briant

Basics and contexts illustrations by Henry Iles

© Maps and street plans from *Nueva Guía de España* by ANAYA/*touring*, Spain. Juan Ignacio Luca de Tena, 15, 28027 - Madrid, except for pp.vi–vii, 51, 54–55, 93, 97, 104–105, 145, 150, 162–163, 177, 246–247, 265, 310–311 & 356 © Rough Guides.

Typeset in Linotron Univers and Century Old Style to an original design by Andrew Oliver.

Printed in the United Kingdom by Cox & Wyman Ltd (Reading).

© Geoff Garvey and Mark Ellingham 1994
448pp.
Includes index.
A catalogue record for this book is available from the British Library.
ISBN 1-85828-094-X

Andalucía

THE ROUGH GUIDE

written and researched by
Geoff Garvey and Mark Ellingham

with additional accounts by
Jan Fairley, Teresa Farino,
Pau Sandham, and Chris Stewart

THE ROUGH GUIDES

HELP US UPDATE

We've gone to a lot of effort to ensure that this first edition of *The Rough Guide to Andalucía* is accurate and up-to-date. However, things do change – places get "discovered," opening hours are notoriously fickle, restaurants and rooms raise prices or lower standards, extra buses are laid on or off. If you feel we've got it wrong or left something out, we'd like to know, and if you can remember the address, the price, the time, the phone number, so much the better.

We'll credit all contributions, and send a copy of the next edition (or any other Rough Guide if you prefer) for the best letters. Please mark all letters "Rough Guide Andalucía Update" and send to:

Rough Guides, 1 Mercer Street, London WC2H 9QJ
or, Rough Guides, 375 Hudson Street, 4th Floor, New York NY10014

ADDITIONAL THANKS

Thanks also to readers of the *Rough Guide to Spain* who wrote in offering information and updates on Andalucía. In particular: Pat and Sylvia Bacon, Tim Bradley, TW Buck, Christine and Ian Campbell, Suzannah Carver, AJ Cragg, Jenny Doe, Marja Dullaart, Jan Duvekot, Tom and Thelma Eley, Rebecca Ferguson, Teresa Flower, Neil Froom, Amanda Goldin, A Gough-Yates, Barbara and Mike Harding, Angus Haywood, John Hemingway, Colin Hogarth, Charlotte Hunter, Andrew Knowlman, Uwe Lorentzen, Sally-Ann Lynch, Gordon Macdonald, Duncan Maxwell, John Moore, Phebe Paine, RH Pell, Allen Potter, Wendy Pullem, Liz Raymont, David Rumsey, Gavin Schmidt, Frank Sierowski, Marguerite and Martyn Skinner, GJ and KL Slay, Ciarán Slevin, Sebastian Smedley-Aston, TJ Snow, Pernille Holm Sorenson, Barry C. Smith, Richard Thompson, Gabriella Vergés, Magda Walker, Martin Webber, Juli Wileman, Sarah Williams, Richard Winscoo, Christopher Wood, and Nicola Young.

CONTENTS

Introduction viii

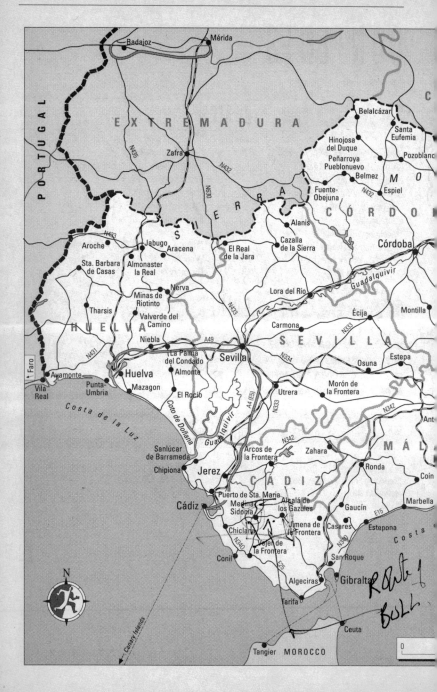

INTRODUCTION

Andalucía is the southernmost territory of Spain and the part of the Iberian peninsula that is most quintessentially Spanish. The popular image of Spain as a land of bullfights, *flamenco*, sherry and ruined castles derives from this spectacularly beautiful region. The influences that have washed over Andalucía since the first paintings were etched on cave walls here more than twenty-five thousand years ago are many – Phoenicians, Carthaginians, Greeks, Romans, Visigoths and Vandals all came and left their mark. And the most influential invaders of all, **the Moors**, who ruled the region for seven centuries and named it *al-Andalus*, have left an enduring imprint on Andalucian culture and customs.

The sight and sound of **flamenco**, when the guitar laments and heels stamp the boards, or *cante jondo*, Andalucía's blues, as it mournfully pierces the smoke-laden gloom of a backstreet *café*, also tell you there's something unique about the people here. The Muslim influence on speech and vocabulary, a stoical fatalism in the face of adversity, and an obsession with the drama of death, are all facets of the modern Andalucian character. The *andaluz* love a party, and the colour and sheer energy of the region's countless and legendary **fiestas** – always in traditional costume worn with pride – make them among the most exciting in the world. The **romerías**, wild and semi-religious pilgrimages to honour local saints at country shrines, are yet another excuse for a jamboree. And in quieter moments there are few greater pleasures than to join the drinkers at a local bar winding down over a glass of traditional *fino* (dry sherry from Jerez), while nibbling *tapas* – Andalucía's great titbit invention.

Few places in the world can boast such a wealth of **natural wonders** in so compact an area. The mighty Guadalquivir river which crosses and irrigates the region from its source in the Cazorla mountains of Jaén in the northeast, reaches the sea 250 miles away at the dune-fringed beaches and *marismas* of the **Coto Doñana National Park**, Europe's largest and most important wildlife sanctuary. To the east and towering above Granada, the peaks of the **Sierra Nevada** include Spain's highest mountain, snow-capped for most of the year, while twenty miles away and close to the sweltering beaches, sugar cane thrives. This crop was another contribution to Europe by the Moors, along with oranges, almonds, aubergines, saffron and most of the spices now used to flavour the region's cooking – which features an astonishing variety of **seafood**. Nestling in the folds of the same mountains are the valleys of the Alpujarras, a wildly picturesque region dotted with dozens of mountain villages, many of them little changed since Moorish times. Further east again come the gulch-ridden badlands and lunar landscapes of Almería's deserts, sought out by film-makers and astronomers for the clearest skies in Europe.

On **the coast** it's easy to despair. Extending to the west of **Málaga** is the **Costa del Sol**, Europe's most developed resort area, with its beaches hidden behind a remorseless density of concrete hotels and apartment complexes. But even here the real Andalucía is still to be found if you're prepared to seek it out; go merely a few kilometres inland and you'll encounter the timeless Spain of white villages and wholehearted country fiestas. Travel further, both east and west, along the coast and you'll find some of the best beaches in all Spain, along the **Costa de la Luz**, near Cádiz, or the **Costa de Almería**.

Andalucía's sunshine image – projected across the world in advertising campaigns and the much-hyped Expo '92 held in Sevilla – belies the fact that this is also Spain's poorest region where an economy rooted in near-feudal landownership stifles investment and is the cause of desperate poverty. Rural life is bleak; you soon begin to notice the appalling **economic structure** of vast absentee-landlord estates, and landless peasants. The *andaluz* villages saw little economic aid or change during the Franco years, or indeed since, even though the ruling Socialist party has its principal power base here. Tourism has brought some respite in coastal areas to the alarmingly high levels of unemployment, and Spain's growing importance as a member of the European Community promises to speed up progress, but there is still a mighty long way to go.

Where to go: some highlights

Andalucía's manageable size makes it easy to take in something of each of its elements – inland cities, extensive coastline and mountainous *sierras* – even on a brief visit. The main characteristics and appeal of each province are covered in the chapter introductions, but the more obvious and compelling highlights include:

Sevilla. Andalucía's capital city, the home of *flamenco* and all the clichés of the Spanish south has beautiful quarters, major Christian and Moorish monuments and extraordinary festivals at Easter and, afterwards, at the April *feria*.

Moorish monuments. Granada's Alhambra palace is perhaps the most sensual building in Europe; the exquisite Mezquita, a former mosque, in Córdoba, and the Alcázar and Giralda tower in Sevilla, are also not to be missed.

Castles. Niebla in Huelva and Baños de Encina in Jaén, as well as those in the cities of Málaga and Almería are the outstanding Moorish examples; the best Renaissance forts are at La Calahorra in Granada and Vélez Blanco in Almería, whilst hilltop Segura de la Sierra in Jaén has the most dramatic location.

Cathedrals. Sevilla's Gothic monster is the biggest, but those of Cádiz, Granada, Jaén, and Almería are all worthy of a visit.

Renaissance towns and hill villages. Small-scale towns and villages, once grand, now hardly significant are an Andalucian forte. Baeza and Úbeda in Jaén are remarkable treasurehouses of Renaissance architecture, while Ronda and the White Towns to the west are among the most picturesque hill villages in Andalucía.

Baroque. The Baroque splendours of Andalucía are without equal; towns such as Écija and Osuna in Sevilla province, and Priego to the south of Córdoba have clusters of stunning Baroque churches and mansions.

Roman and prehistoric ruins. Italica near Sevilla, Baelo Claudia near Tarifa and Carmona's Roman necropolis are all impressive Roman sites, while for an atmospheric "lost city" Mulva, in the hills of the Sierra Morena, is hard to beat. Andalucía also has some of the most important prehistoric sites in Europe, including a group of third millennium BC dolmens at Antequera, and the remarkable Los Millares site near Almería.

Beaches and resorts. For brashness and nightlife it has to be the Costa del Sol, but you'll find the more authentic resorts such as Nerja, Almuñecar and Mojácar are less frenzied. The region's best beaches lie along the Atlantic coast and to the east of Almería.

Hiking. The Sierra Nevada and the nearby foothills of Las Alpujarras in Granada are excellent places for hiking, as are the densely wooded hills of the Sierra de Cazorla and the Sierra de Morena – including the latter's less well-known offshoot, the Sierra de Aracena, in the north of Huelva.

Seafood. This is Andalucía's speciality and is excellent all along the coast but particularly so in Málaga and seafood-crazy Cádiz. The many good places to try it are listed in the relevant chapters throughout the *Guide*.

Bars. Spain has the most bars of any country in Europe, and Andalucía has more than its share of these. For sheer character and diversity, the bars of the cities of Córdoba, Sevilla and Cádiz are some of the best anywhere.

Offbeat. Among the more curious things to see in Andalucía are a self-styled "pope" who has built a "New Vatican" near Utrera in Sevilla province; a rosary museum at Aroche in Huelva displaying beads once owned by the famous; a nineteenth-century English-designed housing estate in the middle of the city of Huelva; a mini-Hollywood in Almería which preserves the film-set of famous "paella westerns"; the spectacular mines of Río Tinto in Huelva, and Andalucia's oldest inn, complete with highwayman's cell at Alfarnate, in the rugged Axarquia district of Málaga.

When to go
In terms of **climate** the question is mainly one of how much heat you can take. During the **summer** months of July and August temperatures of over 40°C (104°F) on the coast are normal and inland they rise even higher in cities such as Sevilla, generally reckoned to be the hottest in Spain. The solution here is to follow the natives and get about in the relative cool of the mornings and late afternoons finding somewhere shady to rest up as the city roasts in the midday furnace. The major resorts are busy in July and packed in August (the Spanish holiday month) when prices also are at their highest.

Better times to visit are the **spring** months of April, May and early June when lower temperatures combine with a greener landscape awash with wild flowers. The **autumn** is good, too, although by this time much of the landscape looks parched and the resorts have begun to wind down. The **winter** months – particularly December and January – can often be dismal and wet, although Almería sees only one day of rain a year on average and in winter has many days of perfect crystal visibility.

AVERAGE TEMPERATURES (°C)		Feb	April	June	Aug	Oct	Dec
Almería	av. max temp	16	20	26	29	23	17
	av. min temp	8	12	18	22	16	9
Cádiz	av. max temp	16	21	27	30	23	16
	av. min temp	9	12	18	20	16	9
Córdoba	av. max temp	16	23	32	36	24	14
	av. min temp	5	10	17	20	13	5
Granada	av. max temp	14	20	30	34	22	12
	av. min temp	2	7	14	17	9	2
Huelva	av. max temp	18	22	29	32	25	17
	av. min temp	7	11	16	18	14	7
Jaén	av. max temp	14	20	30	34	22	12
	av. min temp	5	10	17	21	13	5
Málaga	av. max temp	17	21	28	30	24	17
	av. min temp	8	11	17	20	15	9
Sevilla	av. max temp	17	23	32	36	26	16
	av. min temp	6	11	17	20	14	7
Tarifa	av. max temp	17	20	24	27	23	17
	av. min temp	11	13	17	20	17	1

To convert °C to °F, multiply by 9/5 and add 32

PART ONE

THE BASICS

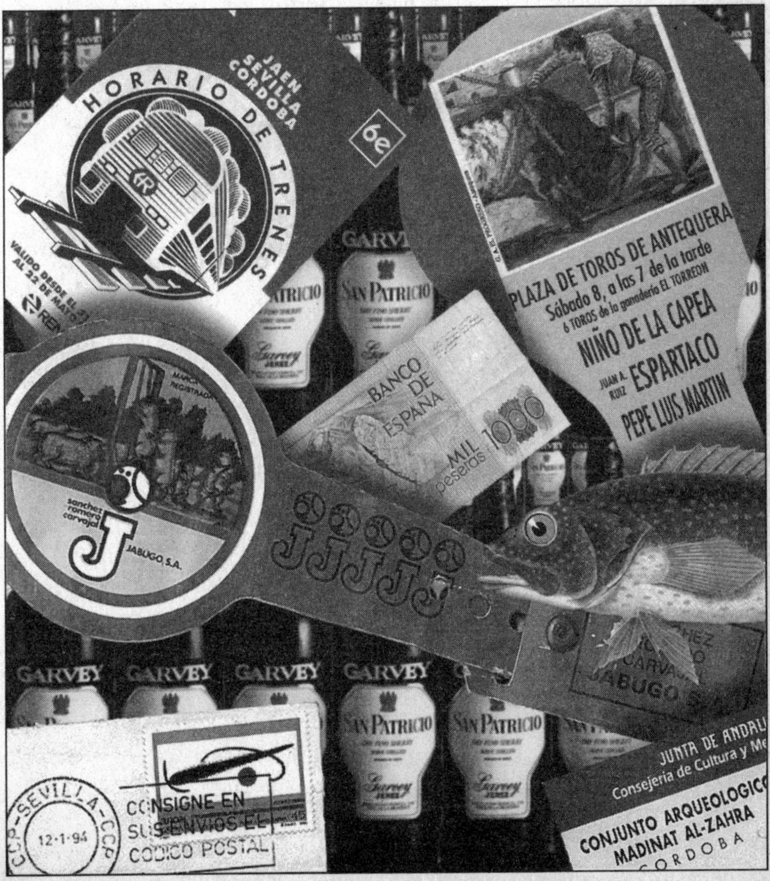

GETTING THERE FROM NORTH AMERICA

There is a fair variety of scheduled and charter flights from most parts of the US to Madrid, with connections on to Sevilla and Málaga – Andalucía's main airports. Occasionally, however – and especially if you're travelling from Canada – you'll still find it cheaper to route via London, picking up an inexpensive onward flight from there (see "Getting There from Britain", p.7 for all the details). If Spain is part of a longer European trip, you'll also want to check out details of the Eurail pass, which must be purchased in advance of your arrival and can get you by train from anywhere in Europe to Spain.

FROM THE US

Leaving aside discounted tickets, the cheapest way to travel is with an **Apex** (Advance Purchase Excursion) ticket, although these carry certain restrictions: you have to book your seat – and pay for it – at least 21 days before departure, spend at least seven days abroad (maximum stay three months), and you tend to get penalized if you change your schedule. There are winter **Super Apex** tickets, sometimes known as "Eurosavers" – slightly cheaper than an ordinary Apex, but limiting your stay to between 7 and 21 days. Some airlines also issue **Special Apex** tickets to those under 24, often extending the maximum stay to a year.

However, discount outlets can usually do better than any Apex fare. They come in several forms. **Consolidators** buy up large blocks of tickets that airlines don't think they'll be able to sell at their published fares, and sell them at a discount. Besides being cheap, consolidators normally don't impose advance purchase requirements (although in busy times you'll want to book ahead just to be sure of getting a ticket), but they do often charge very stiff fees for date changes. Also, these companies' margins are pretty tiny, so they make their money by dealing in volume – don't expect them to entertain lots of questions. **Discount agents** – such as *STA*, *Council Travel*, *Nouvelles Frontières*, or others listed on p.6 – also wheel and deal in blocks of tickets offloaded by the airlines, but they typically offer a range of other travel-related services such as travel insurance, rail passes, youth and student ID cards, car rentals, tours and the like. These agencies tend to be most worthwhile to students and under-26s, who can often benefit from special fares and deals. You should bear in mind, however, that discount agents tend to concentrate on high-volume routes to major cities; they'll give you a good deal on Madrid, but they won't be able to help you with any of the lesser destinations in Andalucía. **Travel clubs** are another option for those who travel a lot – most charge an annual membership fee, which may be worth it for discounts on air tickets, car rental and the like. You should also check the travel section in the Sunday *New York Times*, or your own major local newspaper, for current bargains, and consult a good travel agent.

Regardless of where you buy your ticket, the fare you pay will depend on season. Fares to Spain (like the rest of Europe) are highest from around early June to the end of August, when everyone wants to travel; they drop during the "shoulder" seasons, September–October and April–May, and you'll get the best deals during the low season, November through March (excluding Christmas). Note that flying on weekends ordinarily adds $50 to the round-trip fare; price ranges quoted here assume midweek travel.

DIRECT FLIGHTS

Obviously Madrid is the main air destination in Spain, and the best fares are usually found on flights into the capital – but don't assume this

AIRLINES IN NORTH AMERICA

Air France ☎800/237-2747
Flies from many cities to Paris and then on to Madrid, Málaga and Sevilla.

American Airlines ☎800/433-7300
Dallas and Miami to Madrid.

British Airways ☎800/247-9297
(in Canada ☎800/668-1059)
Flies from many cities to London, with connections to Madrid and Málaga.

Continental Airlines ☎800/231-0856
Newark to Madrid.

Iberia ☎800/772-4642
Flies direct from New York, Miami, LA, Toronto and Montréal to Madrid, Málaga and Sevilla; many other internal connections possible.

KLM ☎800/374-7747
Numerous flights, via Amsterdam, to Madrid and Málaga.

Lufthansa ☎800/645-3880
Flights from many cities to Madrid and Málaga via Frankfurt.

Sabena ☎800/955-2000
Flights from East Coast cities to Brussels and on to Madrid and Málaga.

TAP Air Portugal ☎800/221-7370
New York, Boston, Toronto and Montréal to Madrid via Lisbon.

TWA ☎800/892-4141
New York to Madrid.

United Airlines ☎800/538-2929
Washington DC to Madrid.

always to be the case. In the summer many airlines will throw in a connecting flight to **Sevilla** or **Málaga** (Andalucía's main airports) on *Iberia* for free; during the winter, these add-ons will cost an extra $150 round-trip, which still isn't bad. A third possibility in Andalucía is **Almería**, a more obscure destination that will add $50–200 to the fare to Madrid, depending on the season.

Iberia has the widest selection of transatlantic routes into **Madrid**, with direct flights departing from New York, Miami and Los Angeles. For an APEX ticket (book 14–21 days in advance, stay for a minimum of seven days, maximum three months), expect to pay around $1000 round-trip from New York JFK, travelling midweek in the high season. From Miami the fare is $1050, and from Los Angeles $1250; figure around $450 less in low season.

As for other carriers, *Continental* and *TWA* offer direct flights from New York/Newark to Madrid at much the same price; *United* has flights out of Washington, DC (also around $550 in low season, $1000 peak); and *American* flies regularly out of Miami (figure on $650/$1100), Chicago ($650/$1100) and Dallas-Ft. Worth ($700/$1300); and *Delta* flies to Madrid out of its Atlanta hub (about $650/$1200). Coming from anywhere else in the US, a connecting flight on the same airline should add only $50–200 from Midwest cities, $150–200 from the West Coast (a connecting flight with a different carrier may run to $300–500).

FLIGHTS VIA OTHER EUROPEAN CITIES

Discount travel agents might have cheaper deals on routings to Madrid **via other major European cities** with the airlines of those countries: *KLM* via Amsterdam, *Lufthansa* via Frankfurt, *TAP* via Lisbon, *British Airways* via London or *Sabena* via Brussels. Competition is intense, so look out for bargains, especially out of season. *TAP* also has flights from Lisbon to Málaga (usually with a stop in Madrid).

FROM CANADA

From Canada, you've got considerably less choice of direct flights to Spain – in fact, at the time of writing there's only one, *Iberia*, which has a daily service to **Madrid** originating in Toronto and stopping in Montréal. The APEX fare, at around CDN$750 in low season, CDN$1100 in peak season, isn't bad, and this fare also entitles you to a free connecting flight to **Málaga** or **Sevilla** in the high season (add $150 in low season). A connection to **Almería** is also available (add $50–200, depending on season).

Flights from other Canadian cities to Toronto or Montréal will add about $200–500 to the above fares. West of the Rockies you're probably better off flying Vancouver–London (from CDN$750–1050 return) and then continuing on to Madrid, or alternatively getting a flight from Seattle.

Discount travel agents deal mainly in flights **via London** (using a combination of airlines) or via Lisbon (on *TAP*). There are several other possibilities using other European national airlines via their respective capitals (see airlines box). Fares are generally in line with those of *Iberia*.

Travel CUTS is the most reliable student/ youth agency, with some deals for non-students, too; or check the travel ads in your local newspaper and consult a good travel agent.

CITY BREAKS AND PACKAGE TOURS

Package tours may not sound like your kind of travel, but don't dismiss the idea out of hand. It's true that tours arranged in North America tend to be of the everybody-on-the-bus group variety, but many agents can put together very flexible deals, sometimes amounting to no more than a flight plus car or rail pass and accommodation; if you're planning to travel in moderate or luxury style, and especially if your trip is geared around special interests, such packages can work out cheaper than the same arrangements made on arrival. A package can also be great for your peace of mind, if only just to ensure a worry-free first week while you're finding your feet on a longer tour (of course, you can jump off the itinerary any time you like). Most companies will expect you to book through a local travel agent, and since it costs the same you might as well.

A number of American outfits offer tours that focus on Andalucía. For the most part they boil down to two basic formulas: escorted **historic city tours**, making a circuit of Granada, Córdoba and Sevilla; and accommodation-only packages on the **Costa del Sol**. Some operators allow you to build your own itinerary with a few nights in each of various cities. Any way you slice it, though, going with a tour company will land you in fairly expensive hotels, in the neighbourhood of $100 a night per person – even more if you're staying in *paradores*. In addition, a few American companies organize biking and trekking trips in Andalucía, which cost at least as much as city tours due to all the logistics involved.

RAIL PASSES

The *Eurail Pass* is not likely to pay for itself if you travel only in Spain, though if you're planning a longer European trip it may prove useful. The pass, which must be purchased before arrival in Europe, allows unlimited free train travel in Spain and sixteen other countries. The *Eurail Youthpass* (for under-26s) costs US$578 for one month or $768 for two; if you're 26 or over you'll have to buy a first-class pass, available in 15-day ($498), 21-day ($648), one-month ($798), two-month ($1098) and three-month ($1398) increments.

TOUR OPERATORS IN NORTH AMERICA

Abercrombie & Kent
1520 Kensington Rd, Oak Brook, IL (☎800/323-7308). *Bike tours.*

Cosmos Tourama
92–25 Queens Bvd, Rego Park, NY 11374 (☎800/338-7092). *Budget tours.*

Discover Spain
2200 Fletcher Ave, Fort Lee, NJ 07024 (☎800/227-5858). *Costa del Sol packages, parador tours.*

EC Tours
10153 1/2 Riverside, Toluca Lake, CA 91602 (☎800/388-0877). *Historic city tours, paradores, pilgrimages.*

Escapade Tours
2200 Fletcher Ave, Fort Lee, NJ 07024 (☎800/356-2405). *Costa del Sol packages for seniors.*

Friendly Holidays
575 Anton Blvd, #790, Costa Mesa, CA 92626 (☎800/221-9748). *City packages and parador tours.*

Himalayan Travel
112 Prospect St, Stamford, CT 06901 (☎800/225-2380). *Trekking in the Sierra Nevada and Alpujarras.*

MI Travel
450 7th Ave, Suite 1805, New York, NY (☎800/848-2314). *Historic city tours, Costa del Sol packages, paradores.*

Mountain Travel-Sobek
6420 Fairmount Ave, El Cerrito, CA 94530 (☎800/227-2384). *Trekking in the Sierra Nevada.*

Petrabax
6464 Sunset Blvd, #570, Hollywood, CA 90028 (☎800/634-1188). *Historic city tours, paradores.*

Sun Holidays
26 6th St, Stamford, CT 06905 (☎800/243-2057). *City tours, Costa del Sol packages, paradores.*

Welcome Tours
99 Tulip Ave, Suite 208, Floral Park, NY 11001 (☎800/274-4400). *City and regional tours, Costa del Sol packages, paradores.*

You stand a better chance of getting your money's worth out of a *Eurail Flexipass*, which is good for a certain number of travel days in a two-month period. This, too, comes in under-26 and first-class versions: 5 days cost $255/$348; 10 days, $398/$560; and 15 days, $540/$740.

A further alternative is to attempt to buy an *InterRail Pass* after you arrive in Europe (see "Getting There From Britain") – most agents don't check residential qualifications, but once in Europe it's too late to buy a *Eurail Pass* if you have problems. North Americans are also eligible to purchase the more specific **Spain Flexipass** (see "Getting Around", p.23). All these passes can be reserved through *Rail Europe*, 226 Westchester Ave, White Plains, NY 10604 (☎800/438 7245) or youth-oriented travel agents (see below).

DISCOUNT AGENTS, CONSOLIDATORS AND TRAVEL CLUBS IN NORTH AMERICA

Council Travel
Head Office, 205 E 42nd St, New York
NY 10017 ☎800/743-1823
Nationwide US student travel organization with branches (among others) in San Francisco, Washington DC, Boston, Austin, Seattle, Chicago, Minneapolis.

Discount Travel International
Ives Bldg, 114 Forrest Ave, Suite 205, Narberth
PA 19072 ☎800/334-9294
Discount travel club.

Encore Travel Club
4501 Forbes Blvd, Lanham
MD 20706 ☎301/459-8020
East Coast travel club.

Interworld
800 Douglass Rd, Miami
FL 33134 ☎305/443-4929
Southeastern US consolidator.

Moment's Notice
425 Madison Ave, New York
NY 10017 ☎212/486-0503
Discount travel club.

New Frontiers/Nouvelles Frontières
12 E 33rd St, New York
NY 10016 ☎800/366-6387
also at:
1001 Sherbrook East, Suite 720
Montréal, H2L 1L3 ☎514/526-8444
French discount travel firm. Other branches in LA, San Francisco and Québec City.

STA Travel (nationwide) ☎800/777-0112
Worldwide specialist in independent travel with offices in Los Angeles, San Francisco, Boston.

Stand Buys
311 W Superior St, Chicago
IL 60610 ☎800/255-0200
Midwestern travel club.

Travel Cuts
* Head Office: 187 College St, Toronto
ON M5T 1P7 ☎416/979-2406
Others include:
MacEwan Hall Student Centre, University of
Calgary, Calgary, AL T2N 1N4 ☎403/282-7687
12304 Jasper Av, Edmonton
AL T5N 3K5 ☎403/488 8487
6139 South St, Halifax
NS B3H 4J2 ☎902/494-7027
1613 rue St Denis, Montréal
PQ H2X 3K3 ☎514/843-8511
1 Stewart St, Ottawa
ON K1N 6H7 ☎613/238 8222
100–2383 CH St Foy, St Foy
G1V 1T1 ☎418/654 0224
Place Riel Campus Centre, University of
Saskatchewan, Saskatoon
S7N 0W0 ☎306/975-3722
501–602 W Hastings, Vancouver
V6B 1P2 ☎604/681 9136
University Centre, University of Manitoba,
Winnipeg R3T 2N2 ☎204/269-9530
Canadian student travel organization.

Travelers Advantage
49 Music Sq West, Nashville
TN 37204 ☎800/344-2334
Reliable travel club.

Travac
989 6th Ave, New York
NY 10018 ☎800/872-8800
US consolidator.

Unitravel
1177 N Warson Rd, St Louis
MO 63132 ☎800/325-2222
US consolidator.

Worldwide Discount Travel Club
1674 Meridian Ave, Miami Beach
FL 33139 ☎305/534-2082
Florida-based travel club.

GETTING THERE FROM BRITAIN

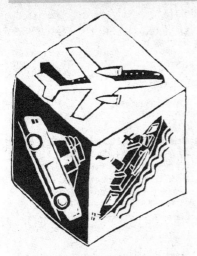

The most convenient way of getting to Andalucía is to **fly** – flights take around two and a half hours to Sevilla and Málaga compared with a gruelling 35 hours-plus by train to Málaga. Driving to Spain will become even easier with the opening of the *Le Shuttle* cross-Channel service and there are also two **direct ferry services** from Britain: Plymouth to Santander, and Portsmouth to Bilbão. However, whether you enter Spain here or by crossing the Pyrenees, you'll still face a journey of around 400 miles (650km) to the Andalucian border.

BY PLANE

There's a vast number of flights from Britain to Andalucía throughout the year, mostly serving the Costa del Sol. Out of season, or if you're prepared to book at the last minute, they can be very good value indeed – often as little as £80–100 return to Málaga, though more likely £150 in the height of summer.

CHARTER FLIGHTS
Charters are usually block-booked by package holiday firms, but even in the middle of August they're rarely completely full and spare seats are often sold off at discounts. For an idea of current prices and availability, contact any high street travel agent, or a specialist agency or operator.

The widest selection of ads for London departures is invariably found in the classified pages of the London listings magazine *Time Out*. For departures **from other British airports** check the local evening papers and *The Sunday Times* and *Observer*. The agents and operators listed on p.8 make a good start.

The independent travel specialists *STA Travel* offer a range of special discount flights, most frequently on the Madrid and Barcelona routes, while students – and anyone else under 26 – can also try *Campus Travel*. Student union travel bureaux can usually fix you up with flights through one of these operators, and they're both worth calling for charters, whether you're a student or not.

The major disadvantage of charter flights is the fixed return date – a maximum of four weeks from the outward journey. Some return charters are good value even if you only use half, but for more flexibility you'll probably want to buy a ticket for a scheduled flight.

SCHEDULED FLIGHTS

Spain's national airline, *Iberia*, and *British Airways* have the widest range of **scheduled flights** including regular services to Sevilla and Málaga. *GB Airways* (part of *BA*) also flies direct to Gibraltar.

Scheduled flights are rarely the cheapest option but some of their special offers can be highly competitive, especially if you need the greater **flexibility** of a scheduled airline. They offer, for example, open-jaw flights (fly in to one airport, back from another); Fly-Drive deals; and inexpensive connections from most regional UK airports. The cheapest tickets with *Iberia* or *BA* go by various names at different times of the year, but they are usually valid for one month only, require you to stay at least one Saturday night, and don't allow for change or cancellation. Consequently there's no great difference between these and a charter ticket but prices are competitive: fares start from around £175 return from London to Málaga in low season up to £245 in July and August; it's worth shopping around the various operators as there can sometimes be significant differences in their fares for the same destination. For a more flexible ticket, such as *BA*'s "Excursion" fare, which is valid for six

AIRLINES, AGENTS AND OPERATORS

AIRLINES

Iberia 29 Glasshouse St, London W1R 5RG (☎071/830 0011); Birmingham ☎021/643 1953; Manchester ☎061/436 6444; Glasgow ☎041/248

British Airways 156 Regent St, London W1R 5TA (☎081/897 4000).

AGENTS AND OPERATORS

APA Travel 138 Eversholt St, London NW1 (☎071/387 5337). *Spanish flight specialists.*

Aventura 42 Greenlands Rd, Staines, Middlesex TW18 4LR (☎0784/459 018). *Horse-riding and mule-trekking in the Sierra Nevada.*

B&B Abroad 5 World's End Lane, Green Street Green, Orpington, Kent BR6 6AA (☎0689/857 838). *Specialist operator with a wide range of bed and breakfast accommodation from rustic farmhouses to luxurious country manors. Also has hotel accommodation.*

Blackheath Wine Trails, 13 Blackheath Village, London SE3 9LA (☎081/463 0012). *Tours of the wine bodegas of the region from a base at Jerez de la Frontera.*

Campus Travel 52 Grosvenor Gdns, London SW1 (☎071/730 3402); 541 Bristol Rd, Selly Oak, Birmingham (☎021/414 1848); 39 Queen's Rd, Clifton, Bristol (☎0272/292 494); 5 Emmanuel St, Cambridge (☎0223/324 283); 53 Forest Rd, Edinburgh (☎031/668 3303); 166 Deansgate, Manchester (☎061/273 1721); 13 High St, Oxford (☎0865/242 067). Also in *YHA* shops and on university campuses throughout Britain. *Youth/student specialist.*

Cox & Kings, St James' Court, Buckingham Gate, London SW1E 6AF (☎071/834 7746). *Specialized trips including the Al Andalus Express, the Andalucian version of the Orient Express calling at Sevilla, Granada, Córdoba, Ronda and Jerez.*

Exodus Expeditions 9 Weir Rd, London SW12 0LT (☎081/675 5550). *Walking and riding in Andalucía, Majorca and the Pyrenees.*

Explore Worldwide Ltd, 1 Frederick St, Aldershot, Hants GU11 1O (☎0252/344 161). *Walking in Andalucía, Sierra Nevada and Picos de Europa.*

Keytel International 402 Edgware Rd, London W2 1ED (☎071/402 8182). *Main agents for the paradores.*

Magic of Spain 227 Shepherd's Bush Rd, London W6 7AS (☎081/748 7575). *High quality, out-of-the-way hotels and paradores.*

Mundi Color 276 Vauxhall Bridge Rd, London SW1 (☎071/828 6021). *Spanish specialists for flights, packages and city breaks.*

Owners Abroad Astral Towers, Bettsway, London Road, Crawley, West Sussex (☎0293/554 444). *Charter flights.*

Sherpa Expeditions 131a Heston Rd, Hounslow, Middlesex TW5 0RD (☎081/577 2717). *Trekking in the Sierra Nevada, the Alpujarras and Pyrenees.*

Springways Travel 258 Vauxhall Bridge Rd, London SW1 (☎071/976 5833). *Good prices on charters.*

STA Travel 86 Old Brompton Rd, London SW7 (☎071/937 9921); 117 Euston Rd, London NW1; 25 Queen's Rd, Bristol BS8 1QE (☎0272/294 399); 38 Sidney St, Cambridge CB2 3HX (☎0223/66966); 36 George St, Oxford OX1 2OJ (☎0865/792 8000); 75 Deansgate, Manchester M3 2BW (☎061/834 0668). *Independent travel specialists; discounted flights.*

Time Off 2a Chester Close, Chester St, London SW1 (☎071/235 8070). *City breaks.*

Travellers Way Hewell Lane, Tardebigge, Bromsgrove, Worcs B60 1LP (☎0527/836 791). *Tailor-made holidays and city breaks all over Spain, especially Andalucía.*

Waymark Holidays 44 Windsor Rd, Slough SL1 2EJ (☎0753/516 477). *Good range of walking holidays in Andalucía.*

months, can be upgraded and is fully refundable, you're looking at paying around £393 from London to Málaga (£505 from Manchester) and £393 from London to Sevilla (£423 from Manchester).

PACKAGES AND CITY BREAKS

Package holiday deals, too, can be worth looking at. Certainly if you book late – or out of season – you'll often find incredible prices. While

SAMPLE SCHEDULED FLIGHT PRICES TO SPAIN

	Low	High
From **London** to:		
Madrid	£157	£230
Málaga	£175	£245
Sevilla	£196	£254
Gibraltar	£189	£219
From **Manchester** to:		
Madrid	£175	£232
Málaga	£206	£264
Sevilla	£206	£264
Gibraltar	£209	£239

these may seem to restrict you to some of the worst parts of the coast, remember that there's no compulsion to stick around your hotel. Get a good enough deal and it can be worth it simply for the flight – with transfer to a reasonably comfortable hotel laid on for a night or two at each end. Bargains can be found at virtually any high street travel agent – look for *Skytours'* brochure which offers most of the Costa del Sol resorts. Prices for two weeks in a self-catering apartment on the Costa del Sol (based on four people sharing), including flights, start at around £220 per person (low season) and rise to around £400 in July and August. Fly-Drive deals are well worth considering as a combined air ticket and car rental arrangement can be excellent value.

City breaks are available to several Spanish cities, with Sevilla and Granada the most popular destinations in Andalucía. Flying from London or Manchester, prices start at around £187–212 for three days (two nights) for both destinations; adding extra nights or upgrading your hotel is possible, too, at a reasonable cost. The prices always include return flights and bed and breakfast in a centrally located one-, two- or three-star hotel. Again, ask your travel agent for the best deal, and check the addresses in the Agents box.

BY TRAIN

From **London to Barcelona** takes just under 24 hours by train with an additional 11 hours to **Málaga**, though once through trains from London to Paris are in operation using the Channel Tunnel (see below), you can expect the time to drop a

little. Currently, departures are from Victoria station at around 9am, changing trains (and stations, from Nord to Austerlitz) in Paris around 6–8pm and again at the Spanish border (Cerbere/Port Bou) around dawn. It's an efficient approach, and can be an interesting one if you stop over en route.

TICKETS AND PASSES

A **standard rail ticket** from London to Málaga, Sevilla or Granada will currently cost you around £230 return, depending on whether you use the Madrid (via San Sebastián) or the slightly pricier Barcelona route. An interesting round trip is possible going out on one route and coming back on the other, but this has to be booked in advance. Details and tickets are available through some travel agents or at *British Rail International* (see box below).

The alternative for **under-26s** is a discounted BIJ ticket from *Eurotrain* (through *Campus Travel*) or *Wasteels*. These can be booked for journeys from any British station to any major station in Europe; like full-price tickets, they remain valid for two months and allow as many stopovers as you want along a pre-specified route (which can be different going out and coming home). The current return fare from London to Málaga, Sevilla or Granada is £217 – demonstrating that these tickets offer very small savings.

If you're under 26, however, or if you plan to use Spanish trains extensively, there are better value options than simply buying a return ticket. The best known is to buy an *InterRail* pass from *British Rail* or a travel agent; the only restriction is that you must have been resident in Europe for at least six months. The pass comes in two forms: either an *InterRail Global* pass, valid for one month's unlimited travel in 26 European

TRAIN INFORMATION

British Rail European information line ☎071/834 2345

Eurotrain 52 Grosvenor Gdns, London SW1 ☎071/730 3402

Wasteels, Victoria Station, London SW1 ☎071/834 7066

BUS INFORMATION

Eurolines *National Express*, 164 Buckingham Palace Rd, London SW1 ☎071/730 0202

countries including Spain (£249), or an *InterRail Zonal* pass, whereby the 26 countries are split into seven zones and you choose which countries you want the pass to be valid for – Spain is grouped with Portugal and Morocco. A fifteen-day pass for any one zone costs £179; any two zones, valid for one month, costs £209; any three, also for one month, £229. In addition, all *InterRail* passes offer discounts on rail travel in the UK, on Channel ferries, and on ferries from Spain to the Balearics and Morocco. Since Spain has an extensive rail network this is basically a bargain, though be prepared (see p.22) to pay various and unpredictable supplements on some of the Spanish services; there are also one or two private lines on which passes are not valid.

BY BUS

The main **bus route** from Britain to Spain is from London to Barcelona (daily in season, 3 times a week out; 26hr) and Alicante (3 times a week; 35hr) via the Costa Brava. There are also two buses a week to Algeciras (43hr), via Paris, Madrid (32hr; more buses run this far in season), Málaga and the Costa del Sol (38hr). Typical peak season fares to the Costa del Sol are around £85 single, £149 return with a ten percent reduction if you're under 26. All these routes are operated by *Eurolines* in Britain and by *Iberbus/Linebus* and *Julia* in Spain. In both Britain and Spain tickets are bookable through most major travel agents; *Eurolines* sells tickets, and through-transport to London, from all British *National Express* bus terminals.

To Barcelona the journey south is long but quite bearable – just make sure you take along enough to eat, drink and read, and a small amount of French and Spanish currency for coffee, etc. There are stops for around twenty minutes every four to five hours and the routine is also broken by the Dover–Calais/Boulogne ferry (which is included in the cost of a ticket). However, doing the whole trip to Andalucía in one go starts to lose its appeal after 24 hours in a bus and you may want to consider an overnight stop inside the Spanish border. These considerations mean that you may well find air tickets compare very favourably price- and comfort-wise.

BY CAR, FERRY AND LE SHUTTLE

The coach routes follow the most direct road routes from London to southern Spain: if you plan to **drive** them yourself, unless you're into non-stop rally motoring, you'll need to roughly double their times. There are now two **direct ferry sailings** to **Bilbão** and **Santander** from Britain which are worth considering as a way of cutting down on fatigue and avoiding expensive *autoroute* tolls crossing France. See the box for ferry company addresses, or contact your local travel agent for the latest ticket and sailing details.

LE SHUTTLE AND CROSS-CHANNEL SERVICES

The opening of **Le Shuttle** service through the Channel Tunnel won't significantly affect travel times for drivers to Spain, though it will of course speed up the cross-Channel section of the journey. *Le Shuttle* will operate trains 24 hours a day carrying cars, motorcycles, coaches and their passengers, taking 35 minutes between Folkestone and Calais. At peak times, services will operate every 15 minutes, making advance bookings unnecessary; during the night, services will still run hourly. Through trains will eventually connect London with Paris in just over three hours. Return fares from May to August will cost £280–310 per vehicle (passengers included), with discounts in the low season on either side.

The alternative cross-Channel options for travellers heading to Andalucía via Barcelona are the conventional **ferry** or **hovercraft** links between **Dover** and Calais or Boulogne. With more time you might want to consider one of the ferries to Le Havre (from Portsmouth), Cherbourg (from Portsmouth and Weymouth), St-Malo (from Portsmouth) or even Roscoff (from Plymouth). Any of these cuts out the trek round or through Paris, and opens up some interesting detours around Brittany and the French Atlantic coast. Ferry prices vary according to the time of year and, for motorists, according to the size of your car. The Dover–Calais/Boulogne runs, for example, start at about £70 one-way for a car, two adults and two kids, but this figure doubles in high season. Foot passengers should be able to cross for about £20–30.

TO SANTANDER AND BILBÃO

Alternatively, though it's expensive, you can use one of the two direct **ferry services** from England to Spain, an option which also gives you a choice of some interesting and scenic routes across country (through Extremadura, for example) en route to the south.

FERRY COMPANIES AND LE SHUTTLE

Brittany Ferries Millbay Docks, Plymouth (☎0752/221 321); Wharf Rd, Portsmouth (☎0705/827 701); New Harbour Rd, Poole (☎0202/671 100).
To Santander, St Malo, Roscoff, Cherbourg and Caen.

Hoverspeed International Hoverport, Dover, Kent (☎0304/240 101); also in London (☎081/554 7061).
To Boulogne and Calais.

P&O European Ferries Channel House, Channel View Rd, Dover (☎0304/203 388); Continental Ferry Port, Mile End, Portsmouth (☎0705/772 244);

also in London (☎081/575 8555).
To Calais, Cherbourg, Le Havre and Bilbão.

Sally Line Argyle Centre, York St, Ramsgate, Kent (☎0843/595 522); 81 Piccadilly, London W1 (☎081/858 1127).
To Dunkerque.

Stena Sealink Line Charter House, Park St, Ashford, Kent (☎0233/647 047).
To Calais, Cherbourg and Dieppe.

Le Shuttle Customer Services Centre (Information and ticket sales ☎0303/271 100).

The car passenger ferry from **Plymouth to Santander** is operated by *Brittany Ferries*, takes 24 hours and runs twice weekly for most of the year (less often from December to mid-March). Ticket prices vary widely according to season and number of passengers carried; one-way fares start at £111 for a car plus £48 per person mid-season. Foot passengers will pay around £50 one way, and everyone has to book some form of accommodation; cheapest is a pullman seat (from £3.50 off-season), and there are two- and four-berth cabins for around £50–70 each. Tickets are best booked in advance, through any major travel agent.

P&O has recently started a twice-weekly ferry service from **Portsmouth to Bilbão**. The journey takes approximately 30 hours, leaving Portsmouth on Saturdays and Tuesdays. A mid-season return for a car and up to five passengers costs £638;

foot passengers pay £129 (children £54). All prices include a cabin.

HITCHING

Hitching on major French routes – and Spanish ones too – can be dire and stopping people in cafés and asking directly for lifts is about the only technique that works. At all events don't try to hitch from the Channel ports to Paris (organize a lift while you're still on the ferry) nor (worse still) out of Paris itself. If you can afford it, perhaps the best approach is to buy a train ticket to somewhere south of Paris and set out from there.

Freewheelers (☎091/222 0090) is a Newcastle-based **lift-sharing service**, which can arrange lifts from the UK to Spain. It is free to drivers and costs passengers a few pounds in fees plus any arrangements with the driver.

GETTING THERE FROM IRELAND

Summer charter flights to the Costa del Sol are easy to pick up from either Dublin or Belfast, while year-round scheduled services operate to Madrid and Barcelona. However, other package holidays or city breaks are often routed via London, with an add-on fare from Ireland for the connection. Students, and anyone under the age of 31, should contact *USIT*, which generally has the best discount deals on flights and train tickets. For *InterRail* details, see p.9.

Iberia has direct **scheduled flights** from Dublin to Madrid costing from IR£225 return in the low season (Jan–Feb) to IR£271 in July and

August, and to Barcelona costing from IR£197 to IR£237. These cheapest fares have several restrictions – you must stay at least one Saturday night, and can only stay for a maximum of one month – and if you want to change your departure date you can do so only once by paying an upgrade fee of IR£30.

There are direct once-a-week summer **charter flights** to Málaga from Belfast (around £269 return) and Dublin (IR£239–269), with prices reaching their highest during August and dropping a little in the months either side. If you're prepared to book at the last minute, you'll often get much better flight-only deals, though obviously you can't guarantee the departure date you want.

For a two-week **package** to the Costa del Sol (based on four people in a self-catering apartment), you can expect to pay from £315 (low season) to £409 (high) from Belfast; from IR£285

to IR£395 from Dublin. **City breaks** out of Belfast run from £209–285 for three days (two nights) in Barcelona and from £189–289 in Madrid; you can book a city break from Dublin, but it basically means sorting out a city break deal from London with your travel agent, which will then be able to sell you a connecting, add-on Dublin–London flight – from IR£59–89, depending on which London airport you fly into.

If you're really trying to get to Andalucía in the cheapest possible way, you might find that budget flights from Dublin (with *Ryanair*, *Aer Lingus* and *British Midland*) or Belfast (*British Airways* and *British Midland*) to London, plus a last-minute London charter flight, will save you a few pounds, but don't count on it. Buying a *Eurotrain* ticket (from *USIT*) from Dublin to London will slightly undercut the plane's price, but by this time you're starting to talk about a journey of days and not hours.

USEFUL ADDRESSES IN IRELAND

AIRLINES

Aer Lingus, 42 Grafton St, Dublin (☎01/637 0011); 46 Castle St, Belfast (☎0232/245 151).

British Airways 60 Dawson St, Dublin (☎800/ 626 747); 9 Fountain Centre, College St, Belfast
Iberia 54 Dawson St, Dublin 2 (☎01/677 9846).

AGENTS AND OPERATORS

Joe Walsh Tours 8–11 Baggot St, Dublin (☎01/ 678 9555). *General budget fares agent.*

Thomas Cook, 118 Grafton St, Dublin (☎01/677 1721); 11 Donegall Place, Belfast (☎0232/240 833). *Package holiday and flight agent, with occasional discount offers.*

USIT O'Connell Bridge, 19–21 Aston Quay, Dublin 2 (☎01/778 117); 10–11 Market Parade, Cork (☎021/270 900); 31a Queen St, Belfast (☎0232/ 242 562) *Student and youth specialist for flights and trains.*

GETTING THERE FROM AUSTRALASIA

There are no direct flights to Spain from Australia or New Zealand, but by combining services some airlines now offer travel to Madrid (and sometimes Barcelona) in conjunction witrh a stopover in Europe. While this means around 24 hours' flying time – not counting time spent waiting for connections – this is a good way to see places on the way if you're not rushed for time. British Airways, Aeroflot and Japanese Airlines provide the most direct services.

As destinations in Europe are "common rated" – you pay the same fare whatever your destination – some airlines offer free flight coupons, car rental or accommodation if you book these extras with your ticket. Choose carefully, though, as such perks are impossible to alter later.

Alternatively, you could buy the cheapest possible flight to anywhere in Europe and make your way to Spain using standby flights, trains or buses, but this would rarely work out as cheaply

AIRLINES AND AGENTS IN AUSTRALASIA

Aeroflot 388 George St, Sydney (☎02/233 7911). *Low fares from Sydney via Moscow to Madrid twice a week; for a little more you can fly to Singapore on Singapore Airlines and connect with Aeroflot there.*

Air France 12 Castlereagh St, Sydney (☎02/233 3277); 57 Fort St, Auckland (☎09/303 1229). *One flight weekly from Sydney and Auckland to Madrid or Barcelona via Pacific islands.*

British Airways 64 Castelreagh St, Sydney (☎02/258 3300). *Use the free European flight included in the London ticket price to reach Madrid or Barcelona. Daily to London from Sydney.*

Garuda 120 Albert St, Auckland (☎09/366 1855). *Combined services with KLM; flights to Madrid via Jakarta and Amsterdam.*

Japanese Airlines 17 Bligh St, Sydney (☎02/233 4500). *Flies from Sydney via Tokyo to Madrid three times a week, and includes one night's accommodation in Tokyo.*

KLM 5 Elizabeth St, Sydney (☎02/231 6333). *Combines services with Singapore Airlines or Lufthansa/Air Lauda for Madrid via Amsterdam.*

Lufthansa 143 Macquarie St, Sydney (☎02/367 3800). *Combines with KLM and Air Lauda to Europe; use the free flight coupons (booked with main ticket and not alterable) from hub European cities to reach Spain.*

Malaysian Airlines 388 George St, Sydney (☎02/231 5066). *Once weekly to Madrid via Kuala Lumpur and London.*

Qantas Qantas House, 154 Queen St, Auckland (☎09/303 2506). *Three times a week from Auckland via Rome to Madrid.*

Singapore Airlines 17 Bridge St, Sydney (☎02/236 0111). *Combined services with KLM (see above).*

Thai International, Kensington Swan Building, 22 Fanshawe St, Auckland (☎09/377 0268). *Spanish connections from Bangkok via London.*

AUSTRALIAN DISCOUNT AGENTS

Anywhere Travel 345 Anzac Parade, Kingsford, Sydney (☎02/663 0411).

Brisbane Discount Travel 360 Queen St, Brisbane (☎07/229 9211).

Discount Travel Specialists Shop 53, Forrest Chase, Perth (☎09/221 1400).

Flight Centres Circular Quay, Sydney (☎02/241 2422); Bourke St, Melbourne ☎03/650 2899; plus other branches nationwide except the Northern Territory.

Passport Travel 320b Glenfarrie Rd, Malvern, Melbourne (☎03/824 7183).

STA Travel 732 Harris St, Sydney (☎02/212 1255); 256 Flinders St, Melbourne (☎03/347 4711); other offices in Townsville and state capitals.

Topdeck Travel 45 Grenfell St, Adelaide (☎08/410 1110).

Tymtro Travel Suite G12, Wallaceway Shopping Centre, Chatswood, Sydney (☎02/411 1222).

NEW ZEALAND DISCOUNT AGENTS

Budget Travel PO Box 505, Auckland (☎09/309 4313).

Flight Centres National Bank Towers, 205–225 Queen St, Auckland (☎09/309 6171); Shop 1M, National Mutual Arcade, 152 Hereford St, Christchurch (☎09/379 7145); 50–52 Willis St, Wellington (☎04/472 8101); other branches countrywide.

STA Travel Traveller's Centre, 10 High St, Auckland (☎09/309 9995); 233 Cuba St, Wellington (☎04/385 0561); 223 High St, Christchurch (☎03/379 9098); other offices in Dunedin, Palmerston North and Hamilton.

as buying a discounted flight that will take you all the way. For more extended trips, Round the World (RTW) tickets, valid for up to a year, are a good option – especially from New Zealand, where airlines tend to offer fewer bonuses to fly with them.

FARES

Fares change according to the time of year you travel. December and January is high season; February, and October through to mid-November the low season; and the rest of the year the shoulder season. The current lowest standard return fares to Madrid (low/high season) are around A$2000/2200 from eastern Australia; A$1990/2200 from Perth; NZ$2200/2600 from Auckland.

While charging heavily for cancellations or alterations, **discount agents** can usually provide far better prices than these – from A$1700/ NZ$2155 for a low-season fare. Full-time students, and those under 26 or over 60, can also make big savings through specialist agents. Check the box on p.13, and you'll find others in the travel sections of the major Saturday papers.

RED TAPE AND VISAS

Citizens of most EC countries (and of Norway, Sweden, Finland and Iceland) need only a valid national identity card to enter Spain for up to ninety days. Since Britain has no identity card system, however, British citizens do have to take a passport. US citizens require a passport but no visa and can stay for up to six months; other Europeans, Canadian and New Zealand citizens also require a passport and can stay for up to ninety days. Australians need a visa, but can get one on arrival which is valid for thirty days. Everyone else should consult their local Spanish embassy or consulate for details of particular entry requirements.

To stay for longer periods, EC nationals (and citizens of Norway, Sweden, Finland and Iceland) can apply for a *permiso de residencia* (residence permit) once in Spain. You'll have to either produce proof that you have sufficient funds (officially 5000ptas a day) to be able to support yourself without working – easiest done by keeping bank exchange forms when you change money – or produce a contract of employment (*contrato de trabajo*) or become self-employed (eg as a teacher), which involves registering at the tax office. Other nationalities will need to get a special visa from a Spanish consulate before departure (see box below), or can apply for one ninety-day extension, showing proof of funds.

CUSTOMS

Customs and duty-free restrictions vary throughout Europe, with subtle variations even within the European Community, at least for the moment. For instance, since the inauguration of the EC Single Market, travellers coming into **Britain** directly from Spain do not have to make a declaration to Customs. In other words British residents can effectively take home as much duty-paid wine or beer as they can carry (the legal limits being 90 litres of wine or 110 of beer). However, there are still restrictions on the volume of tax- or duty-free goods you can bring into the country.

In general, **residents of EC countries** travelling to other EC states are allowed a duty-free allowance of 200 cigarettes, one litre of spirits and five litres of wine; for non-EC residents the allowances are usually 200 cigarettes, one litre of spirits and two litres of wine.

Residents of the USA and Canada can take up to 200 cigarettes and one litre of alcohol back into their country, as can **Australian citizens**, while **New Zealanders** must confine themselves to 200 cigarettes, 4.5 litres of beer or wine, and just over one litre of spirits. Again, if in doubt consult the relevant – or your own – embassy.

INSURANCE

As an EC country, Spain has free reciprocal health agreements with other member states. To take advantage, British and other EC citizens will need form E111, available over the counter from main post offices. For details of what to do and where to go in a medical emergency, see p.25.

Even with an E111, some form of travel insurance is still all but essential. With insurance you'll be able to claim back the cost of any drugs prescribed by pharmacies, and European policies generally also cover your baggage/tickets in case of theft.

EUROPEAN COVER

In Britain and Ireland, travel insurance schemes (from around £20 a month) are sold by almost every travel agent and bank – or consider a specialist insurance firm. Policies issued by *Campus Travel* (see p.8 for address), *Endsleigh Insurance* (97–107 Southampton Row, London WC1; ☎071/436 4451), *Frizzell Insurance* (Frizzell House, County Gates, Bournemouth, Dorset BH1 2NF; ☎0202/292333) or *Columbus Travel Insurance* (17 Devonshire Square, London EC2; ☎071/375 0011) are all good value. If you're going climbing or skiing in the Sierra Nevada, or engaging in any other high-risk outdoor activity, you'll probably have to pay an extra premium; ask your insurers for advice.

NORTH AMERICAN INSURANCE

In the **US and Canada**, insurance tends to be much more expensive, and may be medical cover only. Before buying a policy, check that you're not already covered by existing insurance plans. **Canadians** are usually covered by their provincial health plans; holders of **ISIC cards** and some other student/teacher/youth cards are entitled to $3000 worth of accident coverage and sixty days ($100 per diem) of hospital in-patient benefits for the period during which the card is valid. **Students** will often find that their student health coverage extends during the vacations and for one term beyond the date of last enrollment. Bank and credit cards (particularly *American Express*) often have certain levels of medical or other insurance included, and travel insurance may also be included if you use a major credit or charge card to pay for your trip. **Homeowners' or renters'** insurance often covers theft or loss of documents, money and valuables while overseas, though conditions and maximum amounts vary from company to company.

Only after exhausting the possibilities above might you want to contact a specialist travel insurance company; your travel agent can usually recommend one. Travel insurance offerings are quite comprehensive, anticipating everything from charter companies going bankrupt to delayed or lost baggage, by way of sundry illnesses and accidents. **Premiums** vary widely, from the very reasonable ones offered primarily through student/youth agencies (*STA*'s policies range from about \$50–70 for fifteen days to \$500–700 for a year, depending on the amount of financial cover), to those so expensive that the cost for anything more than two months of coverage will probably equal the cost of the worst possible combination of disasters. Note also that very few insurers will arrange on-the-spot payments in the event of a major expense or loss; you will usually be reimbursed only after going home. If you're planning on doing any **hiking, mountaineering or skiing** while abroad, you'll need to take out an additional rider to cover these activities – this will add an extra 30–50 percent to the premium.

None of these policies insure you against **theft** of anything at all while overseas. (Americans have been easy pickings for foreign thieves – a combination of naivete on the part of the former, an all-Americans-are-rich attitude among the latter – and companies were going broke paying robbery/burglary claims.) North American travel policies apply only to items **lost** from, or **damaged** in, the custody of an identifiable, responsible third party – hotel porter, airline, luggage consignment, etc. Even in these cases you will have to contact the local police to have a complete report made out so that your insurer can process the claim. If you are travelling via London it might be better to take out a British policy, available instantly and easily (though making the claim may prove more complicated).

TRAVELLERS WITH DISABILITIES

Spain is not by any means at the forefront of providing facilities for travellers with disabilities. That said, there are accessible hotels in each of the major cities and resorts. By law, all new public buildings are required to be fully accessible. The staging of the 1992 Paralympic Games in Barcelona has done a great deal towards helping attitudes and facilities there; and there are also a number of active and forceful groups of disabled people: *ONCE*, **the Spanish organization for the blind, is particularly active, its huge lottery bringing in a great deal of money.**

Transport is still the main problem, since buses are virtually impossible for wheelchairs and trains only slightly better (though there are wheelchairs at major stations and wheelchair

spaces in some carriages). *Hertz* has cars with hand controls available in Madrid and Barcelona (with advance notice), and taxi drivers are usually helpful. The *Brittany Ferries* crossing from Plymouth to Santander offers good facilities if you're **driving to Spain** (as do most cross-Channel ferries).

Once out of the cities and away from the coast, the difficulties increase. Road surfaces in the mountain regions can be rough and toilet facilities for disabled motorists are a rare sight. If you've got the money, *paradores* are one answer to the problem of unsuitable **accommodation**. Many are converted from castles and monasteries and although not built with the disabled guest in mind, their grand scale – with plenty of room to manoeuvre a wheelchair inside – tends to compensate.

CONTACTS FOR TRAVELLERS WITH DISABILITIES

General

Spanish National Tourist Office (See p.18 for addresses). *Publishes a fact sheet, listing a variety of useful addresses and some accessible accommodation.*

Organización Nacional de Ciegos de España (*ONCE*), c/de Prado 24, Madrid (☎91/589 46 00); c/Calabria 66–76, Barcelona 08015 (☎93/325 92 00). *Sells braille maps and can arrange trips for blind people; write for details.*

Institut Municipal de Disminuits c/Comte d'Urgell 240, 3°/A, Barcelona (☎93/439 66 00)

Britain

Holiday Care Service 2 Old Bank Chambers, Station Rd, Horley, Surrey RH6 9HW (☎0293/774535). *Information on all aspects of travel.*

Mobility International, 228 Borough High St, London SE1 1JX (☎071/403 5688). *Information, access guides, tours and exchange programmes.*

RADAR 25 Mortimer St, London W1N 8AB (☎071/637 5400). *A good source of advice on holidays and travel abroad.*

North America

Information Center for People with Disabilities Fort Point Place, 27–43 Wormwood St, Boston, MA 02210 (☎617/727-5540). *Clearing house for information, including travel.*

Jewish Rehabilitation Hospital 3205 Place Alton Goldbloom, Montréal, Québec H7V 1R2 (☎514/688-9550). *Guidebooks and travel information.*

Kéroul 4545 Ave Pierre de Coubertin, CP 1000, Montréal H1V 3R2 (☎512/252-3104). *Travel for mobility-impaired people.*

Mobility International USA Box 10767, Eugene, OR 97440 (☎503/343-1284). *Information, access guides, tours and exchange programmes.*

Travel Information Center Moss Rehabilitation Hospital, 1200 West Tabor Rd, Philadelphia, PA 19141 (☎215/456-9900). *Access information.*

INFORMATION AND MAPS

(addresses are detailed in the *Guide*) and from these you can usually get more specific local information and useful free maps. They vary enormously in quality of service, but while generally extremely useful for local information, they cannot be relied on to know anything about what goes on outside their patch. Turismo hours are usually Mon–Fri 9am–1pm and 3.30–6pm, Sat 9am–1pm – but there are wide variations across the region and you can't always rely on the official hours, especially in the more out-of-the-way places, which are known to close without notice; on the other hand, the major coastal resorts often have enthusiastic offices staying open until nine at night and even later in season.

The Spanish National Tourist Office (SNTO) produces and gives away an impressive variety of maps, pamphlets and special interest leaflets. Visit one of their offices before you leave and stock up, especially on city plans, as well as lists of hotels, hostales and campsites.

INFORMATION OFFICES

Throughout Andalucía you'll find *Junta de Andalucía* (regional government) tourist offices – called **Turismo** – in virtually every major town

MAPS

In addition to the various free leaflets, the one extra you'll probably want is a reasonable **road map**. This is best bought in Spain, where you'll find a good selection in most bookshops (*librerías*) and at street kiosks or petrol stations. Among the best are those published by *Editorial Almax*, which also produces reliable indexed street plans of Sevilla and Granada. The best **single map** for Andalucía is the *Michelin Andalucía* (1:400,000), which includes a plan to get you in and out of Sevilla, the region's only serious traffic headache. Good alternatives, especially if you're shopping before arrival, are the 1:300,000 *RV* (Reise und

SNTO OFFICES ABROAD

Australia 203 Castlereagh St, Suite 21a, PO Box A685, Sydney, NSW (☎02/264 79 66).

Belgium 18 Rue de la Montagne, 1000 Bruxelles (☎02/512 57 35).

Britain 57–58 St James's St, London SW1A 1LD (☎071/499 0901 or 499 1169). *The number is invariably engaged; write or visit.*

Canada 102 Bloor St W, 14th Floor, Toronto, Ontario (☎416/961 31 31).

Denmark Store Kongensgade 1–3, Kobenhavn (☎33/15 11 65).

France Ave Pierre 1er de Serbie 43, 75381 Paris (☎61 47 23 37).

Netherlands Laan Van Meerdevoort 8, 2517 Den Haag (☎070/46 59 00).

Norway Ruselökkveien 26, 0251 Oslo 2 (☎22 83 40 92).

Portugal Rua Camilo Costelo Branco 34, 1000 Lisbon (☎01/54 19 92).

Sweden Grev Turegatan 7, 1TR, 114-46 Stockholm (☎08/611 41 36).

USA 665 Fifth Ave, New York, NY 10022 (☎212/759 88 22); 8383 Wiltshire Boulevard, Suite 960, Beverly Hills, CA 90211 (☎213/658 7188); Water Tower Place, Suite 915 East, 845 North Michigan Ave, Chicago, IL 60611 (☎312/642 1992); 1211 Brickell Ave #1850, Miami, FL 33131 (☎305/358 1992).

MAP OUTLETS

IN THE UK

London *National Map Centre*, 22–24 Caxton St, SW1 (☎071/222 4945); *Stanfords*, 12–14 Long Acre, WC2 (☎071/836 1321); *The Travellers Bookshop*, 25 Cecil Court, WC2 (☎071/836 9132). **Edinburgh** *Thomas Nelson and Sons Ltd*, 51 York Place, EH1 3JD (☎031/557 3011).

Glasgow *John Smith and Sons*, 57–61 St Vincent St (☎041/221 7472).

Note: maps by **mail or phone order** are available from *Stanfords* (☎071/836 1321).

IN NORTH AMERICA

Chicago *Rand McNally*, 444 N Michigan Ave, IL 60611(☎312/321-1751).

Montréal *Ulysses Travel Bookshop*, 4176 St-Denis (☎514/289-0993).

New York *British Travel Bookshop*, 551 Fifth Ave, NY 10176 (☎1-800/448-3039 or 212/490-6688); *The Complete Traveler Bookstore*, 199 Madison Ave, NY 10016 (☎212/685-9007); *Rand McNally*, 150 E 52nd St, NY 10022 (☎212/758-7488); *Traveler's Bookstore*, 22 W 52nd St, NY 10019 (☎212/664-0995).

San Francisco *The Complete Traveler Bookstore*, 3207 Fillmore St, CA 92123 (☎415/923-1511); *Rand McNally*, 595 Market St, CA 94105 (☎415/777-3131).

Santa Barbara *Map Link, Inc*, 25 E Mason St, CA 93101 (☎805/965-4402).

Seattle *Elliot Bay Book Company*, 101 S Main St, WA 98104 (☎206/624-6600).

Toronto *Open Air Books and Maps*, 25 Toronto St, M5R 2C1 (☎416/363-0719).

Vancouver *World Wide Books and Maps*, 1247 Granville St (☎604/687-3320).

Washington DC *Rand McNally*, 1201 Connecticut Ave NW, Washington DC 20036 (☎202/223-6751).

Note: *Rand McNally* now has 24 stores across the US; call ☎1-800/333-0136 (ext 2111) for the address of your nearest store, or for **direct mail** maps.

IN AUSTRALIA AND NEW ZEALAND

Adelaide *The Map Shop*, 16a Peel St, Adelaide, SA 5000 (☎08/231 2033).

Brisbane *Hema*, 239 George St, Brisbane, QLD 4000 (☎07/221 4330).

Melbourne *Bowyangs*, 372 Little Bourke St, Melbourne, VIC 3000 (☎03/670 4383).

Perth *Perth Map Centre*, 891 Hay St, Perth, WA 6000 (☎09/322 5733).

Sydney *Travel Bookshop*, 20 Bridge St, Sydney, NSW 2000 (☎02/241 3554).

Verkehrsverlag) *Andalucía*, distributed in the UK by *Roger Lascelles* and by *Plaza y Janés* in Spain, as well as the less detailed *Firestone* and *Rand McNally*. The most comprehensive city **street plans** are the somewhat unwieldy *Plano Callejeros* by *Editorial Everest*, which cover all the major towns in Andalucía and have street indexes; they are obtainable from most *librerías*, but outside Sevilla the free maps handed out by most tourist offices serve just as well. For Sevilla, the best street plan is *La Guia Verde;* the fold-out *Falkplan Sevilla* is also good.

Serious **hikers** can get more detailed maps from the offices and stores listed in the city sections of the *Guide*. All the provincial capitals have a *CNIG* (National Geographical Information

Centre), which stocks the full range of topographical maps issued by two government agencies: the *IGN* (*Instituto Geográfico Nacional*) and the *SGE* (*Servicio Geográfico del Ejército*). The maps are available at scales of 1:200,000, 1:100,000, 1:50,000, and even occasionally 1:25,000. The various *SGE* series are considered to be more up-to-date and accurate by those in the know, although no Spanish maps are up to the standards that British or North American hikers are used to. The *CNIG* offices in Sevilla, Córdoba, Granada and Málaga are detailed in the respective "Listings" sections; the local Turismo will provide addresses for the others should you need them. If you are likely to be passing through Madrid, *La Tienda Verde*, c/Maudes 38

(☎91/535 38 10) has all the maps listed above and many more and is also willing to do business through the post.

A Catalunya-based company, *Editorial Alpina*, produces 1:40,000 or 1:25,000 map **booklets** for most of the mountain and foothill areas of interest, and these are also on sale in many bookshops. Other guidebooks dealing with hikes in specific areas (mostly in Spanish) are noted in the text where appropriate.

COSTS, MONEY AND BANKS

Although people still think of Spain as a budget destination, hotel prices have increased considerably over the last three or four years, and if you're spending a lot of your time in the cities of Andalucía you can expect to spend easily as much as you would at home, if not more. However, there are still few places in Europe where you'll get a better deal on the cost of simple meals and drink.

On average, if you're prepared to buy your own picnic lunch, stay in inexpensive *pensiones* and hotels, and stick to local restaurants and bars, you could get by on £15–20/US$23–30 a day. If you intend to upgrade your accommodation, experience the city nightlife and eat fancier meals then you'll need more like £40/$60 a day. On £50–60/$75–90 a day and upwards you'll only be limited by your energy reserves – though of course if you're planning to stay in four- and five-star hotels or any of Andalucía's magnificent *paradores*, this figure won't even cover your room.

Room prices vary considerably according to season. In the summer you'll find little below 1500ptas (£7/$11) single, 2000ptas (£9/$14) double, but 1800ptas single, 2500ptas double (£11.50/$18) might be a more realistic average.

Campsites start at around 400ptas (£2/$3.30) a night per person (more like 600ptas in some of the major resorts), plus a similar charge for a tent.

The cost of **eating** can vary wildly, but in most towns there'll be restaurants offering a basic three-course meal for somewhere between 750 and 1500ptas (£3.50–7/$5.50–11). As often as not, though, you'll end up wandering from one bar to the next sampling *tapas* without getting round to a real sit-down meal – this is certainly tastier though rarely any cheaper (see "Eating and Drinking"). Drink, and wine in particular, costs ridiculously little: £3/$5 will see you through a night's very substantial intake of the local vintage.

Most of the **journeys** you'll be making inside Andalucía will rarely be longer than 250km (the distance between Sevilla and Granada) and unless you plan to travel daily your **transport** budget should not prove a major expense. Sevilla to Granada, for example, on the cheapest *regional* train (see below) currently costs around 1600ptas one-way, 2400ptas for a return, or 2900ptas one-way by bus. Urban transport almost always operates on a flat fare of 150–250ptas (70p–£1.20/$1–1.80).

All of the above, inevitably, is affected by where you are and when. The larger cities such as Sevilla and Granada, as well as the tourist resorts, are invariably more expensive than remoter areas, and prices are hiked up, too, to take advantage of special events like *Semana Santa*. Despite official controls, you'd be lucky to find a room in Sevilla during Easter week or the April *feria*, which follows on its heels, at less than double the usual rate. As always, if you're travelling alone you'll end up spending much more than you would in a group of two or more – sharing rooms saves greatly. An *ISIC* **student card** is worth having – it'll get you free or reduced entry to many museums and sites as well as occasional other discounts – and a *FIYTO* youth card (available to anyone under 26) is almost as good.

One thing to look out for on prices generally is the addition of sales tax – **IVA** – which may come as an unexpected extra when you pay the bill for food or accommodation, especially in more expensive establishments.

MONEY AND THE EXCHANGE RATE

The Spanish currency is the **peseta**, indicated in this book as "ptas". **Coins** come in denominations of 1, 5, 10, 25, 50, 100, 200 and 500 pesetas; **notes** as 1000, 2000, 5000 and 10,000 pesetas. The only oddity is that in a shop when paying for something, you'll often be asked for a *duro* (5ptas) or *cinco duros* (25ptas), and even, in country districts, *quince* (fifteen) *duros* – which can test your mental arithmetic.

The exchange rate for the Spanish peseta is currently around 210 to the pound sterling, 140 to the US dollar. You can take in as much money as you want (in any form), although amounts over one million pesetas must be declared, and you can take out up to 500,000 pesetas, unless you can prove that you brought more than this with you in the first place. Not that this is likely to prove a major worry.

TRAVELLERS' CHEQUES AND CREDIT CARDS

Probably the safest and easiest way to carry your funds is in **travellers' cheques** – though watch out for occasional outrageous commissions; 500–600ptas per transaction isn't unusual. If you have an ordinary British bank account (or virtually any European one) you can use **Eurocheques** with a Eurocheque card in many banks and can write out cheques in pesetas in shops and hotels. Most Eurocheque cards, many *Visa*, *Mastercard* (*Access*) or British automatic bank cards, and US cards in the *Cirrus* or *Plus* systems, can also be used for **withdrawing cash from ATMs** in Spain: very useful at night, weekends or on the frequent public holidays when banks can sometimes close down for days at a time. Using cards also cuts out waiting in time-consuming queues –

something that happens often in the more popular destinations. Check with your bank to find out about these reciprocal arrangements – the system is highly sophisticated and all Spanish machines now give instructions in a variety of languages.

Leading **credit cards** are recognized too, and are useful for such extra expenses as car rental, as well as for cash advances at banks. *American Express*, and *Visa*, which has an arrangement with the *Banco Bilbão*, are the most useful; *Mastercard* is less widely accepted.

CHANGING MONEY

Spanish **banks** and *cajas de ahorro* (equivalent to a building society) have branches in all but the smallest towns, and most of them should be prepared to change travellers' cheques (albeit occasionally with reluctance for certain brands, and almost always with hefty commissions). The *Banco Central Hispano* and *Banco Bilbão Vizcaya* are two of the best and most widespread; all handle Eurocheques, change most brands of travellers' cheques, and give cash advances on credit cards; commissions at the *Banco Central Hispano* are generally the lowest. Elsewhere you may have to queue up at two or three windows, a twenty- to-thirty-minute process.

Banking hours are Mon–Fri 9am–2pm, Sat 9am–1pm (except from June to September when banks close on Saturday). Outside these times, it's usually possible to change cash at larger hotels (generally bad rates, low commission) or with travel agents, who may initially grumble but will eventually give a rate with the commission built in – useful for small amounts in a hurry.

In tourist areas you'll also find specialist *casas de cambio*, with more convenient hours (though the rates vary), and most branches of *El Corte Inglés*, a major department store found throughout Spain, have efficient exchange facilities open throughout store hours (until late evening) and offering competitive rates and generally a much lower commission than the banks (though they're worse for cash). *American Express* offices can also be useful, particularly in Málaga, Sevilla and Granada.

GETTING AROUND

Most of Andalucía is well covered by both bus and rail networks and for journeys between major towns there's often little to choose between them in cost or speed. On shorter or less obvious routes buses tend to be quicker and will also normally take you closer to your destination; some train stations are several miles from the town or village they serve and you've no guarantee of a connecting bus – these instances are noted throughout the *Guide*. Approximate journey times and frequencies can be found in the "Travel details" at the end of each chapter, and local peculiarities are also pointed out in the text of the *Guide*. Car rental may also be worth considering, with costs among the lowest in Europe.

BUSES

Unless you're travelling on a rail pass, **buses** will probably meet most of your transport needs; many smaller villages are accessible only by bus, almost always leaving from the capital of their province. Service varies in quality, but on the whole the buses are reliable and comfortable enough, with prices pretty standard at around 600ptas per 100km. The only real problem involved is that many towns still have no main bus station, and buses may leave from a variety of places (even if they're heading in the same direction, since some destinations are served by more than one company). Where a new terminal has been built, it's often on the outer fringes of

town. As far as possible, departure points are detailed in the text or the "Travel details".

One important point to remember is that all public transport, and the bus service especially, is drastically reduced on **Sundays and holidays** – it's best to not even consider travelling to out-of-the-way places on these days. The words to look out for on timetables are *diario* (daily), *laborables* (workdays, including Saturday), and *domingos y festivos* (Sundays and holidays).

TRAINS

RENFE, the Spanish rail company, operates a horrendously complicated variety of train services. An ordinary train, much the same speed and cost as the bus, will normally be described as an *expreso* or *rapido*. *Semi-directos* and *tranvías* (mostly short-haul trains) are somewhat slower. Intercity expresses, in ascending order of speed and luxury, are known as *Electrotren*, *Talgo* or *Pendular*. The last two categories, complete with muzak and air conditioning, are the most expensive, costing as much as 60–70 percent more than you'd pay for a standard second-class ticket; *Electrotren* tickets cost 40–50 percent more. The new high-speed train from Madrid to Sevilla, the *AVE*, costs just under double the basic fare.

In recent years many bona fide train services have been phased out in favour of buses operated jointly by *RENFE* and a private bus company. This is particularly the case when the connection is indirect or when the train departure is at an inconvenient time. On some routes the rail buses outnumber the conventional departures by a ratio of four to one. Prices are the same as on the trains, and these services usually leave from and arrive at the bus stations/stops of the towns concerned.

RAIL PASSES

InterRail (see p.9) and *Eurail* (p.5) passes, and **BIJ** tickets, are valid on all *RENFE* trains, but there's a supplement payable for travelling on any of the intercity expresses, and sometimes on *expresos* and *rapidos* too. The apparently random nature of these **surcharges** – which seem to depend on the individual train guard – can be a source of considerable irritation. It's better to know what you're letting yourself in for by reserving a seat in advance, something you'll be obliged to do on some trains. For 400ptas (including a 200ptas *suplemento fijo*), you'll get a large, computer-printed ticket which will satisfy even the most unreasonable of guards.

If using the trains extensively in Spain, but not outside the country, you might consider a **RENFE Tarjeta Turistica**, accepted on all trains – and currently the only pass available within Spain. Three days' second-class travel in any 30-day period costs 15,400ptas (£72/$110); 5 days' costs 24,200ptas (£112/$173); and 10 days' 37,400ptas (£173/$267). First-class passes are also available, for around 30 percent more. North Americans can also buy a **Spain Flexipass** before arrival, allowing 3 days' ($145) or 5 days' ($225) travel in a month, or 10 days' in two months ($345). See p.6 for details of where to buy the pass.

TICKETS AND FARES

RENFE also offers a whole range of **discount fares** on its *días azules* ("blue days" – which cover most of the year, with the exception of peak holiday weekends). If you're over 65, travelling with children under 12, in a group of eleven or more, or planning a return to be done on the same or another "blue day", you can get between twelve and fifty percent off.

Tickets can be bought at stations between sixty days and fifteen minutes before the train leaves, from the *venta anticipada* window, or in the final two hours from the *venta inmediata* window. Don't leave it to the last minute, however, as there are usually long lines. There may also be separate windows for *largo recorrido* (long-distance) trains and *regionales* or *cercanías* (locals). If you board the train without a ticket the conductor can charge you up to double the normal fare; if you don't have the cash, they'll call the police.

Most larger towns have a much more convenient *RENFE* office in the centre, which sells **tickets in advance** and has schedule pamphlets – many of these are listed in the *Guide* under the relevant towns; you can buy the *Guia RENFE* timetable here too (and at major stations) – useful if you plan to travel extensively by train. You can also buy tickets at travel agents which display the *RENFE* sign – they have a sophisticated computer system that can also make seat reservations; the cost is the same as at the station. For long journeys, a reserved seat is a good idea, as many trains are very crowded.

You can **change the departure date** of an electronically issued, reserved-seat, long-distance (*largo recorrido*) ticket without penalty up to fifteen minutes before your originally scheduled departure. An actual cancellation and a refund of the same sort of ticket entails losing 15 percent of the purchase price if it's done more than 24 hours in advance.

DRIVING AND VEHICLE RENTAL

Whilst getting around on public transport is easy enough, you'll obviously have a great deal more freedom if you have your **own car**. Major roads are generally good, and traffic, while a little hectic in Sevilla, is, generally well behaved – though Spain does have one of the highest incidences of traffic accidents in Europe. But you'll be spending more (even with a full car); petrol prices are only marginally lower than in Britain (almost double US prices), and in the larger cities you'll probably want to pay extra for the security of a hotel with parking, or be forced to stay on the outskirts.

Also, **vehicle crime** is rampant – never leave anything visible in the car, and in major cities such as Sevilla and Málaga empty it if the car is to be left on the street overnight. A useful tip for rental-car drivers is to get your vehicle as dirty as possible as soon as possible and leave it that way; that shiny new car spells "tourist" to the car thieves, who even know which models are used by the major rental companies. Needless to say, remove any visible stickers bearing the rental company's name or logo and check that all locks are fully functioning when you take delivery. That said, most of the people you'll meet in Andalucía will be shiningly honest, and although car crime is bad in cities such as Sevilla and Málaga, it is rarely accompanied by physical violence against the person.

Tow-cranes or *gruas* are now big business in most Spanish cities as the municipalities attempt to control **illegal parking**. In all cities check carefully where you park, for if you return to find your car gone it will usually be in the pound and the only way to retrieve it is by paying a stiff fine (currently around 15000ptas or £70/$105); no excuses will be accepted and without payment in cash you won't get your vehicle. When parking, look out for the tow-crane symbol on street signs and study the time regulations carefully; if in doubt ask a local. It is also a towable offence to park on a taxi-rank.

Most foreign **driver's licences** are honoured in Spain – including all EC, US and Canadian ones – but an International Driver's Licence (available in Britain from the *AA* or *RAC*) is an easy way to set your mind at rest. If you're bringing your own car, you must have a green card from your insurers, and a bail bond or extra coverage for legal costs is also worth having, since if you do have an accident it'll be your fault, as a foreigner, regardless of the circumstances. Without a bail bond both you and the car could be locked up pending investigation.

Away from main roads you yield to vehicles approaching from the right, but rules are not too strictly observed anywhere. **Speed limits** are posted – maximum on urban roads is 60kph, other roads 90kph, motorways 120kph – and (on the main highways at least) speed traps are common. If you're stopped for any violation, the Spanish police can and usually will levy a stiff on-the-spot fine before letting you go on your way, especially since as a foreigner you're unlikely to want, or be able, to appear in court.

VEHICLE RENTAL AND TAXIS

Renting a car lets you out of many of the hassles, and it's not too expensive. You'll find a choice of companies in any major town, with the biggest ones – *Hertz*, *Avis* and *Europcar* – represented at the airports as well as in town centres. You'll need to be 21 (and have been driving for at least a year), and you're looking at from 5000ptas per day for a small car (less by the week; special rates at the weekend). **Fly-Drive deals** with *Iberia* and other operators can be good value if you know in advance that you'll want to rent a car. The big companies all offer schemes, but you'll often get a better deal through someone who deals with local agents. *Holiday Autos* (see box) are one of the best, substantially undercutting the large companies. If you're going in high season, it's best to try and book well in advance.

Renting **motorcycles** (from 3000–4000ptas a day, cheaper by the week) is also possible. You have to be 14 to ride a machine under 75cc, 18 for one over 75cc and crash helmets are compulsory; there's an on-the-spot fine if you're caught not wearing one. Note that mopeds and motorcycles are often rented out with insurance that doesn't include theft – always check with the company first. You will generally be asked to produce a driving licence as a deposit.

CAR RENTAL AGENCIES
Britain
Avis ☎081/848 8733.
Budget ☎0800/181 181.
Europcar/InterRent ☎0345/222 525.
Hertz ☎081/679 1799.
Holiday Autos ☎071/491 1111.
North America
Avis ☎800/331-1212.
Budget ☎800/527-0700.
Europe by Car ☎800/223-1516.
Hertz ☎800/654-3131.
Holiday Autos ☎800/442-7737.
National Car Rental ☎800/CAR-RENT.

Taxis in city areas are incredibly good value and are certainly the safest way to travel late at night. Make full use of them, particularly in Sevilla, Málaga and Granada.

HITCHING

As in most other countries today, we do not recommend **hitching** in Spain as a safe method of getting around. If you are determined to hitch in Andalucía, be warned that away from the main roads things can become very tedious, often involving long, hot waits. Always carry water with you and some kind of hat or cap – lifts all too often dry up at some shadeless junction in the middle of nowhere. On the other hand, thumbing on back roads in areas such as Las Alpujarras can be surprisingly productive; the fewer cars there are, the more likely they are to stop.

CYCLING

Taking your own bike can be an inexpensive and flexible way of getting around, and of seeing a great deal of the country that would otherwise pass you by. Do remember, though, that Spain is one of the most mountainous countries in Europe and that Andalucía contains its two highest peaks. In searing high summer temperatures, attempting to scale the hills becomes an endurance test: seasoned cycle tourists advise starting out at dawn and covering the main part of the day's schedule by mid-morning, before the temperature peaks. That leaves the rest of the day for sightseeing, picnicking around riverbanks or dipping in the often pleasant village pools, before covering a few more kilometres in the cooler hours before sunset.

The Spanish are keen cycle fans – though their interest is mainly in racing, and active cycling is largely restricted to racing club members – which means that you'll be well received and find reasonable facilities. There are bike shops in the larger towns and parts can often be found at auto repair shops or garages – look for *Michelin* signs. Cars tend to hoot before they pass, which can be alarming at first but is useful once you're used to it. Cycle-touring guides to the better areas can be found in good bookshops – in Spanish, of course.

Getting your bike there should present few problems. Most airlines are happy to take them as ordinary baggage provided they come within your allowance (though it's sensible to check first; crowded charters may be less obliging). Deflate the tyres to avoid explosions in the unpressurized hold. Spanish trains are also reasonably accessible, though bikes can only go on a train with a guard's van (*furgón*) and must be registered – go to the *Equipajes* or *Paquexpres* desk at the station. If you are not travelling with the bike you can either send it as a package or buy an undated ticket and use the method above. Most *hostales* have somewhere safe for overnight storage, but take a strong lock or chain.

FLYING

Both *Iberia* and the smaller, slightly cheaper *Aviaco* operate an extensive network of **internal flights**. While these are quite reasonable by international standards, they still work out very pricey, and are only really worth considering if you're in an extraordinary hurry and need to cross the entire peninsula.

HEALTH MATTERS

No inoculations are required for Spain, though if you plan on continuing to North Africa, typhoid and polio boosters are highly recommended. The worst that's likely to happen to you is that you might fall victim to an upset stomach. To be safe, wash fruit and avoid *tapas* dishes that look like they were cooked last week.

PHARMACIES, DOCTORS AND HOSPITALS

If you fall ill, it's easiest to go to a **farmacia** for minor complaints – see the phone book in major towns; they are also found in almost every village. Pharmacists are highly trained, will give advice (often in English), and can dispense many drugs which would be available only on prescription in most other countries. They keep usual shop hours (ie 9am–1pm & 4–8pm), but some open late and at weekends, and a rota system keeps at least one open 24 hours. The rota is displayed in the window of every pharmacy, or check in one of the local newspapers under *Farmacias de guardia*.

In more serious cases you can get the address of an English-speaking doctor from the nearest relevant consulate, or with luck from a *farmacia*, the local police or Turismo. In emergencies dial ☎091 for the *Servicios de Urgencia*, or look up the *Cruz Roja Española* (Red Cross), which runs a national ambulance service. Treatment at hospitals for EC citizens in possession of form E111 (see "Insurance", p.15) is free; otherwise you'll be charged at private hospital rates, which can be as much as 14,000ptas per visit. Accordingly, it's essential to have comprehensive travel insurance.

EMERGENCY TELEPHONE NUMBER
Dial ☎091 in an emergency.

COMMUNICATIONS: POST, PHONES AND MEDIA

Post offices (*correos*) are generally found near the centre of towns and are open from 8am to noon and again from 5 to 7.30pm, though big branches in large cities may have considerably longer hours and do not usually close at midday. Except in the cities there's only one post office in each town, and queues can be long: stamps (*sellos*) are also sold at tobacconists (look for the brown and yellow *Tabac* sign).

You can have letters sent **poste restante** to any Spanish post office: they should be addressed (preferably with surname underlined and in capitals) to *Lista de Correos*, followed by the name of the town and province. To collect, take your passport and, if you're expecting mail, ask the clerk to check under all of your names – letters are often to be found filed under first or middle names.

American Express in Málaga, Sevilla and Granada will hold mail for at least a month for customers, and have windows for mail pickup.

Outbound mail is reasonably reliable, with letters or cards taking around five days to a week to the UK, a week to ten days to North America.

PHONES

Spanish public **phones** work well and have instructions in English. If you can't find one, many bars also have pay phones you can use. Cabins take 5-, 25-, or 100-peseta pieces or phone cards of 1000ptas or 2000ptas, which you can buy in tobacconists (*Tabac*): in old-style phones, rest the coins in the groove at the top and they'll drop when someone answers; in the newer cabins follow the instructions automatically displayed. Spanish provincial (and some overseas) dialling codes are listed in the cabins. The **ringing tone** is long, engaged is shorter and rapid; the standard Spanish response is *dígame* (speak to me).

For **international calls**, you can use almost any cabin (marked *teléfono internacional*) or go to a ***Telefónica*** office where you pay afterwards. International and domestic rates are slighly cheaper after 10pm, and after 2pm on Saturday and all day Sunday. If you're using a cabin to call abroad, you're best off putting at least 200ptas in

---

PHONING ABROAD FROM SPAIN

To Britain: dial ☎07, wait for the International tone, then 44 + area code minus first 0 + number.

To US: dial ☎07, wait for the International tone, then 1 + area code + number.

PHONING SPAIN FROM ABROAD

From Britain: dial ☎010 + 34 + area code + number.

From US: dial ☎011 + 34 + area code + number.

USEFUL TELEPHONE NUMBERS

Directory Enquiries ☎003

International Operator (Europe) ☎008
International Operator (rest of the world) ☎005

AREA CODES WITHIN ANDALUCÍA

Almeria ☎950	Gibraltar ☎350	Jaén ☎953
Cádiz ☎956	Granada ☎958	Málaga ☎952
Córdoba ☎957	Huelva ☎959	Sevilla ☎954

The code for Madrid is ☎91

to ensure a connection, and make sure you have a good stock of 100-peseta pieces.

If you want to make a **reverse-charge call** (*cobro revertido*), you'll have to go to a *Telefónica*, where you can expect queues at cheap rate times. Some hotels will arrange reverse-charge calls for you, but as with all phone calls from hotels you'll be stung for an outrageous surcharge.

MEDIA

British newspapers and the *International Herald Tribune* are on sale in most large cities and resorts. The main resort areas have their own English-language publications catering to the vast army of (largely elderly) expats. The glossy monthly *Lookout* is one of the best, often with travel articles and background on Spanish affairs. *Sur in English* is a publication by the Málaga daily, *Sur*, cashing in on the same market; its small ads section can be good for picking up odd jobs such as bar work and it carries details of local events and entertainment. The *Marbella Times* is another dismal expat newssheet.

Of the **Spanish papers** the best is *El País* – liberal-left, critically supportive of the current government, and the only one with much serious analysis or foreign news coverage. *El Independiente*, despite its name, is more securely tied to the *PSOE* (ruling Socialist Party) bandwagon. In the last few years, the appearance of *El Mundo* has provided competition for *El País*

as a serious centrist newspaper. The rest are mostly well to the right, notably the dated-format *ABC*, solidly monarchist with a hard moral line against divorce and abortion; the Catholic *Ya*,. *Diario 16* and Barcelona's *La Vanguardia* (available in Andalucía) are both centrist and solid. Best for keeping up with **sport** (including foreign soccer results) are the Madrid sports papers *As* and *Marca* and the Catalan *El Mundo Deportivo*, all widely available in Andalucía, which has a phenomenal number of supporters of the Madrid and Barcelona teams.

TV AND RADIO

You'll inadvertently catch more **TV** than you expect sitting in bars and restaurants, and on the whole it's a fairly entertaining mixture of grim game shows, foreign-language films and TV series dubbed into Spanish. Soaps are a particular speciality, either South American *telenovelas*, which take up most of the daytime programming, or well-travelled British and Australian exports. **Sports** fans are well catered for, with regular live coverage of football and basketball matches – in the football season, you can watch one or two live matches a week in most bars.

If you have a **radio** which picks up short-wave you can tune in to the *BBC World Service*, broadcasting in English for most of the day on frequencies between 12MHz (24m) and 4MHz (75m). You may also be able to receive *Voice of America* and American Forces' stations.

ACCOMMODATION

Simple, reasonably priced rooms are still very widely available in Spain, and in almost any town you'll be able to get a double for around 2000–3000ptas (£9–14/$14–21), a single for 1500–2500ptas (£7–11.50/$11–18). Only in major resorts and a handful of "tourist cities" (like Granada or Sevilla) need you pay more.

We've detailed where to find places to stay in most of the destinations listed in the *Guide*, and given a price range for each (see box on the following page), from the most basic rooms to luxury hotels. As a general rule, all you have to do is head for the cathedral or main square of any town, invariably surrounded by an old quarter full of accommodation possibilities. In Spain, unlike most countries, you don't seem to pay any more for a central location (this goes for bars and cafés, too), though you do tend to get a comparatively bad deal if you're travelling on your own as there are relatively few single rooms. Much of the time you'll have to negotiate a reduction on the price of a double.

It's always worth **bargaining** over room prices, in fact, since although they're officially regulated this doesn't necessarily mean much. In high season you're unlikely to have much luck (although many places do have rooms at different prices, and tend to offer the more expensive ones first) but at quiet times you may get quite a discount. If there are more than two of you, most places have rooms with three or four beds at not a great deal more than the double room price – a bargain, especially if you have children.

FONDAS, PENSIONES, HOSTALES AND HOTELES

The one thing all travellers need to master is the elaborate variety of types and places to stay. Least expensive of all are *fondas* (mostly identifiable by a square blue sign with a white **F** on it, and often positioned above a bar), closely followed by *casas de huéspedes* (**CH** on a similar sign), *pensiones* (**P**) and, less commonly, *hospedajes*. Distinctions between all of these are rather blurred, but in general you'll find food served at both *fondas* and *pensiones* (some of which may offer rooms only on a meals-inclusive basis). *Casas de huéspedes* – literally "guest houses" – were traditionally for longer stays; and to some extent, particularly in the older family seaside resorts, they still are.

Slightly more expensive but far more common are *hostales* (marked **Hs**) and *hostal-residencias* (**HsR**). These are categorized from one to three stars, but even so prices vary enormously according to location – in general the more remote, the less expensive. Most *hostales*

ACCOMMODATION PRICE SYMBOLS

All the establishments listed in this book have been price-graded according to the following scale. The prices quoted are for the **cheapest available double room in high season**; effectively this means that anything in the ① and most places in the ② range will be without private bath, though there's usually a washbasin in the room. In the ③ category and above you will probably be getting private facilities. Remember,

though, that many of the budget places will also have more expensive rooms including en suite facilities. Youth hostels are graded under ① as the price per person is less than half of the category's upper limit.

Note that in the more upmarket *hostales* and *pensiones*, and in anything calling itself a hotel, you'll pay a **tax** (*IVA*) of six percent on top of the room price.

① Under 2000ptas	③ 3000–4500ptas	⑤ 7500–12,500ptas
② 2000–3000ptas	④ 4500–7500ptas	⑥ Over 12,500ptas

offer good functional rooms, usually with private shower, and, for doubles at least, they can be excellent value. The *residencia* designation means that no meals other than perhaps breakfast are served.

Moving up the scale you finally reach **hoteles** (**H**), again star-graded by the authorities (from one to five). One-star hotels cost no more than three-star *hostales* – sometimes they're actually less expensive – but at three stars you pay a lot more, and at four or five you're in the luxury class with prices to match. Near the top end of this scale there are also state-run **paradores**: beautiful places (although there are modern exceptions), often converted from castles, monasteries and other minor Spanish monuments. If you can afford them, these are almost all wonderful (the best ones in Andalucía are detailed in the *Guide*), despite a reputation amongst Spanish critics for blasé service. Even if you can't afford to stay, the buildings are often worth a look in their own right, and usually have pleasantly classy bars.

Outside all of these categories you will sometimes see **camas** (beds) and **habitaciones** (rooms) advertised in private houses or above bars, often with the phrase "*camas y comidas*" (beds and meals). If you're travelling on a very tight budget these can be worth looking out for – particularly if you're offered one at a bus station and the owner is prepared to bargain with you.

If you have any **problems** with Spanish rooms – overcharging, most obviously – you can usually produce an immediate resolution by asking for the *libra de reclamaciones* (complaints book). By law all establishments must keep this and bring it out for regular inspection by the police. Nothing is ever written in them.

YOUTH HOSTELS AND REFUGES

Youth hostels (*Albergues Juveniles*) are rarely a very practical option. Only a few of them stay open all year – the rest operate just for the summer (or spring and summer) in temporary premises – and in towns they tend to be inconveniently located. The most useful are detailed in the *Guide*, or you can get a complete list (with opening times and phone numbers) from the *YHA* or Turismo. However, be warned that they tend to have curfews, are often block-reserved by school groups, and demand production of a *YHA* card (though this is generally available on the spot if you haven't already bought one from your national organization). At 800–1000ptas a person, too, you can quite easily pay more than you would sharing a cheap double room in a *fonda* or *casa de huéspedes*.

In isolated **mountain areas** the *Federacion Español de Montañismo*, c/Alberto Aguilar 3, Madrid 15 (☎91/445 13 82) or Apodaca 16, Madrid 4 (which has a branch in Granada) and three Catalunya-based clubs (the *FEEC*, the *CEC*, and the UEC) run a number of **refugios**: simple, cheap dormitory-huts for climbers and hikers, generally equipped only with bunks and a very basic kitchen.

CAMPING

There are some 120 authorized **campsites** in Andalucía, predominantly on the coast. They usually work out at about 400ptas (£2/$3.30) plus the same again for a tent (once again, discriminating against solo travellers) and a similar amount for each car or caravan, perhaps twice as much for a van. Only a few of the best sited or most popular sites are significantly more expensive. Again we've detailed the most useful in the text, but if you plan to camp extensively then pick up the free *Guía de Camping* published by the Junta de Andalucía, which marks and names virtually all of them; it's available from most Turismos, and in advance from Spanish National Tourist Offices abroad. A complete nationwide *Guía de Campings*, listing full prices, facilities and exact locations, is available from most Spanish bookshops.

Camping outside campsites is legal – but with certain restrictions. You're not allowed to camp "in urban areas, areas prohibited for military or touristic reasons, or within 1km of an official campsite". What this means in practice is that you can't camp on tourist beaches (though you can, discreetly, nearby) but with a little sensitivity you can set up a tent for a short period almost anywhere in the countryside. Whenever possible ask locally first.

If you're planning to spend a lot of your time camping, an **international camping carnet** is a good investment, available from home motoring organizations, or from one of the following: in Britain, the *Camping and Caravan Club*, 32 High St, London E15 2PF (☎081/503 0426); in the US, the *Family Campers and RVers*, 4804 Transit Rd, Building 2, Depew, NY 14043 (☎800/245-9755); and in Canada, *Family Campers and RVers*, 51 W 22nd St, Hamilton, Ontario LC9 4N5 (☎800/245-9755). The carnet is useful identification and covers you for third party insurance when camping.

EATING AND DRINKING

There are two ways to eat out in Spain: you can go to a *restaurante* or *comedor* (dining room) and have a full meal, or you can have a succession of *tapas* (small snacks) or *raciones* (larger ones) at one or more bars. At the bottom line a *comedor* – where you'll get a basic, filling, three-course meal with a drink, the *menú del día* – is nearly always the cheapest option, but they're often tricky to find, and rather drab. Bars tend to be a lot more interesting, allowing you to do the rounds and sample local (often house) specialities.

BREAKFAST, SNACKS AND SANDWICHES

For **breakfast** you're best off in a bar or café, though some *hostales* and *fondas* will serve the "Continental" basics. Traditionally in Andalucía, it's *churros con chocolate* – long tubular doughnuts (not for the weak of stomach) with thick drinking chocolate. But most places also serve *tostadas* (toasted rolls) with oil (*con aceite*) or butter (*con mantequilla*) – and jam (*y mermelada*), or egg dishes (*huevos fritos* are fried eggs). Cold *tortilla* also makes an excellent breakfast.

Coffee and pastries (*pastas*) or doughnuts are available at most cafés, too, though for a wider selection of cakes you should head for one of the many excellent *pastelerías* or *confiterías*. In larger towns, there will often be a *panadería* or *croissantería* serving quite an array of appetizing baked goods besides the obvious bread, croissants and pizza. For the different ways of ordering coffee see p.37.

Some bars specialize in **sandwiches** (*bocadillos*), and as they're usually outsize affairs in French bread, they'll do for breakfast or lunch. In a bar with *tapas* (see below), you can have most of what's on offer put in a sandwich, and you can often get them prepared (or buy the materials to do so) at grocery shops. Incidentally, a *sandwich* is a toasted cheese and ham sandwich, usually on sad processed bread.

TAPAS

Andalucía has more **tapas bars** than anywhere else in Spain and Sevilla seems to have one on every street corner. One of the advantages of eating in bars is that you are able to experiment. Many places have food laid out on the counter, so you can see what's available and order by pointing without necessarily knowing the names; others have blackboards (see the lists below). *Tapas* are small portions, three or four small chunks of fish or meat, or a dollop of salad, which traditionally used to be served up free with a drink. These days you have to pay for anything more than a few olives (although many country districts and not a few city bars retain this generous custom); however, in most of the city-centre places where you do get free food now, it will often be called a *pincho*, or morsel. A single *tapa*

helping rarely costs more than 200–400ptas unless you're somewhere very flashy or you choose one of the expensive kinds of *jamón* (cured ham). *Raciones* are simply bigger plates of the same, and can be enough in themselves for a light meal; *pinchos morunos* (small kebabs) are often also available. Make sure you make it clear whether you want a *racion* or just a *tapa*. The more people you're with, of course, the better; half a dozen *tapas* or *pinchos* and three *raciones* can make a varied and quite filling meal for three or four people.

Tascas, **bodegas**, **cervecerías** and **tabernas** are all types of bar where you'll find *tapas* and *raciones*. Most of them have different sets of prices depending on whether you stand at the bar to eat (the basic charge) or sit at tables (up to 50 percent more expensive – and even more if you sit out on a terrace). **Casinos** are essentially

TAPAS AND OTHER SNACKS

The most usual **fillings for bocadillos** are *lomo* (loin of pork), *tortilla* and *calamares* (all of which may be served hot), *jamón* (York or, much better, serrano), *chorizo*, *salchichón* (and various other regional sausages – like the small, spicy Catalan butifarras), *queso* (cheese), and *atún* (tuna – probably canned).
Standard *tapas* and *raciones* might include:

Aceitunas	Olives	*Hígado*	Liver
Albóndigas	Meatballs, usually in sauce	*Huevo cocido*	Hard-boiled egg
Anchoas	Anchovies	*Jamón serrano*	Dried ham
Berberechos	Cockles	*Jamón York*	Regular ham
Boquerones	Fresh anchovies	*Judias*	Beans
Calamares a la romana	Squid, deep fried in rings	*Mejillones*	Mussels (either steamed, or served with diced tomatoes and onion)
Calamares en su tinta	Squid in ink	*Morcilla*	Blood sausage, or black pudding
Callos	Tripe		
Caracoles	Snails, often served in a spicy/curry sauce	*Navajas*	Razor clams
		Pan con tomate	Bread, rubbed with tomato and oil
Carne en salsa	Meat in tomato sauce		
Champiñones	Mushrooms, usually fried in garlic	*Patatas alioli*	Potatoes in mayonnaise
		Patatas Bravas	Fried potato cubes topped with spicy sauce and mayonnaise
Chipirones	Whole baby squid		
Chorizo	Spicy sausage		
Cocido	Stew	*Pimientos*	Peppers
Croqueta	Fish or chicken croquette	*Pincho moruno*	Kebab
Empanadilla	Fish/meat pasty	*Pulpo*	Octopus
Ensaladilla	Russian salad (diced vegetables in mayonnaise)	*Riñones al Jerez*	Kidneys in sherry
		Salchichón	Cured sausage
Escalibada	Aubergine (eggplant) and pepper salad	*Sardinas*	Sardines
		Sepia	Cuttlefish
Gambas	Shrimps	*Tortilla Española*	Potato omelette
Habas con jamón	Broad beans with ham	*Tortilla Francesa*	Plain omelette

places to drink and relax – quieter and more comfortable than most of the bars – and serve as a kind of club, with locals paying a nominal monthly membership charge. Most small towns have one, and tourists and visitors are always welcome to use the facilities free of charge – worth doing since the membership rule means everybody drinks at reduced prices.

MEALS AND RESTAURANTS

Once again, there's a multitude of distinctions. You can sit down and have a full meal in a *comedor*, a *cafetería*, a *restaurante* or a *marisquería* – all in addition to the more food-oriented bars.

Comedores are the places to seek out if your main criteria are price and quantity. Sometimes you will see them attached to a bar (often in a room behind), or as the dining room of a *pensión* or *fonda*, but as often as not they're virtually unmarked and discovered only if you pass an open door. Since they're essentially workers' cafés they tend to serve more substantial meals at lunchtime than in the evenings (when they may be closed altogether). When you can find them – the tradition, with its family-run business and marginal wages, is on the way out – you'll probably pay around 600–1300ptas for a **menú del día** or **cubierto**, a complete meal of three courses, usually with wine.

Replacing *comedores* to some extent are **cafeterías**, which the local authorities now grade from one to three cups (the ratings, as with restaurants, seem to be based on facilities offered rather than the quality of the food). These can be good value, too, especially the self-service places, but their emphasis is more northern European and the light snack-meals served tend to be dull. Food here often comes in the form of a **plato combinado** – literally a combined plate – which will be something like egg and chips or *calamares* and salad (or occasionally a weird combination like steak and a piece of fish), often with bread and a drink included. This will generally cost in the region of 500–900ptas. *Cafeterías* often serve some kind of *menú del día* as well. You may prefer to get your *plato combinado* at a bar, which in small towns with no *comedores* may be the only way to eat inexpensively.

Moving up the scale there are **restaurantes** (designated by one to five forks – which relate to price, not quality) and **marisquerías**. The latter, serving exclusively fish and seafood, are the most

popular places to eat out in Andalucía. *Restaurantes* at the bottom of the scale are often not much different in price to *comedores*, and will also generally have *platos combinados* available. A fixed-price *cubierto*, *menú del día* or *menú de la casa* (all of which mean the same) is often better value, though: two or three courses plus wine and bread for 600–1500ptas. Move above two forks, however, or find yourself in one of the more fancy *marisquerías* (as opposed to a basic seafront fish-fry place), and prices can escalate rapidly. In addition, in all but the most rock-bottom establishments it is customary to leave a small tip: the amount is up to you, though ten percent of the bill is quite sufficient. Service is normally included in a *menú del día*. The other thing to take account of in medium and top-price restaurants is the addition of **IVA**, a six percent tax on your bill. It should say on the menu if you have to pay this. And to avoid receiving confused stares from waiters in restaurants, you should always ask for "*la carta*" when you want a menu; *menú* in Spanish refers only to a fixed price meal.

You'll find numerous recommendations, in all price ranges, in the main body of the *Guide*. Spaniards generally **eat very late** and the *Andaluzes* eat later still, so most places serve food from around 1 until 5pm (though no one considers lunch until at least 2pm) and from 8pm to midnight and later (but, again, no one eats before 10pm). Many restaurants close on Sunday evening. If you insist on dining at northern European hours you'll often be eating alone, with the waiters looking on. The best thing is to try and adjust to the southern style, and in between do what the locals do – keep going on *tapas*.

WHAT TO EAT

Our food glossary should give you an idea of what's on offer and help you cope when faced with a restaurant menu. Local specialities are highlighted in the *Guide*, too. It's possible to make a few generalizations about Spanish food. If you like **fish and seafood** you'll be in heaven in Andalucía as this forms the basis of a vast variety of *tapas* and is fresh and excellent everywhere. It's not cheap, unfortunately, so rarely forms part of the lowest priced *menús* (though you may get the most common fish – cod, often salted, and hake – or squid) but you really should make the most of what's on offer. Fish stews (*zarzuelas*) and rice-based *paellas* (which also contain meat, usually rabbit or chicken) are often memorable in seafood restaurants. *Paella* comes originally from Valencia and is still best there, but you'll find *arroz marinero*, the Andalucian version, just as good. The coastal strip's obsession with seafood is detailed in the main body of the *Guide*, although Cádiz and the nearby "sherry triangle" of Sanlúcar, El Puerto de Santa María and Jerez deserve top spot for sheer volume and variety.

Meat is most often grilled and served with a few fried potatoes and a couple of salad leaves, or cured or dried and served as a starter or in sandwiches. **Jamón serrano**, the Spanish version of Parma ham, is superb, and a passion in Andalucía. The best varieties, though, from Jabugo in the Sierra de Aracena and Trevélez in the Sierra Nevada, are extremely expensive. If you're tempted, they are best appreciated with a glass of *fino* (see p.36). More meat is eaten in inland provinces than on the coast and Córdoba's *rabo de toro* (stewed bull's tail) is renowned. The Sierra de Aracena is also a good place for cooked pork dishes, with *solomillo de cerdo* (pork sirloin) usually outstanding. In country areas bordering the slopes of the Sierra Morena and in the province of Jaén, game is very much a speciality – venison, partridge, hare and wild boar all feature on menus in these parts, as well as fresh trout.

Vegetables rarely amount to more than a few fries or boiled potatoes with the main dish (but you can often order a side dish à la carte). The provinces of Córdoba and Jaén are again the exceptions, and the latter's *pipirrana jaenera* (salad with green peppers and hard-boiled eggs) is only one of a number of hearty vegetable-based dishes to be found in these parts. It's more usual, though, to start your meal with a simple salad or with Andalucía's most famous dish, *gazpacho*; regional variations include Córdoba's *salmorejo* (with more body) and Málaga's *ajo blanco* (with almonds and grapes).

Dessert (*postre*) in Andalucía tends to be sweet and sticky – another hangover from the region's long period under Moorish dominion. The cheaper places you'll eat at will usually offer little variety: nearly always fresh fruit or *flan*, the Spanish *crème caramel*, often replaced on Andalucian menus by the similar *tocino de cielo* ("heavenly lard") or *natillas*. Keep an eye out in more upmarket places for delicious regional specialities such *peras al vino* (pears in wine and cinnamon) from Málaga, *piononos* (liqueur-soaked cakes) from Granada and *crema de Jerez* (sherry pudding) from Cádiz, as well as *brazo de*

gitano (rolled pastry filled with cream), an Andalucía-wide dessert.

Cheese (*queso*) is always eaten as a *tapa* rather than after a meal in Andalucía. The cheeses of the region don't usually travel beyond their immediate area of production which offers you the chance to make some interesting discoveries, especially in areas such as Las Alpujarras. The best-known brand region-wide is Córdoba province's sheep's milk cheese from Pedroches, although the hard, salty *Manchego* from neighbouring La Mancha is also widespread.

VEGETARIANS

Vegetarians have a fairly hard time of it in Andalucía and Spain generally: there's always something to eat, but you may get weary of eggs and omelettes (*tortilla francesa* is a plain omelette, *con champiñones* with mushrooms). In the big cities you'll find vegetarian restaurants and ethnic places which serve vegetable dishes and these are referred to in the *Guide*. Otherwise, superb fresh produce is always available in the markets and shops, and cheese, fruit and eggs are available everywhere. In restaurants you're faced with the extra problem that pieces of meat – especially ham, which the Spanish don't seem to regard as real meat – are often added to vegetable dishes to "spice them up".

The phrase to get to know is *Soy vegetariano. Hay algo sin carne?* (I'm a vegetarian. Is there anything without meat?); you may have to add *y sin mariscos* (and without seafood) *y sin jamón* (and without ham) to be really safe.

If you're a vegan, you're either going have to compromise or accept weight loss if you're away for any length of time. Some salads and vegetable dishes are strictly vegan, but they're few and far between. Fruit and nuts are widely available, though, nuts being sold by street vendors everywhere.

ALCOHOLIC DRINKS

Vino (wine), either *tinto* (red), *blanco* (white) or *rosado/clarete* (rosé), is the invariable accompaniment to every meal and is, as a rule, extremely inexpensive. Andalucía's winemaking genius lies elsewhere (see below) and so most table wines are imported from outside the region. The most common bottled variety is *Valdepeñas*, a good standard wine from the central plains of New Castile; *Rioja*, from the area round Logroño, is better but a lot more expensive. There are also

SPANISH FOOD AND DRINK TERMS

Andaluz cuisine reflects its history and climate: many of the spices used, like cumin, coriander and saffron, were introduced by the Moors, and the variety of cold dishes such as *gazpacho* are intended to cool you down as much as to nourish. The list below should cover most of your needs, and local specialities are mentioned in the body of the *Guide*. Other things you'll simply see people eating. *Quisiera uno así* (I'd like one like that) can be an amazingly useful phrase.

BASICS

Aceite	Oil	*Huevos*	Eggs	*Sal*	Salt
Ajo	Garlic	*Mantequilla*	Butter	*Verduras/ Legumbres*	Vegetables
Arroz	Rice	*Pan*	Bread		
Azúcar	Sugar	*Pimienta*	Pepper	*Vinagre*	Vinegar
Fruta	Fruit	*Queso*	Cheese		

IN THE RESTAURANT

Botella	Bottle	*Cuchara*	Spoon	*Mesa*	Table
La carta	menu	*Cuchillo*	Knife	*Tenedor*	Fork
Cenar	to have dinner	*La cuenta*	The bill	*Vaso*	Glass
Comer	to have lunch	*Desayunar*	to have breakfast		

SOUPS (*SOPAS*)

Ajo blanco	Creamy *gazpacho* with garlic and almonds	*Sopa de cocido*	Meat soup
		Sopa de gallina	Chicken soup
Caldillo	Clear fish soup	*Sopa de mariscos*	Seafood soup
Caldo verde or gallego	Thick cabbage-based broth	*Sopa de pasta (fideos)*	Noodle soup
Gazpacho	Cold tomato and cucumber soup	*Sopa de pescado*	Fish soup

SALAD (*ENSALADA*) AND STARTERS

Arroz a la Cubana	Rice with fried egg and homemade tomato sauce	*Pimientos rellenos*	Stuffed peppers
Ensalada (mixta/verde)	(Mixed/green) salad	*Verduras con patatas*	Boiled potatoes with greens

FISH (*PESCADOS*)

Anchoas	Anchovies (tinned)	*Merluza*	Hake
Anguila	Eel	*Mero*	Grouper
Angulas	Elvers (baby eel)	*Mojama*	Salted blue-fin tuna
Atún	Tuna	*Pez espada*	Swordfish
Bacalao	Cod (often salt)	*Rape*	Monkfish
Baila	Bass	*Rodaballo*	Turbot
Besugo	Sea bream	*Salmón*	Salmon
Bonito	Tuna	*Salmonete*	Mullet
Boquerones	Anchovies (fresh)	*Sardinas*	Sardines
Chanquetes	Minute goby/used also for whitebait	*Trucha*	Trout
		Urta	Member of the bream family
Lenguado	Sole		

SEAFOOD (*MARISCOS*)

Almejas	Clam	*Gambas*	Prawns/shrimps	*Pulpo*	Octopus
Calamares	Squid	*Langosta*	Lobster	*Puntillitas*	Baby squid
Cangrejo	Crab	*Langostinos*	Giant king prawns	*Sepia*	Cuttlefish
Centollo	Spider-crab	*Mejillones*	Mussels	*Vieiras*	Scallops
Chipirrones	Small squid	*Ostras*	Oysters	*Zamburiñas*	Baby clams
Cigalas	King prawns	*Percebes*	Goose-barnacles		
Conchas finas	Large scallops	*Pescadilla*	Small whiting		

MEAT (*CARNE*) AND POULTRY (*AVES*)

Albóndigas	Meatballs	*Jabalí*	Boar
Callos	Tripe	*Lengua*	Tongue
Cabra	Goat	*Lomo*	Loin (of pork)
Carne de vaca	Beef	*Mollejas*	Sweetbreads
Cerdo	Pork	*Morcilla*	Blood sausage
Chorizo	Spicy sausage	*Perdiz*	Partridge
Chuletas	Chops	*Pollo*	Chicken
Cochinillo	Suckling pig	*Pato*	Duck
Conejo	Rabbit	*Pavo*	Turkey
Codorniz	Quail	*Riñones*	Kidneys
Cordero	Lamb	*Salchicha*	Sausage
Escalopa	Escalope	*Salchichón*	Cured salami-type sausage
Faisán	Pheasant	*Sesos*	Brains
Hamburguesa	Hamburger	*Ternera*	Veal
Hígado	Liver		

SOME TERMS

al ajillo	in garlic	*alioli*	with mayonnaise
asado	roast	*cazuela, cocido*	stew
a la Navarra	stuffed with ham	*en salsa*	in (usually tomato) sauce
a la parilla/plancha	grilled	*frito*	fried
a la romana	fried in batter	*guisado*	casserole
al horno	baked	*rehogado*	baked

VEGETABLES (*LEGUMBRES*)

Aguacate	Avocado	*Judías verdes, rojas, negras*	Green, red, black beans
Alcachofas	Artichokes	*Lechuga*	Lettuce
Berenjenas	Aubergine/eggplant	*Nabos*	Turnips
Champiñones/Setas	Mushrooms	*Palmitos*	Palm hearts
Coliflor	Cauliflower	*Patatas (fritas)*	Potatoes (chips/french fries)
Cebollas	Onions		
Espárragos	Asparagus	*Pepino*	Cucumber
Espinacas	Spinach	*Pimientos*	Peppers
Garbanzos	Chickpeas	*Puerros*	Leeks
Guisantes	Peas	*Repollo*	Cabbage
Habas	Broad beans	*Tomate*	Tomato
Judías blancas	Haricot beans	*Zanahoria*	Carrot

RICE DISHES

Arroz Negre	"Black rice", cooked with the ink of the squid	Paella a la Catalana	Mixed meat and seafood sometimes distinguished from a seafood paella by being called Paella a Valencia
Arroz a banda	Rice with seafood, the rice served separately		
Arroz a la marinera	Paella: rice with seafood and saffron		

DESSERTS (POSTRES)

Alfajores	Honey and almond pastries	Natillas	Custard
Arroz con leche	Rice pudding	Pestiños	Anís or wine fritters
Flan	Crème caramel	Polvorones	Almond cakes
Helados	Ice cream	Tocino de Cielo	Andalucía's rich crème caramel
Melocotón en almíbar	Peaches in syrup	Yemas	Egg-yolk cakes
Miel	Honey	Yogur	Yogurt
Nata	Whipped cream (topping)		

FRUIT (FRUTAS)

Albaricoques	Apricots	Melón	Melon
Chirimoyas	Custard apples	Naranjas	Oranges
Cerezas	Cherries	Nectarinas	Nectarines
Ciruelas	Plums, prunes	Peras	Pears
Datiles	Dates	Piña	Pineapple
Fresas	Strawberries	Plátanos	Bananas
Higos	Figs	Pomelo	Grapefruit
Limón	Lemon	Sandía	Watermelon
Manzanas	Apples	Uvas	Grapes
Melocotónes	Peaches		

scores of other wines to try from regions such as Catalunya (Bach, Sangre de Toro and the champagne-like Cava), Galicia (Ribeiro, Fefiñanes and Albariño), Navarra (Gran Feudo) and even La Mancha (Estola) is now making a name for itself as a producer of quality wines. Andalucía's solitary table-wine area of any volume is the Condado de Huelva zone, which turns out reasonable dry whites. There are also many local wines made in the country districts, such as the costa wine of Las Alpujarras, and these are always worth trying.

Outside the larger towns and cities you'll rarely be given any choice apart from whatever dusty old bottles the proprietor can dig up. Restaurants with a healthy reputation, however, usually have well stocked cellars. Otherwise it's whatever comes out of the barrel, or the house bottled special (ask for caserío or de la casa). This can be great, it can be lousy, but at least it will be distinctively local. In a bar, a small glass of wine will generally cost around 50–100ptas; in a restaurant, if wine is not included in the menú, prices start at around 300–350ptas a bottle. If it is included you'll usually get a whole bottle for two people, a media botella (a third to a half of a litre) for one.

The classic Andalucian wine is **sherry** – Vino de Jerez – which is excellent, widely available and consumed with gusto by Andaluzes. Served chilled or at bodega temperature – a perfect drink to wash down tapas – like everything Spanish, it comes in a perplexing variety of forms. The main distinctions are between fino or Jerez seco (dry sherry), amontillado (medium), and oloroso or Jerez dulce (sweet), and these are the terms you should use to order. Similar – though not identical – are montilla and manzanilla. The first of these dry, sherry-like wines comes from the province of Córdoba, and the latter from Sanlúcar de Barrameda, part of the "sherry triangle" along with Jerez and El Puerto de Santa María. More information about these wines is given in the *Guide* under each production centre.

Cerveza, lager-type beer, is generally pretty good, though more expensive than wine. It comes in 300ml bottles (*botellines*) or, for about the same price, on tap – a *caña* of draught beer is a small glass, a *caña doble* larger. Many bartenders will assume you want a *doble*, so if you don't, say so. Simply asking for *un tubo* (roughly half a pint) avoids these complications. Andalucía's main brand is *Cruz Campo*, produced in Sevilla, which is also the best beer in Spain, easily surpassing the heavily marketed *San Miguel*. *Cruz Campo* is served on draught just about everywhere, although "foreign" brands such as the Castilian *Mahon* or the ubiquitously produced *Estrella Dorada* are making inroads. Granada's *Alhambra* beer is another one to look out for.

Equally refreshing, though often deceptively strong, is *sangría*, a wine-and-fruit punch which you'll come across at fiestas and in tourist bars; *tinto de verano* is basically the same red wine and soda or lemonade combination.

In mid-afternoon – or even at breakfast – many Spaniards take a copa of **liqueur** with their coffee (for that matter many Spaniards drink wine and beer at breakfast, too). One of the best is *anís* (like Pernod) – in its respectable guise – whose coarser brother appears at *romerías* and *fiestas* as the often lethally potent *aguardiente* firewater. *Coñac* (also "*brandy*" in Spanish) is excellent and Andalucía is the main centre of production for Spain's leading brands. Produced by the sherry *bodegas*, the distinctive flavour is imparted by its maturation in old sherry casks. Try *Magno*, *Soberano* or *Carlos III* ("*tercero*") to get an idea of the variety, and *Carlos I* ("primero") and *Gran Duque de Alba* for a measure of the quality. Most spirits are ordered by brand name, since there are generally less expensive Spanish equivalents for standard imports. *Larios Gin* from Málaga, for

instance, is about half the price of *Gordon's Gin*. Specify "*nacional*" to avoid getting an expensive foreign brand. The measures of spirits are generous and usually glugged from the bottle into the glass in front of you with deft skill. Mixed drinks are usually extremely strong – they all seem to be known as *Cuba Libre* or *Cubata*, though strictly speaking this is rum and Coke. Juice is *zumo*; orange, *naranja*; lemon, *limon*; tonic is *tónica*.

SOFT DRINKS AND HOT DRINKS

Soft drinks are much the same as anywhere in the world, but try in particular *granizado* (slush) or *horchata* (a milky drink made from tiger nuts or almonds) from one of the street stalls that spring up everywhere in summer. You can also get these drinks from *horchaterías* and from *heladerías* (ice cream – *helado* – parlours). Although you can drink the **water** almost everywhere it usually tastes better out of the bottle – inexpensive *agua mineral* comes either sparkling (*con gas*) or still (*sin gas*); *Lanjaron* from Las Alpujarras is Andalucía's main brand.

Coffee – served in cafés, *heladerías* and bars – is invariably espresso, slightly bitter and, unless you specify otherwise, served black (*café solo*). If you want it white ask for *café cortado* (a small cup with a drop of milk) or *café con leche* (made with lots of hot milk). For a large cup ask for a *doble* or *grande*. Coffee is also frequently mixed with brandy, cognac or whisky, all such concoctions being called *carajillo*.

Tea (*té*) is also available at most bars, although Spaniards usually drink it black. If you want milk it's safest to ask afterwards, since ordering *té con leche* might well get you a glass of milk with a teabag floating on top. *Manzanilla* (chamomile, not to be confused with the sherry of the same name) is a popular herbal infusion served in most bars.

DRINKS AND BEVERAGES

Hot drinks		Soft drinks		Alcohol	
Coffee	*Café*	Water	*Agua*	Beer	*Cerveza*
Espresso coffee	*Café solo*	Mineral water	*Agua mineral*	Champagne	*Champan*
White coffee	*Café con leche*	. . . (sparkling)	*. . .(con gas)*	Wine	*Vino*
Decaff	*Descafeinado*	. . (still)	*. . .(sin gas)*		
Tea	*Té*	Milk	*Leche*		
Drinking	*Chocolate*	Juice	*Zumo*		
chocolate		Tiger nut drink	*Horchata*		

OPENING HOURS AND PUBLIC HOLIDAYS

Almost everything in Spain – shops, museums, churches, tourist offices – closes for a siesta of at least two hours in the hottest part of the day. There's a lot of variation (and the siesta tends to be longer in the south) but basic summer working hours are 9.30am–1.30pm and 4.30–7.30pm. Certain shops (such as *El Corte Inglés*) do now stay open all day, and there is a move towards "normal" working hours. Nevertheless, you'll get far less aggravated if you accept that the early afternoon is best spent asleep, or in a bar, or both.

Museums, with very few exceptions, follow the rule above, with a break between 1 and 4 in the afternoon. Their summer schedules are listed in the *Guide*; watch out for Sundays (most open mornings only) and Mondays (most close all day). Admission charges vary, but there's usually a big reduction or free entrance if you show an *ISIC* or *FIYTO* card. Anywhere run by the *Patrimonio Nacional*, the national organization which preserves monuments, is free to EC citizens on Wednesday – you'll need your passport to prove your nationality. Most of the sites and museums administered by the Junta de Andalucía are free to EC citizens on production of an identity card (or passport for UK visitors).

Getting into churches can present more of a problem. The really important ones, including most cathedrals, operate in much the same way as museums and almost always have some entry charge to see their most valued treasures and paintings, or their cloisters. Other churches, though, are usually kept locked, opening only for worship in the early morning and/or the evening (between around 6–9pm). So you'll either have to try at these times, or find someone with a key. This is time-consuming but rarely difficult, since a *sacristán* or custodian almost always lives nearby and most people will know where to direct you. You're expected to give a small tip, or donation. For all churches "decorous" dress is required, ie no shorts, bare shoulders, etc.

NATIONAL HOLIDAYS

Official **national holidays** can disrupt your plans. There are fourteen national holidays, listed in the box, and scores of local festivals (different in every town and village, usually marking the local saint's day); any of them will mean that everything except bars (and *hostales*, etc.) locks its doors. In addition, **August** is Spain's own holiday month, when many of the larger cities are semi-deserted, and shops and restaurants, occasionally museums, may close. In contrast, it can prove nearly impossible to find a free bed in the more popular coastal and mountain resorts at these times; similarly, seats on planes, trains, and buses should be booked in advance.

SPANISH NATIONAL HOLIDAYS

January 1, New Year's Day
January 6, Epiphany
Good Friday
Easter Sunday
Easter Monday
May 1, May Day/Labour Day
Corpus Christi (early or mid-June)
June 24, Día de San Juan, the king's name-saint

July 25, Día de Santiago
August 15, Assumption of the Virgin
October 12, National Day
November 1, All Saints
December 6, Día de la Constitución
December 8, Immaculate Conception
Christmas Day

FIESTAS, THE BULLFIGHT AND FOOTBALL

It's hard to beat the experience of arriving in some small village, expecting no more than a bed for the night, to discover the streets decked out with flags and streamers, a band playing in the plaza and the entire population out celebrating the local fiesta. Everywhere in Andalucía, from the tiniest hamlet to the great cities, will take at least one day off a year to devote to partying. Usually it's the local saint's day, but there are celebrations, too, of harvests, of deliverance from the Moors, of safe return from the sea – any excuse will do.

Each festival is different. In Andalucía horses, *flamenco*, fireworks and the guitar are an essential part of any celebration, usually accompanied by the downing of oceans of *fino* – which is probably why the sherry companies seem to provide most of the bunting. And along with the music there is always dancing, usually *sevillanas*, in traditional flamenco costume, and an immense spirit of enjoyment. The main event of most fiestas is a parade, either behind a revered holy image, or a more celebratory affair with fancy costumes and *gigantones*, grotesque giant carnival figures which terrorize children.

Although these festivals take place throughout the year – and it is often the obscure and unexpected event which proves to be most fun – there are certain occasions which stand out. **Easter Week** (*Semana Santa*) and **Corpus Christi** (in early June) are celebrated all over the country with magnificent religious processions. Easter,

particularly, is worth trying to coincide with – head for Sevilla, Málaga, Granada or Córdoba, where huge *pasos*, floats of wildly theatrical religious scenes, are carried down the streets, accompanied by weirdly hooded penitents atoning the year's misdeeds.

Among the biggest and best known of Andalucía's other **popular festivals** are: the Cádiz *carnavales* (mid-February); Sevilla's enormous *April Feria* (a week at the end of the month); Jerez's *Feria del Caballo* (Horse Fair, April/May); the *Romería del Roció*, an extraordinary pilgrimage to El Roció near Huelva (arriving there on Whitsunday) and Málaga's boisterous and good-humoured *Feria* (mid-August).

The list is potentially endless, and although you'll find more major events listed in the accompanying box, we can't pretend that this is an exhaustive list. The Junta de Andalucía publishes an annual *Ferias y Fiestas de Andalucía* guide, available from local tourist offices. Outsiders are always welcome at these festivals, the one problem being that during any of the most popular you'll find it difficult and expensive to find a bed. If you're planning to coincide with a festival, try and book your accommodation well in advance.

THE BULLFIGHT

Bullfights are an integral part of many Spanish festivals. In Andalucía, especially, any village that can afford it will put on a *corrida* for an afternoon, while in big cities like Madrid or Sevilla, the main festivals are accompanied by a week-long (or more) season of prestige fights.

Los Toros or *La Lidia*, as Spaniards refer to bullfighting, are big business. Each year an estimated 24,000 bulls are killed before a live audience of over thirty million, and many more on television. It is said that 150,000 people are involved, in some way, in the industry, and the top performers, the *matadores*, are major earners, on a par with the country's biggest pop stars. There is some opposition to the activity from animal welfare groups but it is not widespread: if Spaniards tell you that bullfighting is controversial, they are likely to be referring to practices in the trade. In recent years, bullfighting critics (who you will find on the arts pages of the newspapers) have been expressing their perennial outrage at the widespread but illegal shaving

FIESTAS

Listed below are some of Andalucía's main fiestas, all worth trying to get to if you're going to be in the area around the time; more are listed under locations covered in the *Guide*. Note that saints' day festivals – indeed all Spanish celebrations – can vary in date, and are often observed over the weekend closest to the dates given.

JANUARY

1–2 *La Toma* – celebration of the entry of the *Reyes Católicos* into the city – at Granada.

5 *Cabalgata de los Reyes Magos* – Epiphany parade at Málaga.

6 *Romería de la Virgen del Mar* – pilgrimage procession from Almería.

17 *Romería del Ermita del Santo* – similar event at Gaudix.

FEBRUARY

1 *San Cecilio* – fiesta in Granada's traditionally gypsy quarter of Sacromonte.

Mid-month: *Carnaval* is an extravagant week-long event (leading up to Lent) in all the Andalucían cities. Cádiz, above all, celebrates with fancy dress, *flamenco*, spectacular parades and street-singers' competitions.

MARCH

5–15 El Puerto de Santa María (Cádiz) celebrates its *carnaval*.

Holy Week (*Semana Santa*), following Palm Sunday, has its most elaborate and dramatic celebrations in Andalucía. You'll find moving and memorable processions of floats and penitents at (in descending order of importance) Sevilla, Málaga, Granada and Córdoba, and to a lesser extent in smaller towns like Jerez, Arcos, Baeza and Úbeda. All culminate with the full drama of the Passion on **Good Friday**, with **Easter Day** itself more of a family occasion.

APRIL

Last week (2 weeks after Easter, but always in April) Week-long *Feria de Abril* at Sevilla: the largest fair in Spain, a little refined in the way of the city, but an extraordinary event nonetheless. A small April fair – featuring bull running – is held in Vejer.

Last Sunday Three-day *Romería de Nuestra Señora de Cabeza* at Andujar (Jaén) culminates in a huge procession to the sanctuary of the Virgin in the Sierra Morena.

MAY

1–2 *Romería de Nuesta Señora de la Estrella* at Navas de San Juan – Jaén province's most important pilgrimage.

3 "Moors and Christians" carnival at Pampaneira (Alpujarras).

First Week *Cruces de Mayo* (Festival of the Patios) in Córdoba – celebrates the Holy Cross and includes a competition for the prettiest patio and numerous events and concerts organized by the local city council.

Early May (usually the week after Sevilla's fair) Somewhat aristocratic Horse Fair at Jerez de la Frontera.

17 *San Isidro Romería* at Setenil (Cádiz).

Pentecost (7 weeks after Easter) *Romería del Rocío* – Spain's biggest: a million (often inebriated) pilgrims in horse-drawn carriages and processions converge from all over the south on El Rocío (Huelva).

Corpus Christi (variable – Thursday after Trinity). Bullfights and festivities at Granada, Sevilla, Ronda, Vejer and Zahara de la Sierra. At Sevilla, *Los Seises* (six choirboys) perform a dance before the altar of the Cathedral.

Third weekend *Romería de Santa Eulalia* at Almonaster La Real in the Sierra de Aracena – pilgrimage, fireworks, parades and *fandangos* in honour of the village's patron saint.

JUNE

Second week *Feria de San Bernabé* at Marbella – often spectacular since this is the richest town in Andalucía.

13–14 *San Antonio Fiesta* at Trevélez (Alpujarras)

---

of bulls' horns prior to the *corrida*. Bulls' horns are as sensitive as fingernails, and shaving just a few millimetres deters the animal from charging; they affect the creature's balance, too, reducing the danger for the *matador* still further.

Notwithstanding such abuse (and there is plenty more), *Los Toros* maintain their *aficionados* throughout the country. Indeed, in some areas they are on the rise, with the elaborate language of the *corrida* quite a cult among the

– includes mock battles between Moors and Christians.

23–24 *Candelas de San Juan* – bonfires and effigies at Vejer and elsewhere.

23-26 *Feria* of Alhaurin de la Torre (Málaga) – processions, giants and an important *flamenco* competition.

30 Conil (Cádiz) *feria.*

End June/early July International Festival of Music and Dance: major dance groups, chamber orchestras and *flamenco* artistes perform in Granada's Alhambra palace, Generalife and Carlos V palace.

JULY

Early July International Guitar Festival at Córdoba – brings together top international acts from classical, *flamenco*, and Latin American music.

9–14 Around feast of *San Francisco Solano* Montilla (Córdoba) celebrates its annual *feria.*

End of month Almería's *Virgen del Mar* summer fiesta – parades, horse-riding events and usually a handful of major jazz and rock concerts in its Plaza Vieja.

AUGUST

3 *Colombinas* at Huelva celebrate Columbus's voyages of discovery with a fiesta.

First week Berja (Almería) holds its annual fiesta in honour of the Virgin of Gádor.

5 Trevélez (Granada) observes a midnight *romería* to Mulhacén.

13–21 *Feria de Málaga* – one of Andalucía's most enjoyable fiestas for visitors, who are heartily welcomed by the ebullient *malagueños.*

15 Ascension of the Virgin – fair with *casetas* (dance tents) at Vejer and elsewhere.

15 *Noche del Vino* at Competa (Málaga) – a riotous wine festival with dancing, singing and endless drinking.

17–20 The first cycle of horse races along Sanlúcar de Barrameda's beach, with heavy official and unofficial betting; the second tournament takes place exactly a week later.

19–21 *Vendimia* – grape harvest fiesta at Montilla (Córdoba).

Third week The Algeciras fair and fiesta, another major event of the south.

Third weekend *Fiesta de San Mamés* at Aroche (Huelva) in the extremeties of the Sierra de Aracena – unpretentious and fun, everything a village fiesta should be.

22–25 *Feria de Grazalema* (Cádiz).

23–25 *Guadalquivir festival* at Sanlúcar de Barrameda – bullfights and an important *flamenco* competition.

25–30 *Fiestas Patronales* in honour of San Agustín at Mojacar (Almería).

SEPTEMBER

7 *Romería del Cristo de la Yedra* at Baeza (Jaén) – singing and dancing in the streets.

8 *Feria de Nuestra Señora de Regla* at Chipiona (Cádiz).

8 *Romería de Nuestra Señora de los Angeles* at Alajar (Huelva) – lots of colour and horse races to the peak sanctuary of Arias Montano.

8–9 *Fiesta de la Virgen de la Cabeza* at Almuñecar (Granada).

First/second week *Vendimia* (celebration of the vintage) at Jerez – starts with the blessing of the new grapes, after which everyone gets sozzled on the old.

6–13 Celebration of the *Virgen de la Luz* in Tarifa – street processions and horseback riding.

First two weeks Ronda bursts into life with a *feria*, *flamenco* contests and the *Corrida Goyesca*, bullfights in eighteenth-century dress.

24–25 *Dia del Señor* (Lord's Day) at Orgiva (Granada) – celebrated with impressive fireworks and processions.

28–4 October Ubeda's (Jaén) *Fiesta de San Miguel* with a fair and *casetas.*

OCTOBER

1 *San Miguel* fiesta in Granada's Albaicín quarter and dozens of other towns, even at Torremolinos.

6–12 Fuengirola's *Feria del Rosario* – horseriding events and *flamenco.*

15–23 *Feria de San Lucas*; Jaén's major fiesta, dating back to the fifteenth century.

---

young, as the days of Franco's patronage of bullfighting are forgotten, and TV stations pay big money for major events. To *aficionados* (a word that implies more knowledge and appreciation than "fan"), the bulls are a culture and a ritual – one in which the emphasis is on the way man and bull "perform" together – in which the art is at issue rather than the cruelty. If pressed on the issue of the slaughter of an animal, they generally fail to understand. Fighting bulls are, they will tell you, bred for the industry; they live a reasonable life before they are killed; and, if the bullfight went, so too would the bulls.

Whether you attend a *corrida*, obviously, is down to your own feelings and ethics. If you spend any time at all in Spain during the season (which runs from March to October), you will encounter *Los Toros*, at least on a bar TV, and that will as likely as not make up your mind. If you decide to go, try to see the biggest and most prestigious that is on, in a major city, where star performers are likely to despatch the bulls with "art" and a successful, "clean" kill. This happens much less frequently than many *aficionados* would have you believe and the beginners' fights, or *novilladas*, are often little more than a gruesome repetition of botched jobs. And even in the senior *corridas*, there are few sights worse than a *matador* making a prolonged and messy kill, while the audience whistles. Established and popular **matadores** include Enrique Ponce, Cesar Rincon, Victor Mendes, Joselito, Litri, Paco Ojeda, Ortega Cano, José María Manzanares and Finito de Córdoba. Two new stars in the headlines are El Cordobes – a young pretender of spectacular technique who claims to be his legendary namesake's illegitimate son – and Cristina Sanchez, the first woman to make it into the top flight for many decades. The most exciting and skilful performances of all are by mounted *matadores*, or *rejoneadores*; this is the oldest form of *corrida*, developed at Ronda in the seventeenth century. However, they still dismount to despatch the bull.

THE CORRIDA

The *corrida* begins with a **procession**, to the accompaniment of a *paso doble* by the band. Leading the procession are two *algauziles* or "constables", on horseback and in traditional costume, followed by the three *matadores*, who will each fight two bulls, and their *cuadrillas*, their personal "team" each comprising two mounted *picadores* and three *banderilleros*. At the back are the mule teams who will drag off the dead bulls.

Once the ring is empty, the *algauzil* opens the *toril* (the bulls' enclosure) and the first bull appears – a moment of great physical beauty – to be "tested" by the *matador* or his *banderilleros* using pink and gold capes. These preliminaries conducted (and they can be short, if the bull is ferocious), the **suerte de picar** ensues, in which the *picadores* ride out and take up position at

opposite sides of the ring, while the bull is distracted by other *toreros*. Once they are in place, the bull is made to charge one of the horses; the *picador* drives his short-pointed lance into the bull's neck, while it tries to toss his padded, blindfolded horse, thus tiring the bull's powerful neck and back muscles. This is repeated up to three times, until the horn sounds for the *picadores* to leave. For most neutral spectators, it is the least acceptable and most squalid stage of the *corrida*, and it is clearly not a pleasant experience for the horses, their ears stuffed with rags to shut out the noise of the bull and spectators, and their vocal cords cut to prevent any terrified cries from alarming the crowd.

The next stage, the **suerte de banderillas**, involves the placing of three sets of *banderillas* (coloured sticks with barbed ends) into the bull's shoulders. Each of the three *banderilleros* delivers these in turn, attracting the bull's attention with the movement of his own body rather than a cape, and placing the *banderillas* whilst both he and the bull are running towards each other. He then runs to safety out of the bull's vision, sometimes with the assistance of his colleagues.

Once the *banderillas* have been placed, the **suerte de matar** begins, and the *matador* enters the ring alone, having exchanged his pink and gold cape for the red one. He (or she) salutes the president and then dedicates the bull either to an individual, to whom he gives his hat, or to the audience, by placing his hat in the centre of the ring. It is in this part of the *corrida* that judgements are made and the performance is focused, as the *matador* displays his skills on the (by now exhausted) bull. He uses the movements of the cape to attract the bull, while his body remains still. If he does well, the band will start to play, while the crowd *olé* each pass. This stage lasts around ten minutes and ends with the kill. The matador attempts to get the bull into a position where he can drive a sword between its shoul-

---

If you want to know more about the international **opposition to bullfighting**, contact the World Society for the Protection of Animals, 2 Langley Lane, London SW8 1TJ ☎071/793 0540; PO Box 190, Boston, MA 02130 ☎617/522-7000; PO Box 15, Toronto, Ontario, M5J 2HT ☎416/369-0044. Spain's Anti-Bullfight Committee (*Comité Antitaurino*) is at Apartado 3098, 50080 Zaragoza.

ders and through to the heart for a coup de grâce. In practice, they rarely succeed in this, instead taking a second sword, crossed at the end, to cut the bull's spinal cord; this causes instant death.

If the audience are impressed by the *matador*'s performance, they will wave their handkerchiefs and shout for an award to be made by the president. He can award one or both ears, and a tail – the better the display, the more pieces he gets – while if the *matador* has excelled himself, he will be carried out of the ring by the crowd, through the *puerta grande*, the main door, which is normally kept locked. The bull, too, may be applauded for its performance, as it is dragged out by the mule team.

Tickets for *corridas* are 2000ptas and up – much more for the prime seats and prestigious fights. The cheapest seats are *gradas*, the highest rows at the back, from where you can see everything that happens without too much of the detail; the front rows are known as the *barreras*. Seats are also divided into *sol* (sun), *sombra* (shade), and *sol y sombra* (shaded after a while), though these distinctions have become less relevant as more bullfights start later in the day, at 6pm or 7pm, rather than the traditional 5pm. The *sombra* seats are more expensive – not so much for the spectators' personal comfort but because most of the action takes place in the shade.

On the way in, you can rent **cushions** – two hours sitting on concrete is not much fun. It's also something to toss in the ring when there's an especially awful performance – as frequently happens. Beer and soft drinks are sold inside.

FOOTBALL

To foreigners, the bullfight is easily the most celebrated of Spain's spectacles. In terms of popular support in modern Spain, however, it ranks far below *futbol* (soccer). If you want the excitement of a genuinely Spanish afternoon out, a football stadium will usually have more passion than anything you'll find in the Plaza de Toros.

For many years, the country's two dominant teams have been **Real Madrid** and **F.C. Barcelona**, and these have shared the League and Cup honours more often than is healthy. At the time of writing, Barcelona are in the ascendant, having won the league in 1992 and 1993 – each time after Real, in the lead, lost their last game of the season against their bogey-team, Tenerife. Recently, however, both teams have faced a bit more oppositon than usual from clubs like Atletico Bilbao, Sporting Gijón, Atletico Madrid, Real Sociedad (the Basque team from San Sebastián), Real Zaragoza, and, a new force, Deportivo La Coruña (from Galicia).

Sevilla, where Maradona finished his European career, are the main team in Andalucía, though currently in the doldrums. The only other Andalucian sides with any pretensions are **Real Betis**, Sevilla's other club, and **Cádiz**, but they are both currently in an even deeper trough than Sevilla.

With the exception of a few important games – such as when either of the big two plays Sevilla – **tickets** are pretty easy to get; they start at around 1200ptas for First Division games. Trouble is very rare: English fans, in particular, will be amazed at the easygoing family atmosphere and mixed sex crowds. And August is a surprisingly good time to catch games since there's a glut of warm-up matches for the new season, often involving top foreign clubs.

If you don't go to a game, the atmosphere can be pretty good watching on TV in a local bar, especially in a city whose team is playing away. Many bars advertise the matches they screen, which, if they have Canal 5, can include Sunday afternoon English league and cup games.

MUSIC

Andalucía is the home of much Spanish traditional music and you should try to catch all that is going on. At the numerous fiestas and *romerías* (see p.40-41) you can see many of Andalucía's best performers; other likely venues are listed in the body of the *Guide*.

MUSIC

Traditional ***flamenco*** (see *Contexts* p.401), Spain's most famous sound, is best witnessed in its native Andalucía, and particularly at one of the major fiestas. There are also some specifically *flamenco* festivals in the summer, most notably at Córdoba, Jerez and around Granada. Clubs and bars which feature *flamenco* performers tend on the whole to be expensive and tourist-oriented, while the traditional *peñas* (clubs) are often members-only affairs. However, it is possible to find accessible places which cater for *aficionados*, and in Andalucía itself almost any *flamenco* guitarist you come across is likely to be extremely good. Just watch the cost of the drinks. In recent years, there has been an exciting development in the shape of new *flamenco* bands, some of whom have attempted to introduce jazz, rock and African elements into their music. Names to watch out for are Ketama and Pata Negra, two bands featured on the recommended Hannibal Records compilation *Los Jovenes Flamencos*.

If you're anywhere in Andalucía between about December 18 and January 3, look out for performances in local churches of **villancicos**. These are Christmas carols in local style – they can be *flamenco*, waltz or polyphonic – and are sung by fairly large *coral/rondalla* groups of instrumentalists and vocalists. When they're good they're an extremely beautiful spectacle.

Rock music in Spain may tend to follow British and American trends, but the scene is considerably livelier – and less slavishly derivative – than in almost any other west European country, at its best drawing from a broad range of influences in which traditional Spanish and Latin American rhythms play a major part. There are some excellent home-grown bands and regular gigs in most of the big cities.

Thanks to Spain's relatively large expatriate populations, there are also good places to hear **Latin American and African** music – again, keep your eye out for posters and check the club and dance-hall listings in the local papers. **Jazz** also has a considerable following, and most of Andalucía's venues are located in the cities although they tend to close down in August. Worth checking out, too, is the International **Festival of Guitar** in Córdoba (early July), where most of the great classical guitarists put in an appearance along with exponents of Latin American and *flamenco* styles. Among its more adventurous practitioners, *flamenco* (to the outrage of purists) touches on modern jazz – look out especially for the brilliant Paco de Lucía.

TROUBLE, THE POLICE AND SEXUAL HARASSMENT

While you're unlikely to encounter any trouble during the course of a normal visit, it's worth remembering that the Spanish police, polite enough in the usual course of events, can be extremely unpleasant if you get on the wrong side of them.

AVOIDING TROUBLE

Almost all the problems tourists encounter are to do with **petty crime** – pickpocketing and bag-snatching – rather than more serious physical confrontations, so it's as well to be on your guard and know where your possessions are at all times. Sensible **precautions** include: carrying bags slung across your neck, not over your shoulder; not carrying anything in zipped pockets facing the street; having photocopies of your passport and leaving passport and tickets in the hotel safe; and noting down travellers' cheque and credit card numbers. There are also several ploys to be aware of and situations to avoid as you do the rounds of the city.

• **Thieves** often work in pairs, so watch out for people standing unusually close if you're studying postcards or papers at stalls; keep an eye on your wallet if it appears you're being distracted. Ploys (by some very sophisticated operators) include: the "helpful" person pointing out birdshit (shaving cream or something similar) on your jacket while someone relieves you of your money; the card or paper you're invited to read on the street to distract your attention; the move by someone in a café for your drink with one hand (the other hand's in your bag as you react to save your drink).

• If you have a **car** don't leave anything in view when you park it; take the radio with you. When parked overnight in large towns and cities you'd be wise to remove everything. Vehicles are rarely stolen, but luggage and valuables left in cars do make a tempting target and rental cars are easy to spot; see also p.23.

• Looking for **hotel rooms**, don't leave any bags unattended anywhere. This applies especially to blocks where the hotel or *hostal* is on the higher floors and you're tempted to leave baggage in the hallway or ground floor lobby. And check, if you leave your room windows open while you're out, that there's no possibility of "fishing-rod" crime.

This is a new phenomenon where thieves go fishing through even barred windows to "hook" any valuables in sight.

WHAT TO DO IF YOU'RE ROBBED

If you're robbed, you need to **go to the police** to report it, not least because your insurance company will require a police report. Don't expect a great deal of concern if your loss is relatively small – and expect the process of completing forms and formalities to take ages.

In the unlikely event that you're **mugged**, or otherwise threatened, never resist; hand over what's wanted and run straight to the police, who will be more sympathetic on these occasions. There's also a police office – *Centro Atención Policial* – specifically designed to help tourists, with English-speaking officers, legal and medical advice, and practical help if you've lost your money and credit cards.

THE POLICE

There are three basic types of **police**: the *Guardia Civil*, the *Policía Municipal* and the *Policía Nacional*, all of them armed.

The *__Guardia Civil__*, in green uniforms, are the most officious and the ones to avoid. Though their role has been cut back since they operated as Franco's right hand, they remain a reactionary force (it was a *Guardia Civil* colonel, Tejero, who held the Cortes hostage in the February 1981 failed coup).

If you do need the police – and above all if you're reporting a serious crime such as rape – you should always go to the more sympathetic *__Policía Municipal__*, who wear blue-and-white uniforms with red trim. In the countryside there may be only the *Guardia Civil*, though they're usually helpful, they are inclined to resent the suggestion that any crime exists on their turf and you may end up feeling as if you are the one who stands accused.

The brown-uniformed *__Policía Nacional__* are mainly seen in cities, armed with submachine guns and guarding key installations such as embassies, stations, post offices and their own barracks. They are also the force used to control crowds and demonstrations.

OFFENCES

There are a few offences you may possibly commit unwittingly that it's as well to be aware of.

• In theory you're supposed to carry some kind of **identification** at all times, and the police can stop you in the streets and demand it. In practice they're rarely bothered if you're clearly a foreigner.

• **Nude bathing** or **unauthorized camping** are activities more likely to bring you into contact with officialdom, though a warning to cover up or move on is a more probable result than any real confrontation. Topless tanning is now commonplace at all the trendier resorts, but in country areas, where attitudes are still very traditional, you should take care not to upset local sensibilities.

• If you have an **accident** while driving, try not to make a statement to anyone who doesn't speak English. The SNTO in your home country can provide a list of the most important rules on the road in Spain; and see p.24.

• Spanish **drug laws** are in a somewhat bizarre state at present. After the socialists came to power in 1983, cannabis use (possession of up to 8gm of what the Spanish call *chocolate*) was decriminalized. Subsequent pressures, and an influx of harder drugs in recent years, have changed that policy and – in theory at least – any drug use is now forbidden. You'll see signs in some bars saying "no porros" (no joints), which you should heed. However, in practice the police are not too worried about personal use. Larger quantities (and any other drugs) are a very different matter.

Should you be **arrested** on any charge you have the right to contact your **consulate** (see p.48), and although they're notoriously reluctant to get involved they are required to assist you to some degree if you have your passport stolen or lose all your money. If you've been detained for a drugs offence, don't expect any sympathy or help from your consulate.

SEXUAL HARASSMENT

Spain's macho image has faded dramatically in the post-Franco years and these days there are relatively few parts of the country where foreign women, travelling alone, are likely to feel threatened, intimidated, or noteworthy.

Inevitably, the **big cities** – like any others in Europe – have their no-go areas, where street crime and especially drug-related hassles are on the rise, but there is little of the pestering and propositions that you have to contend with in, say, the larger French or Italian cities. The outdoor culture of *terrazas* (terrace bars) and the tendency of Spaniards to move around in large, mixed crowds, filling central bars, clubs and streets late into the night, help to make you feel less exposed. If you are in any doubt, there are always taxis – plentiful and reasonably priced.

The major **resorts** of the *costas* have their own artificial holiday culture. The Spaniards who hang around in discos here or at fiesta fairgrounds pose no greater or lesser threat than similar operators at home. The language barrier simply makes it harder to know who to trust. "Dejame en paz" (leave me in peace) is a fairly standard rebuff.

Predictably, it is in **more isolated regions**, separated by less than a generation from desperate poverty (or still starkly poor), that most serious problems can occur. Since the last edition of this book, we have had two reports of women being followed and attacked in remote parts of Andalucía. You do need to know a bit about the land you're travelling around.

In some areas you can walk for hours without coming across an inhabited farm or house, and you still come upon shepherds working for nothing but the wine they take to their pastures. It's rare that this poses a threat – help and hospitality are much more the norm – but you are certainly more vulnerable. That said, **hiking** is becoming more popular in Spain as a whole and in Andalucía many women happily tramp the footpaths of the Sierra Nevada. In the south, especially, though, it is worth finding rooms in the larger villlages, or, if you camp out, asking permission to do so on private land, rather than striking out alone.

WORK

Unless you've some particular skill and have applied for a job advertised in your home country, such as au pair work, the only real chance of long-term work in Spain is in language schools. However, there is much less work about than in the boom years of the early 1980s – schools are beginning to close down rather than open – and you'll need to persevere if you're to come up with a rewarding position. You'll need a TEFL (Teaching English as a Foreign Language) or ESL (English as a Second Language) certificate to give yourself any kind of chance.

TEACHING AND OFFICE WORK

Finding a teaching job is mainly a question of pacing the streets, stopping in at every language school around and asking about vacancies. For the addresses of schools look in the Yellow Pages under *Idiomas* or *Escuelas Idiomas*.

If you intend to stay in Spain longer than three months, you'll also need a visa (see p.14). A word of warning: police are cracking down on people without visas and may ask for passport/residence papers on the spot, especially out of tourist season.

You could also try advertising private lessons (better paid at 1500–2500ptas an hour, but harder to make a living at) on the *Philologia* noticeboards of university faculties.

Another possibility, so long as you speak good Spanish, is **translation work**, most of which will be business correspondence – look in the Yellow Pages under *Traductores*. If you intend doing agency work, you'll usually need access to a fax and a PC.

TEMPORARY WORK

If you're looking for **temporary work** the best chances are in the **bars and restaurants** of the big resorts. This may help you have a good time but it's unlikely to bring in very much money; pay (often from British bar owners) will reflect your lack of official status or work permit. If you turn up in spring and are willing to stay through the season you might get a better deal – also true if you're offering some special skill like windsurfing (there are "schools" sprouting up all along the coast). Quite often there are jobs at **yacht marinas**, too, scrubbing down and repainting the boats of the rich; just turn up and ask around, especially from March until June.

DIRECTORY

ADDRESSES are written as: c/Picasso 2, 4° *izda.* – which means Picasso street (calle) no. 2, 4th floor, left- (*izquierda*) hand flat or office; *dcha.* (*derecha*) is right; *cto.* (*centro*) centre; s/n (*sin número*) means the building has no number. Other confusions in Spanish addresses result from the gradual removal of Franco and other fascist heroes from the main avenidas and plazas. Avenidas del Generalísimo are on the way out all over the country (often changing to "Libertad", "España", or frequently "Andalucía"); so too are José Antonios, General Molas, Falanges and Caudillos. Note that a lot of maps – including the official ones – haven't yet caught up.

AIRPORT TAX You can happily spend your last pesetas – there's no departure tax.

CONSULATES Practically every nation has an embassy in Madrid: there are also British consulates at Málaga (c/Duquesa de Parcent 8; ☎952/217571), Sevilla (Plaza Nueva 8; ☎954/228875), and of course Gibraltar (65 Irish Town; ☎350/78305). US consulates are based in Fuengirola (c/Martínez Catena 6, Apt 5B, Complejo Sol Playa; ☎952/479891) and Sevilla (Paseo de las Delicias 7; ☎954/231885).

ELECTRICITY Current in most of Spain is 220 volts AC (just occasionally it's still 110V): most European appliances should work as long as you have an adaptor for European-style two-pin plugs. North Americans will need this plus a transformer.

FEMINISM The Spanish women's movement, despite having to deal with incredibly basic issues (like trying to get contraception available on social security), is radical, vibrant, and growing fast. Few groups, however, have permanent offices, and if you want to make contact it's best to do so through the network of feminist bookshops in the major cities. Two of the more established in Andalucía are: *Librería Feminista*, c/ Zaragoza 36, Sevilla, and *Librería Mujer*, c/ Carnicería 1, Granada.

FISHING Fortnightly permits are easily and cheaply obtained from any *ICONA* office – there's one in every big town (addresses from the local Turismo). For information on the whereabouts of the best trout streams and other wrinkles contact the Spanish Fishing Federation, Navas de Tolosa 3, 28013 Madrid (☎91/225 59 85).

GAY LIFE The largest gay communities in Andalucía are in Cádiz and Torremolinos and attitudes in both places, as well as the major cities and resorts, are fairly relaxed. Sevilla and Cádiz in particular have large permanent gay communities and a thriving scene. The age of consent is 18. Two guides to the Spanish scene worth getting hold of are *Spartacus España*, available in the UK and US, and *Guía Gay Visado*, a regularly updated Spanish guide to gay and lesbian activities and entertainment across Spain.

KIDS/BABIES don't pose great travel problems. *Hostales*, *pensiones* and *restaurantes* generally welcome them and offer rooms with three or four beds; *RENFE* allows children under three to travel free on trains, with half price for those under seven; and some cities and resorts – the Costa del Sol is particularly good – have long lists or special pamphlets on kids' attractions. As far as babies go, food seems to work out quite well (*hostales* often prepare food specially – or will let you use the kitchen to do so), though you might want to bring powdered milk – babies, like most Spaniards, are pretty contemptuous of the UHT (ultra heat-treated) stuff generally available. If you're likely to be travelling out of season, however, bear in mind that *hostales* (as opposed to more expensive hotels) often don't have any heating systems – and it can get cold. Disposable nappies and other standard needs are very widely available. Many *hostales* will be prepared to baby-sit, or at least to listen out for trouble. This is more likely if you're staying in an old-fashioned family-run place than in the fancier hotels.

LANGUAGE COURSES are offered at most Spanish universities, and in a growing number of special language schools for foreigners. For details overseas and a complete list write to a branch of the Spanish Institute: the London one is at 102 Eaton Square, London SW1 (☎01/235 1484) – other addresses from the nearest tourist office. Many American universities have their own courses based in Spain – or try the Education Office of Spain, 150 Fifth Ave #600, New York, NY 10011 (☎212/741-5144).

LAUNDRIES You'll find a few self-service launderettes (*lavanderías automáticas*) in the major cities, but they're rare – you normally have to leave your clothes for the full (and somewhat expensive) works. Note that you're not allowed by law to leave laundry hanging out of windows over a street. A dry cleaner is a *tintorería*.

LUGGAGE After a long period of absence following terrorist actions in the late 1970s, self-service *consignas* are back at most important Spanish train stations. You'll find lockers large enough to hold most backpacks, plus a smaller bag, which cost about 200ptas a day. (Put the coin in to free the key.) These are not a good idea for long-term storage, however, as they're periodically emptied by station staff. Bus terminals have manned *consignas* where you present a claim stub to get your gear back; cost is about the same.

SKIING Andalucía's main ski centre is the Sierra Nevada, detailed in the *Granada* chapter. The SNTO's *Skiing in Spain* pamphlet is also useful. If you want to arrange a weekend or more while you're in Spain, *Viajes Ecuador* (the biggest travel firm in the country, with branches in most cities) is good for inexpensive all-inclusive trips.

SWIMMING POOLS Most Andalucian towns – and even quite small villages – have a *piscina*, a lifesaver in the summer and yet another reason not to keep exclusively to the coast. Many of these, along with river swimming spots, are detailed throughout the *Guide*.

TIME Spain is one hour ahead of the UK, six hours ahead of Eastern Standard Time, nine hours ahead of Pacific Standard Tme, except for brief periods during the changeovers to and from daylight saving. In Spain the clocks go back in the last week in March and forward again in the last week in September.

TOILETS Public ones are averagely clean but rarely have any paper (best to carry your own). They're often squat-style. The most common euphemisms are *baños* (literally "bathrooms"), *aseos*, *servicios*, *retretes* or *sanitarios*. *Damas* (Ladies) and *Caballeros* (Gentlemen) are the usual signs, though you may also see the confusing *Señoras* (Women) and *Señores* (Men).

> *"The Andalucían sun starts singing a fire song, and all creation trembles at the sound."*
>
> Federico García Lorca

GUIDE

CHAPTER ONE

MÁLAGA AND CÁDIZ

The smallest of Andalucía's eight provinces, **Málaga** is also its most populous, swelling to bursting point with sheer weight of visitors in high summer. Although primarily known as the gateway to the Costa del Sol and its unashamedly commercial resorts such as **Torremolinos** and **Marbella**, the province has much more to offer than just its coastline. To most incoming tourists the **provincial capital Málaga** is merely "the place by the airport", but it is also a vibrant city of half a million people in its own right. Easily the most enjoyable, if not the most scenic, of all the coastal capitals, with plenty of harbour life and more than enough in the way of sights to keep you busy for a couple of days, it's well worth getting to know. Away from the beaches, in the west of Málaga's provincial heartland, lies the **Sierra de Ronda** – a series of small mountain ranges sprinkled with gleaming villages hugging the peaks beneath ancient Moorish castles. Andalucía is dotted with these small, brilliantly whitewashed settlements – the **pueblos blancos** or "white towns", all of which look great from a distance, though many are rather less interesting on arrival. **Ronda**, located astride a stunningly beautiful *tajo*, or gorge, is justly the most famous of these *pueblos blancos*.

To the north lies the appealing market town of **Antequera** with its remarkable prehistoric dolmens and sumptuous Baroque churches, and from here it's just a quick hop south to the natural wonders of **El Torcal**, where vast limestone outcrops have been eroded into a landscape of weird natural sculptures. Another possible trip from Antequera is to the spectacular **El Chorro Gorge**, which, along with the Guadalhorce lake, has become a major climbing and camping centre. Nearby, the saline **Laguna de Fuente de Piedra** is Europe's only inland breeding ground for the greater flamingo, whose flying flocks make a spectacular sight in summer.

Northeast of the city of Málaga is the largely unknown and little visited **Axarquía** region, an area of rugged natural beauty and once the haunt of mountain bandits. Now the domain of the *cabra hispanica*, a distinctive Iberian long-horned goat, the area's magnificent scenery and earthy villages contrast starkly with the crowded **beaches** to the south. Economically, Málaga's coastal hinterland is undergoing a gradual resurgence, in contrast to the general decline in the rest of Andalucía. In recent years the cultivation of subtropical fruits including mangoes and lychees has replaced the traditional orange, lemon and almond trees. Most farm labourers, however, can't afford coastal land; those who buy are often former migrants to France and Germany who have been forced to return because of the unemployment there.

With a 200km coastline fronting both the Atlantic and the Mediterranean **Cádiz** is the most southerly province of Andalucía. The sea has played a large part in the history of the province, and most of Cádiz's dozen or so major conurbations are within easy distance of a beach. Founded by the Phoenicians, the **city of Cádiz** itself makes up for in sheer elegance, atmosphere and sea-girthed location what it lacks in the way of irresistible sights.

After the tumult of the Costa del Sol, the bracing Atlantic winds and broad, white, dune-lined beaches of the **Costa de la Luz** – great stretches of which have so far survived the developers' attentions and which are often deserted – can come as a

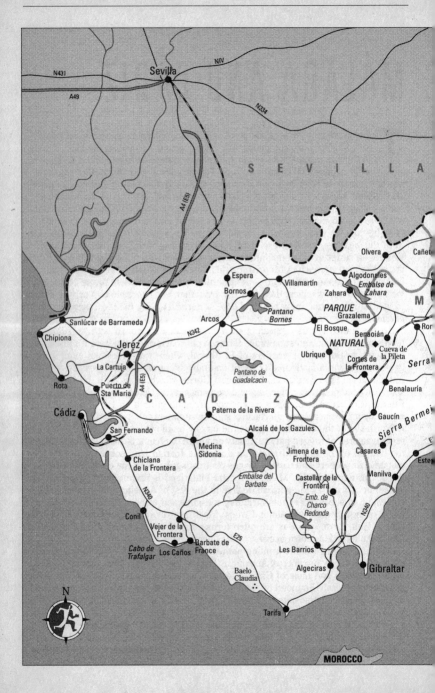

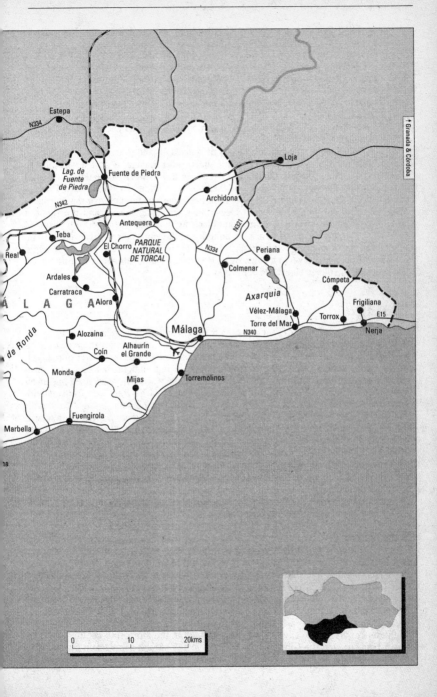

welcome relief. Resorts such as **Conil**, **Chipiona** and **Sanlúcar de Barrameda** possess a low-key charm, while at the southern tip of the coast, **Tarifa** – also with miles of fine beaches – has become a major windsurfing centre. The entire 30km stretch between Tarifa and Algeciras (Andalucía's main port for sailings to Morocco) has been designated a "potential military zone". This sounds off-putting – and in parts, marked by "*Paso Prohibido*" signs, it is – but the ruling has also had happier effects, placing strict controls on Spanish developments and preventing foreigners from buying up land. Flanked by La Linea and Algeciras, the British colony of **Gibraltar** sits beneath its daunting mountain of rock, uneasily regarded by Spaniards and a strange, hybrid curiosity to almost everyone else.

Inland, Cádiz offers a fascinating variety of landscapes and towns. The mountainous region in its northeastern corner, which it shares with Málaga, is dotted with hill-top white towns such as **Zahara**, **Olvera** and **Arcos de la Frontera**, while the green oasis of **Grazalema**, the wettest point in Andalucía, is surrounded by its **Natural Park**, a paradise for walkers and naturalists. South of here sharp countours give way to rolling hills covered with clumps of walnut trees, pines and Spanish firs, and the ranches around **Medina Sidonia** where ominous black fighting bulls graze in the shade of cork oaks. To the west, the hills are left behind and the vines take over, covering thousands of acres of dazzling white chalk soil, and forming the famous **sherry triangle** between **Jerez**, a fine town in its own right, **Puerto de Santa María** and **Sanlúcar de Barrameda**, the oldest vineyards in Europe.

Málaga

First impressions of **MÁLAGA** are generally disappointing. A large and ugly town, it's the second city of the south (after Sevilla) and also one of the poorest: *official* unemployment figures for the area estimate the jobless at one in four of the workforce. Yet, though many people get no further than the train or bus stations, put off by the grim clusters of high rises, it can be a surprisingly attractive place. The town itself has many intriguing corners, and around the old fishing villages of **El Palo** and **Pedregalejo**, now absorbed into the suburbs, is a series of small beaches and a *paseo* lined with some of the best fish and seafood cafés in the province. Overlooking the town and port, the Moorish citadels of the **Alcazaba** and **Gibralfaro** give excellent introductions to what you can expect to see at Córdoba and Granada, and while *sevillanos* loudly proclaim that there is only one *Semana Santa* worthy of the name, *malagueños* – and with reason – furiously disagree. The processions are celebrated here with great fervour and with much larger *pasos* (or floats) than those of Sevilla, carried by up to 150 sober-suited males.

Incidentally, **Picasso** was born in Málaga, and although the artist moved away in his early teens, you can still visit his birthplace.

Some history

The **Phoenicians** founded the settlement they called *malaka* in the eighth century BC, building a fortress on the summit of the hill today dominated by the Alcazaba. Later incorporated into the Roman province of Baetica in the wake of Rome's victory over Carthage, Málaga prospered as a **trading port** exporting iron, copper and lead from mines in the hills near Ronda, as well as olive oil, wine and *garum*, a relish made from pickled fish to which the Romans were particularly partial. When the city fell into the hands of the **Moors** early in the eighth century Málaga was soon flourishing again as the main port for the city of Granada. Although in the fourteenth century the ruler Yusuf I constructed the Gibralfaro as defence, in 1487 Málaga was taken by Christian forces following a bitter siege, after which the large Moorish population was persecuted and its property confiscated on a grand scale; the city's main mosque was also transformed into a cathedral, and another twenty into churches. Málaga entered into a decline only exacerbated by a revolt of the Moors in 1568 which resulted in their complete expulsion.

It was not until the nineteenth century that real prosperity returned – and then only briefly. Middle-class families arriving from the north invested in textile factories, sugar refineries and shipyards, and gave their names to city streets such as Larios and Heredia, while Málaga **dessert wine** became the favourite tipple of Victorian ladies. Then, in the early part of this century the bottom fell out of the boom as the new industries succumbed to foreign competition and the phylloxera bug got to work wiping out the the vines. A number of radical revolts leading up to the Civil War also brought the city an unhealthy reputation.

Given its volatile nature it was inevitable that Málaga would be staunchly Republican during the **Civil War**. In six years of struggle, churches and convents were burned while Italian planes bombed the city, destroying much of its ancient central area, and mass executions of "reds and anarchists" by the conquering Franco forces were to leave enduring emotional scars.

The 1960s finally brought an economic lifeline in the form of **mass tourism** and the exploitation of the Costa del Sol. Coastal nightmares, however, hardly touch the heart of Málaga. The airport lies west of the city, with the result that most of the millions of visitors attracted to the beach resorts are hardly aware of the existence of a vibrant metropolis nearby. All that may be about to change, however, as Málaga embarks on a costly face-lift which has already reclaimed two miles of beach, with plans in hand to create an enormous hotel-lined promenade. It remains to be seen whether the city's unique character will survive.

Arrival and information

From the airport (☎2240000), the **electric train** provides the easiest, and cheapest approach into town (every 20–30min; 190ptas), though note that in the evening it gets very full. Cross via the pedestrian walkway (baggage trolleys allowed) to the unmanned *Ferrocarril* station; the sweet kiosk, if open, sells tickets, or you can buy one on the train. Make sure you're on the Málaga platform and stay on the train right to the end of the line (about 30min), the *Guadelmedina* stop, just across the bridge at the end of the Alameda. The stop before this is *RENFE*, Malagá's main **train station**, from where it's a slightly longer walk into the heart of town (bus #3 runs from here to the centre every 10min or so).

All buses (run by a number of different companies) operate from the one **bus station**, a little northwest of the *RENFE* station. A useful machine in the station saves waiting in line at the (usually helpful) information desk: indicate your destination and it will tell you the connections and departure time of the next bus. If you're heading on to Granada, it's best to arrive an hour or so early, as tickets occasionally sell out.

Going **out to the airport**, trains leave the *Centro/Alameda* station on the hour and half-hour (daily 6.30am–11pm). Remember that there are two airport stops; first *Nacional*, for domestic flights, then *Internacional* for international departures.

Information

The helpful **Turismo**, Pasaje de Chinitas 4 (Mon–Fri 9.30am–1.30pm & 4–6pm, Sat 9.30am–1pm; ☎213445) can provide full accommodation lists and a larger, more detailed map of the city than the one printed here. They also have lots of information on the Costa del Sol; their bi-lingual listings guide *Que Hacer? Donde Ir?* is a great source of information on current events along the coast. There's another branch at the bus station – see above – and a kiosk (summer only) in Plaza Merced.

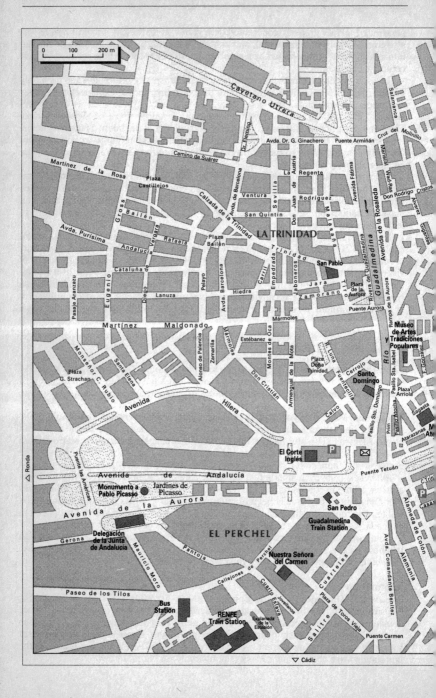

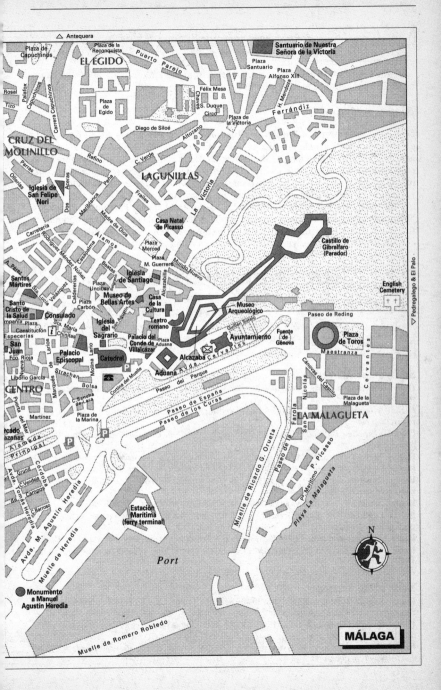

> The **telephone area code** for Málaga is ☎952

Train information and tickets are available from the *RENFE* office at c/Strachan 2, near the front entrance to the Cathedral.

Accommodation

Málaga boasts dozens of **fondas** and **hostales**, so budget rooms are rarely hard to come by, and there are some real bargains in winter. You may well get offers at the train and bus stations, and so long as the rooms are fairly central these will probably be as good as any. **Places to avoid** include the cheap but extremely dingy *casas de huéspedes* on c/de Cuarteles between the main train station and the *Centro/Alameda* station.

Numerous possibilities are to be found in the grid of streets just north and south of the Alameda, which is probably the best place to start looking. For those who want a little more luxury, we've listed a couple of places further out. The cheapest options are the **youth hostel** and the single **campsite**, though neither of these are particularly convenient for the centre, lying out in the eastern suburbs.

ACCOMMODATION PRICE SYMBOLS

The symbols used in our hotel listings denote the following price ranges:

① Under 2000ptas	③ 3000–4500ptas	⑤ 7500–12,500ptas
② 2000–3000ptas	④ 4500–7500ptas	⑥ Over 12,500ptas

See p.28 for more details.

South of the Alameda

Hostal Alameda, c/Casas de Campos 3 (☎222099). Friendly place, with good-value rooms, some with bath. ③.

Hostal Avenida, Alameda Principal 5 (☎217729). Right on the Alameda but not too noisy. Some rooms with bath. ③.

Casa Huéspedes Bolivia, c/Casas de Campos 24 (☎218826). Clean and simple with a friendly proprietor. ③.

Hostal El Cenachero, c/Barroso 5 (☎224088). A clean, quiet and excellent value place with friendly proprietors; in a quiet street just off the seafront end of c/Córdoba. ③.

Hostal Córdoba, c/Bolsa 9–11 (☎214469). Inexpensive, simple rooms in a family-run establishment near the cathedral. ②.

Hostal Indalo, c/Casas de Campos 5 (☎211974). Clean, airy rooms without bath. ③.

Hostal El Ruedo, c/Trinidad Grund 3 (☎215820). Clean, but basic. If you want air, make sure to get a room at the front. ②.

Hotel Sur, c/Trinidad Grund 13 (☎224803). Quiet, efficient hotel with some mod cons plus TV. ④.

Hotel Venecia, Alameda Principal 9 (☎213636). Central new hotel with all facilities and satellite TV. ④.

North of the Alameda

Hostal Aurora II, c/Cisneros 5 (☎224004). Spacious rooms, all with bath in renovated house. Same owners also have slightly cheaper *Aurora I* around the corner in c/Muro Puerta Nueva. ④.

Hostal Buenos Aires, c/la Bolsa 12 (☎218935). Clean, light rooms on a reasonably quiet street near the cathedral. ③.

Hostal Cisneros, c/Cisneros 7, west of Plaza Constitución(☎212633). Pleasant rooms with bath and friendly proprietors. ④.

Hostal Cordoba, c/Bolsa 9-11, near the cathedral (☎214469). Simple rooms in family run establishment. ②.

Hostal Derby, c/San Juan de Dios 1 (☎221301). Excellent value fourth-floor establishment, on a tiny street north of the Plaza de la Marina, with some rooms overlooking the harbour. Very friendly proprietors. ③.

Hostal Lamperez, c/Santa Maria 6, off Pasaje Chinitas (☎219484). Basic but clean. ②.

Hostal La Palma, c/Martínez 7 (☎226772). Pleasant and clean place run by a friendly couple. Sometimes willing to give discounts. ③.

Hostal Ramos, c/Martinez 8, just above the Alameda (☎227268). Clean and basic rooms without bath.②.

Hostal Victoria, c/Sancha de Lara 3 (☎224223). Pleasant, serviceable place with good value single rooms. ④.

Hostal Viena, c/Strachan 3 (☎224095). Simple rooms in a quiet street near the cathedral. ②.

Out of the centre

Parador de Málaga–Gibralfaro, Monte de Gibralfaro (☎221903). You won't get a better panoramic view of the coast than from this eagle's nest on top of the Gibralfaro hill; however, despite its rates, it's quite small as *paradores* go, and the service sometimes lacks grace. Well worth calling in for a drink or a meal, though (see under "Eating"). ⑤.

Hotel Las Vegas, Paseo de Sancha 22 (☎217712). A smart hotel, east of the bullring and reasonably close to the beach; with its own swimming pool. ⑤.

Campsite

Camping Balneario del Carmen, Paseo Salvador Rueda (☎290021). Three kilometres out of town towards El Palo, this site is a rather gritty affair set amid the decaying and elegant remains of an old "bathing station", but it's well positioned for the Pedregalejo *paseo*. Get there on bus #11 from the centre of town.

Youth hostel

Albergue Juvenil Málaga, Plaza de Pio XII (☎308500). Pleasantly modern, complete with sunterrace. The #18 bus (heading east across the river) from the Alameda will drop you nearby. ①.

The Town

Divided into two by the seasonal Guadalmedina torrent, all Malagá's major sights lie to the east of this and below the **Alcazaba**. The cathedral is easy to find, from where the **Museo de Bellas Artes** and a clutch of **churches** all lie within a few minutes' walk.

The Alcazaba

Malaga's magnificent **Alcazaba** (Mon–Sat 10am–1pm & 5–8pm, Sun 10am–2pm; 20ptas) is an exuberant contrast to the dour fortresses of Castile. At its entrance stands a lost-looking **Roman theatre**, accidentally unearthed in 1951 during the construction of the Casa de Cultura, which now cuts into the orchestra pit giving the restored banks of seating a rather meaningless focus. From here a path winds upwards, lined by the cypresses and flower encircled arbours so loved by the sybaritic Moors. The citadel too, is Roman, and interspersed among the Moorish brick of the double- and triple-arched gateways are recycled blocks and columns of classical marble.

Although the main structures were begun by the Moors in the 700s, the palace higher up the hill dates from the early decades of the eleventh century. It was the residence of the Arab Emirs of Málaga, who carved out an independent kingdom for themselves upon the break-up of the Western Caliphate. Their independence lasted a mere thirty years, but for a while the kingdom grew to include Granada, Carmona and Jaén. The palace, restored as an **archeological museum**, is scattered chaotically with fragments of statuary and mosaics, and is not always easy to make sense of. And although the prehistoric, Phoenician and Roman artefacts testify to the city's antique pedigree, the simple truth is that they are not very inspiring. The Moorish section is altogether better, with some striking examples of the ceramics for which Málaga was renowned during the thirteenth and fourteenth centuries, particularly its gilded work exemplified by the **Barco plate**. Note, too, the more recent fine stucco work in the museum, and 1920s Moorish-style ceilings (a big vogue at that time in Spain).

Above the alcazaba, and connected to it by a long double wall, is the **Gibralfaro castle** (free access). By far the most appealing approach is to take the road to the right of the alcazaba, then a path up through gardens, a ramble of towers, bougainvillea-draped ramparts and sentry-box-shaped Moorish wells (you can also approach from the town side, as the tourist coaches do, but this is a rather unattractive walk). Built by Yusuf I of Granada in the fourteenth century and last used in 1936 during the Civil War, the heavily restored castle, with its formidable walls and turrets, affords terrific views over the city and the complex fortifications of the alcazaba. A pleasant place to take refreshment is at the nearby **parador** with its terrace overlooking the city. It's reached by following the road leading out of the car park for 500m. If you're feeling lazy, take bus #35 from the Paso del Parque.

The Cathedral and the Museo de Bellas Artes

Dominating the views from the Gibralfaro is Málaga's peculiar, unfinished **Catedral** (Tues–Sun 10am–1pm & 4–5.30pm; 100ptas). It lacks a tower on the west front, the result of a radical Malagueño bishop having donated the earmarked money to the American War of Independence against the British. Despite this curiosity, which has resulted in the building's popular nickname *La Manquita* ("the one-armed lady"), the cathedral lacks much else of interest. The interior is distinguished only by an intricately carved and naturalistic seventeenth-century *sillería* (choirstall) with outstanding sculptural work – in particular *St Francis* and *John the Baptist* – by Pedro de Mena. However, the **Iglesia del Sagrario**, on the cathedral's northern flank, is worth a look, if only for its fine Gothic **portal**, dating from an earlier, uncompleted Isabelline church. Inside, the restoration of a magnificent **Plateresque retablo** has closed the church to visitors for the foreseeable future. Just along the street (c/Cister) from here, you could take a look at the exterior of the house where **Pedro de Mena** – often described as Andalucía's Michelangelo – lived during his years in Málaga; a crumbling place marked by a plaque, it's in a small cul-de-sac named c/Afligidos.

The **Museo de Bellas Artes** (Mon–Fri 10am–1.30pm & 5–8pm; 250ptas) just round the corner from the cathedral on c/San Agustín, is housed in an impressive sixteenth-century mansion with an elegant patio. The early rooms have exhibits of silver work, furniture and polychromed medieval wood sculpture among which two striking sixteenth-century pieces by Luis de Morales stand out – the *Virgen de los Dolores* and an *Ecce Homo*. Room 3 includes two works by Zurburan, *San Benito* and *San Jerónimo* together with a fine *San Francisco de Paula* by Murillo. In Room 5 there's a wonderfully lifelike eighteenth-century head of *San Juan de Dios* in painted wood by Fernando Ortiz. Upstairs, Room 8 is devoted to the surprisingly tedious works of Muñoz Degrain, Picasso's first tutor. Degrain's pupil is represented by collections of engravings, *Mes dessins d'Antibes* and *Faunes et flore d'Antibes*, as well as *Tauromaquia*, a series of twenty-six aquatints inspired by the *corrida*. Most interesting here for the casual visitor, however, are some **juvenile works by Picasso** including a drawing of his father, Ruiz, executed at age nine, betraying sure signs of a burgeoning and mighty talent. Among the other modern works on this floor there's a poignant wood sculpture of a beggar, *Mendiga Canaria*, by Manuel Ramos, as well as the preposterously mawkish ...*Y tenía corazón* ("...And she had a heart") depicting an autopsy being carried out on a beautiful young woman, by Enrique Simonet.

Casa Natal de Picasso

Picasso's birthplace and family home during his early years, the **Casa Natal de Picasso**, Plaza de la Merced 15, is now the headquarters of the Picasso Foundation (open office hours). It was during his formative years in Málaga that Picasso's prodigious talent for drawing was first noticed – "When I was a child I could draw like Raphael," he later wrote; "it took me all my life to learn to draw like a child." – and it was in the cafés around the square that the boy saw the first solid shape that he wanted to commit to paper: *churros*, those oil-steeped fritters that Spaniards dip into their breakfast chocolate. The foundation is not strictly a museum as yet – though it is hoped that the Picasso family apartment upstairs from the foundation will soon be turned into one – but the friendly staff will nevertheless allow you in to look around. Apart from a couple of notebooks containing some early sketches and one or two paintings there is little to actually see and most visitors are scholars and art historians come to research.

Pasaje de Chinitas and the Parque Picasso

Tucked behind the Plaza de la Constitución is one of Málaga's most evocative corners, the **Pasaje de Chinitas**. In the last century, when Málaga was a thrusting industrial town, this narrow white-walled street was filled with *tascas*, or bars, where businessmen would meet to discuss deals over fine wines before slinking off to the *Café de Chinitas* to hear some of the best *flamenco* in town. In the 1920s and 1930s the fame of this *flamenco* shrine, now a mundane textile store, grew as it became a noted meeting place of artists and writers, bullfighters and singers. Lorca loved the place and composed a poem in its honour, part of which appears on a plaque fixed to the former café, close to the statue of the girl-with-jar:

> *In the café de Chinitas*
> *Said Paquiro to his brother:*
> *"I'm more valiant than you,*
> *more brave and more gitano."*

West of here, Málaga has honoured its most famous son with a modern garden, the **Parque Picasso** at the end of the Avda. de Andalucía 100m or so beyond the *El Corte Inglés* department store. In 1978 the country's first monument to the artist was erected here, a curiously restrained abstract work by Ramon Calderón. Second thoughts were in a much more monumental vein and Ortiz Berrocal was commissioned to produce something of the size required: a wonderfully intestinal bronze, flanked by two magnificent dragon trees which are fairly remarkable sculptures in their own right. Don't hang around here at dusk or after dark, however, as the area has a dubious reputation.

Museo de Artes y Tradiciones Populares

Housed in a seventeenth-century inn, the entertaining **Museo de Artes y Tradiciones Populares**, c/Pasillo Santa Isabel 10 (Mon–Fri 10am–1pm & 5–8pm, Sat 10am–1pm; free) uses the former stables and stores on the lower floor as well as the lodging rooms above to mount displays of arts, crafts and furniture from previous eras. These include a collection of *barros malagueños* – typical painted clay figurines – as well as boats, carriages, farming and wine-making implements and rooms furnished in period style.

Mercado Atarazanas

Lying at the heart of an area that bustles with life, the nineteenth-century wrought-iron, Mudéjar-style **Mercado Atarazanas,** just north of the Alameda on c/Atarazanas incorporates a little-known gem of which the thousands of shoppers who pass beneath it daily are hardly aware. The remarkable **fourteenth-century Moorish arch** on its southern facade was built for Yusuf I of Granada – incidentally the ruler also responsible for that other great gateway, the Puerta de la Justicia in the Alhambra – when Málaga was part of the Nasrid kingdom. In those days it formed the entrance to the Moorish arsenal, and the original building's purpose is preserved in the market's present name: Atarazanas in Arabic translates as "the house that guards the arsenal." Note the two coats of arms in the upper corners inscribed in Arabic with the confidant proclamation, "There is no Conquerer but God. All Praise to Him."

Paseo del Parque

An ideal place for a stroll, especially on summer evenings when the air has cooled, the **Paseo del Parque** is an elegant palm-shaded avenue laid out at the turn of the century on land reclaimed from the sea as a result of the construction of the Cánovas Harbour. Along its length are a number of architectural delights as well as a **botanical garden** containing hundreds of exotic plants and flowers and many varieties of fig, bamboo, jacaranda and yucca trees. Discreet plaques placed at intervals along the esplanade identify the different species. Among the buildings of note are the Neoclassical **La Aduana** (the former customs house) started in 1788, with an austerely impressive patio and, further along, **El Correo**, or the old post office. And don't miss the Paseo's star turn a little further on, the exhuberant **Ayuntamiento**, a delightful cream and brown Art Nouveau pile, constructed to coincide with opening of the esplanade. At the Paseo's eastern end you'll come to the **Fuente Genovesa**, or Genoa fountain, now encircled by traffic and difficult to appreciate. An Italian Renaissance work, it was captured during the reign of Carlos V by pirates while being transported to its Spanish buyer; when finally retrieved the king awarded it to the city by royal edict. Finally, just south of here at the entrance to the port are two of Málaga's best loved **sculptures**, Pimentel's *El Cenachero* (the fish seller) and *El Jazminero* (the jasmine seller); characters who, with their trays of blooms and baskets of fish, used to be a common sight on the city's streets.

The English Cemetery

Flanked by carved stone rampant lions, the **English Cemetery**, 150m east of the bullring (Mon–Fri 9am–6pm, Sat 9am–noon; free) dates from the era when gunboats flying Union Jacks held the world in awe. This did not, however, disturb the Spanish authorities from their post-*reconquista* custom of denying Christian burial to all "infidels" unlucky enough to die on Iberian turf. Thus British Protestants – who were included in this grouping – suffered the indignity after death of burial upright in the sand below the tide line to their necks. Málaga's expatriate population, which increased during the early nineteenth century, was, understandably, not amused when some of these "shore burials" were washed up on the beach or seen bobbing on the waves. Thus in 1830 the British consul, William Mark, finally persuaded the authorities to let him found the English Cemetery. In the early days and to get the place established, it seems that Mark pursued corpses with the zeal of bodysnatchers Burke and Hare, hardly waiting for the deceased to expire before carting them off to the new graveyard. Traveller Richard Ford, whose wife's frailty was his original reason for coming to Spain, became alarmed when Mark began to make overtures. "Hearing of my wife's ill health, he tried all in his power to get me to Málaga to have a pretty female specimen in his sepulchral museum," he wrote to a friend.

The cemetery itself, once an isolated site overlooking the sea but now enveloped by urban sprawl, is still nevertheless a leafy and tranquil oasis. Follow the path from the Paseo de Reding up to the modest redstone church of St George where, just before it, stands the sepulchre of William Mark. Further up the hill you'll see the original walled cemetery containing the oldest graves, among them a number studded with sea-shells (an ancient symbol of immortality), marking the passing of child victims of fever and consumption, the scourge of that age. The tombstone of Gamel Woolsey, poet and wife of Gerald Brenan is inscribed with the poignant message "Fear no more the heat o' the sun." Many of the other tombstones with their dedications to the wives, loyal servants and men of military zeal, most of them in English, make fascinating reading.

Málaga's churches: Nuestra Señora de la Victoria, Iglesia de Santiago and Iglesia de San Juan

Sited on the spot where Fernando and Isabel pitched their tent during the 1487 seige of Málaga, **Nuestra Señora de la Victoria**, at the north end of c/Victoria, is, after the cathedral, Málaga's most prestigious church, where the city's Virgin patron is venerated. The fifteenth-century building was substantially rebuilt in the seventeenth century by the Count of Buenavista, whose remains, along with those of his descendants, lie in an eerie **subterranean crypt** decorated with symbolic stucco skeletons and skulls. Above, the main altar's centrepiece is an image of the virgin in a *camerín* attributed to Pedro de Mena. Legend has it that the *reja*, or altarscreen, was wrought from the chains wrested off the liberated Christian slaves after the city was taken.

Other churches with interesting features are the **Iglesia de Santiago**, c/Granada, with an original fifteenth-century Mudéjar tower – note the intricate *sebka* brickwork reminiscent of the Giralda in Sevilla – and the **Iglesia de San Juan** founded in 1487, but with the addition of a curious Baroque tower-portal. The heavily restored interior contains a fine seventeenth-century sculpture of *San Juan* by Francisco Ortiz.

Eating

Málaga has a justified reputation for its splendid **fried fish**, served everywhere and acknowledged as among the best in Spain. You'll find many fish restaurants grouped around the Alameda, although for the very best you need to head out to the suburbs of Pedregalejo and El Palo, served by bus #11 from the Paseo del Parque. On the seafront *paseo* at **Pedregalejo**, almost any of the cafés and restaurants serves terrific fish – though a few are beginning to get very overpriced, and you should check the menu before you enter. Further on, as the *paseo* trails away, you find yourself amid fishing shacks and smaller, sometimes quite ramshackle, cafés. This is **El Palo**, an earthier sort of area for the most part, with a beach and fishing huts, and an even better place to eat. Bear in mind that good fish is rarely cheap and wherever you're eating it's as well to ascertain the price before you dine to avoid a nasty shock when the bill arrives.

To stock up on food for trips or **picnics**, your best bet is the *mercado*, and for a sweet treat, the nuns at the Abadia (Abbey) of Santa Clara, c/Cister 11 (between the Cathedral and the Alcazaba) sell their *dulces* between 9am and 1pm. Specialities are coconut and quince cakes. The *Convento de las Clarisas* does the same at c/Zumaya 1.

CONVENT DULCES

Many convents throughout Andalucía and Spain are in the business of supporting their orders by making "**convent dulces**"; cakes and pastries which they can then sell to the community. Many recipes date back to the Arabs, who used rich combinations of eggs, almonds, sugar and honey to concoct their Moorish goodies. Each convent guards its recipes jealously, and many are so good that they supply local restaurants. The **sherry manufacturers** also had an influence on the development of *convent dulces*, for they traditionally used egg whites to clarify their wines and donated the leftover yolks to the nuns. This is the origin of many egg yolk-based creations such as *tocino de cielo* (Andalucía's richest flan) and *yemas* (sweet cakes), two of the region's most popular pastries.

In most places you pay your money and are served with the sweets of your choice through a *turno* – a kind of revolving dumb waiter – which means you never see the nun who serves you.

Fish restaurants

Antonio Martín, Paseo Maritimo. One of Málaga's most celebrated fish restaurants, a century-old establishment and the traditional haunt of matadors celebrating their successes in the nearby bullring. Expensive, but probably the best in town.

Casa Vicente, c/Comisario. Livley *marisquería* in a narrow alley on the northern side of the Alameda.

Los Culitos, c/Circo 1, just above Plaza Victoria, at the end of c/Victoria. An exceptional fish bar that's inexpensive and deservedly popular, serving the best *mero* in town. Slightly disconcerting, though, if you're travelling there by taxi – the Plaza Victoria is popularly known as Plaza de los Monos, and the address thus translates as "the little bums on the square of the monkeys". Closed Thurs.

La Lonja, c/Cervantes 5. Facing the eastern wall of the Plaza de Toros (and heavily patronized by fight fans when there's a *corrida*), this place serves up a wide variety of seafood. When you've chosen your fish from the chilled display you can eat inside or, more atmospherically, at tables on the pavement. The *parrillada* (selection of grilled fish) is recommended.

Bar El Puerto, c/Comisario. A good *marisquería* a shrimp shell's throw away from the *Casa Vicente* (see above).

Mesón El Rincon, junction of c/Marmoles and c/Armengual de la Mota. Neighbourhood restaurant well worth seeking out across the dry Río Guadalmedina in the old *gitano* quarter of El Perchel. A real *malagueño* fish place, it may seem like two establishments, but one is a bar with outdoor tables (for *tapas* and *raciones*) while the other (under the same ownership) is a great restaurant. Take care in this area at night as it's slightly off the tourist beat.

El Tintero II, El Palo. Right at the far end of the seafront, just before the *Club Náutico* (stay on bus #11 and ask for "Tintero Dos"), this is a huge beach restaurant where the waiters charge round with plates of fish (all costing the same for a plate) and you shout for, or grab, anything you like. The choices to go for are, above all, *mero* (a kind of gastronomically evolved cod) and *rosada* (equally indefinable), along with Andalucian regulars such as *boquerones* (fresh anchovies), *gambas* (shrimp), *calamares, chopos, jibia* (different kinds of squid) and *sepia* (cuttlefish).

Non-fish restaurants

Al-Yamal, c/Blasco de Garay 3. A good Arab restaurant serving up pricey, but authentic meat in spicy sauces, *couscous* and other typical dishes.

Restaurante Arcos, Alameda 31. Efficient central place behind a garish neon exterior on the south side of the Alameda, towards the Tetuán bridge. Recommended for its all-day *platos combinados* and late-night meals – for breakfast they also serve *pan tostada* with wholemeal bread, *pan integral*.

La Cancela, c/Denis Belgrano 3, off c/Granada. A reasonably priced *menú* served at outdoor tables in a pleasant pedestrian street – there's also a good stand-up *tapas* bar next door.

El Corte Inglés department store, Avda. de Andalucía 4. Worth a mention for its top-floor restaurant with reasonably priced dishes, especially good at lunchtime.

Mesón Danes, c/Barroso 5. Just up the street from the *Al-Yamal*, this long-established Danish restaurant does an interesting combination of Spanish and Scandinavian dishes served on traditional Nordic red tablecloths.

El Mesón Gallego, c/Casas de Campos 23. A Galician restaurant with a medium-priced *menú* and regional specialities such as *caldo gallego* (cabbage and bean soup) and *caldeirada* (fish stew).

Mesón de Jamon, Plaza María Guerrero 5, just off Plaza de la Merced. Good value *menú* and a selection of *jamon* and cheese *tapas*.

Maite, c/Esparteros 5. A rock-bottom *menú*. Located in a difficult-to-find alley just west of c/Larios.

El Mesón, c/Trinidad Grund. Traditional medium-priced *malagueño* restaurant south of the Alameda. Serves typical provincial dishes such as *ajo blanco con uvas* (gazpacho with grapes) and *lomo al ajillo* (pork loin in garlic sauce).

Parador Gilbralfaro, Monte Gilbralfaro. Superior terrace dining with spectacular views over the coast and town. Definitely worth a splurge, or try the *menú* (around 3000ptas) for excellent value. If you can't face the climb, bus #35 heading east along the Paseo del Parque will take you there.

Bar Los Pueblos, c/Atarazanas, opposite the *mercado*. Serves satisfying, inexpensive food all day – bean soups and *estofados* are their speciality; *gazpacho* is served in half-pint glasses.

Bar San Agustín, c/San Agustín 11. A central place for *tapas* and *raciones*, near the cathedral. Especially good for lunch.

Drinking: cafés and bars

Málaga has a variety of places to drink, from bustling breakfast cafés for *churros* and morning coffee to atmospheric bars where you can while away an evening. The best of the breakfast places are clustered around the Atarazanas market, where the daily bustle starts at dawn. **Bars** for more serious drinking – usually with *tapas* thrown in – are concentrated north of the Alameda and around the cathedral. A number of traditional bars serve the sweet **Málaga wine**, made from muscatel grapes and dispensed from huge barrels; other options include the new wine, *Pedriot*, which is incredibly sweet, and the much more palatable *Seco Añejo*, which has matured for a year.

Cafés
Casa Aranda, c/Herrería del Rey just east of the market. One of the best of the market cafés, renowned for its excellent *churros*, served at outside tables. There are actually two bars here, owned by the same family and operating as one.

Bar Central, east side of Plaza de la Constitución. A cavernous old institution in the centre of town, one of the city's favourite meeting places for generations. It not only serves *tapas* but also has an enticing *pastelería* counter.

Bar la Nueva Cubana, c/Calderia 6, off c/Granada. Stylish place for coffee and tea later in the day.

Bars
Antigua Casa Guardia, corner of c/Pastora, on the Alameda. Great old nineteenth-century spit-and-sawdust bar. Picasso frequented this place when he was in town, and a photo on the wall shows him toting one of the bar's *jarras*. Try the mussels with Málaga wine.

Antigua Reja, Plaza de Uncibay, off c/de Méndez Núñez. Lively bar with seafood *tapas*.

Boqueron de la Plata, c/Marin García 11. Simple place serving beer and seafood *tapas*.

Bar Don Jamon, Alameda 11. Typical *tapas* bar specializing in excellent *fino*.

Bar Lo Güeno, c/Marin García 9, off c/Larios. A smartish haunt with a wide range of *tapas*; try their *pincho* (spicy shrimp) or *habas* (broad beans with black sausage).

La Manchega, c/Marin García 4. Another fine old drinking den; *jibias guisadas* (stewed cuttlefish) is a speciality.

Rincon de Oliva, c/Don Cristián 1. Typical neighbourhood *tapas* bar round the back of *El Corte Inglés* with tasty *jamón serrano*.

Rincon de Pepe Luis, c/Vendeja 29. Good *fino* a couple of streets south of the Alameda.

Bar la Tosca, c/Marín Garcia 12. Popular city centre bar with a wide *tapas* selection and excellent *jamón serrano*.

Nightlife

You'll find most of Málaga's limited nightlife northeast of the cathedral along and around **calles Granada and Beatas**, as well as in Malagueta, south of the bullring. At weekends and holidays dozens of youthful **disco–bars** fill the crowded streets in these areas with a cacophany of sound, and over the summer – though it's dead out of season – the scene spreads out along the seafront to the suburb of **Pedregalejo**. Here the streets just behind the beach host most of the action, and dozens of **discos** and smaller **bars** lie along and off the main street, Juan Sebastián Elcano.

Genuine **flamenco** is, as always, hard to come by and the few shows there are in Málaga aren't up to much. Many of the *peñas* where it is performed are private, but you could try *La Lecheria*, Paseo de Sancha 25, east of the bullring, where live *flamenco* takes place on Wednesday evenings.

Barsovia, c/Belgrano 3. Restrained music bar open till late.

Bobby Logan, c/Juan Sebastián Elcano, Pedregalejo. A disco in a beautiful building but with lousy music.

Café Teatro, c/Afligidos 5. Stylish bar at the bottom of a cul-de-sac with unobtrusive live music most nights and pub theatre at weekends.

La Chancla, the beach, Pedregalejo. One of a recent rash of bars on the beach; bursts forth at midnight and continues until 3am or later.

Bar CTB, c/Don Juan de Málaga. Málaga's dope crowd gather in this alley behind the cathedral, nominally at the tiny bar, enveloped in a hashish haze, but more usually on the pavement around it.

Duna, c/Juan Sebastián Elcano, Pedregalejo. Big, overdecorated and pricey place with dancing.

El Pimpi, c/Granada 62. Cavernous place with flashing TV screens and a wide selection of recorded music.

Ragtime, c/Reding 12. Specializes in jazz, blues and rock, often with live performers. In the Malagueta area.

Salsa, at the top of c/Denis Belgrano, off c/Granada. Salsa, karaoke, samba and mambo on week-day nights. Next door to the *Barsovia*.

Terral, junction c/Cister and c/Toledo. Low-key bar near the cathedral, frequented by Málaga's (mostly foreign) artist colony, and mounting occasional exhibitions.

Listings

Banks Numerous places with cash machines along c/Larios and on the Plaza de la Constitución.

Books/newspapers The *El Corte Inglés* department store stocks most foreign newspapers and periodicals. *Librería de Ocasion*, c/Salinas 7, has a selection of English second-hand books as does *Librería Malagueña*, c/Mártires 5.

Camping/climbing/hiking Equipment and advice available from two excellent shops in c/Carretería (north of Plaza de la Constitucíon) *El Campista* (no. 71; ☎222 93 23) and *La Trucha* (no. 100; ☎221 22 03) who also sell top brand Spanish walking and climbing boots at bargain prices and provide information on a variety of courses: rock climbing, hang-gliding, canoeing, caving etc.

Car Rental Cheap deals available from *Autos Rent Málaga*, Paseo Ciudad de Melilla 17, south of the bullring(☎221 00 10). Especially good for a one or two day hire, but be sure to pay additional accident insurance.

Consulates *Britain*, c/Duquesa Parcent 8 (☎217571); *Netherlands*, c/Linaje 3 (☎260 02 60).

Ferries Daily sailings (except Sunday) to the Spanish enclave of Melilla in Morocco only, generally leaving around 1pm; the crossing takes ten hours. Tickets from *Compañía Aucona* at c/Juan Díaz 1(☎224391).

Flea Market Every Sunday morning along the Paseo de los Martiricos on the west bank of the river near the football stadium.

Hiking Maps 1:50,000 1:100,000 and 1:200,000 maps are available from CNIG (National Geographical Insitute) branch office: Avda. de la Aurora, 47–7º, near the Jardines Picasso, (☎312808).

Hospital *Cruz Roja*, Avda. José Silvela 64 (☎250450).

Motorcycle/Scooter Rental *Victoria Racing* c/Victoria 6 (☎222 04 83). Daily or weekly rates.

Police Phone ☎215005; for emergencies dial 091.

Post Office Avda. de Andalucía, across the bridge at the end of the Alameda. Mon–Fri 9am–1pm & 4–6pm; Sat 9am–2pm.

Telephones c/Molina Larios 11, near the Cathedral. Open Mon–Sat 9am–9pm; Sun 10am–1pm.

El Chorro Gorge and around

Inland, some 50km north of Málaga, **El Chorro Gorge** (*Garganta del Chorro*) is an amazing place. It's impressive in itself – an immense cleft cut through a vast limestone massif by the Río Guadalhorce – but the real attraction is a **concrete catwalk**, *El Camino del Rey*, which threads the length of the gorge hanging precipitously halfway up its side. Built in the 1920s as part of a burgeoning hydroelectric scheme and opened by king Alfonso XIII who walked its whole length and gave it his name, it used to figure in all the guidebooks as one of the wonders of Spain; today it's largely fallen into

WALKING EL CHORRO GORGE

From the train station take the road below you, signposted *Pantano de Guadalhorce*, crossing over the dam and turning right, then following the road north along the lake towards the hydroelectric plant. After 10km you'll come upon the bar-restaurant *El Mirador*, poised above the various lakes and reservoirs of the Guadalhorce scheme. From the bar a dirt track on the right (just manageable by car) covers the 2km to an abandoned power plant at the mouth of the gorge. The footpath to the left of this will take you into the chasm and to the beginning of **El Camino**. Although it is marked "No Entry" you'll probably come upon a number of young Spaniards exploring the catwalk. The first section, at least, seems reasonably safe – despite places where it is only a metre wide and where parts of the handrail are missing – and this is in fact the most dramatic part of the canyon. Towards the end, where the passageway gets really dangerous, the gorge widens and it's possible to climb down and follow the riverbank or have a swim.

disrepair, and will probably collapse completely unless (unlikely) renovation takes place. But at present, despite a few wobbly – and decidedly dangerous – sections, with the occasional hole in the concrete through which you can see the gorge hundreds of feet below, it's still possible to walk much of its length. You will, however, need a very good head for heights, and at least a full day starting from Málaga. If you've neither, it's possible to get a glimpse of both gorge and *camino* from any of the trains going north from Málaga – the line, slipping in and out of tunnels, follows the river for quite a distance along the gorge, before plunging into a last long tunnel just before its head.

To explore the gorge, head for **EL CHORRO**, served by direct trains from Málaga. The village is rapidly becoming a centre of outdoor activities for the gorge, particularly rock climbing and para-gliding, and has two **places to stay**. At the southern end of the station platform the *Bar-Restaurante Garganta del Chorro* (☎952/497219; ③) has pleasant rooms inside a converted mill, while following the signs for 2km along the track beyond here will lead you to *Finca La Campana* (☎952/950934; ①/③), a farmhouse set in scenic surroundings with overnight accommodation in a bunkhouse or weekly accommodation in an apartment or cottage. The Yorkshire proprietor John Bell can provide information on walking, climbing, and para-gliding in the area and sells walking and climbing boots.

From the station it's about 12km to the **start of the path** and the gorge, and to some magnificent lakes and reservoirs for swimming, such as the *Embalse del Guadalhorce*. You can camp along the rocky shore; alternatively, the tiny village of Ardales (see p.71), 4km beyond the lake, has shops, bars, a lone *hostal* on the main square and two daily buses to and from Ronda. The walk is beautiful, and hitching is also feasible with hundreds of cars passing along here in summer.

Bobastro

A few kilometres beyond El Chorro, amid some of the wildest scenery in the whole peninsula, lies **BOBASTRO**, the mountain-top remains of a Mozarabic (Arabized Christian) fortified settlement. Famous as the isolated eyrie of colourful ninth-century rebel, Ibn Hafsun, the castle was said to be the most impregnable in all Andalucía, but only a ruined **church**, carved into an enormous boulder, remains of the once-great fortress.

Situated outside the original fortified area, and below some cave dwellings of uncertain date, the church is typically Mozarabic in style, its nave and two aisles separated by horseshoe-arched arcades. The transept, and a deep apse chapel flanked by two side chapels, can clearly be seen making the edifice one of the few identifiable traces of building from the period.

IBN HAFSUN

Ibn Hafsun was a *muwallad* (of mixed Christian-Arab parentage) who after killing a man fell out with the Ummayad caliphate at Córdoba and resorted to a life of brigandage. Gathering around him a formidable army, he built his stronghold at Bobastro, and during the years 880–917AD scored a number of spectacular victories over the many Ummayad forces sent to defeat him. At the height of his power Hafsun controlled an area between the straits of Gibraltar in the west and Jaen in the east. His defence of the poor against excessive Ummayad taxation and forced labour further served to increase the popularity of this Robin Hood-style figure, especially among his fellow *muwalladin*, who believed they were getting a raw deal from their pure-blooded Arab rulers. After he converted to Christianity in 899 the church was constructed to receive his remains, which were interred at Bobastro upon his death in 917.

Nearby and to the west is the **Cueva de Doña Trinidad** with Paleolithic cave paintings; to see them you'll need to get a key from the *Ayuntamiento* at Ardales.

You can **get to Bobastro** from El Chorro by crossing the dam from the train station and turning right along the road to *El Mirador* (see box on p.69). After a couple of kilometres a signed turn-off (on the left and easy to miss) indicates a twisting route to another sign (marked "Iglesia Mozárabe") pointing to a slope on the left. Leave your transport here and follow the path for 400m through the pine woods to the site.

Álora, Carratraca, Teba and Ardales

While in this area there are possible detours to the **white towns** of Álora, Carratraca and Teba.

Álora

Located by the road to Antequera, 12km south of El Chorro, **ÁLORA** is a sparkling cluster of whitewalled dwellings nestling between three rocky spurs topped by the ruins of a Moorish alcazaba. It's relaxing simply to stroll through the delightful narrow, cobbled streets – take a look at the eighteenth-century church of **La Encarnación** on the main square or climb up to the castle, now the town graveyard. Monday is market day, when the village becomes a lively mass of stallholders and shoppers. If you want to **stay**, try the *Hostal Durán*, c/La Parra 9 (☎952/496642; ③), or the more economical *fonda* at c/General Mola 56 (②).

Carratraca

Surrounded by some excellent **walking country**, the village of **CARRATRACA** 5km southwest of Ardales, is famous for its sulphur spa, used since the times of the Greeks and Romans. The *balneario*, or baths, which, during the last century attracted kings, princesses and literary big-names such as Lord Byron and Alexander Dumas, have recently reopened (June–Sept) after a long closure, but the three casinos where these socialites used to while away their time between plunges in the stinking, sulphurous waters which gush from the rocks are long gone.

The Regency-style *Ayuntamiento* on the edge of the village was the residence of Doña Trinidad Grund, a local benefactress who donated funds for the excavation of the cave near Bobastro which bears her name, as well as La Pileta near Ronda (see p.119). She also provided funds for the curious bullring nearby, hacked out of solid rock and the scene of the village passion play during *Semana Santa*.

Should you fancy an **overnight stay** Carratraca has one of the most exotic *hostales* in Andalucía. A royal palace built by the tyrannical King Fernando VII early in the last century to accommodate himself and his retinue (although he probably never used it) while visiting the spa, the *Hostal El Príncipe*, c/Antonio Rioboo 11 (☎952/458020; ③) is an elegant old place with an attractive patio, as well as a bar and restaurant (for guests only) but no en-suite bathrooms, which explains the low price. Another good restaurant is *El Trillo*, on the main street.

Ardales

At the southern point of the third of the lakes that comprise the Guadalteba-Guadalhorce reservoir, **ARDALES** tumbles down the hill below *La Peña*, a rocky outcrop topped by remains of the Iberian settlement of Turóbriga as well as a Roman fort and Moorish *alcázar*. On the way up to the summit, look out for the fifteenth-century Mudéjar **church** with its distinctive, partly tiled, tower.

Activity in Ardales revolves around a wide and animated central plaza, where you'll find the *Ayuntamiento* (collect keys to the nearby Paleolithic Cueva de Doña Trinidad here), as well as comfortable **rooms** at the friendly *Hostal Bobastro*, La Plaza 13 (☎952/458081; ②). While there's a lively bar scene, with *tapas* to be had on the square, **to eat** more substantially you'll have to cross the bridge at the bottom of the village to the *Hostal-Restaurante El Cruce*, which serves a good value *menú*.

El Burgo

An unpaved road leaves Ardales for the tiny settlement of **EL BURGO**, 15km southwest. It's a beautifully scenic drive – and a fine three- to four-hour **walk** – through the rugged valley of the Río Turón which gurgles beneath the heights of the Sierra de Ortegicar. There's plenty of birdlife, and, halfway along the route, a deserted village with a ruined mill to explore. This was, until relatively recently, bandit country, where travellers needed to be constantly on their guard against robbers and kidnappers. One particularly ruthless *bandolero* named Pasos Largos (Big Steps) worked this stretch in the 1930s and ended his days in a shoot-out with the Guardia Civil – his memory is still fresh around El Burgo where he was born. El Burgo, when you finally reach it, is a pleasant enough place with another ruined Moorish fort, and few facilities – although it does have a **fonda**; the *Berrocal*, c/Heredia 5 (☎952/872945; ②). You can also get rooms at **YUNQUERA**, 7km to the south, where there's a good *hostal*; the *Asencio*, c/Mesones 1 (☎952/480543; ②).

The paved C344 from El Burgo meanders through more ruggedly picturesque, uninhabited terrain until, after 20km, it reaches the suburbs of Ronda (see p.110).

Teba

About 15km north of Ardales, the village of **TEBA** spreads itself out below a hill crowned by a striking **Moorish castle** built on Roman foundations. There's a well-preserved dungeon in the castle, but you'll need either matches or a flashlight to find your way around. The castle battlements give wonderful **views** over the surrounding countryside; you can also glimpse the municipal **swimming pool**, close by.

On the plain below the castle, a battle against the Moors took place in 1331 when the forces of Alfonso XI recovered Teba for Christian Spain. In this battle fought Sir James Douglas, who had been commissioned by a dying Robert Bruce to carry the Scottish king's heart to the Holy Land "to be carried in battle against the enemies of Christ". Douglas took the long way round, via Spain, and ended up getting involved at the siege of Teba. He wore the royal heart in a silver case around his neck and – at a difficult moment in the battle – to spur on his men he threw it into the fray charging after it to his death. The heart was recovered and taken back to Scotland to be buried in Melrose Abbey. Near the centre of the village, in the Plaza de España, a block of Scottish granite has been set up to mark Teba's illustrious connection with Robert Bruce and the exploits of Douglas, and was unveiled by one of Douglas' descendants in 1989.

The lower square you come upon as you arrive in Teba has all the **places to stay**: three clean, friendly and good-value *fondas*. Progressing up the hill to the heart of the town you are left in no doubt as to Teba's political persuasions – there's an enormous hammer and sickle painted on the tarmac in the middle of the crossroads. Aside from this and the parish church, with its frescoes and Flemish paintings, there's little to see in this calm and prosperous little place.

About 3km to the east of the village lies the small but picturesque Garganta de Teba or **Teba Gorge**, where the oleander-fringed Río la Venta cuts through the limestone hills to join the reservoir. A haven for all kinds of butterflies, there's also plenty of bird-life along the river banks and the gorge is a nesting site for the Egyptian vulture and Bonelli's eagle, along with plenty of other varieties such as black kites and choughs. To reach the gorge, descend the track which leaves the roadside by the bridge over the Río la Venta on the edge of the reservoir.

El Torcal Natural Park

EL TORCAL, 13km south of Antequera, and 32km north of Málaga, is the most geologically arresting of Andalucía's natural parks. A massive high plateau of glaciated limestone, tempered by a lush growth of hawthorn, ivy, wild rose and thirty species of orchid, it's quite easily explored using the **walking routes** that radiate from the centre of the park. Try to leave your explorations until late afternoon, when not only is it quieter, but you will have the added benefit of the setting sun throwing the natural sculptures into sharp relief.

The best designed and most exciting trail is the 3km path picked out in yellow arrows and climaxing with suitable drama on a cliff edge with magnificent views over a valley. This is the most popular walk in the park, and in summer you may find yourself competing with gangs of schoolkids who arrive en masse on vaguely educational trips, excitedly trying to spot "La Copa" (the wineglass), "El Lagarto" (the lizard) and "La Loba" (the she-wolf) as well as other celebrated rock sculptures. More peaceful, at all times, is the **red route** (5km; allow 5hr), which gives fantastic vantage points of the looming limestone formations, eroded into vast, surreal sculptures. Griffon vultures with their huge wingspans often make a spectacular sight as they glide overhead.

Though **no buses** link El Torcal to Antequera, it's an easy enough 13km walk (take the C3310 road to Villanueva de la Concepción and head down the second signed turning on the right to El Torcal). You've got good chances of hitching a lift, especially on weekends, when it may possible to persuade one of the school buses to take you back. Failing this, you might consider a taxi (approximately 1500ptas one way) or the daily buses which run on workdays from Antequera to Villanueva de la Concepcíon (1pm & 6.30pm) and ask the driver to drop you at the road for El Torcal. The return bus should pass the same turn-off at 7.45am and 3.30pm, which is not much use unless you plan to stay overnight. It's quite acceptable to **camp** in the park – but take plenty of provisions.

Antequera

Sited on two low hills in the valley of the Río Guadalhorce, **ANTEQUERA** is an attractive market town with some important ancient monuments and a clutch of fine churches. On the main train line to Granada and at the junction of roads heading inland to Córdoba, Granada and Sevilla, it's easy to get to, and makes a good day trip from Málaga. Travelling from Málaga, the bus takes you along the fastest (but least interesting) route, the recently constructed N331 which follows the Guadalmedina river valley. If you're hitching or driving, however, it's far nicer to take the older, more picturesque

The telephone area code for Antequera is ☎952.

road that meanders through **Almogía**, a small hill town with tortuously narrow streets. It's a sleepy place except on Friday, market day, when the whole place spills over with shoppers. From here the road climbs on through hills of baked red earth dotted with wild olives to **Villanueva de la Concepcíon**. Nearing Antequera you pass a turning to El Torcal (see opposite) which is quickly followed by a **spectacular view** over the sea plain to the south.

Arrival, information and accommodation

Antequera's *RENFE* station, c/Divina Pastora 8, is rather out of the way, a 3km walk or bus-ride to the centre of town. The bus from Málaga brings you closer in, disembarking at the **bus station** near the bullring. For information on the town, or help with finding a room, the **Turismo** has two offices: one at the Museo Municipal, and a sub-office on the main Alameda at c/Infante Don Fernando 1 (both Tues–Fri 10am–1.30pm, Sat 10am–1pm, Sun 11am–1pm; ☎842180).

Places to stay are limited. Two worth trying first, however, are *Hostal Reyes*, c/Tercia 4 (☎841028; ③), or the friendly *Pension-Bar Madrona*, c/Calzada 25 (☎840014; ③) near the market. On the opposite side of the market there's the tranquil *Pension Toril*, c/Toril 3 (☎843184; ③) with its rooms arranged around a leafy patio. A little further away – towards the Málaga road – lies another good option *Hostal Bella-Vista,* Cuesta de Archidona 27 (☎841997; ③). There's also the modern *Parador de Antequera*, c/Garcia del Olmo s/n (☎840261; ⑥) and several *hostales* on the roads in and out of town. The nearest **campsite** is in El Torcal.

The Town

A bustling agricultural centre where farmers from the surrounding *Vega* come to stock up on everything from tractor tyres to seeding attachments, Antequera has a modern appearance that belies its history. In Roman times *Anticaria* ("ancient city") seems to have had a substantial population; much later, in 1410, the town was the first in Andalucía to fall to the Christian forces, who in this battle introduced gunpowder to Spanish warfare for the first time.

Antequera divides into two zones: a **monumental quarter** situated at the foot of the hill dominated by the alcazaba, and the mainly nineteenth-century **commercial sector** concentrated around the Alameda de Andalucía. This end of town is where modern Antequera works and plays, and there's not much in the way of sights, though the nineteenth-century bullring is worth a look. Probably the most famous sights, however, are the prehistoric Dolmen Caves, on the northern edge of town.

The Museo Municipal

At the heart of the monumental quarter, the **Museo Municipal**, c/Coso Viejo s/n (Mon–Sat 10am–1.30pm, Sun 11am–1pm; hourly guided tours 100ptas) is located in a striking eighteenth-century ducal palace. It's just as well that the palace is worth visiting for itself, because the exhibits do little justice to the setting, despite the efforts of a guide who tries his best to enliven the proceedings with a few time-worn jokes. Largely a hotchpotch of church vestments, silver plate and indifferent paintings, the collection is, however, distinguished by two works of sculpture; a fine **first century AD Roman bronze** of a youth known as the "Efebo de Antequera", and an eerily lifelike carving in wood of **Saint Francis of Assisi** by the seventeenth-century Andalucían sculptor and

painter, Alonso Cano. More fragments of ancient statuary and tombstones are dotted around the courtyard, and a room on the ground floor devotes itself to the artworks of a modern painter born in Antequera, Cristóbal Toral.

Just to the east of the museum, on the way to the alcazaba, the eighteenth-century **Carmelite nunnery** on Plaza de las Descalzas has a good selection of *dulces*. The entrance is behind the small fountain. Inside, the sweets available are displayed in a window; a *surtido* (sampler) gets you a bit of everything. When you've decided, ring the bell and call your order into the *torno* – you won't see the nun who serves you, but she may ask you to pay first – a sign of changing times.

Nuestra Señora del Carmen

The nearby Cuesta de los Rojas climbs steeply to the Postigo de la Estrella, an old postern gate. To the east of this – and not to be missed – lies the seventeenth-century Mudéjar church of **Nuestra Señora del Carmen**, whose plain facade little prepares you for the eighteenth-century interior, recently and painstakingly restored to its former glory. The main altar's sensational forty-feet high **retablo** – one of the finest of its kind in Andalucía – is a masterly late-Baroque extravaganza of carved wood, its centrepiece a Virgin in a *camarín* flanked by a bevy of polychromed saints and soaring angels.

The Alcazaba

Further up Cuesta de los Rojas lies the ruined medieval Alcazaba, with its thirteenth-century century Islamic fortification, the **Torre Mocha**. The first fortress to fall to the Christians during the Reconquest of the Kingdom of Granada, the ruined alcazaba now encloses a municipal Garden, giving **fine views** over the town towards the curiously anthropoid **Peña de las Enamorados** ("Lovers' Rock") resembling the profiled head of a sleeping giant. The outcrop acquired its name from two lovers (a Christian girl and a Moslem youth) during the Moorish period, who are said to have thrown themselves from the top when their parents forbade their marriage.

Adjoining the alcazaba, the sixteenth-century **Arco de los Gigantes** preserves stones and inscriptions embedded in its walls which were rescued by antiquaries from the destruction of the Roman town in the same period. Large parts of the town were still standing – including a fine theatre – until used for the construction of many churches in the seventeenth and eighteenth centuries.

East of the castle, in the spacious Plaza Alta, the sixteenth-century church of **Santa María** boasts a great Plateresque facade inspired by a Roman triumphal arch. Should you be able to gain entry – which isn't easy as the church now serves as a concert hall – you'll also see a superb Mudéjar coffered ceiling.

Antequera's churches

Walking from the alcazaba back into the town centre you'll pass a number of **churches**. The seventeenth-century **San Sebastian**, in the elegant plaza of the same name, possesses a striking brick steeple that dominates the town. Note the carved angels on the tower – one of them has the remains of Antequera's patron saint, Santa Euphemia, in a reliquary hung around its neck. This church also has some beautifully carved choirstalls, as does the nearby eighteenth-century **San Augustin**, at the start of c/Infante Fernando. At the western end of this street and close to the **Palacio Consistorial** – a stylish seventeenth-century mansion now functioning as the *Ayuntamiento* – lies the Renaissance church of **San Juan de Dios**, constructed (or so Richard Ford maintained), almost entirely with stone taken from the demolition of a perfectly preserved Roman theatre. Slightly further away at the southern end of the town, the whitewalled Baroque chapel of **Santa María de Jesús** contains Antequera's most revered image, Nuestra Señora del Socorro (Our Lady of Succour).

The Plaza de Toros

The western end of town has little in the way of sights, though the nineteenth-century **Plaza de Toros**, on the Alameda de Andalucía, is well worth a look – access is usually available when the restaurant (see "Eating and drinking") is open. This bullring staged its first *corrida* on 20 August 1848, and whatever your view about the morality of this "sport", it's difficult not to pick up on the atmosphere that the old place generates, especially when you view the amphitheatre from the matador's position in the centre of the burning sand.

The Dolmen caves

On the town's northern outskirts – an easy 1km walk along the Granada road – lie a group of **prehistoric dolmens** (Tues–Fri 10am–2pm & 3–5.30pm, Sat–Sun 10am–2pm; 200ptas), which rank among the most important in Spain. The most impressive of these megalithic monuments is the **Cueva de Menga**, its roof formed by massive stone slabs, among them an immense 180-ton monolith. Dating from c2500BC, the columned gallery leading to an oval burial chamber was probably the final resting place of an important chieftan. On the final stone slab of the left wall you'll see some engraved – and probably symbolic – forms; the star, however, is a more recent addition. If you stand just inside the entrance to the Menga dolmen you will be able to see the Lovers' Rock, precisely framed in the portal – something that cannot have been accidental and suggests that the rock may have had some religious or ritual significance. This is underlined by the fact that the sun rises behind the "head" of the rock at the summer solstice and penetrates into the burial chamber, much as happens in the New Grange passage grave in Ireland.

The **Cueva de Viera**, dating from a century later, has better cut stones, forming a long narrow tunnel leading to a smaller burial chamber. To the west of here it is possible to make out the quarry on the peak of a nearby hill (topped by a rather incongruous school) from where the stone used to construct the dolmens was hewn before being hauled across the intervening valley. The cave guardian will point it out on request.

The third dolmen, **El Romeral**, is a further 2km down the road on the left behind a sugar factory (easily identified by its chimney). Once you've crossed the train line, the road to it is signed on the left; if it's locked you'll have to return to the Cueva de Menga for the key. Built more than half a millennium later than the other two dolmens and containing dual chambers roofed with splendid corbel vaulting, El Romeral has something of an eastern Mediterranean feel, and bears an uncanny resemblance to the tholos tombs constructed in Crete at around the same time.

Should you turn up outside the official opening hours, pause outside the garage beside the main entrance; you may be approached by a couple of rum old characters who have spare keys and will allow you to see the dolmens for a consideration.

Eating and drinking

Antequera, unlike its neighbours on the coast to the south, has little in the way of exciting food or entertainment options. You'll trail past a variety of fast food places, bars and *heladerías* along the Alameda, but a far better bet, during the day at least, is to head for the many **places to eat** around the market on Plaza Abartos, catering for the traders and customers who flock in from miles around. Among numerous good *tapas* bars here, there's also a good restaurant, *Madrona*, c/Calzada 25, which serves a hearty and inexpensive *menú*. This bar-restaurant also opens in the evenings and even has rooms (see "Arrival, information and accommodation").

Nearer the centre, the *Meson Noelía*, Alameda 12, serves medium-priced *platos combinados* and has pavement tables – only really feasible once the traffic has died down. A quieter location to sit out is at the **Plaza de Toro**. The bullring's very own restaurant, *La Espuela* ("the spur") offers a medium-priced *menú*, which includes wine, as well as more expensive meals – the bar here is also a good place to stop for lunchtime *tapas*.

Around Antequera

Within easy distance of Antequera are trips to the important flamingo breeding grounds of **Fuente de Piedra** and the hill town of **Archidona** set in the midst of olive groves.

Laguna de Fuente de Piedra

About 20km northwest of Antequera lies **Laguna de Fuente de Piedra**, the largest natural lake in Andalucía and a celebrated site for observing birdlife. The shallow water level and high saline content of the lake, and the crustaceans that these conditions breed, attract a glorious flock of **Greater Flamingo** each spring, making this Europe's only inland breeding ground for the species. Unfortunately the droughts of recent years and the demands for more water by local farmers who have cashed in on an asparagus boom in the nearby Sierra de Yeguas, have led to the lake almost drying up completely in the summer months, thus placing many of the young flamingos in peril. This resulted in rescue missions being mounted by teams from the Coto Doñana (see p.221) who transferred many young birds back to the wetlands of Huelva. Andalucía's environmental agency, the *Agencia del Medio Ambiente*, has been working urgently on a system to prevent this happening again.

Besides supporting a variety of waders at all times of the year, in winter the lake is often a haven for cranes, and the surrounding marshes provide a habitat for numerous amphibians and reptiles. Remember that because this is a sanctuary, the beaches are strictly out of bounds (ruling out swimming) and because many sections are privately owned, limiting access, it's not possible to make a complete circuit of the lake.

Easy to get to, the village of **Fuente de Piedra** is on the train route from Málaga to Córdoba, while the lake itself lies a twenty-minute walk east of the station. The village has two **places to stay**, the *Hostal La Laguna* (☎952/735292; ③) and the *Hostal D'Málaga* (☎952/735093; ②), both close to the main Sevilla–Málaga road. There's also a **campsite**, c/Camino de la Rabita s/n (☎952/735294) on the edge of the village with a view over the lake.

Archidona

ARCHIDONA, 15km east of Antequera and surrounded by olive groves, lies beneath a mountain spur topped by a *castillo* and an ancient hermitage. Called by the Romans *Arx Domina*, referring to its impregnable position, the town was also of strategic importance to the earlier Iberian Túrduli tribe, as well as the later Moors who built a solid alcazaba on the remains of the Roman walls. In 756 Abd ar-Rahman I was proclaimed emir at Archidona, and went on to found the great Ummayad dynasty, later based at Córdoba. Conquered by the Christian forces in 1462, the town became the feudal fief of the Counts of Ureña and Dukes of Osuna – which it remained until the last century.

The Town

Archidona has two parts: the older monumental quarter at its eastern end is connected by one long main street to the more recent *polygano industrial*. It's well worth calling in on the exceptionally friendly **Ayuntamiento**, Paseo de la Victoria s/n, housed in the fine **Edificio de la Cilla**, the sixteenth-century tax collection centre for the ducal lands, which doubles up as a **Turismo** and will provide maps and information about the area.

A little to the west of here and flanking either side of the main street are the **Convento de las Minimas** and, off to the right, the **Plaza Ochavada**. Closed to the public, the sixteenth-century convent has an elegant early Baroque facade and a wonderful polygonal brick tower topped by a green and white tiled spire. Just along from the main entrance a small door opens on to a lobby where, from behind a *torno* the nuns will serve you with their fattening *dulces*.

Across the road and just behind the main street, the remarkable **Plaza Ochavada** is a late eighteenth-century octagonal square, inspired by French styles but incorporating local Andalucian features based upon the use of brickwork and the traditional patio. Designed by Francisco Astorga and Antonio González Sevillano, the plaza was built partly to alleviate the terrible unemployment of the period as well as bringing better housing and drains to a previously run down quarter. Recent additions such as the hedgerows and a central fountain have provoked criticism from purists.

On the hill overlooking the town and approached by a road which ascends from its eastern end, the **Ermita de la Virgen de Gracia** is built over a much altered ancient mosque. Little remains of the Moorish structure apart from an underground water cistern, although in the chapel is preserved a superb Mudéjar **baptismal font** in glazed green earthenware. From the vestiges of the alcazaba above there are terrific **views** to be had over the town as well as back to Antequera and the Peña de los Enamoradas (Lovers' Rock).

Practicalities

Archidona's **train** station is 6km northwest out of town. As for **places to stay**; close to the turn off for the hermitage on the main street, the *Hostal Cervera* (☎952/714827; ②) offers clean **rooms** and a restaurant. Another *hostal* with similar facilities, *Hostal Las Palomas* (☎952/714326; ②), lies on the western approach to the town. However, by far the most glamorous place to stay in the area lies east of town, towards the uninspiring town of **Loja**. A turn off after 10km along the C334 to Rute will bring you to the grandiose *La Bobadilla*, Finca La Bobadilla (☎958/321861; ⑥). Surrounded by acres of woodland and built on the model of a "typical" Andalucian village it has appealed to guests as diverse as Tom Cruise and King Juan Carlos. To stay at this Iberian Xanadu will cost you a king's ransom and dinner at the *à la carte* restaurant – supplied by its own farm on the estate – doesn't come cheap either. Call in for a drink if you're curious.

East from Málaga: the coast to Torre del Mar

The dreary eastern stretch of the **Costa del Sol** – the beaches within easy distance of Málaga – is a largely unbroken landscape of urbanization and uncharming holiday towns, packed to the gunnels in summer with day-tripping *malagueños*. There are enough places of interest, however, to warrant stopping off en route, before arriving at the unremarkable resort of **Torre del Mar**.

With your own transport it's possible to avoid the Málaga suburbs by using the N331 *circunvalación* – picked up on the northern edge of town – which comes out just beyond Rincón de la Victoria (see below). Otherwise, heading out of Málaga the N340 traverses the suburbs of Pedragalejo and El Palo where for most of the summer the beaches are covered with a forest of day-trippers' parasols.

Cueva del Tesoro and Rincón de la Victoria

Just beyond Cala del Moral, a signed road on the left indicates the **CUEVA DEL TESORO** (Mon–Fri 10am–2pm & 3–7pm, Sat & Sun 11am–7pm; 200ptas), a spectacular network of underground caves less commercialized than the caves at Nerja (see p.87). A series of seven chambers, spiked with stalagmites and stalactites, leads to the eighth, the **sala de los lagos**, a Gaudí-esque rock cathedral with natural underground pools. Paleolithic cave paintings were discovered here in 1918 (presently not on view) as well as other prehistoric remains indicating almost continual human habitation. The cave's name ("tesoro" means treasure) derives from the legend that five fleeing Moorish kings took refuge in its depths and stashed a large quantity of gold; the gold is long gone but the cave retains its name.

Two kilometres further on, **RINCÓN DE LA VICTORIA** is a no-nonsense, scruffy sort of place, and another local resort for *malagueño* families. It's a functional spot to swim if you've a day to fill before catching a plane home, but nothing more. A seafood speciality in the *marisquerías* here are *coquinas*, tasty small clams.

Macharaviaya

To break the monotony along this strip you could follow a small road north at the featureless suburb of Torre de Benagalbón which winds up into the hills and approaches the hamlet of **MACHARAVIAYA**.

Surrounded by slopes covered with olive and almond trees, the village was built up in the eighteenth century by the Galvéz family, one of Andalucía's great imperial dynasties. Count Bernardo de Galvéz became governor general of Spanish North America and gave his name to Galveston in Texas after laying siege to the town during the American War of Independence in 1777. Today, even taking into account its impressive Baroque church (a Galvéz construction), it's hard to credit that this tiny cobble-streeted village was once known as "little Madrid". It was a wealthy place, benefiting from the extensive Galvéz family vineyards as well as a playing-card factory which had a monopoly for supplying cards to the Americas. This was all to end, however, when the phylloxera plague of the 1870s wiped out the vines, the card monopoly lapsed and the Galvéz line died out. The family title died with them, and the last Visconte de Galveston is buried in the church crypt among the tombs and alabaster statues of his ancestors.

At the entrance to the village is a rather proprietorial whitewashed brick temple erected by the family in 1786 and, at its centre, the once crumbling but now over-restored – as part of the *Expo 92* celebrations – exterior of the **church of San Jacinto**. To enter you'll need to get two keys from the mayor's house, up a ramp beside the *Ayuntamiento* – as it's a private house, avoid calling in at siesta time. Inside the single nave church, altars dedicated to various Galvéz family members are decorated with fine marble, and inscriptions express the ultimately vain hope that mass would be said on certain days for their souls *in perpetuum*.

Don't miss the eerie crypt behind the church, where a remarkable collection of sombre **alabaster family busts** face each other around an alcove and seem about to start up a gloomy conversation. The great marble tomb of Don José Galvéz, Marquis of Sonora and Minister for the Indias during the eighteenth-century reign of Carlos III, stands nearby. Facing the church is the old playing-card factory, now converted into dwellings, and including the *Bar Sonora*. Should this be closed and you need refreshment, follow the sign to the simple *Taberna El Candil* around the corner, which will serve you *tapas* if pushed.

Two kilometres to the north of Macharaviaya, the village of **Benaque** has a Mudéjar church whose tower has conserved the minaret of the Moorish mosque it replaced. It's also possible to **walk** from here across the ridge of the Montes de Málaga west to Olías or alternatively, east to Almayate and the sea, about a two-hour trek in either direction.

Torre del Mar

Back on the main coast road, the chain of localities with "torre" in their names refers to the numerous *atalayas* or watchtowers which have been used to guard this coast since Roman and Moorish times, many strikingly visible on the headlands. There is little to detain you between Torre de Benagalbón and Almayate – though the latter has a reasonable campsite, *Almayate-Costa* (☎952/540272) with limited shade – from where it's only a couple of kilometres to **TORRE DEL MAR**. A line of concrete tower blocks on a grey, pebble beach, this resort is Torremolinos without the latter's money or fun. But it's quiet, and recent improvements include a paved promenade area, El Copo, in an attempt to swoop the place upmarket. Numerous **restaurants and bars** here fill up in the evenings, but it never really takes off.

If you want to **stay**, head for the central *Hostal Generalife*, c/Patrón Veneno 22 (☎952/254 33 09; ②), a *pensión* with an ebulliently friendly owner and just 30m from the beach. Like everywhere else around here, though, rooms are at a premium in high season and your best hope then will probably be the basic **campsite** *Torre del Mar* (☎952/540224) on the Paseo Marítimo. Otherwise the helpful **Turismo**, Avda. de Andalucia 92 (☎952/541104) may be able to advise.

The Axarquia

If you have your own transport, a trip up into the often spectacularly beautiful region of **Axarquia** makes a refreshing change from the sunbed culture of the Costa del Sol. Bounded by the coast, the Sierra de Tejeda to the north and, on its eastern flank, the mountainous edge of the province of Granada, this rugged, ham-shaped wedge of territory offers excellent walking country and abundant wildlife, as well as a host of attractive mountain villages that make easy-going stop-offs. Long a breeding ground for *bandoleros* who preyed on traders carrying produce from the coast to Granada, Axarquia was also a notorious guerrilla encampment during the Civil War – which fought on against Franco's *Guardia Civil* until the early 1950s: it is only in recent times that the area has become safe for travellers.

Vélez-Málaga

Frequent buses head the 4km inland from Torre del Mar to **VÉLEZ-MÁLAGA**, a bustling market town, supply centre for the region's farmers and capital of Axarquia. In the fertile valley of the Río Vélez, Vélez-Málaga (often simply referred to as Vélez) was important in both Roman – under the name of *Menoba* – and Moorish times, when as *Ballix-Malaca* ("Fortress of Málaga") it had an important role in subduing what has always been a turbulent zone. A number of Phoenician cemeteries and tombs discovered recently nearby testify to a much older pedigree still. When Fernando conquered the town in 1487, the Christian flag was raised on the castle's battlements as the Moors were ejected. This victory, which drove a wedge through the kingdom of Granada dividing it in two, paved the way for the fall of the Nasrid city five years later.

The Town

Vélez climbs up a slope from the main street, **Avenida Vivar Téllez** – where you'll arrive whether you're travelling by bus or car – towards the **castillo**, as good a place as any to start a tour of the sights. What's left of it clings to a rocky outcrop overlooking the town and from its dominant position above the white-walled barrio of San Sebastián, gives good views out over the coast. Now reduced to a keep and a few chunks of wall surrounded by gardens, it suffered badly during the War of the Spanish Succession when the English went down to the French here after a bitter struggle in 1704. Visible from the castillo is the sixteenth-century Mudéjar church of **Santa María la Mayor** whose beautiful sectioned tower still holds the minaret of the mosque that preceded it. Inside, Moorish arches separate a triple nave, and there's a fine Mudéjar ceiling. Immediately below the castillo another church, **Nuestra Señora de la Encarnación**, has a history reflecting that of Andalucía itself. Beginning life as a Visigoth bishopric, the building was transformed into a mosque during the Moorish period, and back into a church again following the *reconquista*. The late-Gothic **San Juan Bautista**, on Plaza de España, is also worth a look, featuring an elegant tower and, inside, a superbly naturalistic sculpture *Cristo Crucificado* ("Christ Crucified") by Pedro de Mena.

The recently restored **Palacio del Marques de Beniel**, Plaza Palacio 1, is an elegant sixteenth-century mansion – formerly the town hall – which now hosts the *International Summer School of the Axarquia* covering all aspects of culture, including poetry and theatre as well as *flamenco* and classical guitar. A prestigious annual guitar competition is held here in July, and, as the free concerts all take place in the *palacio's* delightful patio, are well worth taking in. The reception desk here will provide details of a varied programme of cultural activities throughout the summer.

Less attractively, Vélez is also one of the last bastions of **cock-fighting** in Europe, and the Sunday fights held in the town in winter pull in crowds of *aficionados* from miles around to bet on the outcome as the feathers fly.

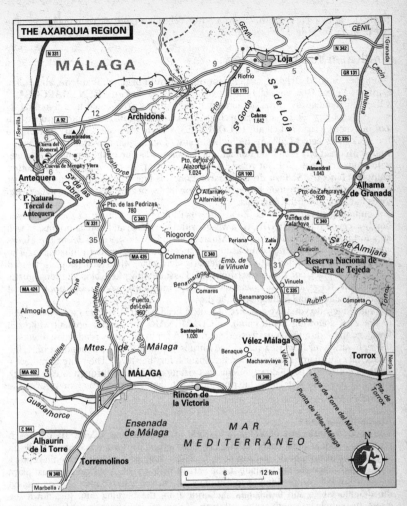

THE AXARQUIA REGION

Practicalities

Vélez-Málaga's **bus station** is on Avda. Vivar Téllez, the main street leading out of town towards the sea. Many places to **eat and drink** line the avenida, including the excellent medium-priced *Meson Los Migueles*, at no. 83, serving a variety of fish and meat dishes and a good-value *menú*.

Finding a place to stay isn't usually a problem, except possibly at the end of July when every *hostal* bedroom seems to be twanging furiously as the young competitors go through their exercises in preparation for the guitar competition. Best of the bunch is the friendly *Casa los Martinez*, c/Cristo 58, on the main crossroad as you approach the centre from Avda. Vivar Téllez (☎952/504287; ②); they also have a good **restaurant**. Just across the road, the surly *El Cañizo*, Avda. Vivar Téllez 11 (☎952/250 05 20; ③) is another accommodation possibility, while the local **campsite**, *Valle Niza* (☎952/

513181), on the edges of town on Avda. Vivar Téllez is a more pleasant option than the one down in Torre del Mar (see p.79).

North from Vélez to Alfarnate

A number of **good driving routes around Axarquia** begin at **Trapiche**, about 3km north of Vélez. One possibility is to veer northwest towards **BENAMARGOSA**, a village surrounded by citrus orchards and olive groves. You could take a look at its sixteenth-century Gothic-style **church of La Encarnación** before moving on to **La Zubía**, where a road left climbs to **COMARES**, a white town spectacularly clinging to the peak of its conical hill. At the highest point of all, beside a charming cemetery, a ruined Moorish fort – built on Roman foundations – was one of the strongholds, along with Bobastro (see p.79), of rebel leader Ibn Hafsun. In the village is yet another church of **Nuestra Señora de la Encarnación**, this time a sixteenth-century Mudéjar building with a picturesque tower. A **mirador** in the nearby Plaza del Ayuntamiento gives fine views over the Axarquia.

Continuing north out of La Zubía the road follows the course of the Río Cueva, finally ascending to **RIOGORDO**, a village with Phoenician and Roman origins, as well as a fortified stronghold during the Moorish period. After the *reconquista* the Moors were replaced by settlers from Castile, the ancestors of the modern inhabitants. The *Semana Santa* celebrated here is a particularly vivid affair, when local people – dressed for the part – act out the scenes from the Passion with often bloodcurdling gusto. Incidentally, the village also boasts an attractive **municipal swimming pool**, a great place to splash around in the heat of the day.

From Riogordo you have a choice of routes: head east to Alfarnate (see opposite) or to the west, following a stiff climb, to **COLMENAR**, yet another brilliant white hill town and the Axarquia's most westerly outpost. A centre of honey production thanks to the rich variety of flowering plants and shrubs growing in the surrounding hills; the village takes its name from *colmena*, the Spanish for "bee-hive". The route from here – via the Puerto del León – down to Málaga, twisting and turning through forests of cork oaks and pines, is wonderful, offering, during its latter stages, great views over the Costa del Sol.

Alcaucín and Zalía

The **second route out of Vélez** forks right at Trapiche and follows the old coach route from Málaga to Granada. **VIÑUELA**, 7km beyond the fork, was originally a *venta* stop and the **atmospheric old inn** here, *La Viña* – dating from the eighteenth century – still stands opposite the fountain in the narrow main street. A spit-and-sawdust place today, it's usually jammed full on midsummer afternoons with old men arguing around the domino tables and farmhands sheltering from the burning sun. Just down the street, the simple sixteenth-century **church of San José** has a finely worked sculpture of the *Pietá*.

At the Puente de Don Manuel, 3km further on, a road cuts off on the right and ascends to the village of **ALCAUCÍN**. On the way up keep an eye to your left where, across a valley you will be able to make out the ruins of the deserted medieval village of Zalía (see below) and beyond, the Puerto de Zaffaraya, a great "U" shaped cleavage in the Sierra de Alhama through which passes the ancient route to Granada. Alcaucín itself, perched on the slopes of the Sierra de Tejeda, is beautiful little village with wrought-iron balconies ablaze with flowering geraniums and a web of narrow white-walled streets reflecting its Moorish origins. As befits a mountain village there are numerous spring-fed fountains, among which the five-spouted Fuente San Sebastian has been restored very much in the Moorish style, complete with *azulejos*.

Continuing north from the Puente de Don Manuel, the C335 takes you to the dauntingly impressive **Zaffaraya Pass** (where in 1983 Neanderthal remains were found in a nearby cave), passing on the way the ruins of the fort and the deserted medieval village of **ZALÍA**. Local legend has it that the Moorish village was attacked by a plague of vipers after Patricio, a *malagueño* church minister, came in an attempt to convert the inhabitants to Christianity and they spurned him. The more likely explanation, though, is that the population of the village was put to the sword during the uprisings following the *reconquista*. Throughout most of the Moorish period Zalía's fortress, together with those at Comares and Bentomiz (near Arenas to the south) formed a defensive triangle to control this central sector of the Axarquia region. From here it is possible to continue to Granada via the Puerto de Zaffaraya and Alhama de Granada (p.338).

Alfarnatejo and Alfarnate

Pressing on along the C340 to **Periana** – a noted centre of peach growing and *anis* production – leads into the Axarquia's remoter extremities. About 3km beyond Periana you'll reach a fork; if you don't want to face a tortuous switchback secondary road which is unmade for the last few kilometres, ignore the sign for "Alfarnate 15km" and continue along the road signed to Riogordo and Colmenar. A further 4km will bring you to a right turn and an easier route to the village of **ALFARNATEJO** and, a little beyond this, the Axarquia's most northerly outpost, **ALFARNATE**. Although they lie a mere couple of kilometres apart, it would be difficult to find two places in Andalucía with less in common. Alfarnatejo, the smaller of the two is staunchly right-wing, while Alfarnate has always been on the left, and, unable to agree or cooperate on anything, they have built up a strong mutual animosity, which even discourages marriages between the two communities. In truth, neither village would win any beauty prizes, though Alfarnate, set on a plain covered with wheatfields is worth a visit for its attractive church, **Santa Ana**, a sixteenth-century edifice with a graceful Mudéjar tower.

However, Alfarnate's real claim to fame is the thirteenth-century **Venta de Alfarnate** (☎952/730544) on the village's western edge, which maintains – with some justification – to be the **oldest inn in Andalucía**. Situated in an isolated spot in the midst of brooding hills, it's not hard to see what attracted the various brigands and highwaymen to the place. Indeed, the interior, as well as being a bar/restaurant, is also a **museum** dedicated to keeping alive the memory of such outlaws as Luis Candelas who spent a night in the *venta*'s well-preserved **prison cell** en route to justice in Málaga. By far the most terrifying *bandolero* of all, however, was El Tempranillo, who in the 1820s arrived one hot day unannounced and, when there were no spoons for him to eat with, ordered the dining clients to eat their wooden ones at gunpoint, cracking their teeth in the process. The place is more civilized these days and serves a hearty mountain speciality, *huevos a lo bestia* (fried eggs with local sausage, ham and black pudding). Although it no longer has rooms, the amiable landlord, Fernando Nuño, rents out a fully equipped house in the village nearby (three day minimum let; ring in advance; ③) which is a good base for exploring the excellent walking terrain in the vicinity. He also has plans to open a more basic walkers' *hostal* and will provide information on this, too. Keep your eyes peeled in this area for the amazingly agile *cabra hispanica*, the rare Spanish goat; the long-horned male is a spectacular sight as he effortlessly scales almost vertical cliff faces.

From here you could backtrack to the C340 and continue along a spectacularly scenic road – flanked by great rock peaks and gorges filled with clumps of violets and pink oleander in summer – to Riogordo, eventually returning to Vélez by way of Benamargosa village.

East from Torre del Mar: the coast to Motril

The coast east from Torre del Mar is a nondescript stretch of faceless towns and the occasional concrete resort, dotted with more ancient *atalayas* or watchtowers. The first town of any real interest is **Nerja**, with some fine beaches and a relatively slow pace, while further east, **Almuñécar**, and even better **Salobreña**, are the city of Granada's Mediterranean playgrounds, flanked by numerous coves and inlets where for most of the year you can have a beach all to yourself.

Competa and Torrox

Leaving Torre del Mar the coast road climbs slightly to Algorrobo-Costa, an unappealing highrise beach resort. It's worth ignoring this and heading inland for a stretch, making the scenic 20km climb to the village of **COMPETA**. Keep your eyes peeled just after turning off the coast road for some well conserved **Phoenician tombs** (signposted on the right) dating from the eighth century BC. Originally these tombs formed part of an extensive cemetery, built of stone blocks and roofed in wood – the main tomb produced rich finds now in the Alcazaba museum at Málaga (see p.61). Beyond the village of Algorrobo the road toils on upwards as the fruit orchards of the coastal strip give way to the olive groves and vineyards. The road passes Sayalonga and ascends again, twisting and turning until it reaches Competa itself, a huddle of brilliant white boxes tumbling down a hillside, and surrounded by vineyards. A Moorish settlement in origin, and now discovered by migrants from northern Europe, Competa retains a relaxed atmosphere, and the easy-going villagers don't seem too worried about being swamped by foreigners. The sweet – and potent – wine made from the area's Moscatel grapes is renowned as the best in the whole province. You can try it for yourself at a tiny bodega, *La Buena Uva*, on Avda. de la Constitución close to the main plaza below the bell-tower of the church of La Asunción. On 15 August each year Competa rolls out the barrels – hundreds of them – during its annual fiesta, the *Noche del Vino*, when the square is filled with revellers determined to sink as much of the free *vino* as they can hold. Above the plaza to the left a street leads to a shrine with a **superb view** over the valley to the west and the sea beyond. If you decide to stay, the centrally located *Hostal Los Montes*, Plaza Almijara 2 (☎952/251 60 15; ②) has economical **rooms**.

Back on the coast, the **road** continues east through the dismal complexes of Lagos and El Morche until it enters Torrox Costa, a largely German and Scandinavian timeshare resort. More interesting than this concrete corral is the hamlet of **TORROX** proper, some 4km inland. Historically, Torrox reached the height of its prosperity during the Moorish period due to its pivotal role in the silk trade between Granada and Near Eastern cities such as Baghdad and Damascus. Now a permanent haven for colonies of expat Germans and Scandinavians, its centre is pretty enough, with brilliant whitewalled houses clinging to the steep slope on which the town is built. In high season – when there's little chance of finding a room or a place for your towel on the overcrowded beach – your best bet is to take a quick look at the remains of a **Roman necropolis and villa** immediately to the west of the lighthouse, before moving straight on to Nerja.

Nerja

Although **NERJA**, 8km along the coast from Torrox, cannot claim to have been bypassed by the tidal wave of post-1960s tourist development, this attractive resort has, nevertheless, held out against Torremolinos-type tower blocks, and its mainly villa and *urbanizaciones* construction has been more in keeping with its origins. Its setting, too, is spectacular, nestling among the foothills of the Almijara range and with some attractive **beaches** – Burriana to the east of the town is the best. There's also a series of coves within walking distance if you want to escape the crowds.

Arrival and information

The main **bus station** is on c/San Miguel close to Plaza Ermita; buses also leave from here for the hill village of Frigiliana and the Nerja Caves (see p.87). It's a five minutes' walk south from the station to the beach and centre, or old town. From the bus station locate the nearby **Plaza Cantarero**, slightly east, and then follow c/Pintada south towards the sea. Many of the room options lie to the east and west of this street, which will eventually bring you to the helpful **Turismo**, c/Puerta del Mar 2 (summer 10am–2pm & 5–9pm; ☎952/252 15 31), just to the east of the Balcón de Europa – be sure to pick up their useful town map. There's more maps and plenty of other information at *W H Smiffs* bookshop, next to the post office on c/Puerta del Mar; they also have a notice board which often lists job offers if you're looking for employment.

If you'd like to do some **walking** in the area, the Turismo has reference copies of the excellent *Twelve Walks around Nerja, Frigiliana and Maro* by Elma and Denis Thompson, which you can buy from the newsagent opposite. Elma is a chirpy Mancunian who – when not struggling with the apathetic authorities to keep footpaths open and make them easier to use – offers guided walks from November to May (call for details; ☎952/530782). **Bike rental**, by the day or the week, is available at both *Bici Nerja*, Pasaje Cantarero 1, off Plaza Cantarero near the bus station, and *Mountain Bike Holidays*, c/Cristo 10.

Accommodation

There is usually no problem finding **rooms** in Nerja except in August, when you should book in advance if you want to avoid the desperate twilight scramble for what's left. The lowest-priced possibilities are in the streets south of the bus station heading towards the sea. If everything's full, one solution may be to stay inland at Frigiliana (see p.87) or you could always try renting an apartment – which may even be a more economical bet for a group in high season. The Turismo can help out with information on apartments, and many of the *hostales* listed below have arrangements with numerous *casas particulares* to soak up the overflow.

Nerja's **campsite** (*Nerja Camping*; ☎952/656896) with shade, pool, bar and restaurant lies 4km east of the town, just beyond the turn-off for the caves on the left-hand side.

Hostal Alhambra, c/Antonio Millón s/n, on the junction with c/Chaparil (☎952/522174). Immaculate rooms, some with balcony, in a pleasant *hostal* a little west of the centre. ③.

Hostal Atambeni, c/Diputación 12 (☎952/521341). Friendly place close to the Turismo. ③.

Hostal Azahara, c/Avda. de Pescia 1 (☎952/520426). Serviceable place within a short distance of the bus station. ③.

Hotel Berlin, c/Carabeo 22 (☎952/521621). A range of options including some rooms with sea-view balcony and jacuzzi, as well as a pool, sauna and access to the beach. ④.

Hotel Cala-Bella, c/Puerta del Mar 10 (☎952/252 07 00). Almost on the Turismo's doorstep, with some rooms giving superb sea views. Guests get reductions in its restaurant, also overlooking the Calahonda beach. ③.

Hostal Estrella del Mar, c/Bella Vista 5 (☎952/520461). Quiet and clean place with balcony rooms which, because of its slightly out of the way location, on the eastern side of town, sometimes has space when others are full. ③.

Pensión Florida, c/San Miguel 33 (☎952/252 07 43). Clean little place with bar and patio, around the corner from the bus station. ②.

Hostal Miguel, c/Almirante Ferrandiz 31 (☎952/252 27 25). Atmospheric place with balcony rooms in the heart of the old town. This street can get noisy at night. ③.

Pensión Montesol, c/Pintada 130 (☎952/252 00 14). Clean, friendly *pensión* run by an ebullient *señora*. Across the nearby Plaza Cantarero from the *Florida*. ③.

Parador de Nerja, c/Almuñecar 8 (☎952/252 00 50). Modern parador which, despite an exterior resembling an open prison, has a pleasant plant-filled garden and patio, as well as a small park fronted by a bar (worth a visit even if you're not staying) overlooking the sea, plus an elevator down the cliff to Burriana, one of Nerja's most popular beaches. There's also a restaurant, serving a good value *menú*. ⑥.

Hostal Nerjasol, c/Arropiero 4 (☎952/252 12 47). On a quiet street, with sparkling rooms and a roof patio; this *pensión* will also direct you to a *casa particular* if they're full. ③.

The Town

Nerja's **old town** fans out to the north of the **Balcón de Europa**, a natural palm lined belvedere which offers magnificent views over the rocky coastline. The tangle of pretty narrow streets are crowded with visitors all summer long, but the brash shops which service them have yet to suffocate the town's easy-going tranquility. Nerja's obvious charm has attracted the inevitable colony of migrants – in this case the English – who make their presence felt in the numerous foreign-owned shops and bars as well as on the airwaves with their own stultifyingly expat *Radio Coastline*. Sights, as such, are few, and once you have strolled along the Balcón and taken a look at the nearby seventeenth-century whitewashed **iglesia El Salvador** – which has a fine *Dolorosa* – you should head for the beach or make a short excursion out of town.

Incidentally, Nerja does boast one of the best second-hand bookshops on the coast, **The Book Centre**, at c/Granada 30. It's a huge place, and well worth a visit, especially for rare and out-of-print paperbacks.

Eating

In the old town prices tend to be high and standards indifferent, and you'll do better to head further out for good, reasonably priced **restaurants**. On the western side of town, there are many authentic Spanish places concentrated around Plaza Marina. As for *tapas*, three of the best are *Marisquería la Familia*, c/Diputacíon 17, *Las 4 Esquinas*, on c/Pintada, and *El Chispa*, c/ San Pedro 12, which specializes in fried fish.

Cafetería Carlos, c/Los Huertos 52. Good, cheap *platos combinados*.

Cala-Bella, c/Puerto del Mar 10. One of the best restaurants in town, with balcony dining and a great sea view.

Casa Paco y Eva, c/El Barrio 50. Central restaurant where a medium-priced *à la carte* menu includes some regional specialities.

El Chispa, c/San Pedro 12. *Tapas* place specializing in fried fish.

Meson Gallego, c/Manuel Marin 12. Galician restaurant near Plaza Marina serving an economical *menú* as well as specialities such as *pulpo à la Gallega*, octopus in a paprika sauce.

Bodega del Jamón Casa Pepe, Plaza Marina. Where Nerja's Andalucían heart beats most firmly, run by Pepe, the swarthy giant. In a bar hung with hams and stacked with barrels the *fino* is excellent and is always served *al-Andaluz* – with a complimentary *tapa*. The *jamón serrano* is recommended, as is Pepe's speciality, *La Bomba* ("the bomb") resembling a potato croquette. Things really liven up around 10pm when the *flamenco* karaoke starts, something not to be missed. The bar goes mad as various diners – and sometimes staff – get up to take off *flamenco* greats such as Camaron and El Cabrero. On Thurs nights there's live *flamenco* with professionals.

Marisquería Jiminez, at the corner of Plaza Marina. The best *marisquería* in town, serving sea-fresh *tapas* and *raciones*. There's a sister branch at c/Ingenio 1, off Plaza Ermita.

Restaurante de Miguel, c/Pintada 2. Stylish place near the Turismo, with outdoor tables and an international menu.

Meson Pata Negra, Plaza Marina. Authentic regional dishes, a little more expensive than the other restaurants on the square.

Bar-Restaurante El Puente, c/Carretera 4. Good value place with a terrace, serving a cheap *menú*. On the town's western flank – walk to the bridge on the main road into town from Málaga.

Restaurante Rey Alfonzo, below the tip of the Balcon de Europa. This has the best sea view in town, though it can get a bit too briny in hot weather.

Bar-Restaurante Los Trillizos, c/Los Huertos 38. Excellent-value *menú* in attractive restaurant with a terrace at the back. On the eastern side of town, not far from the *Cafetería Carlos*.

Nightlife

Most of Nerja's **bars and disco bars** – many of them almost carbon copies of places you'd find in England – are concentrated east of the centre around Plaza Tutti Frutti and especially along the nearby c/Antonio Millon.

Los Amigos, c/Antonio Millon. Noisy live music bar.

Bar Cavana, Plaza Cavana. One of Nerja's traditional old bars, a tranquil place serving food behind the iglesia El Salvador.

Restaurante Bar-El Colono, c/Granada 6, just north of Plaza Cavana. Entertaining free *flamenco* show for diners and people just there for a drink.

Bodega del Jamón Casa Pepe, Plaza Marina. Reasonably authentic *flamenco* on Thurs nights.

Around Nerja

Cynics might find the "accidental" discovery in 1957 of the **Cuevas de Nerja** (daily 10.30am–2pm & 3.30–6.00pm; 400ptas) – neatly coinciding with the arrival of mass tourism – a little suspect. Immediately they were revealed, the series of enormous caverns scattered with Paleolithic and Neolithic tools, pottery and cave paintings stretching back 30,000 years, became a local, then national, sensation. Nowadays, however, the fairy lights, piped muzak, and cave theatre – which hosts various shows from rock to ballet and *flamenco* – have more in common with Disneyland than a spectacular natural wonder, and the cave paintings are currently not on public view and possibly never will be. The **restaurant** serves an economical buffet, but can resemble a train station in the busy high season. A far better place to eat is the *Hostal al Andaluz*, down the hill, which serves an excellent-value *menú* often featuring *paella* and *pera en vino* (pear in wine); there's a balcony terrace here, too.

From Nerja the caves are an easy 3km walk east along the main coast road, or as an alternative, there's also a bus service running approximately hourly from the Nerja bus station.

Another excursion that most visitors to Nerja end up making is the 6km trip north to **FRIGILIANA**, a pretty Moorish hill village clinging to the lower slope of Monte Coscoja. Six **buses** per day leave from the bus station in Nerja, the earliest of which give you enough time to take a walk in the area and get back before the last bus returns at 7.30pm.

After the *reconquista*, Frigiliana became a Mudéjar settlement where only those Moors who had converted to Christianity were allowed to live. Although a little of the atmosphere of this period survives in the steep, narrow streets, the place is prettified today by the addition of geranium pots and historical plaques, no doubt the reason why it won the Andalucía's Most Beautiful Village award in 1988.

In keeping with the village's status as a tourist draw, the restaurants and bars here tend to be overpriced, but if you want to **stay over**, the hospitable *Hotel Las Chinas*, Plaza Capitan Cortes 14 (☎952/253073; ③) is a good bet. They also have a good restaurant, and the proprietor, Miguel Agudo, will advise on walking in the area.

East of Nerja, the coast road zigzags around the foothills of the Sierra Almijarra, climbing above a number of tiny coves. The first settlement, the coastal hamlet of **MARO**, is a sparkling cluster of white-walled houses set above an attractive cove beach. Lying close to the ancient Roman settlement of *Detunda*, the town was revitalized in the eighteenth century by the construction of a sugar factory, now a ruin behind the simple church of Nuestra Señora de las Maravillas, which dates from the same period.

WALKS AROUND FRIGILIANA

One easy walk is to follow the 15km dirt track through the foothills of the **Almijara range**, leading from Frigiliana to the Axarquia village of Competa (p.84), which has good facilities and a variety of accommodation.

Another circular 8km walk covers the **hill country** to the northwest of Frigiliana. Follow the road north out of the village towards the pleasant *Venta de Frigiliana* (summer daily 11am–4pm) which you'll reach after 3km. Turn left down the dirt track just beyond the entrance, which leads down the ridge, passing some old cottages and villas. Ten minutes or so further on you'll pass the gates of the *Peñones* and the *Cortijo del Peñon* farmhouses on the right. Continue down this track between pine woods and crags until you reach a crossroads, with a walled villa on the far side. Fork sharply left at this point, passing some more old cottages on the right. One of these has a single palm tree, the ancient Moorish sign of welcome. At the first fork, below a large villa, continue left, uphill. The road winds round the villa wall, swings right and crosses the lower Pedregal valley, from where it climbs up the hill to the col on the Loma de la Cruz. Just below the crest of the ridge, where a *carril* (track) comes up from the right, keep straight on up, passing a villa. In front of this villa, a water-cover stamped "SAT no 7196 Monte Ariza" will confirm that you're on the right road. At the col, go straight across at the cross-tracks marked with red paint and follow the track down and round, keeping left of the fork on the next ridge. This will bring you down past the *Casa del Valle*, on the left. A little further on, round the bend, you'll see some tumbledown houses on the right; the first of these contains an old olive or wine press which is worth a look. The *carril* now passes through open country, then through *huertas*, rejoining the Torrox road at Casa Fernando. A right and then a left turn will you to the upper car park on the edge of Frigiliana.

The Costa Tropical

The **Costa Tropical** is the name given to Granada province's 60km of coastline, much of it refreshingly tranquil after the concrete sprawls along the Costa del Sol. Beyond Nerja, the N340 passes more tracks leading down to inviting coves with quiet **beaches**, a few of which have welcoming bars. One, the Torre Caleta, lies just below the bridge which marks the border of Málaga and Granada provinces. Entering Granada province, the road then launches into one of the most panoramic stretches along the whole coast, climbing and twisting inland before running along sheer cliffs high above the jagged coast. Eventually it surfaces at **LA HERRADURA**, a fishing village-resort suburb of Almuñécar, and for anyone with their own transport a good place to stop off and swim. **Rooms**, however, don't come cheap here – *Hostal La Herradura*, c/Red 5 (☎958/640658; ④) is the most reasonable, although there's also a summer campsite, *La Herradura* (☎958/640056). The next headland, the Punta de la Mona, gives way to a fine view of the spur of Almuñécar, crowned by its castle.

Almuñécar

ALMUÑÉCAR is the city of Granada's flagship seaside resort and although marred by a number of towering holiday apartments, has made some admirable attempts to preserve its Andalucian character. Founded by the Phoenicians – believe it or not – as *Sexi*, it possesses ruins both from this and its later Roman and Moorish periods. The town's pebble beaches, it has to be said, are rather cramped and not improved by the greyish sand, but the esplanade, **Paseo Puerta del Mar** (aka Paseo del Altillo), behind them, with palm-roofed bars (many offering free *tapas*) and restaurants, is fun, and the *casco antiguo*, or old town, is attractive.

Arrival and information

The **bus station** – with frequent connections to Granada and Málaga – is located at the junction of Avda. Juan Carlos I and Avda. Fenicia, northeast of the centre. Inconveniently, the **Turismo**, Avda. Europa s/n, one block in from the Playa San Cristobal (Mon–Sat 10am–2pm & 4–9.30pm), is located at the opposite end of town (a good ten-minute walk away) near the sea. Following Avda. de Andalucía from the bus station through the oldo town will take you by or near many of the town's *hostales* and *fondas*.

ACCOMMODATION PRICE SYMBOLS

The symbols used in our hotel listings denote the following price ranges:

① Under 2000ptas   ③ 3000–4500ptas   ⑤ 7500–12,500ptas

② 2000–3000ptas   ④ 4500–7500ptas   ⑥ Over 12,500ptas

See p.28 for more details.

Accommodation

The pressure on **accommodation** in Almuñécar is not quite as acute as back at Nerja. Half a dozen good value **fondas** and **hostales** ring the central Plaza de la Rosa in the old part of town, as well as, just east of here, in the streets off the Avda. de Andalucía. Almuñécar's **campsite**, the inaccurately named *El Paraiso* (☎958/632370) on the eastern edge of town is, despite being in sight of the beach, a claustrophobic hell-hole with cars and tents jammed in like sardines during high-season. Hang on for Salobreña.

Fonda Heredia, c/San José 15 (☎958/630021). Simple, clean rooms above a restaurant. Near the Plaza de la Rosa in the old town. ②.

Hostal Plaza Damasco, c/Cerrajos 8 (☎958/630165). Cosy place just off the plaza it's named after. Very near the *Fonda Heredia*. ②.

Hostal Rocamar, c/Córdoba 3 (☎958/630023). Pleasant French-owned place which has rooms with bath. Near the bus station. ③.

Hostal Trinidad, c/Cerveteri s/n, off Avda. de Andalucía (☎958/630274). Close to the sea, but some of the interior rooms are a bit sombre. ③.

Hostal Victoria, Plaza de la Victoria 6, off Avda. de Andalucía (☎958/630022). Impersonal, hostel-style place owned by the more expensive *hostal* of the same name a few doors away, but the rooms (with bath) are clean. ②.

The Town

Almuñécar's **castillo**, sitting atop a headland which bisects the resort's two bays, replaced the Moorish alcazaba in the time of Carlos V. It's distinctive for its massive tower, known, for some reason, as La Mazmorra ("the dungeon"), and it also contains the town graveyard. Nearby, the **Parque Ornitológico** (daily 11am–2pm & 6–9pm; 300ptas) is an aviary with a squawking collection of international specimens.

In town, it's well worth stopping off at the small **Archeological Museum** (Tues–Sat 11am–2pm & 6–8pm; 100ptas), located above the elegant Plaza Ayuntamiento (officially the Plaza de la Constitución, a name which nobody uses) in the Cueva de los Siete Palacios or "Cave of the Seven Palaces" – an ancient structure that may well have been a water reservoir. The museum exhibits finds – mostly discovered locally – from the Phoenician, Roman and Moorish periods, including an inscribed seventeenth-century BC **Egyptian vase** which shows not only the oldest piece of written text discovered on the Iberian peninsula, but also the only known reference to the late seventeenth-century BC Pharaoh Apophis I, a ruler during Egypt's hazy Hyksos period when foreign usurpers grasped the throne.

RETURN TO CASTILLO OF THE SUGAR CANES

After being trapped in Spain during the Civil War, in the 1950s Laurie Lee revisited some of the places he knew well, one of which was Castillo (a pseudonym for Almuñecar). He describes the pain of this experience in *A Rose for Winter*.

"Everything now was as it had been before – though perhaps a little more ignoble, more ground in dust. As I walked through the town time past hung heavy on my feet. The face of a generation had disappeared completely. A few old women recognized me, throwing up their hands with an exclamation, then came running towards me with lowered voices as though we shared a secret. But of the men I had known there was little news, and such as there was, confused. Most of them, it seemed , were either dead or fled. The old women peered up at me with red-rimmed, clouded eyes, and each tale they told was different. My ex-boss, the hotel keeper, who used to pray for Franco in his office, had been shot as a red spy; he had died of pneumonia in prison; he had escaped to France. Lalo, the hotel porter, had been killed on the barricades in Málaga; he ran a bar in Lyon; he was a barber in Jaén. Young Paco, the blond dynamiter of enemy tanks, was still a local fisherman – you could run into him at any time; no, he had blown himself up; he had married and gone to Mallorca. Luiz, the carpenter, had betrayed his comrades and been stoned to death; he lived in Vélez Málaga; he sold chickens in Granada . . . In the end I gave up. There was no point in making any further inquiries. Nobody lied deliberately, but nobody wished to seem certain of the truth. For the truth, in itself, was unendurable."

Eating and drinking

There are countless **places to eat** lining the Paseo Puerta del Mar, many of them offering cheap if unspectacular, *menús*. But the town's more interesting possibilities lie away from the seafront hurly-burly in the *casco antiguo*. For **breakfast**, head for the cafés around the Plaza Ayuntamiento in the old town.

Antonio, Paseo Maritimo 12. Great fish restaurant with a good value *menú*.

Casa Paco, Playa Velilla seafront, east of the centre. Pricey, but well worth it for the excellent seafood. Try their house speciality for dessert, *tarta de chirimoya* (custard apple tart) made from the tropical fruit grown along this stretch of the coast.

Restaurante-Meson Curro Muralla, c/Angel Gamay s/n. An excellent *bodega* serving a range of cheap *tapas* and *comidas*, a stone's throw away from the Corral del Carbon in a tiny alley off c/San Jose.

Los Geranios, Plaza de la Rosa 4. A good-value, medium-priced restaurant in the heart of the old quarter.

La Ultima Ola, Paseo Puerto del Mar s/n. Seafront restaurant also serving *tapas*..

Nightlife

Almuñecar's nightlife centres around the **bars and discos** circling Plaza Rosa and Plaza del Teatro.

Discoteca Coliseo, Plaza Teatro s/n. Packs them in to dance to *flamenco*-rock and *bacalao*, frenetic tecno-stuff.

Corral del Carbon Flamenco Bar, c/San José 23. A raucous *flamenco* bar; one of the best free entertainments in town. The party starts around 10pm when locals gather to consume *tapas* and get up on the stage to show what they can do. It veers from the ludicrous to the sublime, but is always fun. Sometimes the crowd even lets the musicians have a go.

Bodega Francisco, c/Real 15, north of Plaza Rosa. A wonderful old bar with barrels stacked up to the ceiling behind the counter and walls covered with ageing *corrida* posters and mounted boars' heads. The *fino* and *Montilla* on offer are both excellent, and the bar offers a wide range of *tapas* and *platos combinados*.

Salobreña

The road east from Almuñécar crosses the Río Verde and slowly makes its way upwards past slopes dotted with almond and *chirimoya* (or custard apple) trees until, 13km later, a spectacular vista opens up to reveal **SALOBREÑA**, a white town tumbling down a hill topped by the shell of its Moorish castle and surrounded by fields of sugar-cane. Comparatively little developed, it's set back a 2km hike away from the sea, and thus less marketable for mass tourism, making it a far more relaxed destination than Almuñécar. Beginning life as a Phoenician city dedicated to Salambo, the Syrian name for the goddess of love, the town retained some importance in Moorish times – as is evidenced by the much restored alcázar – but then languished in poverty until rescued by more recent prosperity generated, in part, by its new trickles of tourism.

On the eastern side of town, the **Alcázar** (daily 10am–2pm & 5.30–9.30pm; 100ptas) is worth a look, not least for the fine views from its crenellated towers. Below this, down at the foot of the hill, the sixteenth-century church of **Nuestra Señora del Rosario** stands on the site previously occupied by a Moorish palace. There's a mildly interesting collection of **archeological finds** in the *Biblioteca* (library) close to the Casa de la Cultura on Carretera de la Playa (daily 10am–2pm), and a lively **market** each Monday to Saturday morning in the central Plaza del Mercado, and that's about as far as sightseeing goes.

Practicalities

Buses arrive and leave from the Plaza de Goya, close to the **Turismo**, Plaza de Goya s/n (Tues–Sun 11am–1.30pm & 5–9pm; ☎958/610314). To get their rather feeble town map you'll have to fork out 100ptas. There's usually no problem in finding **accommodation** in Salobreña, even in high season, and the lack of demand is reflected in lower prices. Most of the budget accommodation is on the western side of town. Close to c/ de Hortensia, the main avenue that winds down from the town to the beach, a few good value possibilities include the *Pensión Arnedo*, c/Nueva 15 (☎958/610257; ②), which has terraces in some rooms and gives delightful sea-views across the canefields. Over the road, the *Pensión Mari Carmen* c/Nueva 32 (☎958/610906; ②) is equally nice, with fans in the rooms. Around the corner from here, *Pensión Palomares*, c/Fabrica Nueva 44 (☎958/610181; ②) is a well-run family establishment with simple rooms above a restaurant. Three more possibilities lie just south of here, along and off the Carretera de la Playa: *Hostal Miramar*, c/Arrabal Villa 112 (☎958/828534; ②) which has rooms with bath, *Hostal Mary Tere,* Cta. de la Playa 94 (☎958/610126; ②) and *Pensión Lopez*, Cta. de la Playa 17 (☎958/610053; ②). On its black sand beach – a fair strip, only partially flanked by hotels – is a good **campsite**, *El Peñón* (April–Oct; ☎958/610207).

Places to eat in town are limited, although the *Pensión Palomares* serves a cheap *menú*. Otherwise, the best bet is one of the many *chiringuitos* lining the seafront, among which *La Bahia*, facing the promontory at the western end, is good value. When *salobreñanos* want to eat in style they usually make for the *Hotel Salambina*, Ct. de Málaga s/n, perched on the head to the west of the town, where the dining room has a balcony overlooking the Peñon de Salobreña. The *menú* here is medium-priced and *tapas* are served in the bar.

Motril

Four kilometres beyond Salobreña, **MOTRIL** lies inland on a coastal plain planted with sugar cane, which long ago earned it the name of "Little Cuba". The crop was introduced to Spain by the Carthaginians in the third century BC when they attempted to

---

THE CARRETERA NACIONAL N340

A special note of warning has to be made about the Costa del Sol's main highway, which is one of the most dangerous roads in Europe. Nominally a national highway, it's really a 100-kilometre-long city street, passing through the middle of towns and *urbanizaciones*. Drivers treat it like a motorway, yet pedestrians have to get across, and cars are constantly turning off or into the road – hence the terrifying number of accidents, with, on average, over a hundred fatalities a year. A large number of casualties are inebriated British package tourists who are unfamiliar with left-hand-drive vehicles and traffic patterns. The first few kilometres, between the airport with its various car rental offices and Torremolinos, are among the most treacherous, but worse still is the stretch heading west from Marbella: around thirty accidents a year occur on each kilometre between Marbella and San Pedro.

Plans have been approved for a new motorway which will link the Costa del Sol with Madrid and Sevilla, and so reduce traffic on the N340. In the meantime, don't make dangerous (and illegal) left turns from the fast lane; be particularly careful after a heavy rain, when the hot, oily road surface sends you easily into a skid; and **pedestrians** should cross at traffic lights, a bridge or an underpass if possible.

---

set up an empire here, but typically it was the Moors who developed the process of refining the cane into sugar. Prior to this, the raw cane was sold in the streets. Motril's other great earner is a burgeoning chemical industry which – when coupled with a beach cluttered with "activities" and escaping *granadinos* – may suggest that the best thing to do is to have a *cerveza* and get straight out.

Buses north to Granada follow the panoramic N323 which leaves the coast between Salobreña and Motril to follow the Río Guadalfeo valley into the mountains of the Sierra Nevada, eventually descending via the fertile Lecrin valley to the city of Granada (p.309). This is also the way to Las Alpujarras (p.343) where, after 25km, a turn-off at Béznar to Lanjarón provides a good starting point. For the coast east of Motril see the "Costa Tropical" (p.369).

The Costa del Sol resorts

West of Málaga – or more correctly, west of Málaga airport – the real **Costa del Sol** gets going. If you've never seen this level of touristic development before, it's going to come as quite a shock, not least when you see how grit-grey the sands are; you have to keep going, around the corner to Tarifa before you reach the golden sands of the tourist brochures. With their faceless banks of 1960s' and 70s' concrete tower blocks, these are certainly not the kind of resorts you find in Greece or even Portugal. Since the 1980s boom in time-share apartments and leisure complexes, it's estimated that 300,000 foreigners live on the Costa del Sol, the majority of them retired and British. However, the cheap package-tour industry – which largely created the Costa del Sol from the poverty-stricken fishing villages that dotted the coastline until the 1950s – has suffered a few lean years recently and resorts such as Torremolinos are beginning to wonder whether the tourists will ever return in the numbers reached during the past two decades.

Approached in the right kind of spirit it is possible to have fun in **Torremolinos**, and at a price in **Marbella**. The sea, at least, is reasonably clean around here, after a lot of work on the sewerage systems. But if you've come to Spain to discover Spain, or even just to forget what inner-city housing looks like, put on the shades and stay on the coach at least until you reach **Estepona**. You are not going to make any new discoveries. It is all far too late.

Torremolinos

The approach to **TORREMOLINOS** – easiest on the electric railway – is a depressing trawl through a drab, soulless landscape of kitchenette apartments and half-finished developments. The town itself – rechristened "Torrie" by English package tourists – it has to be said, is certainly an experience: a vast, grotesque parody of a seaside resort with its own kitschy fascination. This bizarre place, lined with sweeping (but crowded) beaches and infinite shopping arcades, crammed with genuine Irish pubs and real-estate agents, has a large permanent expat population of British, Germans and Scandinavians. It's a weird mix, which, in addition to thousands of retired people, has attracted – due to a previous lack of extradition arrangements between Britain and Spain – a notorious concentration of British Jack-the-lad crooks. Torremolinos' social scene is strange, too, including, among the middle-of-the-road family discos, a thriving, pram-pushing gay transvestite scene.

To get the flavour of the place, take a stroll along Calle San Miguel, the main pedestrian mall east of the train station. Cutting through the "old" quarter (which even has a fourteenth-century Moorish tower), the street is lined with garish illuminated signs, tatty amusement arcades and boutiques, and even tattier restaurants serving steak and

CENTRAL TORREMOLINOS

kidney pie and all its variations. All in all it's an intriguing blend of the smart and the squalid, bargains and rip-offs. One haven of tranquillity in the middle of all this is **George's Secondhand Bookshop**, on the first floor at no. 26; an excellent source of used paperbacks.

The more elegant (and slightly saner) part of the resort lies east of the main conurbation at **La Carihuela**, a former fishing village with a decent beach and a number of good fish restaurants on the seafront. There's a pleasant *hostal* here, too (see "Practicalities").

Practicalities

It's easy enough to **stay** in Torremolinos. There are few *hostales*, but you can walk into almost any travel agent and, for remarkably little, get them to book you into one of the concrete monsters. The **Turismo**, c/Casablanca 25 (☎952/371159) can provide more information on what's available. One haven of sanity amid the highrise blocks is *Hotel Miami*, c/Aladino 14, west of the centre (☎952/385255; ④), which has a nice patio and small pool. Torremolinos' **youth hostel** (☎952/380882) is at Avda. Carlota Alessandri 127, a couple of blocks in from the beach. Further out, at **La Carihuela**, *Prudencia*, Paseo Carmen 41 (☎952/238 14 52; ④) is a great place with a restaurant and sea-views. Be wary of accepting free accommodation from the Torremolinos evangelists (who often invite hitchhikers to their villa), as it's not always so easy to leave their community after a week or two of heavy, "religious" mind games.

The sheer competition between Torremolinos' **restaurants, clubs and bars** is so intense that if you're prepared to walk round and check a few prices you can have a pretty good night out on remarkably little.

Hydrofoils to Tangier (summer only) leave from **Benalmádena**, halfway to Fuengirola. Fairly forgettable as a resort, Benalmádena is not quite as hectic as its neighbour to the north and the beach is usually less crowded.

Mijas

Often grouped with the more famous "White Towns" further north (see p.110), the once tranquil hill town of **MIJAS**, 8km off the road between Benalmádena and Fuengirola, is sited a little too close to the Costa del Sol for its own good, making it an obvious target for coach tours in search of the "typical" Andalucian village. However, despite a host of tacky gift shops and the numbered *burro* (or donkey) taxis which transport visitors around the main square, the village isn't devoid of charm. There are fine views towards the coast, while the ancient Plaza de Toros which claims (wrongly) to be Andalucía's only rectangular bullring is worth a look.

Above the square, the ludicrous *Carromato de Max*, a wagon full of junk, claims to house "the smallest curiosities in the world". If items such as Churchill's head sculpted from a stick of chalk, a copy of Leonardo's *Last Supper* painted on a grain of rice, or the shrunken head of a white man retrieved from South American indians and "certified genuine by the FBI" grab you, then it's well worth the 300ptas entry fee.

After dusk, when the day trippers have gone, the village is far more peaceful. Should you fancy staying overnight, the excellent value *Pensión Romana*, c/Coín 47 (☎952/248 53 10; ②) has apartment-style rooms including fridge and stove. To get there, find your way to Plaza de la Constitución, a small square with a fountain below the bullring, and ask for directions. The house itself has no sign.

Fuengirola

FUENGIROLA, a thirty-minute train journey from Torremolinos, is very slightly less developed and infinitely more staid, middle-aged and family-oriented than "Torrie". Fuengirola's two sights are easily located: on the road west out of town there's the restored but impressive **castillo**, a tenth-century fortress built by Abd ar-Rahman III of Córdoba, as well as the scanty remains of a **Roman temple** at the eastern end of the Paseo Maritímo. Further in, the rather dull Plaza de la Constitución is Fuengirola's effective centre, but most people are here for the **beach**; a huge, long strand divided into restaurant-beach strips, each renting out lounge chairs and pedal-boats. At the far end is a windsurfing school.

Practicalities

Accommodation in Fuengirola is only a problem in August when you'll struggle to find anything at all. Your best bet is around the Plaza de la Constitución. *Hostal Italia*, c/de la Cruz 1 (☎952/474193; ③) has rooms with balcony, bath and room-safe; if that's full, try next door at the British-run *Hostal Coca*, c/de la Cruz 3 (☎952/247 41 89; ③), where basic rooms without bath cost a little less. Round the corner, *Hostal Sedeño*, c/ Don Jacinto 1 (☎952/247 47 88; ④) has balcony rooms overlooking a leafy garden, and for a sea view with balcony try *Hostal Buenavista,* Paseo Maritímo (☎952/800137; ④) which does good bargain deals out of season.

The streets to the south of Plaza de la Constitución are lined with **restaurants** of a rather depressing similarity. A variety of "as much as you can eat" places prove good value, however; two of the best, with fixed prices around 650ptas, are *Versalles*, Paseo Maritímo 3, at the western end of the seafront and *Buffet Las Palmeras*, Paseo Maritímo s/n, nearer the harbour with its fake Moorish towers. Alternatively, *Mesón Salamanca*, c/Capitán 2; just off the Plaza, is a pleasant little Spanish outpost in the middle of it all with an economical *menú*. If you're looking for something a bit more refined, *Bar La Paz Garrido* on the Avda. de Mijas just north of the Plaza de la Constitución serves some of the best seafood on the coast. **Nightlife** is centred around the bars and discos to the north of the harbour and, sharing space with some good *chiringuitos* on the seafront, a fair number of expat **singalong bars** boom after sunset with the bellows of English and Dutch.

Marbella

After another dull sequence of apartment-villa *urbanizaciones*, **MARBELLA**, undisputedly the "quality resort" of the Costa del Sol, stands in considerable contrast to most of what's come before. Sheltered from the winds by the hills of the Sierra Blanca, it has a couple of excellent beaches which first brought it to the attention of the 1960s smart set. However, should you feel like doing a bit of celebrity spotting nowadays, don't bother. The only time the mega-rich descend from their villas in the hills is to attend a private club or put in an appearance at glitzy places like the *Puente Romano Hotel* on the way to San Pedro, where a *beluga caviare* starter in the restaurant will set you back the price of a good hotel room. In an ironic twist of history, there's been a massive return of Arabs to the area, especially since King Fahd of Saudi Arabia built a White House lookalike, complete with adjacent mosque, on the town's outskirts.

Marbella's notoriety in the rest of Spain today, however, springs not from its glitterati but from the activities of its over-the-top mayor Jesus Gil y Gil, a wildly eccentric businessman whose property development schemes landed him in jail after one of his buildings collapsed killing several people. Gil's extreme right-wing ideas win him landslide victories and, despite frequent stunts – such as marching through the marina flanked by police and yelling abuse at the "drunkards, dissolutes and drug addicts" in the open-air bars and cafés – still the vote from the silent majority holds up. His boundless megalomania projected him onto the national stage when he became chairman of football team Atletico Madrid (who now rather confusingly carry the name "Marbella" on their shirts), and he has recently founded his own national political party, *Grupo Independiente Liberal*, whose acronym says it all.

Arrival and accommodation

The **bus** will drop you at the main station on Avda. Ricardo Soriano. Turn left out of here, walk straight for about 500m, and a left will bring you into the old part of town, the *casco antiguo*. The **Turismo**, Avda. Miguel Cano 1 (daily summer 9.30am–9.30pm; winter 9.30am–8pm; ☎952/771442) has excellent street maps and can help with accommodation – though you shouldn't have too much difficulty finding a room anyway, outside the month of August.

All Marbella's budget **hostales** are in the old town, many of them on or around c/ Luna. A couple of streets further west there are more places along the pretty c/San Cristobal, the street of a thousand plants carefully tended by its residents; not for nothing has it has won Marbella's annual "best street" competition more than once. There's also a good **hostel**, the **Africa Youth Hostel**, c/Trapiche s/n (☎952/771491; ①), which usually has space.

Hotels

Hostal Enriqueta, c/los Caballeros 18 (☎952/827552). Comfortable and quiet place above the Plaza de los Naranjos. ④.

Hostal la Estrella, c/San Cristobal 36 (☎952/774252). Very nice *hostal* in lovely street. ④.

Hostal Internacional, c/Alderete 7 (☎952/770295). Good option close to the heart of the old quarter, off Plaza de Tetuán, offering rooms with bath. ③.

Hostal Isabel de Pachecho, c/Luna 24 (☎952/771978). Friendly, low-priced and clean. ②.

Hostal Juan, c/Luna 18 (☎952/779475). One of the nicest *hostales* on this popular street, with clean rooms and a friendly atmosphere. ③.

Hostal La Luna, c/Luna 7 (☎952/825778). Good value, with a fridge in each room. ③.

Hostal La Pilarica, c/San Cristobal 31 (☎952/774252). Pretty *hostal* in lovely location. ③.

The Town

Spared the worst excesses of concrete architecture which have been inflicted upon Torremolinos, Marbella itself is decidedly tasteful, retaining the greater part of its old town or **casco antiguo**. Slowly, this original quarter is being bought up and turned over to "quaint" clothes boutiques and restaurants, but you can still sit in an ordinary bar in a small old square and look up beyond the whitewashed alleyways to the mountains of Ronda.

The *casco antiguo*, partially walled, is set back from the sea and hidden from the main road. Here the main sights are clustered in the web of streets surrounding the picturesque **Plaza de los Naranjos**. On the plaza itself is the striking sixteenth-century **Ayuntamiento** with, inside, fine coffered ceilings. Also worth a look here is the church of **Nuestra Señora de la Encarnación**; built in the sixteenth century it was later remodelled in the Baroque style and has an interesting *retablo*. The **archeology museum** with Neolithic and Roman finds from the surrounding area – including the Roman villa at Río Verde (see p.98) – is currently closed while a new site is found to house it; the Turismo will have the most up-to-date information. In the meantime its former home – a fine Renaissance hospital founded by Alonso Bazán, then mayor of Marbella – now hosts a mildly interesting **museum of contemporary Spanish engraving**, c/Hospital Bazán s/n, with works by Miró and Picasso. Northeast of the Plaza de los Naranjos you'll find Spain's one and only **Bonsai tree museum**, Arroyo de la Represa s/n (daily 11.30–2pm & 5–8.30pm; 300ptas) with 150 examples of this arboreal curiosity.

The real jet-set don't hang around Marbella itself. They prefer to stretch out on the decks of large and luxurious yachts at the marina and casino complex of **PUERTO BANÚS**, 6km out of town towards San Pedro. You can get **work** here, if you so desire, scrubbing and repairing yachts, but you probably won't earn enough to join your employers in the harbourside boutiques and phenomenally expensive restaurants from where they survey all they master.

Eating and drinking

When it comes to **food and drink** you'd be better off in any of Marbella's numerous *tapas* bars than dining at the touristy and overpriced restaurants around the Plaza de los Naranjos. Late night **bars** to check out the local scene are clustered around the Puerto Deportivo, the seafront yacht harbour.

Cafés and bars

Bar Altamirano, Plaza de Altamirano 4. Authentic *casco antiguo* bar with a terrace.
El Chipirón, c/Valencia 8. *Tapas* bar serving enormous portions.

MARBELLA OLD TOWN

Bar Guerra, Avda. Ramón y Cajal 5. Excellent place just south of the old quarter, serving delicious *boquerones fritos al limón*.

Lepanto, Avda. Puerta del Mar s/n. Great café just south of the old quarter, which devotes itself to chocolate confectionary creations.

Los Mellizos, Plaza del Marqués del Turia 9. Slightly out of the way, east of town, but worth the trip to eat good *tapas* on a pleasant terrace.

Restaurants

El Bodegon Charron, c/Charron. Reasonably priced restaurant away from the tourist strip, a few streets north of the Plaza de los Naranjos.

Caféteria-Restaurante Coq d'or, c/Ortega y Gasset, at the junction with c/Gomez. Pricier place serving delicious French-influenced food at the western end of town.

La Fonda, Plaza San Cristo 9, north of Plaza de los Naranjos. Medium priced restaurant with an admirably wide selection of dishes.

San Michel, c/Marques de Najera, off Plaza Tetuán. Cosy restaurant with a good value *menú*.

Triana, c/Gloria 11, just south of Plaza de los Naranjos. Superb fish restaurant specializing in *paella de mariscos*.

San Pedro de Alcántara

About the only place on the Costa del Sol which isn't purely a holiday *urbanización* is the small town of **SAN PEDRO DE ALCÁNTARA**, a none too inspiring resort striving to go the way of Marbella but hindered by the fact that it's set back from the sea. What little activity there is centres on the tranquil palm fringed Plaza de la Iglesia – at its most lively during the Thursday morning flea market – but there's little else to disturb the calm. If you have your own transport, however, you can get to three remarkable **ancient ruins** in the area (see below). The helpful **Turismo**, behind the nineteenth-century church of San Pedro on the Plaza de la Iglesia (daily 9.30am–8pm; ☎952/785252) will supply the keys and a map detailing the route; simply leave them your passport as a deposit.

Should you require **accommodation** in San Pedro, *Pensión Avenida*, c/19 Octubre 53 (☎952/278 11 90; ②) has rooms with bath near the main square, or there's the more basic *Pensión Marta*, c/Lagasca 21 (☎952/278 33 36; ②) a couple of streets away.

Three ancient sites

Four kilometres back along the road east to Marbella is a second-century **Roman villa** at Río Verde. To get there from San Pedro, pass the turn-off for Puerto Banús and, after crossing the river, take a right before the *Puente Romano Hotel* and follow the signs. Constructed in the late first or early second century, the rooms are decorated with an unusual series of black and white **mosaics** depicting not classical themes or intricate designs as elsewhere, but everyday kitchen equipment. The kitchen utensils are a delight, and the shoes portrayed by the door are evidence of the Roman custom of leaving one's footwear outside the *triclinium*, or dining room. One of the amphoras displayed is so accurately portrayed that its style has helped to date the villa almost precisely. Note also the hanging fowl and fish, ready for the pot. The mosaic's theme leads you to wonder who may have been the villa's occupant; perhaps a grand gourmet, or a even wealthy restaurateur (Río Verde was a prosperous area in Roman times) made rich from catering to the ancient predecessors of nearby Puerto Banús.

The sixth-century **Visigothic Christian basilica** of Vega del Mar, is easier to get to and lies close to the sea at the bottom of the Avda. del Mediterráneo, the main road out of San Pedro to the ocean. Take the last road on the right before the beach and you'll come to the railed-off site in the midst of a stand of eucalyptus trees. The remains enable you to make out clearly a rectangular basilica with a double-apse, unique in

Spain. Large boulders cemented with lime-mortar were used in its construction along with still-visible brickwork at the corners. A wonderful **baptismal font** is especially well preserved and was deep enough for total immersion, the custom of the time. In and around the basilica is a cemetery of some two hundred tombs (which yielded a wealth of artefacts) most with the head to the north, the orientation of the church. Note the graves lined with marble, evidence of social stratification even in death.

The third site, the **Roman bath house** of Las Bovedas, lies a litle way west of here, almost on the beach. Leave any transport at the beach *chiringuito* (good for a drink and a *tapa* if it's hot) and walk the fifty metres along the beach to the site. The substantial remains belong to an octagonal third-century Roman baths. Seven chambers, which would have served as a series of heated "steam" rooms, surround the well preserved central bath (parts of the underfloor hypocaust system are visible). Above the central pool was a skylight surrounded by a roof terrace. Because the complex was constructed with a special lime – which, when mixed with sand and pebbles from the beach set to a granite-like hardness – the building has defied the elements impressively.

Estepona

West of San Pedro the coast road is littered with more depressing *urbanizaciones* bearing names such as *Picasso* or – taking irony to the limit – *Paraiso* (paradise), each served by its *centro comercial*. Should you feel an irresistible urge to stop, **ESTEPONA** is about the only good bet, a more or less Spanish resort with much of its identity still intact. Lacking the enclosed hills that give Marbella character, it is at least developed on a human scale; the hotel and apartment blocks which sprawl along the front are restrained in size, and there's a pleasant EC blue-flagged beach in town, as well as the Costa del Sol's oldest nudist beach to the west.

One of the best, and busiest, times to visit Estepona is at the beginning of July, when the *Fiesta y Feria* week brings out whole families in *flamenco*-style garb and the town is transformed into a riot of colour.

Arrival and information

Estepona's **bus station**, on Avda. de Espana, lies west of the centre behind the seafront. Half a kilometre east of here on the same road, the efficient seafront **Turismo** (Mon–Sat 9.30am–1.30pm & 5–8pm; ☎952/800913) will supply town maps and can help you find a room if need be.

Accommodation

Outside August there is usually no problem finding somewhere **to stay** in Estepona. The nearest **campsite**, *Chullera III* (☎952/890196) lies 8km south of town just beyond the village of San Luis de Sabanillas.

Pensión La Malagueña, c/Castillo s/n (☎952/800011). Reliable *pensión* around the corner from the Plaza Las Flores. ③.

Pensión San Miguel, c/Terraza 16 (☎952/802616). Friendly establishment with its own bar a little west of the Plaza Las Flores. ②.

Hostal El Pilar, Plaza Las Flores (☎952/800018). Atmospheric old place on charming plaza. ③.

Pensión Vista al Mar, c/Real 154 (☎952/803247). Barely squeezes in a sea view, thus justifying its name. At the western end of the central zone. ②.

The Town

Estapona is the last stop on the Costa del Sol and one of the most pleasant. By no means as picturesque as Marbella, it makes up in enthusiasm and warmth what it lacks in architecture. The seafront is attractive, with a promenade studded with flowers and palms, and behind this, the older part of the town has some charming corners with cobbled alleyways and two delightful squares, the **Plaza las Flores** and **Plaza Arce**. Calle Terraza bisects the centre and around this are to be found most of the eating and drinking options.

The **fish market** is also worth seeing: Estepona has the biggest fishing fleet west of Málaga, and the daily dawn ritual in the port at the western end of the promenade, where the returning fleets auction off the fish they've just caught, is worth getting up early for – be there at 6am, since by 7am it's all over. Afterwards you can head for the lively covered **market**, on c/Castillo, also at its best in the morning. Estepona's **nudist beach**, the Costa Natura, is located a short bus ride away, 4km to the west of town. From May onward, the town's **bullfighting** season gets underway in a modern bullring reminiscent of a Henry Moore sculpture.

Eating and drinking

Estepona is well provided with **places to eat**, among them a bunch of excellent **freidurías** and **marisquerías**. Worth trying are *La Gamba* and *El Chanquete* on c/ Terraza. *El Barquito*, just off here in c/Reyes, is another good bet, as is *El Rey del Pescado* on the Plaza Arce. **Restaurants** are less distinguished, although *Bar La Trocha* further up c/Terraza on the left serves good *platos combinados* and the French *Costa del Sol*, c/San Roque 23, near the bus station, does a very good value *menú*.

Of the Estepona bars serving **tapas**, *Mesón Genaro* in c/Lozano (off c/Terraza) and *La Jerezana* in c/Estremadura nearby, are two of the best, while for an after dinner **ice-cream**, *Heladería Vitin* in Plaza Las Flores has the edge, if only for location. The bars in the same plaza – who spread their tables around the central fountain – are good places to take **breakfast**, sitting al fesco on a sunny morning. Another option for this time of day is an excellent *churrería* towards the southern end of c/del Mar (one block back from, and parallel to, the promenade) – get there before 11am as they sell out early. For **picnic supplies** try the market and, if you're self-catering, the fish market.

You could, if sufficiently motivated, head **out of town** to eat. Go south along the coast for 10km until you pass the new Puerto de la Duquesa marina, a clone of Puerto Banús (see p.96) but with fewer fat cats; just under a kilometre further on, behind a small castle, is the tiny – and earthy – fishing village of **La Duquesa**, which has a couple of excellent fish restaurants, *Restaurante Antonio* being the better of the two. Old Antonio, the owner, is a real character and the *tapas* in the bar here must be the best value on the coast. The other is *Bar Domingo* with tables fronting a dilapidated seafront.

When it comes to **nightlife**, Estepona has a gratifyingly varied range of possibilities. The **flamenco bar**, *Ría–Pitá*, c/Caridad 93, east of c/Terraza, may not be the most authentic but with free entry, reasonably priced drinks and a friendly proprietor it can be a lot of fun. Weekends are the best nights to go, but not before 10pm. Nearby in the same street *Scorpío*, c/Caridad 109 (open from 10pm) often has live music, including jazz. **Discos** and disco-pubs are mostly grouped around the Puerto Deportivo where you can take your pick from *Bronx*, *Ya te lo dije*, *Mambo*, *Willys Salsa* and others. In town are *Niagara*, Avda. Juan Carlos 1, and the teeny-bopper *Delfos*, c/Caridad 91.

Casares

The greyish coast west of Estapona is dotted with watch towers used by people as diverse as Phoenicians, Romans and Arabs to protect themselves from pirate attacks. There's little reason to stop along here, but one worthwhile detour is to head to **CASARES**, 18km inland from Estepona. One of the lesser known of Andalucía's white towns, it's a beautiful place, clinging tenaciously – and spectacularly – to a steep hillside below a castle, and attracting its fair share of arty types and expatriates.

The village is reputed to take its name from Julius Caesar, who is said to have used the **sulphurous springs** nearby to cure a liver complaint. More concrete historical evidence attributes the impressive alcázar (built on Roman foundations) to the Moorish period, from the ruins of which there are spectacular **views** as far as Gibraltar on clear days. There's little else in the way of sights, but it's satisfying enough simply to wander around, losing yourself in the twisting and narrow whitewalled streets – another vestige of the Arab period. Flanked by an eighteenth-century church, the central plaza is a good place to sit and have a drink, cooled by breezes off the sierra.

The surrounding hill country, richly wooded with cork oaks and pine as well as stands of pinsapo, the rare Spanish fir, offers a verdant contrast with the arid plains below and is fine **walking terrain** with plenty of dirt-tracks winding through the folds of the Sierra Bermeja.

Back on the coast road, to the west and inland from the village of **Manilva**, are the remarkably well-preserved **Roman sulphur baths** supposedly so beloved of Caesar; now enclosed beneath a hideous mustard-yellow concrete canopy resembling a bomb-shelter. If you want to partake of these health-giving waters you'll have scramble – or dive if you're bold enough – into the murky subterranean cavern beneath, from where you can see evidence of the original Roman brickwork. One dubious souvenir you'll definitely be taking away with you is the smell of the place – the sulphurous stench coming from the waters is overpowering, and guaranteed to cling to your swimwear for weeks. To **reach the baths** follow the road out of Manilva for about 3km until you pass a quarry on the left, immediately after which there's a popular bathing pool beside the road. Leave any transport here and walk for about a kilometre along a track away from the pool. Pass the campsite beyond a ford on the right, and the *Bar Alamo*, again on the right, and at the top of a rise, the small chapel of San Adolfo. The baths are a little further beyond this.

Casares practicalities

Only two buses a day leave for Casares from Estapona (1.15pm & 7pm; return 7am & 4pm) meaning, if you're without transport, a very brief visit, a difficult hitch back on a quiet road, or an **overnight stay**. On the central plaza, *Hostal Plaza* (☎952/289 40 88; ②) has rooms above a bar. There are more bars than restaurants in Casares, but **places to eat** include *La Terraza*, a restaurant just outside the village on the Estapona road which has great views from its terrace.

San Roque

SAN ROQUE, 35km south of Estapona, was founded in 1704 by the people of Gibraltar fleeing the British, who had captured the Rock and looted their homes and churches. They expected to return within months, since the troops had taken the garrison in the name of the Archduke Carlos of Austria, whose rights Britain had been promoting in the War of the Spanish Succession. But it was the British flag that was raised on the conquered territory – and so it has remained.

There are few sights, but c/San Felipe, which leads up from the main square to the mirador, has some fine reja-fronted houses. From the **mirador** you can see the Rock of Gibraltar and the hazy coast of Africa beyond – you'll have to ignore the ugly oil refinery. Nearby, the *Ayuntamiento* displays a banner given to the earlier Spanish Gibraltar by Fernando and Isabel, while the eighteenth-century **iglesia Santa María Coronada** – built over the ancient hermitage of San Roque – has a fine image of the Virgin also rescued from the Rock in the flight from the British invaders. And don't miss taking a look at San Roque's dilapidated **bullring**. Built in the middle of the last century it's now a crumbling pile, with still-inhabited dwellings built into its outer walls reminiscent of the middle ages. Surprisingly, it still stages *corridas* during the town's summer *feria*.

Practicalities

San Roque's campsite, *Camping San Roque* (☎956/780100) is on the N340 highway just east of the town. Far better, though, if you want to stay is **LOS BARRIOS** 10km to the west, an atmospheric, tranquil place away from the depressing nature of this industrial zone. There's an excellent cheap *hostal* here on the palm-lined main street, *El Semáforo*, c/Alhóndiga 5 (☎956/620129; ①) and plenty of places to eat and drink.

La Línea

Obscured by San Roque's huge oil refinery, the **"Spanish-British frontier"** is 8km south of San Roque at **LA LÍNEA**. After sixteen years of (Spanish-imposed) isolation, the gates were reopened in February 1985, and crossing between here and Gibraltar is now routine. There are no sights as such; it's just a fishing village which has exploded in size due to the employment opportunities in Gibraltar and Algeciras.

Practicalities

The **bus station** and **Turismo** (daily 9.30am–1.30pm & 5–8pm; ☎956/769950) are both on Avda. 20 Abril just off the main **Plaza de la Constitución**, a large modern square at the heart of La Línea. The closest main-line train station is San Roque-La Línea, 5km west of town from where you can pick up a train to Ronda and beyond.

La Línea is a better bet than Gibraltar for accommodation, although even here prices have risen since the border opened, and it's more expensive than many neighbouring towns. The Turismo has a useful **map** showing all the main **hostales**; the best of which are concentrated around the Plaza de la Constitución. In the Plaza de Iglesia, at the end of c/Real, *La Giralda* (②) is good value and has a friendly owner, free hot showers and a hotplate in the kitchen for preparing simple meals. Almost directly opposite, there's the *Hostal Sevilla*, c/Duque de Tetuán (☎956/764796; ②) and three or four others nearby: *La Esteponera*, c/Carteya 12 (☎956/106668; ②), just off the plaza between c/Cervantes and c/Aurora, is one of the lowest-priced; the *Hostal Bahía*, c/Granada 54 (☎956/101725; ③) is more modern and cleaner.

Calle Real, the main pedestrianized shopping street leading off the Plaza de la Constitución, has plenty of reasonably priced **bars** and **restaurants** – try the *Bar Jerez* for good value *tapas*. A couple of streets north, the *Blanco y Negro*, c/Isabel la Católica 12, specializes in shellfish; *La Económica*, c/del Flores, is an inconspicuous *comedor* with a cheap *menú del día*. Calle Clavel, signposted from the main plaza to the Plaza de Toros, has more options: *Bar Almendra* at the far end is excellent value. Pick up picnic supplies at the **market**, north of c/Real.

Gibraltar

GIBRALTAR's interest is essentially its novelty: the genuine appeal of the strange, looming physical presence of its rock and the increasingly dubious one of its preservation as one of Britain's last remaining colonies. This enormous hunk of limestone, five kilometres long, two wide and 450 metres high – a land area smaller than the city of Algeciras across the water – has fascinated and attracted the people of the Mediterranean basin since Neanderthal times, confirmed by the finds of skulls and artefacts in a number of the Rock's many caves.

The Rock is a curious place to visit, not least to witness the bizarre process of its opening to mass tourism from the Costa del Sol. Ironically, this threatens both to destroy Gibraltar's highly individual society and at the same time to make it much more British, after the fashion of the expat communities and huge resorts up the coast.

The frontier opening has benefited most people: locals can buy cheaper goods in Spain, while expats living on the Costas can pick up from stores like *Safeway* such familiar essentials as baked beans and sliced bread. The resulting boom the Rock is witnessing (after a long recession) should benefit the whole surrounding Campo area.

Some history

New discoveries in a cave on the southeast tip of the Rock – flint tools and evidence of camp-fires and cooked meals – are regarded as one of the most important prehistoric finds in modern times. The cave appears to have been inhabited both by **Neanderthals** and **Homo Sapiens**. It's hoped that further excavations here may provide vital evidence as to the extinction or amalgamation of our species with the earlier race.

The Phoenicians called the rock *Calpe* and had a fortified naval base here, barring the way to jealously guarded Atlantic trading destinations such as Tartessus. In Greek mythology this was the northernmost of the two pillars erected by Heracles. Following the demise of the Roman Empire, the Rock became the bridgehead for a Berber assault on the Visigothic domains of southern Spain. In 711 Tariq ibn Ziryab, governor of Tangier, crossed the straits at the head of an army, defeated the Visigoths and named the Rock "Jabal Tariq" or the Mountain of Tariq, the name – albeit garbled – it still has today. Gibraltar remained in Moorish hands until taken in 1309 by Guzmán el Bueno, but it was not long before it was recovered. The end finally came when another Guzmán, the Duke of Medina Sidonia, claimed it for Spain in 1462. Apart from the raids of Barbarossa, which caused Carlos V to fortify the Rock, Spanish possession was undisturbed until the War of the Spanish Succession, when Britain sided with Spain against the French. The outcome of this was the seizure of the Rock in 1704 by the British forces whose admiral, Sir George Rooke gave the inhabitants the choice of swearing allegiance to the Habsburg claimant to the throne – Archduke Charles of Austria – or getting out. Those that left to found San Roque (see p.101) thought their absence would be temporary. But in 1715 the British contrived to have Gibraltar ceded to them "in perpetuity" in the Treaty of Utrecht, no doubt having calculated the military advantages of such a strategic bastion. Despite military and diplomatic attempts by Spain to recover the Rock since, however, the British have maintained their grip, and Gibraltar played an important strategic role in both World Wars. General Franco mounted persistent campaigns to get it back and closed the access link with Spain in 1969, which only reopened in 1985.

The Rock, it seems, is destined to be a recurring cause of friction between the two nations; in 1988 three IRA suspects were gunned down by British agents near the petrol station at the entrance to the town. The British government – which went to enormous lengths to obscure the facts of the case – produced a version of events much at odds with that of the Spanish police and once more the issue of a "foreign power on Spanish soil" sparked a national debate. For more on the history of Gibraltar, see *Contexts*.

GIBRALTAR MONEY

Gibraltar is a good place to change **money**, since the exchange rate is slightly higher than in Spain and there's no commission charged. The currency used here is the Gibraltar pound (the same value as the British pound, but different notes and coins); if you pay in pesetas, you generally fork out about five percent more. Gibraltar pounds can be hard to change in Spain.

Note that the prices we've quoted for **accommodation** on the Rock are in Gibraltar pounds.

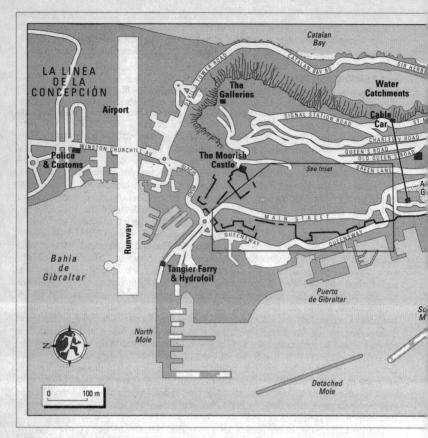

Arrival and information

If you have a car, don't attempt to bring it to Gibraltar – the queues at the border are always atrocious, and parking on the Rock is a nightmare, due to lack of space. Use the underground car parks in La Línea instead (it's worth paying for the extra security) and **walk across**. If you do join the queue to drive in, ignore the people who will attempt to sell non-European visitors a "visa" – it's usually an old bus ticket. From the frontier, where passport checking is a formality, it's a short bus ride or about a fifteen-minute walk across part of the airport's runway to **Main Street** (La Calle Real), which runs for most of the town's length a couple of blocks back from the port. Most of the shops – cheap, duty-free whisky is a major attraction – are clustered in and around Main Street, along with nearly all of the British-style pubs and hotels.

For information, the main **tourist office** (Mon–Fri 10am–6pm, Sat 10am–2pm) is in Cathedral Square, with sub-offices at the airport, the Gibraltar Museum, Market Place and the Waterport coach park (all Mon–Fri 10am–6pm, Sat 10am–2pm). The John Mackintosh Hall at the south end of Main Street is also a useful resource – it's the

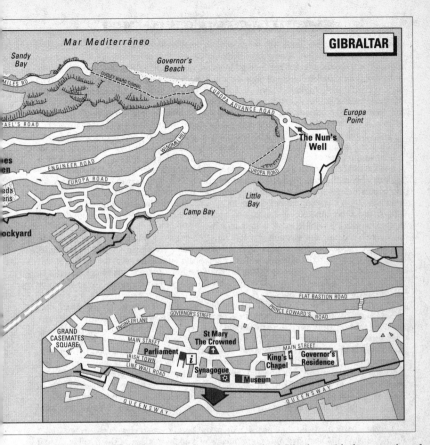

cultural centre, with exhibitions and a library. Much of Gibraltar, with the exception of the cheap booze shops, closes down on Saturday afternoon, but the tourist sites remain open, and this can often be a quiet time to visit. Virtually everything closes down on Sunday.

Accommodation

Shortage of space on the rock means that **accommodation** is at a premium, especially in summer. It's really not worth your while searching out a good place to stay unless you have to: your best bet is to visit on day trips from Algeciras (buses on the hour and half-hour, journey time 30min) or La Línea.

The only budget accommodation is at the *Toc H Hostel* on Line Wall Rd (☎350/73431; about £11 a person) – though rooms here are none too comfortable and almost always occupied by long-term residents – or the tiny *Seruya's Guest House* in Irish Town, a street west of and running parallel to, Main St (☎350/73220; about £15 a double), which is also invariably full. Otherwise, you're going to have to pay standard

SOVEREIGNTY OF GIBRALTAR

Sovereignty over the Rock will doubtless eventually return to Spain, but at present neither side is in much of a hurry. For Britain it's a question of precedent – Gibraltar is in too similar a situation to the Falklands/Malvinas, which conflict pushed the Spanish into postponing an initial frontier-opening date in 1982. For Spain too, there are unsettling parallels with the *presidios* (Spanish enclaves) on the Moroccan coast at Ceuta and Melilla – both at present part of Andalucía. Nonetheless, the British presence is in practice waning, and to this end the government seems to be running down the significance of the military base on the Rock, reducing the number of British troops by half in 1990.

The Gibraltarians see all these issues as irrelevant in light of their firmly stated opposition to a return to **Spanish control** of the Rock. In 1967, just before Franco closed the border in the hope of forcing a quick agreement, the colony voted on the issue – rejecting it by 12,138 votes to 44. Most people would probably sympathize with that vote – against a Spain that was then still a dictatorship – but more than twenty years have gone by, Spanish democracy is now secure, and the arguments are becoming increasingly tenuous. Despite its impressive claims to law and order, Gibraltar is no model society either; its dirty jobs, for instance, are nearly all done by Moroccans on one-year contracts, who are housed in old army barracks.

March 1988 saw the election of Gibraltar's first-ever **Socialist government**, but its leader, Joe Bossano – re-elected in 1992 with a whopping 73 percent majority – continues to oppose back-room deals between Britain and Spain on the future of the colony. A wily ex-trade union leader, he is attempting to make the Rock more self-reliant, encouraging its status as an "offshore" base. Already, some 24,000 companies, many somewhat dubious, are registered in Gibraltar.

Gibraltarians feel very vulnerable, caught between the interests of two big states; they are well aware that both governments' concerns have nothing to do with their own personal wishes. Until very recently people were sent over from Britain to fill all the top civil service and Ministry of Defence jobs, a practice which, to a lesser degree, still continues. Large parts of the Rock are no-go areas for "natives"; the South District in particular being taken up by facilities for the armed services. Space is at a premium and the biggest social problem is housing, but as at home, the British government will give no money for new homes. The withdrawal of British forces, however, is set greatly to improve the housing situation: there's a huge new development in the reclaimed land of the port, and much former army housing is due to be handed over to the local government.

Locals – particularly on the Spanish side of the border – also vigorously protest about the Royal Navy nuclear-powered submarines which dock regularly at the naval base, and secrecy surrounds the issue of whether nuclear warheads and/or chemical and biological weapons are stored in the arsenal, probably deep inside the Rock itself. Yet Gibraltarians still cling to British status and all their institutions are modelled on English lines. Contrary to popular belief, they are of neither mainly Spanish nor British blood, but an ethnic mix descended from Genoese, Portuguese, Spanish, Minorcan, Jewish, Maltese and British forebears. English is the official language, but more commonly spoken is what sounds to an outsider like perfect Andalucian Spanish. It is, in fact, *yanito*, an Andalucian dialect with borrowed words which reflect its diverse origins – only a Spaniard from the south can tell a Gibraltarian from an Andalucian.

British hotel prices: the *Queen's Hotel* on Boyd St (☎350/74000) and the *Bristol* in Cathedral Square (☎350/76800) each charge over £40 for double, often interior facing, rooms. No **camping** is allowed, and if you're caught sleeping rough or inhabiting abandoned bunkers, you're more than likely to be arrested and fined. This law is enforced by Gibraltar and Ministry of Defence police, and raids of the beaches are regular.

Around the Rock

Near the end of Main Street you can hop on a **cable car** (Mon–Sat 9.30am–7.15pm, last trip down 7.45pm; £3.50 return) which will carry you up to the summit – **The Top of the Rock** as it's logically known – via **Apes' Den** halfway up, a fairly reliable viewing point to see the tailless monkeys and hear the guides explain their legend. The story goes that the British will keep the rock only so long as the apes remain too; Winston Churchill was suspicious enough to augment their numbers during World War II when they started to decline. The Top gives good views over to the Atlas Mountains and down to the town, its elaborate water catchment system cut into the side of the rock.

From the Apes' Den it's an easy walk south along Queens Road to **Saint Michael's Cave**, an immense natural cavern which led ancient people to believe the rock was hollow and gave rise to its old name of *Mons Calpe* (Hollow Mountain). Used during the last war as a bomb-proof military hospital the cave nowadays hosts occasional concerts. You can arrange at the tourist office for a guided visit to **Lower Saint Michael's Cave**, a series of chambers going deeper down and ending in an underground lake.

Although it is possible to be lazy and take the cable car both ways, you might instead walk up via Willis's Road to visit the fourteenth-century **Tower of Homage**. This is the most visible survival from the old Moorish Castle, today filled with wax dummies of British soldiers hacking at the stone and doing battle with the Spanish. Further up you'll find the **Upper Galleries**, blasted out of the rock during the Great Siege of 1779–82, in order to point guns down at the Spanish lines. To walk down, take the **Mediterranean Steps** – they're not very well signposted and you have to climb over O'Hara's Battery, a very steep descent most of the way down the east side, turning the southern corner of the Rock. You'll pass through the Jews' Gate and into Engineer Road. From here, return to town through the Alameda Gardens and the **Trafalgar Cemetery**, overgrown and evocative, with a good line in epitaphs.

Back **in town**, incorporated into the **Gibraltar Museum** (Mon–Fri 10am–6pm), are two well-preserved, beautiful fourteenth-century **Moorish Baths**. Resembling the ancient Roman model, the baths had a cold room and hot rooms heated by a hypocaust. Note the star shaped-skylights, and the pillars used in the construction: one Roman, two Visigothic and four Moorish. Otherwise, the museum's **collection** is an odd assortment including an incongruous Egyptian mummy washed up in the bay, a natural history display of stuffed birds in glass cages, and a rather dreary military section documenting how the British came to rule the roost here. The museum's star exhibit should be a female skull, dating from around 100,000 years ago and unearthed in 1848 on the Rock's north face. Ironically, because the find was then stored away, it was the later discovery of a skull in Germany's Neander Valley that gave its name to the era we know as Neanderthal, which could just as easily have been termed "Gibraltarian". The museum now retains only a copy, the original having been removed to the research collection of the Natural History Museum in London.

The best **beach** is at the tiny fishing village at **Catalan Bay**, whose inhabitants like to think of themselves as distinct from the townies on the other side of the Rock.

ADMISSION TO GIBRALTAR ATTRACTIONS

The grand tour of the Rock takes a half to a full day, and all sites on it are open from 10am to 7pm in summer, 10am to 5.30pm in winter; if you visit all the attractions, buy a reduced-price ticket from the tourist office who also have a reduced price **key card**, which allows free entry to all the sights providing you stay overnight.

Eating and drinking

Eating is a bit of a loss in Gibraltar, and relatively expensive by Spanish standards. Pub snacks or fish and chips are the norm. Main Street is crowded with touristy places, although *Smiths Fish and Chip Shop*, 295 Main St, is worth a try. Other choices are the *Penny Farthing* on King Street, off Cathedral Square, always busy for home-cooked food (take-away too); *Corks Wine Bar*, Irish Town, and *La Cantina*, a Mexican place on Governor's St at the end of Cornwall's Lane. The *Market Café* in the public market and *Splendid Bar* in George's Lane both do *tapas*. *Saccarello's Coffee House* in Irish Town is an interesting place to have a drink – upstairs there's a collection of old postcards showing the development of Gibraltar. Further afield, at Marina Bay, try *Biancas*, for reasonably priced seafood, or *Da Paolo* which serves not-bad Italian food.

Gibraltarian **pubs** mimic traditional English styles (and prices), but are often open late. Unlike in Spain, there's hardly anywhere to sit outdoors, which often means drinking beer in the equivalent of a sauna during high summer. For pub food, the *Royal Calpe*, 176 Main St; *Calpe Hounds* on Cornwalls Lane, and *Clipper*, Irish Town, are among the best, all fixing substantial meals. Of the pubs grouped together on Main Street – all of them rowdy, full of squaddies and visiting sailors – the *Gibraltar Arms*, *Royal Calpe* and *The Horseshoe* all have outdoor seating, and *The Horseshoe* shows music videos. The *Prince of Wales* in John Mackintosh Square or the *Canon Bar* in Canon Lane beside the cathedral are quieter.

ONWARD TRAVEL

Two decidedly functional attractions of Gibraltar are its opportunities for reasonably cheap **flights to Britain** (standby one-way fares are about £80; call *GB Airways* ☎350/79200), and its role as a **port for Morocco**. The trip is invariably very rough, and the timetable is erratically subject to weather conditions even at the best of times. In season, though, there's a *Gibline* **catamaran** to Tangier daily: this takes just one hour, making day trips a possibility. There are occasional sailings also to **Mdiq**, near Tetouan on Morocco's Mediterranean coast, which gives a gentler introduction to the country. Buy tickets from *Beagle Travel*, 9B Georges Lane – prices start at around £30 with substantial reductions for day returns or fixed date tickets. A new Moroccan **ferry** runs to Tangier on Friday evening and Monday morning: return fare from £28 for a two-hour trip; tickets from *Tourafrica* in the International Commercial Centre, Casemates Square.

If you're looking for really exotic destinations, at the end of summer the yacht marina fills up with boats heading for the **Canaries**, **Madeira** and the **West Indies** – many take on crew to work in exchange for passage.

For travelling on through Spain, **RENFE** tickets can be bought from *Pegasus Travel* (☎350/72252).

Algeciras

ALGECIRAS occupies the far side of the bay to Gibraltar, spewing out smoke and pollution in its direction. The last town of the Spanish Mediterranean, it was once an elegant resort; today it's unabashedly a port and industrial centre, its suburbs sprawling out on all sides. When Franco closed the border with Gibraltar at La Línea it was Algeciras that he decided to develop to absorb the Spanish workers formerly employed in the British naval dockyards, thus breaking the area's dependence on the Rock.

Most travellers are scathing about the city's ugliness, and unless you're waiting for a bus or train, or heading for Morocco, there's admittedly little reason to stop. However, Algeciras has a real port atmosphere, and even if just passing through it's hard to resist the urge to get on a boat south. Algeciras is the main port for Moroccan migrant workers, who drive home every year during their holidays from the factories, farms and mines of Northern Europe. In summer, the port bustles with groups of Moroccans in transit, dressed in flowing *djelabas* and yellow slippers, and lugging unbelievable amounts of possessions. Half a million cross Spain each year, often becoming victims of all levels of racial discrimination, from being ripped off to being violently attacked.

Once you start to explore, you'll also discover that the old town has some very attractive corners which seem barely to have changed in fifty years, especially around the **Plaza Alta**. This leafy square, arguably the town's only sight of any note, lies a five-minute walk from the bus station/port area and if you're killing time provides a much more pleasant place to sit out than around the port. On the square, the eighteenth-century church of **Nuestra Señora de la Palma** and the Baroque chapel of **Nuestra Señora de Europa** – with a fine facade – are worth a look.

Nearer the port, the romantic **Hotel Reina Cristina**, Paseo de la Conferencia s/n, south of the harbour (☎956/603323; ⑥), set in a park and built in the last century in English colonial style, is a wonderful throwback to the days of the Grand Tour and steam trains. Call in for a drink in the bar and take a look at the plaques on the reception desk bearing the signatures of famous guests, such as Sir Arthur Conan Doyle, WB Yeats and Cole Porter.

Practicalities

The **main bus station** is in c/San Bernardo, 250m or so behind the port, beside the *Hotel Octavio* and just short of the **train station**. If you need any information about the town, or want to pick up an accommodation list, make for the **Turismo**, c/Juan de la Cierva, on the south side of the train track (Mon–Fri 9.30am–1.30pm & 5–8pm, Sat 9.30am–1.30pm). Room rates tend to go up dramatically in midseason, but Algeciras has plenty of low-priced **hostales** and **pensiones** in the grid of streets between the port and the train station, and lots of simple *casas de huéspedes* clustered round the market. There are several in c/Duque de Almodóvar, where options include *Levante* at no. 21 (☎956/651505; ③), or along c/José Santacana – *Vizcaíno* at no. 9 (☎956/655756; ②) or the more comfortable, brand-new *González* at no. 7 (☎956/652843; ③) – and c/ Rafael de Muro, its continuation on the north side of Plaza Palma, the market square. On the square there's the surprisingly spruce *Hostal Nuestra Señora de la Palma* (☎956/632481; ③); *Casa Sanchez* (☎956/696557; ②) also does rooms if you get stuck. The most romantic place to stay in town must be the nineteenth-century *Hotel Anglo-Hispano*, Avda. Villanueva 7 (☎956/572590; ④), its marble-tiled lobby dripping faded grandeur; it's on the south side of the train track near the port.

The huge number of people passing through the town also guarantees endless possibilities for **food and drink**, especially around the port/harbour area. Among them, across the railway line from the Turismo and invariably crowded, is the good value *Casa Gil* at c/Sigismundo Moret 2, and 50m further in along the same street, *Casa Sanchez* (at the corner of c/Río) with a cheap *menú*. A little north of the bus station *Restaurante Montes*, c/Juan Morrison 27, is a more upmarket place, and they have a cheaper *tapas* bar lower down the hill on the same street. The **markets** are useful places to buy food, too, as well as vibrant and fascinating to visit; the main one is on Plaza Palma, down by the port.

Onward travel

At Algeciras the **train line** begins again, heading north to Ronda, Córdoba and Madrid. The **train route to Ronda** is one of the best journeys in Andalucía; there are six departures a day. For Madrid (and Paris) there's a night express, currently leaving at 11pm, and also low-priced *Linebus/Iberbus* coaches to Paris and London. For Málaga, hourly **buses** leave from *Empresa Portillo*, Avda. Virgen del Carmen 15; from here too,

---

ON TO MOROCCO

Morocco is easily enough visited from Algeciras: there are three or four **crossings to Tangier** each day (a 2hr 30min-trip), and six or seven to the Spanish *presidio* of **Ceuta** (1hr 30min), little more than a Spanish Gibraltar with a brisk business in duty-free goods, but a relatively painless way to enter Morocco. Alternatively you can go by **hydrofoil** to Ceuta (daily; 30min). Tickets are sold at the scores of travel agents along the waterside and on most approach roads; they all cost the same, though some places may give you a better rate of exchange than others if you want to pay in foreign currency. Wait till Tangier – or if you're going via Ceuta, Tetouan – before buying any Moroccan currency; rates in the embarkation building kiosks are very poor. Make sure that your ticket is for the next ferry, and beware the ticket sellers who congregate near the dock entrance wearing official Ceuta/Tangier badges: they add a whopping "commission" charge. *InterRail/Eurail* card holders should note that they're entitled to a twenty percent discount on the standard ferry price: if you have trouble getting this go to the official sales desk in the embarkation building.

---

less frequently, are direct connections to Granada. Buses to Barcelona leave from *Empresa Bacoma* in front of the harbour offices, but the journey is appallingly slow at 21 hours (versus a theoretical 20 on the train), and you have to change in Málaga. For Tarifa, Cádiz, Sevilla and most other destinations you'll need the **main bus station**. The bus to La Línea also goes every thirty minutes from here.

Ronda and the White Towns

Though Andalucía boasts many pretty *pueblos blancos*, the best known are the **"White Towns"** – unfeasibly picturesque places, each with its own plaza, church and tavern – set in the roughly triangular area between Málaga, Algeciras and Sevilla. At their centre, in a region of wild mountainous beauty, is spectacular **Ronda**, very much the transportation hub and a great attraction in its own right. From Ronda, almost any route north or west is rewarding, taking you past a whole series of lovely little villages, among cherry orchards and vines, many of them fortified since the days of the Reconquest – hence the mass of "de la Frontera" suffixes. Of these, **Arcos de la Frontera**, a truly spectacular White Town perched on a high limestone spur, comes close to Ronda as the best place to spend a few days in the region.

Described here are two of the major "White Town" routes – the first roughly north-east from Ronda and the second veering southwest towards Cádiz.

To Ronda from the coast

Of several possible approaches to Ronda from the coast, the route up from Algeciras is the most rewarding – and worth going out of your way to experience. From Málaga most of the buses to Ronda follow the coastal highway to San Pedro de Alcántara before turning into the mountains: dramatic enough, but rather a bleak route, with no villages and only limited views of the dark rock face of the Serranía. The train ride up from Málaga is better, with three connecting services daily, including a convenient 6pm departure after the last bus leaves.

You can follow the **Algeciras route** – via Gaucín – by either bus or train, or, if you've time and energy, on a four- or five-day walk. En route, you're always within reach of a river and there's a series of hill towns, each one visible from the next, to provide targets for the day; Casares (see p.100) is almost on the route, but more easily reached from Estepona.

CASTELLAR, JIMENA AND GAUCÍN/111

Castellar de la Frontera

The first "White Town" on the route proper is **CASTELLAR DE LA FRONTERA**, a bizarre hill village within a thirteenth-century Moorish castle, whose population, in accord with some grandiose scheme, was moved downriver in 1971 to the "new" town of La Almoraima. The relocation was subsequently dropped and a few villagers moved back to their old houses, but most of the dwellings were taken over by retired hippies (mainly German, mainly affluent). Perhaps not surprisingly, the result wasn't totally successful, and the two groups didn't exactly gel – not helped by the scandal a couple of years back when the artificial lake below the village was drained, revealing the corpses of two Germans joined together by a rope. Agitation to clean out what local graffiti called "drug addicted swine" started up and there is presently only an uneasy truce between the two sides. Recent plans to rebuild the town as a tourist centre, complete with *parador* appear to have ground to a halt. Reflecting this tension, the place has a brooding, claustrophobic feel, and although there are a couple of German-run bars and a solitary *hostal* (*El Pilar*; c/León Esquivel 4; ☎956/693022; ②), you may want to move on after a brief look around.

Jimena de la Frontera and Gaucín

JIMENA DE LA FRONTERA lacks the traumas of Castellar; again, it's a hill town but it's far larger and more open, rising to a grand Moorish castle with a triple-gateway entrance. In recent years it has become home to a considerable contingent of British expats who probably feel the need to be within working and shopping distance of umbilical Gibraltar. In town are several bars and a beautiful old **fonda** (which has no sign and isn't easy to find – ask for the *Casa María*; ①); there's also the *Hostal El Anon* (②) on c/Consuelo, and, a *fonda* a little way out at the train station, *Los Arcos* (☎952/640328; ③). The best place for a **meal** is *Restaurante Bar Cuenca*, Avda. de los Deportes on the way into town, which also serves *tapas*.

Beyond Jimena it's quite a climb through woods of cork oak and olive groves to reach **GAUCÍN**, though there are bars halfway at the hamlet of San Pablo. Just beyond the Málaga border, Gaucín, almost a mountain village and perched on a ridge below

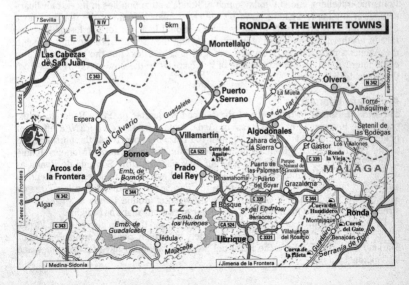

yet another Moorish fort, commands tremendous views (to Gibraltar and the Moroccan coast on a very clear day) and makes a great place to **stop over**. It has a charming *fonda*, the *Nacional*, c/San Juan de Dios 8 (①) and a slightly plusher *hostal*, the *Moncada*; c/Luis Armiñán s/n (☎952/151156; ②). **Food** is available from the *Venta El Soccorro* on the main highway. You can reach the village by bus, but far more rewarding is the 13km walk from its train station. Though it's now known as Gaucín, this station is actually at El Colmenar, on the fringes of the Cortes nature reserve: if you need to rest up before the hike (getting on for 3hr, mostly uphill) there's a *hostal* and several bars here.

Between Gaucín and Ronda is a cluster of tiny villages such as the beautifully sited Algatocín, that could be incorporated into an enjoyable walking route over a number of days. However, there are few official places to stay and if you're not planning on sleeping under the stars you'll need a list of the *casas particulares* in the Serranía de Ronda from the Turismo at Ronda. Alternatively, take the train to the station of Benaoján-Montejaque: from here it's an hour's hike to the prehistoric **Cueva de la Pileta** (see p.119). From Benaoján, Ronda is just three stops (and thirty minutes) down the line.

Ronda

Rising amid a ring of dark, angular mountains, the full natural drama of **RONDA** is best appreciated as you enter the town. Built on an isolated ridge of the sierra, it's split in half by a gaping river gorge (*El Tajo*, though the river itself is the Guadalévin) that drops sheer for 130m on three sides. Still more spectacular, the gorge is spanned by a stupendous eighteenth-century arched bridge, while tall whitewashed houses lean perilously from its precipitous edges.

In Moorish times a provincial capital embellished with lavish mosques and palaces, Ronda is also notable for having been the birthplace of the Maestranza, an order of knights who laid down the rules for early bullfights performed on horseback. During the nineteenth century the town became an increasingly popular destination for Romantic travellers, and still today much of Ronda's attraction lies in its extraordinary setting, or in simply walking down by the river, following one of the donkey tracks through the rich green valley. Bird-watchers should look out for the lesser kestrels, rare in northern Europe, nesting in and launching themselves from the cliffs beneath the Alameda park. Lower down you can spot crag martins. But the town itself is of equal interest and has sacrificed little of its character to the flow of day-trippers from the Costa del Sol.

Arrival and information

The **bus station** is in the north of the Mercadillo quarter on Plaza Redondo, while **trains** pull in a couple of blocks east on Avda. Andalucía. There's a *RENFE* office for tickets and timetables at c/Infante 20, near the Plaza del Socorro. At the northern end of the Plaza de España, Ronda's helpful and enthusiastic **Turismo** (Mon–Fri 10am–2pm; ☎952/871272) has maps and walking information on the Serranía de Ronda as well as details on all kinds of outdoor activities and events in the area. At weekends a **sub-office** operates the same hours from the Palacio de Mondragón on the Plaza de Mondragón. Incidentally, it can be confusing walking around Ronda as many of the streets have **multiple names**: if in doubt, refer to as many maps as possible.

The main **telefónica office** is located in c/Sevilla, and the main **correos** is at Virgen de la Paz 20, near the Plaza de Toros. A variety of **foreign press** is available from c/Mariano Souviron 5 (above the Plaza del Socorro), who also have fax machines and international phones.

Accommodation

The best **places to stay** in Ronda are in the heart of the Mercadillo quarter, and to the east of the Plaza del Socorro off c/Borrego and its continuations, c/Cristo and then c/Almendra. The most upmarket options are to be found near the Plaza de Toros.

Ronda's **campsite**, *Camping El Sur* (☎952/875939) with swimming pool, bar and a good value restaurant, lies 2km out of town along the road to Algeciras. You can rent **bungalows** here, too. It's not served by bus, so if you don't fancy the walk (especially from the train and bus stations which adds an extra kilometre) a taxi is the best bet.

Hostal Aguilar, c/Naranja 28 (☎952/871994). Clean and friendly family-run place off c/Cristo. ②.

Hostal Andalucía, c/Martínez Astein 19 (☎952/875450). Tranquil *hostal* near the train station. All rooms have bath. ③.

Pensión La Española, c/José Aparicio 3 (☎952/871052). In the alleyway just off the the Plaza de España behind the Turismo, with amazing views from some rooms. ②.

Hotel Polo, c/ Mariano Soubiron (c/Benitez on some maps) 8 (☎952/872447). Swish place beyond the bullring; very good value for the price, and with worthwhile off-season deals. ④.

Hotel Reina Victoria, c/Jerez 25 (☎952/871240). Although it has seen better days, this place has a certain decaying grandeur; ask for one of the corner rooms with a spectacular view over the Serranía de Ronda. ⑤.

Hostal Ronda Sol, c/Cristo 11, near the intersection with c/Sevilla (☎952/874497). A budget option, although some of the interior rooms are a bit claustrophobic. ②.

Hotel Royal, c/Virgen de la Paz 42 (☎952/871141). Comfortable rooms in an ugly modern building opposite the Alameda. ③.

Hostal San Francisco, c/María Cabrera (c/Prim on some maps) 18 (☎952/873299). Excellent value place where all rooms have bath. ②.

Hotel El Tajo, c/Cruz Verde 7, off c/ Almendra (☎952/874040). Very comfortable hotel with its own economical restaurant. ④.

Hotel Virgen de los Reyes, c/Borrego 13 (☎952/871140). Good-value hotel with en suite bath and TV included. ③.

Hostal Virgen del Rocío, c/Nueva 18 (☎952/877425). Clean, no-frills place one street off the eastern side of the Plaza de España. ②.

The Town

Ronda divides into three parts: on the northwest side of the gorge is the largely modern **Mercadillo** quarter, while across the bridge is the old Moorish town, the **Ciudad**, and its **San Francisco** suburb.

The **Ciudad** retains intact its Moorish plan and a great many of its houses, interspersed with a number of fine Renaissance mansions. It is so intricate a maze – not helped by the fact that many streets in Ronda are known by more than one name – that you can do little else but wander at random. However, at some stage, make your way across the eighteenth-century **Puente Nuevo** bridge, peering down the walls of limestone rock into the yawning *Tajo* which claimed the bridge's architect, Martín de Aldehuela, as he clambered over the parapet to inspect his finished work, and clutching for his hat in the wind fell to his death. Hemingway, in *For Whom the Bell Tolls*, recorded how prisoners were thrown alive into the gorge. These days, Ronda remains a major military garrison post and houses much of the Spanish Africa Legion, Franco's old crack regiment, who can be seen wandering around town in their tropical green coats and tasselled fezes. They have a mean reputation.

CASA DEL REY MORO AND BAÑOS ÁRABES

Over the bridge, a left turn along the c/Marqués de Parada (or c/Santo Domingo), winds round to the somewhat arbitrarily named **Casa del Rey Moro** ("house of the Moorish king") at no. 17, an early eighteenth-century mansion built on Moorish foundations. Local legend has it that this was the palace of the Moorish emir Badis, an

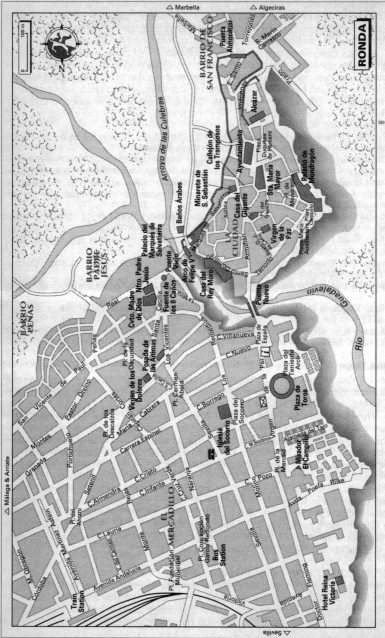

Arabian Bluebeard, who was reputed to drink his wine from the skulls of the victims he had beheaded. The house is not open to the public, but from its garden a remarkable underground stairway (the *Mina*) descends to the river; these 365 steps, guaranteeing a water supply in times of siege, were cut by Christian slaves in the fourteenth century.

Further down the same street is the **Palacio del Marqués de Salvatierra** (Mon–Wed, Fri & Sat 11am–2pm & 4–7pm, Sun 11am–2pm; 150ptas), a splendid Renaissance mansion with an oddly primitive, half-grotesque frieze of Adam and Eve on its portal together with the colonial images of four Peruvian indians; the house is still used by the family but can usually be visited on mildly interesting guided tours. Just down the hill you reach the two old town bridges – the **Puente Viejo** of 1616 and the single-span Moorish **Puente de San Miguel** and nearby, on the southeast bank of the river, are the distinctive hump-shaped cupolas and bizarre glass roof-windows of the old **Baños Árabes** (Tues–Sat 10am–2pm & 4–7pm, Sun 10am–2pm; free). Dating from the thirteenth century and wonderfully preserved, these are truly remarkable structures, with star-shaped windows set in a barrel-vaulted ceiling and beautiful octagonal brick columns supporting horseshoe arches. A channel from the nearby river fed the water into this complex which was formerly surrounded by plant-filled gardens.

IGLESIA DE SANTA MARÍA AND PALACIO DE MONDRAGÓN

At the centre of the Ciudad quarter in Ronda's most picturesqe square stands the cathedral church of **Santa María Mayor**, originally the Arab town's Friday mosque. Externally it's a graceful combination of Moorish, Gothic and Renaissance styles with the belfry built on top of the old minaret. Inside (100ptas) you can see an arch covered with Arabic calligraphy, and just in front of the current street door a part of the old Arab *mihrab*, or prayer niche, has been exposed. Just east of the church along the Callejon de los Tramposos stands the **Minarete de San Sebastián**, a tower that survives from a fourteenth-century mosque. In the opposite direction and a short distance west from Santa María Mayor is the most important of Ronda's palaces, the fourteenth-century **Palacio de Mondragón** (daily 10am–2pm; free) on the plaza of the same name. Probably the real "palace of the Moorish kings", following the *reconquista* it was much altered in order to accommodate Fernando and Isabel who lodged here when they visited Ronda. Inside, three of the patios preserve original stucco work and mosaics and there's a magnificent carved wood ceiling; the palace also houses a small **museum**. From the garden there's a fine **view** over the *Tajo* and the valley.

Just north of here at c/Tenorio 20, you can visit a nineteenth-century **mansion** (100ptas) stuffed full of heavy mahogany furniture. The house itself is dull and oppressive, but the reconstructed Mudéjar gardens with fountain and mosaics are a delight, offering more great views over the *Tajo*. Near the southern end of the Ciudad are the ruins of the **Alcázar**, razed by the French in 1809 and now partially occupied by a school. Once it was virtually impregnable – as indeed was this whole fortress capital, which ruled an independent and isolated Moorish kingdom until 1485, just seven years before the fall of Granada – now it's full of litter and stray sheep.

The principal gate of the town, the **Puerto del Almocabar**, through which passed the Christian conquerors (led personally by Fernando), stands to the southeast of the alcázar at the entrance to the suburb of San Francisco.

THE MERCADILLO QUARTER AND THE PLAZA DE TOROS

When Ronda was retaken from the Moors in 1485, the impoverished governors imposed such heavy taxes on all goods and foodstuffs entering it that the merchants set up their own quarter outside the Ciudad to avoid paying them. This area, the **Mercadillo**, has effectively become the centre of the modern town, and is currently undergoing a face-lift after years of neglect. Many buildings in and around the Plaza de

PEDRO ROMERO: FATHER OF THE CORRIDA

Born in Ronda in 1754, Pedro Romero is the father of the modern **bullfight**; previously they had been killed only on horseback with a *rejón* or spear, as a patrician pastime. However, he was not the first to fight bulls on foot: legend has it that this accolade goes to his grandfather Francisco Romero, who leapt into the ring when an aristocrat had been dismounted by a bull and began to distract it with his hat, delighting the crowd in the process. The hat was changed for the red *muleta*, or cape, and the bullfight was born. Once the *corrida* had been created however, it was Pedro Romero who laid down the pattern for all future contests with his passes and moves, many still in use today, and the invention of the almost mystical *arte* – the union of animal and man in a form of ballet. In the newly constructed Ronda ring Romero killed over 5,000 bulls and fought into his eighties, passing on to his students his soberly classical Ronda style, which is markedly different from the more flamboyant styles of Sevilla and Córdoba. A statue honouring Romero stands in the Alameda del Tajo.

España are being renovated, and there's a new *parador* under construction, overlooking the *Tajo*.

The barrio's major monument has to be the **Plaza de Toros**, to the north of the Plaza de España (10am–6.30pm; 150ptas), the oldest, the largest and the most venerated bullring in Spain. Opened in 1785, it became the stage upon which the father of the modern bullfight, Pedro Romero, laid down and demonstrated the rules of fighting bulls on foot. Once you've passed through the elaborate Baroque doorway, it's possible to wander around the arena with its unusual stone barriers and an elegant double tier of seats supported by stone Tuscan columns. The **museum** gives an illuminating history of the *corrida* or bullfight; besides posters advertising the first *corrida* held here on May 19th, 1785, and Pedro Romero's "suit of lights", there are photos of Hemingway and Orson Welles, two regular visitors. Welles' last wish was to have his ashes buried in Ronda and they are now interred on the nearby estate of his friend and one of Spain's greatest *toreros*, the *rondeño* Antonio Ordóñez. The artist Goya made a number of paintings here of the *matadores* in action, and each September in a tribute to Goya and Romero the *corridas goyescas* are staged (supervised by Ordóñez), when the fighters participate in eighteenth-century-style gear similar to those in the paintings.

AROUND THE ALAMEDA DEL TAJO

To the north of the bullring lies the **Alameda del Tajo**, a pleasant park completed in the early nineteenth century with fine views over the Serranía de Ronda. The garden is said to have been laid out at no cost to the local council, the funds raised by fines on those using "obscene language in public, thereby causing a scandal". Continuing in the same direction will bring you to the Carmelite **Convent** on the Plaza de la Merced, its doors flanked by two great palms. Inside, the nuns sell their *dulces*.

You could continue along Avenida Fleming to the **Hotel Reina Victoria**, built by an English company in the first decade of the century to house British visitors, many of whom came from the military base at Gibraltar. The German poet Rainer Maria Rilke put up here in 1913, and his room (no. 208) has been preserved as a museum which the management will allow you to view on request. The hotel **bar** has a terrace with fine views and a swimming pool in the leafy grounds which, while officially for guests only, is easy enough to enjoy using a little discretion.

Finally, a couple of blocks in from the Plaza de España is the remarkably preserved inn where Miguel Cervantes once slept, the sixteenth-century **Posada de las Ánimas** ("Inn of Souls") on c/Cecilia. Today, although this is officially the town's *Hogar del*

Pensionista, or old people's home, the building looks every bit the ancient inn, with a skull and crossbones carved in the keystone above the door which may have something to do with the building's name. The elderly residents are only too happy to let you see inside, and, if you're lucky, will show you the giant guitar that hangs on the wall on the second floor. Nearby, the eighteenth-century **Virgen de los Dolores** in the street of the same name, is a chapel with a curious porch projecting into the street. Carved on the porch's pillars are some weird bird-like creatures, as well as others that are part beast, part human with ropes fastened around their necks. The site of the church was formerly a gallows for condemned prisoners and this strange imagery may be connected with the representation of these unfortunates.

Eating and drinking

A great many of Ronda's best **eating and drinking** options are on or around the Plaza del Socorro. There are numerous good places for **breakfast** along c/Espinel, and a couple of good restaurants in the **Ciudad quarter**, but few of the touristy restaurants along the c/Virgen de la Paz, fronting the bullring, are worth bothering with.

Café Alba, c/Espinel 44. Piping hot *churros* and delicious breakfast coffee.

Restaurante El Campillo, Plaza del Campillo 4. Ciudad quarter restaurant, close to the Palacio de Mondragón, with a charming terrace and garden, and offering a medium priced *menú*.

Don Miguel, Plaza de España. Splendid restaurant with *rondeño* specialities such as *perdiz estofada* (partridge stew) and *arroz con conejo* (rabbit with rice) as well as a medium priced *menú*. The main attraction here, though, is the terrace, with a marvellous view of the *Tajo*.

Doña Pepe, Plaza del Socorro. Decent family-run restaurant with – on the near side of the intervening Pasaje Correos – a seperate Cafeteria-Bar serving *bocadillos* and freshly squeezed orange juice.

Bodega La Esquina, c/Los Remedios 24. Wholly traditional bar serving excellent *jamon serrano*, *tapas* and *fino*.

Bar Faustino, c/Santa Cecilia 4, just off Plaza Carmen Abela. A good and lively local bar – with patio – serving *tapas* and *raciones*.

Bodega La Giralda, c/Nueva 19. Hugely popular bar serving up superb *tapas* in a great setting – you'll have trouble finding somewhere to sit.

Bar-Restaurante Jerez, Plaza Tenerife Arce. Terraced restaurant, flanking the bullring, which serves *tapas* and *raciones* to a high standard. Best of the lot round here.

Marisquería Paco, Plaza del Socorro 8. The best *tapas* place round here without question. The seafood is fresh and the *tapas* – washed down with a beer at outdoor tables – are excellent.

Peking, c/Los Remedios 14. Reasonably priced Chinese food if you're desperate for a change.

Bar Picasso, Plaza de la Merced. *Tapas* bar with a low-priced, rather eccentric, restaurant attached.

Rico, c/Espinel 42, south side of the Plaza del Socorro. The best *heladería* in town – also good for afternoon tea and in winter, steaming cups of hot chocolate.

Restaurante Tenorio, c/Tenorio 1. Faintly baronial Ciudad quarter restaurant with a terrace.

Todo Natural, Pasaje Correos. Health food shop with a vegetarian restaurant (lunch only).

Bar Valencia, c/Naranja 6. Good *platos combinados* in an earthy and authentic atmosphere.

Nightlife

Unfortunately, Ronda's most atmospheric **bar** operates only seasonally. In summer you'll find it in the middle of the Puente Nuevo bridge – reached by a stairway in the plaza. The bar was originally the town prison and last saw use during the Civil War, when Ronda was the site of some of the south's most vicious massacres. Otherwise, **nightlife** tends to be provincial and low key.

Bodega Siete de Copas, Paseo Blas Infante, behind the bullring. A nice place to hear jazz music (albeit recorded).

Tobalo, on the Sevilla road. *Flamenco peña*; the Turismo will let you know if there are any *juergas* (shindigs) in the offing.

Around Ronda

Ronda makes an excellent base for exploring the superb countryside in the immediate vicinity or for visiting more of the White Towns; one of the most unusual is **Setenil**, 15km away.

Arriate

Eight kilometres from the northern end of town, across a plain of olive groves, the village of **ARRIATE** is reached by turning off the C341 to Campillos on the outskirts. This charming place is home to the Campaneros del Amanacer ("bell-ringers of the dawn"), who rise at dawn every Saturday and tour the streets until 7am singing hymns to the accompaniment of bells, guitars and cymbals. They continue on their way pausing at the doors of houses who have "pre-booked" numbers from the repertoire. *Salves,* which last ten minutes, cost the most, or you could ask for a quick cheap blast (called a *Pater Noster*). You can get **rooms** at *Pensión El Chozo*, Avda. Andalucía s/n (☎952/165344; ②) or the *fonda, Central,* c/Ronda 30. **Trains** to Ronda leave from the station on the southern edge of the village.

Ronda la Vieja

Twelve kilometres from the town are the ruins of **Ronda la Vieja**, the first-century Roman town of Acinipo, set in the midst of beautiful hill country. The ruins are reached by turning right 6km down the main road to Arcos/Sevilla, and following the signed way to a farmhouse where the friendly farmer will present you with a plan (in Spanish only) and record your nationality for statistical purposes. Entry to the site, which sprawls away up the hill to the west, is free.

Based on Neolithic foundations and an outpost of the Phoenicians, it was as a Roman town in the first century AD that Acinipo reached its zenith. The piles of stones interspersed with small fragments of glittering marble strewn across the hillside once formed the forum, baths, temples and other edifices of a prosperous agricultural centre, which also had access to iron ore, marble, good building stone and a fine potters' clay in close proximity.

Today only a **Roman theatre** – of which just the stage backdrop and some seating survives – alludes to the importance of Acinipo, to where (inscriptions found here tell

---

WALKS AROUND RONDA

Walks around Ronda are pretty limitless. One of the best is to take the path down to the gorge from the Mondragón palace terrace. In the fields below there's a network of paths and some stupendous views, although unfortunately there are also several ferocious dogs. One path leads to the **Ermita de la Virgen de la Cabeza**, an ancient and ruined hermitage, and nearby is the **Casa de la Virgen de la Cabeza** where the English artist David Bomberg lived in the 1950s. His dramatic paintings of Ronda and Toledo are now recognized as some of the finest Spanish landscapes ever. From here, a couple of hours' walk brings you to the main road to the northwest where you can hitch or walk back the 4–5km into the Mercadillo.

Another excursion is to an old, unused **aqueduct** set in rocky pasture – from the market square just outside the Ciudad in the San Francisco area, take the straight residential street which leads up and out of town. After about an hour this ends in olive groves, by a stream and a large water trough. A path through the groves leads to the aqueduct.

You can also explore the Serranía de Ronda on horseback; **guided horse treks** are available from *Finca La Puentezuela* (☎952/874195; English spoken).

us) crowds once flocked to see the chariot races. Immediately west of the theatre, the ground falls away in a startlingly steep escarpment and from here there are fine **views** all around, taking in also the hill village of Olvera to the north (see p.122). For reasons not entirely clear, Acinipo declined in the third century and in the fourth, ceded its power in the area to the nearby Arunda (modern Ronda). On your way out take a look at the foundations of some recently discovered prehistoric stone huts beside the farmhouse. From here a track leads off towards the strange "cave village" of Setenil de las Bodegas (see p.122).

Cueva de la Pileta

Probably the most interesting trip out from Ronda is to the prehistoric **Cueva de la Pileta** (daily 9am–2pm & 4–7pm; 500ptas), set in a deep valley and surrounded by a spectacular wall of white rock. These fabulous caverns, with their remarkable Paleolithic paintings of animals, fish and what are apparently magic symbols, were discovered by a local farmer in 1905 when hunting for guano fertilizer for his fields, and are still supervised by the same family, the Bullóns, one of whom will be your guide. After the usual jokes, as various "cauliflowers", "castles", and a "Venus de Milo" are pointed out among the stalactites and stalagmites en route, the paintings in the depths of the caves, when you reach them, are genuinely awe-inspiring, particularly those in the central chamber.

These etchings – in charcoal, and red and yellow ochres – depict an abundance of wildlife including fish, the *cabra hispanica* and a pregnant mare, all painted on walls which bear the scorch marks of ancient fires. Other abstract signs and symbols have been interpreted as having some magical or ritual purpose. The occupation of the caves, and the earliest red paintings, date from about 25,000 BC, thus predating the more famous caves at Altamira near Santander, down to the end of the Bronze Age. The section of the caves (and paintings) open to view is but a small part of a more massive subterranean labyrinth, and archeologists will be kept busy for many years to come documenting this Paleolithic art gallery. Tours lasts one hour on average, but can be longer (endlessly so if you haven't brought a pullover to keep warm), and are in Spanish – though the guide may speak a little English. There are hundreds of bats in the cave, and no artificial lighting (a flashlight is useful), so visitors carry lanterns with them, only adding to the sense of adventure and privilege at being able to view something so stupendously old.

To **reach the caves** by public transport, take an Algeciras-bound local train (4 daily) to the Estación Benaoján-Montejaque (35min; departures times vary with season); or a bus, which drops you a little closer, in Benaoján. There's a bar at the train station where you can stock up on drink before the hour-long walk to the caves. Follow the farm track from the right bank of the river until you reach the farmhouse (approximately 30min). From here a track goes straight uphill to the main road just before the signposted turning for the caves.

Benaoján and Montejaque

The nearby villages of **Benaoján** and **Montejaque**, 3km apart, are both worth a visit. The former has a sixteenth-century church built on the site of an earlier mosque (this was a Moorish stronghold well into Christian times) as well as **rooms** at the *Pensión Pepita*, c/Padre José Moreno s/n (☎952/167246; ②); **food** is available at bars in the centre or, near the station the *Molino del Santo* serves a medium priced *menú*. Montejaque, cradled between two rocky crags, has a great, typically Spanish square – with its own sparkling white church – fringed with bars, any of which will rustle you up *raciones* if asked. The friendly *Bar Aleman* in the opposite corner to the church tower, is the best.

Northeast from Ronda to Cañete

Looping through the rocky contours of the last foothills of the Cordillera Subbética mountain range, much of which is covered in pine forest, this route travels from Ronda through the **Sierra de Grazalema Natural Park**.

Grazalema

The N344 winds away from Ronda into the Sierra de Sanguijuela, forking left after about 12km to cross the provincial border into Cádiz. Another 13km from the turning, the road arrives at **GRAZALEMA**, the central point of the Sierra de Grazalema, now a **Natural Park**. The town itself is a pretty white village beneath the craggy peak of San Cristobal, with lots of sloping narrow streets and windowboxes full of blooms in summer. This is the spot with the country's highest rainfall – and there's quite a bit of snow here in winter too – a fact which explains the lush vegetation covering the surrounding park, home to a spectacular variety of flora and fauna. Quite apart from the attractions of the park, the village itself is pretty in its own right, with a simple main square – adorned with a *pinsapo* fir tree – and the eighteenth-century **iglesia San Jose**, a former Carmelite convent.

Grazalema's lethargic **Turismo** (Tues–Fri 10.30am–1pm & 6–8pm, Sat & Sun 9.30am–2pm; ☎956/132225) just off main square, can give you information about the park and the surprisingly limited **accommodation** available in the town. If you're considering a longer stay here – and it's certainly worth taking time to explore the park – the Turismo also has information on renting *casas de labranza* (farm cottages). Otherwise the only choices are the rather sterile *Hotel Grazalema*, 500m along the Ronda road (☎956/132136; ④) or the overpriced *Fonda García*, c/Las Piedras 32 (☎956/132014; ③), above the main square – both places have restaurants. There's a **campsite**, *Tajo Rodillo* (☎956/132063), located above the village at the end of c/Las Piedras, whose office has literature on the Natural Park and will provide information

---

SIERRA DE GRAZALEMA NATURAL PARK

Bounded by the towns of Grazalema, Ubrique, El Bosque and Zahara, the **Sierra de Grazalema Natural Park** is an important mountain wilderness, unique to Andalucía. The limestone mass of the Sierra was formed in the Jurassic and Triassic periods and the close proximity of the range to the sea – which traps many of the clouds drifting in from the Atlantic – has produced a microclimate where many botanical species dating from before the Ice Age have survived. The most famous of these is the rare **pinsapo**, or Spanish fir, native only to this area of Europe, which grows at an altitude of between 1000 and 1700 metres. The high rainfall here, plus the wet, cool summers are essential to its survival. The Sierra also supports a feast of bird life and eagles (Bonelli's, booted, and golden), vultures (griffon and Egyptian), as well as various owls and woodpeckers are all common. The streams and riverbanks are the domain of water voles and otters, the latter of whom are not popular with a number of fish farms in the area. On the Sierra's higher reaches the magnificent Spanish ibex has been reintroduced to a craggy habitat where its numbers are increasing.

The best way to appreciate the park is by walking, but to protect wildlife and nesting birds access is restricted to different sections at certain times. The park's **Information Offices** in Grazalema, c/Las Piedras 11 (Thurs–Fri 9am–2pm & 4–6pm, Sat–Sun 9am–2pm; ☎956/132230) or El Bosque, Avda. de la Diputación s/n (daily 9am–2pm & 3–8pm; ☎956/716063) can provide access, as well as maps with **walking routes** – the *Itinerario del Pinsapar* takes you through the major stands of the *pinsapo* Spanish fir. More walks are detailed in the Spanish *Andar por el Macizo de Grazalema* (Penthalon), sold in most large bookshops.

about walks and horse-treks in the Sierra. The **bars and restaurants** on the square are reasonably priced for *raciones* and *menú* meals, and if the weather's warm enough, you may feel inclined to try out the village **swimming pool** which is spectacularly sited below the village.

El Bosque

Located on the Natural Park's western flank, the village of **EL BOSQUE** surrounded by slopes of planted pine, is easily reached via a delightfully wooded drive along the C344 which bisects the park. When travel writer Richard Ford passed through here in the 1830s he described it as a "robbers lair" and counted "fifteen monumental crosses in the space of fifty yards," victims of the ruthless bandits who preyed on travellers. He advised his readers to make sure they carried a watch to buy off these brigands, preferably one with a gaudy gilt chain, "the lack of which the bandit considered an unjustifiable attempt to defraud him of his right." Today it's a far more peaceful place, although the tranquillity is interrupted in August, when nearby summer camps increase the 2000-odd population threefold.

El Bosque provides an alternative to Grazalema as a **base** for visiting the Natural Park: there's usually space at *Hostal Enrique Carillo*, Avda. Diputación 5 (☎956/716105; ③) in the centre. Close by, the aptly named *Hotel Truchas*, Avda. Diputacíon 1 (☎956/716061; ④) has a **restaurant** where fresh trout features strongly on the menu, often with a slice of *jamon serrano* tucked inside; El Bosque has the most southerly trout river in Europe, the nearby Río Majaceite.

One scenic **walk** along the Río El Bosque is best started from Benahoma, 4km east: the steep descent is easier this way. On the edge of the Natural Park, there's plenty of opportunities for bird spotting and picnicking as you make your way back.

Zahara de la Sierra and Algodonales

It's worth going back to Grazalema to take the spectacular CA531 road which climbs to the Puerto de las Palomas (Pass of the Doves, at 1350m the highest pass in Andalucía). Just before the pass you'll see on the left an entrance to the forest of the *pinsapo* Spanish fir – this is the start of the *Itinerario del Pinsapar* walking route (see opposite). Once through the pass the road embarks on a dramatic descent to **ZAHARA DE LA SIERRA** (or *de los Membrillos* – "of the Quinces") today surrounded by olive groves. This is perhaps the most perfect of Andalucía's fortified hill *pueblos*, a landmark for miles around, its red-tiled houses huddled round a church beneath a ruined castle on a stark outcrop of rock. Once an important Moorish town, its capture by the Christians in 1483 opened the way for the conquest of Ronda – and ultimately Granada. The heart of the village – the whole of it was declared a national monument in 1983 – is a cobbled main street which connects **iglesia San Juan** and the eighteenth-century Baroque **iglesia Santa María de Mesa**, which has a fine *retablo* with a sixteenth-century image of the Virgin. The surviving tower of the twelfth-century Moorish fort – constructed over a previous Roman one – looms over the village and incorporates the remains of an early church.

Along the main street, c/San Juan, are a couple of **places to stay** – the homely *Pensión Gonzalo* (②) with rooms overlooking the church, as well as the good-value *Hotel Marqués de Zahara* (☎956/123061; ③) which has balcony rooms, a shady patio and a **restaurant** serving an excellent *menú* of local specialities. Nearby, at c/San Juan 1, is the office of **Turismo Rural de Bocaleones** (☎956/123114), a cooperative organization dedicated to "green" tourism and catering for a variety of **outdoor activities** in the Natural Park of the Sierra de Grazalema. They offer horse-trekking, mountain bike tours, guided walks and Land Rover trips – as well as rugged stuff such as parascending, potholing, climbing and canoeing – and conduct a variety of wildlife and birdwatching excursions. They'll even arrange accommodation for you.

Enclosed by the folds of the Sierra de Líjar **ALGODONALES**, 4km north, is a pleasant enough place with a long, central plaza dominated by the tower of the eighteenth-century Neoclassical **iglesia de Santa Ana**. Should you wish to stay the night, there are **rooms** at *Hostal Sierra Líjar*, c/Ronda 5 (☎956/137065; ②), just below the square.

Olvera

OLVERA, 18km beyond Algodonales in an area thick with olives (from which the town's name may derive), couldn't look more dramatic – a great splash of whitewashed houses tumbling down a hill below the twin towers of its church and a fine Moorish castle. You can ascend the hill along the town's long main street – the church, **La Encarnación**, is disappointing, when you get up close, as it's actually a nineteenth-century version of an earlier, fifteenth-century edifice. More interesting is the twelfth-century **Moorish castle**, reached by a path from the square fronting the church, which formed part of Nasrid Granada's line of defence against the Christian lands. There are great **views** from here both over the town and to the surrounding hill villages. If the gate to the castle is locked, ask at Plaza de la Iglesia 2 for the key.

Should you want to **stay** and explore the region with its river, olive groves and stark backdrop of the Sierra de Líjar, options include the excellent value *Hostal Maqueda*, c/Calvario 35 (☎956/130733; ②), *Hostal Olid*, c/Llana 13 (☎956/130102; ②) and the plusher *Hotel Sierra y Cal*, Avda. Ntra. Sra. de los Remedios 4 (☎956/130303; ④), all around the centre. For **food** there's a good-value *menú* at *Casa Manolo* in Plaza Andalucía, below the castle, or, just try your luck at any of the places along the main street. At the foot of the hill, the bar on the square does good *tapas*.

Setenil de las Bodegas

SETENIL DE LAS BODEGAS, 12km south of Olvera on a minor road, is the strangest of all the White Towns, its cave-like streets formed from the overhanging ledge of a gorge carved through the tufa rock by the Río Trejo. Many of the houses – sometimes two or three storeys high – have natural roofs in the rock which, in places, block out the sky completely. This was once a major wine-producing centre; the caves made good wine cellars, and thus the town's name. The phylloxera plague of the last century destroyed the vines, however, and brought economic ruin in its wake, from which Setenil has only recently recovered.

Sights in Setenil are limited, but if you can get into the church of **La Encarnación** (ask the neighbours) – a sixteenth-century Gothic structure devastated in the Civil War – you'll see a fine twelve-panelled Flemish painting that survived. The ruins of the nearby Moorish **castillo** are worth a look, too, and below the church, the **Ayuntamiento** has a superb Mudéjar *artesonado* ceiling. There are a couple of **bars** – *Las Flores,* near the river at the opposite end of the town from the church, has great views – and a **pensión**, *El Almendral* (☎956/134029; ③) on the road just outside town.

Don't take the **train** from Ronda to Setenil station: the station's a good 8km from Setenil village itself. If public transport lets you down, the roads around here are pleasant for walking or hitching, and rides aren't usually hard to come by. From Setenil it's possible to **walk** the 8km to the ruins of Ronda la Vieja (see p.118) via the hamlets of Campiña and Venta de Leche.

Cañete la Real

Twenty-five kilometres northwest of Setenil lies **CAÑETE LA REAL** (the 2pm bus from Ronda to Almargen passes through), famed around these parts for a monumental century-old feud with its enemy Olvera over the custody of the **sacred image of the Virgen de los Cañosantos**. The result has been a bitter Andalucian compromise: Cañete grabbed the work's head and arms and quickly locked them up – no doubt to thwart any sneaky sorties from Olvera – in the town's impressive Baroque church. To see the revered fragments you'll need to raise the priest who lives behind the church, and who can be a little deaf. Should you not succeed, there's always the medieval castle to divert you, and a municipal swimming pool (close to the entrance to the town before the main square) but unfortunately, nowhere to stay.

From Ronda to Cádiz

One truly spectacular White Town route is from Ronda **to Cádiz** via the villages of Ubrique, Alcalá de los Gazules and Medina Sidonia, cutting its way across the Sierra de Grazalema Natural Park, and winding through rocky hills, deep gorges and dense cork oak forests.

Villaluenga del Rosario

Perching about ten kilometres northeast of Ubrique on a winding secondary road, the tiny village of **VILLALUENGA DEL ROSARIO**, is the highest in Cádiz province. Tucked beneath a great crag, it's a simple place, with narrow streets, flower-filled balconies and pan-tiled roofs, frequently enveloped by mountain mists. When the Córdoban Caliphate fell it was taken by forces under the Duke of Arcos and repopulated with settlers from Arcos and Villamartin. Its curious **Plaza de Toros** partly hacked out of the rock, is worth a look and sees action once a year each October 7, when the feast of the Virgen Del Rosario is celebrated with a *corrida*. The friendly *Hostal Villaluenga* (☎956/461912; ③) has **rooms**.

Benaocaz

From Villaluenga the road continues through the Manga Pass, an area which has yielded many prehistoric artefacts and dolmens, to the farming settlement of **BENAOCAZ**, another ancient village founded by the Moors in the eighth century. There's little to see here, but a Baroque **church** built over the former mosque, which used part of its minaret to make its tower, and a small **museum** documenting the life of the Sierra. The **Turismo** is just off the main square.

If you want to stretch your legs, a 4km **walk** to the northwest along the Río Tavizna brings you to the ruined Moorish castle of the same name, one of a string of defensive bastions that once gave protection to these isolated hamlets. There's a good chance of seeing choughs, booted eagles and griffon vultures patrolling the crags here. You can get **rooms** – and apartments for a longer stay – at *Hostal San Antón*, Plaza de San Antón 5 (☎956/440764; ④); there's also a **campsite**, *Camping Tavizna* (☎956/463011) near the entrance to the village, with a restaurant.

Ubrique

From Benaocaz the road corkscrews down from the mountainous sierra until the snow-white vista of **UBRIQUE** comes into view below, spreading along the valley of the Río Ubrique with the daunting knife-edged crag of the Cruz de Tajo rearing up behind. Despite this stunning first appearance, on closer contact it's a rather large and disappointingly dull industrial centre, but there are enough features to divert you for a while.

A place which has always bred tenacious guerrilla fighters and fought dourly against the French in the War of Independence (actually defeating a contingent of the Imperial Guard near Guacín), Ubrique is a natural mountain fortress which was one of the last Republican strongholds in the Civil War. According to Nicholas Luard's book, *Andalucía*:

> It proved so difficult for the besieging nationalists to take they eventually called up a plane from Sevilla to fly over the town and drop leaflets carrying the message: "Ubrique, if in five minutes from now all your arms are not piled in front of the Guardia Civil post and the

roofs and terraces of your houses are not covered in white sheets, the town will be devastated by the bombs in this plane". The threat was effective, although not quite in the way the nationalists had intended. Without spreading a single white sheet or leaving a gun behind them Ubrique's citizens promptly abandoned the town and took to the hills behind.

This is a Civil War story typical of these parts. More unusual, however, is that the town today is relatively prosperous, surviving largely on its medieval guild craft of leather making. It's worth stopping in at the seventeenth-century **Convento de los Capuchinos** and the **Nuestra Señora de la O**, a Baroque edifice with a fine image of the Virgin. Otherwise, after a stroll along the main street where most of the bars, restaurants and leather shops are, you'll probably want to get on your way. There's only one **place to stay**; *Hostal Ocurris*, Avda. Solis Pascual 49 (☎956/110973; ④).

Alcalá de los Gazules

The road from Ubrique towards Alcalá, 44km to the southwest, runs through some magnificently rugged but sparsely populated mountain scenery, in parts densely wooded with forests of cork oak and pine. Close to the Sierra de Aljibe to the south, the road skirts the frontier with Málaga before joining the valley of the Río Barbate for the final descent into the the the sleepy White Town of **ALCALÁ DE LOS GAZULES**, the geographical centre of the province of Cádiz. When the Romans were conquering this area early in the second century BC, they tried to divide and rule the Iberian tribes by granting the status of *colonia* to selected settlements – a crucial first step on the way to full Roman citizenship and all the privileges such status could bestow. One such settlement was the Iberian *Turris Lascutana* – as Alcalá then was – in an attempt to win its allegiance away from the Turditanian tribal capital at Hasta Regia near Jerez. A surviving bronze plaque (in the archeological museum in Madrid) records the decree of the Roman governor, Lucius Aemelius Paullus in 189 BC, which granted *Turris* possession of the fields and town which they had formerly held as a fief of Hasta. Little remains – apart from the winding, narrow streets – of the later Moorish settlement founded by the Berber family the Gazules, who gave their name to the town in the twelfth century when this was a *taifa* state of the kingdom of Granada.

Gathered beneath its ruined alcázar, Alcalá is a sleepy little place. In town there's the fifteenth-century gothic church of **San Jorge**, with an imposing tower, beautifully carved choir and an effigy attributed to Martínez Montañes, but not much else. (Somewhat blasphemously given the surrounding bull-breeding country, the **bullring** has been turned into a disco.) You could make the trip out to the nearby Laja de los Hierros with its prehistoric **cave paintings**; the *Ayuntamiento* will advise on visits. Towns like Alcalá are the real heart of Andalucía and, once you've adjusted to the slower pace, make great places to **stop over**. Try the *Hostal Pizarro*, Paseo de la Playa 9 (☎956/420103; ③), which also has a superb **restaurant**.

Tajo de las Figuras and El Cuervo Monastery

An alternative route to Medina Sidonia from here would take you 17km south-west to **Benalup de Sidonia** where the **Tajo de las Figuras** caves have important **prehistoric cave paintings**. The caves lie a further 7km south of Benalup along the CA212, are signed on the left and the *abrigos*, or rock shelters can be seen from the road. As the opening hours had not been fixed at the time of writing, enquire at the *Ayuntamiento* in Benalup to save yourself a wasted journey.

Roughly 6km further east on the same road there's a delightful **walk** leading to the **abandoned monastery of El Cuervo**. When you come to the top of the hill here, look out on the right for a clump of trees and a white wooden gate. Beyond the gate, a track follows the trickling Río Celemín, bringing you – after about an hour's steady pace – to the ruined monastery. You'll need to turn sharply left when you reach an old mill – a little beyond which there's a pool where you can swim – and climb a steep path. A poignant sight, the monastery was started in the eighteenth century by the Carmelite order, occupied by the French troops during the War of Independence and abandoned in 1835. The tranquillity of the spot makes it an ideal place for a picnic.

La Ruta del Toro

Heading towards Medina Sidonia by the direct C440 route you'll join, beyond Alcalá, what is known as **La Ruta del Toro** ("route of the bull"), passing many of the ranches that breed the mean, black *toros bravos*, or fighting bulls used in the *corridas*. The mighty beasts, grazing on the pastures shaded by olives and holm oaks, are tended by mounted *vaqueros* who guard them while noting their potential for valour. This will eventually be tested in the *tienta* or trial ring, an important first step in deciding whether the bull will die in the *corrida* or the abattoir.

About 6km east of Medina Sidonia, a turn-off on the right leads to another White Town – or village in this case – **Paterna De La Rivera** set among rolling hills. Famous for its *ganaderías* (cattle ranches) and horse breeding studs, it's celebrated among gourmets for the quality of its asparagus and its snails. Nearby, the **Castillo de la Gigonza**, an ancient Moorish fort, lies a walkable 4km to the northeast. Take care, however, not to cross the paths of any bulls – it may be safer to follow the circuitous route via the hamlet of La Parrilla. Returning from here via the minor road east will bring you to the main C440 road from Jerez to Medina Sidonia where – at the cross-roads – there's a *venta*, the *Ventorillo de Carbón* which has excellent *tapas* and makes an ideal lunch stop.

Medina Sidonia

Following its reconquest by Alfonso X in 1264, **MEDINA SIDONIA**, another ancient hilltop town, was to become one of Spain's most prestigious ducal seats and supplied the admiral who led the Armada against England. The title of Duque de Medina Sidonia was bestowed upon the family of Guzmán El Bueno for his valiant role in taking the town, a line which continues and is currently led by the firebrand socialist Duchess of Medina Sidonia (see p.151), whose actions and pronouncements probably have some of her ancestors spinning in the family vault.

Not unlike the ducal house, the town, depopulated and now somewhat ramshackle, has seen better days. Nevertheless, the tidy narrow streets still offer glimpses of sixteenth-century grandeur. Monuments are few but well worth a look; among them the church of **Santa María la Coronada**, at the top of the steep main street, fronting a charming square and built over an earlier mosque. Inside, an enormous **retablo** – 15m high – depicting scenes from the life of Christ, is a stunning work of craftsmanship in the Plateresque style. Medina Sidonia also boasts three **Moorish gates** of which the Arco de la Pastora, close to the Jerez road, is the best preserved. Otherwise, enjoy a stroll along the cobbled streets with their rows of *reja*-fronted houses, and make sure you see the spacious and pleasant main square half way up the hill. The town is unused to tourists and has a distinct shortage of places to stay; your only hope for a **room** here is at the *Fonda García*, c/Medina 95.

Arcos de la Frontera

From whichever direction you approach it, your first view of **ARCOS DE LA FRONTERA** – the westernmost of the White Towns – will certainly be fabulous. In full sun the town shimmers magnificently on its great double crag of limestone high above the Río Guadalete. This dramatic location, enhanced by low, white houses and fine sandstone churches, gives the town a similar feel and appearance to Ronda – only Arcos is poorer and, quite unjustifiably, far less visited.

Dating from Iberian times and known as *Arco Briga* to the Romans, it was as a Moorish town that Arcos came to prominence as part of the Cordoban Caliphate. When Córdoba's rule collapsed in the eleventh century Arcos existed as a petty *taifa* state, until its annexation by al-Mu'tamid of Sevilla in 1103. The fall of Arcos to the Christian forces under Alfonso El Sabio (the Wise) in 1264 – over two centuries before Zahara fell – was a real feat against what must have been a wretchedly impregnable fortress.

Arrival and information

The **bus station** is in the new town on c/Corregidores (☎956/702015), served by the *Comes* company with regular buses to Cádiz and Jerez. With all Ronda's potential but none of its energy, Arcos de la Frontera is pitifully equipped to cater for tourists, especially those on a limited budget. An apathetic **Turismo** (open in theory Mon–Sat 10am–2pm but often closed) on the Cuesta de Belén is indicative of the problem.

Accommodation

Quite in keeping with Arcos' lackadaisical attitude to tourists, there's little budget **accommodation** in the **old town**. Lower down, the new town has more options: you'll find the best places on either side of the main street, c/Corredera. The **campsite** (*Arcos de la Frontera*; ☎956/700514) is east of town on the sandy riverbank.

Hostal Andalucía, Carretera Nacional 342 (☎956/702718). The best mid-range option, on the edge of town, close to the Jerez road and with a decent restaurant. ③.

Parador de Arcos de Frontera, Plaza de España (☎956/700500). Wonderfully situated next to the Santa María de la Asunción, and perched on a rock pedestal – reassuringly enough they've recently reinforced the foundations to prevent it from sliding over the cliff. Delightful patio, and the "crow's nest" terrace gives the best views for miles. ⑥.

Mesón Las Callejas, c/Callejas 19 (☎956/701773). Tiny *hostal* east of San Pedro's church, with its own restaurant and great views. ③.

Fonda del Comercio, Debajo del Corral, no sign (☎956/700057). Budget option off c/Corredera in the new town. Very basic, and there's always a queue for the shower, but rooms are clean. ②.

Hotel El Convento, c/Maldonado 2 (☎956/702333). Upmarket option housed in an old convent whose rooms share the spectacular view over the *vega* with the *parador*. ⑤.

Cortijo Faín, 5km out of town along the road to Algar (☎956/701167). A converted seventeenth-century pan-tiled farmhouse with swimming pool, gardens and plenty of white-walled tranquillity. ⑤.

Hotel Marqués de Torresoto, c/Marqués de Torresoto 4 (☎956/700517). Converted seventeenth-century mansion near the Plaza de España, complete with colonnaded patio and Baroque chapel. ⑤.

Los Olivos c/San Miguel 2 (☎956/700811). Restored *casa antigua*, behind the Turismo and close to the Paseo de Andalucía gardens. ⑤.

The Town

By far the best thing to do in Arcos de la Frontera is take a stroll around the tangle of narrow Moorish streets, lined with a mix of Moorish and Renaissance buildings. At the heart of the **monumental quarter** is the Plaza de España, easily reached by following the signs for the *parador*, which occupies one whole side of it. Flanking another two sides are the castle walls and the large Gothic-Mudéjar church of **Santa María de la Asunción**, built over an earlier mosque; the last side is left open, offering plunging views to the river valley and the *vega*.

The fifteenth-century (with later additions) church's **plateresque south facade** is a stunning work, although an unfinished bell tower unbalances the whole – the original was destroyed by the Lisbon earthquake of 1755 and the plan was to raise this new one to 58m, second only in height to Sevilla's Giralda. Three years later, however, the money ran out and the tower rested at a rather feeble 37m. The gloomy **interior** (daily 10am–1pm & 4–7pm; 150ptas) has fine gothic vaulting as well as some exquisitely carved **choirstalls** by Pedro Roldán, and a **treasury** with all the usual collection of church silver and some dubiously attributed artworks.

East of here along c/Nunez de Prado, the Gothic church of **San Pedro** (open service times only) is perched precariously on the cliff-edge, and was rebuilt in the sixteenth century over an original Moorish fort. The later Baroque exterior and tower are in strong contrast to the interior, where a fine fifteenth-century **retablo** documents the life of San Pedro and San Jerónimo and an **image of the Virgin** is attributed to La Roldana, the sculptor daughter of Pedro Roldano. You can climb the tower, but you'll need a good head for heights, as there are few guard rails on the top to prevent a nasty fall. Other monuments in this quarter include the **Palacio del Mayorazgo**, c/de Maldonado, with a Renaissance facade, and further east still, the convent of **San Agustín**, on the narrow neck of the spur, whose church contains a fine seventeenth-century **retablo**. Nearby, in c/Cuna, there's **Casa Cuna**, formerly the synagogue of the old Jewish ghetto, and further east again in the Plaza de la Caridad lies the **Iglesia de la Caridad**, a sixteenth-century church built in ornate colonial style.

Near the church of Santa María, the **Convento de la Encarnación**, c/de las Monjas, is worth a look, though only the church – with a sixteenth-century Plateresque facade – survives. Close by, next to the privately owned castle, the **Ayuntamiento** boasts a superb Mudéjar coffered ceiling, while lower down along the Cuesta de Belén, the fourteenth century ducal palace **Casa del Conde de Águila** has the town's oldest facade. At the end of this street, just before it joins the Paseo de Andalucía, the **Hospital de San Juan de Dios** incorporates a charming early Baroque church with a sixteenth-century image of the crucified Christ.

Each September 29, Arcos' narrow streets echo to the screams of hundreds of children when they run the bulls in the **Feria de San Miguel** honouring the town's patron saint. To see these girls and boys leap up to grab a *reja* or overhanging balcony to lift themselves clear of the horns of the rampaging *toro* is a fantastic, truly nail-biting sight, and remarkably few seem to get injured.

East of town, the road to Ronda leads down to a couple of sandy **beaches** on the riverbank (buses every 30min). If you swim in the Bornos reservoir, or further along toward its namesake village, take care – there are said to be whirlpools in some parts.

Eating and drinking

When it comes to **eating and drinking** in Arcos de la Frontera, there's little variety, but a couple of good restaurants are worth seeking out.

Café-Bar El Faro, c/Debajo del Corral 14. Good *platos combinados* and an economical *menú*.

Mesón Las Callejas, c/ Callejas 19. Great little *hostal* restaurant with a *menú* and balcony views.

Camino del Rocío, c/Debajo del Corral 8. New town restaurant, which despite its name, is an Arab place, offering some interesting north African dishes and a *menú*.

El Convento, c/Marqués de Torresoto 7. Pricey option in the old town, owned by the hotel of the same name, and renowned for its kitchen; there's a medium-priced *menú* here as well as specialities such as *perdiz con salsa de almendras* (partridge with almond sauce) and a tasty house-soup with pine nuts and cheese.

Mesón Los Murales, Plaza de Boticas 1. One of the best low-priced options in the old town, close to the church of San Pedro, and serving an economical *menú*.

La Terraza, c/Muñoz Vásquez. Below the monumental quarter, in the gardens of the Paseo de Andalucía, this is a pleasant place to sit out and serves a wide variety of *platos combinados*.

The Costa de la Luz

The villages along the **Costa de la Luz** – the stretch between Algeciras, over the bay from Gibraltar, and Cádiz – are in a totally different class to the resorts along the Costa del Sol. West from Algeciras the road climbs almost immediately into the rolling green hills of the Sierra del Cabrito, a region lashed for much of the year by the ferocious *Levante* (east) and *Poniente* (west) winds which vie continuously, it seems, for the upper hand. From these heights there are fantastic views down to Gibraltar and across the straits to the just-discernible white houses and tapering mosques of Moroccan villages. Beyond, the Rif Mountains hover mysteriously in the background and on a clear day, as you approach Tarifa, you can distinguish Tangier on the edge of its crescent-shaped bay.

Tarifa

TARIFA, spilling out beyond its Moorish walls, was until the mid-1980s a quiet village, known in Spain, if at all, as the southernmost point on the European landmass and for its abnormally high suicide rate – attributed to the unremitting winds that blow across the town and its environs. Occupying the site of previous Carthaginian and Roman cities, Tarifa takes its name from Tarif Ibn Malik, leader of the first band of Moors to cross the straits in 710, a sortie that tested the waters for the following year's all-out assault on the peninsula. Today it's a prosperous, popular and at times very crowded, resort, following its discovery as Europe's prime **windsurfing** locale. Indeed, according to windsurfing *aficionados*, Tarifa now ranks alongside Hoopika in Hawaii, and Fuerta Ventura in the Canaries as one of the top three windsurfing beaches in the world. Equipment rental shops line the main street, and in peak season crowds of windsurfers pack out every available bar and *hostal*. Even in winter, there are windsurfers to be seen – drawn by regular competitions held year-round. Development continues at a rapid rate as a result of this new-found popularity, but for the time being Tarifa remains a fairly attractive place.

Arrival and information

On the main Algeciras–Cádiz road you'll find the **bus station**, a supermarket, a **laundromat**, fried fish and *churro* stalls and many of the largest hotels. Near here, south of the Avda. de Andalucía, the **Turismo** has a summer kiosk with variable hours. If you find it open they should be able to provide a useful map and information. If it's closed, however, the kindly owner at the *Villanueva fonda-restaurante* nearby (see "Accommodation") is not averse to lending you his window map to photocopy at the shop over the road.

Due to its international fame (and journalists needing to send copy worldwide), Tarifa is well endowed with privatized **phone kiosk and fax offices**; there's one next door to the photocopy shop on Avda. de Andalucía should you wish to avail yourself.

Accommodation

Tarifa has plenty of **places to stay**, though finding a bed in August can be a struggle.

Hostal La Calzada, c/Justino Pertiñes 7 (☎956/680366). Popular place in the centre of the old town, by San Mateo's church. Fine except on weekends when a nearby disco blasts the street outside. ④.

Pensión Correo, c/Coronel Moscardó 8 (☎956/680206). A reasonably tranquil option in the old town; this charming place is in the old post office just south of the cathedral entrance. ②.

La Mirada, c/ San Sebastián 43 (☎956/684427). Attractive hotel with sea views. ④.

Hostal Tarik, c/San Sebastián 32/36 (☎956/685240). Outside the walls in the northern part of town and overlooking the coast, this place is very clean and has helpful owners. ④.

Villanueva, Avda. Andalucía 11 (☎956/684149). Excellent-value *fonda-restaurante* built into the north wall of the old quarter. ②.

The Town

There's great appeal in wandering the crumbling ramparts of Tarifa's old walls, gazing out to sea or down into the network of lanes that surround the fifteenth-century church of **San Mateo**. Don't be fooled by a Baroque exterior here, fine though it is; inside, the body of the church is late Gothic with elegant rib-vaulting in the nave as well as some interesting stained-glass windows.

The **castle** – in origin the tenth-century Moorish *alcázar* constructed by the great Abd ar-Rahman III, ruler of Córdoba – was the site of many a struggle for this strategic foothold into Spain. Known today as El Castillo de Guzman, the appendage refers to Guzmán el Bueno (the Good), Tarifa's infamous commander during the Moorish siege of 1292, who earned his tag for his role in a superlative piece of tragic drama. Guzmán's nine-year-old son had been taken hostage by a Spanish traitor and surrender of the garrison was demanded as the price of the boy's life. Choosing "honour without a son, to a son with dishonour," Guzmán threw down his own dagger for the execution. The story – a famous piece of heroic resistance in Spain – had echoes in the Civil War siege of the Alcázar at Toledo, when the Nationalist commander refused similar threats; an echo much exploited for propaganda purposes.

Also worth a look is the charming Plaza de Santa María, behind the castle, on which you'll find the *Ayuntamiento* and a small museum. A **mirador** to the east of the square offers more views of the African coast. The daily covered **market** – close to the Puerta de Jerez and inside the walls – with Moorish-style arches is worth a visit; while the market's in full swing the bars in the vicinity do a roaring trade.

Tarifa Beach

Heading northwest from Tarifa, you find what are perhaps the best **beaches** along the whole Costa de la Luz – wide stretches of yellow or silvery-white sand, washed by some magical rollers. The same winds – the eastern *Levante* and western *Poniente* – that have created such perfect conditions for windsurfing can, however, be a problem for more casual enjoyment, sandblasting those attempting to relax on towels or mats and whipping the water into whitecaps.

The beaches beckon immediately west of the town. They get better as you move past the tidal flats and the mosquito-ridden estuary – until the dunes start, and the first campervans lurk among the bushes. At **TARIFA BEACH**, a little bay 9km from town, there are restaurants, campsites and a *hostal* at the base of a tree-tufted bluff. Germans have started a windsurfing school here, which acts as the local centre for the sport. For more seclusion head for one of the numerous **beach-campsites** on either side, signposted from the main road or accessible by walking along the coast. All of these – the main ones are *Río Jara* (☎956/643570), *Tarifa* (☎956/684778), *Torre de la Peña* (☎956/684903) and *Paloma* (☎956/684203) – are well equipped and inexpensive.

Eating, drinking and nightlife

Though Tarifa has some good places to **eat**, there's little in the way of entertainment except the bars. However, the *Peña de Flamenco de Tarifa* holds regular sessions in the neo-Moorish Miguel de Cervantes infants' school, alongside the *Ayuntamiento* in Plaza Santa María. The club gathers here most weekends and you may be lucky enough to hear some live **flamenco**; visitors get a warm welcome and the bar serves *tapas* as well. In addition to the bars and clubs listed below is the German-run **Bistro Point**, a windsurfers' hangout, which as well as being a lively bar, is also a good place for finding long-term accommodation as well as picking up secondhand windsurfing gear.

Bar Alameda, the Alameda. Popular, pleasant place outside the western wall, which does reasonable *platos combinados*.

Mesón El Cortijo, c/General Copons. Alongside San Mateo's church in the old town, this vaguely upmarket restaurant serves a good value *menú*; its walls are hung with bullfighting trophies.

Bar Silos, c/Silos 19. Interesting bar close to the Puerta de Jerez, serving food and mounting occasional art exhibitions.

El Trato, c/Sancho El Bravo. Bar wired for international communications with phone booths and fax cabin two steps from your bar stool.

EUROPE'S AFRICAN TIME-BOMB

Above the town, in Tarifa's cemetery, lines of unmarked headstones mark where deceased lie three deep. Most of these corpses, usually washed up on the beach, are unknown Africans. This is the darker side of the emergence of a federal Europe whose individual borders must be sealed to protect all. Europe's high standard of living – beamed all over Africa by satellite TV – is an irresistible attraction to would-be illegal migrants suffering the economic and social privations of north and sub-Saharan African countries.

In recent years the trickle of "wet-backs" eager for a share of this prosperity has turned into a flood as gangs operating in Tangier play on the fears of the poor who see Spain (backed by EC money) applying increasing resources, in the form of helicopters and powerful motor-launches equipped with Infra-Red and satellite technology, to the problem of illegal immigration. Wet-backs come across on *pateras*, the flimsy, easily capsized, flat-bottomed fishing boats designed to carry six people but packed with as many as thirty – who pay up to £400 each to be dropped close to the Spanish shore – before making the hazardous trip across one of the most treacherous straits of water in the world. Gangster skippers often tip these unfortunates into the water too far out and many non-swimmers drown. More often though, the boats themselves don't make it and the toll of bodies washed up along Spanish beaches is rising to alarming levels. Of those that do get safely across the straits, many are picked up by the authorities and held in the detention centre on Tarifa's harbourside, pending extradition. The few that do wriggle through the police-net face a life without papers as non-citizens, drifting between illegal and low-paid jobs or street-selling.

As conditions in Africa worsen, the temptation to migrate becomes ever stronger: three million illegal immigrants are already reckoned to be living in those EC countries with a Mediterranean seaboard, and current projections see this increasing to beyond five million by the end of the century. The alarming implications of this exodus for Europe's social fabric – political extremism included – has led the Governor of Cádiz Province, Señor Placido Conde, to describe the immigrant problem as "Europe's African time-bomb". In the meantime, Tarifa's gravediggers are kept busy as more of these "boat people" perish on the way to El Dorado.

The coast west of Tarifa

Around the coast from Paloma and almost on the beach at Bolonia Cove, are the extensive ruins of the Roman town of **BAELO CLAUDIA**, (guided tours 10am, 11am, noon, 1.15pm, 4pm, 5pm & 6.15pm; free with EC passport, otherwise 100ptas). Established in the second century BC, the town's prosperity – rather like that of modern Zahara and Barbate nearby – was founded upon the exploitation of tuna and mackerel fish to make a sauce or relish called *garum* of which the Romans were passionately fond. The town reached the peak of its prosperity during the first century AD when it was raised to the status of a *municipium* or self-governing township by the Emperor Claudius, and the buildings you see today date from this period.

Excavations began here in 1917 and have gradually revealed remains which confirm the importance of the ancient town. A **tour of the site** starts with a well-preserved rectangular forum best viewed from the platform at the northern end supporting a row of **three temples** to Jupiter, Juno and Minerva, the great gods of Imperial Rome. Just west of here is a smaller temple dedicated to the Egyptian goddess, Isis, and directly ahead, occupying the whole south side of the forum are the remains of the **basilica**, or law court. At the eastern end of this building stood a colossal white marble statue of the second-century emperor, Trajan, the head of which is now preserved in the museum at Cádiz. On the forum's eastern flank stood a line of *tabernae* or shops, which seem to have been superseded by the later *macellum* or **market** built to the west of the basilica. The **main street**, the *decumanus maximus*, runs east–west behind the basilica and is crossed to the east of the forum by the *cardo maximus* which cuts through the centre on a north–south axis. Much of the town still remains beneath the ground to the north and east where a well-preserved **theatre** (just visible but presently closed to the public) has been unearthed.

Probably the most interesting series of buildings stand to the south of the site proper, actually on the beach. Here has been revealed a **fish factory** which produced the famous *garum*, a sort of "Gentleman's Relish". You can clearly make out the great stone vats used to make this concoction; they were always located as near to the sea – and as far away from the town – as possible because of the putrid stench. This arose from a process whereby the heads, entrails, eggs, soft roes and blood of the fish were removed and then layered in the vats with salt and brine and left for weeks to "mature." The resulting mixture was then slopped into amphorae and shipped all over the empire, particularly to Rome where the poet Martial droolingly described it as "made of the first blood of a mackerel breathing still, an expensive gift". The mackerel sauce was the Roman equivalent of beluga and they paid the earth for small quantities of it; the tuna based sauce, however, was less of a luxury and much cheaper.

Baelo Claudia lies sheltered by the cape known as Punta Camarinal, and can be reached down a small side road (signed) which turns off the main Cádiz road 15km beyond Tarifa. There's a great beach here with a scattering of **bars and eating places** open in summer. You can also walk here along the coast from either Paloma or, from the west, Zahara de los Atunes (3–4hr with a couple of natural obstacles en route).

Eight kilometres north, **ZAHARA DE LOS ATUNES**, a small fishing village beginning to show signs of development, has a fabulous 8km-long beach. There's a smallish plush hotel next to the beach, the *Gran Sol*, c/Sánchez Rodríguez s/n (☎956/439301; ⑤) and three *hostales*, all of which are usually full until at least the end of September; *Hostal Castro* (close to the *Gran Sol*; ☎956/439358; ③) and *Hostal Nicolás*, c/María Luisa 13, by the lagoon (☎956/439267; ④) are probably the best value. **Sleeping on the beach** is also feasible, but don't forget the insect repellent.

BARBATE DE FRANCO, next along the coast and linked by a daily bus (except Sun), is an ugly little town dominated by its harbour and canning industry which fills the air with a fishy pong. There is, however, **camping** on an extensive beach to the west of the town, which has the distinct advantage of being shaded by pines.

LOS CAÑOS DE MECA, (not served by buses) a small village surrounded by pine groves, is connected to Barbate by a tiny road that loops round by the sea. A favourite summer escape for *sevillanos*, it has a long, beautiful beach lined with rocky coves and freshwater springs, only marred by some unfortunate "egg-box" hotel developments.

ON TO MOROCCO

Tarifa offers the tempting opportunity of a quick approach **to Morocco** – Tangier is feasible as a day trip on the once-daily seasonal hydrofoil (presently suspended but check with the Turismo or local travel agents). Normally this leaves at 9.30am, returning at 4.30 or 6pm (Spanish time – which is 1hr ahead of Moroccan). The trip takes just thirty minutes; tickets are available from the embarkation office on the quay or in advance from travel agents. If you're planning to do a day trip you'd be wise to book a few days in advance – or you may find that a tour company has taken over more or less the whole boat. This crossing is a lot more expensive than the one from Algeciras (see p.110) but might be a better bet if the latter is chock-a-block in summer or when Moroccans are returning home for the two major Islamic festivals (in April and June). There's also a **car ferry**, which leaves at 10am (Mon–Sat only), returning from Tangier at 3pm.

TUNA FISHING

The catch of the bluefin tuna – the largest of the tuna family weighing in at around 200 kilos each – is a ritual which has gone on along the Costa de la Luz for a thousand years. The season lasts from April to June as the fish migrate south towards the Mediterranean, and from early July to mid-August when they return, to be herded and caught by huge nets. The biggest market is Japan and Japanese factory ships can often be seen waiting offshore in season ready to buy up as much of the catch as they can. Once the tuna are on board, the fish are rapidly gutted, washed, filleted and frozen ready to cross another ocean to be eaten raw as sushi. In recent years tuna numbers have been declining and the season shortening – probably the result of overfishing – much to the concern of the people of Barbate, Conil de la Frontera and Zahara de los Atunes, since the catch represents an important source of local employment in the canning factories nearby.

There used to be a huge hippy colony here and, although this crowd has now gone, some of the atmosphere lingers on, especially among the groups of naturist Germans who swim out to the more secluded coves along the coast. If you want to **stay**, two mid-range *hostales* on Avda. Trafalgar, the *Miramar* (③) and *Residencia William* (③) may have rooms outside August. Nearer to the lighthouse, a number of slightly less expensive places include the friendly *Casa Pedro* (③). Just west of town, towards Cape Trafalgar, is a **campsite** (*Caños de Meca*; ☎956/450405), but don't bother with the small, grotty and misnamed *Camping Camaleón* (chameleon), which never changes.

Los Caños has lots of **bars**, lively in season; *El Pirata* is a good one in the centre and *Las Dunas* – a big log cabin with *copas* and music – and *Macondo*, another music bar, are two worth trying in the lighthouse zone.

Vejer de la Frontera

While you're on the Costa de la Luz, be sure to take time to head inland and visit **VEJER DE LA FRONTERA**, a classically white, Moorish-looking hill town set in a cleft between great protective hills that rear high above the road from Tarifa to Cádiz. If you arrive by bus, it's likely to drop you at two *hostal-restaurantes* well below the town; *La Barca de Vejer* (☎956/450369; ③) does superb *bocadillos de lomo*. The road winds upwards for another 4km but just by one of the bus-stop cafés there's a donkey path that gets you to town in only about twenty minutes. This is a perfect approach – the drama of Vejer is in its isolation and its position, which gradually unfold before you. If you don't fancy the walk, though, taxis are usually available.

Until the last decade, the women of Vejer wore long, dark cloaks that veiled their faces like nuns' habits; though trotted out in most guidebooks, this custom seems now to be virtually extinct, but the town has a remoteness and Moorish feel as potent as anywhere in Spain. There's a castle and a church of curiously mixed styles (mainly Gothic and Mudéjar) but the main fascination lies in exploring the brilliant white and labyrinthine alleyways, wandering past iron-grilled windows, balconies and patios, and slipping into the bars. At one of these, *Peña Flamenca Aguilar de Vejer*, you can sample *manzanilla* from the barrel and take in weekend *flamenco* performances. Try, too, the *Bar Chirino* on Plaza España, which contains a photographic history of the town.

Limited **accommodation** makes finding a room in high season hard work, and late in the day it's all but impossible. If you don't want to end up searching for equally hard to find *casas particulares*, try calling ahead. The lowest-priced places include *Hostal La Posada*, c/Los Remedios 2 (☎956/450258; ③) above a restaurant near the top of the hill as you enter the town, and the excellent *Hostal la Janda*, Cerro Clarisas s/n (☎956/

450142; ③). There's also the delightful, upmarket *Hotel Convento San Francisco*, La Plazuela s/n (☎956/643570; ⑤); the latter two are rather tucked away, so ask for directions. Both the *Convento* and *Posada* will direct you to rooms in private houses should you get really stuck.

Conil

Back on the coast, a dozen or so kilometres further on, is **CONIL** – an increasingly popular resort threatening to become a little too much so for its own good. Outside July and August, though, it's still a good place to relax, and in mid-season the only real drawback is trying to find a room. Conil town, once a poor fishing village, now seems entirely modern as you look back from the beach, though when you're actually in the streets you'll find many older buildings too. The majority of the tourists are Spanish (with a lesser number of Germans), so there's an enjoyable, if rather family, atmosphere, and if you are here in mid-season, a very lively nightlife.

The **beach**, Conil's *raison d'être*, is a wide bay of brilliant yellow stretching for miles to either side of town and lapped by an amazingly, not to say disarmingly, gentle Atlantic – you have to walk halfway to Panama before it reaches waist height. The area immediately in front of town is the family beach: up to the northwest you can walk to some more sheltered coves; across the river to the southeast is a topless and nudist area. The beach here is virtually unbroken until it reaches the cape, the **Trafalgar**, off which Lord Nelson achieved victory and death on 21 October, 1805. If the winds are blowing, this is one of the most sheltered beaches in the area. You can get there by road, save for the last 400m across the sands to the rock.

Practicalities

Most **buses** let you out at the *Transportes Comes* station: walk towards the sea and you'll find yourself in the centre of town, where there's a very helpful **Turismo** at Alameda Cristina 7. Conil has numerous hotels and **hostales** – *Mesón de las Quince Letras*, Plaza de España 6 (☎956/441053; ②) is one of the few reasonable ones, though others may be worth trying out of season – and a great number of private **rooms**. The easiest way to find one of these is to go to the first "supermarket" on the right-hand side of the road to Playa Fontanilla (opposite the *Rinkon Way* open-air disco), where they have a complete list; there are good ones at c/Velásquez 1. If you **camp** you've less to worry about; nearby **campsites** include *Fuente del Gallo* in the nearby *urbanización* Fuente del Gallo, a 3km walk despite all signs to the contrary (March–Oct; ☎956/440137).

Conil has lots of good **seafood restaurants** along the front; try the *ortiguillas* – deep fried sea anemones – which you only find in the Cádiz area. For an excellent, modestly priced meal, search out the *Bar-Restaurante Peña Federata de Caza*, on the road uphill towards Barbate.

Towards Cádiz

Beyond Conil's beaches there's little on the coast to attract you before you reach Cádiz. **CHICLANA DE LA FRONTERA** is nothing special, though a useful road junction with sporadic buses to Medina Sidonia (see p.125). Beyond Chiclana you emerge into a weird landscape of marshes, dotted with drying salt pyramids, in the midst of which lies the town of **SAN FERNANDO** – once an elegant place (and still so at its centre) but quickly being swallowed up by industrial suburbs. These extend until you reach the long causeway that leads to Cádiz, an unromantic approach to what is one of the most extraordinarily sited and moody towns of the south.

Cádiz

Cádiz, from a distance, was a city of sharp incandescence, a scribble of white on a sheet of blue glass, lying curved on the bay like a scimitar and sparkling with African light.
Laurie Lee, *As I Walked Out One Midsummer Morning*

Founded about 1100 BC by the Phoenicians as Gadir, a transit depot for minerals carried from the mining areas of the Río Tinto to the north, **CÁDIZ** has been one of the Spanish peninsula's principal ports ever since, and lays claim to being the oldest city in Europe. Sited on a tongue of land enclosing a bay and a perfect natural harbour with some fine beaches besides, it has – you would think – all the elements that make for an appealing place to visit. But despite a charming old town, oddly enough the place seems unable to shake off a brooding lethargy when it comes to entertaining visitors, and the world of tourism has largely passed it by.

Historically Cádiz served as an important base for the navies of Carthage, Rome and later – following a long decline under the Moors – imperial Spain. Always liable to attack because of its strategic importance, the city's nose was bloodied on numerous occasions, especially by the English. It was here that Drake's "singeing of the king of Spain's beard" occurred in 1587, followed not long after by Essex's ransacking of the port in 1596, and in 1797 Nelson's bombardment.

The city's greatest period, however, and the era from which much of **Inner Cádiz** dates, was the eighteenth century. Then, with the silting up of the river to Sevilla, the port enjoyed a virtual monopoly on the Spanish-American trade in gold and silver, and on its proceeds were built the golden-domed (in colour at least) **cathedral** – almost Oriental when seen from the sea – public halls and offices, broad streets and elegant squares as well as a clutch of smaller churches. This wealth spawned Spain's first modern middle class which, from early on was free thinking and liberal, demanding such novelties as a free press and open debate. One historian has claimed that political dialogue in Spain originated along the Calle Ancha, Cádiz's elegant central thoroughfare where politicians met informally.

In the early nineteenth century the city made arguably its greatest contribution to the development of modern Spain, when a group of radicals set up the short-lived Spanish Parliament or **Cortes** in 1812 during the Peninsular Wars. The Cortes drew up a constitution that upheld the sovereignty of the people against the throne and set down a blueprint for a liberal Spain that would take a further century and a half to emerge. Later, and loyal to its traditions, the city relentlessly opposed General Franco during the Civil War, even though this was one of the first towns to fall to his forces, and was the port through which the Nationalist armies launched their invasion. Later, when Franco often referred in power to the forces of "Anti Spain" he had the sentiments expressed in the Cádiz Constitution of 1812 in mind, ramming home his disapproval by renaming the city's major plazas after himself and other members of the Falangist pantheon. Left-wing Cádiz merely bided its time and now, in the new democracy, these landmarks have regained their original designations. The city's tradition of liberalism and tolerance is epitomized by the way *gaditanos* (as the inhabitants of the city are known) have always breezily accepted a substantial gay community here – who are much in evidence at the city's brilliant *carnaval* festivities.

Cádiz is, above all, a city that knows how to enjoy itself. It has always been noted for its vibrant fiestas – the ancient Roman poet Martial was among the many who commented on the sensuous and swirling dances of the townswomen, implying a pre-Moorish origin for *flamenco*. Although settled after the *reconquista* with immigrants from the northern city of Santander, Cádiz maintains its Roman reputation for joviality with its **annual Carnival** in February, acknowledged to be the best – and wildest – in Spain.

¡CARNAVAL!

Claiming to be saltier than the carnivals of Havana and Río de Janeiro rolled into one, each February Cádiz launches into its riotous *Carnaval*, the most important and wittiest in Spain. Largely a disorganized series of fiestas in origin, it was given its present shape in the late nineteeth-century by Manuel Rodriguez, now known by his nickname "El Tío de la Tiza" ("Chalky"), who was improbably employed as a customs official in the port. He organized the *murgas* or bands – a major feature of *Carnaval* – into four categories:

Coros: These are (recently mixed) groups of about thirty who tour the city on flamboyantly decorated floats singing to the accompaniment of guitars, lutes and mandolins.

Comparsas: Groups of around fifteen people who parade on foot with guitars and drums.

Chirigotas: Arguably the most popular with *gaditanos*, these are groups of around ten people accompanied on an impish reed whistle or *pito*, who tour the bars singing hilarious satirical songs about people and events in the public eye.

Trios, Cuartetos, Quintetos: These smaller groups not only sing, but also act out parodies and satirical sketches based upon current events as they tour the town in costume.

Illegales: Given the city's innate anarchy these bands do not compete officially (see below), but take to the streets for the sheer hell of it with whatever instruments they can lay their hands on. They include whole families, groups of friends and even collections of drunks, staggering about as they attempt to make music.

The above groups provide only the focus, however, for the real *Carnaval* which takes place on the streets with everyone dressed up in carnival costume and apparently drunk for ten whole days. The "legal" groups compete before judges in the Teatro Falla in between sessions on the streets and are symbolically awarded "*un pelotazo*" (good shot) for a bitingly witty composition and "*un cajonazo*" (a box drum) for a bomb. The various groups work at their repertoire for months before and, during the two weekends prior to *Carnaval*, road-test their compositions (but not in costume, which is regarded as bad form) at the warm-up shindigs of the *Erizada* (hedgehog party) or the *Ostionada* (oyster party), great street fiestas which feature sea-urchin and oyster tasting.

ATTENDING THE CARNAVAL

During *Carnaval* there are no rooms to be had in town at all unless you've made reservations well in advance. One way round this is to see it on day trips from Sevilla, catching an evening train (a couple of hours journey) and returning with the first train the next day, around 5.30am. These trains are a riotous party in themselves and, packed as they are with costumed carnival-goers from Sevilla, you'd be well advised to get dressed-up yourself if you don't want to stand out like a sore thumb. The opening and final weekends are the high points of the whole show.

Arrival and information

Arriving by train you'll find yourself on the periphery of the old town, close to the Plaza de San Juan de Dios, busiest of the many squares. By **bus** you'll be a few blocks to the north, along the water – at the *Los Amarillos* terminal, Avda. Ramón de Carranza 31 (serving Rota, Chipiona and resorts west of Cádiz) or a few blocks north again at the *Estación de Comes*, Plaza de Independencia, near Plaza de España (serving Sevilla, Tarifa and other destinations toward Algeciras). *Los Amarillos* also runs a twice-daily service through Arcos to Ubrique, with a connection there to Ronda – by far the best route.

Timetables as well as general information and a detailed street map are available from the **Turismo**, c/Calderon de la Barca 1 (Mon–Fri 9am–2pm & 5–7pm, Sat 10am–1pm; ☎956/211313), which is effectively on Plaza de Mina close to the Museo de Bellas Artes. There's also a **municipal Turismo** at c/Marqués de Iñigo, a few blocks east, as well as a **kiosk** at the Playa de la Victoria which is open during high season.

△ Punta de San Felipe

CÁDIZ

0 ————— 150 m

Plaza de las Tres Carabelas

Estación Marítimo

Plaza de Filipinas

Bus Station (Comes)

Plaza de la Hispanidad

Plaza de Argüelles

Plaza de España

Bahía de Cádiz

Palacio de la Diputación Provincial

Av

Rar

Museo de Bellas Artes y Arqueológico

Iglesia y claustro de San Francisco

Pl. de San Agustín

Alameda de Apodaca

Plaza de Mina

Plaza de San Francisco

Santa Cueva

San

Varga

Baluarte de Candelaria

Iglesia del Carmen

Rosario

Castillo

Cánovas

del

Ancha

Plaza de San Antonio

Pza. Gral. Varela (del Palillero)

Plaza Cand

Iglesia de San Antonio

Plaza de M. Núñez (del Mentidero)

Plaza de Viudas

Torre Tavira

Columna

Plaza de las Flores

Sacramento

Iglesia oratorio de San Felipe Neri

Museo Histórico Municipal

Plaza Manuel de Falla

Mercado Central

Parque Genovés

Gran Teatro Falla

Hospital de las Mujeres

Plaza de la Cruz Verde

Cruz

Benito Pérez Galdós

Plaza del Tío de la Tiza

Parroquia de la Palma

BARRIO DE LA VIÑA

Doctor Marañón

Baluarte del Bonete

Castillo de Santa Catalina

Balneario de la Palma y del Real

Av.

Duque de Nájera

Campo

Playa de la Caleta

▽ Castillo de San Sebastián

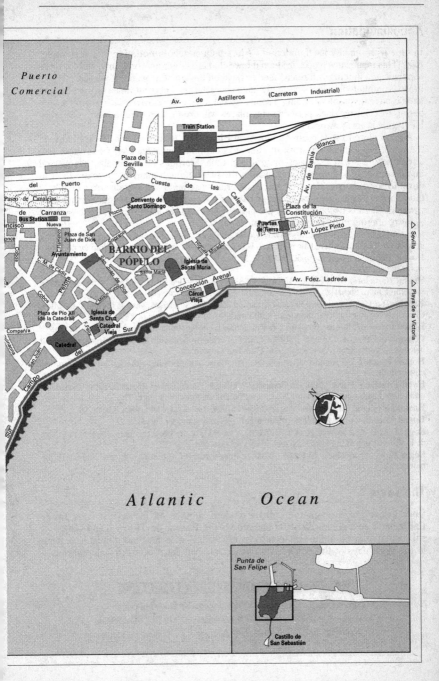

Accommodation

In tune with the city itself, much of Cádiz's budget **accommodation** has seen better days. This means few places in the old town that are either new or comfy, and for more sophisticated lodging you really need to head off towards the beach. However, many of these crumbling old places certainly have character, and at most times of the year you should have no problem finding a room, except during the *carnaval*. It's worth remembering that during slack periods many places will drop prices to fill a room – an amiable haggle is always worth a try.

A good place to start room hunting is in **Plaza San Juan de Dios**. Arrayed around the square is a dense network of alleyways crammed with *hostales*, *fondas* and, less attractively, a few dosshouses or brothels. Calle Marqués de Cádiz also has several budget options, as does c/Plocia, east of the plaza, though many of these are too run down to sensibly consider. The more salubrious *pensiones* and *hostales* are a couple of blocks away, towards the cathedral or **Plaza de Candelaria** and beyond. Further west again, the area between here and the plazas **San Antonio and Mina** is the best value in town, offering good rooms at reasonable rates.

Hotel Atlántico, Parque Genovés 9 (☎956/226905). Functional modern *parador*, somewhat lacking in romance, but it does have balcony rooms with Atlantic views and an outdoor swimming pool. ⑥.

Hostal Bahia, c/Plocia 5 (☎956/259061). By far the most pleasant place along here, and well worth the price. ④.

Hostal Barcelona, c/Montañés 10 (☎956/213949). Basic – despite credit card stickers implying something more upmarket – but clean. Near the Plaza de Candelaria. ③.

Pensión La Catalina, c/San Francisco, just off Plaza San Francisco, east of the Plaza de Mina. Clean, comfortable and charming place with very low rates. ②.

Hostal Colón, c/Marqués de Cádiz 6 (☎956/285351). Good option with spacious rooms. ②.

Pensión del Duque, c/Ancha 13 (☎956/222777). Friendly place with attractive rooms, many with balconies, overlooking c/Ancha. Close to Plaza San Antonio. ③.

Hostal Fantoni, c/Flamenco 5 (☎956/282704). Clean and friendly, although some rooms are cramped. ③.

Hotel Francia y París, Plaza San Francisco 2, close to Plaza de Mina (☎956/222348). Luxurious, quiet *Belle Époque* hotel with some rooms overlooking an attractive square. ⑤.

Hostal La Isleña, Plaza San de Dios 12 (☎956/287064). Good-value and clean, if basic. ②.

Hostal Manolita, c/Benjumeda 2 (☎956/211577). Family-run, friendly place. ②.

Regio I, Avda. Ana de Viya 11 (☎956/279331). The older of the two *Regio* hotels behind the Playa de la Victoria; one of the town's most luxurious options. ④.

Regio II, Avda. Andalucía 79 (☎956/353008). More upmarket of the *Regio* hotels, and worth the money. ⑤.

The Town

Once you've got through the tedious modern suburbs on its eastern flank **Inner Cádiz**, built on a peninsula-island entered via the **Puerta de Tierra** (Land Gate) – a substantial remnant of the eighteenth-century walls – looks much as it must have done in the great days of the empire, with its grand open squares, sailors' alleyways and

---

ACCOMMODATION PRICE SYMBOLS

The symbols used in our hotel listings denote the following price ranges:

① Under 2000ptas	③ 3000–4500ptas	⑤ 7500–12,500ptas
② 2000–3000ptas	④ 4500–7500ptas	⑥ Over 12,500ptas

See p.280 for more details.

SHIPS FROM CÁDIZ

Before the decline of passenger **ships** it was possible to sail to London or South America from Cádiz. Today you can go only as far as the Canary Islands of Tenerife (36hr) and Las Palmas (43hr). A ship makes this round trip every two days in season and every five out; tickets, which cost about the same as for flights, can be obtained from the *Ancona* office, near the port at Avda. Ramón de Carranza 26.

More locally – and for a nominal charge – you can get a boat (or "*vapor*" as it's known locally, alluding to the old steamboats) to **El Puerto de Santa María**, a forty-minute trip across the bay. Departures are at 8.30am (summer only) 10am, noon, 2pm and 6.30pm (returning at 7.30am in summer only and 9am, 11am, 1pm & 3.30pm) from the Estación Maritima, opposite the *Comes* bus station near to the Plaza de España, with extra ones in season according to demand (especially in the evening).

high, turreted houses. Literally crumbling from the effect of the sea air on its soft limestone, it has a tremendous atmosphere – slightly seedy, definitely in decline, but still full of mystique. Unlike most other ports of its size, the city seems immediately relaxed, easy-going, and not at all threatening, even at night. Perhaps this is due to its reassuring shape and compactness, the presence of the sea making it impossible to get lost for more than a few blocks.

Although there are plenty of **sights** to aim for, including an excellent museum, a Baroque cathedral and some memorable church art, Cádiz is more interesting for its general ambience and for its vernacular architecture – elegant *mirador*-fronted facades painted in pastel shades, blind alleys and cafés, and ancient *barrio* backstreets, imprisoned behind formidable fortifications – than for any particular buildings.

Museo de Bellas Artes y Arqueológico

The **Museo de Bellas Artes y Arqueológico**, Plaza de Mina 5 (Tues–Sun 9.30am–2pm; free with EC passport, otherwise 250ptas), housed in an imaginatively restored Neoclassical mansion just across from the Turismo, is an ideal place to start a tour of the city. The ground floor **archeological collection** includes some fine Phoenician jewellery excavated in the city as well as two superb **Phoenician carved sarchophagi**. In the same section there's a display of ancient glassware from Phoenician, Greek and Roman periods. Notable among the Roman statuary is an enormous marble sculpture of the second-century **emperor Trajan**, which prior to excavation stood in the forum of Román Bolonia, near Tarifa.

The second floor **fine arts museum** is one of the best in Andalucía. The kernel of the collection is a group of twenty-one canvases by **Zurbarán**, including a quite exceptional series of saints brought here from La Cartuja, the Carthusian monastery at Jerez and one of only three such sets in the country (the others are at Sevilla and Guadalupe) preserved intact, or nearly so. With their sharply defined shadows and intense, introspective air, Zurbarán's saints are at once powerful and very Spanish – even the English figures such as Hugh of Lincoln, or the Carthusian John Houghton, martyred by Henry VIII whom he refused to accept as head of the English Church. Perhaps this is not surprising, for the artist spent much of his life travelling round the Carthusian monasteries of Spain and many of his saints are in fact portraits of the monks he met. Among the many other works on display highlights include Murillo's *Ecce Homo* and *San Pedro y San Paulo*, as well as his final work, the *Mystic Marriage of Santa Catalina* – during the painting of which he fell from a scaffold to his death – and a *Sagrada Familia* by Rubens. The museum's third floor has an interesting **ethnological collection** which includes some antique marionettes, part of a section covering the long tradition of *Tía Norica*, or satirical marionette theatre, in Cádiz. The city still holds an annual marionette theatre festival.

Incidentally, while you are in this area you should take a look at three fine **Goya frescoes** in the eighteenth-century **iglesia de Santa Cueva** (usually Mon–Fri 10am–1pm; if closed during these times try ringing at c/San Francisco 11, one block north; 50ptas) a short walk away on c/Rosario. The elliptical chapel is divided into two parts, in the upper of which, beneath an elegant painted ceiling and flanked by lofty jasper columns, are the three Goya frescoes representing the *Miracle of the Loaves and Fishes*, the *Bridal Feast* and the *Last Supper*, an intriguing depiction of Christ and the disciples dining sprawled on the floor, eastern style.

The Cathedral and around

The huge **Catedral Nueva** (Mon–Sat 10am–1pm; 250ptas) so-titled because it replaced the former cathedral, Santa Cruz is one of the largest churches in Spain. Begun in 1722, it took 110 years to get it finished, and even then the towers – shortened when the money ran out – were only completed in 1853 in an unsympathetic white stone whose patchwork effect jars with the original brown. What is more, on closer inspection you'll see that the distinctive "gilded" dome, which appears so impressive from afar, is in fact made from glazed yellow tiles.

Even if you don't normally go for High Baroque, it's hard to resist the attraction of the austere interior, which has more of the architect Vincente Acero's original design. From inside, the soaring 170ft-high dome is illuminated by a powdery violet light, the whole, perfectly proportioned building decorated entirely in stone with no gold or white in sight. Artworks include a sculpture of *San Bruno* by Montañes in the chapel of San Sebastian and some other polychromed sculptures including an *Ecce Homo* attributed to Lusia Roldán ("La Roldana"), the daughter of Pedro Roldán. Also worth a look are the wonderful **choirstalls** dating from 1702 which were originally in the Cartuja of Sevilla and moved here upon the latter's Disentailment in 1835. In the **crypt** (same hours) is buried Manuel de Falla, the great *gaditano* composer of such Andalucía–inspired works as *Nights in the Gardens of Spain* and *El amor brujo*. The Cathedral's **museum** holds some dubiously attributed paintings as well as a rather tedious collection of ecclesiatical silver enlivened only by a monster monstrance – a 13ft-high bejewelled custodia nicknamed the *Millón* (million), a reference to the number of precious gems set into the work.

The best view of the cathedral is from the **waterfront** behind, where the golden dome is perfectly set off by the pastel tinted facades of the adjacent houses along c/Campo del Sur. To the east of the Plaza de la Catedral fronting the cathedral lies the **Barrio del Pópulo**, a poor, run-down area of narrow alleyways and decaying tenements, a surviving remnant of the thirteenth-century medieval city. Many of its streets are graced by the odd crumbling *palacio*, formerly residences of merchants made wealthy by empire trade, and now split up into residential blocks. An ancient seventeenth-century inn, the **Meson del Populo** on c/Meson Nuevo is worth a look, and Calles Sopranis and Santa María are other good places to sample the typical atmosphere of this quarter.

Iglesia de Santa Cruz and other churches

A little further east of the cathedral stands the "Old" Cathedral, the iglesia de **Santa Cruz**. Originally a thirteenth-century church built on top of the former mosque, it was almost destroyed by the Earl of Essex during the English assault on Cádiz in 1596, and is effectively a seventeenth-century rebuild with only odd vestiges such as the entrance arch surviving from the earlier Gothic structure. The *retablo*, a beautiful work with sculptures by Martínez Montañes is well worth a look, as is the Capilla de los Genoveses, its *retablo* of red, white and black Italian marble.

From here you could follow the waterfront west to the **capilla de Santa Catalina** (presently closed), a shrine for Murillo fans. This seventeenth-century church was where – during the completion of a commission for the former Capuchin proprietors – the painter fell from a scaffold while finishing the *Mystic Marriage of Santa Catalina* on the high altar *retablo*. He was carried back to Sevilla where he died from his injuries a few days later, and the painting was completed by one of his pupils. Currently this work, together with an *Immaculada* and a stunning *Stigmata of San Francisco,* which also used to hang here, are displayed in the Museo de Bellas Artes.

And, lastly, there are two churches of note for the paintings and sculptures they contain. Foremost of these is the chapel of the **Hospital de las Mujeres** (daily 9am–6pm; ask the porter for admission) on the street of the same name, and one of the most impressive Baroque buildings in the city. Quite apart from its two elegant patios, the hospital's chapel has a brilliant El Greco of *San Francisco in Ecstasy*. The other church, the **iglesia y claustro de San Francisco** just east of Plaza de Mina on a tiny square of the same name, has in its sacristy two sculptures of *San Diego* and *San Francisco* attributed to Martinez Montañes.

Oratorio de San Felipe Neri and Museo Histórico Municipal

The eighteenth-century oratory of **San Felipe Neri**, c/San Jose, south of Plaza de Mina (daily 8.30–10am & 7.30–10pm) is one of the most important historical buildings in Spain. It was here, on 29 March 1812, that a group of patriotic radicals defied the Napoleonic blockade and set up the Cortes, framing a liberal Constitution – the nation's first – which, although it was to be over a century and and a half before Spain was ready to embrace its ideas, nevertheless had a major impact on the development of European liberal politics. The church itself, a charming oval structure, has a double tier of balconies which would once have rung with the roars of fierce debate, and above which eight *ventanillas* in the dome allow the brilliant light to illuminate the sky-blue decor and the central nave punctuated by seven chapels. The high altar's *retablo* is crowned by a fine *Immaculada* by Murillo.

Next door to the oratory in c/Santa Inés, the **Museo Histórico Municipal** (Tues–Fri 9am–1pm & 5–8pm, Sat–Sun 9am–1pm; free) was set up in 1912 to commemorate the first centenary of the 1812 Constitution. The highlights of the museum are a large Romantic-style **mural** depicting the events of 1812 together with a number of the original documents of the Cortes, and an enormous eighteenth-century **scale model of the city** – almost filling a room – made of mahogany and ivory at the behest of King Carlos III. Further north, Plaza España is dominated by a rather pompous **monument to the 1812 Constitution**, also set up in 1912. *Gaditanos* like to claim that it's the only monument in the world topped by a book – a representation of the 1812 Constitution.

Just east of here, on c/Sacramento the **Torre Tavira**, Marqués de Valdeíñigo 4, above Plaza Candelaria, is an eighteenth-century mansion with one of the tallest towers in the old city, which you may climb to get a great view over the white roofs below and the sea beyond. To go inside contact the Turismo. A couple of blocks north the Calle Ancha – the historic thoroughfare that is today a charming pedestrianized street – has another impressive mansion, the nineteenth-century **Casa Mora** (Tues 10am–1pm) at no. 26, which retains the furnishings and style of the period.

Barrio de la Viña

Squeezed between c/Campo del Sur and the Playa de la Caleta to the west of the Cathedral, lies the **Barrio de la Viña**, the old fishermen's quarter, typically *gaditano* and traditionally renowned for the spirited and sarcastic humour of its inhabitants. Its main street is the c/Virgen de la Palma, close to the eastern end of which lies the tiny **Plaza Tío de la Tiza**, a charming square (with a terrace for *tapas* in summer) named after the man who, in the late nineteenth century gave the famous *carnaval* the form it has today (see p.135).

The beaches

The barrio's southern flank faces the **Playa de la Caleta**, a popular – though none too clean – **beach** in a small bay sandwiched between the most impressive of Cádiz's eighteenth-century sea fortifications, the **Castillo de Santa Catalina** and the **Castillo de San Sebastian**, the latter constructed on an islet and reached by a causeway. This is believed to be the site of the ancient Phoenician harbour where, tradition has it, there once stood an impressive temple to the Phoenician god, Kronos. The fort now houses a small **Museo del Mar** (Tues–Sun 10am–1.30pm & 5–6.30pm; free) whose exhibits cover the city's illustrious maritime past. A **walk along the seafront** here can be wonderfully bracing day or night (when cooling breezes blow in off the Atlantic and many of the monuments are floodlit) with the possibility of a stroll through the Parque Genovés planted with palms and cypresses, as far as the bastion of Candelaria or onwards to the Alameda Apodeca, another waterfront garden, beyond. Across the road from the Parque Genovés near the bus stop there's a mammoth **dragon tree**, a centuries-old piece of natural sculpture.

An alternative **beach** to La Caleta is the **Playa de la Victoria**, longer, cleaner and usually less crowded. It's an easy thirty-minute walk from the old town – just find the seafront on the south side of the peninsula and head east – or there's a bus from Plaza de España which follows the interior route along the Avenida de Andalucía; ask for the *"Residencia"* (an enormous hospital that you can't miss) stop, or get off anywhere after five or six stops as the beach is a long one.

Eating and drinking

Cádiz's best cafés and restaurants tend to be clustered around its many grand squares, among them the animated and palm-fringed **Plaza de San Juan de Dios**, protruding across the neck of the peninsula from the port and dominated by the wonderful wedding-cake facade of the late eighteenth-century *Ayuntamiento* (whose bells sound the hour with notes from de Falla's *El amor brujo*). Heading west into the old town, **Plaza de Mina** is another pleasant square with plenty of places to eat, while across the old town there are more places to hunt down in and around the adjoining **Plaza de las Flores** and **Plaza de la Libertad**, the latter of which contains the market. The *gaditanos* summer playground, **Paseo Marítimo** – the long boulevard fronting the Playa de la Victoria – is lively and fun all season.

Fried fish is excellent everywhere, especially from stands around the beach; for sit-down dishes there are plenty of places east of Plaza San Juan de Dios, where specialities include *almejas* (shellfish) and *urta al horno*, a tasty white member of the bream family that's a great favourite along the Cádiz coast. As befits a seaport with great maritime traditions, Cádiz is full of excellent *tapas* bars, too, particularly in the streets around the **Plaza de Mina** and towards the Alameda Apodeca. Calle Zorilla, on the plaza's northern side, has several bars which are full of atmosphere, both day and night. In the Barrio de la Viña, the charming **Plaza Tío de la Tiza** has tables outside in summer where seafood *tapas* predominate, including *caballa* (barbecued mackerel). One tasty speciality is *tortilla de camarones*, a shrimp omelette.

Again, the major squares are the places to head for **breakfast** snacks, while *the* most tempting *heladerías* are dotted about the Paseo Marítimo. The *Heladerías Ibense Bornay* chain are renowned for their *batidos* (milkshakes) with *turrón* (nougat) and *pistacho* flavours among the most popular.

Restaurants

El Anteojo, c/Apodaca 22. Classy, expensive bar–restaurant with an upstairs dining room with sea-views; it also serves *raciones* on its promenade terrace overlooking the bay – a wonderful place to watch the sun set over the Atlantic.

La Caleta, Plaza de San Juan de Dios. The interior is built like the bow of a ship, where you can eat excellent *champiñones al Jerez* (mushrooms in sherry), *chipirones en su tinta* (squid in ink) and other hearty *raciones*. It also has a *comedor* with good value *menús*.

El Faro, c/San Felix 15. In the heart of the Barrio de la Viña, near the Plaza Tío de la Tiza, this is one of the best fish restaurants in Andalucía. House specialities here include *pulpo* (octopus), *merluza* (hake), *urta* (sea bream), and a delicious *arroz marinero* (Andalucian *paella*), and there is a reasonably priced *menú* for those on a tighter budget.

Las Flores, Plaza Las Flores. One of the best *freidurías* in town.

El Fogón, c/Sacramento 39. One of the few outposts for carnivores in this fish crazy city. The lamb dishes, especially, are excellent, and watch the menu for the dish of the day; they also have "*pinchitos*," a type of *tapa* which allows you to try a few dishes out. Roughly in the centre of the old town.

El Madrileño, Plaza de Mina. Tables outside on the square, and a good value *menú*.

Méson Miguel Angel, Plaza de Mina. Outdoor seating and a good *menú*.

Pasaje Andaluz, Plaza de San Juan de Dios. Outdoor tables and a good, low-priced *menú*.

Bars, heladerias and tapas

Bar Achuri, c/Plocia, east of the Plaza San Juan de Dios. Atmospheric traditional establishment with good fish and seafood *tapas* and *raciones*.

Bar Atlántida, c/Pelota, close to the southeast corner of the Plaza San Juan de Dios. Comfortable café-style establishment which serves very good *tapas* – the *croquetas* (rissoles) are superb.

Bahia, Avda. Ramon Carranza 29. Quality place serving delicious *guisos* – *tapas* in sauce; there's no frying here. Try the *costillas de cerdo* (pork ribs) or *papas aliñas* (potatoes in sauce).

Cafétería-Heladería Andalucía, Plaza Libertad. A good and popular place for coffee and ice cream. Locals buy their breakfast *churros* from the stalls on the plaza here and take them to this or other bars to eat with a *café* or chocolate.

Mesón de Churrasco, c/San Francisco (just off Plaza San Francisco, east of the Plaza de Mina). Excellent atmospheric *tapas* bar.

Cervecería Gaditana, c/Zorilla. Probably Cadiz's best *tapas* bar – the tasty "*montaditos*" (or titbits) are wonderful; try the salmon and Roquefort and their "*Bombita*" – (baby bomb) a ball of potato with onion and tuna fish.

Bar Manteca, c/San Felix. Good little place west of the Barrio de la Viña which serves excellent *lomo* (cured pork loin).

Taberna la Manzanilla, c/Feduchy 18, north of Plaza Candelaria. Wonderful eighteenth-century *bodega* serving the odd *tapa* in addition to excellent *manzanilla* from nearby Sanlúcar.

Marisquería Joselito, c/San Francisco 38. One of a chain of *tapas* bars, but none the worse for that. There's a sister branch just around the corner and facing the port on Avda. Ramon Carranza.

Merodio, Plaza Libertad on the corner of c/Santa Lucía. Specializes in *erizos de mar* (sea urchins) in season, as well as shellfish.

El Moderno, Plaza Libertad. Excellent seafood *tapas* served at this delightfully old-fashioned place.

Tinte, c/Tinte. Great old institution, though sadly somewhat spoiled by the addition of a blaring TV. Will serve up *tapas* if asked.

Nightlife

Outside of carnival and fiesta times, **nightlife** in Cádiz can be a bit of a damp squib. In summer much of the *marcha nocturna* migrates to the Paseo Maritimo, where you'll find most of the music bars and discos. Another place that *gaditanos* flock to for fresh air and nightlife is the **Punta de San Felipe**, the peninsula beyond the harbour to the north of Plaza de España. Here, there are numerous bars and discos with plenty of frenetic activity in season. The best way to reach it is by taxi.

In town, the area around the **Plaza de España** has a few lively **music bars**, especially along calles Antonio López, Rafael Viesca and Dr. Zurita. **Flamenco** isn't easy to find and is put on irregularly at private *peñas* or clubs. Check with the Turismo for the best places.

El Baluarte de los Mártires, the seafront fort on the eastern flank of the Playa de la Caleta. Regular summer discos – on cooler nights when the wind gets up here you have to dance simply to keep warm.

El Café del Correo, c/Cardenal Zapata 6. Pleasant place close to Plaza Candelaria, with music and a relaxed atmosphere, although it tends to fill up at weekends.

Peña Cultural y Folklorica, c/Fernan Caballero 9 (☎956/225972). Flamenco club in the old town, just above the Plaza San Antonio.

Persígueme Ibañez, c/ Tinte, near Plaza de Mina. Good music bar which gets very lively.

El Poniente, c/R Viesca near Plaza de España. Loud music and a young crowd.

The Cádiz coast

If you fancy a change of beach – Cádiz's two beaches sometimes struggle to cope with the hordes during the summer months – a trip across the bay offers an attractive escape route. The resorts of **El Puerto de Santa María**, **Rota**, **Chipiona** and **Sanlúcar de Barrameda** have fine and spacious beaches and are all within easy distance by bus, boat or train as well as being in striking distance for a visit to the inland sherry capital, Jerez.

El Puerto de Santa María

Just 10km across the bay, **EL PUERTO DE SANTA MARÍA** is the obvious choice for a brief daytrip from Cádiz, a traditional family resort for both *gaditanos* and *sevillanos* – many of whom have built villas and chalets along the fine **Playa Puntilla** which you'll pass as the boat comes in to dock at the Muelle del Vapor in the estuary of the Río Guadalete. The town itself – some distance from the beach – is low key and, despite some ugly modern development on its periphery, surprisingly picturesque. It's well exploring before heading off to the beaches.

Today one of the three centres of wine production (along with Jerez and Sanlúcar) that make up the "sherry triangle", El Puerto de Santa María came to prominence in the eighteenth century as a botanical garden where plants brought from the New World were cultivated for seed. This and other trading enterprises increased prosperity, as the numerous mansions around the town (it was once known as the "*ciudad de los cien palacios*" or "city of a hundred palaces") show.

Arrival and information

Whether you arrive by **bus** (the "station" is little more than a couple of bus stops next to the Plaza de Toros) or *vapor* (quicker, cheaper and more romantic than the bus, though marginally slower than the train), the helpful **Turismo** near the quayside (Mon–Fri 9.30am–1pm and 5–8pm, Sat 9.30am–1pm; ☎956/857545) is handily sited for picking up a **street map** as well as information. From here the heart of the town is within easy walking distance.

Accommodation

Most visitors come to El Puerto for the day, but should you be tempted to stay on there are plenty of **rooms** within easy walking distance of the ferry. Bear in mind that things tend to get tight during high season, when you should fix something up as early as possible in the day, or ask at the Turismo for assistance.

Clean and basic places for an overnight stay include *Pensión Manolo*, c/Jesus de Milagros 18 (☎956/857525; ③), who have pleasant doubles and singles; *Pensión Santa María*, c/Nevería 32 (☎956/853631; ②); the friendly *Pensión Pina*, c/Larga 130; ☎956/

853532; ②) and *Pensión Las Columnas*, c/Vicario 2 (☎956/852729; ②). *Hostal Puerto Sur*, c/Vicario 9 (☎956/852338; ④) is a little more plush, while the loveliest place to stay in town must be the *Monasterio San Miguel*, c/Larga 27 (956/540440; ⑥), a sixteenth-century monastery beautifully converted into a luxurious hotel. It's well worth stopping here, if only for a drink at the bar.

El Puerto has two **campsites**, both close to beaches. *Camping Playa Las Dunas* (☎956/870112) just behind the Playa Puntilla is the best of the two, with the advantage of plenty of shade. Take the bus from Plaza de España. The other campsite, *Camping Guadalete* (☎956/561749) lies 1km inland from the Playa Valdelgrana and buses to it leave from the ferry dock, the Muelle del Vapor.

The Town

If you're arriving by ferry, as soon as you get off the boat you'll see a fine four-spouted eighteenth-century fountain, **El Fuente de las Galeras**, constructed – as the Latin inscription on it states – to provide galleys leaving for the Americas with water. West of here and a couple of blocks in – behind the elegant old fish market, now a restaurant –

will bring you to the **Castillo San Marcos**, c/Federico Rubio, a thirteenth-century fort built by Alfonso X on the site of a former Moorish watchtower and mosque. The towers of the castle still bear the stirring proclamations of devotion to the Virgin, a symbol of the victory over the vanquished Moors. So besotted was the king with her that he sang the Virgin's praises in a surviving poetical work, *Las Cantigas* and renamed El Puerto after her. Inside the fort Alfonso also constructed a charming triple-naved **Mudéjar church**, in which the mosque's ancient *mihrab* can still be identified.

Following c/Luna into town from the ferry quay will bring you to El Puerto's **Plaza Mayor**, fronted by the **iglesia Mayor Prioral**. A thirteenth-century gothic edifice, it has suffered much rebuilding and the shell is now largely Baroque, but don't miss its superb Plateresque **south entrance**. Inside there's a nice *retablo* and the seventeenth-century images of *Christ* and *San Juan* are attributed to the *sevillano* sculptor Pedro Roldán. Note also some fine choirstalls richly carved in walnut and cedar.

A few blocks west lies the **Plaza de Toros** (Mon–Fri 10am–1pm), one of the largest (second only to Madrid and Sevilla) and – among *aficionados* – most celebrated in Spain. Opened in 1880 with a capacity of 15,000, the bullring has hosted all the great names. A mosaic at the entrance records the words of the legendary *sevillano* bullfighter, Joselito who fought here: "He who has not seen bulls in El Puerto does not know what bullfighting is."

Scattered all over town are the **palacios** left behind by the great eighteenth-century families of El Puerto and decorated with their escutcheons. Near the ferry dock are the remains of the **Palacio Medinaceli**, on Avda. Amburu de Mora, formerly occupied by the powerful ducal family whose gardens once stretched to the river. Others worth seeing are the eighteenth-century **Palacio Purullena**, c/F Rubio 92, east of the bullring, **Casa de Vizarrón**, Plaza de Polvorista, and **Palacio de Aranibar**, near the Castillo San Marcos, as well as the **Palacio de Cadenas** slightly closer to the river.

The **Museo Municipal**, c/Pagador 1, just off the Plaza Mayor (Mon–Sat 9am–2pm & 5–9pm) is housed in another mansion, the Casa de la Marquesa de Candia, and contains archeological finds from the surrounding area.

Another monument tucked away upstream and behind the train station is the poignant **Monasterio de la Victoria**, a beautiful sixteenth-century monastery founded by the Medinaceli family and now in a semi-ruined state after having been sacked by the French during the Napoleonic wars.

The closest **beaches**, Playa La Puntilla and Playa Valdelgrana, are a little way out from the town (30min walk or a local bus) and are pleasant places to while away an afternoon with lots of friendly beach bars where, for ridiculously little cash, you can nurse a litre of icy *sangría* (bring your own picnic).

Eating and drinking

The best area in town for **places to eat** is the Ribera del Marisco, a street near the ferry dock lined with a variety of seafood restaurants and bars serving *tapas* and *raciones*. You should also try the beaches of La Puntilla and Valdelgrana for a cluster of friendly bars.

El Faro de El Puerto, 0.5km out, along the Rota road. Truly wonderful seafood in this twin establishment to the restaurant of the same name in Cádiz (see p.143).

Bodega Jerezana, Valdelgrana seafront. Sea-salty bar where you can try all the regional sherries.

El Puerto, c/Guadalete 2, near the Turismo. Excellent *pescado frito* .

Rincon del Jamon, Valdelgrana seafront. Great place to eat, specializing in cured hams.

Romerijo, Ribera del Marisco. Popular seafood bar where you can get a take-away in a paper funnel, or sit at an outdoor table; the *coctel de mariscos* (seafood cocktail) is splendid.

La Tortillería, c/Palacios 4, near the Plaza Mayor. Loads of different *tortillas* to try, and offers a cheap *menú* too.

THE SHERRY BODEGAS OF EL PUERTO DE SANTA MARIA

The long, whitewashed warehouses flanking the streets and the banks of the Río Guadalete belong to the big **sherry bodegas**: *Luis Caballero, Terry, Osborne* and *Duff Gordon*, the last three founded in the eighteenth and nineteenth centuries by Irish and English families. *Osborne* and *Duff Gordon* are now co-owned after a take-over by *Osborne*, although separate production is maintained. *Osborne* is also the largest producer of Spanish brandy and its black-bull billboard perched on hills, has become a familiar part of the country's landscape.

In sherry, El Puerto is noted for a lighter, more aromatic *fino* with more *flor* aroma imparted due to its humid geographical location, close to the sea (see p.155 for details of sherry styles). It's easy enough to visit the bodegas; *Osborne* and *Duff Gordon*, c/Fernan Caballero 3 (Mon–Fri 9am–2pm; ☎956/855211), *Fernando de Terry*, c/Santísima Trinidad 2 (Mon–Fri 9am–2pm; ☎956/857700) situated in a beautiful, converted, seventeenth-century convent, as well as the smaller *Luis Caballero* (☎956/861300) all welcome visitors for free tours and tastings, although you'll need to **call in advance** to book a place (the afternoon before is usually enough notice). As English is very much the second language of the sherry world, you should have no problems in being understood.

Nightlife

Nightlife in El Puerto centres around the bars in the areas mentioned above under "Eating and drinking". For a change of scene a couple of *copas* bars you may want to have a look at are *La Kama* and *El Rancho*, both on Avda. Aramburu de Mora, down river from the ferry dock. *Taberna Gambribus* at c/La Palma 22, above the Castillo San Marcos stages occasional live bands, sometimes jazz.

The smart set gravitate to *Centro Comercial Vistahermosa,* 2km out on the Rota road, a complex full of bars, discos and late night shops constructed inside a hideous toytown version of a "typically *andaluz*" *urbanización*. It must be said, however, that the nightmarish ambience has a kitschy fascination. Two *flamenco* places, *Tertulia Flamenca Tomás El Nitri* and *Peña Flamenca El Chumi*, put on superb but irregular performances at their magnificent old venues – the Turismo can supply details about any performances in the offing.

Rota and Chipiona

Two of the best beaches along this stretch flank the resorts of **Rota** and **Chipiona**, both popular weekend retreats from Cádiz and Sevilla, and during July and August pretty much packed.

Rota

Outside the town of **ROTA** is one of the three major **US bases** in Spain – installed in the 1950s as part of a deal in which Franco exchanged strips of Spanish sovereign territory for economic aid and international "respectability" – surrounded by a seemingly endless barbed-wire fence and bristling with the technological gadgetry of war. Recently, when some Bronze Age cave dwellings were found on the territory of the base, archeologists were not allowed in, and since their discovery the caves have been looted by treasure-hunters. Some fairly nasty long-standing resentments between locals and US Marines flare up from time to time, too, and travelling around here you will frequently see posters emblazoned with the words *USA Nos Usa* (The USA Uses Us), slightly ironic when you consider that half the town's population either work on or gain remuneration from the base.

That said, however, the town itself isn't a bad little place, quite apart from its excellent **beach**, the Playa de la Costilla. Trade with the base has brought profits for Rota's businesses, and although locals find it irksome that the dollar is as common currency in the shops and bars here as the peseta, they do persist in reminding their American neighbours that they are still in Spain. The town, in the way you'd expect, is dotted with pancake houses and pizza parlours, but there are still pockets of a more authentic Andalucía among it all. Sights here include a thirteenth-century **castle** – the much-restored Castillo Luna – as well as a sixteenth-century Gothic **church**, Nuestra Señora de la Expectación (known locally as Nuestra Señora de la O).

If the bizarre nature of the place or, more likely, its beach, induces you **to stay**, *Hostal La Española*, c/García Sánchez 9 (☎956/810098; ③) and *Hostal Macavi*, c/Ecija 11, off the main Avda. Sevilla (☎956/813336; ③) are hospitable and central places. For **food**, *Bar Ramón* has authentic *tapas* and *platos combinados* and *Restaurante La Almadraba* is also excellent, but more expensive; both are on the Avda. de la Constitución. As regards **bars**, *El Cliché*, and *El Dorado* – the latter playing 1960s stuff – are popular, while *El Dardo* and *La Década* are places with a more relaxed *andaluz* ambience.

Chipiona

From Rota the road north winds inland behind a coast lined with more golden sand beaches to **CHIPIONA**, on a point at the edge of the estuary of the Guadalquivir. A modest, straightforward seaside resort crammed with family *pensiones,* what genuine charms the place may have are all but submerged in summer beneath an annual onslaught of mainly Spanish visitors. Older tourists come here for the spa waters, channelled into a fountain at the church of **Nuestra Señora de Regla**, which incorporates a Gothic cloister adorned with seventeenth-century Triana *azulejos.* But for most it's the **beaches** that are the lure; south of the town and lighthouse is the long **Playa de Regla**, where for much of the year it's possible to leave the crowds behind, but probably best avoided in July or August. Northeast, towards Sanlúcar, are sand bars and rocks with fine views towards the Marismas de Doñana and the Guadalquivir estuary.

If you're planning on **staying** (and in high summer without an advance reservation you can forget it), the *hostales* along the beach are the most attractive, and the most expensive; *Hostal Andalucía*, c/Larga 14 (☎956/370705; ④) and *Hostal Gran Capitán*, c/Fray Baldomero González 3 (☎956/370929; ③) are the most economical. During July and August you will probably have to fall back on rooms in *casas particulares* – which also go fast – offered by the troop of women who meet new arrivals at the bus station. The **campsite** *Pinar de Chipiona* (☎956/372321), is 3km out of town towards Rota.

For **eating and drinking** *El Club de Vela*, Avda. Rocío Jurado, is a good place specializing in meat and fish dishes and does *tapas*, too. *La Pañoleta* on c/Isaac Peral near the beach also serves good fish and *mariscos*. You can eat well at the *Bodega El Chusco*, c/General Mola, near the *correos*; the house speciality is *coquinas* (a type of small clam). Plenty of **bars** cluster around the centre and seafront. Places with a good atmosphere are *Bar Ajedrez,* Avda. de la Regla 15, *Bar Moustaki,* Avda. de Sevilla, and *Bar Tani* and *Bar Kaipions* both in c/Isaac Peral, and nice places for an *aperitivo*. A good music venue is *Bar Tarsis* on Avda. de Sevilla.

Sanlúcar de Barrameda

Like El Puerto de Santa María, **SANLÚCAR DE BARRAMEDA** is a major sherry town. A substantial place with an attractive old quarter set at the mouth of the Guadalquivir, it is the main depot for **Manzanilla** wine – a pale dry *fino* variety with a salty tang – highly regarded by connoisseurs and much in evidence in the bars round here. Sanlúcar is also one of the best places in Andalucía for **seafood**, for which *manzanilla* is the perfect accompaniment.

Although there was a small settlement here in Roman times and the Moors built a fort to guard the vital Gaudalquivir estuary from sea raiders, it was after the recapture of the town in 1264 by Alfonso X that Sanlúcar grew to become one of Spain's leading ports in the sixteenth century. **Columbus** sailed from here on his third voyage to the Americas and it was also from here in 1519 that Magellan set out to circumnavigate the globe. Decline in the eighteenth century, however, was excacerbated by the War of Independence and the town only revived in the mid-nineteenth century when the Duke of Montpensier built a summer palace here, since when Sanlúcar has grown into the popular resort it is today.

Arrival, information and orientation

Sanlúcar's two **bus stations** are close to each other in the Barrio Alto; that of *Los Amarillos* serving Chipiona, Cádiz and Sevilla is on Plaza de La Salle, while *La Valencia* at c/San Juan 12, has buses to Jerez.

Sanlúcar is split into two distinct halves, the older and formerly walled **Barrio Alto** on the hill, and the **Barrio Bajo** fronting the river. The monuments are all in the higher town, and as you ascend the tree-lined Alameda leading from the river to the Plaza del Cabildo – the effective centre of the town – there's a pleasant a hint of sherry in the air. Just before the plaza you'll pass the **Turismo**, Calzada del Ejército s/n, towards the top of this avenue, who can provide you with a street map.

Accommodation

There's a serious shortage of budget **accommodation** in Sanlúcar, and in high season you'll be pushed to find anything at all. One off-beat possibility is to put up with the Duchess of Medina Sidonia who has three economical guest rooms (see "The Town" p.151).

If you were thinking about a longer stay, new **apartments for rent** (minimum three nights; ③) are available at Avenida Cerro Falón 18, east of and parallel to, the Alameda. The Turismo will supply more addresses should you need them.

Pensión Blanca Paloma, Plaza San Roque (☎956/363644). Good-value *pensión* in a magnificent position in the Barrio Alto. ③.

Pensión Bohemia, c/Don Claudio 1 (☎956/369599). Comfortable rooms near the church of Santo Domingo in the Barrio Alto. ③.

Hotel Los Helechos, Plaza Madre de Dios 9 (☎956/361441). Upmarket hotel with two charming patios and lots of traditional features. ④.

Hostal Las Marismas, Plaza de La Salle (☎956/366008). Good place next to the bus station. ④.

SANLÚCAR'S MANZANILLA BODEGAS

The delicate taste of Sanlúcar's distinctive *manzanilla*, is created by the seaside environment where the wine is matured. The humid conditions necessary for the growth of the dense *flor* inside the wine butts is added to by the moist *Poniente* wind which blows across the Coto Doñana, imparting the characteristic saltiness to this driest of all sherries.

Most of Sanlúcar's *bodegas* are open for **visits and tastings** – you should ring in advance to book a place on the tour. The town's major producer, *Antonio Barbadillo*, c/ Eguilaz 11 (Mon–Fri 7.30am–3pm; ☎956/365103) which produces seventy percent of all *manzanilla* also makes *manzanilla pasada*, an exceptional fifteen-year-old wine (as against the normal four for standard *fino*), besides one of Andalucía's best white table wines from the same Palomino grape. Other bodegas to try are *Vinícola Hidalgo*, Banda de Playa 24 (☎956/360516; Mon–Fri 8am–2.30pm) producers of the *La Gitana* brand, and *Bodega Hijos de A. Pérez Mejía*, c/Farina 56 (Tues–Sat 11am–1pm).

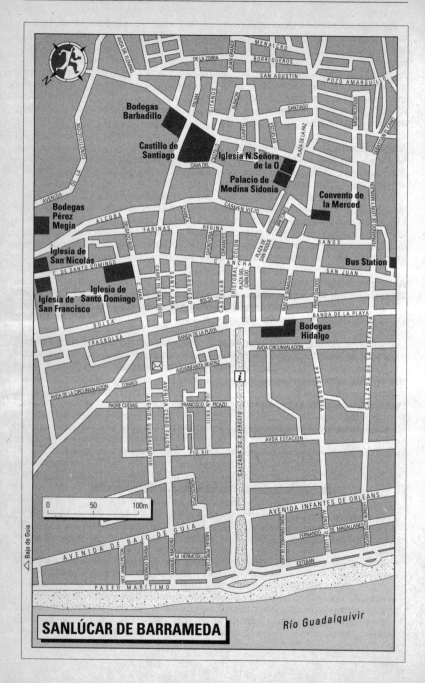

SANLÚCAR DE BARRAMEDA

Río Guadalquivir

The Town

The **Plaza del Cabildo**, a charming palm-fringed square with plenty of bars is as good a place as any to start your explorations of the town. Directly north of the square, Plaza de San Roque adjoins the **market**, one of the town's great sights when it's in full swing. Just off this square, the interior of the fifteenth-century **iglesia de La Trinidad** has a fine Mudéjar ceiling. Following c/Bretones north from the plaza, passing the seventeenth-century **Convento de la Merced** – currently undergoing restoration – will eventually lead you to the neo-Mudéjar nineteenth-century palace of the Dukes of Montpensier, now occupied by the police station. Taking a left at the top of this hill will bring you to – on the right – **Plaza de la Paz**, another delightful small square and further on, the church of **Nuestra Señora de la O**, founded in the thirteenth century but much altered since. The church has a fine Gothic-Mudéjar **portal** depicting lions bearing coats of arms, and inside, a superb *artesonado* ceiling.

The church is connected to the *palacio* of the **Duques de Medina Sidonia** (erratic hours, though usually open Sun afternoons – at other times ring the bell) whose sixteenth- to eighteenth-century interior, which also houses the family's historical archive, offers wonderful views over the Coto Doñana. The Duchess of Medina-Sidonia – a descendant of Guzmán El Bueno of Tarifa – still lives here and is one of Sanlúcar's most controversial characters. Small in stature and fiery in temprament she is known as *la duquesa roja* ("the Red Duchess"), with a long history of defending the poor and oppressed of the region, even once serving time in jail for leading a demo demanding compensation for the peasants affected by the Palomares H-bomb. Over another issue she challenged the mayor of Sanlúcar to a duel, brandishing her own dagger outside the *Ayuntamiento* while taunting him to come out and fight like a man; the terrified official locked himself inside the building. The Duchess has three inexpensive guest rooms to rent, if you want to try your luck.

Continuing along c/Eguilaz eventually brings you to the semi-ruined Moorish **Castillo de Santiago** which is pretty inaccessible unless you fancy scrambling up the side. A little further along the same street the sherry *bodega* of *Barbadillo* allows public visits (see below). A flight of steps beside the castle leads back down to the Barrio Bajo.

East of the Plaza del Cabildo, c/Ancha is the site of a colourful spectacle each August 15, the fiesta of the Virgen de la Caridad, when the street is laid with a carpet of colourful "flowers" – actually tinted sawdust – from end to end. A short way along here, the sixteenth-century convent church of **Santo Domingo** is worth a look, while at the end of the same street lies the church of **San Francisco** with an elegant facade, built in the sixteenth century by Henry VIII of England – while he was married to Catherine of Aragón – as a hospital for British sailors. Just off the Plaza San Roque at c/Truco 4 (and signposted) is the **Museo del Mar Las Caracolas** (all day; donations), an oddball lifetime collection of objects retrieved from the sea by the eccentric proprietor.

At the small port of **Bonanza** 4km upstream, a great **fish auction** takes place when the fishing fleet returns in late afternoon. This is the very spot where Columbus and Magellan actually set sail. Finally, if you're tempted by the Turismo's map to toil up the hill to the botanical gardens don't bother, as they are not open to the public.

Sanlúcar's shell-encrusted **river beach** – unfortunately marred by a huge and ugly concrete esplanade – a couple of kilometres' walk from the town centre is nevertheless a nice place to while away some time, and usually quite deserted. The beach is also the setting for some exciting **horse races**, a tradition dating from the nineteenth century, in the last two weeks of August. A motor boat from the Bajo de Guía will also ferry you to the opposite bank where waiting Landrovers drive you to the **Coto Doñanas beaches**, none too clean unfortunately due to pollution from the Guadalquivir. There are absolutely no facilities should you go, so take along liquid refreshment and food.

THE COTO DOÑANA NATURE RESERVE

Access to the vast, marshy expanses of the **Coto Doñana Nature Reserve** (see p.221) on the opposite shore from Sanlúcar is strictly controlled to protect Europe's largest wild-life sanctuary and a vital wetland for a variety of migrating birds. However, a new **boat cruise** aboard the *Real Fernando* has been inaugurated to allow visitors to see the park and, while it doesn't allow you to get into serious exploration, it's a wonderful introduction to this remarkable area. Lasting approximately four hours, the boat – which has a *cafetería* on board – leaves from the Bajo de Guía (daily summer 8.30am & 4.30pm; winter 10am; 2000ptas, 1000ptas kids and senior citizens; ☎956/363813). The trips allow two short guided walks inside the park.

Eating and drinking

Sanlúcar is known the length of Andalucía for the quality of its **seafood**. The place to head for is the **Bajo de Guía**, the old fishing district upstream from where the Alameda meets the river. Numerous bars and restaurants lining the waterfront serve excellent food. In the **Barrio Alto** the Plaza del Cabildo has a number of good *tapas* bars, and higher still, Plaza de la Paz is a tranquil little square with various bars serving *tapas* and excellent *manzanilla*. Probably the highest concentration of **places to drink** is along c/Alonso Nuñez and at the foot of the Alameda, where it meets the river.

Bar Restaurant El Bigote, Bonanza. Celebrated establishment with its own fishing fleet. You can eat *tapas* in the bar, or more formally in the restaurant where the house *arroz de marisco* (seafood *paella*) is outstanding. You must try the succulent *langostinos* (prawns).

Casa Balbino, Plaza del Cabildo. Typical *taberna* with an outdoor terrace. The *patatas rellenas* (stuffed with tuna) are especially good.

Bar Correos, c/Banda de la Playa where it crosses Avda. Cerro Falcón. Economical place serving good *platos combinados*.

Mirador de Doñana, Bajo de Guía s/n. One of the best places in town for seafood – try their "*Mi Barca Doñana*", white fish in a tomato sauce, or in season, *Sopa de Galeras* (a cross between a crab and a shrimp) a special *marisco* soup of which they're deservedly very proud.

Jerez de la Frontera

Encircled by vines planted in the chalky, *albariza* soil, **JEREZ DE LA FRONTERA**, 20km inland from Sanlúcar towards Sevilla, is the home and heartland of **sherry** (itself an English corruption of the town's Moorish name – *Xerez*) and also, less known but equally important, of Spanish brandy. Once you've penetrated some architecturally bleak suburbs, the town centre possesses a charming *casco antiguo* and a number elegant palm-fringed squares, as well as a handful of notable Renaissance and Baroque churches and palaces.

Santiago, a fascinating and authentic white-walled *gitano* quarter to the north of the cathedral, contrasts sharply with the great *bodegas* of the sherry houses sited, rather surprisingly, in the heart of the town. The sherry dynasties that own these companies are renowned as some of the biggest snobs in Spain, and take a haughty pride in apeing the traits and customs of the English upper-middle classes, such as strutting around on polo horses, wearing tweeds and speaking Spanish with an affected accent. This has earned them the derisive nickname of *señoritos* or "toffs" among their fellow countrymen. Jerez's innate sobriety is thrown to the wind, however, during one of the two big **festivals** – the May Horse Fair (perhaps the most refined – or snooty – depending on your viewpoint, of Andalucian *ferias*), and the celebration of the vintage towards the end of September.

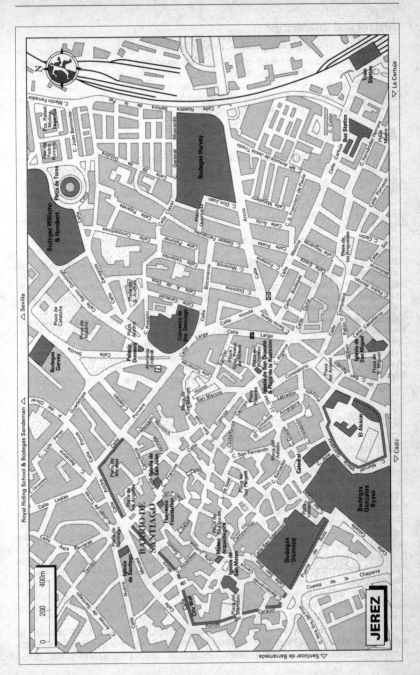

Arrival and information

Jerez's points of arrival are located east of the centre. The **train** and **bus stations** are more or less next door to each other, eight blocks east of the alcázar and the town's central square, the **Plaza del Arenal**. If you want to buy train tickets in advance, *RENFE* has an office at c/Tornería 4, near the Turismo. The town's main street, **c/ Larga**, heads north from the Plaza del Arenal to the Alameda Cristina where a well-stocked **Turismo**, at no. 7 (Mon–Fri 8am–2pm & 5–8pm) has detailed maps.

Accommodation

Most of the budget **accommodation** in Jerez is conveniently located within a few minutes' walk of the bus and train terminals. More possibilities are to be found close to the church of San Miguel, along c/Caballero. Jerez's **Albergue Juvenil**, Avda. Carrero Blanco 30 (☎956/3428900; ①) lies out in the suburbs and is on the L8 bus line from the centre, with a stop close to the bus station.

Pensión Los Amarillos, c/Medina 30 (☎956/342296). Lowest prices in town, for rooms without bath. To get there, turn left from the bus station and walk three blocks. ②.

Hotel Capele, c/Corredera 5 (☎956/346400). Fairly upmarket option with all facilities, close to Plaza Arenal. ④.

Hostal Nuevo, c/Caballero 23 (☎956/331600). Attractive *hostal* in a charming old mansion, with good-value rooms. ④.

Hostal Las Palomas, c/Higueras 17 (☎956/343773). Clean rooms in quiet street off c/Medina. ②.

Hostal San Andres, c/Morenos 12 (☎956/340983). Rooms both with and without bath, as well as a pleasant plant-filled patio. ②.

Hostal San Miguel, Plaza San Miguel 4 (☎956/348562). Good value place with lots of character and a great location opposite the church of San Miguel . ③.

Hostal Sanvi, c/Morenos 10 (☎956/345624). Basic, friendly option near the *Hostal San Andres*. ②.

Hostal Torres, c/Arcos 29 (☎956/323400). Excellent value, with two pretty patios. ③.

Hotel Trujillo, c/Medina 36 (☎956/342438). Comfortable, air-conditioned rooms. ④.

Hostal Zaragoza, c/Zaragoza 2 (☎956/334427). Straightforward, family-run place with friendly proprietors. Close to the Alameda Cristina. ②.

The Town

Quite apart from the **sherry bodegas**, indisputably Jerez's biggest draw, the town has many sights which warrant a look, not least the gypsy quarter, **Barrio de Santiago**, which is a fascinating place to stroll around. Conveniently, all the major sights and most of the *bodegas* are just a few minutes walk of the central Plaza del Arenal.

The Alcázar and the Cathedral

The substantial **Alcázar** (daily 10.30am–2pm & 5–7pm; Aug 10.30am–2pm only) lies just to the south of the Plaza del Arenal. Constructed in the eleventh century by the Almohads, though much altered since, it contains a well-preserved **mosque** from the original structure, now converted into the church of Santa María la Real.

East of the same plaza, the **Cathedral of San Salvador** (daily 5.30–8.00pm) was rather harshly dismissed by Richard Ford as "vile Churrigueresque" because of its mixture of Gothic and Renaissance styles. The most exciting time to be here is September, when on the broad cathedral steps below the free-standing belltower – actually part of an earlier fifteenth-century Mudéjar castle – the wine harvest celebrations begin with the crushing of grapes.

Northeast of the alcázar is the most charming square in town, the **Plaza de la Asunción** (known as Plaza San Dionisio to *jerezanos*) where a delightful sixteenth-century former *Ayuntamiento* features ornamental statues of Hercules and Julius

SHERRY – JEREZ'S LIQUID GOLD

It's believed that the Phoenicians brought the vine to this area early in the first millenium BC. The Romans shipped wine from here to all parts of their empire, and the Roman *Asido Caesaris* may well be the town from which Jerez derives its name, later corrupted to *Xerez* (pronounced "Sherrish") by the Moors.

British merchants were attracted here in the fourteenth century and, following the expulsions of Moors and Jews in the wake of the *reconquista*, established firms that first traded, and later produced, Falstaff's "sack". Some of the *bodegas*, or cellars, were founded by British Catholic refugees, barred from careers at home by the sixteenth-century Supremacy Act, and the names of the great sherry firms today testify to the continuing love affair of the British with this wine. Britain still consumes up to seventy percent of all exports.

It's a particular combination of climate, soil and grape variety that gives the distinctive style of sherry wine. The chalky, white *albarizo* soil of the triangle is the natural habitat for the Palomino sherry grape, and though the wine that results from this grape is ordinary stuff, it is what happens inside the *bodegas* that transforms it into sherry. Here the wine is transferred to oak butts with loose stoppers to let in air. Then the *flor* – a puffy layer of scum (actually yeast) – magically appears on the surface of the wine not only preventing oxidization, but feeding on it too, in the process adding a special flavour and bouquet. It is the subtle nature of the *flor*, the ingredient that cannot be duplicated by competitors, that imparts a different flavour to the sherrys of Jerez, El Puerto de Santa Maria and especially Sanlúcar where it absorbs the salty breezes off the sea, producing the most delicate *fino* of all, *manzanilla*. The *bodegas* of Jerez, unlike in other wine producing areas, are situated above ground in order to maintain the humid conditions – helped by sprinkling the sand-covered floors with water – necessary to the growth of this *flor*.

The final stage in the creation of sherry is the fortification of the wine with alcohol (up to fifteen percent in the case of *fino* sherry) before it enters the *solera* system. Because sherry is not a vintage, or yearly, wine it is always blended with older wines through the *soleras* and *criaderas*, as many as six rows of butts placed on top of each other from which the wine is gradually transferred from the topmost to the bottommost over a period of time. This process, mixing the new, younger, wine with the greater quantity of mature older wine "educates" it to assume its character. The wine drawn off at the end for bottling has an even consistency year after year, conveniently with none of the problems of "good" and "bad" years. The classic sherry is the bone dry *fino*, but variations on the theme include *amontillado* (where the flor is allowed to "die" in the butt, imparting a nutty flavour), *oloroso* (produced as *fino* but minus the *flor*) and *cream* – pronounced "cray-am" in Andalucía – a purely British concoction where sweet grapes are blended with *oloroso* .

Caesar on its facade. It's flanked by the fifteenth-century Mudéjar **parroquia de San Dionisio** with an elegant bell-tower and an interior which underwent some later Baroque alterations.

Barrio de Santiago

Part of the attraction of Barrio de Santiago, the *gitano* quarter facing the cathedral, is its many fascinating churches. The sixteenth-century Gothic **parroquia de San Mateo** (Saint Matthew), with a fine *retablo* and superb vaulting over the chapels, is one of a quartet of churches dotted around the barrio dedicated to the four Evangelists (saints Marcos, Lucas and Juan are also worth seeking out). Facing the church, the Plaza del Mercado centres on the **Museo Arqueológico**, currently closed for restoration. When it re-opens, be sure to see a Greek military helmet dating from the seventh-century BC, and found on the banks of the nearby Río Guadalete.

Just west of here along c/Muro is a bit of the original **Moorish city wall**, which you can follow north to another Gothic church, the **parroquia de Santiago**, which has a beautifully ornate Baroque *retablo* with a celebrated sixteenth-century sculpture of the *Prendimiento* – or **arrest of Christ** – attributed to La Roldana, the daughter of sculptor Pedro Roldán.

Fronting the Plaza de San Juan, the **Andalucian Flamenco Foundation** (Mon–Fri 9.30am–1.30pm; free) is housed in a stylish eighteenth-century mansion, the Palacio de Pemartín. As one of the founding centres of the dance, Jerez has created this library of "*flamencología*" as well as a sound and vision archive, to preserve the works and performances of past greats in the art. There's also an interesting audiovisual presentation, *El Arte Flamenco* (hourly on the hour) which – if you know little about *flamenco* – will give you a grasp of the basics and an understanding of why it is so important to Andalucians.

The Bodegas

The **tours of the sherry and brandy processes** in Jerez can be a fascinating insight into the mysteries of sherry production, although sampling – nowadays restricted to a couple of tots at the end of a tour – is hardly as much fun as when Richard Ford was here in the last century and saw visitors emerging "stupified by drink".

There are a great many *bodegas* to choose from and, with the exception of August when all but a few firms close down, most welcome visitors throughout the year. Some houses insist that you book a place a day in advance; if your Spanish isn't too hot don't worry about making yourself understood, as English is very much the second language in Jerez's sherry fraternities. Below are a selection of *bodegas* offering tours throughout the whole or part of August; should you wish to visit some of the smaller establishments, get hold of a complete list from the Turismo or town centre travel agents.

The most central *bodega* and one of the two giants of Jerez – whose establishments are almost small towns in their own right – is **González Byass**, c/Manuel González s/n (English-language tours Mon–Fri 10.30am & 1pm; 250ptas; ☎956/340000) behind the alcázar. The González cellars are perhaps the oldest in Jerez and, though no longer used, preserve an old circular chamber, *La Concha*, designed by Eiffel (of Tower fame). Each *bodega* has its celebrity barrels signed by famous visitors: Martin Luther King, Orson Welles, Queen Victoria, Cole Porter and Franco (protected by a glass screen) are some of the big names in the González collection. Another popular attraction here are the performing mice that climb ladders to reach their favourite tipple; perhaps more relevant is a transparent butt which allows you to see the action of the magical *flor* on the sherry. The other major firm is **Domecq**, c/San Ildefonso 3 (closed first three weeks of Aug; otherwise tours daily 10am, 11am & noon; free; ☎956/331900) while **Sandeman**, c/Pizzaro 10 (daily 9am–2pm; free; ☎956/301100) have pleasant gardens and **Williams and Humbert**, c/Nuño de Cañas s/n (closed mid-July to mid-Aug; 300ptas; ☎956/331300) near the bullring, are a smaller more intimate outfit.

Most of the *bodegas* have their own shop where you can buy the house brands. In town, *La Vinoteca*, c/Santo Domingo 13, north of the Convento de Santo Domingo, is one store that stocks them all.

The Convento de Santo Domingo and the Palacio Domecq

At the northern end of c/Larga – which passes, at the junction with c/Santa María, the **Café Cena Cirullo**, a fine turn-of-the-century building which used to be the great meeting place of Jerez's salon society – one side of the Alameda Cristina (opposite the Turismo) is dominated by the august frontage of the **Convento de Santo Domingo** (7.30–10am & 5.30–9.30pm). Although badly damaged by fire in the Civil War, it has since been diligently restored and, in common with many of the town's other religious buildings, has a curious a mixture of styles: in this case Mudéjar, Romanesque and Gothic. The church's seventeenth century *retablo mayor* is an orgy of gilded wood, with the *Virgen de la Consolación* – the patron of the city carved in Italian marble – as its centrepiece. At the far end of this square stands the eighteenth-century **Palacio Domecq**, a grand pile erected by the sherry family. Behind an entrance flanked by barley-sugar pillars, an exquisite marble-floored **Baroque patio** is occasionally open.

The Museo de Relojes and the Riding School

At the northern end of town, the **Museo de Relojes**, c/Cervantes (Mon–Sat 10am–1.30pm; 300ptas) claims to have the largest collection of antique clocks and watches in Europe, while nearby, north of the Alameda Cristina, at the **Royal Andalucian School of Equestrian Art**, Avda. Duque de Abrantes s/n, you can see teams of horses performing to music (Thurs noon; 1750ptas; ☎956/311111). Training and practice takes place on other weekdays between 11am–1.00pm, when admission is a more affordable 425ptas.

La Cartuja

The remarkable Carthusian monastery of **LA CARTUJA** (Tues, Thurs & Sat 5–6.30pm) lies 4km along the road out of town towards Medina Sidonia (see p.125) in the midst of lush countryside and surrounded in summer by a sea of sunflowers. The monastery was founded in 1477 and, following great destruction by billeted French troops in 1810, was abolished in 1835 during the Liberal backlash against the church and male religious orders.

After serving as a military barracks for almost a century the monastery was restored to the Carthusians in 1949, since when the handful of monks here have dedicated themselves to restoring and maintaining this beautiful building. The Baroque facade you see today – added in the 1660s – is one of the most spectacular in the whole of Spain. Unfortunately, access is restricted to the building's exterior (with a magnificent main doorway), gardens and cloister; other parts of the monastery and its artworks may be seen by prior arrangement, and then only by men.

The Laguna de Medina

If you have transport, you could make another excursion from Jerez to the **LAGUNA DE MEDINA**, a small freshwater lake which – from late August on – attracts a great number of migrating birds returning from northern Europe to Africa. Under the care of ICONA (*Instituto para Conservación de la Naturaleza*), two paths skirt the lake from where, among a variety of waders, it's possible to spot white-headed duck, spoonbills and the greater flamingo in season. Fringed with reeds and tamarisk trees, the shallow lagoon is also home to numerous frogs, snakes and lizards. Because of its close proximity to the Coto Doñana across the Guadalquivir, many birds – particularly flamingos – use this as an alternative food source, especially if the Doñana's *marismas* are drier than normal towards the end of the summer.

To get there take the C440 out of Jerez for about 11km towards Medina Sidonia; the entrance to the lake area is signposted (immediately opposite a cement factory) and there's a small car park.

Eating and drinking

Befitting the capital of sherry production, Jerez has a clutch of great **bars** where *fino* – the perfect partner for *tapas* – can be sampled on its own turf. You could also do as the locals do: buy some take-away fried fish from a *freiduria* and take it to a nearby bar.

Bars and marisquería

Cervecería Antonio, c/Pajarete 9, south of the bullring. Tasty seafood *tapas*.

Bar Bodoski, c/Comandante Paz Varela 1, north of the bullring. Excellent fish *tapas* and *finos*.

El Boqueron de Plata, Plaza Santiago. One of the best *freiduria* in town.

Marisquería Cruz Blanca, c/Consistorio 16, close to Plaza Asunción. A good place, with outdoor seating. You buy your seafood by weight and then get drinks from the bar; try their *cañadillas*, or *murex*, a spiky shellfish whose purple dye was used to stain the clothes of Mediterranean aristocrats three thousand years ago.

Bar Juanito, c/Pescadería Vieja 4. In a small passage behind Plaza del Arenal, this is a good place to drink *fino* and nibble the famous seafood *tapas*.

Bar La Venencia, c/Larga 3. Central bar with a wide *tapas* selection – try the *pimientos rellenos* (stuffed peppers); it's aptly named after the curious long-handled implement used to draw wine from the sherry butt.

Restaurants

Mesón Alcazaba, c/Medina 19, east of c/Larga. Low-priced *menú* and an attractive patio.

El Bosque, Avda. Alvaro Domecq 28, north of the bullring. Quite upmarket restaurant with a garden and serving Andalucian specialities.

Gaitán, c/Gaitán 3. Pricey place behind the Turismo; a wide range including excellent seafood.

La Habichuela, c/San Marcos 1. A good value *menú*, near the church of San Marcos.

Tendido 6, c/Circo 10. Popular restaurant on the bullring's doorstep, which, predictably, has *rabo de toro* as one of its special dishes.

Nightlife

Much of Jerez's **nightlife** centres around the bars and discos north of the bullring.

Cairo, c/José Cádiz Salvatierra. Stylish place north of the bullring frequented by Jerez's young bloods and *chicas guapas*.

El Camino del Rocío, c/Velazquez. Curious bar which commemorates the memory of the famous pilgrimage to El Rocío – every night. Rocío memorabilia covers the walls, and at midnight the lights go down, candles are lit and the singing of the *gitano Ave María* begins another night of frenzied dancing. Buried in the northern suburbs, you'll need a taxi to get there and back for one of life's more memorable experiences.

Mudéjar, c/Canto. North African bar near the church of San Lucas; frequent live Arab music.

Raíces, c/Zaragoza 20. Live music venue east of the bullring towards the centre.

FLAMENCO IN JEREZ

Given Jerez's great **flamenco** traditions it's worth trying to hear some of the real thing at one of the many *peñas* or clubs concentrated in the old gypsy quarter of Santiago, north of the cathedral. The following are some of the best; turning up at around 10pm should provide an opportunity to hear some authentic performances. Otherwise consult the Turismo who also have details of the special *flamenco* festivals held in town over the summer.

Centro Andaluz de Flamenco, Plaza San Juan 1, Santiago.

Peña Antonio Chacón, c/Salas 2, Santiago.

Peña La Buena Gente, c/Lucas 9, Santiago.

Peña Tío José de Paula, c/La Merced 11, Santiago.

travel details

TRAINS

Algeciras to: Córdoba (4 daily; 1hr 45min–2hr); Granada (2 daily; 5hr 30min–6hr); Madrid (3 daily; 12hr 30min–15hr); Málaga (2 daily; 5hr); Sevilla (2 daily; 6-7hr).

Cádiz to: Granada (3 daily; 6hr); Jerez de la Frontera (18 daily; 45min–1hr 30min); Sevilla (8 daily; 2hr).

Málaga to: Antequera (2 daily;1hr 30min); Córdoba (8 daily; 2hr 30min–3hr 30min, via Bobadilla); Fuengirola (every 30min; 14min, via Málaga airport); Granada (2 daily; 3hr 30min, via Bobadilla); Madrid (5 daily; 7hr); Ronda (3 daily; 3hr, via Bobadilla); Sevilla (5 daily; 3hr 30min–4hr, via Bobadilla); Torremolinos (every 30min; 28min, via Málaga airport).

BUSES

Algeciras to: Cádiz (9 daily; 3hr); Jerez (6 daily; 2hr 15min); La Línea (for Gibraltar: hourly; 30min); Madrid (1 daily; 10hr); Málaga (11 daily; 5hr 30min); Sevilla (6 daily; 3hr 30min); Tarifa (11 daily; 30min).

Cádiz to: Algeciras (8 daily; 2hr 45min); Arcos de la Frontera (7 daily; 2hr); Chipiona (9 daily; 1hr 30min); Conil (6 daily; 1hr); Granada (2 daily; 8hr); Jerez de la Frontera (8 daily; 45min); Málaga (3 daily; 5hr); Puerto de Santa María (18 daily; 40min); Sanlúcar de Barrameda (8 daily; 1hr 15min); Sevilla (11 daily; 1hr 30min); Tarifa (1 daily; 2hr).

Jerez to: Arcos de la Frontera (17 daily; 30min); Cádiz (18 daily; 1hr); Sevilla (7 daily; 1hr 30min).

Málaga to: Algeciras (10 daily; 3hr 30min);

Almería (5 daily; 4hr 30min); Antequera (9 daily; 1hr); Córdoba (2 daily; 4hr); Granada (14 daily; 2hr 30min); Madrid (1 daily; 8hr); Marbella (every 30min; 1hr 30min); Motril (10 daily; 2hr 30min); Nerja (10 daily; 1hr 30min); Osuna (2 daily; 3hr); Ronda (4 daily; 3hr 30min); Sevilla (9 daily; 4hr 30min); Torremolinos (every 30min; 30min).

Ronda to: Arcos de la Frontera (3 daily; 1hr 45min); Cádiz (2 daily; 3hr 30min); Jerez (3 daily; 2hr 30min); Málaga (5 daily; 2hr 30min); Marbella (6 daily; 2hr); Olvera (1 daily; 30min); San Pedro de Alcántara (6 daily; 2hr); Setenil (1 daily; 15min); Sevilla (4 daily; 3hr 15min); Ubrique (2 daily; 45min).

Sanlúcar de Barrameda to: Cádiz (8 daily; 1hr 15min); Chipiona (17 daily; 15min); Jerez (17 daily; 40min); Sevilla (12 daily; 2hr).

FERRIES

Algeciras to: Ceuta (ferry boats 9 daily; 1hr 30min. Seasonal hydrofoil 1 daily; 30min); Tangier (ferry boats 5– 6 daily; 2hr 30min. Seasonal hydrofoil 1 daily; 1hr).

Benalmádena to: Tangier (Seasonal hydrofoil).

Cádiz to: Las Palmas (every 2 days in season, every 5 out; 43hr); Puerto Santa María (4 daily; 20min); Tenerife (every 2 days in season, every 5 out; 36hr).

Gibraltar to: Tangier (ferry boats twice weekly; 3hr. Seasonal hydrofoil 1 daily; 1hr).

Málaga to: Melilla (daily except Sun; 7hr 30min).

Tarifa to: Tangier (ferry boats daily except Sun; 2hr. Seasonal hydrofoil daily; 30min). Note that the hydrofoil does not run in bad weather and has been temporarily suspended; enquire locally.

CHAPTER TWO

SEVILLA AND HUELVA

With the major exception of the ebullient and irresistable city of **Sevilla**, the centre and western region of Andalucía – consisting of the city's province and the neighbouring province of **Huelva** – are not much visited. This is a great pity, as these areas are capable of springing a variety of surprises, both scenic and cultural, on those visitors prepared to wander off the beaten track to find them.

The **city of Sevilla**, Andalucía's capital, has many of the region's most beautiful monuments: the **Giralda** tower, a magnificent Gothic **Cathedral** and a rambling Mudéjar **Alcázar** with fabulous ornamentation are only the highlights of a marvellous architectural feast. Add to these a stunning and revamped **Museo de Bellas Artes**, the Roman site of **Italica** and a number of remarkable Renaissance mansions such as the **Casa de Pilatos**, and you're looking at a stay of at least two days. The most exciting parts of Sevilla, however, are its various **barrios**, each with its own strong character and traditions. These are atmospheric places to explore, warrens of delightful vernacular buildings and churches, plant-filled patios and welcoming *tapas* bars.

East of Sevilla rewards include a clutch of smaller towns on the way to Córdoba; in particular Moorish **Carmona**, which possesses a remarkable Roman cemetery, and Baroque **Écija**, with its striking churches and mansions. Also in Sevilla's **Campiña** – the name given to this broad and fertile agricultural plain watered by the Guadalquivir – are the towns of **Osuna** and **Estepa**, both with their own Renaissance architectural gems. To the north, the wooded hills of the **Sierra Morena** offer welcome respite from the intense summer heat, with charming small towns making excellent base-camps for hikes into the surrounding oak- and pine-covered slopes and river valleys.

The **province of Huelva** stretches from Sevilla to the Portuguese border, and hardly deserves its reputation as the least visited province of Andalucía. True, it does not have the spectacular sights that you associate with Sevilla or Granada and the countryside south of the lush Sierra de Aracena is not outstandingly beautiful. Huelva's greatest glory, – especially compelling if you're into bird-watching or wildlife – is the huge nature reserve of the **Coto Doñana National Park**, spreading back from the Guadalquivir estuary in vast expanses of *marismas* – sand dunes, salt flats and marshes. The largest roadless area in western Europe, the park is vital to scores of migratory birds and to endangered mammals including the Iberian lynx, and is also home to Andalucía's most rumbustious Whitsuntide pilgrimage and fair, the **Romería del Rocío**.

Huelva, the provincial capital, although scarred by its industrial surrounds, tries its best to be welcoming and does have a number of interesting sights; it also makes a convenient base for trips to local sites associated with the **voyages of Columbus** which set out from here. It was at the nearby monastery of **La Rabida** that the explorer's 1492 expedition was planned and from the tiny port of **Palos** that he eventually sailed for the New World. The province of Huelva was also the site of ancient **Tartessus**, a legendary kingdom rich in minerals that attracted the Minoans, Phoenicians and Greeks in ancient times. Minerals are still extracted from the hills to the north of the city – the awesome **Río Tinto Mines** display evidence of man's quest for minerals stretching back over five thousand years.

Among the most beautiful, and neglected, parts of this region are even further north, in the dark, ilex-covered hills and poor rural villages of the **Sierra de Aracena**. Perfect walking country, with its network of streams and reservoirs between modest peaks, this is a botanist's dream, brilliant with a mass of spring flowers. Here also, along a sierra rich in cork oaks, chestnuts and poplars, some of the finest *jamón* in Spain is produced from acorn-eating black pigs.

While the landlocked province of Sevilla takes its relaxation along the banks of the Guadalquivir, Huelva has a sea coast that harks back to pre-Costa del Sol tranquility. This section of the **Costa de la Luz** has some of the finest **beaches** in Andalucía with long stretches of luminous white sand and little sign of development. Here, between low-key coastal resorts all noted for their seafood, you'll find space to breathe along expansive beaches backed by shady pine woods.

Sevilla

"Seville," wrote Byron, "is a pleasant city, famous for oranges and women". And for its heat, he might perhaps have added, since summers here are intense and start early, in April. But the spirit of the quote, for all its nineteenth-century chauvinism, is about right. What is captivating about the city, as much as the monuments and works of art, is its essential romantic quality – the greatest city of the Spanish south, of Carmen, Don Juan and Figaro, and the archetype of Andalucian promise. It has a reputation for gaiety and brilliance, for theatricality and intensity of life, which seems well deserved. *Sevillanos* are world leaders in the art of street theatre. During **Semana Santa**, for example, a century of sandalled and helmeted Roman soldiers somberly escorts the *paso*, or effigy, of the condemned Christ through the crowded but silent streets in the grey dawn of Good Friday morning. Typically, the mood changes dramatically a couple of weeks later when the rags of mourning are cast off for *flamenco* costumes, and the city launches into the wild exhuberance of the **Feria de Abril** which also inaugurates the start of the bullfight season, another *sevillano* passion. Either is worth considerable effort to get to. Sevilla is also Spain's second most important centre for **bullfighting**, after Madrid.

Despite its considerable elegance and charm, however, and its wealth, based on arms industry and lucrative export trade to Latin America, the city lies at the centre of a depressed agricultural area and has an unemployment rate of nearly forty percent – one of the highest in Spain, along with Jaén and Málaga. You do not need to travel far into the suburbs to find slums of a third world standard. The total refurbishment of the infrastructure boosted by the **1992 Expo** – held to celebrate the 500th anniversary of Columbus's discovery of the New World – including new roads, seven bridges, a high-speed train link and a revamped airport may ultimately help in attracting much needed employment to the city, but the long-term effects will take a while to assess.

Petty crime is a notorious problem. Theft is usually drug-related and bag-snatching is common (often Italian-style, from passing *motos*). Non-*sevillanos* make much of the city's special breed, *semaforazos*, who break the windows of cars stopped at traffic lights and grab what they can. You'd be very unwise to leave anything in a car parked on the street overnight; the guarded underground car-parks are a possible alternative. Be careful in Sevilla, but don't be put off. Violent crime is rare.

Sevilla's most famous present-day native son is Prime Minister **Felipe González**; his deputy Alfonso Guerra also hails from here. Another, more bizarre *sevillano* is one **Gregorio XVII**, who calls himself the true Pope, in defiance of his excommunication by the Vatican. "Pope Greg" is leader of a large ultra-reactionary order which has made the dead Franco a saint, gives out free beer and *churros* to all who call at its headquarters,

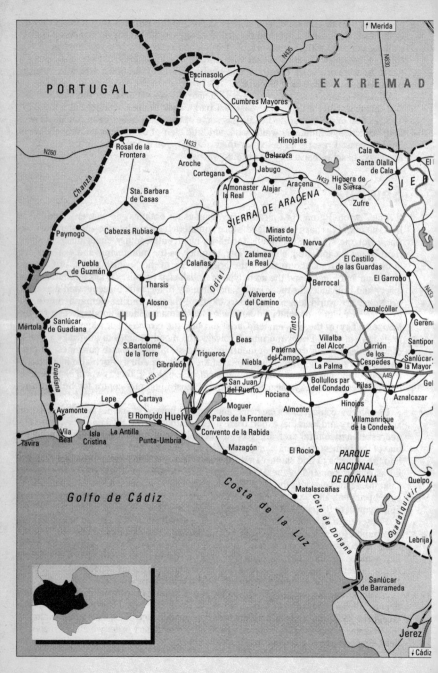

PORTUGAL

EXTREMAD

↑ Merida

Encinasolo
Cumbres Mayores
Hinojales
Galaroza
Cala
Santa Olalla
de Cala
Rosal de la
Frontera
Aroche
Cortegana
Jabugo
Almonaster
la Real
Alajar
Aracena
Higuera de
la Sierra
Zufre
SIER
SIERRA DE ARACENA
Sta. Barbara
de Casas
Paymogo
Cabezas Rubias
Minas de
Riotinto
Nerva
Puebla
de Guzmán
Calañas
Zalamea
la Real
El Castillo
de las Guardas
El Garrobo
Tharsis
Berrocal
Alosno
Valverde
del Camino
Aznalcóllar
HUELVA
Gerena
Sanlúcar
de Guadiana
Beas
Villalba
del Alcor
Santipor
Mértola
S.Bartolomé
de la Torre
Trigueros
Paterna
del Campo
Carrión
de los
Cespedes
Sanlúcar
la Mayor
Gibraleón
Niebla
La Palma
Lepe
Cartaya
San Juan
del Puerto
Bollullos par
del Condado
Pilas
Gel
Ayamonte
El Rompido
Huelva
Moguer
Rociana
Almonte
Hinojos
Aznalcazar
Vila
Real
Palos de la Frontera
Villamanrique
de la Condesa
Tavira
Isla
Cristina
La Antilla
Punta-Umbria
Convento de la Rabida
Mazagón
El Rocio
PARQUE
NACIONAL
DE DOÑANA
Quelpo
Golfo de Cádiz
Matalascañas
Costa de la Luz
Coto de Doñana
Lebrija
Sanlúcar
de Barrameda
Jerez

↓ Cádiz

N435
N630
N260
N433
N433
N431
A49
N435

Chanza
Odiel
Tinto
Guadiana
Guadalquivir

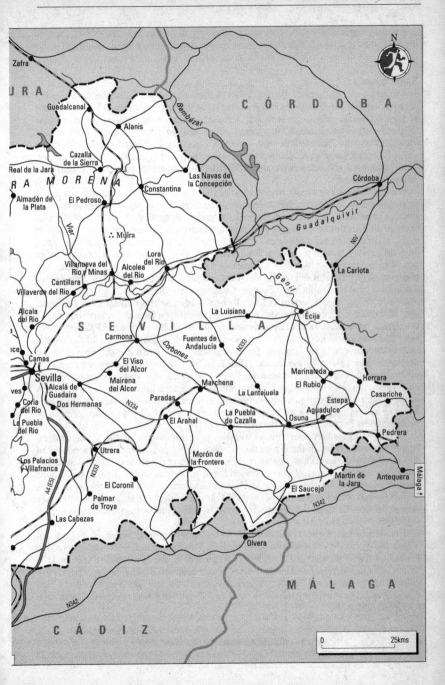

and is building a mammoth "Vatican II" 40km south of the city (see p.207). Despite being blinded in a road accident, Gregorio conspicuously enjoys the good life and stalks the city's bars dressed in silken regalia, along with his "papal" entourage.

Some history

Sevilla began when ancient Iberian tribes settled on the banks of the Guadalquivir perhaps early in the first millenium BC. The settlement grew into the town now known as **El Carámbalo**, whose great wealth derived from the minerals from the mountains to the north. The demand for copper, silver and gold lured in the Greeks and Phoenicians, who traded their own ceramics, jewellery and ivory goods. It was the same Phoenicians, or perhaps their successors the Carthaginians, who attacked and then conquered the settlement around 500BC, subsequently renaming it **Hispalis**, meaning "flat land".

When the **Romans** finally wrested Spain from Carthage the Roman general Scipio founded **Italica** in 206 on a hill overlooking the river. The conquest of Spain cost the Romans two hundred years of dogged campaigning against the ferocious Iberian peoples, and in the latter stages of this struggle **Julius Caesar** captured Hispalis in 43BC and renamed it Julia Romula ("little Rome"). As the capital of the Roman province of Baetica (roughly modern Andalucía) the city flourished and nearby Italica provided Rome with two of its greatest second-century Emperors, **Trajan** and **Hadrian**. The city later fell to the Visigoths, whose Christian archbishop **San Isidro** made sixth-century Sevilla into a European centre of learning.

Conquered by the **Moors** in 712, Sevilla briefly became **the capital of al-Andalus**. The Moors left an indelible imprint on the city, not only in its architecture, but also in the Arabic-influenced local dialect, renaming the River Baetis *Wadi El Kabir* ("great river"), a title it still keeps as the Guadaquilvir. The **Almohad** dynasty of the twelfth and thirteenth centuries brought great prosperity and when Sevilla was captured during the *reconquista* by **Fernando III** in 1258 the city became a favoured residence of the Spanish monarchy, in particular Pedro the Cruel who was responsible for the construction of the outstanding Mudéjar alcázar. Religious intolerance racked the city in the wake of the Reconquest, however, and in 1391 the Jewish quarter in the *barrio* Santa Cruz was sacked – a harbinger of the banishment of all Jews from Spain, to be proclaimed by Fernando and Isabel a century later.

The fifteenth century also saw, as well as the **construction of the Cathedral**, an event that would catapult the city to the forefront of Spanish affairs – the **discovery of the New World**. Sevilla's navigable river, with access to the Atlantic made it a natural choice for the main port of commerce with the Americas. In the 1500s, as fabulous wealth poured in from the empire, Sevilla was transformed into one of the great cities of Europe and, with a population of over 150,000, one of the largest. The cultural renaissance that accompanied this prosperity attracted artists and writers – Cervantes spent some time here — from far and wide.

The **silting up of the Guadalquivir** in the 1680s deprived Sevilla of its port and with it the monopoly of trade with the Americas. The merchant fleet was transferred to Cádiz and the city went into a decline exacerbated by the great earthquake of 1755 which, although centred on Lisbon, caused much destruction. The city was largely bypassed by the industrial revolution and it was only in the nineteenth century that Sevilla was rediscovered by travellers such as Richard Ford who declared it to be "the marvel of Andalucía".

The **telephone area code** for Sevilla is ☎954.

Arrival and orientation

Split in two by the Río Guadalquivir, Sevilla is fairly easy to negotiate and a delight to explore on foot (though hell if you're driving). If you are going to be spending more than a fleeting visit, try and get hold of a copy of the invaluable *La Guía Verde* street guide (available from bookshops), which will help you unravel the city's more convoluted corners.

The **old city** – where you'll spend most of your time – takes up the east bank. At its heart, side by side, stand the three great monuments: the **Giralda tower**, the **Cathedral** and the **Alcázar**, with the cramped alleyways of the **Barrio Santa Cruz**, the medieval Jewish quarter and now the heart of tourist life, extending east of them. North and west of the *barrio* is the main shopping and commercial district, its most obvious landmarks the **Plaza Nueva** and **Plaza Duque de la Victoria**, and the smart pedestrianized **Calle Sierpes** which runs between them. To the north of the area enclosed by the medieval walls lies the gritty **Macarena quarter** from whose church the *paso* of the bejewelled Virgin of Macarena – the most revered in Sevilla – sails forth on the Maundy Thursday of *Semana Santa* to enormous popular acclaim. Just beyond the walls here in the converted sixteenth-century Hospital de las Cinco Llagas ("five wounds of Christ") is the new permanent seat of the **Andalucian Parliament**.

Across the river – where the great April *feria* takes place – is the very much earthier, traditionally working-class district of **Triana,** flanked to the south by **Los Remedios**, now transformed into the city's business zone. Also on this bank lie the remains of the *Expo 92* Exhibition Ground, at Isla de la Cartuja.

Points of arrival and information

Sevilla's **airport** is 12km northeast of town along the NIV towards Córdoba – from here the #EA airport bus runs down Avda. Kansas City, the airport road, and drops you at the Puerta de Jerez, close to the cathedral. In addition, *Iberia* buses run to their office, also very close to the cathedral on c/Almirante Lobo.

Expo resulted in a long-overdue update of Sevilla's transport links, with the introduction of the high-speed **AVE train** between the city and Madrid. This is expensive, but very impressive, with a journey time cut from seven to two-and-a-half hours. Sevilla's new **train station**, Santa Justa, is a long way out northeast of the centre, on Avda. Kansas City. The aforementioned #EA, the airport bus, terminates in the centre at the Puerta de Jerez, at the top of Avda. Roma between the Turismo and the Fábrica de Tabacos. For **train information** and tickets go to the *RENFE* office, off the Plaza Nueva at c/Zaragoza 29, which saves the long trek out to the station (☎441 41 11 for information, ☎442 15 62 for reservations).

The **main bus station** is at the Prado de San Sebastián (☎441 71 11), a short bus-ride from the train station on #70. Most companies, to most destinations go from here: exceptions include buses for **Badajoz**, **Extremadura** and **Huelva** which are served by the *La Estrella* and *Empresa Damas* companies, operating out of the new station at Plaza de Armas (☎490 80 40) by the Puente del Cachorro, on the river.

You can get good city maps at Sevilla's **Turismo**, just south of the Cathedral at Avda. de la Constitución 21 (Mon–Fri 9.30am–7.30pm, Sat 10am–2pm; ☎422 14 04). While you're there, pick up a copy of their excellent free monthly listings guide, *El Giraldillo*, which details the month's cultural activities in the city and updates any changes in museum and monument opening hours, especially useful around holiday periods.

One good way to get to grips with the city and orientate yourself is on an **open top bus tour** – especially if you're pressed for time. Buses – operated by British company *Guide Friday* – leave hourly from the Torre del Oro and tour the main sites, including a peer into *Expo 92*. Tickets are 1000ptas and half-price for kids.

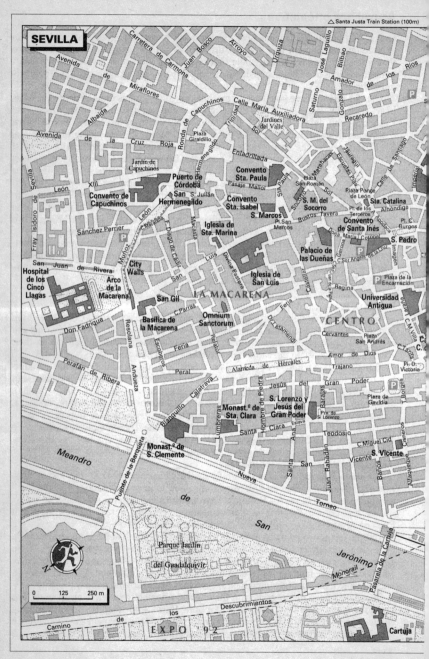

SEVILLA

Carretera de Carmona

Avenida

de

Miraflores

Juan Bosco

Arroyo

Urquija

José Laguillo

Bilbao

Amador de

Recaredo

los Ríos

Saturno

Gonzalo

Avenida

de

la

Cruz Roja

Ronda de Capuchinos

Calle María Auxiliadora

Jardines del Valle

Albaida

León

XIII

Convento de
Capuchinos

Jardín de
Capuchinos

Plaza
Giraldillo

Pasaje Mallol

Enladrillada

Trinidad

Sol

San Julián

Convento
Sta. Paula

Plaza
San Román

Escuelas Pías

Fray Isidoro de Sevilla

Puerto de
Córdoba

San
Hermenegildo

S. Julián

Convento
Sta. Isabel

Sta. Paula

S. M. del
Socorro

Plaza Ponce
de León

Sta. Catalina

Sánchez Perrier

Convento
de Santa Inés

S. Pedro

Iglesia de
Sta. Marina

S. Marcos

Pl. San
Marcos

Bustos Tavera

Pt. de los
Terceros

Alhóndiga

Pl. C.
Burgos

Muñoz

F. Diego de Cádiz

Macasta

Luis

Doña María Coronel

Palacio de
las Dueñas

San Juan de Rivera

City
Walls

Divina Pastora

Iglesia de
San Luis

Castellar

C. Sor Angela

Plaza de la
Encarnación

Imagen

Hospital
de los
Cinco
Llagas

Arco
de la
Macarena

San Gil

C. Parras

Regina

Universidad
Antigua

Don Fadrique

Resolana

Basílica de
la Macarena

Omnium
Sanctorum

Feria

Relator

CENTRO

Peraflán de Ribera

Andueza

Escoberos

Feria

Palacio

Cervantes

Amor de Dios

Plaza
San Andrés

C. Villa

C.

Peral

Alameda de Hércules

Trajano

Pl. D.
Victoria

Calatrava

Blanquillo

Jesús del

Gran Poder

Meandro

Lumbreras

Monast.ª de
Sta. Clara

Hombre de Piedra

S. Lorenzo y
Jesús del
Gran Poder

Santa

Clara

Baraja

Pza. de
S. Lorenzo

Plaza de
Gavidia

Teodosio

C. Miguel Cid

Cisneros

Puente de la Barqueta

Monast.ª de
S. Clemente

Santa

Ana

San

Vicente

S. Vicente

Baños

Alhóndiga

Nueva

Juan Rabadán

Tomeo

Meandro

de

San

Jerónimo

Parque Jardín
del Guadalquivir

Pasarela de la Cartuja

Monorail

0   125   250 m

Descubrimientos

Camino

de

los

E X P O ' 9 2

Cartuja

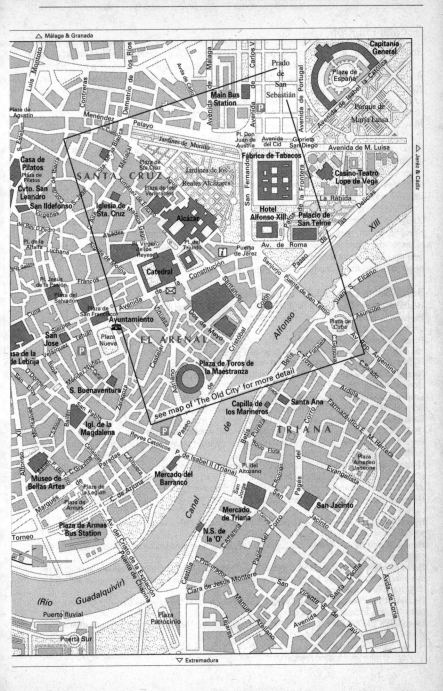

△ Málaga & Granada

Capitania General

Plaza de España

Parque de Maria Luisa

Avenida de M. Luisa

△ Jeréz & Cádiz

Luis Montoto

Contreras

Avda. de los Rios

Demetrio

Avda. de Carlos V

Avenida de Málaga

Avenida de Portugal

Avenida de Isabel la Católica

Plaza de Agustín

Menéndez

Pelayo

Main Bus Station

Prado de San Sebastián

Pl. Don Juan de Austria

Avenida del Cid

Glorieta San Diego

Santa María Blanca

Jardines de Murillo

Fábrica de Tabacos

Casa de Pilatos

Plaza de Pilatos

Cvto. San Leandro

San Ildefonso

SANTA CRUZ

Plaza de Sta.Cruz

Jardines de los Reales Alcázares

Casino-Teatro Lope de Vega

La Rábida

Iglesia de Sta. Cruz

Plaza de los Venerables

Alcázar

Hotel Alfonso XIII

Palacio de San Telmo

del Rey D.Pedro

Pl. de la Alfalfa

Luchana

Virgenes

Abades

Pl. Virgen de los Reyes

Pl. del Triunfo

Puerta de Jerez

Av. de Roma

Pl. Jesús de la Pasión

Francos

Catedral

Constitución

Plaza del Salvador

Cuna

Plaza de San Francisco

Ayuntamiento

Puente de San Telmo

Plaza de Cuba

San Jose

Sierpes

Tetuán

Plaza Nueva

EL ARENAL

Colón

Alfonso

Av. Rep. Argentina

asa de la de Lebrija

Velázquez

S. Buenaventura

Plaza de Toros de la Maestranza

see map of 'The Old City' for more detail

Capilla de los Marineros

Santa Ana

TRIANA

Igl. de la Magdalena

Reyes Católicos

P. de Isabel II (Triana)

Pl. del Altozano

Museo de Bellas Artes

Mercado del Barranco

Mercado de Triana

San Jacinto

Plaza de Armas Bus Station

N.S. de la 'O'

Canal

(Río Guadalquivir)

Puerto fluvial

Plaza Patrocinio

Puerta Sur

▽ Extremadura

Accommodation

Rooms in Sevilla are relatively expensive; in mid-season or during the big festivals you can find yourself paying ridiculous amounts for what is little more than a cell. By far the most attractive **area to stay** in Sevilla is undoubtedly the **Barrio Santa Cruz**, an appeal reflected in its prices – lower-priced options are concentrated around its periphery (especially immediately north, and southeast towards the bus station). Slightly further out, another promising area is to the north of the **Plaza Nueva** and the **Maestranza bullring**, and especially the streets beyond c/Reyes Catolicos towards the Museo de Bellas Artes. More central options are to be found in the streets and squares surrounding the churches of **Santa Catalina** and **San Pedro**, and to the south of the **Alameda de Hercules** – areas possessing much of the charm of the older *barrio*s without the tourist hurdy-gurdy or prices. Further out still, but walkable from the centre, the solidly working-class *barrio* of **La Macarena** can be a wonderful introduction to the real Sevilla.

When you do hit on a place it's worth trying to bargain the price down a little, especially out of high season, though you may not always succeed. In mid-season (and *Semana Santa*) you may face quite a walk to find a bed; ringing ahead if your plans allow could spare you some hassles. **Hostelling** or **camping** are by far the cheapest options, but not exactly handy: the youth hostel is out in the university district; the nearest **campsite** some 6km from the centre.

Barrio Santa Cruz and Cathedral Area

Hostal Águilas, c/Águilas 15 (☎213177). Small, quiet place near the Casa de Pilatos. ④.

Pensión Alcázar, c/Deán Miranda 12 (☎228457). Tiny place in a tiny street off the Plaza de la Contractación beside the Alcázar. ④.

Hotel Álvarez Quintero, c/Álvarez Quintero 12 (☎221298). This newly converted former *bodega* has a delightful seventeenth-century patio and great views from some rooms (especially nos. 201–6). Just to the north of the cathedral and excellent value. ⑤.

Hostal Bien Venido, c/Archeros 17, east of c/Santa María la Blanca (☎413655). Small rooms but nice roof terrace. ④.

Casa de Huéspedes Buen Dormir, c/Farnesio 8, off c/Santa María la Blanca on the cathedral side (☎217492). Friendly but scruffy; so check the room first. ③.

Casa Diego, Plaza Curtidores 7, near Iglesia de Santa María La Blanca at the end of c/Archeros (☎413552). The best value of several similar establishments around here. ③.

Casa Moreno, Avda. Cádiz 15 (☎421460). Not the prettiest place in the world, but in a convenient location very close to the bus station. ③.

Hostal Córdoba, c/Farnesio 12 (☎227498). A very good option, close to Iglesia de Santa Cruz. ④.

Hostal Dulces Sueños, c/Santa María La Blanca 21 (☎419393). Hostal "sweet dreams" is reasonably low-priced and shouldn't give you too many nightmares. ③.

Hostal Fabiola, c/Fabiola 16 (☎218346). Comfortable rooms, on a quiet street with a pleasant patio. ④.

Hostal Goya, c/Mateos Gago 31 (☎211170). Good value, with a range of rooms, in a street with several possibilities. ④.

Hostal Marco de la Giralda, c/Abades 30 (☎228324). Very good value for a place so close to the cathedral. ④.

Hotel Murillo, c/Lope de Rueda 7 (☎216095). Traditional hotel in restored mansion with all facilities plus amusingly kitsch features such as suits of armour, heavy leather chairs and paint palette key rings. ⑤.

Pensión Pérez Montilla, Plaza Curtidores 13 (☎421854). On the eastern edge of Santa Cruz, with many facilities include air-conditioning. ⑤.

Hostal San Pancracio, c/Cruces 9 (☎413104). A range of room options here so check what's available. Close to Plaza Santa Cruz. ③.

Hostal Santa María, c/Hernando Colón 19 (☎228505). Small place on a noisy street, but in the Giralda's shadow and a good price. ③.

ACCOMMODATION PRICE SYMBOLS

The symbols used in our hotel listings denote the following price ranges:

① Under 2000ptas   ③ 3000–4500ptas   ⑤ 7500–12,500ptas
② 2000–3000ptas   ④ 4500–7500ptas   ⑥ Over 12,500ptas

See p.28 for more details.

Hostal Santa María, c/Santa María la Blanca 28 (☎421174). Newly refurbished *hostal* above a shop through which you gain entry. ④.

Hostal Sierpes, Coral del Rey 22, northeast of the cathedral (☎224948). One of the better value places for rooms with bath in this area, and also has a restaurant (serving breakfast) and garage. ④.

Hotel Simón, c/García de Vinuesa 19 (☎226660). Well-restored eighteenth-century mansion with attractive patio and excellent position across Avda. de la Constitución from the cathedral. Can be a bargain out of season. The charming, Moorish-inspired dining room is open to non-residents. ⑤.

Hostal Toledo, c/Santa Teresa 15 (☎215335). Atmospheric old *pensión* in Santa Cruz. ④.

Plaza Nueva, Reyes Catolicos, Museo de Bellas Artes

Hotel Bécquer, c/Reyes Católicos 4 (☎228900). Efficient and comfortable central hotel with air-conditioning and garage. ⑤.

Hostal Cataluña, c/Doña Guiomar 1, just off c/Zaragoza, near the bullring (☎216840). Friendly place and delightful rooms, but haggle for a lower price. ④.

Estoril, c/Gravina 78 (☎225095). Spotless single-rooms-only *hostal* in quiet street off c/Reyes Catolicos. ③.

Hostal Granadina, c/Gravina 82 (☎213122). Only a small number of rooms here, but they're all pleasant and quiet. ④.

Hostal Gravina, c/Gravina 46 (☎216414). Friendly, family run place in quiet street off c/Reyes Catolicos. ③.

Hostal La Gloria, c/San Eloy 58 (☎222673). Simple rooms in a wonderful neo-Moorish building above the *Café Zafiro*. This street has several other possibilities. ④.

Hostal Paco's, c/Pedro del Toro 7, off c/Gravina (☎217183). Run by the owners of the *Hostal Gravina* but with slightly better facilities. ④.

Hostal Plaza-Sevilla, c/Canalejas 2, to the north of c/Reyes Catolicos (☎217149). Worth staying here for the stunning Neoclassical facade alone. Facilities include air-conditioning and on-site hairdresser. ⑤.

Hostal Regi, c/Carlos Cañal 42 (☎215764). Small, clean and reliable place west of Plaza Nueva. ③.

Hostal Rivero, c/Bailen 67 (☎216231). This eighteenth-century former bishop's residence with an attractive plant-filled patio is run by two sprightly sisters. Situated in a quiet street, it's on the doorstep of the Museo de Bellas Artes. ④.

Hostal Romero, c/Gravina 21 (☎211353). Efficient, reliable place. ④.

Hostal Suiza, c/Méndez Núñez 16 (☎220813). Just off Plaza Nueva – a range of rooms and prices, so look first. ⑤.

Pensión Zahira, c/San Eloy 43 (☎221061). Comfortable rooms with bath. ⑤.

Hostal Zaida, c/San Roque 26, just south of Museo de Bellas Artes (☎211138). Charming *hostal* with a fine exterior and an interior replete with Moorish inspired decor. ⑤.

Santa Catalina, San Pedro, Alameda de Hercules

Hostal Alvertos, c/Cervantes 4, backing on to the Iglesia San Andrés (☎385710). Engagingly eccentric *hostal*. The ramshackle patio crammed with plants, leather armchairs, piano and TV is a work of art. ③.

Hotel Corregidor, c/Morgado 17, off c/Amor de Dios (☎385111). Stylish, serene and recently renovated hotel with a nice patio and all you'd expect for the price. ⑥.

Hostal Don Gonzálo, c/Jesús del Gran Poder 28 (☎381409). Another good, middle-of-the-road *hostal*. ⑤.

Hostal Duque, c/Trajano 15, south of the Alameda de Hercules (☎387011). Friendly, comfortable establishment with pretty tiled patio. ⑤.

Hostal La Posada, c/Relator 49 (☎374768). Small, simple place; to the east of the northern end of the Alameda de Hercules. ③.

Hotel San Andrés, c/Angostillo 6, by the Iglesia de San Andrés (☎562856). Attractively refurbished mansion on a pleasant and quiet *plazuela* facing the crumbling church of San Andrés. ⑤.

Hostal Unión, c/Tarifa 4, south of the Alameda de Hercules (☎211790). Clean, economical rooms with bath and friendly management. One of the best value places in this area. ③.

La Macarena

Hostal Galatea, c/San Juan de La Palma 4, northwest of the Iglesia de San Pedro (☎563564). Friendly new *hostal* in a restored town house situated on a charming (and peaceful) *plazuela*. ④.

Hostal Macarena, c/San Luis 91, near the Iglesia de San Luis (☎370141). Clean and economical rooms in the centre of a vibrant quarter. ③.

Hostal La Muralla, c/Macarena 52 (☎371049). Cosy, residential *hostal* near the medieval walls. ⑤.

La Rábida, c/Castellar 24 (☎220960). Friendly, modern hotel with superb patio. Near the Iglesia de San Marcos. ⑤.

San Gil, c/Parras 28 (☎906811). This apartment-hotel – in a beautifully restored turn-of-the century *palacio* close to the Puerta de la Macarena – is listed in the top hundred major buildings of Sevilla. There's a garden with palms and cypresses, rooftop pool, and an interior decorated with mosaics and azulejos. You'll need plenty of cash for even one night's stay here; it's at the very top of the range. ⑥.

Youth hostel and campsites

Albergue Juvenil Sevilla, c/Isaac Peral 2 (☎613150). Crowded youth hostel some way out; take bus #34 from Puerta de Jerez or Plaza Nueva.

Camping Sevilla (☎514379). Right by the airport, so very noisy but otherwise not a bad site. The airport bus will drop you there.

Camping Villsom, 12km out of town on the main Cádiz road. Benefiting from an overhaul this place has a brand new pool. Half-hourly buses from the bus station.

Club de Campo, 12km out of town in Dos Hermanas (☎720520). A pleasant shady site with a pool.

The Giralda

Beyond doubt the most beautiful building in Sevilla, the Moorish **Giralda** (Mon–Sat 11am–5pm, Sun 10am–4pm; 500ptas; same ticket valid for the cathedral), named after the sixteenth-century *giraldillo* or weather vane on its summit, dominates the skyline. In character with the city below, whose much-loved symbol it has become, with all its contradictions the Giralda remains in its perfect synthesis of form and decoration one of the most important monuments of the Islamic world.

The **minaret** – according to Ford built on a foundation of destroyed Roman statuary – was the culmination of Almohad architecture, and served as a model for those at the imperial capitals of Rabat and Marrakesh. It was used by the Moors both for calling the faithful to prayer (the traditional function of a minaret) and as an observatory, and was so venerated that they wanted to destroy it before the Christian conquest of the city. This they were prevented from doing by the threat of Alfonso (later King Alfonso X) that "if they removed a single stone, they would all be put to the sword." Instead the Giralda went on to become the bell tower of the Christian cathedral. Incidentally, the **Patio de Los Naranjos**, the old entrance to the mosque, also survives intact; access is through the cathedral.

You can ascend to the **bell chamber** for a remarkable view of the city – and, equally remarkable, a glimpse of the Gothic details of the cathedral's buttresses and statuary. Keep an eye out, too, for the colony of kestrels which has long nested in the tower – the descendants no doubt of the "twittering, careering hawks" seen by Ford

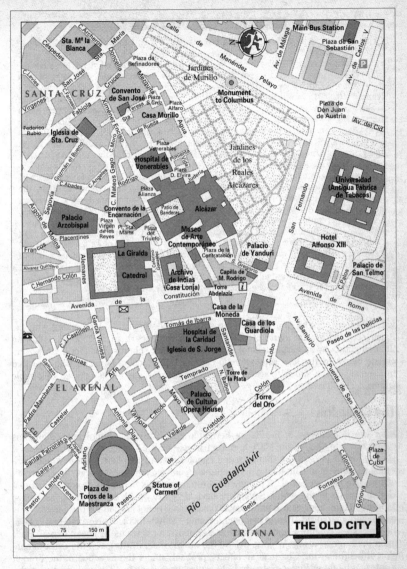

THE OLD CITY

when he climbed up here in the 1830s. Most impressive is the tower's inner construction, a series of 35 gently inclined ramps wide enough for two mounted guards to pass.

The Moorish structure took twelve years to build (1184–96) and derives its firm, simple beauty from the shadows formed by blocks of brick trelliswork or *ajaracas*, different on each side, and relieved by a succession of arched niches and windows. The harmony has been spoiled by the Renaissance-era addition of balconies and, to a still

MOORISH SEVILLA

Sevilla was one of the earliest **Moorish conquests** (in 712) and, as part of the Caliphate of Córdoba, became the second city of *al-Andalus*. When the Caliphate broke up in the early eleventh century it was by far the most powerful of the independent states (or *taifas*) to emerge, extending its power over the Algarve and eventually over Jaén, Murcia and Córdoba itself. This period, under a series of three Arabic rulers from the Abbadid dynasty (1023–91), was something of a golden age. The city's court was unrivalled in wealth and luxury and was sophisticated too, developing a strong chivalric element and a flair for poetry – one of the most skilled exponents being the last ruler, al Mu'tamid, the "poet-king". But with sophistication came decadence, and in 1091 Abbadid rule was usurped by a new force, the **Almoravids**, a tribe of fanatical Berber Muslims from North Africa, to whom the Andalucians had appealed for help against the threat from the northern Christian kingdoms.

Despite initial military successes, the Almoravids failed to consolidate their gains in *al-Andalus* and attempted to rule through military governors from Marrakesh. In the middle of the twelfth century they were in turn supplanted by a new Berber incursion, the **Almohads**, who by about 1170 had recaptured virtually all the former territories. Sevilla had accepted Almohad rule in 1147 and became the capital of this last real empire of the Moors in Spain. Almohad power was sustained until their disastrous defeat in 1212 by the combined Christian armies of the north, at Las Navas de Tolosa. In this brief and precarious period Sevilla underwent a renaissance of public building, characterized by a new vigour and fluidity of style. The Almohads rebuilt the Alcázar, enlarged the principal **mosque** and erected a new and brilliant minaret, a tower over 100m tall, topped with four copper spheres that could be seen from miles round: the Giralda.

greater extent, by the four diminishing storeys of the belfry – added, along with the Italian-sculpted bronze figure of "Faith" which surmounts them, in 1560–68, following the demolition by an earthquake of the original copper spheres. The fact that a weathervane blown by the four winds should epitomize the ideal of constant faith – or that this female figure should possess a masculine name – has never seemed to trouble whimsical *sevillanos*.

The Cathedral

After the Reconquest of Sevilla by Fernando III (1248), the Almohad mosque was consecrated to the Virgin Mary and kept in use as the Christian cathedral. Thus it survived until 1402, when the cathedral chapter dreamt up plans for a new and unrivalled monument to Christian glory: "a building on so magnificent a scale that posterity will believe we were mad." To this end the mosque was demolished, and the largest Gothic church in the world, Sevilla's **Catedral** (entry on Plaza Virgen de los Reyes; Mon–Sat 11am–5pm, Sun 10am–4pm; 500ptas; same ticket is valid for the Giralda) was completed, extraordinarily, in just over a century (1402–1506). As Norman Lewis says, "it expresses conquest and domination in architectural terms of sheer mass." Built upon the huge, rectangular base-plan of the old mosque, it was given the extra dimension of height by the Christian architects, probably under the direction of the French master architect of Rouen Cathedral. Its central nave rises to 42 metres, and even the side chapels appear tall enough to contain an ordinary church. The total area covers 11,520 square metres and was previously reckoned to be the third largest church in the world after Saint Paul's in London and Saint Peter's in Rome. However, new calculations based on cubic measurements have now placed it the number one position, a claim upheld by the *Guinness Book of Records*, a copy of whose certificate is proudly displayed at the entrance.

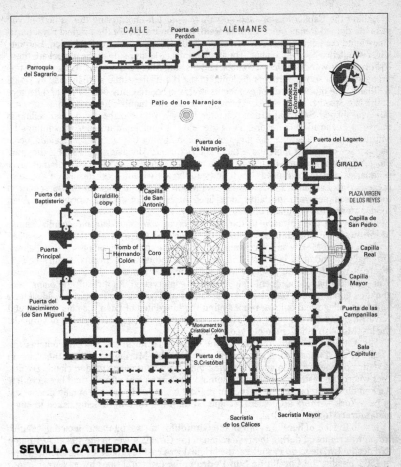

SEVILLA CATHEDRAL

Sheer size and grandeur are, inevitably, the chief characteristics of the cathedral. But as you grow accustomed to the gloom, two other qualities stand out with equal force: the rhythmic balance and interplay between the parts, and an impressive overall simplicity and restraint in decoration. All successive ages have left monuments of their own wealth and style, but these have been limited to the two rows of side chapels. In the main body of the cathedral only the great box-like structure of the *coro* (choir) stands out, filling the central portion of the nave.

The *coro* extends and opens on to the **Capilla Mayor**, dominated by a vast Gothic **retablo** composed of 45 carved scenes from the life of Christ. The lifetime's work of a single craftsman, Pierre Dancart, this is the supreme masterpiece of the cathedral – the largest and richest altarpiece in the world and one of the finest examples of Gothic woodcarving. The guides provide staggering statistics on the amount of gold involved. Above the central tabernacle, the **Virgen de la Sede** (Virgin of the Chair) is a stunning thirteenth-century Gothic figure of silver plated cedar – just to the right, a panel depicts an **image of the Giralda** as it appeared prior to any Renaissance additions.

Behind the Capilla Mayor (and directly to your left on entering the cathedral) you pass the domed Renaissance **Capilla Real**, built on the site of the original royal burial chapel and containing the body of Fernando III (*El Santo*) in a suitably rich, Baroque silver sepulchre before the altar. The large tombs on either side of the chapel are those of Fernando's wife, Beatrice of Swabia, and his son, Alfonso the Wise. At the end of this first aisle are a series of rooms designed in the rich Plateresque style in 1530 by Diego de Riano, one of the foremost exponents of this predominantly decorative architecture of the late Spanish Renaissance. Through a small antechamber here you enter the curious oval-shaped **Sala Capitular** (Chapter House), whose elaborate domed ceiling is mirrored in the marble decoration of the floor. It contains a number of paintings by Murillo, a native of Sevilla, the finest of which, a flowing *Concepción Inmaculada*, occupies a place of honour high above the bishop's throne. Alongside this room is the grandiose **Sacristía Mayor** which houses the treasury. Amid a confused collection of silver reliquaries and monstrances – dull and prodigious wealth – are displayed the keys presented to Fernando by the Jewish and Moorish communities on the surrender of the city; sculpted into the latter in stylized Arabic script are the words "May Allah render eternal the dominion of Islam in this city."

Just beyond the entrance to the sacristy is an enormous late nineteenth-century **Monument to Christopher Columbus** (*Cristóbal Colón* in Spanish), by Sevillian sculptor Arturo Mélida and which may or may not be the navigator's tomb (see below). Originally intended to be erected in the Cuban cathedral of Havana, Spain's colony, where it would become a sepulchre for Columbus's remains, the Spanish-American War – and Cuba's subsequent independence – intervened. As a result the plans were changed and the work was placed in the cathedral. The mariner's coffin is held aloft by four huge allegorical figures, representing the kingdoms of León, Castile, Aragón and Navarra; note how the lance of Castile is piercing a pomegranate, symbol of Granada, the last Moorish kingdom to be reconquered.

The **Capilla de San Antonio** in the cathedral's northwest corner contains the *Vision of St Anthony*, another magnificent work by Murillo, depicting the saint in ecstatic pose before an infant Christ emerging from a luminous golden cloud. Try and spot where the restorers joined San Antonio back into place after he had been crudely hacked out of the picture by thieves in the last century. He was eventually discovered in New York – where art dealers recognized the work they were being asked to buy – and returned to the cathedral.

Just to the left of here is a copy of the **Giraldillo**, the weathervane depicting "Faith", which was removed during the restoration of the Giralda tower in the 1980s. Attributed to a design by Diego de Pasquiera, the original was cast in bronze by Bartolomé Morel in 1568. Finally, the **Capilla de San Pedro** in the cathedral's northwest corner (close to the entrance to the Giralda tower) has a fine seventeenth-century **retablo** by Diego López Bueno with nine Zurburán scenes (except for the image of God which is a later replacement) depicting the life of Saint Peter. Also here, within a niche, lies the tomb of Columbus's friend and advisor, Archbishop Fray Diego de Deza, of the monastery of La Rábida, near Huelva. Should you be inspired by the Columbus saga, or have a fervent interest in Columbus's travels, visit the **Lonja**, opposite the cathedral. This, the city's sixteenth-century *Casa de Contractación* (commercial exchange) for trade with the Americas, now houses the remarkable **Archives of the Indies** (Mon–Sat 10am–1pm; free). Among the selection of documents on display are Columbus's log and a changing exhibition of ancient maps and curiosities.

The Patio de los Naranjos

All that remains today from Sevilla's great Almohad mosque – apart, of course, from the Giralda – is the **Patio de los Naranjos**, the Moorish entrance court where ritual ablutions were performed prior to worship. Today you can only enter the Patio from

WHERE LIES CHRISTOPHER COLUMBUS?

The dispute about Christopher Columbus's birthplace – claimed by both Italy and Spain – is matched by the labyrinthine controversy surrounding the whereabouts of his remains.

After his death in Valladolid in 1506, Columbus was buried in that town, but not for long. Three years later the remains were removed to Sevilla and interred at the monastery of Santa Maria de la Cuevas, across the river on La Cartuja island. Then, when Columbus's eldest son Diego passed away, his remains were buried in the same tomb. After this Columbus's widow declared that she wished to have both bodies transferred to the Carribean island of Hispaniola (the modern Haiti and the Dominican Republic), the site of Columbus's first landfall in 1492 and then – as Santo Domingo – capital of Spanish America. Following some bureaucratic resistance and an intervention by the emperor, Carlos V, in 1544 the remains of both bodies were packed into lead coffins and shipped to the island where they were placed in the cathedral. Then Columbus's grandson, Luis, was buried in the same cathedral in 1783.

Later, during repairs to this building it seems that the coffins were mislaid, then opened, and the names mixed up. It did not take the authorities long to resolve the dilemma of which was which, by having all three sets of remains placed in one coffin. Shortly after 1795, when Spain was forced to cede Santo Domingo to the French, the remains were moved to the cathedral in Havana, still Spanish territory. When Cuba was lost in 1898 the remains were transported back across the Atlantic and placed in the tomb prepared by Mélida. The lingering uncertainty lies in the accidental discovery in 1879 of another lead coffin in the cathedral in Santo Domingo bearing a silver plate inscribed with Columbus's name. This box of remains then disappeared, but numerous coffins of bones claiming to be the same have made frequent appearances at auction houses ever since.

Were the correct remains despatched from Santo Domingo to Havana in 1795? Was the discovery of 1879 a fraud? Are the remains in the tomb today really those of Christopher, Diego and Luis? We can only gaze into the inscrutable expressions of the coffin bearers and wonder. However, it is certain that one member of the Columbus family, at least, was buried in the Cathedral and has stayed here – Christopher's bookish son Hernando, who wrote a biography of his father and donated his large library to what became the cathedral's Biblioteca Colombina. His tombstone lies in the centre of the pavement towards the west door, flanked by smaller slabs portraying sailing vessels.

the Cathedral, but you can also glimpse it from c/Alemanes through the magnificent Puerta del Perdón, the mosque's original main gateway, sadly marred by Renaissance embellishments.

Of special note here is the exquisite Almohad plasterwork and the original great doors made from larchwood faced with bronze. Minute Cufic script inside the losenges proclaims that "the empire is Allah's." The beautiful pierced bronze door-knockers are also the twelfth-century originals. In the centre of the patio a **Moorish fountain** incorporates a sixth-century carved marble font, a surviving remnant of the earlier Visigothic cathedral levelled to make way for the mosque.

The Alcázar

Rulers of Sevilla have occupied the site of the **Alcázar** (Tues–Sat 10.30am–6.00pm, Sun 10am–2pm; 600ptas) from the time of the Romans. The fortified palace was probably founded in the early eighth century on the ruins of a Roman barracks, with the surrounding walls being added in the ninth. In the eleventh century it was expanded to become the great court of the Abbadid dynasty who turned the wealth gained from the production of olive oil, sugar-cane and dyes (extracted from the kermes beetle) into a palace worthy of their hubris. This regime reached a peak of sophistication and exaggerated sensuality under the cruel and ruthless al-Mu'tadid – a poet-ruler who further enlarged the Alcázar in order to house a harem of 800 women and decorated the terraces with flowers planted in the skulls of his decapitated enemies. Later, in the twelfth and thirteenth centuries under the **Almohads**, the complex was turned into a citadel, forming the heart of the town's fortifications. Its extent was enormous, stretching to the Torre del Oro on the bank of the Guadalquivir. Parts of the Almohad walls survive, but the present structure of the palace dates almost entirely from the Christian period following the fall of the city in 1248.

VISITING THE ALCÁZAR

The pressure of visitors to the **Alcázar** has resulted in the introduction of a flow-control system whereby every twenty to thirty minutes 750 people are allowed in. This seems to be working and while it has reduced the unholy scrums which used to take place in the past, you would still be advised to visit during early morning or late afternoon to savour the experience in relative calm.

Sevilla was a favoured residence of the Spanish kings for some four centuries after the Reconquest – most particularly of **Pedro the Cruel** (1350–69) who, with his mistress María de Padilla, lived in and ruled from the Alcázar. Pedro embarked upon a complete rebuilding of the palace, utilizing fragments of earlier Moorish buildings in Sevilla, Córdoba and Valencia. Pedro's works form the nucleus of the Alcázar as it is today and despite numerous restorations necessitated by fires and earth tremors it offers some of the best surviving examples of **Mudéjar architecture** – the style developed by Moors working under Christian rule. Later monarchs, however, have left all too many traces and additions. Isabel built a new wing in which to organize expeditions to the Americas and control the new territories; Carlos V married a Portuguese princess in the palace, adding huge apartments for the occasion; and under Felipe IV (c.1624) extensive renovations were carried out to the existing rooms. On a more mundane level, kitchens were installed to provide for General Franco, who stayed in the royal apartments whenever he visited Sevilla.

Entry – the Casa del Océano

The Alcázar is entered from the Plaza del Triunfo, adjacent to the cathedral. The gateway, flanked by original Almohad walls, opens on to a courtyard where Pedro (who was known as "the Just" as well as "the Cruel", depending on one's fortunes) used to give judgment; to the left is his **Sala de Justicia**. The main facade of the palace stands at the end of an inner court, the **Patio de la Montería**; on either side are galleried buildings erected by Isabel. This principal facade is pure fourteenth-century Mudéjar and, with its delicate, marble-columned windows, stalactite frieze and overhanging roof, is one of the finest things in the whole Alcázar.

It's a good idea to look round the **Casa del Océano** (or *de las Américas*), the sixteenth-century building on the right, before entering the main palace. Founded by Isabel in 1503, this gives you a standard against which to assess the Moorish forms. Here most of the rooms seem too heavy, their decoration ceasing to be an integral part of the design. The only notable exception is **the chapel** with its magnificent *artesonado* ceiling inlaid with golden stars. Within is a fine early sixteenth-century altarpiece by Alejo Fernández depicting the *Virgin of the Navigators* spreading her protective mantle over the conquistadors and their ships. Columbus (dressed in gold) is flanked by the Pinzón brothers who sailed with him on his first voyage to the New World, while

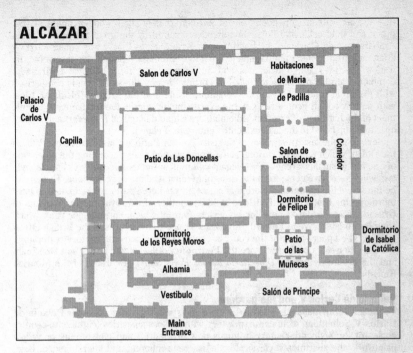

ALCÁZAR

Palacio de Carlos V

Capilla

Salon de Carlos V

Habitaciones de Maria de Padilla

Patio de Las Doncellas

Salon de Embajadores

Comedor

Dormitorio de Felipe II

Dormitorio de los Reyes Moros

Patio de las Muñecas

Dormitorio de Isabel la Católica

Alhamia

Vestibulo

Salón de Principe

Main Entrance

Carlos V (in a red cloak) shelters beneath the Virgin. In the rear to the left are portrayed the kneeling figures of the Indians to whom the dubious blessings of Christianity had been brought by the Spanish conquest. The painting synthesizes the sense of a divine mission – given to Spain by God – prevalent at the time. Beside the altarpiece stands a model of the *Santa Maria*, Columbus's first flagship.

The Palace

Entering the **main Palace** the "domestic" nature of Moorish and Mudéjar architecture is immediately striking. This involves no loss of grandeur but simply a shift in scale: the apartments are remarkably small, shaped to human needs, and take their beauty from the exuberance of the decoration and the imaginative use of space and light. There is, too, a deliberate disorientation in the layout of the rooms which makes the palace seem infinitely larger and more open than it really is. From the entrance court a narrow passage leads straight into the central courtyard, the **Patio de las Doncellas** (Patio of the Maidens), its name recalling the Christians' tribute of one hundred virgins presented annually to the Moorish kings. The court's stuccowork, *azulejos* (tiles) and doors are all of the finest Granada craftsmanship. Interestingly, it's also the one room where Renaissance restorations are successfully fused – the double columns and upper storey were added by Carlos V, whose *Plus Ultra* ("Yet still further") motto recurs in the decorations here and elsewhere.

Past the **Salon de Carlos V**, distinguished by a truly superb ceiling, are three rooms from the original fourteenth-century design built for María de Padilla (who was popularly thought to use magic in order to maintain her hold over Pedro – and perhaps over other gallants at court, too, who used to drink her bath water). These open on to the **Salon de Embajadores** (Salon of the Ambassadors), the most brilliant room of the Alcázar, with a stupendous *media naranja* (half-orange) wooden dome of red, green and gold cells, and horseshoe arcades inspired by the great palace of Medina Azahara outside Córdoba. An inscription in Arabic states that it was constructed by craftsmen from Toledo and completed in 1366. Although restored, for the worse, by Carlos V – who added balconies and an incongruous frieze of royal portraits to commemorate his marriage to Isabel of Portugal here – the salon stands comparison with the great rooms of Granada's Alhambra. Note also the **original Mudéjar tiles**, with their Moorish geometric patterns expressing artistically the fundamental Islamic tenet of the harmony of creation. Adjoining are a long dining hall (*comedor*) and a small apartment installed in the late sixteenth century for Felipe II.

Beyond is the last great room of the palace – the **Patio de las Muñecas** (Patio of the Dolls), which takes its curious name from two tiny faces decorating the inner side of one of the smaller arches. The elegant columns in the tenth-century Caliphate style are believed to have come from the ruins of Medina Azahara near Córdoba. Thought to be the site of the harem in the original palace, it was here that Pedro is reputed to have murdered his brother Don Fadrique in 1358; another of his royal guests, Abu Said of Granada, was murdered here for his jewels (one of which, an immense ruby which King Pedro later gave to Edward, the "Black Prince", now figures in the British crown jewels). The upper storey of the court is a much later, nineteenth-century restoration. On the other sides of the patio are the **bedrooms** of Isabel and of her son Don Juan, and the arbitrarily named *Dormitorio del los Reyes Moros* (Bedroom of the Moorish Kings).

Palacio de Carlos V and the gardens

To the left of the main palace loom the large and soulless apartments of the **Palacio de Carlos V**. Something of an endurance test, with endless tapestries (eighteenth-century copies of the sixteenth-century originals now in Madrid) and pink-orange or yellow paintwork, the apartments' classical style asserts a different and inferior mood. Best, then, to hurry through to the beautiful and rambling **Alcázar gardens**, the confused but enticing product of several eras, where you can take a well-earned rest from your exertions. Here are the vaulted baths in which María de Padilla was supposed to have bathed (actually an auxiliary water supply for the palace), and the tank specially built for Felipe V (1733), who whiled away two solitary years at the alcázar fishing in this pool and preparing himself for death through religious flagellation. In the gardens proper – and close to an unusual maze of myrtle bushes – lies the **pavilion of Carlos V,** the only survivor of several he built in the gardens. This one, designed by Juan Hernández, was completed in 1543 and has the the king's motto *Plus Ultra* displayed on the tiles of the steps leading to the pavilion's entrance.

The Plaza de España and María Luisa Park

Laid out in 1929 for an abortive "Fair of the Americas", the Plaza de España and adjoining María Luisa Park are among the most impressive public spaces in Spain. They are an ideal place to spend the middle part of the day, just ten minutes' walk to the east of the cathedral and centre. En route you pass a number of buildings of note: the **Hotel Alfonso XIII**, the **Palacio de San Telmo** and the **Fábrica de Tabacos**, the city's old tobacco factory and the setting for Bizet's *Carmen*.

Hotel Alfonso XIII and Palacio de San Telmo

The *Hotel Alfonso XIII*, Sevilla's grandest, is worth a look inside – no one minds as long as you aren't dressed too outrageously. Built to house the more important guests attending the 1929 exhibition, an elegant neo-Baroque facade conceals one of the city's most beautiful patios, best enjoyed over a beer (or afternoon tea) from the bar.

Slightly west of here, the **Palacio de San Telmo**, built as a marine training academy for the Indies fleet and completed in 1734, is another expression of Sevilla's full-tilt Baroque period. During the mid-nineteenth century as Sevilla's naval importance declined, it was purchased by the dukes of Montpensier a member of whose family – the Dowager Duchess Maria Luisa – in 1893 presented part of the palace's vast grounds to the city, which became the park now named after her. The palace's **main facade** overlooks Avda. de Roma and has a marvellous **Churrigueresqe entrance arch** topped – in a central niche – by San Telmo (of Saint Elmo's fire fame) patron saint of navigators. The building's interior is presently closed to the public.

Antigua fábrica de tabacos

The **Tobacco Factory**, just behind, was where Carmen – in the nineteenth-century story by Mérimée made into an opera by Bizet – worked as a cigar maker. A beautiful and sensual *gitana,* she falls in love with Don José, a corporal. He deserts his regiment to join her band of smugglers but she tires of him and transfers her affections to the toreador Escamillo, and is finally stabbed to death by an insanely jealous Don José outside the bullring where a statue of "Carmen" now stands. Afterwards legions of foreign travellers made pilgrimages to Sevilla in search of their own Carmen. The disillusion of the 1930s Irish traveller Walter Starkie is typical: he said that he had never seen "an uglier collection of women in my life", and was then hounded out of their workshops with a chorus of obscene abuse.

Now part of the university, this massive structure – 250m long by 180m wide – was built in the 1750s and still retains its position as the largest building in Spain after El Escorial. Above the main entrance – facing Avda. del Cid – perches a marble angel, a trumpet to its lips, which malicious popular legend has it would only sound when a virgin entered the factory for the first time. The entrance arch below aptly incorporates medallion busts of Columbus (discoverer of the tobacco lands) and Cortés (reputedly Europe's first smoker), in effect the factory's founding fathers.

The building was divided into a residential quarters below with the work areas on the upper – and lighter – level. The entrance leads through a vestibule into the Clock Patio off which, to the right, a short passage will bring you to the University's **cafetería,** open to all and offering a wide range of food at budget prices during term time. At its peak in the nineteenth century the factory was also the country's largest single employer, with a workforce of some 10,000 women *cigarreras* – "a class in themselves" according to Richard Ford, and forced to undergo "an ingeniously minute search on leaving their work, for they sometimes carry off the filthy weed in a manner her most Catholic majesty never dreamt of." Production of cigars, cigarettes and snuff – originally ground by 200 donkey-driven rolling mills – continued here until 1965 when its operations were moved to a new factory across the river close to the Puente del Generalíssimo.

Plaza de España

The **Plaza de España** lies beyond the Avenida del Cid – also incidentally the site of the Inquisition's *quemadero*, or burning platform, and where convicted heretics were put to death for three hundred years until the last witch was was burned here in 1781. The vast semicircular complex was designed as the centrepiece of the Spanish Americas Fair (which was somewhat scuppered by the Wall Street crash), with fountains, majestic stairways and mass of tilework – its flamboyance would seem strange in most Spanish cities but here it looks entirely natural, carrying on the great tradition of civic display. At the fair, the Plaza de España was used for the Spanish exhibit of industry and crafts, and around the crescent are *azulejo* scenes and maps of each of the provinces – an interesting record of the country at the tail-end of a moneyed era.

Locals and tourists alike come out to the plaza – slightly shabby now – to potter about in the little boats rented out on its tiny strip of canal, or to hide from the sun and crowds amid the ornamental pools and walkways of the **Parque de María Luisa**. The park is designed, like the plaza, in a mix of 1920s Art Deco and mock-Mudéjar. Scattered about, and round its edge, are more buildings from the fair, some of them amazingly opulent, built in the last months before the Wall Street crash undercut the scheme's impetus – look out, in particular, for the stylish **Guatemala building**, off the Paseo de la Palmera.

Towards the end of the park, the grandest mansions from the fair have been adapted as museums, of which, the **archeology museum** (Tues–Sun 10am–2pm; 250ptas) is the most important of its kind in Andalucía. The collection's wide remit, divided between twenty-seven rooms, spans the period from prehistory to the end of the Moorish age.

Following the prehistoric sections, Room 4 displays a collection of funerary stelae from the Iberian period, while Room 5 has a unique Phoenician bronze **statuette of Astarte-Tanit**, the virgin goddess once worshipped throughout the Mediterranean. A darkened Room 6 contains the stunning **Carambalo Treasures** discovered in the Sevilla suburb of Camas in 1958. This remarkable hoard of gold jewellery further fuelled the debate surrounding the whereabouts and existence of the ancient land of Tartessus, known to the Greeks and mentioned in the Bible as Tarshish. The legendary mineral wealth of Tartessus probably indicates a location in the area between Sevilla and the mineral-rich hills of Huelva, but despite investigations by archeologists for most of this century it has never been found.

Rooms 10 through to 24 contain the substance of the Roman collection with an interesting display of kitchen equipment in Room 12, including what appears to be a modern-looking fork apparently contradicting the theory that the implement was a medieval invention. Room 13 has a fine third-century mosaic from Écija depicting a chariot and tigers and in Room 17 there's a sensitive second-century sculpture of Venus from Itálica. There's still more statuary in Rooms 19 and 20, as well as portrait busts of the emperors Augustus and Nero and local boys Trajan and Hadrian, the latter particularly striking. Finally, Rooms 26 and 27 display post-Roman finds including early Christian tombstones and Mudéjar ceramic works among which a fifteenth-century green-glazed **baptismal font** stands out.

Opposite is the fabulous-looking **Popular Arts Museum** (Tues–Sat 10am–2pm; 250ptas), which has absorbing displays of costumes, furniture, photos, and posters describing life in eighteenth- and nineteenth-century Andalucía, along with a lively section devoted to *Semana Santa* and the April *feria*.

Barrio Santa Cruz

The **Barrio Santa Cruz** is very much in character with the city's romantic image, its streets narrow and tortuous to keep out the sun, the houses brilliantly whitewashed and festooned with flowering plants. Many of the windows are barricaded with *rejas* (iron grilles) behind which girls once kept chaste evening rendezvous with their *novios* who were forced to *comer hierro* ("eat iron") as passion mounted. Almost all of the houses have patios, often surprisingly large, and in summer these become the principal family living room. Most of the time they can be admired from the street beyond the wrought-iron screen inside the doorway, something the residents don't appear to mind. One of the most beautiful is within the Baroque **Hospicio de los Venerables Sacerdotes** (guided tours only Tues–Sun 10am–2pm & 4–8pm; 500ptas), near the centre in a plaza of the same name. Built around the patio and originally a home for infirm clerics, the hospice and church now form a gallery of outstanding artworks. These include sculptures by Montañes, Pedro and Luisa Roldán, a painting of the *Last Supper* by Roelas plus some wonderfully restored frescos by Lucás Valdés and Valdés Leal.

A walk around the Barrio Santa Cruz

The *barrio* is a great place for a stroll and you'll soon discover your own favourite nooks and crannies along the tangle of narrow streets with their beautiful patios and tiny squares. There's no set route around this fascinating area; the following **walk** highlights just a few of the *barrio*'s many features.

Starting out from Plaza Virgen de los Reyes, behind the cathedral, the **Palacio Arzobispal** (access to its patio free) conceals behind a Baroque facade a remarkable staircase made entirely of jasper. Along c/Mateos Gago **Bar Giralda**, at no. 2, incorporates part of a Moorish *hammam* or steam baths while over the road, at no. 20, is one of Sevilla's institutions, the hole-in-the-wall **bodega of Juan García Aviles** with its prized gleaming bar counter of Spanish mahogany, over a century old and one of the few remaining in the city.

When you've downed a *manzanilla*, continue east and turn right into c/Mesón del Moro, where the slightly incongruous *San Marco Pizzeria*, at no. 4, is another establishment operating inside a splendid **Moorish bathhouse**. Further up c/Mateos Gago, a left turn will bring you into c/Guzmán el Bueno where, at no. 10, the charming sisters at the **Convento de San José** will allow you to view some remarkable **Mudéjar plaster decoration** (its ornate appearance is on a par with the alcázar) in what was the salon, and is now the chapel, of this former fourteenth-century palace. This street is an especially good one for patio hunting – **no. 17** with plants, azulejos, wall-mounted bulls' heads and Roman statuary is a picture.

Retracing your steps and following the c/Meson del Moro will bring you – via c/Ximinez de Enciso – to c/Santa Teresa where, at no. 8, you'll find the **Museo de Murillo** (Tues–Sat 10am–2pm & 5–8pm; Sun 10am–2pm; free). Located in the artist's seventeenth-century home, this house-museum is furnished with contemporaneous artworks, craftsmanship and furniture, but, somewhat disappointingly, none of Murillo's original paintings.

Continuing along this street will bring you to the delightful **Plaza Santa Cruz** where, until the French burned it down in 1810, stood the church which gave the square (and the *barrio*) its name and in which Murillo was buried. Of three possible directions from here a route east would bring you to the church of Santa María La Blanca, on the street of the same name, which has, built into its south wall in c/de los Archeros, the **entrance to the original synagogue**, the only surviving architectural remnant of the Jewish quarter. Directly south from Plaza de Santa Cruz are the **Jardines de Murillo**, another peaceful oasis and a place to get your breath back in the midst of shady arbours decorated with Triana tiles. Alternatively, the Callejón del Agua will take you west back towards the town centre where, at no. 6, the **Corral del Agua** restaurant has yet another fine patio quickly followed by the sweet, plant-bedecked c/Pimienta (Pepper Street), thought to take its name from a Jewish spice merchant who once lived here.

The River and Museo de Bellas Artes

Down by the **Guadalquivir** – just below the Plaza de Toros – are more pedal-boats for idling away the afternoons, and at night a surprising density of local couples. The main riverside landmark here is the twelve-sided **Torre del Oro**, built by the Almohads in 1220 as part of the Alcázar fortifications. It was connected to another small fort across the river by a chain which had to be broken by the Castilian fleet before their conquest of the city in 1248. The tower later saw use as a repository for the gold brought back to Sevilla from the Americas – hence its name. It now houses a small, mildly interesting **naval museum** (Tues–Sun 10am–1pm; 100ptas), which exhibits charts and engravings of the port in its prime.

Hospital de la Caridad

One block east of the Torre del Oro is the **Hospital de la Caridad** (Mon–Sat 10am–1pm & 3–6pm; 200ptas) founded in 1676 by Don Miguel de Manara, who may well have been the inspiration for Byron's Don Juan. According to the testimony of one of Don Miguel's friends, "there was no folly which he did not commit, no youthful indulgence into which he did not plunge . . . (until) what occurred to him in the street of the coffin." What occurred was that Don Miguel, returning from a wild orgy, had a vision in which he was confronted by a funeral procession carrying his own corpse. He repented his past life, joined the Brotherhood of Charity (whose task was to bury the bodies of vagrants and criminals), and later set up this hospital for the relief of the dying and destitute, for which it is still used. Touchingly, whenever a patient dies here, the chapel is closed on the day of the funeral.

Between 1660–74 Don Miguel commissioned a series of eleven paintings by Murillo for the chapel, six of which remain after Marshal Soult looted five of them during the Napoleonic occupation, and which were never returned. Murillo always created pictures "made to measure" for the available light, and it's a real treat to see the pictures in the place they were originally intended to hang. Of the surviving works are a colossal *Loaves and Fishes* depicting Christ feeding the Five Thousand, and "a *San Juan de Dios* equal to Rembrandt" as Richard Ford, a fervent Murillo fan, described it. Mañara himself posed as the model for the saint. Alongside them hang two *Triumph of Death* pictures by Valdés Leal. One, portraying the fleeting nature of life, features a skeletal image of Death pointing to the message *in ictu oculi* ("in the blink of an eye") while the other depicts a decomposing bishop being eaten by worms (beneath the scales of justice labelled *Ni más, Ni menos* – "No More, No Less"). Murillo found this so powerfully repulsive that he declared that "you have to hold your nose to look at it." The mood of both works may owe a lot to the vivid memory of the plague of 1649 which killed almost half the population of the city.

Museo de Bellas Artes

To the north of c/Reyes Catolicos on the Plaza del Museo, the **Museo de Bellas Artes** (Tues–Sun 10am–2pm; 250ptas, free with EC passport), housed in recently modernized galleries in a startlingly beautiful former convent, ranks second only to the

---

MURILLO IN ALL HIS GLORY

Born in Sevilla in 1618 and orphaned ten years later, Bartolomé Estebán Murillo grew up in the home of his brother-in-law. After enrolling as a student under Juan de Castillo he came to the attention of another *sevillano*, Velázquez, who was by then established in Madrid. Murillo studied with Velázquez for three not very happy years in the capital, where he found the social scene oppressive, but was apparently much impressed by the works of the Flemish and Italian schools he saw in the royal collections there.

Once back in his native city Murillo started work in earnest, often using poor *sevillanos* from districts such as the Macarena as his models. In 1682, still at the height of his powers, he was painting an altarpiece for the Capuchin church in Cádiz when he fell from the scaffold suffering serious injury. He was brought back to Sevilla where he died in the Convent of San José near to his home in the *barrio* Santa Cruz.

Downgraded by critics in the nineteenth century for his sentimentalism – a view largely based on the genre paintings of rosy-faced urchins that had found their way across Europe – Murillo's reputation has since been restored. A greater familiarity with the powerful works that remained in Sevilla, such as those in the Caridad, substantiates Ford's proclamation: "At Sevilla Murillo is to be seen in all his glory . . . a giant on his native soil."

Prado in Madrid. Among the highlights of an outstanding collection is a wonderful early sixteenth-century sculpture in painted terracotta in Room 1, *Lamentation over the Dead Christ*, by the Andalucian **Pedro Millan**, the founding father of the Sevilla school of sculpture. A marriage of Gothic and expressive naturalism, this style was the starting point for the outstanding seventeenth-century period of religious iconography in Sevilla – a later example, in Room 2, is a magnificent *San Jeronimo* by the Italian **Pietro Torregiano,** who spent the latter years of his life in Sevilla. Ever his own man, Torregiano once broke the nose of his contemporary Michelangelo in a quarrel and eventually died at the hands of the Inquisition in Sevilla, condemned for impiety after he had smashed his own sculpture of a Virgin when the Duke of Arcos refused to pay the price asked.

Room 3 has a **retablo** of the Redemption, c.1562, with fine woodcarving by **Juan Giralte**. Originally made for the Convento de Santa Catalina in Aracena, tableaux six (the crowning with thorns) and ten (Mark writing his gospel) are especially fine. A monumental *Last Supper* by **Pachecho** covers an end wall of Room 4 – note the lack of forks – while the grisly terracotta sculpture of the severed head of *John the Baptist* by **Núñez Delgado** may not be something you want to see too soon after lunch. Dated 1591, this work is a prototype of the Baroque images later to be carried on the *pasos* during *Semana Santa*.

Room 5 is located in the monastery's former church and the newly restored **paintings on the vault and dome** by the eighteenth-century *sevillano,* Domingo Martinez, are spectacular. Here also is the nucleus of the collection: **Zurburan's** *Apotheosis of St Thomas Aquinas* as well as a clutch of **Murillos** in the apse crowned by the great *Immaculate Conception* – known as *"la colosal"* to distinguish it from two other of his works here with the same name. In an alcove nearby you'll see the same artist's *Virgin and Child.* Popularly known as **La Servilleta** because it was said to have been painted on a dinner napkin, the work is one of Murillo's finest. In the same room are also works by Roelas and Velázquez as well as **El Greco's** portrait of his son. There's more sculpture in Rooms 9 and 10, this time by **Montañes**, the sixteenth-century "Andalucian Lysippus", whose *Saint Dominic in Penitence* and *San Bruno* show mastery of technique. Here also is another outstanding canvas by **Zurbarán** of San Hugo visiting the Carthusian monks at supper. The collection ends with a rather lacklustre selection of works from the Romantic and Modern eras, not a terribly inspiring end to an otherwise remarkable museum.

The Expo 92 site

The staging of **Expo 92** secured a year of publicity and prosperity for Sevilla during which the sybaritic *sevillanos* started to believe their own hype, billing it as the "event of the century". However, after the fuss died down, the city was left with financial scandals, endless recriminations, and a dilapidated site which no one seems sure what to do with. Latest thinking suggests that the exhibition ground may be transformed into a scientific Disneyland, but don't count on it.

Today, all that remains of the mammoth Expo 92 **site** at La Isla de la Cartuja, northwest of the centre across the river (Tues–Thurs 7pm–2am; Fri–Sun 11.30am–4am; 2000ptas) is a hotchpotch of Spanish pavilions plus gimmicks such as the **monorail** – hardly worth the stiff entrance fee. If you're determined to take a look, however, get a promenade ticket (500ptas) which, although it will not allow you to enter the pavilions, gives you access to the lakeside bars and weekend entertainments.

Inside this complex lies the **Santa Maria de las Cuevas** monastery in which Columbus lodged on his visits to Sevilla, and where for 37 years he was buried. The core of the fifteenth-century Carthusian monastery suffered eighteenth-century Baroque additions and was made the headquarters of the notorious Marshal Soult's garrison during the Napoleonic occupation of 1810–12. A final indignity was visited on

---

BOAT TRIPS TO THE COTO DOÑANA NATIONAL PARK

A new boat service down the Guadalquivir from Sevilla allows visitors to make restricted visits to the remarkable wildlife reserve of the **Coto Doñana National Park** (see p.221). You could either take the morning boat from Sevilla to the park and return by bus in the evening, or take the bus in the morning, returning by boat. The morning boat leaves the Torre del Oro at 9am, and arrives at Sanlúcar de Barrameda – a wonderful river trip in itself – at 1pm. Then it follows a cruise around the southerly waterways of the Coto Doñana, with a couple of stops inside the park for guided tours with a chance to see some wildlife. The bus drops you back in Sevilla at 9.30pm. Doing it the other way round gets you back to Sevilla at 9.00pm.

The trip costs 2900ptas for adults and 1500ptas for children and you can get tickets from a small office next to the Torre del Oro (*Cruceros Turisticos*; ☎211396). Access to the National Park is sometimes limited, and it would be wise to check with the office above before making any plans.

---

the place when, after Disentailment, it was purchased by a Liverpudlian, Charles Pickman, and turned into a pottery. The whole thing – including the towering brick kilns which can be glimpsed from outside the site, and are now regarded as industrial history – was restored for *Expo 92* at enormous cost.

Barrio Triana

Over the river is the **Triana** *barrio*, scruffy, lively and not at all touristy. Generally believed to have taken its name from the Roman emperor Trajan who was born at nearby Italica, this was once the heart of the city's gypsy community and, more specifically, home of the great *flamenco* dynasties of Sevilla. Most of these were kicked out by developers earlier this century and are now scattered throughout the city. The gypsies lived in extended families in tiny, immaculate communal houses called *corrales* around courtyards glutted with flowers; today only a handful remain intact. Triana is still, however, the starting point for the annual pilgrimage to El Rocío (at the end of May), when a myriad of painted wagons leave town, drawn by elephantine oxen. And one of the great moments of *Semana Santa* occurs here in the early hours of Good Friday when the candlelit *paso* of the Virgin *Esperanza de Triana* is carried back over the Puente de Triana (Isabel II) to be given a rapturous welcome home by the whole *barrio* assembled on the other side. Triana has long been a centre of **glazed-tile production**, and you'll see plenty of examples of this fine ceramic work as you take a gentle stroll around the streets.

A walk around the Barrio Triana

There are any number of ways to explore and enjoy Triana, taking time to stop off in some of the scores of wonderful *tapas* bars on the way (for more on which see "Eating, drinking and nightlife"). This particular **walk** starts out from the Plaza de Cuba, reached by crossing the Puente de San Telmo to the river's western bank. From here head down c/Genova to the Plaza de la Virgen de la Milagrosa. In the centre of this square is a modern statue to **Roderigo de Triana**, a sailor on Columbus's initial voyage who was the first European to set eyes on the New World. In spite of his name, however, more recent research suggests that he hailed not from Triana, but Lepe, in the neighbouring province of Huelva. Determined not to be put off by this academic meddling with their history, the *barrio* erected the sculpture anyway with the laconic "Tierra" ("land") inscribed on its base, the word an unidentified Rodrigo is presumably yelling as he clings to the mast.

Take a right along c/Troya to c/Betis which fronts the river and preserves its Roman name. This was the **old docklands area** of Triana, before it was tarted up in the earlier part of this century and planted with trees. To the right, in c/Gonzalo Segovia, was the location of the gunpowder factory which supplied the vessels of the Indies fleet. An enormous explosion here in 1579 not only destroyed half of Triana but also blew the stained-glass windows out of the cathedral across the river.

In Roman times, clay was collected from this riverbank to make the amphorae used to transport cereals, wine, oil and pickled fish to the imperial capital; much of the broken pottery piled up in ancient Rome's towering rubbish dump at Monte Testaccio has now been identified as coming from Triana. The same clay also made the bricks for the Giralda and many more of the city's houses and monuments. Behind the *Río Bravo* restaurant, which has great terrace views, there are **pedalos** and rowing boats for rent should you want to give the river a closer look.

Further along, a left turn at c/Duarte will bring you to Triana's main church of **Santa Ana**, the oldest parish church in Sevilla. Built for Alfonso X in the thirteenth century, it includes many later additions – note, for example, the Mudéjar tower with blocked lobed windows topped by a Renaissance belfry. Should you be able to gain entry – as ever, early evening is your best bet – look out for the fine sixteenth-century **retablo** of the *Virgen de la Rosa* by Alejo Fernández. The church's baptismal font – **Pila de los Gitanos** – is the source, according to tradition, where the gifts of *flamenco* singing and dancing are bestowed on the newborn infants of the *barrio*. Take c/Pureza (at the church's eastern end) north to no. 53, the **Capilla de los Marineros**, an eight-eenth-century chapel now famous as the seat of the Cofradía de Jesus de las Tres Caidas y Nuestra Señora de la Esperanza (Brotherhood of Jesus of the Three Falls and Our Lady of Hope), one of the major brotherhoods who march in the *Semana Santa* processions (see p.196). The chapel's Baroque *retablo* incorporates the figure of the Virgin known as the **Esperanza de Triana** to which the *barrio* is devoted and which is carried triumphantly through the streets of the city by the brotherhood during the same Easter processions.

Continue north, turning left along calles Rocío and Flota – streets which still have a few of the typical Triana dwellings – and then right crossing c/San Jacinto into c/Alfarería, where there are more *corrales*. A left turn a short way along here into c/Antillano Campos brings you to *Bar Anselma* (fronting c/Pages), a great old tiled place where you might be lucky enough to catch an impromptu *flamenco*. Still heading north along c/Alfarería, take a right along c/Procurador to the sixteenth-century church of **Nuestra Señora de la "O"** at c/Castilla 30, with its splendid tiled tower. The interior, as well as holding more ceramics, contains a seventeenth-century sculpture of **Jesús Nazareno** by Pedro Roldán.

Heading south, with the river now on your left, and just before a twist in the street, a small alley bears the name Callejón de la Inquisición. This was the site of the former Castilla de Triana (or Triana Castle), the original **residence of the Inquisition** until it was forced out by a flood in 1626 or, as Ford colourfully puts it, until "the Guadalquivir, which blushed at the fires and curdled with the bloodshed, almost swept it away as if indignant at the crimes committed on its bank." Almost opposite, *Cervecería Ruiz* is a welcoming tiled and oak-beamed bar serving good *tapas*, with a restaurant in the back. Continuing around the corner you'll come to the spectacular tiled facade of **Ceramica Santa Ana** at Plaza Callao 12. The city's oldest working ceramics factory, over a century old, this is a good place to buy hand-painted Triana pots and tiles, many depict-ing traditional, geometric Moorish designs. On the right, continuing south, is the old Triana market, after which you arrive in Plaza Altozano where there's a monument to one of Triana's great *toreros*, Juan Belmonte, as well as – nestling against the Puente de Triana which will take you back to the centre – the celebrated *Kiosko de los Flores Freiduría*, where you'll get some of the best fried fish in town.

The Centro

The **Centro**, or central zone, lies north of the cathedral at the geographical heart of the city. It contains the main shopping areas, including **Calle Sierpes**, the city's most famous and fashionable street. Here, too, you'll find many of Sevilla's finest churches, displaying a fascinating variety of architectural styles. Several are converted mosques with belfries built over their minarets, others range through Mudéjar and Gothic (sometimes in combination), Renaissance and Baroque. Most are kept locked except early in the morning, or in the evenings from about 7pm until 10pm – a promising time for a church crawl, especially as they're regularly interspersed with bars.

Casa de Pilatos

Of Sevilla's numerous mansions, by far the finest is the so-called **Casa de Pilatos** (daily 9am–6.00pm; 500ptas) in the Plaza de Pilatos, on the northwestern edge of Santa Cruz. Built by the Marqués de Tarifa of the Ribera family on his return from a pilgrimage to Jerusalem in 1519, the house was popularly – and erroneously – thought to have been in imitation of the house of Pontius Pilate, supposedly seen by the Duke on his travels. In fact it's an interesting and harmonious mixture of Mudéjar, Gothic and Renaissance styles, featuring brilliant *azulejos*, a tremendous sixteenth-century stairway and the best domestic patios in the city. After the Civil War the Dukes of Medinaceli returned to live here and inaugurated a programme of restoration which has gradually brought it back to its original splendour.

Entering by the Apeadero, where the old carriages were boarded, and which for most of the year has a riot of magenta bougainvillea cascading over its arcade, brings you to a gateway leading into the wonderful **Patio Principal**. Here, Muslim elements such as the irregular arches, plasterwork and glazed tiles combine with Gothic tracery on the upper balustrades and an Italian Renaissance fountain and columns below. The imposing statues in each corner of the patio are classical originals, of which the **Athene** (bearing a spear) is attributed to the fifth-century BC school of the Greek master, Phidias; the others are Roman. Antique Italian busts of Roman emperors and men of letters such as Augustus and Cicero occupy niches in the arcades.

The Salón Pretorio is notable for its coffered ceiling, incorporating the Ribera family's coat of arms. The Roman sculptures – collected in Italy by the sixteenth-century Duke of Alcalá – in the nearby Zaquizamí corridor are extremely fine, especially the **slumbering Venus** and a marble relief fragment, depicting weapons, above. Passing the Jardín Chico (Small Garden), the Chapel of the Flagellation (its central column is supposed to represent the one at which Christ was scourged) and Pilate's "study", you reach the **Jardín Grande**, a verdant oasis with palms, pavilions and a bower, not to mention its wonderful abundance of orange trees. A tradition associated with this garden relates that the first Duke of Alcalá obtained from Pope Pius V the ashes of the Emperor Trajan, which were then displayed in a vase in the library. Later, a servant is supposed to have dumped them in the garden thinking the urn to be full of dust. The legend grew that an orange tree sprouted up wherever the ashes had fallen.

The upper floors – reached via the fine tiled staircase with a gilded, semi-circular dome – feature various frescoes, artworks and *objets d'art* collected by the family. Oustanding here is the **Salón de Pachecho** with a ceiling depicting the *Apotheosis of Hercules* painted in 1603 by the Sevillan artist after whom the room is named. A sixteenth-century oak bench carved in the Plateresque style is also worth a look. As you leave the house, note a rather curious bust of **Julius Caesar** at the entrance to the toilets. It's a fine portrait and, given the wealth of artefacts the family have hauled back from classical parts, is probably a two-thousand year old original deserving a more seemly location.

Churches and convents in the Centro

Leaving the Casa de Pilatos, a circuit of the churches in the area will take you first via c/Caballerizas to **San Ildefonso**, a fourteenth-century church later rebuilt in the Classical style. Inside, behind the altar on the north aisle there's a **fresco of the Virgin** dating from the original building. The church also has some seventeenth-century wood sculptures by Roldán and a bas-relief, *The Trinity*, by Montañes dated 1609.

Not far away, and still heading in a more or less westerly direction, c/Boteros will bring you to **Plaza Alfalfa**, a good place for *tapas* bars. Just north of here on Plaza del Buen Suceso lies the **convent** of the same name. Inside, there's a marvellous sculpture of **Saint Anne with the Virgin and Child** by Montañes. North again, c/Velilla leads to the Gothic **San Pedro** with a Mudéjar tower modelled on the Giralda, and where a marble tablet records Velázquez's baptism. A stroll west along c/Imagen passes the Renaissance chapel of the **Anunciación** on c/Larana leading to c/Cuna on the left where, at no. 8, stands the eighteenth-century **Palacio Lebrija** (Mon–Fri 5–7pm; free) which has some fine Roman mosaics from Italica built into its three patios. A route directly north from here brings you to the **Alameda de Hercules**, once a swamp and converted in the sixteenth century into a promenade. The southern end has two pillars taken from a Roman temple to Hercules, which give the promenade its name. Once fashionable, this area has now gone to seed and has become the city's red-light district.

West of the Alameda, on Plaza San Lorenzo lies the church of San Lorenzo and, next to it, the modern church of **Jesús del Gran Poder**. In the latter's **retablo** is displayed the much venerated figure of *Christ Bearing his Cross* by Juan de Mesa, carved in 1620. This image is borne in procession in the small hours of Good Friday morning. Continuing north along c/Santa Clara, make for the convent of the same name at no. 40. The convent's charming patio leads to the **Torre de Don Fadrique** (Mon–Fri 10am–5pm) a medieval tower from the thirteenth century. Originally a defensive bastion protecting the palace of Don Fadrique, eldest son of Alfonso X, it is Romanesque-Gothic in style. As you climb to the top, note the slits in the walls through which arrows could be fired. The **view** from the top of the tower is not to be missed. On your way out, should the convent's church be open, try to catch the splendid **retablo** by Montañes.

Plaza de San Francisco and Calle Sierpes

Due to its Muslim origins – whose vernacular architecture was primarily designed to keep out the sun – Sevilla had, until relatively recent times, no great squares on the European model. Most of the plazas it does possess are the result of palaces and convents being torn down to make way for them – some, such as the depressing Plaza del Duque, site of the *palacio* of the Guzman family, as recently as the 1960s.

In the shadow of the Giralda, the **Plaza de San Francisco**, slightly north of the cathedral, takes its name from the great monastery that once covered much of this and the Plaza Nueva to the west. During the *Semana Santa* processions, the whole square – filled wall-to-wall with specially constructed grandstands – is *the* prime site where the city's great and good gather to see and be seen. On the plaza's eastern flank, elegant, balconied nineteenth-century houses face the *Ayuntamiento*, constructed in the sixteenth century and noted for its fine and richly ornamented Plateresque facade by Diego de Riaño. Interior features include a vaulted vestibule in the Gothic style and a richly decorated *sala capitular*.

To the north of the Plaza de San Francisco you'll find the true heart of Sevilla, **Calle Sierpes,** where, according to Cervantes – who spent some involuntary time here serving time for his tax debts – "all the social classes of the city come together." This narrow pedestrianized street, lined with antique stores, fan shops, *tapas* bars, private clubs and smart *pastelerías* is a wonderful place to stroll. It's particularly dramatic –

though quite uncharacteristic – during *Semana Santa,* when the brotherhood of El Silencio passes through in total silence in the early hours of Good Friday, watched by an equally hushed crowd lining the route. Features to look out for include Sevilla's most famous *pastelería, La Campana,* at no. 1, while further along at no. 65 a wall plaque indicates the site of the Carcel Real, or royal prison, where Cervantes did time. A short way down on the left, in c/Jovellanos lies the small **Capillata de San José,** one of the best examples of full-blown Baroque in the city with, inside, a beautiful gilded retablo. Just behind here in the parallel c/Tetuan, make a detour to take a look at a wonderful old tiled "billboard" advertising a 1924 Studebaker car. It's opposite the *C&A* deparment store.

Nearby, and to the east of c/Sierpes, the Plaza del Salvador contains the collegiate church of **San Salvador,** built on the site of a ninth-century – and the city's first – Friday mosque. Most of what you see today dates from the seventeenth century, with remnants of the mosque preserved in its tower, formerly the minaret, and its patio, originally the ablutions courtyard. Inside, there's a magnificent Churrigueresque **retablo** as well as a number of sculptures, among them the *Jesús del Pasión* by Montañes.

Barrio Macarena

"The **Macarena,** now as it always was, is the abode of ragged poverty, which never could or can for a certainly reckon on one or any meal a day." Things have changed considerably for the better since Ford was here in the middle of the last century, and since Murillo used the *barrio's* beggars and urchins as models for his paintings. Northwest of the *centro* and enclosed by the best surviving stretch of the city's ancient walls, Macarena's very unfashionability, along with its solid working-class traditions, have helped prevent its wholesale dismemberment at the hands of speculators and builders. The result today is an area full of character, with many cobbled streets and its own local dialect, and not a few jewels to show off in the way of **churches** and **convents** of which it is extremely proud. The Macarena's pride was further enhanced when it was decided that the *barrio* would become the home of the newly autonomous **Andalucian Parliament** in the converted Renaissance hospital of the Cinco Llagas.

A walk around the Barrio Macarena

A good place to start a **tour of the barrio** would be at **Plaza Terceros,** slightly to the northwest of the Casa de Pilatos. Here you'll find the fourteenth-century Mudéjar church of **Santa Catalina** with a tower modelled on the Giralda and topped off with Renaissance embellishments. The interior (access is difficult but try between 6.30–7.30pm) has some interesting Mudéjar features including an elegant panelled ceiling. Within spitting distance of the church (on the corner of c/Gerona) lies another of Sevilla's great institutions, the bar **El Rinconcillo,** founded in 1670 and believed to be the oldest bar in the city, it's just the place for a *fino* and a *tapa.*

Follow c/Sol out of the Plaza Terceros to Plaza San Román where another four-teenth-century Gothic-Mudéjar church, **San Román,** has a fine coffered ceiling. Taking c/Enladrillada along the north side of the church will bring you to the fifteenth century, **Convento de Santa Paula** (Mon–Sat 9.30am–1pm & 4.30–6.30pm; donations welcome), renowned for its beautiful belfry and church. The church is entered through an imposing fifteenth-century **Gothic doorway** built with Mudéjar brickwork and decorated with Renaissance azulejos by Pedro Millán, with ceramic decoration by Niculoso Pisano. Inside there's a sumptuously gilded *San Juan Evangelista* **retablo** by Alonso Cano with a magnificent central figure of **Saint John** by Montañes dated 1637.

The convent **museum,** crammed with treasures, is entered through a small patio to the left of the entrance to the church. Guided tours (in Spanish) are led by one of the covent's forty-eight nuns, given a special dispensation to break the order's vow of silence. The first room has a painting of *San Jerónimo* by Ribera, and, almost as beautiful, a real view out onto a seventeenth-century patio cloister. In Room 2 there's a fascinating **maquette** made by Torregiano before starting on his full-size masterpiece of *San Jerónimo Penitente,* now in the Museo de Bellas Artes. Room 3 holds two outstanding painted **sculptures by Pedro de Mena**, a *Virgin* and an *Ecce Homo*. The unfortunate – and alarming – damage to both works were caused by unruly schoolchildren who pulled off Christ's fingers and knocked both of these works to the floor. The hard-working sisters are famous for the *dulces* and *mermaladas* (including a tomato jam) made in the convent's kitchen, and which you can buy from their small shop. Facing the convent's entrance a wall plaque marks a house described in *La Española Inglesa* by Cervantes.

From Santa Paula, head north along Pasaje Mallol to **San Julian**, yet another fourteenth-century church, with a Gothic-Mudéjar portal. Calle Madre Dolores Marquez will then take you the short distance to the **Puerto de Córdoba** (the Córdoba Gate) with its horseshoe arch and the best surviving section of the **city wall**. The Almoravids constructed the wall in the early twelfth century, possibly on Roman foundations, and it was further strengthened by the later Almohads as wars against the Christians intensified. This stretch of the fortification – which once spanned twelve gates and 166 towers – owes its survival to the poverty and unfashionability of the *barrio* during the nineteenth century when, elsewhere in the city, it was pulled down to allow expansion.

Follow the wall west until you reach the Puerta de la Macarena, the only one of the city's gates to retain its pre-Christian name. Reconstructed in the eighteenth century, just beyond it stands the **Macarena Basilica** (daily 9am–1pm & 4.30–9pm; 300ptas) which, despite an apparently Baroque facade, dates from the 1940s. The basilica's importance, however, derives from the revered image of the *Virgen de la Esperanza Macarena* it was constructed to house. Inside the church, to the left, is the *paso* – made of solid silver – used to carry the image around the city during the *Semana Santa* processions. To the right is a second *paso* (the brotherhoods normally carry them in pairs), *Jesús de la Sentencia*, depicting Pilate washing his hands with a fine, but now cloaked, **Christ**, by the seventeenth-century sculptor, Felipe Morales. The retablo of the main altar is dominated by the seventeenth-century image of **La Macarena**, as she is popularly called by a city which is fanatically devoted to her. Depicted in the trauma of the Passion when her son has been condemned, the work is attributed to La Roldana – largely based on the *sevillano* sentiment that only a woman could have portrayed the suffering of a mother with such intensity. La Macarena's elaborate costume is often decorated with five diamond and emerald brooches bestowed on her by Joselito el Gallo, a famous *gitano torero* of the early part of the century, and on which he spent a considerable fortune. She didn't show him many favours though; he died in the ring in 1920. Despite this mishap, the Virgin is still regarded as the patron of the profession and all *matadores* offer prayers to her before stepping out to do business in the Maestranza. The basilica's **treasury** features a rather gaudy display of the Virgin's other jewels and regalia.

Over the ring road and beyond a small garden lies the sixteenth-century **Hospital de las Cinco Llagas** (aptly, of the five wounds of Christ), one of the first true hospitals of its time and the largest in Europe. Sited outside the walls because hospitals then were places of pestilence and contagion, the restored building is now the seat of **Andalucía's autonomous government**. (Many *sevillano* wags drily comment that nothing's changed.) The enormous edifice, once capable of holding a thousand beds, is noted for a fine Mannerist **facade** with a Baroque central doorway of white marble. The interior is expected to be open to the public in the near future, in which case you will be able to view the hospital's former church, now the debating chamber.

Crossing back to the Puerta de la Macarena, follow c/San Luis to the church of **San Gil** just behind the Macarena Basilica. Badly damaged in the Civil War, the church nevertheless still has a Mudéjar tower, and inside, a timber Mudéjar ceiling. Continuing south along the same street you'll come to the Gothic-Mudéjar church of **Santa Marina**, set back from the road in a *plazuela*. Founded in the thirteenth century, the oldest feature here must be its **doorway** dating from circa 1300 which has Gothic archivolts, or arch mouldings, with Mudéjar star decoration on the outer band. Another church badly damaged in the Civil War, Santa Maria was in ruin for decades, only spruced up for *Expo 92* when the interior was entirely restored.

On the same street, on the right, lies the sad, weed-festooned **San Luis**, a glorious eighteenth-century church waiting for a similar miracle to preserve it from the demolition hammer. That this riot of a **Churrigueresque facade**, topped by glazed-tile domes, could be dealt a death sentence by the same city council that restored the previous church beggars belief. But that is what they did, declaring in 1991 that it was beyond repair and would be abandoned. This caused an outcry from conservationists and while the arguments continue the church's fate still hangs in the balance. San Luis is still **floodlit at night**, a spectacular sight.

Further along you come to the fourteenth-century **San Marcos** in the plaza of the same name. Another fine Macarena church built on the site of an earlier mosque, it has a Mudéjar tower – note the Giralda-style *sebka* brickwork – and a superb **Gothic-Mudéjar entrance**. Although gutted by fire during the Civil War and since restored, its interior uniquely preserves the original Mudéjar **horseshoe arches** dividing nave and aisles. At the head of the north aisle there's a seventeeth-century **sculpture** in painted wood of *San Marcos*, by Juan de Mesa. Cervantes used to climb San Marcos's tower to view the plant-filled and peaceful patio of the convent of **Santa Isabel** just behind the church. You can see why.

Cemetery of San Fernando

One place not on the tourist trail but definitely worth a visit is the **cemetery of San Fernando** to the north of the city, beyond La Macarena. A #10 bus from Plaza Encarnación (ask for Cementerio San Fernando) will drop you outside the gates. Of the cemetery's many fascinating eighteenth- and nineteenth-century monuments, note especially the life-size bronze sculpture over the **tomb of Joselito** the famous *sevillano* bullfighter, killed in the ring in 1920, and whose jewels the Virgin of Macarena still wears.

Outside the city: Roman Italica

The Roman ruins and remarkable mosaics of **ITALICA** (Tues–Sat 9am–5.30pm, Sun 10am–4pm; 250ptas) lie some 9km to the north of Sevilla, just outside the village of **Santiponce**. They're easily reached by bus; departures, about every half-hour, are from the c/Reyes Catolicos end of c/Marqués de Paradas and take about twenty minutes.

As you survey the dusty, featureless landscape of the site today it's hard to believe that this was once one of the major cities of the Roman world. Italica was the birthplace of three emperors (Trajan, Hadrian and perhaps Theodosius) and one of the earliest Roman settlements in Spain. Founded in 206 BC by Scipio Africanus after his decisive victory over the Carthaginians at nearby Alcalá del Río, it became a settlement for many of his veterans, who called the place "Italica" to remind them of home. The city rose to considerable military importance in the second and third centuries AD, when it was richly endowed during the reign of Hadrian (117–138). Grand buildings dripped with fine marble brought from places as far away as Turkey and Egypt, as well as Italy and Greece, and the population swelled to half a million. Italica declined as an urban centre only under the Visigoths, who preferred Sevilla, then known as Hispalis. Eventually the city was deserted by the Moors after the river changed its course, disrupting the surrounding terrain.

In the Middle Ages the ruins were used as a source of stone for Sevilla, and from the eighteenth century onwards, lack of any regulation allowed enthusiastic amateurs to indulge their treasure-hunting whims and carry away or sell whatever they found. The Duke of Wellington spent some time excavating here during the Peninsular Wars and later the Countess of Lebrija conducted her own "digs" to fill her palace in Sevilla with mosaics and artefacts. Somehow, however, the shell of its enormous **amphitheatre** – the third largest in the Roman world – has survived. It's crumbling perilously, but you can clearly detect the rows of seats for an audence of 25,000, the corridors and the dens for wild beasts.

Beyond, within a rambling and unkempt grid of **streets** and **villas**, about twenty **mosaics** have been uncovered in what was originally the northern, richer, sector of the city. The mosaics are presently undergoing a programme of restoration which means, frustratingly, that some may be out of view. If you're in luck, though, you'll be able to see the outstanding **Neptune mosaic** in the house of the same name, as well as the colourful **bird mosaic** in the Casa de Los Pájaros depicting thirty-three different species. Towards the baths, in the Casa del Planetario, there's a fascinating representation of the **Roman planetary divinities** who, in the Roman calendar, gave their names to the days of the week. Finally, the Hadrianic **baths** on the site's western edge are divided into those for males to the centre and right, with the women's baths to the left.

Italica today is at the leading edge of archeological technology as advanced X-ray techniques, ground-penetrating radar and infra-red aerial photography – all linked to computers – are being used to gauge the scope of the subterranean remains. So far a large stretch of fourth-century wall has been identified along with what is believed to have been a great religious complex constructed by Hadrian and dedicated to the worship of his adoptive father Trajan.

There's also a well-preserved **Roman theatre** and **baths** in the village of Santiponce itself – beneath which lies another sizeable chunk of the unexcavated town – signposted from the main road. The **restaurant** opposite the site entrance does good *platos combinados* should you want to eat before or after your visit.

Eating

Sevilla is a tremendously atmospheric place to be in the evening, packed with lively and enjoyable bars and clubs. That Sevilla has never been particularly noted for its **restaurants** may have a lot to do with a strong *tapas* tradition (see "Bars and tapas" below). Great though this is, even the most enthusiastic *sevillanos* eventually tire of "plate-pecking" to seek out a place to sit down for a more conventional meal.

Barrio Santa Cruz and Cathedral area

If you want to **eat** well without breaking the bank you'll generally have to steer clear of the restaurants concentrated around the major sights and in the **Barrio Santa Cruz**. However, as you're probably going to be spending quite a bit of your time here it's worth listing some of the area's more reasonable options. Calle Menéndez Pelayo has quite a few possibilities, as does nearby c/Santa María la Blanca, lined with more bars and cafés.

La Albahaca, Plaza Santa Cruz 9. A charming traditional restaurant with outdoor tables, housed in a converted mansion; fairly expensive, but it has a *menú* for 3,500ptas. Closed Sun.

Alcazabar, c/Mateos Gago 6. Busy no-nonsense place serving *platos combinados*.

Hotel Alfonso XIII, c/San Fernando 2. Sumptuous place near the tobacco factory, offering a lunch menu for 4,500ptas including wine.

Bar-Pizzeria El Artesano, Mateos Gago 11. Good-value and lively; popular with young locals.

Buffet Libre, c/Mateos Gago, about 100m into the *barrio*. All you can eat seafood and *paella*. Extremely reasonably priced – its profits can only come from the drink it sells.

Casa Cobo, c/Menéndez Pelayo 5. Above the Murillo Gardens at the eastern end of the *barrio*, this place serves good *platos combinados* to a mainly local clientele.

Corral del Agua, Callejon del Agua 6. Great restaurant (owned by the same people who run the *Albahaca*), where you can eat in a superb plant-filled patio. Pricey, but well worth it. Closed Sun.

Doña Francisquita, c/Alvarez Quintero 58. Good pizzas near the cathedral.

Las Vegas, c/Alemanes 7. Upmarket restaurant flanking the cathedral.

Bodegón Pez Espada, c/Hernando Colón 8, near the cathedral. Bustling place which is the outstanding bargain in this area; excellent for cheap fried seafood.

Café Sevilla at c/Miguel de Mañara 9. A lunchtime venue which serves *raciones* and salads at outdoor tables in a pedestrianized street behind the Turismo.

The River and Triana

Around c/Garcia Vinuesa to the west of the cathedral there's an abundance of reason-able *boccadillo* bars and delis for picnic food. Across the river, **Triana** offers some excellent possibilities. Near the Puente San Telmo, a number of restaurants along c/Salado cater for workers from the Los Remedios business quarter, and along c/Betis close to the water's edge are a number of restaurants with terraces looking out over the city.

Casablanca, c/Zaragoza 50, east of the Maestranza bullring. Luxurious restaurant noted for its fish and, unsurprisingly given the location, its *rabo de toro*.

Bar-Pizzeria Don Camillo e Peppone, c/Salado 11. Excellent Italian pizzas, made by Italians.

La Mandragora, c/Albuera 11. One of Sevilla's two exclusively vegetarian restaurants, just to the north of the Maestranza bullring.

Ox's Restaurante, c/Betis 61. Renowned for its pricey Basque fish dishes.

Bodega La Primera del Puente, c/Betis 66. Terrace restaurant with great views over the city.

Rio Grande, c/Betis 70. One of the best places in town for a splurge. The lunchtime *menú* costs 3000ptas and – whether you're seated behind panoramic windows or on the terrace – the tremen-dous view over the river to the Torre del Oro and Giralda beyond, illuminated at night, more than compensates for the rather ordinary food.

Bodegon Torre del Oro, c/Santander 15. A decent 1500ptas *menú*.

Café-Bar Veracruz, opposite the Torre del Oro near the river. Does a very good 1000ptas *menú* including wine.

Centro and La Macarena

This area is seedy, especially in its southern reaches, but you'll find low-priced *comidas* in and around streets such as c/San Eloy which runs into Plaza Duque de la Victoria.

Alboronia, c/Alhondiga 51. Pleasant *barrio* restaurant east of the church of San Pedro, with an excellent value 850ptas *menú*.

Ciudad Dong Hai, c/Aponte 4. Budget Chinese *menú*.

Restaurante Los Gallegos, c/Capataz Franco. Friendly, buzzing place tucked away in a tiny alley-way off c/Martín Villa, and well worth the trouble to find. *Sevillanos* wait in line to eat here.

Jalea Real, c/Sor Angela de la Cruz 37. Excellent vegetarian restaurant run by a friendly and enthusiastic *sevillana*.

Misericordia at c/Pérez Galdos 20. Good restaurant in an eighteenth-century mansion close to Plaza Alfalfa, serving many traditional dishes at a slightly higher cost than many in the city.

Mesón del Rociero, round the side of *El Corte Inglés* department store in the Plaza del Duque. There's a reasonably inexpensive *menú* here; it's a small place, that fills quickly, notably with Latin American researchers from the Archivo de las Indias.

Mesón San Andrés Plaza San Andrés. Andalucian specialities served at a terrace, in this attractive square south of the Alameda de Hercules.

Bodeguita San Eloy, c/San Eloy. Locally famed for its *pringá bocadillos* – tasty, if best unspecified, grilled meats.

Rincón San Eloy, c/San Eloy 24. Fairly ordinary food, but a colourful decor replete with *corrida* posters.

Bars and tapas

As the city which claims to have invented *tapas*, Sevilla knocks spots off the competition. There is simply nowhere else in Andalucía – or even Spain – with the sheer variety of places to indulge this culinary art. **Good tapas bars** are scattered all over town – a high concentration of them with barrelled sherries from nearby Jerez and Sanlúcar, the perfect accompaniment to the various plates. Many locals drink the cold, dry *fino* with their *tapas*, especially shrimp; a *tinto de verano* is the local version of *sangría* – wine with lemonade, enjoyed in summer. Finally, don't think that because the servings are small they are always low-priced. Some seafood *tapas* can be pretty pricey, as can the cured *jamon*, and the plates have a tendency to mount up . . . to avert a nasty shock confirm prices before ordering.

Santa Cruz and the Cathedral area

One of the liveliest places in **Santa Cruz** is *La Gitanilla* in c/Ximénez de Enciso (cheap drinks, expensive *tapas*), but perhaps the best *tapas* bar in the city, with just about every imaginable snack, and pavement tables, is *Bar Modesto*, c/Cano y Cueto 5, up at the north corner of the quarter by Avda. Menéndez Pelayo – ask for it by name, it's well known.

Close by at c/Doncellas 8, is another fine old hole-in-the-wall place, *Bar Lucas*. Off the Plaza Santa Cruz, c/Santa Teresa has a couple of bars worth searching out. *Las Teresas* is a "ham gallery" with cured hams lining the beautiful, tiled walls – enticing and pricey – and serving good, cold beer. It's also a nice place to relax over breakfast the morning after. *Bar Giralda*, c/Mateos Gago 1, has a wide selection of *tapas*, but even better, especially if you're on a tight budget, is *Bodega Santa Cruz* nearby at c/Rodrigo Caro 1, where portions are generous. Closer to the cathedral on c/Placentines, *Bar Placentines* has a good view of the cathedral from its rooftop bar, and a couple of streets away on c/Alvarez Quintero *Bar Las Gadas* does superb *riñones al jerez* (veal kidneys with sherry).

Moving west, *La Moneda* is a lively student bar off Avda. de la Constitución, while off that street at c/García de Vinuesa 11, *Casa Morales* is an ancient bar serving barrelled

---

SEVILLA'S TOP TEN TAPAS

The origin of the *tapa* (literally "cover" or "lid") is generally believed to have originated with the bartender's generous custom of placing a slice of ham or cheese over the top of a glass of *fino* before serving it to a customer. Many bars in remoter areas still continue this tradition, but most city establishments now charge for the much more elaborate *tapas* provided. Below is a selection of some of the outstanding taste-treats on offer:

Caracoles – snails.

Chanquetes – tiny fish similar to whitebait; dunked in flour, deep fried and eaten whole.

Cola de Toro – bull's tail in a winey sauce.

Espinacas con Garbanzos – spinach with chick peas.

Frito Variado de Pescado – all kinds of different fried fish. A *tapa* gets you a piece but most people order the better value *ración*.

Jamón – slices of cured ham on bread; simple but traditional and delicious.

Pincho moruño – mini meat kebab usually grilled over charcoal.

Puntillitas fritas – tiny baby squid, deep fried.

Revueltos – scrambled egg with a variety of fillings ranging from asparagus to mushrooms and garlic or even all three.

Solomillo al Whisky – small pork or beef steak in a Highland sauce probably made with Spanish grog.

wine. Unusually, they don't serve *tapas* or food here, but the clientele merely hop to the *freiduría El Arenal* on the corner to bring back a fried fish take-away. Fans of the famed Jabugo *jamon iberico* from the mountains of Aracena have a bar all to themselves at c/Castelar, named appropriately *Jabugo 1* to differentiate it from its sisters in the suburbs. Here again, be careful as the king of hams doesn't come cheap.

The River and Triana

Owing perhaps to its *gitano* traditions, **Triana** is another excellent hunting ground for *tapas*. In addition to the bars on the riverfront along c/Betis there are a few atmospheric places to try further into the *barrio*. On the doorstep of the Maestranza bullring at c/López de Arenas 5, is the "foreign" *tapas* bar *Jamon Real* specializing in delicious Extremaduran *jamón serrano* and cheese from Sevilla's neighbouring province to the north. Over the river and next to the church of Santa Ana on c/Correa are *Bar Bistec*, whose speciality is *cabrillas*, or spicy snails, and its neighbour *Bar Siglo XVIII*, another solid Triana establishment with plenty of tiles and *corrida* posters. Slightly further in, at c/Pages del Corro 76, *Bar Kika* is a workers' bar with its own *tapas* specialities such as *solomillo* (beef in garlic). To the north on the same street, *Bodega Triana*, c/Pages del Corro 5, is an entertaining shack specializing in rabbit and kid *tapas*.

Deeper into the *barrio* a detour west along c/San Jacinto would bring you to Avda. de Santa Cecilia where, at no. 2, *Bar Casa Ruperto* has specials such as *cabrillas* (snails) and *Pincho moruño* (marinated kebabs). Just north of the church of San Jacinto, at the junction of c/Pages and c/Antillano Campos, lies *Bar Anselma*, a fine old place with a great neo-Moorish facade and where you might be lucky enough to catch an impromptu *flamenco* in the evenings.

Nearer to the river on c/Castilla, and oppposite the church of Nuestra Señora de la O, *Bar Sol y Sombra* is another Triana favourite, and finally, the *Kiosko de las Flores freiduría*, tucked into the side of the Puente Triana (Isabel II) with views over the river is the perfect place to say goodbye to the *barrio*. With *tapas* served at the bar, and *raciones* – the *fritura mixta* (mixed fried fish) is recommended – at outdoor tables near the river, this is just the place on a summer night. It's closed on Monday.

Centro and La Macarena

To the west of the Alameda de Hércules in the Plaza San Lorenzo – fronting the church of the same name – *Varrales de Plata* is a friendly neighbourhood bar with a good *tapas* selection. Nearby, *El Retablo* at c/Eslava 3 is a family-run place serving excellent *espinacas con garbanzos* (spinach with chick-peas), and not far away, near Plaza Duque del la Victoria, c/San Eloy is another street full of possibilities; no. 5 (with wine straight from the barrel) and no. 9 are the best.

East of here, off c/Larana, *Bodegon San Lucar* at c/Arguijo 5 is another lively establishment with tables in the small street outside. *Bar Alicantina* in Plaza del Salvador has tables on the square and excellent, though pricey, seafood *tapas* – lower priced is *El Refugio* at c/Huelva 5, close to the same plaza, where they serve up a wide variety including **vegetarian** *tapas*.

Close by, along c/Alcaicería, at the junction with c/Siete Revueltas the refurbished *Bar Europa* is another good place. Slightly further, in and around the **Plaza Alfalfa** is a lively, young area with loud music in many of the bars: *Sopa de Ganso* in c/Pérezand, *El Lamentable* in c/Pérez Galdos, *Alcaicería* in c/Empecinado and *Berlin* in c/Siete Revueltas are all worth stopping by. Many of the **bars** here serve *tapas*, of which the more tranquil *Bar Alfalfa* (on the square at the corner of c/Candilejo) is recommended. Sevilla's oldest bar (founded 1670), *El Rinconcillo*, c/Gerona 32, lies a short walk away near Plaza Los Terceros. This is an atmospheric old place, with lots of wooden beams, *azulejos*, a few cobwebs and great *tapas*.

Breakfast, cakes and convent dulces

Sevilla's **breakfast bars** bustle with life on working days and you're bound to find your own favourites. The best are concentrated around the **centro** and **La Macarena**; some to look out for are *Bar Santa Marta*, c/Angostillo, in a plazuela planted with orange trees hard by the church of San Andrés or, not far away, there's *Cafe Zafiro* on the vibrant c/San Eloy at no. 58. At the end of this street you can get excellent *churros* – an essential part of the streetwise *sevillano's* breakfast – and *chocolate* at *Jerez en Sevilla*, and at the *Bar Rubí* opposite. Another place that turns out great churros is *Esperanza* at c/Feria 108, east of the Alameda de Hercules.

, For the best **cakes and pastries** in town, the *pastelerías* along c/Sierpes are the places to head for. *La Campana*, at no. 1, is the most celebrated, with its smartly uniformed waitresses, although many of the others, such as *Ochoa* at no. 45, are just as good. Another, slightly unusual, possibility is an Egyptian tea-bar, *Jan El-Jalili*, c/Descalzos, near Plaza de Alfalfa, which serves its own cakes as well as *tapas*.

Many of Sevilla's *conventos de clausura*, or enclosed orders of nuns, are today a small industry in themselves turning out a spectacular assortment of **dulces**. This took off in a big way when, in the 1950s, the pope gave permission for the struggling convents to earn money to support themselves. Some convents take in laundry, others perform tasks such as bookbinding, but most of them turn out the *dulces* which the city's population consumes with a passion equalled only by its contempt for calorie-counting and cholesterol. So skilled have the nuns become at turning out these delicious sweets that they even supply many of the city's leading restaurants with their desserts. Among convents only too willing to lead you into temptation are the *Convento de San Leandro*, at Plaza Ildefonso 1, renowned for its *yemas*, a sugar and egg-yolk concoction that defies description, or the *Convento de Santa Inés*, c/Doña Maria Coronel 5, near the church of San Pedro, whose speciality is *bollitos* (sweet buns). The *Convento de Santa Clara*, c/Santa Clara 40, west of the Alameda de Hercules, has a shop where you can buy *pasteles de cidra* (cider cakes). In the heart of Macarena, *Santa Paula* – more famous for its jams and marmalades – also gets into the *dulces* business with another mouth-watering egg-yolk confection, *tocino de cielo* (translated, inadequately, as "heavenly lard").

Nightlife

Sevilla has plenty to offer in the way of **nightlife**; from expensive, touristy *flamenco* shows to atmospheric, tucked-out-of-the-way drinking holes. Major **concerts**, whether touring international bands or big Spanish acts like Paco de Lucía or Miguel Ríos, usually take place in one or other of the football stadiums (see "Listings" on p.199). The local press and *El Giraldillo* list possibilities.

> Official agents for many concerts, in Sevilla and elsewhere in Spain, are *Viajes Meliá*, Avda. de la Constitución 30, opposite the cathedral.

Through the summer the Plaza San Francisco (by Plaza Nueva) and other squares host occasional **free concerts**.

Flamenco
Flamenco – or more accurately *sevillanas* – music and dance are offered at dozens of places in the city, some of them extremely tacky and over-priced. Finding *flamenco*

SEMANA SANTA AND THE FERIA DE ABRIL

Sevilla boasts two of the largest festival celebrations in Spain. The first, **Semana Santa** (Holy Week), always spectacular in Andalucía, is here at its peak with extraordinary processions of masked penitents and lavish floats carried bodily by young males. The second, the **April Feria**, is unique to the city: a one-time market festival, long converted to a week-long party of drink, food and *flamenco*. The *feria* follows hard on the heels of Semana Santa. If you have the energy, experience both.

SEMANA SANTA

Semana Santa may be a religious festival, but for most of the week solemnity isn't the keynote – there's lots of carousing and frivolity, and bars are full day and night. In essence, it involves the marching in procession of brotherhoods of the church (*cofradías*) and penitents, followed by *pasos*, elaborate platforms or floats on which sit seventeenth-century images of the Virgin or of Christ depicted in eerily lifelike scenes from the Passion. For weeks beforehand the city's hundred-plus *cofradías* painstakingly adorn the hundred or so *pasos* (each brotherhood normally carries two; Christ and a Virgin), spending as much as six million pesetas (£30,000) on flowers, costumes, candles, bands and precious stones. The bearers (*costaleros*) walk in time to stirring traditional dirges and drumbeats from the bands, which are often punctuated by impromptu street-corner *saetas* – short, fervent, *flamenco*-style hymns about the Passion and the Virgin's sorrows.

Each procession leaves its district of the city on a different day and time during Holy Week and finally ends up joining the official route at La Campaña (off Plaza Duque de la Victoria) to proceed along c/Sierpes, through the cathedral and around the Giralda and the Bishop's Palace. **Good Friday** morning is the climax, when the *pasos* leave the churches at midnight and move through the town for much of the night. The highlights then are the procession of **El Silencio** – the oldest *cofradía* of all, established in 1564 – in total silence, and the arrival at the cathedral of **La Esperanza Macarena**, an image of the patron Virgin of bullfighters, and by extension of Sevilla itself.

The pattern of events changes every day; and while newsstands stock the official programme – *Guia de Semana Santa* – they quickly sell out. A loose **timetable** is issued with local papers and is essential if you want to know which events are where – the ultra-Catholic *ABC* paper has best listings, though the Turismo's *El Giraldillo* listings

puro, the real thing, isn't easy, possibly because – like good blues or improvized modern jazz with which *flamenco* shares an affinity – its spontaneous nature is almost impossible to timetable. Visitor demand for this romantic Spanish art form has resulted in a form of "theatre *flamenco*", where you can pay to see two shows a night – a far cry from the time when the *gitanos* sang in their *juergas* or shindigs for as long and as often as the mood took them. The agents of every *flamenco* "show" or *tablao* will leap to assure you that you're lucky to have alighted on them before rubbishing the competition. Unless you've heard otherwise, avoid these fixed "shows", many of which are a travesty, even using recorded music. If you're only here for a while, however, and are determined to catch something of the flavour of this wonderful art form, we've listed a few of the better places below. But if you want the real thing it really is best to stick to the **bars** already mentioned in this chapter and below; here you'll have a fair chance of hitting upon an impromptu performance that you won't forget.

La Carbonería, c/Levíes 18. An excellent bar which often has spontaneous *flamenco* – Thurs is the best night to try, but not before 10pm. It used to be a coal merchant's building (hence the name) and is a large, simple and welcoming place – with its own patio at the back – run by Paco Lira, an engaging expert on the whole subject of *flamenco*. While you're there take a look at the enormous carved mahogany mantel around the fireplace. The wood was brought back from Cuba in the early sixteenth century, and is thus one of the first fruits of the *conquista*. Tricky to find, slightly to the northeast of the Iglesia de Santa Cruz, but well worth the effort.

magazine also prints a programme. On Maundy Thursday women dress in black and it's considered respectful for tourists not to dress in shorts or T-shirts. Triana is a good place to be on this day when, in the early afternoon, **Las Cigarreras** (the *cofradía* attached to the chapel of the new tobacco factory) starts out for the cathedral with much *gitano* enthusiasm, its band playing marches in *flamenco* rhythm. To see the climax of the processions there's always a crush of spectators outside the cathedral and along c/Sierpes, the most awe-inspiring venue. However without a seat (the best of which are rented by the hour) or an invitation to share someone's balcony, viewing spots near the cathedral are almost impossible to find. As most of the crowd want to see the processions *enter* the cathedral, a good place to stand is at the rear, beneath the Giralda, where they exit into Plaza de la Virgen de los Reyes but even here it gets chaotic. The best way of all to see the processions is to pick them up on the way from and to their *barrio*s. And here you'll see the true *teatro de la calle* – theatre of the streets.

THE FERIA DE ABRIL

The non-stop, week-long *Feria de Abril* takes place in the second half of the month. For its duration a vast area on the far bank of the river, the *Real de la Feria*, is totally covered in rows of *casetas*, canvas pavilions or tents of varying sizes. Some of these belong to eminent *sevillana* families, some to groups of friends, others to clubs, trade associations or political parties. Each one resounds with *flamenco* singing and dancing from around 9pm at night until perhaps 6am or 7am the following morning. Many of the men and virtually all the women wear traditional costume, the latter in an astonishing array of brilliantly coloured, flounced gypsy dresses.

The sheer size of this spectacle makes it extraordinary, and the dancing, with its intense and knowing sexuality, is a revelation. But most infectious of all is the universal spontaneity of enjoyment; after wandering around staring you wind up a part of it, drinking and dancing in one of the "open" *casetas* which have commercial bars. Among these you'll usually find lively *casetas* erected by the anarchist trade union *CNT* and various leftist groups.

Earlier in the day, from 1pm until 5pm, Sevillana society **parades** around the fairground in carriages or on horseback. An incredible extravaganza of display and voyeurism, this has subtle but distinct gradations of dress and style; catch it at least once. Each day, too, there are **bullfights** (at around 5.30pm; very expensive tickets in advance from the ring), generally reckoned to be the best of the season.

Los Gallos, Plaza de Santa Cruz. *Flamenco* show using a professional group of singers and dancers who sometimes get close to the real thing. But it doesn't come cheap (3000ptas including one drink), and even here there's a nagging feeling that the performers are going through the motions as bow-tied waiters serve up drinks in an atmosphere not helped by the inevitable flashbulbs and chattering over attempts at *cante jondo,* the emotional and unaccompanied "deep song".

La Garrocha, c/Salado in Triana. The interior resembles a combination of a youth hostel and a milk bar, and there's a horrendous amplification system, but gritty *flamenco* is known to take place here when the mood grabs them.

Puerto de Triana, or *Sevilla y Olé*, depending on which name it happens to be using, c/Castilla 137. Larger and less intimidating *flamenco* show than some other places. No entry charge, but you must pay for at least one drink (first drink 1200ptas; succeeding drinks 700ptas).

Bar Quita Pesares, Plaza Jerónimo de Córdoba, near the church of Santa Catalina. Run by the *flamenco* singer Peregil, this is a chaotic place where there's often spontaneous music. Things get lively around midnight and, more importantly, when the owner is on song. If he isn't, he'll sell you a cassette of an occasion when he was – almost as good, but not quite.

Discos and live music

Earlier on in the evening, Sevilla's **discos** attract a very young crowd; the serious action starts after midnight and often lasts till well beyond dawn. Fashions in music change rapidly – the current rage is *bacalao* (literally "codfish") a furious synthesized beat music which generates frenzied gyrating. For **rock music** the bars around Plaza Alfalfa and the Alameda de Hercules have most of the best action – although be very wary in the latter quarter after dark. More music bars are to be found in c/Tarifa (at the end of c/Sierpes) and in c/Trastamara, near Plaza de Armas, where you'll also find a concentration of **gay clubs**.

Antigüedades, c/Argote de Molina 10. Arty live music bar with paintings and sculptures hanging from roof, walls and balconies, many created by its owner.

B60, c/Betis 60. Lively, youthful Triana disco.

Bestiario, Plaza Nuevo end of c/Zaragoza. Disco-bar with manic *bacalao* music.

Bluemoon, c/JA Cavestany s/n, near the Santa Justa train station. Run by affable jazz guitarist "Pitito" Maqueda, with live jazz at weekends (closed Aug).

Catedral, c/Cuesta del Rosario, near the Iglesia del Salvador. Newly-opened, classy joint with high prices to match.

DOK, c/Trastamara 22. Gay music bar.

Fun Club, Alameda de Hercules 86. Good music bar which gets really packed when live groups play at weekends.

Lamentable, Pérez Galdós 28, just off Plaza Alfalfa. Music bar with a gay ambience but not exclusively so. Occasionally holds exhibitions.

Maracabu, c/Jesus del Gran Poder 71, near the Alameda de Hercules. Popular disco attracting a slightly older clientele.

Poseidon, c/Marques de Paradas, near the Puente de Triana. Small gay disco-bar inside an attractive old building with free entry and reasonable drink prices. Another gay option is *Antena*, directly opposite.

RRIO, c/Betis 67. Cavernous place in Triana with an energetic younger crowd – competes for attention with its neighbour, *B60* (see above).

Sasaya, c/Francos, near the cathedral. Lively *salsa* venue.

El Sol, c/Sol 40 close to the church of Santa Catalina. Good live jazz, with a small cover charge (closed Aug).

Sopa de Gansa, Pérez Galdós 8. Music bar which serves *tapas* till late, with a good selection of vegetarian possibilities.

Trastamara 24, c/Trastamara 24. Music bar with a predominantly gay clientele.

Urbano Comix, c/Matahacas. Popular student bar which stays open late.

Drinking

Sevilla is crammed full of **bars** for *tapas* and *finos*, many of which we've already listed. For a long night of drinking, however, leisurely places to sit out with a river view are the bars near the Plaza de Toros overlooking the Guadalquivir. *El Capote* (beside the Puente de Triana) is an interesting new arrival here. Two more possibilities in this vein – both with terraces – are *Alfonso* and *El Líbano* in the gardens of the Parque de Maria Luisa. A few streets east of the Alameda de Hercules is a new **women's bar**, *Café Sureñas* (open 4pm to midnight) which also puts on exhibitions.

Finally, a few idiosyncratic bars – of which Sevilla has many and which are usually well hidden – are worth a mention. *Taberna Anima*, c/Miguel Cid 80, north of the Museo de Bellas Artes, is a lovely old tiled bar which also mounts periodic exhibitions, while one bar with a strong claim to the title of Sevilla's most eccentric is *El Joven Costalero* at c/Torneo 18, just opposite the spectacular Puente de la Barqueta built for *Expo 92*. This place is devoted to *Semana Santa*, celebrated here for 52 weeks by the artist owner who has covered the walls with hundreds of his renditions of Christ and the Virgin while candles wrapped in tin foil punctuate the darkness and video replays of the real thing light up a TV screen. This weird establishment is named after the young men (*costaleros*) who carry the *pasos* in the *Semana Santa* processions. It's open all night and even serves food – the *potaje de garbanzos* (chickpea broth) is recommended.

Listings

Airport Information (☎451 61 11) for airport flight information. Mainly internal flights run by *Iberia*, c/Almirante Lobo (☎422 96 39). *Iberia* buses leave from the bar opposite their office, bus #EA from the Puerta de Jerez nearby.

American Express *Viajes Alhambra*, c/Coronel Segui 3, off Pl. Nueva (☎421 29 23). Open Mon–Fri 9.30am–1.30pm & 4.30–8pm, Sat 9.30am–1pm.

Banks Numerous places on the Avda. de la Constitución.

Bike Rental You can rent bikes by the day or the week at *El Ciclismo*, Paseo Catalina de Ribera 2, at the north end of the Jardines de Murillo (☎411959).

Books/newspapers The best place for English-language books is the *English Bookshop*, c/M de Nervíon 70, on the doorstep of the Estadio Sánchez Pizjuan football ground. There's also a reasonable selection – mainly on Spain – at *Librería Pascuallazaro*, c/Sierpes 4, and the *El Corte Inglés* department store, Plaza Duque de la Victoria. There's a good newspaper stand at the northern end of c/Sierpes, while British newspapers and the *International Herald Tribune* are also sold in the international bookshop on c/Reyes Católicos.

Bullfights Details and tickets from the Plaza de Toros or (with commission) from the kiosks in c/ Sierpes.

Car Rental Most agents are along the Avda. de la Constitución. One of the lowest-priced operators, represented in the foyer of the *Hotel Alfonso XIII* (by the tobacco factory), is *Atesa*.

Consulates *UK*, Plaza Nueva 8 (☎422 88 75); *USA*, Paseo de las Delicias 7 (☎423 18 84); *Canada*, Avda. de la Constitución 30, 2° 4 (☎422 94 13).

Coto Doñana Details on the procedures for visiting this nature reserve are given under the section on the park (see "Huelva" p.212). If you want to do anything out of the ordinary the office responsible for its administration is the *Estación Biológica de Doñana*, c/Paraguay 1. To book Land Rover tours contact *Centro de Recepción del Acebuche*, Avda. de la Constitución 21 (☎4221440).

Currency Exchange *American Express* (see above); *El Corte Inglés* department store, Plaza Duque de la Victoria, offers good exchange rates, low commission and long hours (Mon–Sat 10am–9pm).

Flea Market A *rastro* takes place on Thursday mornings along the c/Feria past the Plaza Encarnación, and a bigger one on Sunday mornings at the Alameda de Hércules.

Food Market A cheap and cheerful market takes place daily in Triana – at the *Mercado* immediately on the right as you cross Puente Isabel II.

Football Sevilla has two major teams – *Sevilla CF* play at the Sánchez Pizjuan stadium on the east side of town, and *Real Betis* play at Estadio Benito Villamarín in the southern suburbs. Pick up schedules from local or national press.

Hiking Maps 1:50,000, 1:100,000 and 1:200,000 military maps from the *Servicio Geográfico del Ejército* (Plaza de España building, Sector Norte). You can also buy maps from CNIG, Edificio Sevilla, c/San Francisco Javier 9 (☎644256).

Hospital English-speaking doctors available at the *Hospital Universidad*, Avda. Dr. Fedriani; ☎378400. Dial ☎091 for emergency treatment.

Motorbike Rental Motorcycles are available from *Alkimoto*, c/Recaredo 28, east of the Casa de Pilatos (☎441115).

Police Bag snatching and breaking into cars is big business in Sevilla. If you lose something get the theft documented at the Plaza de la Gavidia station (near Plaza Duque de la Victoria; ☎422 88 40). Dial ☎092 in emergency.

Post Office Avda. de la Constitución 32, by the cathedral; for poste restante, the *Lista de Correos* stays open Mon–Fri 9am–8pm, Sat 9am–1pm.

Telephones Plaza de la Gavidia 7, near Plaza Concordia (Mon–Sat 9am–1pm & 5.30–9pm).

East from Sevilla

From Sevilla to Córdoba (see p.245), a distance of some 135km, the direct route by train or bus along the valley of the Guadalquivir is a flat and not terribly exciting journey. There's far more to see following the route just to the south of this, via **Carmona**

and **Écija**, both interesting towns. Plenty of buses run along these roads so there's no real need to stay – Carmona in particular is an easy 30km day trip from Sevilla.

Leaving Sevilla the NIV crosses **La Campiña**, a rich and undulating lowland framed between the Guadalquivir to the north and the hills of Penibétic Cordillera to the south. It's a sparsely populated area, its towns thinly spread and far apart – a legacy of post-*reconquista* days when large landed estates were doled out to the nobility by the crown. The feudal nature of this system of *latifundia* – great estates where the nobles owned not only the towns but also the inhabitants and the serfs on the land – has wrought much bitterness in Andalucía, vividly described in Ronald Fraser's book, *Pueblo*.

Carmona

Sited on a low hill overlooking a fertile plain planted with fields of barley, wheat and sunflowers, **CARMONA** is a small, picturesque town which has burst beyond its ancient walls. Founded by the Carthaginians in the third century BC probably on the

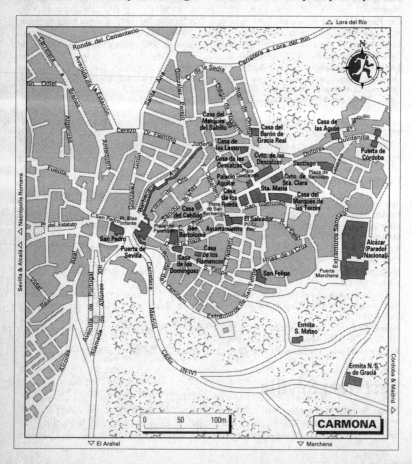

site of a Turditani Iberian settlement, they named it *Kar-Hammon* ("City of Baal-Hammon") after their great deity, the origin – via the Roman *Carmo* – of its present name. A major Roman town (from which era it preserves a fascinating subterranean necropolis) it was also an important *taifa* state in Moorish times, and following the *reconquista* Pedro the Cruel built a palace within its castle, which he used as a "provincial" royal residence, now the modern *parador*.

The Town

The fifteenth-century church of **San Pedro**, near the bus stop, is as good a place as any to start a tour of Carmona. With its soaring tower built in imitation of the Giralda and added a century later, San Pedro evokes a feeling of Sevilla – entirely appropriate since the two towns share a similar history, and under the Moors Carmona was often governed by a brother of the Sevillan ruler. Inside, the church has a superb Baroque **sagrario chapel**, by Figueroa.

The old town – circled by 4km of its **ancient walls** containing substantial Carthaginian, Roman as well as Moorish elements – is entered by the **Puerta de Sevilla**, an impressive double gateway. Of Roman origin too, (though the Moors added the fortified alcázar), through this passed the great Via Augusta on its way from Hispalis (Sevilla) to Corduba (Córdoba). Inside the walls, narrow streets wind upwards past Mudéjar churches and Renaissance mansions. Follow c/Prim uphill to the **Plaza San Fernando** (or Plaza Mayor), modest in size but dominated by splendid Moorish-style buildings including the **Casa del Cabildo** (or old *ayuntamiento*) with a beautiful Renaissance facade. Just off here is the eighteenth-century **Ayuntamiento** (still the town-hall) whose patio contains a striking geometric-patterned **Roman mosaic** with a head of Medusa. Behind the square there's a bustling fruit and vegetable market.

Beyond and east of here is **Santa María la Mayor**, a fine fifteenth-century Gothic church built over the former Almohad Friday (or main) mosque, whose elegant patio, complete with orange trees and horseshoe arches, it retains; like many of Carmona's churches it is capped by a Mudéjar tower, possibly utilizing part of the old minaret. One of the patio's pillars is inscribed with a **Visigothic liturgical calendar**, said to be the oldest in Spain. The church's high-altar has a superb Renaissance **retablo** and, in the first chapel to the left, a fifteenth-century **triptych** by Alejandro Fernández. Dominating the southeastern ridge of the town are the massive ruins of Pedro's **Alcázar**, an Almohad fortress transformed into a lavish residence – employing the same Mudéjar craftsmen who worked on the alcázar at Sevilla – by the fourteenth-century king, but destroyed by an earthquake in 1504. It received further architectural attentions from Fernando (after Isabel's death) but later fell into a pitifully ruined state, until it was recently renovated to become a remarkably tasteful *parador*, entered through an imposing Moorish gate (if you fancy staying here, see "Practicalities"). Just west of here, the Mudéjar church of **San Felipe** is worth a look, if, that is, you can gain entry, as it has a fine **artesonado** ceiling inside.

To the left, beyond and below Pedro's palace, the town comes to an abrupt and romantic halt at the Roman **Puerta de Córdoba**, a second-century gateway with later Moorish and Renaissance additions, from where the old Córdoba road (now a dirt track) drops down to a vast and fertile plain. Following this ancient route will lead you – after a few kilometres – to a five-arched **Roman bridge** on the plain below. The nearby church of **Santiago**, on c/Calatrava, is another impressive fourteenth-century Mudéjar building with an elegant brick tower decorated with *azulejos*. Following c/Dolores Quintanilla (and its continuation, c/López) from the Puerta de Córdoba back to the centre takes you past more *palacios* and churches, among them the fifteenth-century **Convento de Santa Clara** with a mirador tower on the left, and beyond the **Convento de las Descalzas**, the Baroque **Palacio de los Aguilar** on the right with a fine facade.

Roman necropolis

Lying on a low hill outside the walls, as was the Roman custom, Carmona's remarkable **Roman necropolis** (guided tours June–Sept Tues–Sat 9am–2pm, Sun 10am–2pm; Oct–May Tues–Fri 10am–2pm & 4–6pm, Sat & Sun 10am–2pm; free with EC passport, otherwise 250ptas) is one of the most important in Spain. To get there, walk out of town from San Pedro and take c/Enmedio, parallel to the main Sevilla road, for about 450m. Here amid the cypress trees, more than nine hundred family tombs dating from the second century BC to the fourth century AD were excavated between 1881 and 1915. Enclosed in subterranean *columbaria* – chambers hewn from the rock – the tombs are often frescoed in the Pompeian style with images of garlands, birds and fruit and contain a series of niches in which many of the funeral urns remain intact.

Some of the larger tombs, such as the **Tumba del Elefante** (complete with a stone elephant, perhaps symbolic of long life) are enormously elaborate, in preparation for the ceremonies that went with burial and after, when the tomb became a focus for family ritual centred on the dead. Alongside its burial chamber, a bath, pantry, kitchen with chimney as well as stone benches and tables for funeral banquets are wonderfully preserved. Most spectacular is the **Tumba de Servilia** – a huge colonnaded temple with vaulted side chambers and separate *columbaria* for the servants of the family. Tours (English spoken) lead you in gratifying detail round this extraordinary site, pointing out the various types of tombs together with the **cremation pits** where the corpse would have been burned while members of the family (and hired mourners if they were rich) threw clothes and food into the flames for use in the afterlife. The paths between the tombs were used in Roman times, and it doesn't take a lot of imagination to imagine a slow procession of grieving relatives and mourners preceded by flute players or trumpeters making their way to the family vault.

The site also has a small **museum**, whose finds from the tombs include gravestones, mosaics and vases. Opposite is a partly-excavated **amphitheatre**, though as yet you can't see this on the tour.

Practicalities

The bus from Sevilla will let you off by the old Moorish **Puerta de Sevilla**, a grand and ruinous fortified gateway to the old town. From here it's a short walk northeast to the **Turismo**, in the *Casa del Cultura* on the Plaza de Descalzas, near the church of Santa María in the centre of the old town (Mon–Fri 9am–3pm, Sat 9am–1pm; ☎954/142200).

There is a paucity of budget **accommodation** (or accommodation of any kind) in Carmona, and, especially if you arrive late in the day you'd be advised to grab what you can. The first place to try is the *Pensión El Comercio* (☎954/140018; ③), built into the gateway itself. It's got small, clean rooms, there are plenty of fresh flowers around the place, and a terrace overlooking the gate, as well as an excellent restaurant. Close by, and almost opposite the church of San Pedro, *Hostal Hoyos*, c/San Pedro 3 (☎954/141254; ③) is another possibility, as is *Hostal Carmelo* at no. 15 (☎954/140572; ④). Of a number of hotels in the four and five-star bracket, the *Parador Nacional*, Alcázar Rey Don Pedro (☎954/141010; ⑥) with its history, superb location and swimming pool, is the best. It's worth calling in for a drink to enjoy the views from the terrace.

When it comes to **food**, budget possibilities are also limited, especially in the old town. Its best to head for the *tapas* bars – whose outdoor tables are heaving in summer – along c/La Fuente (off to the right before the church of San Pedro) which descends to a famous fifteen-spouted fountain. Try *Juan Mesa Hidalgo* (at no. 2). Beyond San Pedro towards the old gate, *Gamero* is a restaurant with reasonably priced *platos combinados* and *menús*. Two upmarket suggestions are *Restaurante El Ancla* (1km along the Alcalá/El Viso road) which does fine seafood and *tapas*, or the *parador* (see above) which serves a set *menú* for 3,500ptas.

On to Écija

Beyond Carmona the NIV gently undulates across the deserted Campiña passing, after 20km, a turning to **FUENTES DE ANDALUCÍA**, which boasts some fine Baroque mansions, and the church of **San José**, worth a peep for its magnificent *retablo*. After skirting the ancient **castle of Monclova** to the right, the road cuts through the village of La Luisiana, one of a series of settlements founded in the eighteenth century by Carlos III to combat brigandage (see also La Carlota, p.206). Fifty-four kilometres from Carmona the road dips towards Écija, its towers projecting elegantly above the town.

Écija

Sevilla and Córdoba are reputedly the hottest cities in Spain; **ÉCIJA** lies midway between them in a basin of low sandy hills. The town is known, with no hint of exaggeration, as *la sartenilla de Andalucía* ("the frying pan of Andalucía") and once registered an alarming 52°C on the thermometer. Not long ago, during a particularly torrid heatwave, the citizens of Écija were rung up by a radio station and asked to inform the nation how hot it was on their terraces – the scorching temperatures quoted made everybody else feel suddenly much cooler. In mid-August the only possible strategy to avoid this heat is to slink from one tiny shaded plaza to another, putting off sightseeing until late in the day or early evening, or, if you have a burst of energy, to make for the riverbank. It's worth the effort, since Écija is one of the most distinctive and individual towns of Andalucía, with eleven superb, decaying **church towers**, each glistening with brilliantly coloured tiles. It has a unique domestic architecture, too – a flamboyant style of twisted or florid forms, displayed in a number of fine mansions close to the centre.

The Romans knew Écija as *Astigi*, probably the name of an earlier Iberian settlement. It was an important and prosperous town, based on the cultivation of olives, and trading the prized Baetican oil all over the empire during the first and second centuries. In the early Christian era Écija became a bishopric, and in Moorish times sunk into relative obscurity as part of the Caliphate of Córdoba. Conquered by Fernando III in 1240, it was only in the seventeenth and eighteenth centuries that it staged a recovery, when the prosperity brought by the new *latifundia* – harking back to the great slave-worked Roman estates – encouraged the nobility to build impressive mansions in the town. Following the devastation wrought by the Lisbon earthquake of 1755, Écija's ruined churches were restored at great cost; hence the magnificent collection of the late **Baroque towers** that are the glory of the place today.

The Town

Écija's most important churches and palaces are all within a few minutes' stroll of the delightful arcaded and palm shaded **Plaza Mayor** (Plaza de España). At the western end of the plaza the *Ayuntamiento*, as well as housing the Turismo (see "Practicalities"), contains a fine second-century **Roman mosaic** depicting the mythological Dirce being dragged by a bull as a punishment meted out by the two sons of Antiope, Zethus and Amphion – whose mother she had mistreated.

To the west of the Plaza Mayor and just behind the *Ayuntamiento*, the lyrically beautiful tower of **Santa María** – one of the eighteenth-century rebuilds – overlooks the square. Inside, a cloister displays archeological finds from the surrounding area. Behind this church, on c/Castillo, the eighteenth-century **Palacio de Benamejí** – with a fine portal in contrasting tints of stone – must be one of the most impressive army barracks anywhere. Ask the soldiers on guard outside to let you admire the fine

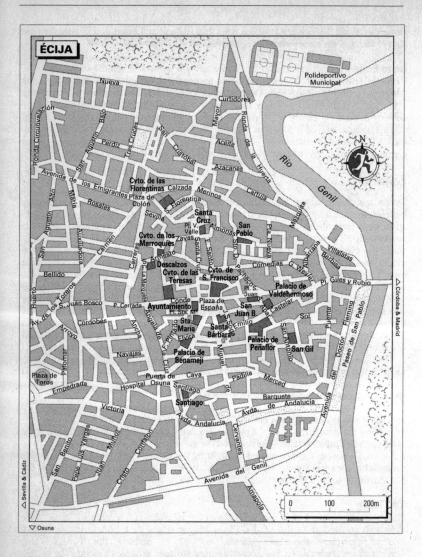

patios and collection of old coaches inside the wonderfully preserved stables; after they've inspected your passport and decided that you're not a subversive, there should be no problem. South of here the fifteenth-century church of **Santiago** has a Mudéjar side facade and, inside, a stunning **Cristo de la Expiración** (crucifixion) by Roldán.

Backtracking to the quarter northwest of the Plaza Mayor, along c/El Conde behind the *Ayuntamiento*, will bring you to the **Convento de las Teresas**, a former Mudéjar palace which, although not open to the public, has been described as a miniature of the Acázar in Sevilla with fine Moorish stuccowork, *azulejos* and doors. Continuing up and

THE NUEVAS POBLACIONES OF CARLOS III

A modern monument on the NIV at **La Carlota** (see p.206) commemorates one of the more curious episodes in Andalucía's history, when thousands of settlers were attracted from Germany, France, Switzerland and the Low Countries to repopulate this corner of Andalucía, whose inhabitants had declined disasterously due to the eviction of the Jews and Moors, as well as a plague around 1600. The government also believed that increasing the population would reduce banditry in an area through which passed the *camino real* (or royal road) transporting the wealth and bullion of the empire from the port at Cádiz to Sevilla and Madrid. But when **Carlos III** – urged on by a radical administrator named **Pablo de Olavide** – added a Utopian wish that these colonies should be egalitarian settlements untramelled by rank, privilege or parasitic religious orders he ran into opposition from the landed class of *señoritos* who were utterly opposed to parting with even the small plots of land.

The scheme was eventually set in train, nevertheless, and twelve **colonies**, stretching from La Carolina in Jaén to La Luisiana, 160km away near Écija, were founded. The foreigners soon came, attracted by grants of free land and cattle. But the scheme ran in to trouble when many of the Germans were found to be Protestants which greatly disturbed the Inquisition, who had them expelled. Others, unable to settle in one of the hottest areas of Europe, packed up and left of their own accord. Within two generations most of the foreign colonists had been either assimilated into Spanish stock or had died out. All that remains of this early attempt at social engineering today are placenames on the map, the geometrical layouts of their streets, the odd German, French and Flemish name listed in the phone books – and now the modern **monument** depicting the king and de Olavide bestowing the document of settlement on another colony.

then right along c/La Marquesa brings you to the church of **Los Descalzos** with its ornate Churrigueresque facade, followed just around the corner on c/Saltaderoto by another exquisite belfry belonging to the **Convento de los Marroquíes**. Zigzagging north along calles Parda and Bizco allows you to take in the **Convento de las Florentinas**, whose church has a fine *retablo* by Roldán. Heading east along c/Pardo then c/Santa Catalina leads to the church of **Santa Cruz**, whose brick tower was once a minaret, and carries tenth-century Arabic inscriptions recording the setting up of public fountains. Inside, there are more superb *retablos*, and an early Christian sarchopagus. The c/Santa Cruz leads back to the Plaza Mayor.

Heading along a narrow street out of the Plaza Mayor's north east corner, you'll soon spot the wonderfully ornate belfry of **San Juan Bautista**, perhaps the best of all Écija's Baroque towers. Continuing east will lead you to the sixteenth-century **Palacio de Valdehermoso**, with a Plateresque facade incorporating Roman pillars and where, almost opposite and running along c/Castellar, is the enormous **Palacio de Peñaflor** where a painted and curved front is complemented by a full-blown Baroque portal topped by twisted barley-sugar columns.

The **bullring**, laid over a Roman amphitheatre on the western edge of town, much impressed a visiting Laurie Lee: "Big empty, harsh and haunted, for two thousand years this saucer of stone and sand has been dedicated to one purpose, and even in this naked daylight it still exuded a sharp mystery of blood."

Practicalities

Écija's *Ayuntamiento* houses the **Turismo** (Mon–Fri 9am–1pm; ☎954/590 02 40), who will provide a complete list of the thirty-plus notable buildings throughout the town. As for **accommodation**; to the east of the Plaza Mayor you'll find the charming *Pensión Santa Cruz*, c/Romero Gordillo 8 (☎954/830222; ③), but you'll need your mosquito repellent if you stay here in summer; a more luxurious option is *Hotel Platería*, c/Garci Lopéz 1, just off the main square (☎954/835010; ⑤). Everything else, all on the expensive side, is on the outskirts, along the depressing Sevilla–Córdoba road. Most of the **restaurants and tapas bars** are here, too: for **meals in the centre** you're limited to the fish and meat dishes at *Cafetería-Pasarelli*, Pasaje V del Rocio, off c/Castelar to the east of the Plaza Mayor, or the more expensive *Bodegón del Gallego*, c/A Aparicio, nearby and near the Palacio de Peñaflor. Otherwise, try the bars on the main square.

Around Écija: La Carlota

Leaving Écija, the NIV towards Córdoba climbs slightly to give you a clear view back towards the town and its basin-shaped depression, which catches the heat. In early summer this road is flanked by fields of waving sunflowers, not quite so beautiful after the harvest when they are transformed into endless kilometres of stubble.

Twenty kilometres on from Écija the village of **LA CARLOTA**, as its name indicates, was one of twelve colonies set up by Carlos III in the 1760s. A tidy, anonymous place today, its eighteenth-century **Ayuntamiento** on the main road is worth a look, as is the **coaching inn**, the *Real Casa de las Postas*, opposite, dating from the same period.

From Sevilla to Osuna and Estepa

The A92 motorway that leaves Sevilla to cut across the Campiña's southern flank bypasses, after 15km, Alcalá de Guadaira, a large and scruffy dormitory suburb of Sevilla, whose only interesting feature is a twelfth-century **Almohad fortress**, its well preserved towers and battlements dominating the hilltop above an unkempt park. Sixteen kilometres further, a turn-off right along a minor road provides a possible detour to **Utrera** with a couple of interesting churches, and 14km on, at **El Palmar de Troya**, the bizarre "new Vatican" of Andalucía's heretic "pope", the self-proclaimed Gregory XVII. The ducal village of **Osuna**, 40km beyond El Arahal, and its smaller neighbour **Estepa**, just 20km or so further east again, are architectural delights not to be missed.

Utrera

UTRERA, surrounded by olive groves – said to produce the best green olives in Spain – is a dull, industrial place which is transformed each June during its famous *flamenco* festival known as the *Potaje gitano*, held in the park alongside a ruined Moorish fort. Nearby, the fifteenth-century church of **Santiago** has a fine, if worn, Plateresque west doorway. As you enter the town, on its northeastern outskirts there's also the seventeenth-century pilgrimage church of **Nuestra Señora de la Consolación** with a fine *artesonado* ceiling and glittering gold *retablo*. Should you need a **room**, *Hostal Las Delicias*, c/Abate Marchena 2 (☎954/861012; ②) is clean and central.

El Arahal

Hard to believe today, but the pleasant agricultural town of **EL ARAHAL**, 20km northeast of Utrera, has long been one of the revolutionary hot spots of the region. Along with Marinaleda (see p.210), it has led the fight against the abuses and injustices of the great landed estates against the *braceros* or day labourers, one of Andalucía's most enduring social problems. The centre is a pleasant place to stop for a drink, where you could also take a look at the fifteenth-century **Hospital de la Caridad** and the Baroque churches of La Victoria and Santa María. For **rooms** try *Hostal Alfaro*, c/ Madre de Dios 33 (☎954/840159; ③).

THE MOUNT OF CHRIST THE KING

South of Utrera along the N333 lies one of the strangest sights in the whole of Andalucía. Across the parched, white fields the amazing towers and domes of the **Palmarian Church** of **EL PALMAR DE TROYA** dominate the horizon. The story goes that in 1968 the Virgin appeared on this spot to a *sevillano*, Clemente Domínguez, whose faith, the Palmarian church's literature states, was "wavering at the time". She apparently instructed him that he must deal with the "heresy and progressivism" which were destroying the church of Rome. Miraculous cures, stigmata and numerous conversions were the means chosen by the Virgin to establish her bona fides. Thus convinced, Clemente began his investigations and found that "freemasonry and communism were actually governing the church" and that Pope Paul VI "was kept under drugs, a prisoner within the walls of the Vatican".

Building work soon started at the "Mount of Christ the King" to create Vatican II, while Clemente headed off to Rome to see if he could persuade the erring church back on to the straight and narrow. It proved a hopeless task and upon his return the Roman Pope (and later the "two villains" that succeeded him) was excommunicated and the Holy See of Saint Peter transferred to Palmar. During the midst of all these adventures General Franco was posthumously canonized as a saint of the new church, and Clemente's "battles with Satan" – more realistically a road accident – left him blinded. This disability has not, however, impeded a racy lifestyle in which he and his bishops are seen touring the bars of Sevilla, often the worse for wear, and he confidently awaits a miraculous recovery of his sight.

It only remained for the leader of the new faith to have himself crowned Pope Gregorio XVII, since when there has hardly been a dull moment at the Mount of Christ the King. Repeatedly attacked by riotous crowds of "true believers" – bussed in by local bishops, claim the Palmarians – walls had to be erected around the "Holy See" to protect the growing community inside from crimson-faced and belligerent Christians irate at the frequent ordinations of new priests (from all parts of the globe) and the daily arrival (from their convent in Sevilla) of the Carmelites of the Holy Face, the new church's order of nuns.

To **visit the complex** (which is open day and night), you'll need to cover all parts of your body – women will be subjected to an obsessive examination by the guards to make sure they are wearing *medias* (tights), without which there is no chance of entry. The impressive building turns out up close to be a hideous mass of concrete and plastered brick. Inside the church the scene is incredible, too, with at least fifty altars – including the main one, often featuring Gregorio himself – simultaneously churning through "masses", day and night.

Morón de la Frontera

Nine kilometres beyond El Arahal, a turn-off left to the north brings you, after 7km, to **Marchena**, a small town with a fifteenth-century Mudéjar church and a number of elegant mansions. Taking the southern turn at the same crossroad here allows you to visit **MORÓN DE LA FRONTERA**, 17km away. Standing on a hill at the southern edge of the Campiña, this is a charming small town with a couple of impressive churches, as well as a ruined castle. Just below the castle you'll see the Gothic and Renaissance church of **San Miguel**, an impressive pile of honey-coloured stone with a Giralda-style tower and ornate west doorway.

Following the street which descends from here to the Plaza de Ayuntamiento (the town's main road junction) takes you close to (down a street on the left) **San Ignacio**, with a another superb Baroque doorway. For **accommodation**, almost on the junction, *Hostal Pasqual*, Plaza Ayuntamiento (②) usually has space, although check that the water's on before you commit yourself, as Morón tends to suffer from severe shortages during the summer when the supply is often turned off at certain times of the day.

Osuna

Another 34km along the A92 (or easily reached by the back roads from Morón), unjustly little-visited **OSUNA** is one of those small Andalucian towns which are great to explore in the early evening: slow and quietly enjoyable, with elegant streets of tiled, whitewashed houses and some of the finest **Renaissance mansions** in the province.

Another settlement of obscure Iberian origin, Osuna first came to prominence as the Roman *Urso*, and ten bronze tablets from this period recording the town's statutes are preserved in Madrid's Archeological Museum. In Moorish times the town was of little note and it was during the post-*reconquista* period, when it became the seat of the Dukes of Osuna with enormous territories, that it was embellished with most of the outstanding buildings that make it so attractive today.

The Town

The best of the **mansions** erected by the aristocrats and wealthy landowners attracted to the town are off c/Carrera, running down from the Plaza Mayor, particularly c/San Pedro which intersects it on the left. Here the **Cilla del Cabildo** (at no. 16) has a superb geometric relief round a carving of the Giralda. Further along, the **Palacio de los Marqueses de Gomera** is another Baroque extravaganza with undulating ornamentation, balcony and solomonic columns beneath the family crest. Calle de la Huerta, off the Plaza Mayor, has more interesting buildings, including the **Palacio de los Cepadas** (now the palace of justice) with an elegant patio, and nearby to the west, on c/Sevilla, the **Palacio de Puente Hermoso**.

Two huge stone buildings stand on the hilltop overlooking the town: the **old university**, founded in 1548 by one of the predecessors of the Dukes of Osuna (later suppressed by the reactionary Fernando VII in 1820) and the lavish sixteenth-century **Colegiata**. This latter (guided tours Mon–Fri 10.30am–1.30pm & 3.30–7.00pm; Sat & Sun 10.30am–1.30pm; 200ptas) is a fine Renaissance building with a damaged Plateresque west doorway caused, so the story goes, by French soldiers in the War of Independence who used it for target practice. Inside, an eccentric female guide (who often lights up as she conducts you around the church) will point out a sumptuous gilded **retablo** and the remarkable seventeenth-century canvas of the **Expiración de Cristo** (crucifixion) by Ribera, one of the artist's finest works. Also in the church some fine sculptures include a superb *Crucified Christ* by Juan de Mesa, from the same period. More Riberas are to be seen in the **sacristia**, which now holds the church's impressive art collection. His *San Jerónimo*, *San Pedro* and a moving *Martirio de San Bartolomé* are all of the highest quality.

The high point of any visit is the descent to the subterranean depths to view the gloomy **pantheon and chapel of the dukes of Osuna**, where these descendants of the kings of León and once "the Lords of Andalucía" are buried in niches in the walls. Some of the **Renaissance ornamentation** is extremely fine, especially the polychromed wooden *Santo Entierro* (burial of Christ), as well as panels from the Flemish school and a fine relief of *San Jerónimo*. The tour ends with the guide demonstrating her skills (often at length) on an antique portable **sixteenth-century organ** – one of few to survive from the period. Its venerable status doesn't deter her from allowing children on the tour to have a go at thumping the keys.

Downhill, opposite the entrance of the Colegiata, is the Baroque convent of **La Encarnación** (Mon–Fri 10.30am–1.30pm & 3.30–7.00pm; Sat & Sun 10.30am–1.30pm; 125ptas) founded in the seventeenth century by a Duchess of Osuna, and where the highlight of the nun-led guided tour is a fine plinth of ninth-century Sevillan *azulejos* (from Triana) round its cloister and gallery depicting curiously secular scenes. After filling up on the tasty **convent dulces** sold here, you could take a pleasant **walk** north, passing the former convent church of La Merced with its stupendous carved **late Baroque tower**, and the ruins of Las Canteras, once a hermitage, on c/Camino de las Cuevas. Further along here you'll find the **excavations of Roman Ursa**, including a **necropolis** with tombs quarried from the sandstone, as well as the vague remains of a theatre and fort. Otherwise, the more direct descent to the town takes you past the **Torre del Agua**, a twelfth-century Almohad tower which houses a small **archeological museum** (daily 10am–1pm & 4–7.30pm; 200ptas) containing finds – and unfortunately many copies of the best items, the originals of which are in Madrid – discovered in the town.

Other churches around the town worth seeking out are the sixteenth-century **Santo Domingo** (at the northern end of c/Carrera) another fine Renaissance church, **Nuestra Señora de la Victoria** nearby, with an impressive Baroque *retablo* by José Mora and to the west, the **Convento del Carmen** on the street of the same name, whose church has a beautiful sixteenth-century *retablo* in carved wood.

Practicalities

Osuna's **Turismo**, on Plaza Mayor (Mon–Fri 9am–3pm, Sat 9am–1pm; ☎954/142200), is worth a visit to collect their map, which makes it easier to locate most of the town's monuments. There are plenty of **places to stay**, although prices tend to be on the high side: the best budget option is *Hostal Cinco Puertas*, c/Carrera 79 (☎954/811243; ③) at the northern end of the main street or, opposite, there's a recently renovated old coaching inn, *Hostal Caballo Blanco*, c/Granada 1 (☎954/810184; ④) which has better rooms with bath. Both of these serve decent meals in their restaurants. Lowest-priced of the bunch is a very basic but friendly **fonda**, *Casa Paco*, c/Asistento Arjona 35 (☎954/810218; ②), through the double arch off the Plaza Mayor, and on the left.

For **food and drink** a good place to start is the marvellous **Casino** on the Plaza Mayor, with 1920s Mudéjar-style decor and a grandly bizarre ceiling: it is open to all visitors and an excellent place for a drink while lounging in the chairs overlooking the square. The best restaurant in town is the *Meson del Duque*, Plaza de la Duquesa 2, with full meals and *tapas* served on its attractive terrace; it's above the same square, and close to the Torre del Agua. Another good place is *Bar Canaletas* on c/Carreras just beyond the *Hostal Cinco Puertas* (see above), serving *tapas* and *raciones* with a reasonably priced *menú*.

Estepa

Another delightful Baroque town, **ESTEPA**, 24km east of Osuna, resembles a miniature version of its larger neighbour. Originally a Carthaginian settlement, it took the side of the north-African state during the Punic Wars with Rome, and when the victorious Romans finally took the city in 208 BC they found that the citizens had burned their possessions and killed themselves rather than surrender. Repopulated, it eventually became the Roman *Ostipo* and later, the Moorish *Istabba*.

Close by the central Plaza del Carmen, the eighteenth-century **Iglesia del Carmen** has an exuberant Baroque facade in black and white stone and a stunningly ornate interior, recently restored. Above, in the *ciudad alta*, the **Iglesia de Santa María** is another fine church, dating from the twelfth century. Lower down in the *ciudad baja*, you'll notice the elegant **Torre de la Victoria** – all that remains of the convent of the same name. Taking c/Mesones (and its continuation, c/Castillejos) from the Plaza del Carmen back through the town, you'll pass one of Estepa's best mansions, the **Palacio de los Marqueses de Cerverales**, a superb eighteenth-century palace with barley-sugar columns supporting its balcony. Near the end of this street, the **Iglesia de San Sebastián** has a sculpture of *San Juan Bautista* by Martínez Montañes.

Marinaleda

Fourteen kilometres north of Estepa, the unassuming agricultural village of **MARINALEDA** seems to have inherited the do-or-die qualities of the early inhabitants of Estepa who resisted the might of Rome. Along with El Arahal to the east, "Red" Marinaleda has become the standard bearer in the struggle of the *braceros*, or day labourers, against their exploitation by the great landowners. The leader in this struggle is Marinaleda's Mayor, Sanchez Gordillo, the village schoolteacher and – like the rest of the village to a man and woman – a committed communist. He came to prominence as the organizer of a "hunger strike against hunger", but since then has moved on to taking over large estates in the area, by force if necessary. A couple of years back he occupied a nearby estate belonging to of one of Andalucía's major landowners, the Duke of Infantado. The scene was vividly described by Michael Jacobs in his book *Andalusia* when he visited the "occupation":

> *Attached to a post at the entrance of the estate were the words 'ESTA TIERRA ES NUESTRA MARINALEDA,' (This land is our Marinaleda). On the long drive up to the cortijo I passed a group of villagers carrying hoes and rakes, the women dressed in black. They could have been straight out of a communist poster of the 1930s, and this impression was reinforced by the political badges they were all wearing. In the middle of all this prowled the leonine and instantly recognizable figure of Sanchez Gordillo, wearing a Tolstoyan suit and a red sash. He addressed me in a slow, solemn voice with no trace of a smile. I could not help feeling, confronted by such a manner and appearance, that I was in the presence of one of the Messianic figures who toured the Andalusian country-side in the nineteenth century. He talked of the inadequacy of the present agrarian reforms, of the great extent of the Duke of Infantado's properties, and of how the land in Andalusia continued to be in the hands of the very few.*

The romantic *cortijos* – brilliant white pantiled farm buildings surrounded by walls and often shaded by a cluster of elegant palms – to be seen dotted across the Andalucian landscape have for generations been the focus of the misery of the landless poor, for these are the homes of the landowners, or more often their overseers on whom the day labourers are dependent for what little seasonal work they can get. From the *Casa de Cultura,* in reality a worker's club, on the main square – Plaza de Libertad – at Marinaleda, the *Sociedad de Obreros Campesinos*, led by Gordillo, is fighting for change and despite recent government measures to give workers compensation when there is no work, they continue to demand the transfer of ownership of the land – something that the Socialist government has so far shied away from.

West from Sevilla towards Huelva

With your own transport available, the fastest – and also the dullest – way from Sevilla to Huelva is via the A49 motorway. You'd be better off using the more tranquil and interesting N431 which cuts through the area to the west of the city called El Aljarafe by the Moors (the "high lands," actually rather flat), planted with olives, vines and orange trees, arriving after 8km at **Castilleja La Cuesta**, a village famous as the place where Hernan Cortés, explorer and conqueror of Mexico, died. It's probably more familiar to most Andalucians, however, as the centre for some of the best pastries in the region – Castilleja's delicious cinnamon-coated *tortas* are exported all over the rest of Spain. Also here is *Restaurante Las Tejas* where at weekends after they've eaten (and drunk a fair deal), *sevillanos* try out their skill in a bullring behind. Although the *toros* are only calves some of them can still prove too much for most of these amateur *toreros*.

Fourteen kilometres further on, **Sanlúcar La Mayor**, a sturdy, rather unexciting place, does nevertheless retain parts of its Roman and Moorish walls and has three Mudéjar churches, the most notable of which is the thirteenth-century **Santa María** –

in origin an Almohad mosque – with horseshoe arches, *artesonado* ceiling and the former mosque's minaret, now the church tower.

The olive-planted valley of the Guadiamar comes next, and 14km further on there's a turn off to the charming Moorish village of **CARRIÓN DE LOS CÉSPEDES**. Once a fief of the Knights of Calatrava, a twelfth-century military order formed to defend the southern frontier of Castile against the Moors, this is still an atmospheric place, its early history almost tangible as you stroll around its narrow streets. Further west still on the N431 the village of Manzanilla looms into view beneath its church tower and, 20km beyond Carrión the wine producing town of **PALMA DEL CONDADO** lies off the road to the left. An area first planted with vines by the Greeks, it's probable that this terrain produced the local wine taken on the voyage to the New World by Columbus when he sailed from nearby Palos. (The wine produced here today is the *Condado de Huelva*, which hardly ranks with Spain's top-drawer vintages, but the dry whites are an excellent partner for seafood.) With its impressive eighteenth-century Baroque church of **San Juan Bautista** overlooking a palm-fringed central plaza, this slow-moving white-walled country town makes a good stopping point for a drink of the local brew at one of the central bars. If you're tempted to **stay**, the *Hostal La Viña* (☎959/400273; ④) on the junction of the N431 with a pool, is better value than the over-priced *Hostal Morenos* nearer the centre. Over the road from *La Viña* the *venta* is a good and economical **place to eat**. Five kilometres south, **Bollullos del Condado** is a one-street town filled with *bodegas* and *ventas*. This road continues to El Rocío and the Coto Doñana (see p.221).

Niebla

Twelve kilometres west from Palma along the N431, the salmon-pink ancient walls and towers of **NIEBLA** make a spectacular sight. The approach is wonderful; almost a medieval fairy tale come true, for this is a real walled town and looks the part. The **Roman bridge** – probably built in the second century during the reign of Trajan – is remarkably well preserved and carried traffic for two thousand years until it was blown up during the Civil War. It has since been meticulously restored.

Little is known about Phoenician settlement here or the possible Iberian village of the Turditanian tribe which may have preceded it. However, coins found dating from the Roman period gave the town's name as *Ilipla*, which is probably derived from the Iberian name. Described by the Roman writer Pliny as a fortified city of strategic importance, it was a crucial link in the massive Roman mining operations carried out upriver at the Río Tinto mines. The metals – mostly silver – were moved down the river by barge and then transferred to galleys here for the voyage to Rome and other parts of the empire. A bishopric under the Visigoths, after the Moorish conquest it became successively part of the Almoravid and then Almohad domains until, as an independent *taifa* state it experienced its greatest period of prosperity during the twelfth century, trading in saffron and raisins. It fell to the Christian forces under Alfonso X in 1262, and after being passed around as a fief of various rulers and their offspring, in 1369 Niebla came into the hands of the Guzmán dynasty, after which it entered a long period of decline.

The Town

Once inside the two-kilometre long encirclement of the walls, Niebla's tidy streets of whitewashed houses and small squares are a delight to explore. The Puerta del Socorro leads from the Sevilla–Huelva road to the Plaza Santa María in the heart of the town dominated by the church of **Santa María de Granada**. The key is available from the genial custodian of the *Casa de Cultura* (the former fifteenth-century Hospital de Nuestra Señora de los Angeles) next to the church. Entered through a splendid

Mozarabic **eleven lobed portal**, the original tenth-century church is believed to have been constructed over a Visigothic cathedral, and was used by Christians during the Almoravid period. Converted into a mosque by the Almohads in the thirteenth century, the **mihrab** now to be seen in the side wall, as well as the elegant **tower** – its minaret – date from this period. The pillars in the second-floor windows of the tower, incidentally, are believed to have come from the original Visigothic church. Among the artefacts dotted around the austere and much restored Mudéjar–Gothic interior are a couple of Roman altars and the **Silla Episcopal**, the throne of the Visigothic bishops. The lectern on the pulpit also seems pretty ancient. Outside the entrance, a patio is dotted with remnants of the building's chequered history: various Visigothic, Christian and Moorish stones and pillars.

Of the ruined church of **San Martín** near to the town's main gate and sliced through by a road, only the apse, bell tower and a chapel survive. It was built in the fifteenth century on the site of a former synagogue donated in more tolerant times by Alfonso X as a concession to the Jews of Niebla, and before the Inquisition began its grisly work. The locked chapel contains a fifteenth-century **sculpture** of Christ being scourged. The town's **four gates** are also worth seeking out, each with its Moorish horseshoe arch and features, as is the **Castillo de Guzmán**, in origin the Moorish alcázar, but much added to by Enrique de Guzmán in the fifteenth century. It later fell into decay and was ruined after Marshal Soult used it as a barracks for French troops during the War of Independence. Today it stages concerts and theatrical productions over the summer months as part of Niebla's **annual festival** of theatre and dance.

Most of the **bars** around the main square serve *tapas*, and should you need **rooms** the *Fonda Hidalgo*, c/Moro 3 (①) and *Hostal Cazadores*, c/Queipo de Llano 4 (☎959/363071; ②) usually have space.

Dolmen de Soto

Five kilometres beyond Niebla the road crosses the A49 motorway and shortly after this a broken sign on the right indicates a dirt track leading to the **prehistoric Dolmen de Soto**. Follow the track for about 1km – in one section it fords a stream and can be tricky after heavy rain – which winds around to a parking area with a curious canopy. To the south of this you'll see a mound (containing the dolmen) and the gate should be open. Discovered in 1923, it dates back to about 2000 BC and consists of a long passage leading to a burial chamber topped by a headstone estimated to weigh some 21 tonnes. Parts of the walls are engraved with schematic symbols. Seven kilometres further towards Huelva a turn-off on the left leads to Moguer, one town on the Columbus Trail (see p.218).

Huelva

Large, sprawling and industrialized, the city of **HUELVA** struggles to present an attractive face to its visitors. Still, once you've got past the messy suburbs with their fish canneries, cement factories and petrochemical refineries, the tidy city centre – perched on a peninsula between the confluence of the Odiel and Tinto river estuaries – comes as a pleasant surprise.

It was as *Onuba* (modern inhabitants still call themselves *onubenses*), a trading settlement founded by the Phoenicians early in the first millennium BC, that Huelva was born. These early merchant traders were attracted by the minerals yielded from the mountainous areas to the north, and by the time the Carthaginians came to dominate the area in the third century BC *Onuba* was an established port, conveying these minerals throughout the Mediterranean world. When Spain fell into Roman hands the mining

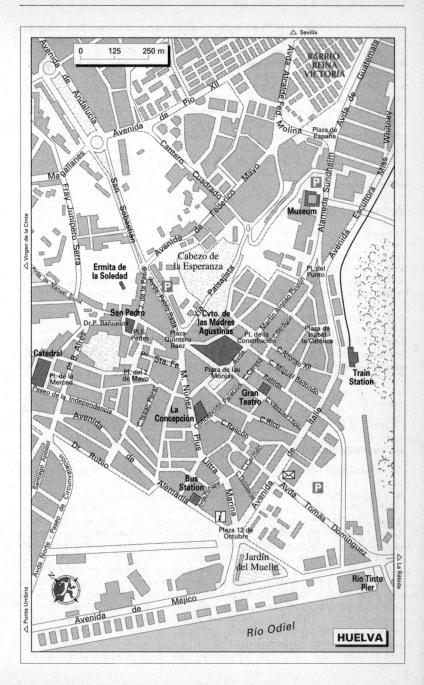

HUELVA

operations at Río Tinto were dramatically expanded to satisfy the empire's insatiable demand for metals such as silver and copper and the city prospered even more. Following Rome's demise the Visigoths and Moors displayed little interest in mineral extraction; the latter concentrated on dominating the seaborne trade with North Africa.

Huelva's maritime prowess gained for the city its crowning glory when **Columbus** set out from across the Río Tinto for the New World in ships manned by hardy Huelvan sailors. The city enjoyed a boom when the Extremadurans to the north of Huelva – the men who conquered the Americas – used the port as a base for their trade with the new territories overseas, but eventually Sevilla, and later Cádiz, came to dominate the silver and gold routes from the Americas and Huelva was squeezed out. Largely flattened by the Lisbon earthquake of 1755, it is only in the last century that the place has begun to regenerate itself: first as the base for mineral exports from Río Tinto at the turn of the century, and later when Franco established a petrochemical industry here in the 1950s.

Arrival and information

Huelva's **bus station**, c/Portugal 9, has frequent services to Sevilla, Ayamonte and Portugal with connections to many other destinations. Frequent trains to Sevilla, and three through trains a day to Madrid leave from the splendid neo-Moorish **train station** (☎959/246666), a short distance south of the centre on Avda. Italia. Completed in 1880 this is a splendid sight, a perfect expression of the self-confidence of that period, and well worth stopping by even if you're not travelling by train.

In summer frequent **boat trips** to Punta Umbría (see p.217) set off from the harbour as well as **cruises** around the **Río Odiel Marismas Natural Park** – a place to spot flamingos, spoonbills and great colonies of herons. For details and bookings contact *Agencia de Medio Ambiente* (☎959/245767).

For information, Huelva's **Turismo**, in front of the Turismo at Avda. Alemania 14 (Mon–Sat 10am–2pm & 4.30–7pm; ☎959/257403) has stacks of brochures and timetables, and hands out full accommodation lists and details on current events.

Accommodation

Accommodation is normally not a problem this far off the tourist trail, and you should be able to fix up a room within a few minutes of arriving. Most places are concentrated near to Avda. Pinzon – the town's main artery – and the pedestrianized shopping street to the south of it. At the lower end of the scale there's the serviceable *Hostal Colon* at c/Rico 20 (☎959/249015; ②) or its slightly more expensive neighbour *Hostal Paris*, c/Rico 6 (☎959/248816; ③). Just around the corner from these two are a couple of clean and simple places which, because they're built around central patios, are pleasantly airy: a welcome bonus on sultry Huelvan nights. The first is *Pensión Calvo* at c/Rascón 33 (☎959/249016; ②) and – a few doors away – *Las Delicias* (☎959/248392; ②) at no. 42. A little west of here, the more expensive *Hostal Virgen del Rocío*, c/Tendaleras 14 (☎959/281716; ④) has rooms with air conditioning. Closer to the pedestrian shopping street you'll find the basic but convenient *Hostal Ruiz*, c/Vásquez López 26 (☎959/247239; ②) and with a few extra mod-cons such as air conditioning, *Pension Andalucía*, c/Vásquez López 22 (☎959/245667; ③). For a touch of luxury try *Hotel Tartessos*, Avda. Pinzón 13 (☎959/282711 ⑤) on the main street, or you may even wish to head further out and join Columbus's ghost at the La Rábida monastery (see p.218) which has five rooms for visitors. Huelva's **youth hostel** (☎959/253793; ①) is at Avda. Marchena Colombo 14; the nearest **campsite** at Punta Umbría is a fifteen-minute bus ride away.

The City

Many of Huelva's key sights are a short walk from **Plaza de las Monjas**, the city's palm-lined main square. Along with a wonderful museum, some important churches and a curious British-built quarter, Huelva also has a couple of buildings of note; the impressive Neoclassical **Gran Teatro**, on c/Vasquez Lopez, and the Art Nouveau **Clínica Sanz de Frutos**, c/Rico 26, both just a short way from the Plaza de Monjas.

The museum

The best place to start a tour of the city – especially if you're pressed for time – is at Huelva's excellent **Museum**, Alameda Sundheim 17 (Tues–Sun 10am–2pm & 5–7pm). Setting the tone, the enormous **Roman water wheel** inside the museum's entrance was discovered during archeological excavations at the Río Tinto mines. Wheels such as this were operated by slaves to raise water to the surface and so prevent the mines from flooding. Often a series of wheels stacked one above the other would be used to haul water from depths of up to 200m and more.

Much thought has gone into the museum's presentation – notice the various coloured lines on the floor which guide you around the different phases of the collection (follow the yellow line for the Paleolithic artefacts, red for the Bronze Age, and so forth). You shouldn't miss the reconstructed **Celtic house** (Room 1) from the north of the province, and, in Room 2, interesting Tartessian artefacts include a wonderfully crafted **bronze jar**.

The **mining section** in the same room offers some fascinating examples of the early history of an activity which has been fundamental to this region for well over three millennia, including a striking **bronze boar** thought to represent one of the early deities connected with mining. A collection of mining artefacts from the Roman period includes a remarkably well preserved length of rope used in the mines. Herodotus, the ancient Greek historian, claimed that ropes of Spanish esparto grass were used by the Persian king Xerxes in building a bridge of boats across the Hellespont in 481 BC. In addition there are a number of terracotta miners' lamps, a wooden tray for washing minerals, as well as a lead pig – a prism-shaped cast of molten lead – stamped with ownership for transportation. The remainder of this room displays items from Huelva's Visigothic and Moorish periods.

The second floor of the museum contains the city's fairly forgettable **fine arts collection**, enlivened only by a number of paintings by the Huelvan artist Daniel Vásquez Diaz, one of Picasso's Paris contemporaries. His **Chico de Nerva** is a typical post-Impressionist work.

The Barrio Reina Victoria

One of Huelva's more bizarre features is a whole quarter designed by English architects. The **Barrio Reina Victoria** (or Queen Victoria housing estate), east of the museum alongside the Avda. de Guatemala, was constructed by the Río Tinto Mining Company in the early years of the century to house its British workers. It's a truly weird experience to stroll along the tree-lined avenues, flanked by bungalows with rose gardens and semis with dormer windows and mock-Tudor gables – more like Acacia Avenue, Essex, than an Andalucian town. Even the street names have a colonial symmetry about them: Calle A, Calle B and so on. Given the drab uniformity it's little wonder that the present native occupants have attempted to relieve these humdrum northern exteriors with a few primary colours.

Río Tinto pier

The **Río Tinto pier**, on east side of the harbour, is a huge nineteenth-century ironwork structure formerly used to ship out the minerals which arrived by train from the mines to the north. Designed by the British engineer George Barclay Bruce and finished in 1874, the redundant pier's decaying ironwork curves gracefully out into the estuary, and today serves as a boardwalk for loungers and courting couples.

The British workers employed in the mines were also responsible, it seems, for the importation of **football** into Spain, helping set up Huelva's league club, which claims to be the oldest in the country. It's a pedigree hardly matched by their record, however, which has been to languish for most of the century in the lower divisions.

Huelva's churches

The **Catedral de la Merced**, just to the north of Plaza de las Monjas off Paseo de Buenos Aires, was one of the few buildings to survive the eighteenth-century earthquake, resulting in its upgrading to Cathedral status which – apart from a brilliant white Baroque interior and an interesting salmon pink colonial facade – it hardly merits. It's worth looking inside at an image of **Virgin de la Cinta** – the city's patron – attributed to Montañes.

A more interesting church and one with Columbus connections is 3km further out, off the coast road heading west towards Portugal. This is the restored **Virgen De la Cinta**, a simple whitewalled sanctuary set on a low hill overlooking the sea, where Columbus is said to have prayed before setting out on his voyage. Inside, beneath the Mudéjar roof, you can see a **medieval fresco of the Virgin**, a fine altar grille, and a series of 1920s' faience tiles by the painter Daniel Zuloaga depicting scenes from the explorer's life. To get there, take the #6 **bus** from Plaza de Monjas, and ask for the "Parada de Santa Marta" stop.

Eating and drinking

Most of Huelva's bars are in the streets around the Plaza de Monjas, particularly the **pedestrianized** c/Concepción through c/Berdigon, lined with modern sculptures.

Bar XII Octobre Brasería, c/Marina 25. Pleasant place with a good *menú*.

Las Candelas, 7km from town at the Aljaraque crossroads on the road to Punta Umbría. An old *venta*, a step up in class and price from anywhere else in town, recommended for its seafood. Without your own transport you'll need to get the Punta Umbría bus to drop you or take a taxi. Closed Sun.

Donaña, Gran Vía, Avda. Pinzón 14, next to the Hotel Tartessus. Specializes in Andalucian dishes, but the cavernous interior can be a bit lifeless if the place is quiet.

Bar-Pizzeria Don Camillo e Peppone, c/Isaac Peral s/n. Genuine Italian pizzas east of the Plaza de las Monjas.

Meson la Esperanza, c/Miguel Redondo 18. Another budget possibility just off c/Carasa.

Freiduria, corner of c/Carasa and c/Alfonso XII. Simply named place with a good value *menú* and a climatized room at the back.

Los Gallegos, c/Carasa. Excellent place serving seafood *tapas* and *raciones*.

Los Gordos, c/Carmen 14. Reasonably priced seafood menu near the bus station; its name, "the fat ones", is a reference to the rumbustious characters who run the place.

El Rinconcito, c/Marina 2. A good value *menú*, often including *paella*.

El Timon, c/Carasa 19. Basic no-nonsense place, though not as cheap as you might expect.

Nightlife

When it comes to **drinking and dancing**, during the summer most Huelvans make their way to Punta Umbría (see below) and the coast. However, c/Concepción through c/Berdigon has numerous bars, cafeterias and ice-cream parlours to serve those left behind.

Two terraced cafeterias where the locals like to sit out are *Café La Taranta*, c/Isaac Peral 5 – to the west of Plaza Monjas, or *Cafetería Laxeira* at Plaza Quintero Báez 5, slightly north. If you like to wash your drink down with **tapas** you could try the seafood specialities at *Bajamar*, c/Miguel Redondo 4, just off the pedestrian street, or the nearby *Las Tinajas*, one block east at c/Alfonso XII 5. Another popular place to drink, with a decidedly Anglo–Saxon ambience, is *Bar Otawa*, c/Berdigon 1.

If you feel the urge to **disco** hop, *Alameda 9*, Alameda Sondheim 9, just below the museum, and two places close by on Gran Vía, Avda. Pinzón – *Discoteca Borsalino* at no. 8 and *Discoteca Génesis* at no. 26 – provide what action there is. Check out that there's a decent crowd before entering, though.

Although Huelva bills itself as a *"flamenco* capital", you'll be lucky to locate any **flamenco** at all in high season. At other times the *Peña Flamenca de Huelva*, c/Nicolás 90 (☎959/230961) or another nameless *peña* (☎959/258752) on Avda. Andalucía are places to try, though ring to check first. The Turismo should also have details of any upcoming performances.

The beaches: Punta Umbría and El Rompido

PUNTA UMBRÍA, 20km away (hourly buses) is Huelva's nearest – and biggest – seaside resort. Hardly an inspiring place, it does, however, make an alternative stopover if you can't bear to stay in the city, although in July and August every room will be taken. Once romantically served by ferries (which still run in the summer months), it is now reached by a long road bridge spanning the water and marshlands of the Río Odiel estuary. A long and sandy beach – lined with tasteless private villas – leads down to the *punta* or point, where you'll find most of the **places to stay**. At the lowest end of the scale (and prices are higher here) there's *Pensión Oliver*, Plaza del Cantábrico 4 (☎959/311535; ③) or *Hostal Manuela*, c/Carmen 6 (☎959/310750; ③). Places with a sea view are a step up again – on the Avda. del Océano there's *Hostal Playa* (☎959/310112 ④) at no. 95 which is recommended, as well as *Hostal Florida* (☎955/311107 ④) next door. High season pressure on rooms could mean that the **youth hostel**, Avda. del Océano 13 (Jun–Oct; ☎959/351650; ①) or Punta Umbría's **campsite** (*Pinos del Mar*, ☎959/310812) on the road out of town towards El Rompido are the only options to spending a night on the beach.

After dark, the place throbs to a dozen **discos** in season and most bars seem to be playing music of some sort or another. When it comes to **food and drink,** *chiringuitos*, open air bars on the seafront serving snacks, are popular, and the resort is full of the usual *freidurías* and *marisquerías*. The central *La Esperanza*, Plaza Pérez Pastor 7, is a good fish restaurant with an economical *menú*, and on the same square, the lower-priced *Las Tinajas* is one of Punta Umbría's most celebrated *marisquerías*. A romantic alternative is to organize your own night party among the marshes – you can **rent a canoe** from *Rosalmi,* down at the canoe pier.

For a more peaceful seaside retreat you might want to move further east along the coast – lined with fine beaches and backed by dunes, pinewoods and a unique juniper grove – to **EL ROMPIDO**, most famous in the past for its oyster beds but now transformed into a smaller resort. There's another campsite here, *Catapum* (☎959/390165), just outside the village as you approach, but it's worth noting that in high summer this can be pretty grim. Further back near the village of **La Bota**, *Camping Derena Mar* (☎959/312004) is a better bet, claiming to be Andalucía's first "ecological" campsite, conserving resources and disposing of rubbish in an environmentally friendly way.

The Columbus trail

Huelva's greatest source of pride lies with the momentous expeditions of **Christopher Columbus** to the New World, the first of which sailed from Palos de la Frontera (or simply Palos), across the Tinto estuary from the city. When he was unable to get the backing for the voyages he wished to make to discover a shorter route to the Indies, Columbus cooled his heels for many years in and around Huelva and the La Rábida monastery until he finally managed to obtain a commission from the king and queen in the spring of 1492. The main sites connected with Columbus – **La Rábida**, **Palos** and **Moguer** – are all within a 30km round trip from Huelva.

La Rábida

The **monastery** of **LA RÁBIDA**, 8km from Huelva, can be reached by bus or, with your own transport, by taking the Mazagón road southeast across the Río Tinto road bridge. At the Punta del Sebo – the tip of land where the Tinto and Odiel rivers meet – there's a **monument to Columbus** donated by the USA. This monster cubist-inspired statue, sculpted by Gertrude Vanderbilt Whitney in 1929, has the navigator looking a bit like a cowled boxer on his way to the ring.

Situated amid a forest of umbrella pines (which serve to mask the petrochemical refineries across the polluted river estuary), the small whitewashed Franciscan **monastery** is a surprisingly pleasant oasis once you reach it. Lying at the end of the Avda. de la América, a road linking it with Palos (see p.219) and lined with ceramic pavement tiles marking all the countries of the New World, the monastery may only be visited by guided tour (Tues–Sun hourly 10am–1pm & 4–8pm). Dating from the fourteenth century, the buildings suffered structural damage during the Lisbon earthquake of 1755 and have been extensively restored.

COLUMBUS AND THE VOYAGES

Probably born in Genoa around 1451 to the son of a weaving merchant, **Christopher Columbus** went to sea in his early teens. After years of sailing around the Mediterranean, in 1476 he was shipwrecked off the coast of Portugal and it was in Lisbon – then the world leader in navigation – that Columbus learned the skills of map-making. In 1479 he married into a high-ranking Portuguese family and spent the following years on trading voyages to the British Isles and elsewhere, including in 1482 a journey down the coast of West Africa to Ghana, a major source of spices, ivory and slaves. During this time the idea germinated in his mind of attempting to sail west to reach the Indies and the Far East; thus shortening the route that Portugal was then exploring around the coast of Africa. He built up an enormous library of ancient and contemporary geographical writings – now preserved in Sevilla, all heavily annotated in his own hand. By some optimistic interpretations of these works and a misreading of an Arab geographer, Alfraganus, Columbus seriously undercalculated the earth's circumference, believing that Marco Polo's fabulous island of Cipangu (Japan) lay a mere 2,400 miles west of the Canaries instead of an actual 10,600. Even so, and had he been correct, this crossing was still further than any ship had sailed before across open sea.

Trying to find backers, when the Portuguese monarch, still more interested in the African route, demurred, Columbus turned to Spain. In 1486 at Córdoba he presented his plan to reach the gold-rich Orient to Fernando and Isabel, still involved in the protracted and costly war of *reconquista* against the Moors. Desirous of the gold to boost their fortunes but wary, after consultations with advisers, of Columbus's calculations they too refused support. Now desperate, Columbus turned to France and then to Henry VIII of England, with no success. During his earlier journey from Portugal to Córdoba,

The tour begins with the room containing stylized modern frescoes of the explorer's life by Vásquez Díaz. At the building's heart is a tranquil fifteenth-century **Mudéjar cloister** filled with pot-plants, opening off which is the monks' **refectory** where Columbus would have dined during his many sojourns here. You will also see the cell where the abbot, Juan Pérez and Columbus discussed the explorer's ideas. Beyond the cloister, a fourteenth-century church contains an alabaster statue of the **Virgin and child** to which the mariner and his men prayed before setting sail. Upstairs, above the refectory, lies the **Sala Capitular** (Chapter House) an impressive beamed room with heavy period furniture where Fray Pérez, Columbus and the Pinzón brothers discussed the final plans before the first voyage set sail. On August 3, 1992 the king and the whole Spanish government gathered in this room to mark the 500th anniversary of the event. In other rooms on the same floor you can see models of the three caravels as well as navigation charts, cases containing various artefacts brought back from the expedition and "team pictures" of the crew. Don't miss the curious **Sala de Banderas** – or Flag Room – where, beneath flags of the various South American nations of the New World is a casket of earth donated by each. If some of these caskets look a bit roughed-up it's probably due to visiting South Americans who, after reverentially handling the soil of their fatherland, often treat the caskets of their neighbours with some disrespect.

The monastery's gardens contain an **information office** as well as a pleasant **bar-restaurant** with terrace tables. You can **stay** here at the *Hostería La Rabida* (☎959/350312; ⑤), although the five rooms are booked well in advance during high season.

Palos de la Frontera

Four kilometres north along the Río Tinto estuary lies **PALOS DE LA FRONTERA**, a rather featureless village but an important site in the Columbus story. It was from the silted-up bay – then a major sea port – below the church of San Jorge that the three

Columbus had stayed at the La Rábida Franciscan monastery. It was to here that he returned frustrated and depressed in the autumn of 1491. The explorer's luck turned when Juan Pérez, the abbot of La Rábida and a former confessor to Isabel, was moved to write to the queen on Columbus's behalf. It was a timely moment. In January of 1492 Granada had fallen, the treasury was empty, and the promise of gold and glory for a resurgent Spain attracted the monarchs.

Columbus set out from Palos on August 3, 1492 with three small vessels, the *Santa María*, the *Niña* and the *Pinta*, carrying a total of 120 men recruited from Palos and Moguer by the Pinzón brothers. Columbus's discovery of the Atlantic wind patterns ranks alongside his other feats; sailing via the Canaries to take advantage of the trade winds, the incredible voyage almost ended in mutiny by crews who believed that they would never find a wind to bring them home. This was avoided when, on October 12, Columbus made landfall on Watling Island (now San Salvador) in the Bahamas. Watched by naked and silent natives he took the island in the name of Spain and gave thanks to God. After leaving a colony of men on Hispaniola (modern Haiti) he returned to Palos on March 15, 1493 to enormous acclaim.

Successsful as a mariner, Columbus was a disaster as a colonizer; epitomized by his forcing of the native population of Hispaniola into the gold mines in a brutal process that reduced their numbers from a quarter of a million in 1492 to 60,000 fifteen years later. In 1500 Columbus was removed from office as governor and sent back to Spain in chains and disgrace. He eventually obtained release and made his final voyage in 1502 – a last desperate attempt to find a strait leading to India – but ended up stranded on Jamaica for a whole year after losing his ships to sea worms. Columbus died at Valladolid in 1506 still believing that he had reached the East Indies.

caravels, the *Niña*, the *Pinta* and the *Santa María* set out to reach Asia by crossing the western ocean.

> *O Palos, no-one can equal your glory.*
> *Not Memphis, nor Thebes nor eternal Rome.*
> *Not Athens nor London.*
> *No city can dispute your historical fame!*

This modern poem fixed to the exterior wall of the fifteenth-century parish **church of San Jorge** leaves you in no doubt of how Palos views its role in world history. It was here that Columbus and his crewmen attended mass before taking on water for their voyage from the nearby **La Fontanilla**, a medieval well recently tarted up as the centrepiece of a dismal park to mark the quincentenary. The harbour lay to the west of the fountain in an area now marshland, and it was due to the the river's silting up that the decline of Palos set in. The church (open only at service times) has a simple, bare brick interior containing some mural fragments as well as an iron pulpit and some thirteenth- and sixteenth-century alabaster **sculptures** of Santa Ana and the Crucifixion.

On that August morning in 1492 Columbus is supposed to have left the church through its southern **Mudéjar portal** flanked by his captains Martín Alonzo Pinzón and his younger brother Vincente, both from Palos. And it is these native sons that Palos today celebrates, even more than its Columbus connection, claiming that their contribution to the epic voyage has been eclipsed. Indeed, at the time the Pinzón family insisted that Martín – a mariner of great local repute – had planned such a voyage long before Columbus. South of San Jorge on the mainstreet, the **house of Martín Alonzo Pinzón** survives, now converted into a **museum** at c/Colón 24. Here you'll see a model of the Spanish plane *Plus Ultra* – the first to fly across the Atlantic in 1927, two years before Lindbergh, who made it to the record books because the Spanish flight made refuelling stops in the Canaries and Ascension Island before reaching Brazil. Incidentally, it was piloted by Ramon Franco, the dictator's brother. Further along the main street and close to the *Ayuntamiento*, **rooms** and **food** are available at *Cafetería-Pensión Rábida* (☎959/350163; ②).

The road north to Moguer runs through **strawberry fields** owned by one of the largest cooperatives in Europe, which has brought welcome prosperity to the area. By playing the market, which entails close scrutiny of weather forecasts for northern European customers such as Germany and Britain – sunshine means high strawberry profits – they decide when is the best moment for picking. Then, loaded with 10,000 kilos of *fresones* apiece, the great refrigerated trucks roll north through the night.

Moguer

The beautiful whitewashed village of **MOGUER**, 8km north of Palos, also takes pride in its Columbus connection: many of the crew members were recruited here. Quite apart from this, it is also a place with plenty to see, and achieved worldwide notoriety in 1956 as the birthplace of the Nobel prize-winning poet Juan Ramón Jiménez.

The Town

Starting from the Plaza del Cabildo in the centre – where there's a bronze statue of Jiménez – it's easy to find your way around. First take a look at the elegant eighteenth-century **Ayuntamiento** on the same square, a quintessentially Andalucian edifice in cream and brown paint described by one art-historian as "the finest Neoclassical building in the whole of Huelva province". It also appears on the 2000-peseta bank note.

Close to here in c/Monjas and to the west of the main square lies the Gothic-Mudéjar **Convento de Santa Clara**. Founded in the fourteenth century, it housed nuns from the order of St Clare until 1898, but is now a **museum** (guided tours on the half hour Tues–Sat 11am–2pm & 5–8pm, Sun 5–8pm; 250ptas). Inside, a splendid Mudéjar cloister leads into the nuns' former quarters which include kitchen and refectory and a large sixteenth-century dormitory. The church possesses some notable alabaster tombs of the Portocarrero family, the convent's founders, as well as – at the entry to the choir – a seventeenth-century diptych of the Sienese school portraying the Immaculate Conception. There are also some fine painted Renaissance choir-stalls and an inscription in the right aisle that tells of Columbus's visit to the convent to offer thanksgiving for his safe return. He is reputed to have spent the whole night in prayer here upon returning from his first voyage in March 1493, in fulfilment of a vow he made in the middle of a terrifying storm.

Other sights in town include the fifteenth-century monastery of **San Francisco** (behind Santa Clara but presently being restored) with its stunning ochre-tinted Mudéjar brick church and from where legions of missionaries were sent out to the New World, and **Nuestra Señora de la Granada** which boasts a scaled-down, whiter version of Sevilla's Giralda tower "which from close up looks like Sevilla's from far away," wrote Jiménez. The house where Jiménez was born, c/Jiménez 5, has been restored as an interesting **museum** (daily 10am–2pm & 4.30–8pm; 100ptas) displaying various mementoes from the poet's life. On the road leading towards the Sevilla–Huelva highway the **cemetery** has the grave of the poet and his wife, Zenobia. His body was returned to the town he loved for burial in 1958 after twenty years spent in exile in Puerto Rico, to where he had emigrated after Franco came to power. The work that most Andalucians remember him for today is *Platero y yo* ("Platero and I") the story of a little donkey who is a "friend of the poet and children" based on his own donkey, Platero, in whose company he often toured Moguer's streets. Glazed plaques on walls around town mark streets or buildings that occur in the story, and to the south of the centre in the grounds of the **Casa de Fuentepiña** – where Jiménez wrote most of it – Platero's grave, beneath a great pine, has become a shrine for generations of children.

Practicalities

Close to the Convento de Santa Clara at the end of c/Monjas there's the delightful and excellent value *Hostal Pedro Alonso Niño*, c/Pedro Alonso Niño 13 (☎959/372392; ②) where all rooms come with shower; get a room overlooking the patio at the back if you can. Around the corner you could also try the more expensive *Hostal Platero*, c/Aceña 4 (☎959/372159; ③). For **food**, *Mesón Restaurante Paralla*, Plaza de Monjas 22, opposite the entrance to Santa Clara, is not only the best restaurant in town but also serves *tapas* and has a bargain *menú*.

Coto Doñana National Park

Sited at the estuary of the Guadalquivir, the vast roadless area of the **COTO DOÑANA** is Spain's largest wildlife reserve, a world-class wetland site for migrating birds and one of Europe's greatest areas of wilderness. The seasonal pattern of its delta waters, which flood in winter and then drop in the spring, leaving rich deposits of silt, raised sandbanks and islands, give the Coto Doñana its special interest. Conditions are perfect in winter for ducks and geese, but spring is most exciting: the exposed mud draws hundreds of flocks of breeding birds. In the marshes and amid the cork oak forests behind you've a good chance of seeing squacco heron, black-winged stilt, whiskered tern, pratincole and sand grouse, as well as flamingos, egrets and vultures. There are, too, occasional sightings of the Spanish imperial eagle, now reduced to just fourteen breeding pairs. In late summer and early autumn, the swamps – or *marismas* – dry out and then support far less bird life. The park is also home to 25 pairs of lynx.

Inevitably, it seems, the park is under threat from development and several lynx have been killed by traffic on the road to Matalascañas. Even at current levels the drain on the water supply is severe, and made worse by pollution of the Guadalquivir by pesticides and Sevilla's industry. Proposals for a huge new tourist centre – to be known

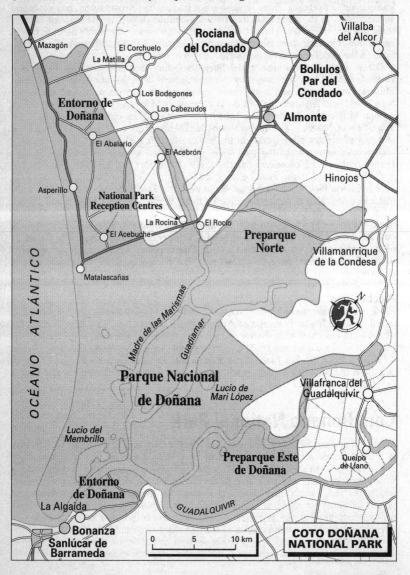

COTO DOÑANA NATIONAL PARK

TOURING THE COTO DOÑANA

The starting point for **Land Rover tours**, and the only place to book them, is at the *Centro de Recepción del Acebuche*, 4km north of Matalascañas towards El Rocío and Almonte (then 1.5km along a dirt track). For details of the tours (daily in spring/summer at 8.30am & 5pm; 2400ptas) call in at the centre or ring (☎959/430432; English spoken). Although the *Centro* has some binoculars available for rent, you'd be advised to bring your own. Outside July, August and holiday periods you should be able to get on to the next day's trip, otherwise you'll need to book at least a week in advance. Tours point out only spectacular species such as flamingo, imperial eagle, deer and wild boar.

If you're a serious ornithologist and just as interested in variations on little brown birds, the tour isn't for you and you should consider a **group booking** which costs a little more than the daily excursion and lets you create your own itinerary (details from the *Centro*).

as the Costa Doñana – on the fringes of the park have now been shelved, but the pressure remains. Bitter demonstrations organized by locals who saw the prospect of much-needed jobs in the new development – accompanied by mysterious outbreaks of vandalism against park property – have abated into an uneasy truce. Some experts have proposed that "green tourism" allowing a greater but controlled public access to the park, and thereby providing an income for the local community, is the only way to bring both sides together.

This area was known to the **Romans** as *Ligur*, and archeologists were recently surprised to discover a Roman quayside three kilometres into the *marismas*, showing just how much the area has expanded in the ensuing two millennia. It was Alfonso X, however, who claimed the territory of Las Rocinas as a hunting reserve for the Spanish crown in 1262 during the *reconquista*. In 1294 his heir, Sancho IV (the Brave), rewarded the "hero" of the siege of Tarifa, Guzmán El Bueno, with the territories of Doñana. The area, still a hunting reserve, remained part of the lands of the Dukes of Medina Sidonia – as the Guzmán line became – for the next five centuries, and the park's hunting lodge was named the palace of Doña Ana in honour of the wife of the seventh duke in 1595. The reserve hit a bad patch when it was sold by the Medina Sidonias in 1897 to sherry baron William Garvey, whose company is still operating in Jerez (see p.152). Garvey turned it into a hunting club and sold off much of the woodland for profit, but saner times followed upon his death in 1909, when people began to realize the unique importance of the area.

In 1957 scientific interest in the park began in earnest and as a result of concern expressed about proposals to carve a highway across it and build tourist developments along its coastline, the **World Wildlife Fund** was set up in 1964. Five years later the Fund persuaded the Spanish government to set up the National Park. Since then the Coto Doñana, now under the management of the National Institute for the Conservation of Nature (ICONA), has expanded to 77,000 hectares. Recently the park's administrators enlisted divine assistance in safeguarding its future when they petitioned the brotherhoods to allow the Virgin of Rocío (see p.224) to become the National Park's patron. The brotherhoods gracefully agreed and the park's future now seems assured.

Doñana practicalities

Visiting the Doñana still involves a certain amount of frustration. At present the heart of the reserve is still only open to brief, organized Land Rover **tours** – four hours at a time along one of five charted, 70km routes. You can also take a boat cruise into the park from Sevilla (see p.161) and Sanlúcar de Barrameda (see p.152).

Day visitors are currently restricted to the **hides** (daily 8am–8pm) at three access centres open to the public. The first of these (moving north from Matalascañas) is the *Centro Recepción del Acebuche* (daily 8am–8pm), where there's also an information office, bookshop, natural history exhibition, a rather tedious audio-visual presentation and a **cafetería**. The five hides adjacent to the *Centro* overlook a lagoon where marbled teal, purple gallinule, various grebes and – around the trees – azure-winged magpies have all been spotted and where with luck, you may even glimpse the extremely rare Audouin's gull. You'll need to bring your own binoculars. At the eastern end of the lagoon you are allowed to view the **aviary** where rescued and recuperating birds enjoy intensive care – another good place for sighting some rare species.

Nine kilometres north, the other two centres are sited off the road close to the El Rocío bridge. **La Rocina** (daily 8am–7pm) has a car park and information centre (get a map here), beyond which a 2km route called the "Charco de la Boca" leads to three hides in marshland, pinewoods and along the riverbank where you might see Cetti's warbler, the spectacular hoopoe, and red-crested pochard as well as – in summer – a plethora of singing nightingales. A minor road leads 7km west from here to **El Acebrón** (9am–6pm) – a former hunting lodge – where there is another car-park and information centre which houses an exhibition called "Man and Doñana". A 1.5km marked route threads from the centre through mainly woodland and offering possibilities to sight the rare hawfinch.

Back on the main road, the **El Rocío bridge** on the village's southern edge has been described by one naturalist as "the best free birdwatching site in Europe". From this spot, red kite – a common sight here – soaring flocks of whiskered terns disturbed by the ominous approach of a majestic booted eagle and migrating greenshank, ruff and sandpiper are all to be seen in season. In high summer though, the marshes dry out and are grazed by horses while the birdlife is restricted to coot and avocets breeding by the river. The **view** across the marshes towards the village of El Rocío from here is superb.

El Rocío

Set on the northwestern tip of the marshes, **EL ROCÍO** – a tiny cluster of white cottages, sandy streets and a church stockade where perhaps the most famous pilgrimage-fair of the south occurs annually at Pentecost – is one of the most atmospheric places in Andalucía. As the cowboy-hatted farmers nonchalantly ride horses along the wide streets and tie up at Wild-West style hitching rails in front of their timber cabins, you half expect to see Clint Eastwood appear from a nearby saloon chewing on a cheroot. And this frontier-like feeling isn't altogether accidental, as it was from this area that many of the colonizers of the New World set out, exporting their vernacular architectural preferences with them. In the evening the lack of street lights only serves to underline the time-warp quality of an area unchanged for centuries.

Centre of the town's Pentecost celebrations, the church of **Nuestra Señora del Rocío** (9am–1pm & 5–7pm) was, despite its Baroque appearance, built in the 1960s on the site of a church which collapsed in the seventeenth-century Lisbon earthquake. It holds the venerated image of the **Virgen del Rocío**, a thirteenth-century work in carved wood.

In the spring, El Rocío is probably the best **bird-watching** base in the area. The *marismas* and pine woods adjacent to the town itself are teeming with birds, and following tracks east and southeast along the edge of the reserve, you'll see many species from white stork, herons and egrets to masked great grey shrike and honking wild geese. The Boca del Lobo ("wolfsbreath") sewage treatment plant is an unlikely sounding birdspotting location, but vultures and storks are frequent patrons here, and the village is even planning to install a hide.

THE ROMERÍA DEL ROCÍO

The **Romería del Rocío**, a Whitsun pilgrimage to the sanctuary of the *Virgén del Rocío* is one of the most extraordinary spectacles in Europe, with whole village communities and some eighty local "brotherhoods" from Huelva, Sevilla and even Málaga converging on the village on horseback and in lavishly decorated ox-carts. The event is part-pilgrimage and part-jamboree as the intense emotions awakened by the two- to four- day journey (not to mention the drinking) often spill over uncontrollably.

The brotherhoods coming from Sanlúcar de Barrameda have a special dispensation to follow their ancient route across the heart of the Parque de Doñana which takes them three nights and four days with all the attendant fire risks en route. The army is employed to get them and their carts over the Guadalquivir safely and the park's rangers set up campsites for them and provide firewood for their great feasts in the woods. Throughout the procession, which climaxes on the Saturday evening, everyone parties in fiesta costume, while by the time the carts arrive at El Rocío they've been joined by hundreds of busloads of pilgrims.

What they have all come for – apart from the fair itself – is the commemoration of the miracle of *Nuestra Señora del Rocío* (Our Lady of the Dew). This is a statue believed to have been found on this spot by a shepherd in the thirteenth century – conveniently after the eviction of the Moors – which, so it is said, resisted all attempts to move it elsewhere. A shrine was built, miraculous healings and events were reported, and El Rocío was suddenly on the map. In the early hours of Pentecost Sunday when many of the revellers are gripped either by religious frenzy or lie prostrate in an alcoholic stupor, the image of the Virgin, credited with all kinds of magic and fertility powers, is paraded before the faithful as she visits each one of the brotherhoods' houses (which lie empty for the rest of the year).

In recent years the sheer size of the Romería has begun to worry the authorities as it has exploded from a few thousand pilgrims in the 1970s to an incredible half a million in the early 1990s. Despite the whole affair having become a spectacular TV event with arc lamps, amplified music and fireworks, popular enthusiasm is undiminished. The brother-hoods fight with each other to carry the *Blanca Paloma* ("the White Dove" as the Virgin is fondly known) one more time in procession before she's returned to her shrine for another year, and the weary homeward trek begins.

El Rocío also makes a nice place to **stay**. *Hostal Vélez*, c/Algaida 2 (☎959/442117; ④) is comfortable while *Hostal Cristina*, c/Real 32 (☎959/442413; ③) is slightly more economical. **Food** is served at most of the bars along the main street – to eat out on their terraces you'll need plenty of mosquito protection after sundown.

Matalascañas

Birds and other wildlife apart **MATALASCAÑAS**, a fast-growing beach resort just outside the reserve is unlikely to excite; with five large hotel complexes and a concrete shopping centre, it looks like it's only recently been built (as indeed it has), and it would be difficult to imagine a more complete lack of character. In summer, the few **hostal rooms** are generally booked solid and unless you plan in advance (any Sevilla travel agent will try to reserve you a room) you'll probably end up **camping** – either unofficially at the resort itself, or at the vast *Camping Rocío Playa* (☎959/430238), down the road towards Huelva. This site is a little inconvenient without your own trans-port if you're planning to take regular trips into the Doñana; if you just want a beach, though, it's not a bad option. Playa Doñana and its continuation Playa Mazagón – with two more campsites *Fontanilla Playa* (☎959/536237) and *Doñana Playa* (☎959/376281) stretch the whole distance to Huelva, with fine beaches backed by dunes and hardly another visitor in sight. This route is covered at present by just one daily bus. Six kilometres east of Mazagón the new *Parador Cristobal Colón* (☎959/536228; ⑥) is set among pinewoods within a stone's throw of the beach. The C442 road west continues beyond some unsightly petrol refineries to the monastery of La Rábida (see p.218) and the city of Huelva (see p.212).

Along the coast to Portugal

This stretch of coast between the Guadiana – which marks the frontier with Portugal – and Tinto rivers is lined with some of the finest beaches in Andalucía and a scattering of low-key resorts that rarely see a foreign tourist. There's no train service, but plenty of buses run along this main route to the frontier, easily crossed by a spectacular new road bridge over the Guadiana estuary.

From Huelva the **coast road to Portugal** loops around the Marisma de San Miguel, passing through the dull towns of Cartaya and **Lepe**. The latter was mentioned by Chaucer in his *Pardoner's Tale* saying that the red and white wine of Lepe "creepeth subtilly." Its main claim to fame today however, is as the butt of hundreds of "did you hear about the man from Lepe..." jokes in which the town's supposedly gormless inhabitants are mercilessly pilloried by the rest of the nation. Taking this notoriety in its stride, Lepe capitalized on its fame by inaugurating an annual Jokes Festival – the last week in May – which now attracts the best comedians in Spain.

Five kilometres south of Lepe on the *marismas* of the Río Piedras, the tiny fishing port of **EL TERRÓN** boasts two of the best **fish restaurants** on the coast. Located on the harbour, both *El Quinto* and *El Ancla* (which specializes in mouthwatering fried and marinated prawns) have economical *menús*. About 2km down the road from here a **campsite**, *La Antilla* (☎959/480829) may be your best bet if rooms are tight.

The road hits the coast at the **PLAYA DE LA ANTILLA**, a not very exciting beach resort with a handful of good *marisquerías*. You won't find a room here in high season but at other times *Hostal La Parada*, c/La Parada s/n (☎959/480811; ③) and *Hostal Playa*, Plaza La Parada (☎959/480726; ④) on the main street – both offer good off-peak prices – enable you to take advantage of an excellent beach. Otherwise there's a **campsite**, *Luz* (☎959/341142) 5km east towards Isla Cristina.

Isla Cristina and Ayamonte

The road passes some pretty awful new beach development on the eastern edge of La Antilla before this clears to provide a pleasant few kilometres of pinewoods and, beyond the dunes, more good beaches. **ISLA CRISTINA**, 9km further on, was, as its name implies, once an island but infilling has transformed it into a pleasant resort surrounded by *marismas* and tidal estuaries.

The commercial centre is concentrated around the port which is the second most important in the province and from where shellfish and wet fish are transported overnight on ice to the markets, bars and restaurants of Sevilla, Córdoba and Madrid. The fish that stays behind is processed in the town's canning and salting plants. At the end of an avenue shaded by giant eucalyptus trees the town's fine sandy beach somewhat makes up for a drab seafront. Along this avenue you'll also find a good fish restaurant, *Casa Rufino*, which does a great *arroz negro de marisco* and a reasonably priced *menú*. **Places to stay** are non-existent in high season without prior reservation; at other times *Hostal Maty*, c/Catalanes 7 (☎959/331806; ③) is basic but central.

Although the sprawling, slightly scruffy border town of **AYAMONTE** lies only 8km away from Isla Cristina as the crow flies, the road has to dogleg 16km around the *marismas* to get there. The warren of narrow streets behind its main square leads up to the old town, where the mildly interesting sixteenth-century **church of San Francisco**, with a beautiful Mudéjar *artesonado* ceiling and fine views from its tower, is the only real monument. The town **beach** at Isla Canela, 2km to the south, though nice enough, is almost impossible to reach without transport. It's not easy to find anywhere to **stay in Ayamonte**. Outside high season you could try *Hostal La Ribera*, c/La Ribera 1 (☎959/320289; ②) or ask at the sleepy **Turismo**, Avda. Ramón y Cajal s/n (Mon–Sat 10am–2pm & 4.30–7pm; ☎959/470988) for addresses of *casas particulares*.

Inland to Río Tinto

Of the potential routes to the mountainous north of the province, the westernmost, from near Ayamonte is the least interesting. Here the road ploughs on endlessly through a dreary landscape dominated by stands of alien and voracious eucalyptus which have sucked the lifeblood from the soil. Far more attractive is the N435 route heading northeast from Huelva city towards Extremadura which offers – with your own transport – an interesting detour to the **mines of Río Tinto**. The **bus** uses the same route to reach Aracena or you could take a **train** which will drop you at Almonaster la Real at the Sierra de Aracena's western end.

Once clear of the Huelva the N435 climbs steadily towards **Trigueros**, a pleasant enough agricultural village which claims propriety over the Neolithic Dolmen de Soto (see p.212), 8km to the south west. Valverde del Camino, 24km north, is a market town noted more for its leather footwear than its charm, and the road continues a further 10km to where a turn on the right towards the hamlet of **El Pozuelo** allows you to see **three dolmens** from the third millennium BC. A couple of kilometres along this road

THE MINES OF RÍO TINTO

The **Río Tinto** (or Red River) takes its name from the oxidized iron minerals which flow down from fissured crags of this strange, forbidding landscape turning the river blood red. Evidence of mineral exploitation here goes back at least five millennia – popular tradition asserts that these were the legendary mines of King Solomon, as seen in place names such as Cerro (or hill) de Saloman and Zalamea la Real. More secure historical evidence shows it was the Phoenicians who encouraged exploitation here early in the first millennium BC, during the age of the fabled kingdom of Tartessus from where they aquired the copper to smelt with the tin of Cornwall to make bronze. It was not copper but silver, however, which attracted the **Romans** in the second century BC. Production was dramatically stepped up during the late Republic and early Empire using remarkable – if brutal – systems to combat flooding, the perennial hazard in deep mining. This they overcame by means of slave-operated *norias*, or waterwheels; in some workings as many as eight pairs of these wheels were used in relays to raise water from a depth of thirty metres. For the shackled slave miners working with primitive tools by the light of small clay lamps in warrens of cramped, dark galleries life must have been wretched. The scale of operations can be judged from the fifty millions of tons of visible slag left behind.

After the Romans had gone the **Visigoths** worked out the Roman shafts and the mines were then run down during the Moorish period – although Niebla built part of its prosperity on its rights of ownership by granting permits. The *conquista* brought further decline in its wake as cheap mineral wealth flooded into Spain from the New World. Loss of empire and hard times induced efforts to restart the industry which, in 1873, resulted in the Spanish government selling the mines to a consortium of British and German bankers. Out of this the **Río Tinto Mining Company** was born, bringing numerous northern Europeans to work here, and in 1954 control of the company returned into Spanish hands.

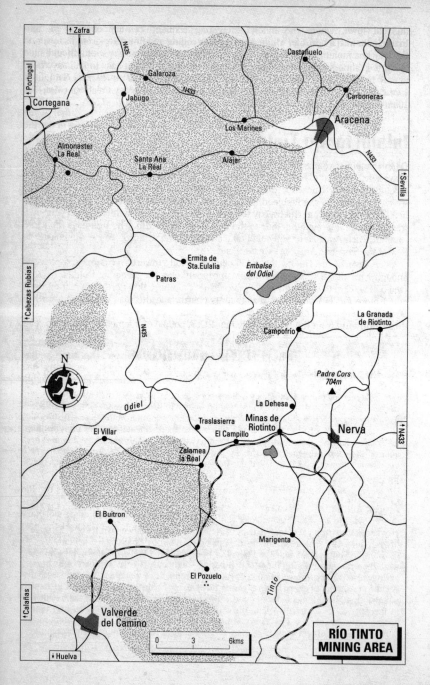

RÍO TINTO MINING AREA

and just before the cemetery on the outskirts of the village, take a dirt track to the right marked "dolmens". Just over two kilometres along this the road forks, with a gate on the left. Leave any transport here and follow the track on the right which ascends the hill through trees for about 100m to the first dolmen, from where the other two can be seen on hills nearby. The first dolmen has three burial chambers, two with their capstones still in place. The second has four burial chambers, and the last is in a ruinous state.

The N435 winds into the wooded hill country of the Sierra Morena until – just beyond Zalamea la Real – a right turn along the C421 leads you into the area of the Río Tinto mines.

Minas de Río Tinto and around

Set in an area dramatically scarred by open cast mineworkings, where the exposed faces of mineral-rich rock are streaked with glinting rivulets of ochre, rust and cadmium, the village of **MINAS DE RÍO TINTO**, 6km east of the N435, was created by the Río Tinto mining company early this century after they had dynamited its predecessor – complete with Baroque church – which stood in the way of mining operations.

As you approach it, watch out on the left for the **Barrio de Bella Vista**, or what the locals refer to as the "English colony". This estate of Victorian villas, complete with neo-Gothic Presbyterian church and village green, was constructed to house the largely British management and engineering staff when the mines passed into Anglo-German hands in the nineteenth century. The attitude of this elite to the surrounding village – where the mineworkers lived – is indicated by the estate's high perimeter wall and once-guarded entry gates intended to rigorously exclude "the natives" as they were disdainfully described. In a company policy with racist overtones these "colonialists" were forbidden from living in Bella Vista if they dared to marry a Spanish woman, thus deterring any dangerous inter-breeding. In the woods beyond the laurel hedgerows surrounding the church, a war memorial records the names of company staff (management only) who fell in the Great War. The estate now houses local people but the clubhouse fronting the village green, which today has a **swimming pool**, still adheres to the fastidious membership rules laid down by the long-departed English; the committee decides who will or will not be allowed to join and many of the old rules still apply, including the restriction of women visitors to certain parts of the premises. The estate can be visited as part of the guided tour from the visitor centre at Nerva (see p.230) or you can usually just wander in for a look around.

The mining museum
In the centre of the village on a hill above the Río Tinto company's offices lies the Río Tinto Foundation's **mining museum**, Plaza del Museo s/n (Tues & Thurs–Sat 10am–2pm; Wed 5–8pm; 200ptas). With transport, continue past the office building – normally flying flags – and at the roundabout take the road ascending to the right. At the next junction turn right and follow the road to the top of the hill where, on the right, you'll see one of the old mine steam trains outside the museum. Alternatively, on foot, you can take the path from opposite the company offices up through the pinewoods .

Housed in the company's former hospital, the museum presents an interesting panorama of mining in the area from prehistoric to modern times. The **Roman period** is the best represented, with exhibits illustrating their mining methods, daily life and burial practices in addition to a variety of coins and statuary. Modern mining is also covered, as well as the geology, flora and fauna of the area. Don't miss the luxurious **wagon of the maharaja**, built in 1892 by the Birmingham Railway Carriage and Wagon Company to be used by Queen Victoria on her proposed visit to India. When this didn't happen it was sold to the Río Tinto company and used for the visit of King Alfonso XIII to the mines. Though compact, the museum is ever expanding, thanks to the energies of its enthusiastic director Pedro Lorenzo Gomez; recent additions include a wonderfully restored **steam train**, and there are plans to install a pit cage and winding gear which will allow visitors to descend to the old underground workings. *Hostal Galán*, c/Romero de Villa s/n (☎959/590840; ③) around the corner from the museum has **rooms**, and a bar below.

La Dehesa and Nerva

Two kilometres north of the village you will pass two spectacular **open cast mines**, the *Corta Atalaya* and – with 5000 years of exploitation behind it – the *Cerro Colorado*, set in an awesome landscape of rock cliffs glittering with iron pyrites, copper, silver and gold. From a **viewing platform** by the roadside you can see into the giant elliptical basin of the *Corta Atalaya*, which at 1200 metres long and 330 metres deep is one of the biggest open-cast mines in the world – far below, enormous trucks are dwarfed by the immense walls of rock.

Another 2km further on, at **LA DEHESA**, the Río Tinto Company headquarters are backed by a recently discovered **Roman graveyard** featuring a number of interesting tombstones. Alarmingly close to the present mining operations which rumble on in the background, the graveyard is only open to the public on guided tours (see below).

NERVA, 4km west of Minas de Río Tinto, is a charming little village, its pedestrianized main street fringed with orange trees and overlooked by a splendid redbrick *Ayuntamiento* with a wonderful minaret-inspired octagonal tower. There's also a good **place to stay**, the friendly and family-run *Hostal El Goro*, c/Reina Victoria s/n (☎959/580437; ②) close to the centre, which also has its own bar.

GUIDED TOURS OF THE RÍO TINTO MINING AREA

You may wish to take the **guided tour** of the mining area organized by the **Nerva Turismo**, Ctra. Sevilla s/n (Mon–Fri 10am–2pm & 5–8pm; Aug 10am–2pm only; ☎959/580073). The 3hr tours (daily 10am, 12.30pm & 3.30pm; 1400ptas, reductions for students and children) cover the *Corta Atalaya* and the *Cerro Colorado* mines, the Bella Vista Victorian housing estate, the Roman mineworkings and cemetery and the steam engine and mining museums.

Leaving the mining area by the H501, beyond Campofrío the landscape softens as the road progresses through verdant forests of cork and holm oaks, chestnut and walnut trees towards Aracena.

The Sierra Morena

The longest of Spain's mountain ranges, the **Sierra Morena** extends almost the whole way across Andalucía from Rosal on the Portuguese frontier to the dramatic pass of Despeñaperros, north of Linares. Its hill towns once marked the northern boundary of the old Moorish Caliphate of Córdoba and in many ways the region still signals a break today, with a shift from the climate and mentality of the south to the bleak plains and villages of Extremadura and New Castile. The range is not widely known – with its highest point a mere 1110m, it is not a dramatic sierra – and even Andalucians can have trouble placing it. All of which, of course, is to your advantage if you like to be alone.

Visiting the Sierra Morena

The Morena's **climate** is mild – sunny in spring, hot but fresh in summer – but it can get very cold in the evenings and mornings. A good time to visit is between March and June, when the flowers, perhaps the most varied in the country, are at their best. You may get caught in the odd thunderstorm but it's usually bright and hot enough to swim in the reservoirs or splash in the springs and streams, all of which are good to drink.

This is an area rich in **wildlife**; if your way takes you along a river, you'll be entertained by armies of frogs and turtles plopping into the water as you approach, by lizards, dragonflies, bees, hares and foxes peering discreetly from their holes – and usually no humans for miles around. Bird fanciers should keep an eye out for imperial and booted eagles, as well as goshawks and the rare black vulture. The sierra is also home to one of two surviving populations of Spanish lynx on the peninsula although, with only thirty or so pairs eking out an existence as their forest habitat is gnawed away, you're unlikely to spot one.

Locals maintain that, while the last bears disappeared only a short time ago, there are still a few wolves in remoter parts. Of more concern to anyone hiking in the Sierra Morena, however, are the **toros bravos** (fighting bulls). Apparently, a group of bulls is less to be feared than a single one, and a single one only if he directly bars your way and looks mean. The thing to do, according to expert advice, is to stay calm, and without attracting the bull's attention, go round. If you even get a whiff of a fighting bull, though, it might well be best to simply drop everything and run.

East–west **transport** in the sierra is very limited. Most of the bus services are radial and north–south, with Sevilla as the hub, although a spasmodic service does run between Aracena and Aroche further west. Tracks are still more common than roads, and tourism, which the government of Andalucía is keen to encourage, has so far led to little more than a handful of signs pointing out areas of special interest. It's not that satisfying to drive around Morena; this is not Michelin car-window-view territory, and the obvious solution if you want to spend any amount of time here is to organize your routes round **hikes** and hitching. In areas like this cars are few and bound to be making for the same place as you, so drivers are often willing to stop. **Cycling**, too, is an option, though you'll need a sturdy bike with plenty of gears, especially on the less frequented hill roads.

Aracena

Clustered beneath its hilltop Moorish castle, the town of **ARACENA** is the highest conurbation in the Sierra Morena as well as the gateway to its own **Sierra de Aracena** to the south. Sheltered by this offshoot of the larger Morena range, Aracena is blessed by remarkably sharp, clear air – all the more noticeable, and gratifying, if you've arrived from the heat of Sevilla.

The Town

Aracena itself is undistinguished but pretty, rambling up the side of a hill topped by the **Iglesia del Castillo** – or, more correctly, Nuestra Señora de los Dolores – a fine thirteenth-century Gothic-Mudéjar church built by the Knights Templar round the remains of a Moorish castle (one of dozens in the sierra). The track up to the church begins from the **Plaza Alta**, where there's the unfinished church of **Nuestra Señora de la Asunción**, with remnants of Renaissance craftsmanship flanked by a sixteenth-century *Ayuntamiento* – the oldest in the province. Not far away, the interior of the **Convento de Santa Catalina**, with its fine fifteenth-century gothic panels, is also worth a look.

The climb to the castle offers good views over the town from an elegant **sixteenth-century brick gate** complete with belfry, which allows access to the castle area. The church's elegant Mudéjar tower was formerly the minaret of the twelfth-century Almohad mosque prior to its destruction by the Templars and its *sebka* brickwork ornamentation echoes the Giralda tower in Sevilla. Inside there's an unusual and finely made **glazed clay tomb** of the sixteenth-century prior, Pedro Vasquez de Miguel.

Aracena's principal attraction, however, must be the **Gruta de las Maravillas** (daily 10am–1pm & 2.30–6pm; 600ptas), the largest and arguably the most impressive cave in Spain. Discovered, so they say, by a local boy in search of a lost pig, the cave is now illuminated and open for guided tours (you may need a sweater). A guide takes you round in hourly groups on busy days or as soon as a dozen or so people have assembled at other times. On Sunday there is a constant procession, but usually plenty of time to gaze and wonder. Although the garish coloured lighting is more Santa's Grotto than geological marvel, the cave is still astonishingly beautiful, and quite a laugh, too – the last chamber of the tour is known simply as the *Sala de los Culos* (Room of the Buttocks), its walls and ceiling an outrageous, naturally sculpted exhibition, tinged in a pinkish orange light. You might care to ponder why this section of the caves did not appear in the film *Journey to the Centre of the Earth,* much of which was shot here. In the plaza outside there's a permanent **outdoor museum of contemporary sculpture**. Sniffily dismissed by many of its critics, despite the vapid nature of some of the works on show it seems an interesting idea – make up your own mind.

Practicalities

For advice and information, Aracena's **Turismo** (Mon–Sat 10am–2.30pm & 3.30–6.30pm; ☎959/110355) is located beneath the Gruta de las Maravillas ticket office. There are numerous **places to stay**; *Hostal Sierpes* at the northern end of the main Plaza de Aracena, c/Mesones 19 (☎959/110147; ③), is a homely place which has rooms with bath and a good, economical restaurant. *Casa Carmen* (☎959/110764; ②), a few doors away has the same facilities but is slightly more spartan. Below the main square, *Casa Manolo,* c/Barberos 6 (☎959/110014; ②) is another budget possibility, while the *Hotel Sierra de Aracena,* Gran Vía 21 (☎959/126175; ④) offers relative luxury. There's also a municipal **campsite**, about 5km out on the Sevilla road, then left towards Corteconcepción; the site is about 500m along this road. It was recently closed for renovation, however, so check with the Turismo to save yourself a wasted journey.

As Aracena is at the heart of a prestigious *jamón*-producing area, you should eat anything with ham in it, and, when they're available, the delicious wild asparagus, mushrooms and local snails. The lowest-priced **places to eat** in town are limited in the evenings to the dining rooms of the two *hostales*; *Sierpes* and *Carmen,* where prices and food are much the same. One place definitely worth a splurge is *Restaurante Sierra,* Avda. Andalucía 51, where patrons gather to savour the five grades of Jabugo *jamón ibérico* (black pig ham) under the approving gaze of owner/chef Vicente Sierra. This delicacy doesn't come cheap, however, and if you're on a budget you may wish to stick to the *menú* which often includes a mouthwatering *solomillo* (pork loin). You can find the restaurant by following the street almost facing the *Hostal Sierpes* for 150 metres – it's on the left opposite the park. Lunchtime (that is, until 5pm) alternatives are provided by the two restaurants close by the entrance to the Gruta de las Maravillas, the outstanding *Casas,* Pozo La Nieve 39, and the nearby *La Serrana,* both slightly extravagant and excellent.

For **breakfast** or evening drinks, sit at the outdoor tables of the *Casino* bar above the main square, from where you get a wonderful view towards the castle. Finally, for superb **dulces** you have to visit *Confitería Casa Rufino* off the main square at c/ Constitucíon 3; the *tocino de cielo, vitorías* (liqueur-soaked iced cakes) and *sultanas* (filled coconut cakes) from this century-old institution are truly memorable.

The Sierra de Aracena

With a few days to spare, the string of rugged villages perched on the hills to the **west of Aracena** make a fine walking tour. Along the route you'll find a number of good places to stay and plenty of tracks to follow through this rich landscape of orange and lemon orchards and forests of cork oaks and gum trees. In spring the profusion of flowers is extraordinary: rosemary, French lavender, peonies, and Spanish irises are most common, and you may also be lucky enough to see the rare brown bluebell and members of the orchid family. You probably won't glimpse the Spanish lynx in its last native habitat (outside the Coto Doñana), but the skies are the place for sightings of black vultures on patrol, and even the occasional imperial eagle, a stirring image as he glides regally above his domain.

Alajar

Leaving Aracena by the minor H521, after about 7km a turn-off left leads to the tiny village of Linares de la Sierra, a fairly simple and impoverished place huddled around its eighteenth-century Baroque church, a typical example of the Sierra style. There's no accommodation on offer in the village, but the bars in the centre serve food. A further 4km along the main road, lined with chestnut orchards and great clumps of oregano, a turning on the left descends to **ALAJAR**, a delightful cobble-streeted hamlet at the foot of the Peña de Arias Montaño. There's another eighteenth-century Baroque church here with the typical spire, besides plenty of places to eat or have a beer, all clustered around the main square. Each September 7 and 8, the village holds a *romería* or pilgrimage to the hermitage of the Virgen de los Angeles – an isolated church or *ermita* – on the Peña de Arias Montano hill, 1km above the village. This involves the young men of the village in the *polleo*, a rite of passage in which these young bloods race horses along the narrow cobbled streets and then up the steep slope to the shrine,

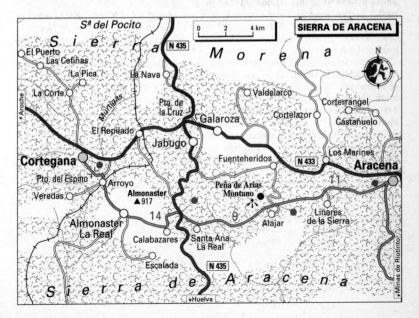

high above. The horses are mercilessly spurred and arrive foaming and bleeding at the top of the climb.

Peña de Arias Montano

On quiet days the **PEÑA DE ARIAS MONTANO**, the rock cliff which towers above the village, is a beautiful leafy spot set among woods of cork oaks, with cold springs surrounding its **shrine**. The Sierra Morena is liberally dotted with these buildings, almost always in isolated spots and dedicated to the Virgin. The site has been hallowed since prehistoric times, and Iberian shamans or priests are reputed to have gained their "second sight" from the hallucinogenic *amanita muscaria* mushroom which grows in the woods here – you are advised against experimenting as some species found in these hills can kill in thirty minutes. The sixteenth-century **hermitage of the Virgen de los Angeles** – filled with ex-votos from pilgrims and distinguished more by the beauty of its setting than for any architectural qualities – is the former retreat of the humanist Benito Arias Montano, confessor and librarian to Philip II, who was born nearby in 1527 and has given his name to the site. The *espadaña*, or belfry, to the side of the church dates from the same period and offers glorious **views** over Alajar beneath, and the Sierra beyond. A **cavern** below the car park is said to be where magical and religous ceremonies were carried out in ancient times and where Philip II is supposed to have meditated during a visit here – giving it the name *Sillita del Rey* (the king's chair), a reference to the huge boulder at the cave's mouth. You reach it by steps from the car park, taking the path to the right at the bottom.

The true peace of the place is best appreciated by leaving the visitors' area with its car park, toilets, café and stalls selling honey, garish pots and religious tack, and heading along the track into the woods of cork oaks where there are plenty of likely picnic spots, and more fine views over the Sierra.

Santa Ana la Real and Almonaster la Real

Six kilometres west of Alájar the modest village of **SANTA ANA LA REAL** has – a couple of kilometres beyond it – a convenient **place to stay**. The modern *Hostal El Cruce* (③), set in fine scenery with a bustling *tapas* bar is located at the junction of the H521 and the N435.

Continuing east for another 6km brings you to the main village of this corner of the Sierra, **ALMONASTER LA REAL**. A sturdy agricultural centre today, Almonaster has an impressive Moorish past and an important tenth-century **mosque** on a hill to the south of the town. The mosque may have Roman and Visigothic antecedents, and after it became Christianized in the thirteenth century was little altered, thus preserving its square **minaret**, the **mihrab** (said to be the oldest in Spain) and beautiful interior of five naves with **brick horseshoe arches** supported by what are probably recycled Roman columns. You can look inside by asking at the *Ayuntamiento*, Plaza de la Constitución, for the key. Tacked on to the mosque/church is the village **bullring** where each August a *corrida* is staged during the annual fiesta (see box). The mosque's tower is a favourite with the kids of the village at this time, as it provides a free view of the ring.

If your Spanish is up to it, it's worth getting hold of *Andar por la Sierra de Aracena* (Penthalon), a **walking guide** which has seventeen clearly described itineraries. Alternatively, the Aracena and Huelva Turismos give out the free *Senderos de la Provincia de Huelva*, with about the same number of walks. And from the *Ayuntamiento* in Almonaster la Real another booklet, *Senderismo*, not only describes a dozen signed walks but also has useful background information on the villages of the western Sierra.

COUNTRY CORRIDAS

Like many other country rings, the **Plaza de Toros** at Almonaster does not see much action. In fact, the prohibitive cost of mounting a *corrida* with six bulls, three matadors and their retinues often restricts a small village to one *corrida* each year, usually in the middle of its annual fiesta. To see a bullfight at places like Almonaster, however, is to get a fascinating insight into many of the secrets of the *corrida* hidden from view in the large city rings. Because the ring itself is barely large enough to hold the arena and a few hundred spectators, just squeezing in a room for the *matadores* and a pen for the bulls, many of the preparations have to take place outside.

First of all, while the arena is doused from a water tanker, the *picadores* select their 8ft-long lances from a couple of dozen leaning against the wall of the ring. When they've chosen, a blacksmith attaches one of three lethal-looking steel points, again selected by the *picador*. Meanwhile, below the walls of the mosque, the grooms prepare the horses – whose vocal chords are severed so as not to alarm the crowd with their terrified shrieks – by fastening on the *peto* or heavy padding, protection against the bull's ferocious horns. Next the horses' ears are stuffed with oil-soaked rags and securely tied to block out the sound of the crowd and the bull. Finally, they are blindfolded over the right eye, the side from which the bull will attack. Fifteen minutes before the *corrida* is due to start the local band marches up the hill playing a lively tune – with the frequent wrong note – before disappearing inside the arena.

Inside, the band strikes up a *paso doble* for the pre-fight parade before the grotesque figure of the helmeted and armoured *picador* is pushed through the small doorway into the ring and a great cheer goes up from the crowd inside. They are soon yelling "fuera!" (away), however, because they don't want the bull too weakened by the lance to be able to put up a decent fight. A few minutes later the trumpets sound and the door opens to allow the *picador* astride the strutting, snorting horse to exit from the arena. With fresh blood dripping from his lance, the image of this warrior is almost medieval. Big name *toreros* appear in these village *corridas* because the pay is good, but equally the risks are high. The primitive facilities in rings such as the one at Almonaster means a long journey to reach a hospital with adequate facilities should the *matador* be seriously gored, a factor which has, in the past, proved fatal.

The village's other main sight is the fourteenth-century Mudéjar-style church of **San Martín** (open service times between 7–9pm), whose most notable feature is a superb sixteenth-century **Manueline portal**, probably Portuguese in inspiration. Also worth a look is the **Ermita de Santa Eulalia**, built over a Roman funerary monument and with late-Gothic frescoes depicting the exploits of Santiago the *matomoros* or "Moorslayer".

A popular event here in early summer is the **Cruz de Mayo** – a *flamenco* festival held over the last weekend in May – at which the celebrated *fandangos* of Almonaster are sung and when the local women parade in the magnificent costume of the *Serrana* (highlands): colourful flounced dresses and tasselled shoes and shawls, complemented by bouquets of wild flowers. The whole affair provides the participants with an excuse to soak up prodigious quantities of the local *aguardiente* firewater, which is misleadingly described as brandy. If you miss this one, similar festivals take place in the surrounding villages all through May.

Almonaster's **train** station – with services to Huelva – is 3km north of the village and is, in fact, nearer to Cortegana (see p.236). Outside the festival period, finding a **place to stay** is usually no problem. At the entrance to the village *Hostal Casa García* (☎959/130409; ③) is good with a great **restaurant** below – try their *tortilla de jamón y espárragos* or the *solomillo* (pork sirloin). Further in, the village's other possibility, *Hostal La Cruz*, c/Los Llanos 8 (☎959/130435; ③) is equally friendly and slightly less expensive.

WALKS AROUND ALMONASTER

There are some superb **walks around Almonaster**, following the old cobbled mule paths and village tracks (*senderos*). The paths are well preserved, on the whole – though you are, at times, forced onto the tarmac road – and are waymarked with paint-splashes on trees and rocks. You need sharp eyes to spot the beginning of the paths, below the road, and, if you can, should try to get hold of the *Senderismo* pamphlet from the *Ayuntamiento* in Almonaster, Cortegana or Jabugo. This has route descriptions and an excellent fold-out survey map.

One of the most enjoyable walks, starting from Cortegana, is the **PRA-5**, which leads off to the left of the Cortegana road, around 1km out of Almonaster. This will take you through woodland, peppered with streams, to the hamlets of **Arroyo** and **Varedas** (2hrs), where there are bars with food, and on to Cortegana (3hrs). Alternatively, if it's just a brief country ramble you're after, follow the sign to Acebuches along the **PRA-5-2** path, under an hour from Almonaster, and again endowed with a small bar.

Another fine walk from Almonaster is to head straight up the hillside northeast of the village, along the **PRA-5-1**. This is actually a paved Roman track, presumably built for some kind of quarrying. It takes a couple of hours' strenuous walking to get up to the summit, and, if you're making a day of it, you could continue on to Cortegana or Jabugo.

Cortegana

A couple of kilometres out of Almonaster the road forks left to **CORTEGANA**, a pleasant and populous hamlet spreading along the valley of the Río Carabaña below a heavily restored castle. Built in the thirteenth century during the frontier disputes with the Portuguese, the **Castillo** (collect the key from the *Ayuntamiento* in Plaza de España) provided a necessary observation post and today gives fine views from its battlements.

Two **churches** here are also worth a look. The **Iglesia del Divino Salvador** (open service times 7–9pm) was started in the late sixteenth century but has elements from much later, such as its bell-tower, added when the original collapsed in the Lisbon earthquake of 1755. The interior has a finely worked Baroque pulpit. Built in Gothic–Mudéjar style, the church of **San Sebastián** (open service times 7–9pm) nearby has interesting Renaissance doors.

If you want to **stay** in Cortegana, try the *Hostal Cervantes*, c/Cervantes 27 (☎959/130092; ②), which is clean and comfortable; a number of bars around the centre serve **tapas** – *Bar España* on Plaza de la Constitución is good. As you are now in the heartland of *jamón* anything anything with pork in it is usually excellent. The best, if slightly pricey, place for **meals** is *Restaurante Titu's* on the main road, or there's the cheaper *Restaurante Jaime*, on c/Eritas, nearer the centre.

Aroche

Heading west for 14km along the N433 brings you to **AROCHE**, in sight of the border with Portugal. Perched on a hill dominated by its castle with a fertile plain below, it's a neat little place, with whitewalled cobbled streets where – because it gets so few visitors – you are sure of a hearty reception. Originally the Roman town of *Arruci Vetus*, many more ancient vestiges of habitation have been discovered here including some giant prehistoric single standing stones, or **menhirs**. (These **Piedras del Diablo** are on private land, so if you're interested in seeing them, enquire at the *Ayuntamiento* in Plaza Juan Carlos.)

Once you have made it up the hill to the village, the obvious place to aim for is the **Castillo** (it should be open; if not, ask at the *Ayuntamiento*, which also provides tourist **information**; ☎959/140201). Constructed by the Almoravids in the twelfth century, it was remodelled after the *reconquista*, but the most bizarre alteration of all was to make the interior into a full-scale **bullring**. A curiosity here are the sallyports – narrow openings in the arena's stone wall – used by the *toreros* to dodge the bull, instead of the normal *barrera* or fence. Despite its primitive facilities many of the big names have fought here, though it's unlikely that they stayed around long after the "kill" to use the ramshackle shower and leaking toilets in their room.

To the left of the entrance to the castle, a small **archeological museum** (Tues–Sun 8am–2.30pm) houses a collection of finds – prehistoric, Roman and Moorish – from Aroche and the surrounding area. If you arrive here outside the opening hours, call at the *Ayuntamiento*, who will usually produce a key. Just below the castle, the parish church of **Nuestra Señora de la Asunción** (again, key from the *Ayuntamiento*) was started in 1483 but added a mixture of Mudéjar, Gothic and Renaissance styles before its completion 150 years later. Behind a dour, buttressed exterior the triple naved church has a fine *retablo*, with a Baroque image of the Virgin, the patron of the town. The church's other treasures include the fifteenth-century crucifix of Cardenal Mendoza of Sevilla, the supporter of Isabel, as well as a seventeenth-century **Russian icon** from St Petersburg.

There are some pretty strange museums in Andalucía, but Aroche's **Museo del Santo Rosario** (Museum of the Holy Rosary) has to be one of the most eccentric. Located in c/Lobos Carlos in a fifteenth-century mansion, the exhibits consist of well over a thousand rosaries donated by such leading religious luminaries as Pope John XXIII and Mother Teresa, in addition to others from bullfighters and soccer players and one each from John F Kennedy and King Juan Carlos. Those sent in by Richard Nixon and General Franco betray suspiciously little sign of wear.

Near the entrance to the town from the N433, *Restaurante Pensión Romero* (☎959/140022; ②) is Aroche's only **accommodation** option, and perfectly adequate. For **food** you could eat here or try the *Centro Social Las Peñas*, c/Carlos Lobos 8, where the bar does a nice *tapas* selection. There's also *El Chino*, c/Bellido 2, near the *Ayuntamiento*, which, despite the name, specialises in local pork dishes.

Jabugo

The mere mention of the name of **JABUGO** is enough to make any Spaniard's mouth water. Once you have tasted what all the fuss is about it's easy to understand what drives this Spanish culinary obsession. As roadside billboards depicting smiling pigs proclaim for miles around, ham – or rather *jamón* – is king in Jabugo. To get stuck into *jamón* sampling, when you approach the village from the N433, ignore the sign directing you to the *centro urbano* and continue straight on. You'll pass half a dozen **bars** all eager to sell you a *bocadillo* stuffed with *jamón de Jabugo* – or even a whole ham should you feel like splashing out. There are *tapas* too, but keep an eye on the prices as the *pata negra* doesn't come cheap.

A WALK FROM EL REPILADO TO LOS ROMEROS

Returning to Aracena from Aroche by the N433 takes you through the hamlet of **El Repilado** from where you could make a picturesque 5km **walk** south along the Río Caliente to the village of Los Romeros. Leave Repilado by the N433 road towards Cortegana and after crossing the bridge over the river, turn left along the H111 going to Los Romeros. Where the road crosses to the east bank of the river, follow the track along the west bank which leads through woods of chestnut and black poplar, and where in spring you'll see a profusion of wildflowers. When the road recrosses the river, use the bridge to gain access to the tiny village of **Los Romeros**. There are few facilities and no accommodation in either Repilado or Los Romeros (which has a bar serving *tapas*), but Jabugo (see below) is close by and has both.

THE KING OF HAMS

Surrounding Jabugo are a scattering of attractive but economically depressed villages mainly dependent on the **jamón industry** and its curing factory, which is the major local employer. Things were little different when Richard Ford passed through here a century and a half ago, describing these mountain villages as "coalitions of pigsties" adding that it was the duty of every good pig to "get fat as soon as he can and then to die for the good of his country".

Sought out by classical writers such as Strabo for its distinctive flavour, and produced since long before by the peoples of the Iberian peninsula, *jamón serrano* (mountain ham from white pigs) is a *bocadillo* standard throughout Spain – the English words "ham" and "gammon" are both derived from the Spanish. Some of the best ham of all, *jamón ibérico* or *pata negra* (both acorn-fed ham) comes from the Sierra Morena, where herds of sleek pigs grazing beneath the trees are a constant feature. In October the acorns drop or are beaten down by their keepers and the pigs, waiting patiently below, gorge themselves, become fat and are promptly whisked off to the factory to be slaughtered and then cured in the dry mountain air. The meat of these black pigs is exceptionally fatty when eaten as pork but the same fat that marbles the meat adds to the tenderness during the curing process. This entails first of all covering the hams in coarse rock or sea salt to "sweat", after which they are removed to cool cellars to mature for up to two years. *Jamón serrano* from mass-produced white pigs is matured for only a few weeks, hence the incomparable difference in taste. At Jabugo the best of the best is then further graded from one to five *jotas* (the letter "J" for Jabugo) depending on its quality – *cinco jotas jamón* comes close to the price of gold.

The king of hams also demands an etiquette all of its own: in bars and restaurants everywhere it has its own apparatus to hold it steady, and carving is performed religiously with a long, thin-bladed knife. The slices must not be wafer thin nor bacon rashers, and once on the plate *jamón ibérico* becomes the classic partner for a glass of *fino*.

Ham apart, the village of Jabugo is a sleepy place for most of of the year, gathered around a charming leafy square with a central dribbling fountain overlooked by the *Casino* and the crumbling Baroque **church of San Miguel**. If you can find a key (try at the *Casino*), the church is worth a look inside for its splendid **retablo** and an original eighteenth-century **organ**. Otherwise, it's back to **eating** and **drinking** at the *Casino* – a relaxing place to call in for a beer. For full meals, *Restaurante Saúco* (with a *menú*) on the main road at the entrance to the town is your best bet, and if you want to **stay**, head for the hospitable *Hostal Aurora*, c/Barca 9 (☎959/121146; ②).

The **villages** around Jabugo – Aguafría, Castaño del Robledo (with decaying mansions, huge Baroque church and the wonderfully rustic *Bar La Bodeguita*), and Fuenteheridos (rooms and food available at the monastery of the **Hermanos Maristas**, but you must call ahead; ☎959/125024; ⑥) – all make rewarding destinations for walks amid splendid wooded hills, though all are equally ill-served by public transport and you may well find yourself in for a walk both ways.

Galaroza

The N433 continues east from Jabugo through country filled with dense oak woods surrounded by dry stone walls, where you may catch a fleeting glimpse of a herd of *cerdos ibéricos*, the celebrated black pigs of the Sierra. **GALAROZA**, encircled by chestnut and fruit orchards seems awash with water which for much of the year splashes and bubbles in its fountains and along the culverts lining the narrow streets. This may explain its annual *Fiesta del los Jarritos* during which everyone – including visitors – gets soaked with water when the town goes *agua* mad. September 6 is the date to avoid if you want to stay dry. The village has another Baroque church as well as

rooms and a number of **places to eat**. *Hostal Toribio*, c/Primo de Rivera 2 (☎959/117073; ③) and the pleasant *Hostal Venecia* (☎959/117098; ③) on the main road, are both good.

Zufre and east to Cazalla

East of Aracena there's more good hiking country – if slightly less wooded – along the northern frontier of Sevilla province, which traverses the **Natural Park of Sierra Norte**. From Aracena one daily **bus** – currently at 5.45pm, connecting with the bus from Sevilla – covers the 25km southeast to Zufre. If you miss it, you'll have to walk, which takes the best part of a day but can be good in itself.

A couple of hours out of Aracena you come upon the **Embalse de Aracena**, one of the huge reservoirs that supply Sevilla, dammed by a massive construction across the southern end of the valley. From here a lovely but circuitous route will take you down towards Zufre along the **Rivera de Huelva**.

Zufre

ZUFRE, about 25km southeast of Aracena, must be one of the most spectacular villages in Spain, hanging like a miniature Ronda on a high palisade at the edge of a ridge. Below the crumbling Moorish walls, the cliff falls away hundreds of feet, terraced into deep green gardens of orange trees and vegetables. In town, and sharing a charming and leafy *plazuela*, the arcaded *Ayuntamiento* and parish **church** – built of brick and pink stone – are both interesting sixteenth-century examples of Mudéjar style, the latter built on the foundations of a mosque. In the basement of the *Ayuntamiento*, too, are a gloomy line of stone seats, said to have been used by the Inquisition. A friendly priest at the house on the other side of the square from the church will usually open it to let you see inside. The focus of town, however, is the **Paseo**, a little park with rose gardens, balcony and a bar at one end and a *Casino* at the other. The villagers gather round here for much of the day – there's little work either in Zufre or the surrounding countryside, and even the local bullring, cleverly squeezed on to a rock ledge, only sees use twice a year; at the beginning of the season in March, and at the town's September *feria*.

Finding **food and drink** shouldn't be a problem – plenty of bars in the warren of Moorish streets above the park serve *tapas*. Although there's no official **accommodation** in Zufre, try asking around and there's a fair chance of fixing up a private room.

Santa Olalla del Cala

There's no bus link between Zufre and **SANTA OLALLA DEL CALA**, 16km to the east, but it's not hard to arrange a lift with one of the many locals who drive the route daily on the way to school and work. If you choose to walk it, you're in for a memorable experience: a flattish route through open country with pigs and fields of wheat and barley, and then a sudden view of the **castillo** – a thirteenth-century Christian construction but incorporating Moorish features – above the town. Half-hearted attempts to reconstruct the castle haven't been helped by its adaptation in the last century as the local cemetery – the holes for coffins in the walls rather spoil the effect. Below the walls, the fifteenth-century parish **church** has a fine Renaissance interior.

Coming from Zufre it's a surprise to find **hostales** in Santa Olalla, but the town is actually on the main Sevilla–Badajoz road and sees a fair amount of traffic (which somewhat dents its charm) – and regular buses between both cities. These stop outside the *Bar Primitivo*, c/Marina 3 (☎959/190052; ②), an admirable place to sleep, eat or just drink, all for a very reasonable price; it's named after the owner, and not meant as a value judgment. Another place to eat which also has rooms is *Casa Carmelo*, c/Marina 23 (☎959/190169; ②), close by.

East to El Real de la Jara

As no buses travel the east–west route, to continue along the Sierra you'll have to walk or hitch the eight kilometres to Real de la Jara. Halfway, after winding through stone-walled olive groves, the road flattens out into a grassy little valley above the **Río Calla** – marking the border of Huelva with Sevilla province and a spot where the villages of Real and Olalla hold their joint *romería* at the end of April. You're bound to receive a great reception if you stumble across one of these country *romerías*, where proceedings start with a formal parade to the local *ermita*, and are followed by feasting and dancing. The young men wobble about on donkeys and mules in a wonderful parody of the grand *hidalgo* doings of Jerez and Sevilla, children shriek and splash in the river, and everyone dances *sevillanas* to scratchy cassettes.

EL REAL DE LA JARA is a village in much the same mould as Santa Olalla: with two ruined Moorish *castillos*, an overpriced and eccentrically run *casa de huéspedes* at c/Real 66 (②), some places to eat, a very welcome public swimming pool, and no buses. To continue hiking east requires persistence and, unless you've a lot of energy, a run back and forth from Sevilla. Cazalla de la Sierra, the next village of any size, is some 45km along a mountainous and lonely route; picturesque if you're driving, but a real test on foot. The one relief is the **Embalse del Pintado**, a huge reservoir from where, starting from the village of El Pintado, you could explore the **Gargantua del Río Viar**, a superb river gorge with plenty of flora and fauna which is also home to an important colony of vultures. Start from the road on the west side of the village where – near a wild fig tree – a track descends into the gorge. At the foot of this you can follow the river's eastern bank. To walk the whole thing would take you a good couple of hours to reach the hamlet of La Ganchosa, and in the high summer heat maybe an amble to see the birdlife would be a better bet. You're also advised not to drink the water here as it contains pollutants.

Cazalla and the Central Sierra

A regional Sierra "capital", **CAZALLA DE LA SIERRA** feels like a veritable metropolis, especially if you arrive on foot. Not only is this one of the few towns on the Sierra served by **bus** (daily between here and Sevilla), but it also boasts a **Turismo**, on Plaza Dr Narcea 1; a couple of **fondas** (the best is in Plaza Iglesia); **hostales** such as *La Milagrosa*, c/Llana 29 (☎954/884260; ②), and a **hotel**, the *Posada del Moro*, c/Paseo El Moro s/n (☎954/884326; ⑤). There are numerous bars and even a pub – pronounced "pa" in Andaluz – where the locals go to drink cocktails and listen to jazz and rock. If this is all too much of a shock, a more traditional bar and restaurant, still lively, is the *Boleras* in Plaza Manuel Nosea – right next to the *Guardia Civil*, who are themselves ensconced in a beautiful former nunnery.

An ancient Iberian settlement, Cazalla became the Roman *Callentum* and later the Moorish *Kazalla* ("fortified city") from which the modern name derives. Its importance in post-*reconquista* days was as a staging post along the route to Extremadura and the north. The place was noted in Roman times for its vines and wines, a tradition which survives in the production of *aguardiente* (eau de vie), sold in *bodegas* around the town.

Cazalla's main sight is the huge church of **Nuestra Señora de la Consolación** at the southern end of town, an outstanding example of *andaluz* "mix and match" architecture which was begun in the fourteenth century in Mudéjar style, and continued with some nice Renaissance touches and finally completed in the eighteenth century. The interior has a fine sixteenth-century *retablo*. Fronting the church's northern door, c/Virgen del Monte leads to the market area, a colourful and bustling place on weekdays. Just by here, along c/Carmelo Meclana, the former monastery church of **San Francisco** has been converted into the sales depot of an *aguardiente* producer, *Miura*, where you can taste the local firewater while contemplating the church's dilapidated

WALKS AROUND CAZALLA

There are some fine spots within easy wandering distance of Cazalla: a walk of just 5km will take you southeast to the **Ermita del Monte**, a little eighteenth-century church on a wooded hill above the Ribera del Huéznar.

From **San Nicolás del Puerto** (see below) you could continue the 12km to **ALANÍS** along the upper reaches of the Huéznar, where it arcs around above San Nicolás through some ruggedly scenic country with meadows dotted with ilex and cork oaks. Take the Alanís road out of San Nicolás, and, after crossing the bridge over the river take a right between some houses. Follow this to the end and continue along a track heading north. If you get confused, remember that you're aiming in a northeasterly direction which will bring you – after 4km – to a dirt track heading left for Alanís. Turn right here (you're not heading for Alanís yet) and after crossing the river, turn left along a track on the opposite bank which follows the river around, passing a hermitage on the right with pines and a barbecue.

Shortly beyond this the charming white village of Alanís appears, its Moorish castle rising above the surrounding terrain. There are places to eat here, but no accommodation; should you not fancy the walk back to San Nicolás, you could hop on the Sevilla **bus** which stops at Alanís, or it shouldn't be too difficult to hitch.

Alternatively, if you're making southwards for **El Pedroso** (see below), you might as well walk from the Cazalla train station – a lovely five-hour route along the banks of the Huéznar flowing through woods of alder, elm and ash with the occasional weeping willow and a fabulous variety of valley flora and fauna. It's an excellent trout river and a wonderful place to swim, and at holiday times and summer weekends can get very crowded with locals. **To start the trail** from Cazalla station take the road towards Constantina, crossing the rail line. Just after this you'll come to a forest track on the right signed for the "Molino de Corcho", an old water mill. A short way downstream, cross the first bridge, and carry on along the prettier east bank of the river. Cross back at the third bridge and continue past the Molino del Corcho (which is open to visitors) and on to the Fábrica de Pedroso (an old factory). From here you can follow the road to El Pedroso, or continuing along the river, at a bridge 4km on you should climb up to the road, and follow the SE190 from where the village lies 3km east.

Baroque interior. The town's fifteenth-century **Cartuja** or Carthusian monastery was, until recently, a near ruin, but funds diverted from *Expo 92* are set to rescue and restore what's left – particularly its beautiful portal and a cupola with Mudéjar frescoes. For refreshment the place to make for is the local *Casino* in **La Plazuela**.

From Cazalla you can take a **bus** (at 6.45am or 1pm) as far as the **Estacíon de Cazalla y Constantina**, 7km east. Here three or four trains a day run northwest to **Guadalcanal** (a pleasant town with three fine Mudéjar churches but lacking accommodation) and Extremadura, and a similar number follow the river down towards El Pedroso and ultimately Sevilla. Taking the train 12km **northwards** brings you to **SAN NICOLÁS DEL PUERTO**, another typical Sierra village with overnight **accommodation** at the *Venta La Salud*, Avda. del Huéznar s/n (☎954/885253; ②) which also has a restaurant.

El Pedroso and Constantina

EL PEDROSO is somewhat less depressed than most towns in the sierra due to the local factory, the *fábrica*, one stop up on the train line, which seems to employ most of the locals, making a nebulous, undefined product. It's a pretty little place, with a notable Mudéjar church; if you fancy **staying the night** ask the woman who runs the station *cantina* for a room. Across the road, an excellent **tapas bar**, the *Serranía*, serves up local specialities such as venison, hare, pheasant and partridge.

Eighteen kilometres further to the east – and perhaps as good a place as any to cut back to Sevilla if you're not counting on hiking the whole length of the range – you reach **CONSTANTINA**, an important and beautiful mountain town with a population of almost 15,000. Founded by the Romans in the time of the Emperor Constantine, hence its name, this is a delightful place to wander around, particularly the old quarter dotted with a number of notable eighteenth-century mansions. High above the town, the **Castillo de la Armada** is an impressive medieval fortress surrounded by shady gardens descending in terraces to the old quarters. At the base you'll find the parish church of **La Encarnación**, once again with a Mudéjar tower – Moorish influence having died hard in these parts – and a splendid, if crumbling, Plateresque portal by Hernan Ruiz. Constantina has a new public **swimming pool**, very welcome to beat the intense summer heat, additionally, if you've got your own transport you can make a trip to **La Pantalla** – a lake for swimming and fishing – east along the road to El Pedroso.

There are two **fondas**, the best of which is the *Pensión Angelita*, c/El Peso 28 (☎954/880438; ②) near the main walking street, c/Mesones, and one dubious *comidas y camas* place in the Alameda. Other possibilities include a spacious **private house**, c/ Jose de la Bastida 25, which rents out rooms, some with bath (②), and a summer-only **youth hostal**, c/Cuesta Blanca s/n (☎954/881054;). Also on c/Mesones *La Farola* (no. 14) is a decent **place to eat** serving *tapas* and a wide range of *platos combinados*. As for **nightlife**; there are plenty of bars as well as three **discos** – *Bonny Dog* is the most central, but *Ja Ja* has better music and goes on till dawn.

Two **buses** a day link Constantina to Sevilla (6.45am & 3pm), but the lovely countryside around the village is best explored using your own transport. One worthwhile excursion is the trip 16km northeast through fine hill country to **LAS NAVAS DE LA CONCEPCIÓN**, a charming hamlet with an eighteenth-century Baroque church containing sculptures attributed to La Roldana.

Lora del Río and Villanueva del Río y Minas

South of Constantina the road descends for 28km through the Sierra de La Cruz until, at the sturdy, rather dull agricultural town of **LORA DEL RÍO**, it joins the fertile valley of the Guadalquivir. The southern banks of the river from Lora are famous for rearing *toros de lidia*, the fighting bulls of the *corrida* who greedily graze on the rich river pastures, and the Miura family, long renowned among *aficionados* as supplying the biggest, meanest beasts has its ranch here.

Heading west towards Sevilla along the C431, 10km further on the flat and monotonous landscape of the river valley is overlooked by the remains of the **Roman ruins** of **Arva**. Not much is visible yet of the first-century town which lies beneath the olive

---

A WALK TO MULVA

To **start out** on the trek to Mulva (and in summer make sure you carry water), take the road opposite the *pensión* and cross the railway line. Then follow a track which twists around the old colliery – with evocative pitwheel, chimneys and a curiously turreted administration building – down to the river. Head north along the river's east bank and then cross at a low footbridge, known locally as the *puente chico*. Now on the west bank, continue north and pass under the large bridge (*puente grande*) ignoring the sign for *Munigua* (Mulva) pointing left – this is a longer road route. Once under the big bridge follow the track into the hills until you come to a farmhouse *La Palmilla*, with green gates. They will give you water. The next part of the walk is important, for in the woods beyond here you must take the **left fork** when the track divides ahead. This will eventually lead you – 3km on – to another gate, beyond which the ruins of **Mulva** (ancient *Munigua*) will eventually appear through the woods, dominating the skyline.

groves, but if you keep your eyes skinned, on the right you'll see the substantial remains of a bathhouse and – if you climb the fence – an impressive stone font smashed in two.

Five kilometres beyond Alcolea del Río a road on the right leads – after 3km – to the old coal mining town of **VILLANUEVA DEL RÍO Y MINAS** a starting point for a fine 7km **walk** to the remarkable Roman ruins of Mulva, buried deep in verdant countryside. A fairly humdrum place, Villanueva is a casualty of the Europe-wide depression in the mining industry and its abandoned pit makes a sad sight on the landscape. You can get **rooms** at the pleasant *Pensión-Bar Reche*, Avda. de la Constitución 179 (☎954/747823; ③); take the balcony room, if it's available. You'll be a source of much hilarity over breakfast – the homemade *churros* are recommended – if you announce your plan to walk to Mulva as no one here seems to have walked further than the main street in their lives. However, they will clarify any queries regarding the route, if asked.

Mulva

The Roman ruins of **MULVA** sit in a dramatic position atop a hill; just to one side of which sits the guardian, protecting the site from plunderers all year round. He will give you a ticket (free) and, if you're lucky, some cool water.

A prosperous city founded by the Romans on top of an earlier Iberian settlement, *Munigua*'s wealth came from iron mining, backed, to judge from the numerous stone olive presses found here, by a flourishing oil industry. Recent excavations have uncovered a **suite of baths** together with some fresco fragments. You can climb the hill to the ruins and explore the **sanctuary** – the heart of ancient *Munigua* and believed to have been a copy of the great temple of Fortuna at Praeneste near Rome – as well as the forum, dwellings, a mausoleum and walls of this impressive "lost" city.

A 2km track from Mulva leads to the train station of **Arenillas**, which is on the Sevilla–Zafra line. Villanueva is also on this line, but check with the site guardian, though, as to whether a train is due. Heading east from Villanueva, the C431 road arcs south along the Guadalquivir passing after thirteen kilometres **CANTILLANA**, a pleasant town with a with a couple of Baroque churches, followed by the farming settlements of Villaverde del Río and Alcalá del Río – the latter's Renaissance church of **Santa María** has a stunning *retablo* – before entering Sevilla (see p.161).

travel details

Trains

Huelva to: Almonaster la Real (2 daily; 3hr); Sevilla (7 daily; 1hr 30min); Zafra (2 daily; 4hr).

Sevilla to: Algeciras (2 daily; 6hr); Cádiz (13 daily; 1hr 30min–2hr); Córdoba (12 daily; 1hr 30min–2hr); Granada (3 daily; 4–5hr); Huelva (7 daily; 1hr 30min); Jaén (1 daily; 3hr 30min); Madrid (9 daily; 6hr 30min–9hr 30min); Málaga (3 daily; 3–4hr); Osuna (3 daily;1hr 30min).

Buses

Huelva to: Aracena (2 daily; 2hr 30min); Ayamonte/Portuguese frontier (6 daily; 1hr); Granada (1 daily; 4hr); Málaga (1 daily; 4hr); Matalascañas (1 daily; 1hr 15min); Sevilla (12 daily; 1hr 30min).

Osuna to: Antequera (6 daily; 1hr); Granada (3 daily; 3hr 30min); Málaga (7 daily; 2hr); Sevilla (12 daily; 1hr 30min).

Sevilla to: Algeciras (5 daily; 3hr 30min); Almería (2 daily; 7–9hr); Aracena (2 daily; 2hr); Arcos de la Frontera (2 daily; 2hrs); Ayamonte (access to Portugal's Algarve – 3 daily); Cádiz (8 daily; 1hr 30min–2hr 30min); Carmona (10 daily; 45min); Córdoba (19 daily; 1hr 45min–3hr 15min); Écija (3 daily; 2hr); El Rocío (5 daily; 2hr 30min); Granada (5 daily; 4–5hrs); Huelva (12 daily; 1hr 30min); Jerez (8 daily; 2hr); Madrid (1 daily; 10hr); Marbella (2 daily; 4hr); Matalascañas (5 daily; 3hr); Ronda (3 daily; 3hr).

CHAPTER THREE

CÓRDOBA AND JAÉN

ndalucía's most northerly province, **Córdoba**, is split in half by the Río Guadalquivir. Sited on the river's northern bank, the provincial capital is a fine city whose outstanding attraction is its twelve-hundred year old Moorish **Mezquita**, one of the world's great buildings. In the tangled lanes of the Judería, the old Jewish quarter, that partially surrounds it, the sense of Córdoba's history, as the centre of a vast and powerful empire, is overwhelming. After the brilliance of the Mezquita the rest of the city, particularly the northern sector of modern Córdoba, can seem like an anti-climax; but persist here and you'll discover a host of striking post-*reconquista* **churches** in addition to a number of elegant **convents and mansions**. Despite a reputation for aloofness and sobriety among its neighbours, Córdoba has some of the most distinctive old **bars** in Andalucía, where taking a drink and a *tapa* is often an excuse to enjoy a particularly unique experience. A few kilometres away there's more lingering Moorish splendour at the ruins of **Medina Azahara**, a once fabulous palace of the caliphs which is being painstakingly restored.

To the south of the river lies Cordoba's **campiña**, a rolling landscape of grainfields, olive groves and vineyards, where *Montilla*, the province's rival to the wines of Jerez, is made. Little visited, the more elevated southern reaches of this area are particularly delightful, with a number of towns and villages such as **Baena**, **Cabra** and **Zuheros** ringed by excellent hiking country. The equally unsung town of **Priego de Córdoba**, further south still, has a clutch of spectacular Baroque churches that are worth a trip in themselves. To the north of the capital, the hardy mining towns in the foothills of the **Sierra Morena** attract even fewer visitors, but there's a rich variety of birdlife here, and the higher slopes are home to deer and wild boar zealously stalked by the hunting fraternity in winter.

The **province of Jaén** has been regarded since Moorish times as Andalucía's gateway – through the **Despeñaperros Pass** – to Castile and the cities of Toledo and Madrid to the north. Although often used as this gateway's doormat and something of a forgotten entity, the region's poorest province has some surprisingly worthy sights to present to those prepared to labour inland. The **city of Jaén** has a fine **Renaissance cathedral** as well as impressive **Moorish baths** but is more often used as a stop on the way to the magnificent twin Renaissance towns of **Baeza** and **Úbeda**. Sharing a similar history, the nobilities of these two conurbations competed in using their sixteenth-century wealth to employ some of the best architects and builders around. These craftsmen such as the great architect **Andrés de Vandelvira** – whose imprint is everywhere – have left behind a monumental treasure in golden sandstone, one of the marvels not only of Andalucía, but of Spain and Europe as well. The province's mountainous eastern flank now forms the heart of the **Cazorla Natural Park** and cradles the source of the Guadalquivir. Extending north-east from the town of **Cazorla**, the park's vast expanse of dense woodlands, lakes, and spectacular crags crowned by eagles' and vultures' nests and patrolled by the agile ibex is a paradise for naturalists and walkers. Its northerly reaches are guarded by many ruined Moorish castles, the most spectacular of which sits on the hill above the village of **Segura de la Sierra**.

The rest is mainly **olive groves**, which cover a vast area of Jaén, and whose exclusive cultivation is the cause of much seasonal unemployment. But there is a beauty in the orderly files of trees stretching across the red and creamy white hills to the horizon which seem "to open and close like a fan," as Lorca poetically put it, as you pass.

Córdoba

CÓRDOBA stands upstream from Sevilla beside a loop of the Guadalquivir, which was once navigable as far as here. It is today a minor provincial capital, prosperous in a modest sort of way, but a mere shadow of its past greatness. The city's name – a possible corruption of the Syrian *coteba* or "oil press" – is believed to be of Phoenician origin dating from the time when these merchant venturers sailed up the river to carry away the region's much prized olive oil.

Córdoba is now principally famous for a single building, the **Mezquita** – the grandest and most beautiful mosque ever constructed by the Moors. It stands right in the centre of the city, surrounded by the Judería, the old Jewish and Moorish quarters, and is a building of extraordinary mystical and aesthetic power. Make for it on arrival and keep returning as long as you stay; its beauty and power increase with each visit.

The Mezquita apart, Córdoba is a place of considerable charm. It has few grand squares or mansions, tending instead to introverted architecture, calling your attention to the tremendous and often wildly extravagant **patios**, yet another Moorish legacy. Filled with potplants, decorative tiles, tinkling fountains and a profusion of flowers in summer, these shady oases can usually be glimpsed beyond a forged iron *verja* or gate, and are indisputably the best to be seen in Andalucía. They are also actively encouraged and often maintained by the city council, which runs a "Festival of the Patios" in May. Besides the city's Moorish treasures, there is another Córdoba, to the **north of the old quarter**, an area rarely touched upon by visitors, but with its own rewarding churches and palaces, not to mention bars.

Some history

Although archeological finds document an antiquity stretching back to Neolithic times, Córdoba's verifiable history begins with a Bronze-Age Iberian settlement at the end of the second millenium BC trading on the mineral wealth – silver and copper – brought down from the Sierra Morena to the north. Apparently of little importance during the next millenium, and largely by-passed by the Carthaginian expansion into Spain, Córdoba rose to prominence under **Rome** in the years following the crushing victories against her north-African enemy at the end of the third-century BC.

Founded as the Roman city of *Corduba* in 152BC, Córdoba flourished as the capital of Hispania Ulterior and, foreshadowing its later brilliance, became famous for its poetry as well as its olive oil. Cicero once cracked that Cordoban poetry sounded as if it had got mixed up with the oil due to its thick style of delivery. Later, after Córdoba had backed the wrong horse in the wars between Caesar and Pompey at the end of the Republic, Caesar sacked the city and an estimated thirty-thousand died. When Augustus reorganized Spain in 27BC, Córdoba's fortunes improved as the capital city of the new province of Baetica, roughly corresponding to modern Andalucía. A brilliant period followed during which the city produced the poets **Lucan** and **Seneca** whilst prosperity – based upon oil, wool and minerals – increased.

As Roman power waned in the fifth century the area was overrun first by **Vandals** and then **Visigoths**. Leovigild took the city in 572 but it was inevitable that the unstable Visigothic territories, riven by civil wars, would not survive.

Córdoba fell to the Moors early in the eighth century, and in 756 became the **capital of Moorish Spain**. The succeeding three centuries – when Córdoba formed the heart of the Western Islamic Empire – were the city's golden age, as it grew to rival Cairo and Baghdad as a centre of Muslim art and learning. Though later its political

power declined, Córdoba remained a centre of culture and scholarship and was the birthplace of the twelfth-century thinkers Averroes, the great Muslim commentator on Aristotle, and Maimonides the Jewish philosopher.

After **conquest by Fernando III** in 1236, Córdoba's glory vanished as the city sank into a long and steady **decline**. Such aspects of civilized life as the elaborate Moorish systems of water supply and sewerage disposal fell into ruin as the mosques were turned into churches. Little of the wealth of imperial Spain found its way here, although the city's leatherworkers, silversmiths and *parfumeurs* (all continuing Moorish traditions) achieved some renown in the sixteenth century. Plagues in the next century decimated the population and when Ford arrived in the 1830s he found "a poor and servile city". The city suffered terrible repression in the wars against the French as it was to do again in this century when, during the Civil War, it was captured by the Nationalists who carried out brutal atrocities.

Córdoba's voters took belated revenge for this in the first post-Franco elections of 1979 when it elected a **communist council** – the only major city in Spain to do so. And the communists remain in power today, although they are no longer led by the immensely popular mayor Julio Anguita who, despite suffering a heart attack during the 1993 election campaign, is now the leader of the national party. Befitting its past, Córdoba is a city of learning once again (the university was re-established in 1971) and the town has built up a modestly successful economy based upon its agricultural wealth and light industry.

> The telephone area code for Córdoba is ☎957

Arrival and information

Finding your way around Córdoba is no problem. From the **train station** on Plaza Guadalhorce, the broad Avda. del Gran Capitán leads down to the old quarter and the Mezquita, a mile to the south. **Bus terminals** are numerous and scattered (see "Listings" for complete details). The main company, *Alsina Graells*, is at Avda. de Medina Azahara 29 (the continuation of c/Gondomar), two or three blocks to the west of the Paseo de la Victoria gardens; they run services to and from Sevilla, Granada and Málaga.

The **Turismo** (Mon–Fri 9am–2pm & 5–7pm, Sat 9.30am–1.30pm; ☎471235) is at the Palacio de Congresos y Exposiciones in c/Torrijos alongside the Mezquita. There's also a small municipal office in Plaza Judá Leví, west of the Mezquita (mornings only) which gives out an illustrated brochure on places to visit, with a town plan. For information on fringe theatre and music, there's a *Casa de la Cultura* at Plaza del Potro 10.

Onward travel

If you're heading for **Sevilla** and **Granada**, you have a choice of using trains or buses, which cost more or less the same but the trains generally take longer. When travelling to Sevilla, however, you can use the new *Ave* super-train but this will cost you four times the price of an ordinary ticket. Going to Granada, be sure you take a train via Bobadilla (5hr) and *not* via Linares-Baeza (7–11hrs).

Accommodation

Places to stay can be found all over Córdoba, but the majority (as well as the priciest) are concentrated in the narrow maze of streets around the Mezquita. If you can resist the urge to lodge on the Mezquita's doorstep, a five-minute walk away in all directions

ACCOMMODATION PRICE SYMBOLS

The symbols used in our hotel listings denote the following price ranges:

① Under 2000ptas   ③ 3000–4500ptas   ⑤ 7500–12,500ptas
② 2000–3000ptas   ④ 4500–7500ptas   ⑥ Over 12,500ptas

See p.28 for more details.

leads to a substantial drop in prices and some real bargains. Finding a room at any time of the year isn't usually a problem, but if you really want to be sure, ring ahead.

Budget options

Hostal Alcázar, c/San Basilio 10, near the alcázar off Plaza Martires (☎202561). Friendly family-run place with nice patio. ③.

Hostal Los Arcos, c/Romeros Barros 14 (☎485643). In a quiet street behind the Plaza del Potro, this is a gem with a superb patio. ③.

Fonda Augustina, c/Zapatería Vieja 5 (☎470872). A rather dingy place, but clean. ②.

Mesón Don Manuel, Corregidor de la Cerda 19 (☎478336). Rooms (some with bath) above a restaurant. ③.

Hostal Esmeralda, c/Lucano 16, near the Plaza del Potro (☎474354). Sparkling new place with many balcony rooms; rooms with bath are good value. This street can be noisy in the daytime. ③.

Hostal El León, c/Cespedes 6 (☎ 473021). Basic facilities immediately north of the Mezquita on a noisy street. ②.

Hostal Mari I, c/Pimentera 6, off c/Caldereros to the east of the Mezquita (☎479575). Pleasant place with garden and clean rooms, some single. ②.

Hostal Mari II, c/Horno de Porras 6 (☎486004). An offshoot of *Mari I* above, though no longer connected with it, this is a friendly, simple place with some budget deals. Ask for the room with a fridge and roof terrace at no extra charge. Only open March–Sept. ②.

Pensión Martinez Rucker, c/Martinez Rucker 14, immediately east of the Mezquita (☎472562). A nice patio conceals Spartan rooms lacking hot water. ②.

Hostal Nieves, c/La Cara 12, a tiny street off c/Corregidor de la Cerda (aka c/Gonzales) near the south-east corner of the Mezquita (☎475139). Another very basic *hostal*. ②.

Fonda Plaza Corredera, at the corner of the Plaza and c/Rodríguez Marin. Old but clean *fonda* on this wonderful ramshackle square with great views over the plaza from some rooms. ②.

Hostal El Portillo, c/Cabezas 2, east of the Mezquita (☎472091). Beautiful old place with an elegant patio and charming management. A few singles; many rooms with balconies. ②.

Hostal Rey Heredia, c/Rey Heredia 26, slightly east of the Mezquita (☎473317). Clean, airy white-walled rooms with plenty of light (at the front). Nice patio and modern bathrooms. ③.

Hostal Seneca, c/Conde y Luque 7, just north of the Mezquita (☎473234). A delightful *hostal* with a stunning patio – complete with original Moorish pavement. Breakfast is available and in summer you'll have to book ahead. ③.

Hostal Las Tendillas, c/Jesus Maria 1, off south side of Plaza Tendillas (☎473029). Two-star *hostal* in the real centre of town, which means it can be noisy at weekends. ②.

Hostal Trinidad, c/Corregidor de la Cerda 58 (aka c/Gonzales). Another basic no frills place, but not bad for the price. ②.

More expensive hostales and hotels

Hotel Albucasis, c/Buen Pastor 11, slightly north of the Mezquita (☎478625). Ivy-clad courtyard, spotless bedrooms and pistols on the walls. ⑤.

Hotel Amistad Córdoba, Plaza de Maimónides 3 (☎420305). A new hotel near the old wall in the Judería incorporating two eighteenth-century mansions with Mudéjar patio and staircase. ⑤.

Parador Nacional Arruzufa, Avda. de la Arrezufa s/n, 5km north of town in the El Brillante suburb (☎275900). Attractive modern *parador* with all mod cons and more, including pool, tennis courts and views over the city. Worth a trip out for a drink in its gardens. ⑥.

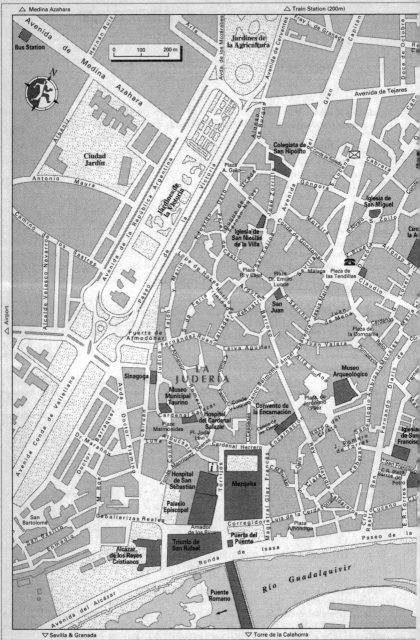

△ Medina Azahara
△ Train Station (200m)

Bus Station

0   100   200 m

Avenida de Medina Azahara

Jardines de la Agricultura

Avenida de Cervantes

Fray L. de Granada

Capitán

Doce de Octubre

Avenida de Tejares

Ciudad Jardín

Antonio Maura

Camino de los Sastres

Alcalde Velasco Navarro

Avenida Conde de Vallellano

Avenida de la República Argentina

Jardines de la Victoria

Plaza A. Grilo

Colegiata de San Hipólito

Conde de Robledo

Gran

Góngora

Iglesia de San Miguel

Iglesia de San Nicolás de la Villa

Plaza Dr. Emilio Luque

Málaga

Plaza de las Tendillas

Claudio

San Juan

Juan de Mena

Plaza de la Compañía

Puerta de Almodóvar

Fernández Ruano

Leiva Aguilar

Juan Valera

LA JUDERÍA

Sinagoga

Museo Arqueológico

Museo Municipal Taurino

Hospital del Cardenal Salazar

Plaza Maimónides

Pl. Judá Leví

Convento de la Encarnación

Plaza de Jerónimo Páez

Cardenal Herrero

Iglesia de San Francisco

Dr. Marañón

Doctor Fleming

Hospital de San Sebastián

Torrijos

Mezquita

Palacio Episcopal

San Bartolomé

Caballerizas Reales

Amador de los Ríos

Corregidor Luis de la Cerda

Plaza Alhóndiga

Paseo de la

San Francisco

Plaza Potro

Triunfo de San Rafael

Puerta del Puente

de Isasa

Ronda

Alcázar de los Reyes Cristianos

Avenida del Alcázar

Puente Romano

Río Guadalquivir

▽ Sevilla & Granada
▽ Torre de la Calahorra

Hotel Gonzaléz, c/Manriquez 3, just northwest of the Mezquita (☎479819). Converted (ruined) Moorish palace with rooms overlooking a brilliant white-walled, geranium-filled patio – entered through the hotel's rather tacky souvenir shop. ⑤.

Hostal Luis de Góngora, c/Horno de la Trinidad 7 (☎438359). A pleasant place which is fair value for the price. ④.

Hostal Maestre, c/Romero Barros, 4–6, behind the Plaza del Potro (☎472410). A fine patio, charming rooms and free underground parking. ④.

Hotel Marisa, c/Cardenal Herrero 6 (☎473142). You won't get closer to the Mezquita than this. Some find it stylish and functional, others soulless. ⑤.

Hostal La Milagrosa, c/Rey Heredia 12, northeast of the Mezquita (☎473317). Pleasant and clean place, but a bit overpriced for what you get. ④.

Youth hostels and campsites

Albergue Juvenil, Plaza Juda Leví s/n, in the heart of the Judería off c/Albucasis (☎290166) Forty-four double rooms with ensuite bath/shower is only for starters at this relaxed, brand new and superbly located hostel. Why can't they all be like this? ①.

Campamento Municipal, Avda. Brillante s/n, 2km north on the road to Villaviciosa (☎472000). Good site with pool. Bus #12 from the Puente Romano.

The Mezquita

As in Moorish times, the **Mezquita** (April–Sept daily 10.30am–7pm; Oct–March 10.30am–1.30pm & 4–7pm; free entrance at side doors 8.30am–10am during services but interior is only illuminated from 10.30am onwards, when prayer niche and cathedral are accessible; 600ptas) is approached through the **Patio de los Naranjos**, a classic Islamic ablutions court with fountains for ritual purification before prayer, which still preserves its orange trees. None of the original ablutions fountains survives, the present ones being purely decorative later additions. Originally, when in use for the Friday prayer, all nineteen naves of the mosque were open to this court, allowing the rows of interior columns to appear an extension of the trees. Today, with all but one of the entrance gates locked and sealed, the image is still there, though subdued and stifled by the loss of those brilliant shafts of sunlight filtering through. The mood of the building has been distorted a little, from the open and vigorous simplicity of the mosque, to the mysterious half-light of a cathedral.

Nonetheless, a first glimpse inside the Mezquita is immensely exciting. "So near the desert in its tentlike forest of supporting pillars," Jan Morris found it, "so faithful to Mahomet's tenets of cleanliness, abstinence and regularity." The mass of supporting pillars was, in fact, an early and sophisticated improvization to gain height. The original architect, Sidi ben Ayub, working under the instruction of Abd ar-Rahman I, had at his disposal columns in marble, porphyry and jasper from the old Visigothic cathedral and from numerous Roman buildings, as well as many more shipped in from all parts of the former Roman empire. This ready-made building material could bear great weight, but the architect was faced with the problem of the pillars' varying sizes: many were much too tall but the vast majority would not be tall enough even when arched, to reach the intended height of the ceiling. The long pillars he buried in the floor, whilst his solution for the short pillars (which may have been inspired by Roman aqueduct designs) was to place a second row of square columns on the apex, serving as a base for the semicircular arches that support the roof. For extra strength and stability (and perhaps also deliberately to echo the shape of a date palm, much revered by the early Spanish Arabs) he introduced another, horseshoe-shaped arch above the lower pillars. A second and purely aesthetic innovation was to alternate brick and stone in the arches, creating the red-and-white striped pattern which gives a unity and distinctive character to the whole design. This architectural *tour de force* was unprecedented in the Arab

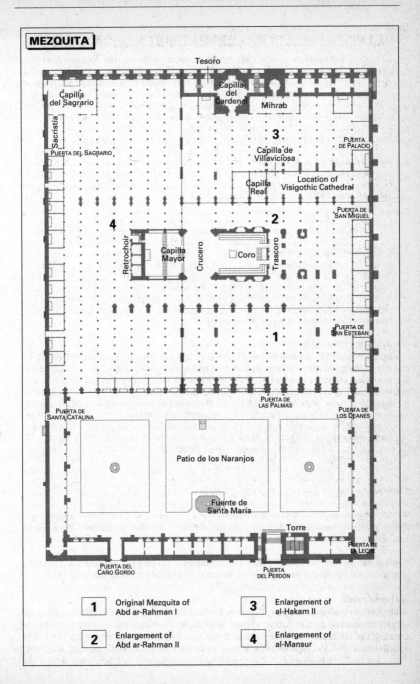

MEZQUITA

Tesoro

Capilla del Sagrario

Sacristía

PUERTA DEL SAGRARIO

Capilla del Cardenal

Mihrab

3

Capilla de Villaviciosa

PUERTA DE PALACIO

Capilla Real

Location of Visigothic Cathedral

4

Retrochoir

Capilla Mayor

Crucero

2

Coro

Trascoro

PUERTA DE SAN MIGUEL

1

PUERTA DE SAN ESTEBAN

PUERTA DE LAS PALMAS

PUERTA DE SANTA CATALINA

PUERTA DE LOS DEANES

Patio de los Naranjos

Fuente de Santa María

Torre

PUERTA DE LA LECHE

PUERTA DEL CAÑO GORDO

PUERTA DEL PERDÓN

1 Original Mezquita of Abd ar-Rahman I

3 Enlargement of al-Hakam II

2 Enlargement of Abd ar-Rahman II

4 Enlargement of al-Mansur

MOORISH CÓRDOBA AND THE BUILDING OF THE MEZQUITA

Córdoba's **domination of Moorish Spain** began thirty years after the conquest – in 756, when the city was placed under the control of **Abd ar-Rahman I**, the sole survivor of the Umayyad dynasty which had been bloodily expelled from the eastern Caliphate of Damascus. He commenced the building of the **Great Mosque** (*La Mezquita*), purchasing the site of the former Visigothic Cathedral of Saint Vincent from the Christians. This building which, divided by a partition wall, had previously served both communities, had itself been constructed on top of an earlier Roman temple dedicated to the god Janus. Demolishing the church as they built, Abd ar-Rahman's architects for reasons of speed and economy, incorporated one of the cathedral's original walls – that facing west – into the new structure and this is the reason why the *mihrab*'s prayer wall is not precisely aligned towards Mecca. This original mosque was completed by his son **Hisham** in 796 and comprises about one-fifth of the present building, the first dozen aisles adjacent to the Patio de los Naranjos.

ABD AR-RAHMAN II

The Cordoban Emirate soon began to rival Damascus both in power and in the brilliance of its civilization. **Abd ar-Rahman II** (822–52) initiated sophisticated irrigation programmes, minted his own coinage and received embassies from Byzantium. He in turn substantially enlarged the mosque. A focal point within the culture of *al-Andalus*, this was by now being consciously directed and enriched as an alternative to Mecca; it possessed an original script of the Koran and a bone from the arm of Muhammad, and, for the Spanish Muslim who could not go to Mecca, it became the most sacred place of **pilgrimage**. In the broader Islamic world it ranked third in sanctity after the Kaaba of Mecca and the Al Aksa mosque of Jerusalem.

ABD AR-RAHMAN III

In the tenth century Córdoba reached its zenith under **Abd ar-Rahman III** (912–67), one of the great rulers of Islamic history. He assumed power at the age of twenty-three after his grandfather had killed his father during a period of internal strife and in his reign, according to a contemporary historian, "subdued rebels, built palaces, gave impetus to agriculture, immortalised ancient deeds and monuments, and inflicted great damage on infidels to a point where no opponent or contender remained in al-Andalus. People obeyed en masse and wished to live with him in peace." In 929, with Muslim Spain and a substantial part of North Africa firmly under his control, Abd ar-Rahman III adopted the title of "Caliph", or successor of the Prophet. It was a supremely confident gesture and was reflected in the growing splendour of Córdoba itself which, with a population approaching (if we take the not always reliable Moorish historians at face value) 500,000, had become the largest, most prosperous city of Europe, and outshone both Byzantium and Baghdad (the new capital of the eastern caliphate) in science, culture and scholarship. At the turn of the tenth century it could boast some 27 schools, 50 hospitals (with the first separate clinics for the leprous and insane), 900 public baths, 60,300 noble mansions, 213,077 houses and 80,455 shops. The construction of a glorious

world and set the tone for all future enlargements – excepting the Christian cathedral – of the building. And it was completed within a year of its commencement in 785.

The Mihrab

The overall uniformity was broken only by the culminating point of al-Hakam II's tenth-century extension – the domed cluster of pillars surrounding the mosque's great jewel, the sacred **Mihrab**. And even here, although he lengthened the prayer hall by a third, al-Hakam carefully aligned the new *mihrab* at the end of the same central aisle which had led to the previous two. The *mihrab* had two functions in Islamic worship: it indi-

new palace at **Medina Azahara** in the 930s as well as further **development of the Great Mosque** paralleled these new heights of confidence and splendour. Abd ar-Rahman III provided the Mezquita with a new minaret (which has not survived), 80m high, topped by three pomegranate-shaped spheres, two of silver and one of gold and each weighing a ton.

AL-HAKAM II

The Caliph's successor **al-Hakam II** (961-76) was a man from another mould to that of his warrior father, best epitomized by his advice to his own son:

> *Do not make wars unnecessarily. Keep the peace, for your own well being and that of your people. Never unsheathe your sword except against those who commit injustice. What pleasure is there in invading and destroying nations, in taking pillage and destruction to the ends of the earth? Do not let yourself be dazzled by vanity; let your justice always be like a tranquil lake.*

In tune with these sentiments, al-Hakam was a poet, historian and the builder of one of the great libraries of the Middle Ages. This cultured ruler was also responsible for the mosque's most **brilliant expansion**, virtually doubling its extent. After demolishing the south wall to add fourteen extra rows of columns, he employed Byzantine craftsmen to construct a new **mihrab** or prayer niche; this remains complete and is perhaps the most beautiful example of all Moorish religious architecture.

AL-MANSUR

Under the vizier-usurper **al-Mansur** (977-1002), who used his position as regent to push al-Hakam's child successor, Hisham II, into the background (see p.266), repeated attacks were carried out on the Christians in the north including the daring expedition to Santiago de Compostela in 997, when the pilgrimage cathedral's bells were siezed. This **military might** was built on the incorporation of thousands of Berbers from North Africa into al-Mansur's army – a policy that was to have devastating implications for the future when the same Berbers turned on their paymasters and sacked and plundered the city, destroying al-Hakam's treasured library in the process. Within less than thirty years the brilliant Caliphate of Córdoba had collapsed in a bloody turmoil as short-lived puppet caliphs attempted to stave off the inevitable.

When he was not away on his military campaigns al-Mansur gave his attention to further embellishing the great mosque. As al-Hakam had extended the building as far to the south as was possible, he completed the final enlargement by adding seven rows of columns to the whole east side. This spoiled the symmetry of the mosque, depriving the *mihrab* of its central position, but Arab historians observed that it meant there were now "as many bays as there are days of the year". They also delighted in describing the rich interior, with its 1293 marble columns, 280 chandeliers and 1445 lamps. Hanging inverted among the lamps were the bells of the cathedral of Santiago de Compostela. Al-Mansur had made his Christian captives carry them on their shoulders from Galicia – a process which was to be observed in reverse after Córdoba was captured by Fernando el Santo (the Saint) in 1236.

cated the direction of Mecca (and hence of prayer) and it amplified the words of the *imam*, or prayer leader. At Córdoba it was also of supreme beauty. As Titus Burckhardt wrote, in *Moorish Art in Spain*:

> *The design of the prayer niche in Córdoba was used as a model for countless prayer niches in Spain and North Africa. The niche is crowned by a horseshoe-shaped arch, enclosed by a rectangular frame. The arch derives a peculiar strength from the fact that its central point shifts up from below. The wedge-shaped arch stones or voussoirs fan outwards from a point at the foot of the arch and centres of the inner and outer circumferences of the arch lie one above the other. The entire arch seems to radiate, like the sun*

or the moon gradually rising over the edge of the horizon. It is not rigid; it breathes as if expanding with a surfeit of inner beatitude, while the rectangular frame enclosing it acts as a counterbalance. The radiating energy and the perfect stillness form an unsurpassable equilibrium. Herein lies the basic formula of Moorish architecture.

The paired pillars which flank the *mihrab* and support its arch were taken from the earlier *mihrab* of Abd ar-Rahman I, their prominent position no doubt a mark of respect by al-Hakam to his great predecessor. The inner vestibule of the niche (which is roped off – forcing you to risk the wrath of the attendants in getting a glimpse) is quite simple in comparison, with a shell-shaped ceiling carved from a single block of marble. The chambers to either side, as well as the dome above the *mihrab* are decorated with exquisite **mosaics** of gold, rust-red, turquoise and green, the work of Byzantine craftsmen supplied by the Emperor Nicephorus II at al-Hakam's request. These constitute the *maksura*, where the Caliph and his retinue would pray, a fitting monument to this scholarly and sensitive ruler.

The Cathedral and other additions

Originally the whole design of the mosque would have directed worshippers naturally towards the *mihrab*. Today, though, you almost stumble upon it, for in the centre of the mosque squats a Renaissance **cathedral coro**. This was built in 1523, nearly three centuries of enlightened restraint after the Christian conquest, and in spite of fierce opposition from the town council. The erection of a *coro* and *capilla mayor*, however, had long been the "Christianizing" dream of the cathedral chapter and at last they had found a monarch, predictably, Carlos V, who was willing to sanction the work. Carlos, to his credit, realized the mistake (though it did not stop him from destroying parts of the Alhambra and Sevilla's Alcázar); on seeing the work completed he told the chapter, "You have built what you or others might have built anywhere, but you have destroyed something that was unique in the world." Some details are worth noting though, particularly the beautifully carved Churrigueresque **choir stalls** by Pedro Duque Cornejo, created with mahogany brought from the New World. To the left of the *coro* stands an earlier and happier Christian addition, the Mudéjar **Capilla de Villaviciosa**, built by Moorish craftsmen in 1371 (and now partly sealed up). Beside it are the dome and pillars of the **earlier mihrab**, constructed under Abd ar-Rahman II. The mosque's original and finely decorated timber-coffered ceiling was replaced in the eighteenth century by the present Baroque cupolas.

The **belfry**, at the corner of the Patio de los Naranjos, is contemporary with the cathedral addition. If it's open after restoration, the climb is a dizzying experience. Close by, the **Puerta del Perdón**, the main entrance to the patio, was rebuilt in Moorish style in 1377. Original "caliphal" decoration (in particular some superb latticework), however, can still be seen in the gates on the east and west sides of the mosque.

The Alcázar and river area

Dating from the time of the *reconquista*, the **Alcázar de Los Reyes Cristianos** (Tues–Sun 9.30am–1.30pm & 4–7pm; May-Sept 5–8pm; 200ptas), a Palace Fortress, was completed in the fourteenth century and now houses a small municipal museum. The original Moorish alcázar stood beside the Mezquita, on the site presently occupied by the Palacio Episcopal. After the Christian conquest it was rebuilt a little to the west and used by monarchs – including Fernando and Isabel who were visited here by Columbus in 1486 – when staying in the city, hence its name. That the buildings retain little of their original opulence today is due to their use as the residence of the **Inquisition** for three centuries prior to 1821, and later as a prison until as recently as 1951. The palace underwent extensive Mudéjar rebuilding during the fifteenth century, when the attractive **Moorish-style gardens** were added. From the tower's belvedere there are great **views** over the town and river where, to the west of the **Puente Romano**, it's possible to see one of the ancient **Moorish waterwheels**, the Albolafia. This is the reconstructed sole survivor of a number of mills which crossed the river here and which, besides grinding flour, pumped water to the alcázar's gardens. So noisy were this wheel's rumblings, that Queen Isabel had it dismantled when it disturbed her sleep.

The **interior** of the alcázar has some mildly interesting fifteenth-century royal baths and some fine **roman mosaics** discovered in the city. The second-century depiction of *Polyphemus and Galatea* is outstanding and the monochrome mosaic beside it is one of the largest complete mosaics in existence. A third-century carved sarcophagus is also worth a look, with its portal ajar indicating that access is open to the person within.

In the gardens across the plaza to the north of the alcázar are the remains of a **Moorish hammam** or bath house, now sadly neglected, filled up with rubbish and scrawled with graffiti. The city intends to protect and restore them; they had better make it soon.

Palacio Episcopal

Opposite the Mezquita's west wall on the site of the former Moorish alcázar lies the **Palacio Episcopal** (Mon–Fri 9.30am–1.30pm & 3.30–5.30pm; Sat 9.30am–1.30pm; 150ptas or free with a Mezquita ticket). This elegant seventeenth-century building with a fine patio and fountain is now a **museum of religious art**, mainly sculpture. The highlights are in the early rooms where there are some outstanding examples of medieval wood sculpture – a great Spanish tradition. The anonymous thirteenth-century *Virgen de las Huertas* in Room 1 is finely worked as is a striking fifteenth-century *Calvario Villaviciosa* or crucifixion. In Room 3, an anonymous early sixteenth-century *pietá*, is another remarkable work with the agonized expressions of the onlookers beautifully portrayed. The remainder of the museum comprises more wood sculpture from later periods, as well as tapestries and furniture. On the ground floor, there's a beautiful **baroque chapel** dedicated to the Virgin and a room containing works by modern Cordoban artists (which may be closed).

Across the river, the **Torre de la Calahorra** (daily 10am–2pm & 5.30–8.30pm; winter all day until 6pm; 350ptas) a medieval tower built to guard the Puente Romano, now houses another museum full of hi-tech gimmicks including weird tableaux, a lit-up Alhambra as well as a model of the Mezquita prior to its Christian alterations. From the tower you get a wonderful panoramic view towards the city.

The Judería and synagogue

Between the Mezquita and the beginning of the Avenida del Gran Capitán lies the **Judería**, Córdoba's old Jewish quarter. A fascinating network of lanes, it's more atmospheric and less commercialized than Sevilla's, though souvenir shops are beginning to gain ground. Near the heart of the quarter, at c/Maimonides 18, is the **synagogue** (Tues–Sat 10am–2pm & 3.30–5.30pm; Sun 10am–1.30pm; 50ptas), one of only three in Spain – the other two are in Toledo – that survived the Jewish expulsion of 1492. This one, built in 1315, is minute, particularly in comparison to the great Santa María in Toledo, but it has some fine stucco work elaborating on a Solomon's-seal motif together with Hebrew texts in the Mudéjar style, and it also retains its women's gallery. Just south of the synagogue in the plazuela named after him, is a statue of Maimonides, the Jewish philospher, physician and Talmudic jurist born at Córdoba in 1135.

Nearby is a rather bogus **Zoco** – an Arab *souk* turned into a crafts arcade – on the site of old mule market. If you're not impressed by the trinkets on offer, there's a bar and and a pleasant patio to enjoy a drink in. Adjoining this, the small **Museo Taurino** (Bullfighting Museum; Tues–Sat 9.30am–1.30pm & 4–7pm, Sun 9.30am–1.30pm; 200ptas, free Tuesdays) warrants a look, if only for the kitschy nature of its exhibits: row upon row of bulls' heads, two of them given this "honour" for having killed matadors. Beside a copy of the tomb of Manolete, most famous of the city's fighters, is exhibited the hide of his taurine nemesis, Islero.

Finally, close to the Mezquita's northeast corner, you shouldn't miss Córdoba's most famous street, the **Callejón de los Flores**. This is a white-walled alley from whose balconies and hanging pots cascades a riot of geraniums in summer and which, when viewed from its northern end, neatly frames the Mezquita's belfry – the picture that decorates every postcard rack in town.

Plaza del Potro

A short walk east from the Mezquita along c/Corregidor de la Cerda is the **Plaza del Potro**, one of Córdoba's more historic landmarks. This fine old square is named after the colt (*potro*) which adorns its sixteenth-century fountain. Originally a livestock market dealing in horses and mules, the area once had a villainous reputation as did the remarkable inn opposite, the **Posada del Potro**, which Cervantes mentions in *Don Quixote*, and where he almost certainly stayed. Sensitively restored, the building, with an atmospheric cattle yard, now houses the *Casa de la Cultura*, municipal education and cultural offices, part of which is used for *artesanía* displays.

Museo de Bellas Artes

On the other side of the Plaza del Potro, is the former Hospital de la Caridad founded in the sixteenth century, which now contains the **Museo de Bellas Artes** (Tues–Sat 10am–2pm & 6–8pm; 5–7pm out of season; Sun 10am–1.30pm; 250ptas). Among a not greatly distinguished collection (rendered even more threadbare by the inexplicable disappearance of the Goyas and Riberas to Madrid) is an *Immaculate Conception* by Murillo as well as works by Valdés Leal and some dubious Zurburáns. A couple of interesting drawings near the entrance by the British artist David Roberts depict the Mezquita's Patio de Los Naranjos and the Puerta del Puente as they were in the last century. The ground floor has a small archeological collection which includes a fine second-century BC **Iberian sculpture** of a she-wolf despatching its victim, as well as a collection of rather humdrum modern sculpture and paintings.

Across the courtyard is a small museum (free) devoted to the Cordoban artist **Julio Romero de Torres** (1885–1930), painter of some sublimely dreadful canvases, most of which depict reclining female nudes with furtive male guitar players. Attacked by feminists and dubbed "the king of kitsch" by critics, the *cordobeses*, however, won't have a word said against him. If you wish to decide for yourself, the nightmarish *Canto Jondo* or the raunchy *Naranjas y Lemones* (Oranges and Lemons) should be enough to give you the measure of Romero's *oeuvre*.

Probably more rewarding would be a visit to *Bodegas Campos*, just east of here, a wonderful rambling old place where they will allow you to see the cellars – stacked with giant oak *botas* (barrels) – in which the company matures its wine through the *solera* system of blending. They'll be only to delighted to offer you a sample in the **bar**, but don't commit the ultimate *faux-pas* by asking for anything from Jerez. Montilla is the brew here, and very good it is, too.

North of the Plaza del Potro

To the north, in an area which was once the *plateros* or silversmiths' quarter you'll find **Plaza de la Corredera**. A wonderful, ramshackle colonaded square, rather like a decayed version of Madrid's or Salamanca's Plaza Mayor, it is unique in Andalucía. The square's complete enclosure occurred in the seventeenth century and presented the city with a suitable space for all kinds of spectacles. These have included burnings by the Inquisition as well as bullfights, from which event the tiny *callejón Toril* (bullpen) on the square's eastern side takes its name. Today, more mundane proceedings take place beneath the balconies of the crumbling tenements when the plaza hosts a small morning **market** with a spectacularly colourful one on Saturdays.

Museo Arqueológico

To the north-west of the Plaza del Potro, on Plaza de Jerónimo Páez, lies the excellent **Museo Arqueológico** (Tues–Sat 10am–2pm & 6–8pm; Sun 10am–1.30pm; 250ptas), essential to gain an understanding of Córdoba's importance as a Roman city in particular, as so little from this period survives above ground today. Housed in the Casa Páez, during its original conversion this small sixteenth-century Renaissance mansion was revealed as the unlikely site of a genuine Roman patio. As a result, it is one of the most imaginative and enjoyable small museums in the country, with good local collections from the Iberian, Roman and Moorish periods.

Starting in Room 3, highlights include, a large number of finds from the excavation of Córdoba's western necropolis among which are a number of inscribed first-century gladiatorial tombstones, whilst Room 5 has a remarkably well preserved set of **bronze horse bridles** from a Roman *quadriga*, or four-horse chariot. Some of the mosaic fragments here, with their geometrical designs, appear to anticipate the later Moorish patterns. Among other cases in this room displaying lamps, pottery and glassware is a fascinating carved stone relief depicting the **olive harvest** – then, as now, Córdoba was renowned for its oil. The stairs leading to Room 7 are flanked by fine mosaics including an outstanding one depicting a *quadriga* in action. The intricate **wooden Mudéjar ceiling** here is worth a look and apparently predates the mansion which was built to incorporate it.

Room 7 contains exhibits from the Moorish period among which is a fine inlaid tenth-century **bronze stag** found at the Moorish palace of Medina Azahara (see p.266) where it was used as the spout of a fountain. On the balcony a collection of wells attests to the Moorish attraction to water – a tradition continued by fountains throughout Andalucía today. The museum's beautiful double patio contains miscellaneous Roman statuary, mosaics and a superb fourth-century Christian marble **sarcophagus**. Also here is a fine second-century **sculpture of Mithras** slaying the bull from a mithraeum excavated at Cabra in the south of the province. This conventional image, which was placed in the *retablo* position in the small mithraic cult temples, shows Mithras plunging his dagger into the bull whose blood, initiates believed, gave birth to all living things, hence the dog and the snake trying to get their share. The ever-present problem of evil is portrayed by the scorpion, its symbol, attacking the bull's vitals.

The rest of the city

Many visitors to Córdoba make a stopover at the Mezquita and then leave without ever discovering the other Córdoba, to the north of the monumental quarter and the Judería, where the city's everyday life is carried on. Here, interspersed between the modern streets – many still built on the ancient grid – are any number of **Gothic churches**, **convents** and **Renaissance palaces** that are little visited but which are well worth an hour or two. Note that churches are usually locked outside service times, and early mornings or evenings (about 7pm–10pm) are the most promising times to catch them open, perhaps visiting a few *tapas* bars en route.

Plaza Tendillas and around

Plaza Tendillas is the vibrant centre of modern Córdoba, as it was in Roman times. Dominated by the bronze equestrian statue of El Gran Capitán, a Cordoban general whose Italian campaigns in the late fifteenth century helped to project post-*reconquista*

Spain on to the world stage, the square is hardly distinguished by its dull, turn-of-the-century buildings.

Off the east side of the plaza, along c/Claudio Marcelo, lies the **Templo Romano**, the tortuously reconstructed remains (mostly pillars) of a first-century Roman temple thought to have been of a similar form to the Maison Carrée at Nîmes. Turning left along c/Capitulares from here brings you to the **Iglesia de San Pablo** fronting the street of the same name, a fine Romanesque-Gothic church. Dating from the period following the *reconquista* – as do many of Córdoba's churches in this part of town – it has undergone numerous later modifications including a Baroque façade. Its interior retains a fine Mudéjar dome and coffered ceiling as well as a seventeenth-century **sculpture of the Virgin**, *Nuestra Señora de las Angustias* (sorrows), a masterpiece by Juan de Mesa, himself a native of Córdoba.

Northwest from here, on c/Alfonso XIII, is the interesting **Circulo de la Amistad**, a *Casino* or social club (founded in 1842) set inside a former convent. Ask the porter to let you see the marvellous Renaissance **patio**, originally the convent's cloister. Continuing east again, beyond San Pablo lies **San Andrés**, another post-*reconquista* church and, further on, at the end of c/Santa María de la Gracia, is the Gothic **San Lorenzo**, whose converted Moorish minaret tower, outstanding **rose window**, and triple-arched portico combine to make it the best-looking church in the city. Inside, the apse has fifteenth-century **frescoes** depicting scenes from the Passion.

Turning north along c/Roelas, passing the nineteenth-century neoclassical Iglesia de San Rafael, you'll come to another *reconquista* church, **San Augustín**, in the plaza of the same name. A Gothic church originally, it was substantially altered in the sixteenth century; inside it has frescoes and another sculpture of the Virgin by Juan de Mesa.

Palacio de Viana

Slightly west of San Agustín in Plaza de Gome you'll find the **Palacio-Museo de Viana** (guided tours daily except Wed; June–Sept 9am–2pm; Oct–May 10am–1pm & 4–6pm; 200ptas), one of Córdoba's finest palaces and seat of the Marquises of Viana until the family sold up to a bank in 1981, after which it was opened – apparently just as the family left it – to the public. Started in the fourteenth century, the building has had numerous later additions tacked on, including most of the **twelve outstanding patios**, filled with flowers, the main attraction for many visitors today.

The compulsory guided tour shunts you around a bewildering number of drawing rooms, gaudy bedrooms (one with a telling Franco portrait), kitchens and galleries, linked by creaking staircases, whilst a commentary delivered in machine-gun Spanish (foreign-language room descriptions available) points out a wealth of furniture, paintings, weapons and top-drawer junk the family amassed over the centuries, giving you little time to take anything in.

More churches, convents and tabernas

North of the Palacio de Viana, the fortress-like **Iglesia de Santa Marina** dates from the thirteenth century (with Baroque modifications) and shares the charming plaza of the same name with a monument to the celebrated Cordoban *torero*, **Manolete**, who was born in the Santa Marina barrio and died in 1947. At the square's eastern end, strictly speaking, the Plaza del Conde Priego, the fifteenth-century Franciscan **convent of Santa Isabel** has a delightful patio with an imposing cypress. The *capilla mayor* inside the convent's church has sculptures by Pedro Roldán. The nuns here also sell their home-made *dulces*.

Calle Conde de Priego leads east again to the Plaza Ruiz de Alda, beyond which, in the simple white-walled Plaza de Capuchinos lies **El Cristo de los Faroles** (Christ of the Lanterns) an eighteenth-century sculpture of the crucifixion which is the centre of much religious fervour. At night, when the lanterns flanking the cross are illuminated, the place has an unearthly, mystical ambience.

North from here are two features – on either side of the Plaza de Colón – worthy of a detour. Close to the north-east corner of this garden-square, the **Torre de la Malmuerta** (bad death) is an early fifteenth-century battlemented tower, once part of the city walls. It takes its name from a crime of passion when a guard posted here is supposed to have killed his adulterous spouse. At the foot of the tower is one of the city's best loved *tabernas*, the *Casa de Paco Acedo* (see p.263), housed in part of a former barracks. The west side of the Plaza de Colón is dominated by the lavishly ornate façade of the eighteenth-century former **Convento de la Merced**, now the seat of the provincial government, and the biggest and best example of full-blown Baroque in town. The porter will allow you inside to view an exquisite Renaissance **patio** with paired columns, elegant staircases and a central fountain. The church, restored after a fire in 1978, has a fine **retablo** by Gómez de Sandoval. Unfortunately, the building is not often open; try service times in the early evening.

Picking up the route south towards the centre, follow c/del Osario until, just before Plaza Tendillas, a left turn brings you into Plaza San Miguel with its charming **Iglesia de San Miguel**, yet another *reconquista* church founded in the thirteenth century by Fernando III. Above the early Gothic entrance there's a magnificent rose window and, inside, a remarkable eighteenth-century *retablo* in red marble depicting the archangels Gabriel, Rafael and Miguel. Tucked behind the church lies one of Córdoba's most atmospheric taverns, the **Taberna San Miguel** (see p.263), a century-old place hung with faded *corrida* posters, the odd guitar and tiled *bon mots*.

Heading back to the Judería you pass another couple of churches: the fourteenth-century **San Nicolás**, at the end of c/Conde de Gondomar, east of Plaza Tendillas, with a spectacular **octagonal bell tower,** and the rather sad **Iglesia de San Juan** in a small square of the same name to the south, where the crumbling minaret of a former ninth-century mosque, complete with elegant horseshoe arches resting on Corinthian pillars, sits precariously beside its later rival.

Eating, drinking and nightlife

Coming from Sevilla or the coast, the nightlife in Córdoba will seem rather tame by comparison. Around eleven, things start to close and, by midnight, the empty streets around the Mezquita, lit by black lanterns, have a melancholy air. Many of the city's bars and restaurants though, when open, are among the best in Andalucía and are worth seeking out.

Restaurants

Córdoba's restaurants are on the whole reasonably priced – you need only to avoid the touristy places round the Mezquita.

El Caballo Rojo, c/Cardenal Herrero 28. One of the city's top restaurants, beneath the Mezquita's belfry, which prides itself on a Moorish-influenced menu serving such specialities as *cordero a la miel* (lamb in honey). Expensive.

El Churrasco, c/Romero 16 (*not* c/Romero Barros) Situated to the north of the Mezquita, this is one of Córdoba's renowned restaurants. It has a long-standing reputation for its *churrasco* (a kind of grilled pork dish, served with pepper sauces) and *salmorejo*, a thick Cordoban version of *gazpacho* with hunks of ham and egg. Prices, together with sometimes snooty service, match its reputation, although there is a set *menú* at 2500ptas.

El Extremeño, Plaza Benevente 1. The enthusiastic owner will guide you through his economical evening meals; Cordoban *migas* (fried savoury breadcrumbs) are a speciality here.

Bar-Restaurante Federación de Peñas, c/Conde y Luque 8. A Moorish-style patio dining room which in spite of its name is open to non-members, and offers a variety of economical *menús*.

Restaurante Cafetín Halal, c/Rey Heredia 28. This restaurant is situated in the Islamic cultural centre and serves excellent, inexpensive dishes with many vegetarian options, but no alcohol.

Restaurante La-La-La, c/Cruz del Rastro 3. On the river by the Paseo de la Ribera, east of the Mezquita, this rather uninspiring place has an inexpensive set *menú*.

Bar-Mesón Rafae, corner of c/Deanes and c/Buen Pastor. North of the Mezquita in the Judería, this pleasant restaurant serves a good, reasonably priced *menú*.

Cafe-Bar Realejo, c/Realejo 89. Much-patronized by locals and east of the church of San Andres, you'll get one of the lowest priced *menús* in town here.

Taberna Santa Clara, c/Oslo 2. A friendly place offering an excellent *menú*.

Mesón El Tablón, c/Luis de la Cerda (aka Cardenal González). The one place close to the Mezquita that is worth trying; very good value.

Méson Restaurante Tania, c/Rodríguez Sánchez 5. To the north, towards Plaza Tendillas, this is a good place for reasonably priced *platos combinados*.

Tabernas and tapas bars

In 1987 Córdoba held a *homenaje*, or tribute, to its treasured *tabernas* – and with good reason, for few places anywhere can match them for sheer character and variety, not to mention *tapas*. Remember, though, when ordering *fino* that the equivalent brew here is *Montilla* and the best way to get up a barman's nose is to ask for any of the wines of Jerez, the product of the upstart province down river. If you're new to *Montilla-Moriles* to give it its full title, named after the villages further south where it's made (see p.269), or have been unimpressed with the insipid concoctions sold abroad under the *Montilla* name, prepare for a pleasant surprise. *Montilla*, which vaguely resembles a mellow, dry sherry, is a giant on its native soil, and is considered a healthier tipple by the *cordobeses*. Whereas Jerez sherry is fortified with alcohol, here the process is totally natural, leading (they insist) to fewer hangovers.

AROUND THE MEZQUITA

Starting **around the Mezquita** there's *Bar Mezquita*, a tiny place beneath the mosque's bell tower, long famous for it's *boquerones in vinagre* (anchovies in vinegar), if not for its comforts. To the north of the Mezquita the *Bar Sociedad Plateros* at c/Deanes 5, is another dusty old place with a good *tapas* range – try *chorizo al vino* – and is part of the the *Plateros* chain (see below). Further west near the Puerta de Almodóvar in the city wall are two more likely spots, *Casa Rubio* at Puerta de Almodóvar 5, and *Casa Salinas* nearby, both serving excellent *Montilla* with their *tapas*. Not far away, *Bodega Guzman* on c/Judíos, and close to the synagogue, is frequented by (bull)fight fans. Good *tapas* and *bocadillos* can be found at the tiny *Casa Elisa*, on c/Almanzor just to the west and *Taberna de Pepe*, c/Romero 1 (the same street's southern continuation), does *tapas* and sometimes meals, too. You might not always get a *tapa* at *Mesón Cabezas*, in the tiny street of the same name at the foot of c/Rey Heredia, but you won't be bothered about that once you've stepped inside the most eccentric bar in town. This crumbling time warp of a place, built around a patio with a wheezing fountain, ludicrous artworks and enormous rope-seat chairs has to be seen to be believed. Excellent *Montilla* though, is served up by the bar's taciturn *patrón*. Long may its fountain splutter.

AROUND THE PLAZA DEL POTRO

East of the Mezquita, behind the **Plaza del Potro**, the *Bodega Sociedad Plateros*, c/San Francisco 6, is the headquarters of the *Plateros* chain, situated in a converted former convent. What started out in 1868 as a mutual benefit society for the workers in Córdoba's silversmith trade eventually branched out into the *bodega* business, presently owning a chain of nine excellent bars around the city (ask for a free map detailing where they are). The bar – now over a century old and serving a wide range of *tapas* – is light and airy with a nice glass-covered patio complemented by hanging plants and *azulejos*. Slightly east of the Plaza del Potro, *Bodegas Campos*, c/Lineros 32, is a full-scale *bodega* with great oak barrels (many signed by celebrities) stacked up in the cellar at the rear. A bar sells their own excellent *Montilla* by the *copita* or the bottle, and *tapas* are on offer as well.

AROUND PLAZA TENDILLAS

North of the Judería, and just above **Plaza Tendillas**, *Taberna San Miguel*, Plaza San Miguel 1, is one of the city's ancient and legendary bars which shouldn't be missed. The Montilla is excellent as are the *tapas*: *rabo de toro* and *callos en salsa picante* (tripe in a spicy sauce) are big favourites here. Heading north again – and into the commercial district – *Bar Gaudí*, Avda. Gran Capitán 22, (near *Galerías Preciados*) is aptly decorated in Art-Nouveau style, and serves a wide range of European beers; along Avda. Tejares close by, *Vanessa* (at no. 10) is a popular *marisquería*. Its neighbour, *La Canda*, Avda. Tejares 18, is another favourite lunchtime venue in this quarter. *Café Central*, nearby at no. 34, also has occasional live jazz. A little to the north-east, but definitely worth the hike, lies *Casa Paco Acedo* beneath the ancient Torre de Malmuerta. Here – in yet another fine old bar – they serve up a superb range of *tapas* and *raciones* including *salmorejo* and all kinds of fried fish. But the house speciality is an unforgettable *rabo de toro* (translating it as "oxtail stew" is an insult), the perfect complement to the *Montilla de la Casa,* and best eaten at the tables outside beneath the tower, once the sun has gone down. The **pastelería** *Café California*, c/Jesús Maria 10 (off Plaza Tendillas) does excellent *churros* as well as other mouthwatering concoctions.

THE EAST OF THE CITY

The eastern part of the city also has a few places worth a visit. Close to the **Plaza de la Corredera**, *Taberna Salinas*, c/Tundidores 3, is an old but revamped place with an excellent range of *tapas*; try their delicious *revuelto* (scrambled eggs) with either *gambas* (shrimps) and *jamón* or salmon. Just east of the Iglesia de San Andrés there's another branch of the *Plateros* chain at c/Realejo 1, and over the road *Casa Castillo* at no. 10, is another good place built around an airy patio serving fine *Montilla* and a hearty *salmorejo* (Córdoba's gazpacho with guts). *Aficionados* of the *Sociedad Platero* empire may want to continue east to visit two far-flung outposts close to the eastern wall at Maria Auxiliadora 25, and around the corner in c/Queso s/n, both worth the walk, with a couple of nice churches to see along the way.

Flamenco and discos

Outside Easter's *Semana Santa* and the annual fiesta at the end of May, the city's nightlife centres around bars and restaurants. The only **late night drinking** you are likely to find is in the north of the city where the bars around Avda. Tejeros and those close to the provincial government building in c/Reyes Católicos tend to stay open after midnight. Córdoba's best non-membership **flamenco** *tablao* is *La Bulería*, c/Pedro López 3, near Plaza de la Corredera, open from 10pm every night (performance starts 10.30pm); being a café-bar there's no entrance fee although your first drink will cost 1000ptas, after which you pay normal prices. The singer El Calli and his family are the core of the show, and compared to some of the dross on offer in Sevilla they get near enough to the real thing, presented in authentic surroundings. Avoid at all costs the *Tablao Cardenal* opposite the Mezquita which is an extortionate parody. Free *flamenco* performances are also mounted by the local council throughout the summer in Plaza de San Hipólito, near the church of the same name off the Avda. del Gran Capitán (details from the Turismo).

Discos are all in the centre of town around c/Cruz Conde (north of Plaza Tendillas). *Plató*, c/Gongora 12, is Córdoba's entertaining attempt at an acid/house venue, while *Zahira*, c/Conde de Robledo s/n, and the nearby *Quo!*, Manuel de Sandoval s/n, play latin and rock until 5am.

Listings

Banks Numerous places (with cash machines) are located along Avda. de los Tejares and the street that crosses this, Avda. del Gran Capitán.

Bullfights Details and tickets from the Plaza de Toros, Avda. Gran Vía Parque (in the north-western suburb). If bullfighting is your thing, it's possible to go on a guided tour of the city's **bull-ring** (tours on the hour, 10am–1pm & 4–7pm); complete with distastefully reverential commentary, this includes even the high-tech emergency room. Ask at the Turismo for further details.

Buses *Alsina Graells*, Avda. Medina Azahara 29 (☎232734) for buses to Granada, Málaga, Almería, Cádiz. *Empresa Urena*, Avda. Cervantes 22 (near train station) for buses to Sevilla and Jaén. *Autocares Priego*, Paseo de la Victoria 29 (☎290158) for Madrid, Valencia and Barcelona.

Car Rental The best deals are to be had from *Europcar* (☎233460), Avda. Medina Azahara 7.

Football Córdoba's team are currently rooted in section B of Division 2. If that doesn't deter you, match details and tickets are obtainable from the stadium, El Arcangel, east of the river.

Hospital Cruz Roja, Avda. del Dr Fleming (☎293411).

Hiking Maps 1:50,000, 1:100,000 and 1:200,000 maps are available from *CNIG* (National Geographic Service) branch office: c/Santo Tomás de Aquino 1–6º; ☎233546.

Markets Plaza de la Corredera has a clothes and crafts market daily (mornings) with the main market – a colourful sight – on Saturday mornings.

Police Avda. del Dr Fleming 25 (☎477500; emergency 091). Just beyond the walls to the west of the Mezquita.

Post Office The *Correos* is at c/Cruz Conde 21 (just north of Plaza Tendillas) and is also the main office for *Lista de Correos* (poste restante).

Telephones The *Teléfonica* office is at Plaza de las Tendillas, 7; open Mon–Fri 9am–1pm & 5–9pm.

Trains The train station is on Avda. de America (☎478221) with a *RENFE* ticket office at Ronda de Los Tejares 10 (☎475884).

Medina Azahara and beyond

Just a few kilometres from the city is the historic site of Medina Azahara, a must for those on the Moorish trail. Continuing west, along the fringes of the Sierra Morena, following the Río Guadalquivir, leads you deep into hunting country via a string of charming rural towns.

Medina Azahara

Seven kilometres to the northwest of Córdoba lie the vast and rambling ruins of **Medina Azahara**, a palace complex built on a dream scale by **Caliph Abd ar-Rahman III**. Naming it after a favourite, az-Zahra (the Radiant), he spent one-third of the annual state budget on its construction each year from 936 until his death in 961.

The **site** (Tues–Sat 10am–2pm & 4–6.30pm; Sun 10am–2pm; free on production of an EC passport, otherwise 250ptas) is entered by the **Puerta Norte**, the typically Moorish "twisted gate" which forced would-be invaders to double back on themselves thus making them easy targets. This leads to **Dar al–Yund**, a large army barracks, fronted by a broad forecourt. To the east of here and beyond the garden, the route leads to the **portico** and **Plaza de Armas**, with a courtyard beyond the portico – which may have been a grand parade ground – still awaiting excavation. Turning south, you can see on the terrace below, the **great mosque**, one of the first buildings to be constructed on the site, oriented towards the southeast and Mecca. It has five clearly defined naves with the central one slightly broader than the aisles. The route now veers west passing the princely baths to the right, beyond which lay the royal apartments.

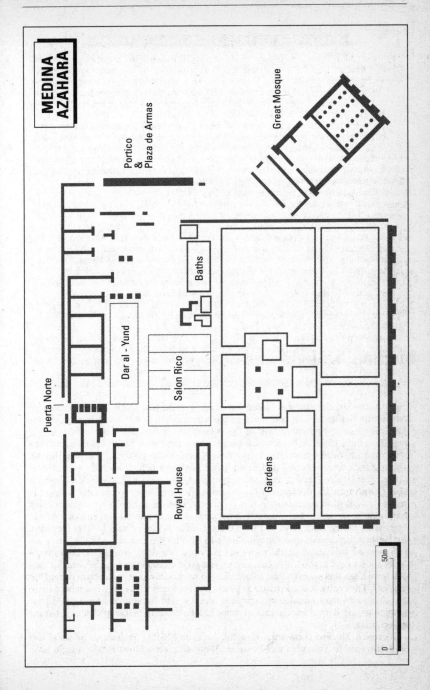

MEDINA AZAHARA

Great Mosque

Portico & Plaza de Armas

Baths

Dar al - Yund

Salon Rico

Puerta Norte

Royal House

Gardens

50m

0

THE RISE AND FALL OF MEDINA AZAHARA

Ten thousand workers and 1500 mules and camels were employed in the construction of Medina Azahara, and the site, almost 2000m long by 900m wide, stretched over three descending terraces above the Guadalquivir valley. Roman masonry was taken from sites throughout Andalucía and re-used, whilst vast quantities of marble were shipped in from north Africa. In addition to the palace buildings, it contained a zoo, an aviary, four huge fish ponds, 300 baths, 400 houses, weapons factories, two barracks for the royal guard as well as numerous baths, markets, workshops and mosques. Visitors, so the chronicles record, were stunned by its wealth and brilliance: one conference room was provided with pure crystals, creating a rainbow when lit by the sun; another was built round a huge shallow bowl of mercury which, when the sun's rays fell on it, would be rocked by a slave, sending sunbeams reflected from its surface flashing and whizzing around the room, apparently alarming guests but greatly amusing the caliph.

Medina Azahara was a perfect symbol of the western caliphate's dominance and greatness, but it was to last for less than a century. **Al-Hakam II**, who succeeded Abd ar-Rahman, lived in the palace, continued to endow it, and enjoyed a stable reign. However, distanced from the city, he delegated more and more authority, particularly to his vizier Ibn Abi Amir, later known as **al-Mansur** (the Victor). In 976 al-Hakam was succeeded by his eleven-year-old son Hisham II and after a series of sharp moves al-Mansur assumed the full powers of government, keeping Hisham virtually imprisoned at Medina Azahara, to the extent of blocking up connecting passageways between the palace buildings.

Al-Mansur was equally skilful and manipulative in his wider dealings as a dictator, and Córdoba rose to new heights of prosperity, retaking large tracts of central Spain and raiding as far afield as Galicia and Catalunya. But with his death in 1002 came swift decline as his role and function were assumed in turn by his two sons. The first died in 1008; the second, Sanchol, showed open disrespect for the caliphate by forcing Hisham to appoint him as his successor. At this a popular revolt broke out and the caliphate disintegrated into civil war and a series of feudal kingdoms. Medina Azahara was looted by a mob at the outset and in 1010 was plundered and burned by retreating Berber mercenaries.

For centuries, the site was looted for building materials; parts, for instance, were used in the Sevilla Alcázar and much of the surrounding town served as a quarry for the fifteenth-century construction of the monastery of San Jerónimo (now privately owned) at the end of the track which climbs above the ruins. But in 1944, excavations unearthed the buried materials from a crucial part of the palace, the **Royal House**, where guests were received and meetings of ministers held. This has been meticulously reconstructed, and though still fragmentary, its main hall, the **Salón Rico de Abd al-Rahman III**, decorated with exquisite marble carvings, must rank among the greatest of all Moorish rooms. It has a different kind of artistic representation than that found in the palaces at Granada or Sevilla – closer to natural and animal forms in its intricate Syrian *Hom* (Tree of Life) motifs. Unlike the later Spanish Arab dynasties, the Berber Almoravids and the Almohads of Sevilla, the caliphal Andalucians were little worried by Islamic strictures on the portrayal of nature, animals or even men – the beautiful hind in the Córdoba museum is a good example (see p.259) – and it may well have been this aspect of the palace that led to such zealous destruction during the civil war. The reconstructed palace gives a scale and focus to the site. Elsewhere there are little more than foundations, gardens and the odd horseshoe arch to fuel your imaginings, amid an awesome area of ruins, hidden beneath bougainvillea and rustling with cicadas.

To reach Medina Azahara, follow the Avda. de Medina Azahara out of town, and on to the road to Villarubia and Posadas. About 4km out of town, make a right turn, after which it's another two or three kilometres to the site. Alternatively, the #1 or #2 **bus** from the Calle de la Bodega station (just south of the train station) will drop you off at the intersection for the final three-kilometre walk. Ask the driver for the "Cruz de Medina Azahara". A taxi will cost you about 3000ptas one way. A good **place to eat** near the site is *Bar-Restaurante Cruce* – often serving *jabilí* (wild boar) – signed at a junction on the way to the entrance.

Almodovar del Río and Hornachuelos

If you have your own transport, it's possible to continue a further 17km west along the C431 to **ALMODOVAR DEL RÍO**, where an impressive **castle** sits on a hill above the town. Dating originally from the eighth century, but with many later additions and restorations it is today privately owned, but can be visited (there are no set visiting hours, you'll just have to turn up). Eighteen kilometres further on, a right turn leads after 8km, to the sturdy hill village of **HORNACHUELOS** and offers the chance to go deep into *caza*, or hunting country. In the wintertime the surrounding terrain, dense with cork and holm oaks, becomes a Mecca for hunters who pay up to 200,000 pesetas each for the chance to secure a trophy for their living room walls. **Walking** in the countryside at this time could be hazardous with these trigger-happy characters on the loose. However, in summer when they are out of action the various river valleys are worth exploring; keep an eye out for members of the colony of Egyptian vultures that breeds near the village. Hornachuelos itself, also has a sixteenth-century Gothic church and a splendid eighteenth-century mansion – **la finca de Morataya** – where the hunting parties of Alfonso XIII stayed in the 1920s. Should you need a **bed**, the *El Alamo*, Ctra. Comarcal 141 (③) has inexpensive rooms in low season, which for this area is high summer.

At **PALMA DEL RÍO**, a small farming town 10km further east, you can spend the night in a converted **fifteenth-century monastery**. *Hospedería de San Francisco*, Avda. Pío XII 35 (☎957/710183; ⑤) preserves much of the former monastic tranquility with a charming cloister, now patio. The excellent Basque-inspired restaurant has an economical *menú*, or you could have a drink in the monastic bar furnished with stone benches and antique paintings.

South of Córdoba – the campiña

To the south of Córdoba, and stretching to the mountains of the province's southern border lies the **Campiña Cordobesa**, a fertile, undulating land full of cornfields, olive groves and vineyards renowned since Roman times. Indeed, the fine relief in Cordóba's archeological museum depicting the olive harvest came from here, and Roman writers such as Pliny and Martial praised its artichokes, fruit, wool and the excellence of its olive oil. The town of **Baena** keeps up the tradition with an oil so good that it carries an official *denominación de origen* label. Each of the villages of the *campiña* has its own interesting castle, church or palace and sometimes a *bodega* – and there are towns such as **Priego de Córdoba**, a Baroque feast, well off the tourist trail, that are undiscovered jewels. The two itineraries described here roughly follow the **bus routes** from Córdoba to Málaga and Granada respectively, making it easy to stop off along the way, as even the smallest villages usually have a *fonda* or *hostal* to provide a **bed** for the night. This opens up the possibility of **walks** exploring some of the *campiña's* delightful countryside, replete with wooded hills and river valleys, areas with a rich variety of flora and fauna. Of course, your own transport – and a little zig-zagging and backtracking – would allow you to combine both routes.

The Ruta del Vino

This itinerary, heading **south** towards **Montilla** and **Iznájar**, also known as the *Ruta del Vino* (wine route), leaves Córdoba by the NIV and, after 14km, forks left along the N331 towards Fernan Nunez, a pleasant hill village a further 14km down the road. Among a number of interesting places along this route are **Montilla**, the centre of Córdoba's wine production, and **Rute** where *anis*, a far stronger brew, is concocted. The itinerary ends at the beautiful lakeside village of **Iznájar** in the midst of some good trekking country.

Montemayor

Just beyond Fernan Nunez **is MONTEMAYOR**, a charming and typical *campiña* hamlet with a fourteenth century **castle**. In the centre of its neat little plaza, there's an amusing copy of the Alhambra's fountain of the lions in Granada. More interesting is the sixteenth-century church of **Nuestra Señora de la Asunción** with a beautifully painted stucco *sagrario* and a sixteenth-century carved baptismal font, still used to initiate the newborn of the parish. You'll need to find the priest, Padre Pablo Moyano, to open the church and he may well be in the *Casino*, a great old institution across the square. When you've looked around the church ask Padre Pablo if you can see his personal **archeological collection**, kept in a vault beneath the church and for which he is famous for miles around. This enormous accumulation of artefacts including coins, agricultural implements, grindstones and jewellery as well as a few pieces of sculpture – most of it from Roman *Ulia*, as Montemayor then was – has been collected in his walks over the years in the surrounding fields. Close to the village, there are **rooms** at *Hostal El Artista*, Carretera Córdoba–Málaga s/n (☎957/384236; ②).

Montilla

The road presses on into the sierra of Montilla and endless rows of vines begin dominating the landscape as you near the heart of Córdoba's **wine producing region**. The tough Pedro-Ximénez vines planted here have to withstand searing summer temperatures, and send their roots deep down into the whitish-grey *albariza* soil searching for moisture. Eleven kilometres beyond Montemayor, **MONTILLA**, the capital of Córdoba's wine country, comes into view. Hardly the region's prettiest town, you may want to call in, however, to visit one of the leading **bodegas**, *Alvear SA*, Avda. María Auxiliadora 1 (visits and tastings Mon–Fri 10am–2pm; ☎957/650135), a picturesque place founded in the eighteenth century.

Almost opposite the *bodega*, the *Barril del Oro*, Avda. de Andalucía 22, makes a good place to stop for *tapas*; try their *flamenquines* (stuffed rolls of veal and *Jamón Serrano*) or the seafood *raciones*. Surprisingly, the excellent *Montilla* served here comes not from the *bodega* over the road, but is bought in by the *patrón* from his own favourite growers. The medium-priced *Restaurante Camachas*, on the main road at the entrance to the town, is also recommended for more substantial fare. If you want **to stay**, *Hostal Nuestra Señora del Carmen*, c/Escuelas 3 (☎957/650734; ②) should be able to provide a room.

Aguilar and the Laguna de Zonar

AGUILAR, 7km further south, perched on top of a hill, is worth a visit to see its wonderful eighteenth-century **octagonal plaza of San José**, probably inspired by the better-maintained one at Archidona in Málaga. The rest of the town is charming with sloping streets lined with white-walled houses, their windows protected by *rejas*, or iron grilles. From the **Torre del Reloj** there are excellent views over the *campiña*. The sixteenth-century **Santa Maria del Soterraño**, with an *artesonado* Mudéjar ceiling and a Plateresque doorway is Aguilar's best church.

There's also a *Montilla* **bodega** here, *Carbonell SA*, on the Puente Genil road (visits Mon–Fri 8am–1pm; ring first ☎957/660643), owned by one of Spain's major olive oil

MONTILLA-MORILES: NO HANGOVER GUARANTEED

The Romans and later the Moors (in spite of the Prophet's prohibition) developed the *campiña* as a **wine region**. The great wine of Córdoba, **Montilla** (often called *Montilla-Moriles*, the latter village being its partner in production to the south) has suffered over the years from its comparison with the wines of Jerez and with which it shares similar characteristics. The reasons for this are largely historical as, prior to the 1940s, much of Córdoba's vintage was sold to the great *fino* houses of Jerez, and eventually marketed as sherry. In 1944 this was made illegal, since when *Montilla* has been granted its own *denominación* and the producers have had to stand on their own feet. But the notion that the wines of this region are merely a less expensive alternative to sherry has been a tag that the industry here has found hard to shake off.

The most visual difference in the production of *Montilla* are the great **tinajas** – huge earthenware urns in which the wine undergoes its fermentation. These Ali-Baba jars, the direct descendants of the Roman *dolium*, have pointed ends which are buried in the earth inside the *bodegas* and are believed to impart a unique character to the wine. As in Jerez the wine in these great vats also develops a *flor* (a thick layer of yeast) which covers the narrow neck of the urns. Later, the *solera* system (see Jerez p.155) during which the wine is aged and blended in oak butts for two years, is used to finish the process. The response you get around these parts should you bring up the subject of comparisons with the *finos* of Jerez is the assertion that *Montilla* is a natural product, whilst the wines of Jerez need to have their alcohol added. The Pedro-Ximénez grape used for *Montilla* is baked in the furnace heat of the *campiña* sun and produces wines of 16 percent proof which, the *bodegas* here like to claim – unlike that synthetic *jerezano* – never gives you a hangover.

producers. Don't let that put you off, however, for it's a beautiful *cortijo* with an ageing-hall modelled on Córdoba's Mezquita. If you're looking for **accommodation**, *Hostal San José*, c/Pescadería 6 (☎957/660222; ③), is clean and central.

Four kilometres southwest of Aguilar along the C329 and easily walkable, the **Laguna de Zonar** is the largest of a group of little-known inland salt lakes. Visited in winter by large numbers of **migrating waterfowl**, this time of the year is best for spotting white-headed duck, a species that once almost disappeared but is now on the increase. Other species which can be seen here include red-crested pochard, mallard, great-crested grebe, tufted duck and marsh harrier. In summer there is less to see, although sometimes flamingos fly in from the Fuente de Piedra in nearby Málaga, for a change of scene. There's an observation **hide** here as well as an **information centre**. Other lakes in this group include the Laguna del Rincon north of Moriles, and the Laguna de Tiscar, north of Puente Genil, both of which, unlike this one, tend to dry up in summer.

Cabra

At Monturque, 9km south of Aguilar there's a turn off to Moriles, the other great *Montilla* name but in truth a dull village, and only to be sought out by wine *aficionados*. Much more rewarding is the C336 road which heads 12km east to **CABRA**, another pleasant *campiña* town. Possessing an old quarter with steep, winding streets lined with *rejas* – many holding pots sprouting colourful geraniums in summer – and a number of Baroque mansions, it's a lovely place to wander for an hour or so. At the end of the town, near the castle, the Baroque **Iglesia de la Asuncíon**, built over a mosque, is surrounded by palms and cypresses. It has a fine portal with twisted marble Solomonic pillars, and inside, an altar of red and black jasper together with fine **choir stalls**. The church of **San Juan Bautista** in the old quarter – Visigothic in origin but much altered since – is reckoned to be one of Spain's oldest with Moorish and Baroque features added. A small **archeological museum** in the *Casa de Cultura*, c/Martin Belda 27, contains finds from the prehistoric, Visigothic, Roman and Moorish periods.

On the road leading east out of town towards Priego de Córdoba, there's a wooded picnic and swimming area, **La Fuente del Río**, centred around a natural spring which is the source of the Río Cabra. Seven kilometres beyond this, a road on the left climbs 6km to the **Ermita de la Virgen de la Sierra**, a hermitage sited at an altitude of over 1200 metres from where there are stupendous **views** west towards the valley of the Guadalquivir, and east to the mountains of the Sierra Nevada.

Places to stay in Cabra are usually easy to come by; try *Hostal Pallares*, c/Alcalá Galiano 2 (☎957/520725; ③) or *Fonda Guzman*, c/ Pepita Jiminez 5 (☎957/520507; ②) both in the centre, or *Hostal San José*, Avda. Fuente del Río 12 (☎957/520368; ②) if you fancy being near the swimming pool. There are numerous bars and **places to eat** around the town; the best is *Mesón El Vizconde*, c/Martín Belda 16, whose *fritura de pescado* (fish fried in the oil of the region), *lubina al hinojo* (sea bass in fennel sauce) and *merluza con salsa de puerros* (hake in leek sauce) are all excellent; there's also a less expensive *menú*.

Lucena

Surrounded by hills covered with vines and olives, **LUCENA**, 11km down the N331 from Monturque, is a large, unsightly industrial town which makes its money from furniture production, and manufacture of the great *tinajas*, or earthenware urns, used in the making of *Montilla*. However, one reason to close your eyes to all of this and stop off is the church of **San Mateo**, sited on the central Plaza Nueva, which houses one of the Baroque glories of the province. The church was started in the fifteenth century over a mosque and has a superb *retablo* and a breathtakingly beautiful eighteenth-century Baroque **sagrario**, with exquisitely painted stucco cherubs and a feast of decorative detail topped off by a remarkable **cupola**, all the work of local artist Antonio de Castro. Nearby, the **Torre del Moral** is the surviving tower of the castle where Boabadil, the last sultan of Granada, was briefly imprisoned by Isabel La Católica in 1483.

Should you need a **place to stay** – although once you've seen the church, there's not much to hang around for – *Hostal Muñoz*, c/Cabrillana 108 (957/501052; ②) is central, clean and has its own *tapas* bar.

Rute

The scenic N331 Málaga road continues to **Benameji**, 20km away, a pleasant agricultural village with a couple of *fondas,* close to the provincial border. However, the more interesting route lies along the road which turns off left 8km south of Lucena, heading towards the small town of **RUTE**. Twelve kilometres from the turn, the town, sited picturesquely on a hill overlooked by the hazy Sierra de Rute behind, comes into view. Beyond a ruined Moorish castle and a Baroque church, it has few monuments to attract visitors and Rute's fame throughout Andalucía is based on a far more potent allure: the manufacture of a lethal **anis**, the local eau-de-vie made with springwater from the Sierra and, at its most potent, an undiluted 96 percent proof. Even the milder *anis seco* at 55 per cent, is fierce enough to have you holding the wall for support after a single glass. The syrupy *anis dulce* (a mere 35 percent) is probably the safest. Different variations on the *anis* theme can be tasted at the twenty or so small *bodegas* scattered around the town. After which you'll probably need a **bed** to sleep it off; *Fonda Francis*, c/Juan Carlos 15 (☎957/526385; ②) and *Fonda Rosales*, c/Toledo 9 (☎957/526097; ②) are both reliable places.

Iznájar

IZNÁJAR, which may also be reached directly along an attractive road from Rute, is a charming white farming village with a spectacular location that belies its poverty, something which the village has long experience of. It was here that a "peasants revolt" ocurred in 1861 against the injustices of the landowning class towards the *braceros*, or

---

A WALK TO IZNÁJAR

From Rute it's possible to make an 18km **walk** around the **Embalse de Iznájar** (reservoir) to the village of the same name, a beautiful white-walled hamlet perched on a promontory below an impressive castle, surrounded by water. There are plenty of opportunities for bird watching and in spring, the flora is quite delightful. The walk should take about three to four hours, depending on how many stops you make and you should be aware that there's no official accommodation at Iznájar (you may be able to hitch the 14km back to Rute), though there are a number of places to eat.

Start by leaving Rute along the road south (the C334) towards Iznájar, veering left at the fork and then taking a track on the right about half a kilometre further on. This slowly descends to the reservoir edge with a pleasant view over the lake. Turn right along the bank following the dirt track in and out of the creeks and coves until you arrive at a rocky promontory where there's a disused mine and from where you can get fine views over the Embalse towards Iznájar. After ascending a hill, the Camorro de la Isla, you arrive at an asphalted road which will bring you around the south side of the Embalse and, across the bridge, to the village of Iznájar, on its scenic peninsula.

---

labourers – an uprising that was viciously suppressed. Of Moorish origin, Iznájar's **alcazaba** was constructed in the eighth century, and the church of **Santiago** built inside it, during the sixteenth. There is no official place to stay here, although **camping** is allowed on the nearby Valdearenas beach on the Embalse. For **food**, there's *Restaurante Rosi* on the road towards Loja as well as two other places, *El Montecillo* and *Mesón Mallas*, near the petrol station.

The Ruta del Aceite

This itinerary towards Priego de Córdoba, known as the *Ruta del Aceite* (oil route), follows the N432 **southeast** out of Córdoba. It takes in the olive-oil producing region centred on **Baena** before visiting some of the province's most picturesque villages, including Luque and Zuheros. The route concludes at the town of **Priego de Córdoba** which has one of the most remarkable collections of Baroque churches in Andalucía.

Espejo

At **ESPEJO**, 41km to the south of Córdoba, an impressive Moorish castle looms above the white-walled village, vineyards and olive groves spread out below. The fourteenth-century Mudéjar **castillo** is the property of the Dukes of Osuna, the great ruling family based in Osuna to the southwest (see p.208), which once owned an enormous tract of Andalucía. The Gothic-Renaissance church of **San Bartolomé** dating from the fifteenth and sixteenth centuries, is also worth seeking out for its fine **retablo mayor** by Pedro Romana and its *artesonado* ceiling.

Castro del Río

Sited on a low hill on the north bank of the Río Guadajoz, **CASTRO DEL RÍO**, 9km down the road, has a **Roman bridge** spanning the river and a ruined **Moorish castle** built on the foundations of a Roman fort. The village also claims a footnote in Roman history as this is believed to be the place where Pompey's troops rested up prior to their showdown battle with Caesar in 45BC at nearby Montilla (Munda) which ended the Roman civil war and, briefly, gave Caesar control of the whole empire. The **Iglesia de la Asunción**, founded in the thirteenth century with later additions, has a fine if somewhat eroded Plateresque portal, and the **Ayuntamiento** preserves the prison in which Cervantes was locked up for a week in 1568 when, then working as a tax collector, he was falsely accused of fiddling the books.

BAENA'S OIL FOR CONNOISSEURS

Spain produces, and probably consumes, more **olive oil** than any other country in the world. However, it wasn't always so, and when the Greeks introduced the olive to the peninsula in the first millenium BC, it was regarded with suspicion by the native Iberians who went on using their traditional lard. Only with the arrival of the Roman legions did they begin to aquire a taste for it, and under Roman supervision Hispanic oil became the finest and most expensive in the Empire. Later, sophisticated Moorish invaders taught the Iberians better cultivation techniques, as well as culinary and medicinal possibilities. The Moorish, and now Spanish, names for oil and the olive, *aciete* and *aceituna* are a legacy of this time.

Today, Spaniards are great connoisseurs of quality oil and **Baena** has its own official **denominación de origen**, backed by an official regulatory body, the *Consejo Regulador*, guaranteeing the standards attained by strict methods of production. Baena's finest oil is claimed by its makers to stand comparison with the best in Europe, and *almazaras* (oil mills) such as that operated for several generations by the Nuñez family in the town, take a great amount of care at every stage in the production process. The olives cultivated on the estate are all harvested by hand prior to being ground to a paste on ancient granite stone mills. The "free run" oil – with no further pressure applied – that results from this process is regarded as the *grand cru* of the oil trade and it takes eleven kilos of olives to yield just one litre of such oil. With a markedly low acid content and an unfatty, concentrated flavour, this oil is far too good (and expensive) for cooking and is sparingly used to flavour *gazpacho* – in Córdoba province, *salmorejo* – or tasted on a morsel of bread as a *tapa*.

The *Nuñez de Prado* mill, c/Cervantes 15 (☎957/670141; 9am–2pm & 4–7.30pm) can be visited, although most of the action takes place in November when the harvested olives are pressed.

Baena

The road continues south into the area geographically known as the **Sierra Subbética Cordobesa**, a rugged, rambling spur of the Cordillera Betica range in the province's south-eastern corner, and now officially a natural park. Beyond Castro del Río the N432 climbs gently through hills covered with olive groves until it reaches Andalucía's most celebrated oil town, **BAENA**. Famous for centuries for the high quality of its olive oil, the huge metal tanks for storing the oil can be seen on the outskirts of town. Baena was an important place in the Moorish period, but has declined as a result of emigration in more recent times. A pleasant and busy town today, there are several interesting monuments located around the **Plaza de la Constitución**, in the upper town. The eighteenth-century **arcaded almacén** or warehouse, is now a cultural centre and, another part of the same building, houses *Mesón Casa del Monte*, a good *tapas* bar.

From the square, c/Henares leads to the early sixteenth-century Gothic church of **Santa María** with a fine portal and a Moorish tower, probably the minaret of a former mosque. The church is a sad testament to the ferocity of the Civil War, when this beautiful building was put to the torch. It has only recently aquired a temporary roof over its burnt-out interior of which a wonderful *reja* (altar screen) survives as a reminder of former days. The image of what was lost, including a precious *retablo*, is preserved in a faded photograph hanging in the sacristy. To look around, enquire at the houses in the vicinity of the church, which should eventually raise the key, possibly accompanied by a young *sacristán* (verger), who will dramatically relate the church's tragic tale. Nearby is the sixteenth-century Mudéjar convent of **Madre de Dios**, with fine late-Gothic porch, *retablo*, *coro* and *artesonados*. The nuns here also sell convent *dulces*, and are noted for their *madalenas*.

Besides oil, Baena is also famous for its *Semana Santa* rituals which include a **drum rolling contest** when the streets are filled with the ear-splitting sound of up to 2000 drums being struck simultaneously. From Wednesday to Friday during Holy Week is the time to avoid, if you forgot to bring ear plugs. Finding **places to stay** outside of this period is normally no problem; *Hostal Rincón*, c/Llano del Rincón 12 (957/670223; ③) is central and comfortable.

Luque

Seven kilometres beyond Baena, a right turn leads to the attractive village of **LUQUE**, spread over a rocky outcrop topped by the almost obligatory castle. Dating from the thirteenth century, the ruins of the Moorish **castle** are worth a look, and beside them is the Gothic-Renaissance church of **La Asunción** with a *retablo* whose central image of San Juan is attributed to Martínez Montañés. For central **accommodation**, the *Hostal Villa de Luque*, Plaza de España s/n (☎957/667136; ③) is a fine old refurbished *casa andaluza* owned by the local council. The *hostal* also has a small **restaurant**, or there's *Bar La Plancha*, across from the church, which is a lively place serving *tapas* and *raciones*.

Zuheros

ZUHEROS, 5km west and nestling in a gorge backed by steep rock cliffs, is another stunningly beautiful *Subbética* village. A cluster of white houses tumbles down the hill below a romantic Moorish **castle** built on and into the rock. Later Christian additions were made after it fell to Fernando III in 1240 and became a frontier bastion against the kingdom of Granada. The nearby early seventeenth-century **Iglesia de los Remedios**, has a fine *retablo* as well as a tower built on the remains of a minaret from an earlier mosque. Downhill from here there's a charming **place to stay**, the *Hotel Zuhayra*, c/ Mirador 10 (☎957/694624; ④) which uses the village's ancient Moorish name, and makes a perfect base to explore the surrounding country. For **food** the *Zuhayra* has a restaurant, and there's also *Mesón Atalaya*, c/Santo 58, a pleasant, medium-priced place.

In the hills behind the village, the **Cueva de los Murcielagos** (cave of the bats – not to be confused with the more important cave of the same name near Albuñol in Granada), contains impressive stalagmites and stalagtites, as well as **Paleolithic cave paintings**. The cave lies about 1km from the village; check access with the *Ayuntamiento*, c/ 18 Julio 2, before setting out.

WALKS AROUND ZUHEROS

With the aid of a good map (1:50,000 IGN; sheet 967), you can follow the Bailón river valley south from Zuheros to the Ermita de Nuestra Virgen de la Sierra near Cabra (see p.270), a splendid **walk** through rugged hill country. The distance is about 14km, with a stiff climb at the end to the Ermita. From here, you could continue 13km to Cabra, taking the train back to Luque station (7km from Zuheros), if you don't want to stay overnight in Cabra itself.

Another walk from Zuheros takes you 14km to the **Laguna del Conde**, the largest of Córdoba's inland salt lakes, and a good place in season to spot flamingo and shelduck. Start out from the village heading east between the Cerro (hill) de los Murcielagos and the road, along an ancient track. This gradually ascends the Cerro de los Cangilones, then descends towards the village of Luque (see above). Leave Luque by the track heading south out of the village towards El Esparragal. Less than a kilometre along this you'll come to a fork where you should bear left in the direction of the *cortijo* (farm) of Las Albercas, which lies in a valley. The road forks again close to the *cortijo* and again you'll need to bear left along the track which descends. Bear right at the next couple of forks – the track eventually meets up with the main C432 road between Baena and Alcaudete. Turn left along the asphalted road and follow it a short way until you come to another track on the right; this will take you the last couple of kilometres to the lake, which in summer tends to dry up considerably leaving behind a salt bed.

Doña Mencía

Not quite as pretty as other villages in the area, **DOÑA MENCÍA**, 5km to the west of Zuheros, is a sizeable oil and wine centre lying at the foot of a slope that's covered with silver-leaved olives, interrupted by the occasional vineyard. There's a fifteenth-century ruined **castle** and, nearby at the end of c/Juan Valera, a small **museum**, c/ Juan Ramon Jiménez 8, in the former house of the nineteenth-century novelist Juan Valera, whose best-known work, *Pepita Jiménez*, was set in Cabra. There are a surprising number of *bodegas* here, and a clutch of **places to eat** around the pleasant Plaza Mayor. For **rooms**, try the village **fonda**, *Casa Morejon*, c/Obispo Cubero 1 (957/☎676169; ①).

Priego de Córdoba

PRIEGO DE CÓRDOBA, 33km southeast of Luque, is one of Andalucía's little-known Baroque wonders which offers a feast of superb churches and a remarkable fountain, making it an interesting and inviting place to stopover. Situated beneath the province's highest mountain, the 1600m La Tiñosa, the northern approach to the town presents a dramatic view of the whitewashed houses and towers of its old quarter, laid out along the edge of a picturesque escarpment known as the Adarve. The centre of this tranquil country town is the Plaza de la Constitución, an elegant square fronted by the **Ayuntamiento**, from where all the monuments are within easy walking distance.

Despite evidence of long prehistoric habitation in nearby caves and a later Roman settlement, it was under the Moors that *Medina Bahiga* as Priego was then known, flourished as part of the kingdom of Granada. Following a tug of war between the Moors and Christians during the fourteenth century, in which the town changed hands three times, it finally fell to the Christians in 1341. Recovery from the aftermath of this turbulent era came only in the eighteenth century when in 1711, Priego became a dependency of the Dukes of Medinaceli. An economic resurgence based on the production of silk and textiles poured great wealth into the town and it was during this time that most of the **Baroque churches**, Priego's outstanding attraction today, were constructed. In the nineteenth century, though, the industry found it hard compete with cheap cotton textiles produced in Catalunya and Britain, and a slow decline set in. The European slump in textiles in the Fifties and Sixties caused by imports from Asia accelerated the problems and as factories closed, many emigrated to seek work elsewhere. Today the remnants of the textile industry, along with farming are the town's main employers.

The Town

Buses arriving in Priego will drop you in the central Plaza de la Constitución although the actual bus station is a five-minute walk to the east of the centre on c/San Marcos.

Your first port of call should be to the extraordinarily helpful **Turismo**, c/Río 33 (Mon–Sat 10am–1pm; ☎957/700625), just south of the Plaza de la Constitución, to collect a copy of the excellent **town map**. It's run by an ebullient human dynamo named José Mateo, who encourages visitors to call at his home, c/Real 46, in the old quarter near the church of the Asunción, for advice and information when the office is closed. He's especially concerned to find budget accommodation for students and young travellers. The building housing the Turismo is itself historic, the birthplace of (and now shrine to) **Niceto Alcalá Zamora**, first president of the ill-fated Spanish Republic from 1931–36. Much of the furniture of this middle-class nineteenth-century family mansion survives intact, and you are free to look around.

Iglesia de la Asunción

From the Plaza de la Constitución head northeast towards the **Barrio Villa**, the old quarter, which contains most of Priego's principal monuments. A good place to begin is with the austere Moorish **castillo**, whose impressive keep dominates the small Plaza de Abad Palomino. Altered in the thirteenth and fourteenth centuries, the interior is now privately owned. In the square's southeast corner lies the first of the Baroque churches, the **Iglesia de la Asunción**, its modest whitewashed exterior dating from the sixteenth century. Inside, however, the surprises begin: an ornate white stucco Baroque interior leads towards a stunningly beautiful carved **retablo** with images attributed to Juan Bautista Vázquez. The greatest surprise of all, though, lies through a door on the left aisle where you enter the breathtaking **sagrario**, one of the masterpieces of Spanish Baroque. Here a dazzling symphony of wedding-cake white stuccowork and statuary, punctuated by scrolls and cornices, climbs upwards beyond a balcony into a fabulous cupola illuminated by eight windows. The frothy depth of the stucco plaster was achieved by the use of esparto grass to lend it additional strength – a material which has played a remarkable part in the craft history of Andalucía, even found in hats, baskets and sandals discovered in the Neolithic caves of Granada. This recently-restored octagonal chapel is the work of Francisco Javier Pedrajas, a native of Priego and one of a number of leading sculptors, carvers and gilders working in the town at this time. The *altar mayor* and the *sagrario* have been declared national monuments.

The church may also have the image of **Jesús Nazareno** (Christ bearing the cross) from the church of San Francisco whilst the latter is being renovated. It's a fine work, attributed to Pedro de Mena.

Barrio de la Villa and Paseo del Adarve

Before taking in more Baroque mastery, the nearby and delightful **Barrio de la Villa** provides a welcome opportunity for a stroll. The ancient Moorish part of the town, a maze of sinuous and whitewashed alleys with balconies and walls loaded with pot plants, leads to a number of typical *plazuelas*. You should eventually stumble on one of the most charming, the **Plazuela de San Antonio**, replete with palms and wrought-iron *rejas*; if you don't, just ask any of the passing locals who are only too pleased to show you around their pride and joy. Behind the church of the Asunción, c/Bajondillo leads to the **Paseo de Adarve** a superb, and originally Moorish, promenade with a spectacular **view** over the valley of the Río Salado and undulating groves of olives stretching to the distant hills.

San Pedro and San Juan de Dios

Just to the west of the castillo, the **Iglesia de San Pedro** is another Baroque treat with more stucco and a wonderful **altar mayor** in painted wood and stucco with a delightful domed *camarín* (side room) behind, which holds a stirring image of the *Immaculada* attributed to *granadino* sculptor Diego de Mora. The side chapel of the **Virgen de la Soledad** with another *camarín*, has an image of the Virgin at the centre of its *retablo* by Pablo de Rojas. To the north of the castillo, and close to the **Carnicerías Reales**, a sixteenth-century abbatoir and meat market with a fine cobbled patio, the church of **San Juan de Dios**, with a finely crafted cupola, is an early example of Priego Baroque, completed in 1717.

La Aurora

Moving south along c/Argentina will lead you to the church of **La Aurora**, yet another Baroque gem, whose exuberant façade with Corinthian and Solomonic pillars topped by a Virgin and flanked by exquisite stone and marble decoration is only an overture for the interior. This, now restored to its full glory, is a single-naved Baroque explosion in painted wood and stucco descending from the grey and white cornices, with polychromed figures on its ceiling, dome and walls, to an animated and sumptuously theatrical **retablo**. This *retablo* is a glittering amalgam of vegetal and geometrical forms, and the crowning achievement of Juan de Dios Santaella, another native Priego talent, born here in 1716. The church is also home to the **Cofradía de la Aurora**, a brotherhood whose sixteenth-century articles of foundation stipulate that they must proceed through the streets in musical procession every Saturday at midnight. Thus, whatever the weather, this band of men, hatted and cloaked, gather behind their banner and a huge lantern to proceed through the streets singing hymns to the *La Aurora* (Our Lady of the Dawn) accompanied by guitars, accordions and tambourines.

Just south of here along c/Buen Suceso, the **Iglesia de San Francisco** on an elegant old square, is another late Gothic church that Santaella had a hand in remodelling. Much deteriorated, it's presently closed whilst undergoing restoration but – once you've admired the **façade and portal** (both by Santaella), employing contrasting tones of marble – a hole considerably drilled in the door allows you to glimpse the *retablo mayor*, a splendid gilded work by Santaella again. You'll need to gain entry, however, to see the beautiful *camarín* and dome (by Santaella) and chapel of Jesús Nazareno which has a gilded and polychromed wood and stucco **retablo** by Pedrajas, the creator of the *sagrario* in the Asunción.

The Fuente del Rey

At the southern end of the town, and easily reached by following c/Río to its end, lies the **Fuente del Rey**, a spectacular sixteenth-century 180-jet fountain (with many later additions) which pours water into a number of basins. The highest of these has a sculpture of a lion struggling with a serpent, whilst the second contains a larger late eighteenth-century depiction of Neptune and Amphitrite, the king and queen of the sea. Amphitrite is clutching the dolphin that returned her to Neptune after her attempted escape, incidentally emphasizing the power of the king, the work's intended ideological message, given that over the border in France, monarchs were losing their heads. There are in fact two fountains here, the second being the **Fuente de la Salud**, to the rear of the plaza, a sixteenth-century Italianate work built on the spot, according to legend, where the conquering Alfonso XI pitched his camp in 1341. One of the most tranquil squares in Andalucía, this leafy area is a wonderful place to relax and get away from it all, which is why there are so many seats.

From just beyond the square you can **walk** to the Ermita de El Calvario from where there are fine **views** over the town. Take the steps to the left of the Fuente de la Salud.

The rest of the churches

When you've seen the main churches, there are many more almost as good. Just off the Plaza de la Constitución at the start of c/Río, the **Iglesia de las Angustias** is a charming small church and another work by Santaella. The interior has a fine cupola with more typically exuberant polychromed stucco decoration. Further along c/Río beyond the Turismo, the **Iglesia del Carmen** has a *retablo* by Santaella, probably an early work. Finally, to the west on Carrera de las Monjas, the **Iglesia del Mercedes** was an ancient hermitage prior to its remodelling in the latter part of the eighteenth century when it was decorated in Rococo style by Pedrajas, highlighted by the four winged archangels at the scalloped corners. Another stunningly ornate snow-white cupola (which is almost Pedrajas' trade mark), is balanced by an elegant *retablo* below. The exterior is an incomplete later addition.

It's encouraging to know that all this splendour, and its maintenance, has brought into being a **crafts academy**, *La Escuela Taller Juan de Dios Santaella*, appropriately named after Priego's Baroque genius. Here the myriad skills and crafts necessary to restore and care for these buildings, as well as others throughout Andalucía, Spain and beyond, will be nurtured and passed on.

Practicalities

Rooms aren't exactly plentiful in Priego, but there's usually no great demand. The best deal in town is *Hostal Rafi*, c/Isabel la Católica 4 (☎957/540749; ③), a charming and friendly place with air-conditioned rooms including TV, in a tiny street east of the main square. This *hostal* also has a separate (and good) restaurant on the ground floor. A more luxurious, but extremely good value option, *Río Piscina* (☎957/700186; ③), is on the western edge of town with a pool, restaurant, tennis court and gardens. Back in town and near the Turismo there's the very basic *Hostal Andalucía*, c/Río 13 (☎957/ 540174; ②), also with a restaurant. Slightly further out *Hostal Andaluz*, c/Jaén 30 (☎957/700044; ①) on the way to the Plaza de Toros, is about the lowest priced in town. Near here, there's a municipal **campsite** (☎957/540135; May–Sept) at the *Poledeportivo Municipal* – which has a restaurant – on Avda. de la Juventud, opposite the bullring.

Eating in town is confined to the bars around the main square most of which are good for breakfast and *tapas*, and the restaurants attached to the *hostales*. The Fuente del Rey makes an ideal place for a picnic lunch between churches. Outside the first week in September when Priego celebrates its annual *Feria Real*, **nightlife** is generally confined to sipping drinks at tables on the Plaza Mayor. However, one interesting diversion is *TES*, a newly-opened **karaoke bar** at c/Río 15 with inexpensive (and lethal) cocktails. If there's a crowd in it can be really fun, especially when groups of Spanish teenagers get up to croon their way through songs like *Blue Velvet* with perfect synch, and lots of wah-wah-woohs. Should you feel like entertaining the natives whilst you make a fool of yourself, they seem to have every number-one pop song back to the Fifties.

Around Priego

With your own transport you could take in a few of the surrounding villages which, although often lacking anything too compelling in the way of sights, are situated in wonderful *Subbética* countryside (see p.272).

CARCABUEY, 7km east of Priego, is a charming place laid out on a hill topped by a ruined castle. The Gothic-Renaissance church of **La Asunción** lower down, has a good portal flanked with Solomonic marble pillars, and inside a superb **retablo** with the central figure of Christ attributed to Pedro de Mena and Alonso Cano. Usually locked, you'll need to enquire at the nearby houses for the key.

ALMEDINILLA, 9km west on the Jaén border is another characteristic *Subbética* village squatting along the valley of the Río Caicena. There are important Roman remains being excavated here (information from the archeological workshop at c/ Franco 5) and the church has a sculpture attributed to Martínez Montañés.

ALCAUDETE, 29km northeast of Priego in Jaén province, tumbles down a hill below an impressive Moorish castle, with a massive keep. There are a few sixteenth-century churches to see here, too.

One of the more spectacularly-sited villages in this part of the country is **MONTE-FRÍO**, 42km southeast of Priego, and just over the Granada border. Cradled between two rocky outcrops, each topped by a church which can be visited, the town has an even bigger neoclassical **Iglesia de la Encarnación** at its heart, with an enormous dome and some bizarre acoustics. Montefrío is known for its *morcilla* (black-pudding) and *chorizo*, both excellent at the *Café Bar la Fonda*, close to the church. Nearby (8km east along the GR222 towards Illora and signposted) is an interesting prehistoric site, **Las Peñas de los Gitanos**. On leaving the road follow a dirt track uphill through a stone quarry to the end, where the site has well preserved dolmens, Iberian stone graves, and ruined dwellings.

North of Córdoba

To the north of Córdoba lies the province's stretch of the Sierra Morena, an area rich in scenery and wildlife but poor in sights. Many of the hardy granite villages are casualties of the Europe-wide depression in mining, and the sad air of many of them is possibly why they see few visitors. Persevere into the region's higher reaches, however, and you enter a landscape most frequented by hunters and anglers; outside the winter hunting season, it's ideal rambling territory as well. This is also another region of the Sierra Morena famed for its *jamón ibérico* or cured ham, and a chance to sample this in the bars and *ventas* along the way shouldn't be missed. For a tour of the area you're at a definite advantage with your own transport and although there are frequent daily buses run by *Alsina Graells, Lopez* and *Ureña* from Córdoba to Peñarroya and Pozoblanco, public transport off the beaten track is minimal.

The main **N432** north out of Córdoba takes the traffic heading for the towns of Badajoz and Cáceres in Extremadura, to the north. Although this road follows a rail line, there are no longer passenger services. After 44km the road forks just before **Espiel**, a small coal mining town, and you can follow the **C411 route** towards Hiñosa del Duque and the valley of Los Pedroches (see below).

Belmez and Peñarroya

From Espiel, the N432 trails the wooded valley of the Río Guadiato until, 21km further on, it passes the grim village of **BELMEZ** with a thirteenth-century **castle** crowning a rocky outcrop, from which there are fine views. Seven kilopmetres further, **PEÑARROYA-PUEBLANUEVO** is the main town of the area, and another sturdy mining centre that would be more at home in northern England than Andalucía. If you're looking for sights, there's an eighteenth-century brick church, but little else to detain you.

Fuente Obejuna

FUENTE OBEJUNA, 16km west of Peñarroya, is famous for its insurrection of 1476 when the population rose against their tyrranical lord, Fernán Gómez de Guzmán, and hacked him to death in the main square. The event was immortalized by the great seventeenth-century playwright, Lope de Vega, in his play *Fuente Ovejuna* and this was performed in the village square in 1933 by the *Barraca* theatre company under the direction of Federico García Lorca. The poet was only too aware that the fundamental injustices portrayed in the work were still true for most of modern Andalucía and the play's Republican-populist theme, and its ecstatic reception in the villages, contributed to making him a marked man by the Right. A journalist who interviewed the mayor of Fuente Obejuna in 1979 found little had changed in five hundred years. "There are those who have a lot, and those who have nothing," said the official bitterly.

Despite its history, the village is hardly an inspiring place today, and in the Plaza Mayor – named after Lope de Vega – a plaque commemorates the playwright for celebrating "the civic virtues" of its citizenry. The fifteenth-century church of the **Virgen del Castillo** was erected on the site of murdered Guzmán's palace, which was pulled down shortly after his death. It's an impressive Gothic building with a fine **retablo** in polychromed wood. The village also has a few Renaissance mansions to seek out in the streets surrounding the square. If you need a **place to stay**, *Hotel El Comendador*, c/ Luis Rodriguez (957/☎582211; ②) is reasonable.

Towards Hinojosa del Duque and Santa Eufemia

Just before it reaches Espiel, the C411 forks right and crosses a number of wooded valleys and watercourses to **Alcaracejos**, where it joins up with the C420. A detour

11km to the east of here allows you to take in **POZOBLANCO**, the sizeable capital of the area known as Los Pedroches. A fairly hum-drum place with a couple of sixteenth-century churches on offer and noted for its *salchichón*, it hasn't changed very much since Gerald Brenan was here in the 1940s gathering material for his book, the *Face of Spain*:

> Although Pozoblanco belongs to the province of Córdoba, it cannot be said to lie in Andalusia. That low step up from the Guadalquivir valley to the meseta lands one in an altogether different geographic and ethnic region. Take architecture. The houses with their deep windows and granite lintels look cold and severe . . . The people too are quite different from the Andalusians. They are hard and dour, with a look of purpose and determination which one certainly does not see south of the Sierra Morena.

Most Andalucians remember the town today as the place where **Francisco Rivera**, or *Paquirri* as he was known, came to a sticky end in the town's bullring during the annual fiesta in 1984. This celebrated *torero's* nemesis appeared in the form of a bull named *Avispado* (Wide-awake) which gored him badly. The town's new hospital, long behind schedule, had not yet opened and the 85km journey to Córdoba was the main reason he died.

Hinojosa del Duque

Turning left at Alcaracejos, the road passes the village of Villanueva del Duque to arrive, 21km futher on, at **HINOJOSA DEL DUQUE**, another sombre town with an outsize church. Popularly known as the *Catedral de la Sierra*, the granite Gothic-Renaissance church of **San Juan Bautista** has a fine **entrance portal** by Hernán Ruiz who designed the belfry for the Mezquita at Córdoba, as well as a superb Gothic interior with beautiful *retablos* and *rejas*. There are a number of other churches here, in addition to the servicable *Hostal Ruda*, c/Padre Manjón 2 (☎957/140778; ③), but not a lot more to hang around for.

Belalcázar and Santa Eufemia

BELALCÁZAR, 9km north and close to the border with Extremadura, has the ruins of a fifteenth-century **castle** with an impressive keep and a sixteenth-century church of **Santiago** with a fine Plateresque *retablo*. Should you need a **room** there's the no-frills *Hostal Morillo*, c/Reina Regente 3 (☎957/146211; ①).

Twenty-eight kilometres to the east, **SANTA EUFEMIA** is a typical north Sierra hamlet with a fifteenth-century Gothic-Mudéjar church and a basic **place to stay**, *Hostal La Paloma*, c/El Calvario 6 (☎957/158076; ②). This is a useful base if you want to go walking in the hills to the north of the village.

A WALK AROUND SANTA EUFEMIA

Head north out of the village along the N502 towards the Pedroches train station. Three kilometres along, you need to veer right at a fork. This road descends parallel to an *arroyo* or dry stream bed, and eventually heads east to a bridge over the Río Guadalmez, the provincial border with Ciudad Real, in a dense wood. From here follow the west bank of the river northwards, along which there are only odd stretches of dirt track. Passing a high hill and some natural ponds on the opposite bank you'll eventually come to a second hill on the east bank topped by the ruins of a castle where you turn left along another dirt track. From the castle ruins, which are an ancient Iberian fortification called *Vioque*, there are fine views of the valley of Los Pedroches to the south. The dirt track heads east to meet up with the road south which brings you back to Santa Eufemia. The walk, about 22km in all (and more easily followed with a 1:50,000 map IGN sheets 833/4) should take from four to five hours depending on how many stops you make.

Northeast from Córdoba

The NIV highway which heads northeast out of Córdoba along the valley of Guadalquivir is the main road to Madrid and one of the great **historical highways** of Andalucía. Not only was this the bullion route between Madrid and its imperial seaports of Sevilla and later Cádiz, but over a millenium and a half earlier, as the Via Augusta, it formed the vital overland link joining Roman Spain with Gaul, Italy and Rome itself. This route has a few delightful stopovers including the village of Montoro, the fine Moorish castle at Baños de Eucina and the historic Despeñaperros Pass. Transport is easy and **buses** link Cordoba with most places on the route. Montoro, Andujar and Bailén are served by **trains** on the Cordoba–Linares–Madrid line.

Montoro

MONTORO lies 43km from Córdoba, past the villages of El Carpio and Pedro Abad, and just off the NIV. Dramatically sited on an escarpment above a horseshoe-bend in the Guadalquivir, the town is a centre of olive-oil production obtained from extensive groves planted in the foothills of the Sierra Morena to the north. A labyrinth of narrow, white-walled streets surrounds the main square, the Plaza de España, dominated by the lofty tower of its Gothic-Mudéjar church, **San Bartolomé**. The interior, behind the red sandstone façade, has a fine *artesonado* ceiling inlaid with mother-of-pearl, recently recovered from under layers of whitewash. Also on this square is the sixteenth-century **Ayuntamiento**, an old ducal mansion with a fine Plateresque frontage, and a historic inn (now closed) at no. 19. A narrow street out of the north side of the square leads into an atmospheric old quarter whose main feature is the thirteenth-century church of **Santa María de la Mota** with some interesting Romanesque capitals. The main street connects Plaza de España with Plaza Benitez along which is a shop selling everything from hats and doormats to bottleholders made from esparto grass, another of the town's industries. The town's other notable monument is the elegant sixteenth-century **bridge of Las Donadas** over the Guadalquivir, paid for by the women of Montoro who, tradition holds, sold their jewellery to place the town on a more direct, and lucrative, route to the north. Across the bridge, the Cardeña road leading up into the hills offers superb **views** back over the town.

If you need a **place to stay**, *Hostal La Paloma*, c/Santos Isasa 42 (☎957/160348; ②) is economical, clean and central. You'll find excellent *tapas* and a pleasant patio at the *Casino*, just off Plaza Benitez.

Andújar

Flanked by the mountains of the Sierra Morena which are visible on the northern horizon, the NIV continues to Villa del Río and enters the province of Jaén. Thirty two kilometres beyond Montoro, **ANDÚJAR** is a simple country town which claims to be the world's biggest centre of sunflower oil bottling. There's also a thriving commercial ceramics industry, as well as a couple of churches worth a visit for their art works.

The road into the town crosses a fifteen-arched **Roman bridge** spanning the Guadalquivir, which has been considerably restored from Moorish times onwards. The central Plaza de España, a baking furnace in the heat of high summer, contains the church of **San Miguel** with Plateresque features, but the more important church is **Santa María** on the plaza of the same name and reached by following c/Feria between the two squares. Built on the site of a former mosque, the free-standing bell tower probably replaced the mosque's minaret. Inside (best to try in the early evening) a chapel on the left has a fine *Christ in the Garden of Olives* by **El Greco**, a startling surprise in a nonedescript country church, highlighted by another painting, an *Immaculada* by Pachecho, the teacher of Velázquez, in a chapel to the the left of the *altar mayor*. The superb *reja* which stands before the El Greco is the work of Master Bartolomé of Jaén, who also created the more famous one in the Capilla Real at Granada.

Of Andújar's traditional ceramics industry, only one exponent survives: José Castillo sells his wares – including the blue and white pottery for which the town is known – from his *alfarería* at c/Alfarero Castillo 7.

Central **places to stay** include the pleasant *Hostal La Española*, c/San Bartolomé 26 (☎953/500150; ③) which has a garden, and *El Turis*, Puerta de la Madrid 23 (☎953/501001; ②) with its own bar. Andújar also has a **campsite**, *Camping Andújar* (☎953/500700) close to the centre, with an on-site restaurant. There are plenty of **bars** in town offering *tapas* or try *Restaurante Don Pedro*, c/G. Zamora 5, which specializes in game.

Around Andújar

A wonderful 30km drive to the north of Andújar along the J501 leads to the thirteenth-century hermitage of **Nuestra Virgen de la Cabeza**, one of the most revered of Andalucía's shrines. There's not much left of the ancient building destroyed in the Civil War when two hundred Guardia Civil officers seized the shrine, declaring their support for Franco's rebellion. Bombarded for eight months by Republican forces, the sanctuary was eventually set alight and the guards captured on May 1, 1937. (Pre-democracy Spanish guide books felt obligated to append an emphatic exclamation mark to the eight months the siege lasted and the more sychophantic compared it to Numancia and Sagunto two of the great Spanish sieges of Roman times – thus turning the episode into a symbol of fascist heroism.) The distasteful rebuild of the hermitage was carried out during the Franco period, but the famous *Romería* – in which brotherhoods and pilgrims converge on the shrine from all over Andalucía and Spain on the last Sunday in April – carries on undaunted.

Just beyond Andújar the NIV turns away from the Guadalquivir valley to head northeast to **Bailén**, a dull town where Napoleon's troops suffered a crushing defeat in 1808, but with little to stop for. From here it pushes on for another 45km to Andalucía's border with La Mancha at the Despeñaperros Pass (see below) and Madrid. Other **possible routes** from this junction lead south to the city of Jaén (see p.283), or to east to Baeza and Úbeda (see p.290) via Linares.

Baños de Encina

6km after Bailén a left turn leads to the village of **BAÑOS DE ENCINA**, which has one of the most impressive Moorish castles in Andalucía. Crowning the low hill above the village, the tenth-century **Alcazár** is a magnificent sight with its fourteen square towers spaced out along a crenellated curtain wall. Built at the behest of al-Hakam II of Córdoba, the fort was completed in 967 no doubt to control the rugged and mountainous territory to the north, the domain of various unruly Iberian clans. Entered through a double horseshoe-arch, where a plaque in Arabic script dates the edifice to year 357 of the *hegira* (967AD), the fort has an oval ground plan and, from the battlements, there are **fine views** towards the Sierra de Cazorla to the east and over the less impressive reservoir behind. Before visting the *alcazár* you should collect the **key** from the **Ayuntamiento** (open office hours), a fine sixteenth-century building on the main square. They can also provide information about a number of caves with prehistoric paintings nearby, as well as a Bronze Age site at **Peñalosa** where an important Iberian mining settlement is being excavated. The village's Gothic-Renaissance church of **San Mateo** is also worth a look, as are its narrow whitewashed streets dotted with señorial mansions. There's no accommodation here, but you can get *tapas* at the bars on the main square.

La Carolina

LA CAROLINA, 20km further to the northeast, is the most important of the new towns set up by Carlos III in the eighteenth century (see p.205) to protect the bullion route from Cádiz to Madrid. As with the other settlements it was named after a member of the royal family – in this case the king himself – settled with foreign immigrants and laid out on a regular grid-pattern street plan which survives today. The town's central square, the Plaza del Ayuntamiento, has the imposing honey-coloured sandstone **Palacio de Pablo de Olavide**, built for Carlos III's radical minister, the force behind the *Nuevas Poblaciones* idea. De Olavide did not long enjoy the fruits of his labours, for the clergy, who were denied access to these new towns, wreaked their vengeance by denouncing him to the Inquisition. Arrested in 1776, he was divested of his property and confined to a covent in La Mancha subject to whatever penances the monks thought appropriate. He subsequently escaped to France "shaking the Spanish dust off his feet for ever", as Ford colourfully put it. Flanking the *palacio*, the parish church of **La Concepción** contains a fine Baroque image of the *Virgen de las Angustias* (sorrows) in alabaster. The town also has a small **archeological museum** which was recently closed for renovation; check with the *Ayuntamiento*.

There are a number of **places to stay**: the basic *El Retorno*, c/Sanjurjo 5 (②) would do for a night, or you could try the more luxurious *La Perdiz* (☎953/660300; ⑤) on the main NIV road at the edge of town. Even if you're not staying, it's worth knowing about their pleasant garden **swimming pool** which you are welcome to use for the price of a drink in the bar.

El Centanillo

A minor road out of La Carolina winds northwest into the hills and ends up at the tiny mountain hamlet of **EL CENTANILLO**, about as far off the tourist trail as it's possible to get in Andalucía. Situated in densely wooded hunting country on the edge of the village, *Bar La Entrada* (②), used by the shooting fraternity in winter, should have a room, although this establishment does have an eccentric streak. It's not unknown for lighting to be exclusively by candlelight when they run out of light bulbs, and the chef has a habit of making up his own mind about what the guests want to eat. You may find that things have improved. Anyway, for **food**, *Bar Alejandro* just along the street with a terrace, is a much better bet and their fish *fritura* cooked up by an ebullient *patrona* is excellent value. There's plenty of good **walking country** around El Centanillo; you could try tracing the Río Grande to its source (about 8km) or, more ambitiously, and with a map (IGN sheet 862), trekking west along the Sierra de los Calderones to the valley of the Río Jándula bordering the province of Ciudad Real.

The Despeñaperros Pass

Two kilometres beyond La Carolina, slightly before the village of Navas de Tolosa, a **roadside monument** marks the site of the important battle which took place in 1212 between the Christian armies under Alfonso VIII and the Almohad forces. The Moors suffered a crippling defeat, opening the way for the Reconquest of Andalucía. The monument depicts the Christian monarchs as well as the shepherd, St Isidore in disguise, who, according to Christian belief, guided them through the well defended Sierra Morena, thus enabling a surprise attack on the Moorish army who fled after defeat through the Despeñaperros Pass. This event, in fact, gave the pass its name – meaning the "overthrow of the dogs" (or Moors).

The **Despeñaperros Pass**, 14km further on, is the dramatic gateway between Andalucía and La Mancha and the only natural breach in the 300-mile length of the Sierra Morena. This narrow defile flanked by daunting crags and slopes covered with dense pinewoods, was for centuries the main point of entry into Andalucía from the north and many travellers have left vivid accounts of arriving in the lush promised land

DON QUIXOTE AND THE DESPEÑAPERROS PASS

Cervantes would have been familiar with the route through the pass, connecting La Mancha with Sevilla and Córdoba, where he lived both as a child and in later life. The brooding and threatening nature of the pass – probably greater before it was blasted to make room for road widening and the rail line – appealed to him, for he used it in two of the most memorable scenes in the adventures of Don Quijote and Sancho Panza. The centre of the pass is where Don Quijote ran mad and played "the desperate, the raving, the furious lover", in order that Sancho could convey news of this penance to his fantasized Lady Dulcinea del Toboso, in reality a slatternly country lass named Alonza Lorenzo:

"Observe the landmarks, and I will try to remain near this spot," said Don Quijote. "And I will even take the precaution of climbing the highest of these crags to look out for you on your return. But your surest way of not missing me, and not getting lost yourself, will be for you to scatter some of the broom that is so plentiful around here. Scatter it at intervals as you go till you get out to open country. The sprigs will serve as landmarks and signs for you to find me by when you come back, just like the thread in Theseus' labyrinth."

This botanical link with the world of Quijote is still strong when, in early summer, the clumps of brilliant yellow flowers are everywhere. About a kilometre further on, the **Venta de Cardenas** was the inn which the delusioned knight errant imagined to be a castle. When, the morning after a night's hospitality the innkeeper demanded payment, Quijote refused with the explanation that knights never paid for their accommodation and made his exit. Sancho, however, was not so lucky and was given a violent tossing in a blanket to teach him a lesson. The old *venta* apparently survived until the last century, when it was seen by Borrow. However, it was subsequently demolished and a characterless hotel now stands on the site. But it's still a stopover on this major transportation route and the lines of articulated lorries parked outside belong to the truck drivers who use this inn today, the successors of the muleteers, drovers and carriers of Cervantes' time.

of the south after traversing the dry and arid plains of La Mancha (from the Moorish *manxa*, or parched earth). George Borrow, however, also related the sense of foreboding due to the pass's evil reputation "on account of the robberies which are continually being perpetrated in its recesses". Ford, when going the other way, described the land beyond the pass as where "commences the *Paño pardo*, the brown cloth, and the *alpargata*, or the hempen sandal of the poverty-stricken Manchegos".

Jaén

Surrounded by olive groves and huddled beneath the fortress of Santa Catalina on the heights above, **JAÉN**, the provincial capital and by far the largest town in the province, is an uneventful sort of place. Derived from the Arabic *Geen*, meaning a stop on the caravan route, the modern town is more northerly than Andalucian in its appearance and character, doubtless stemming from its resettlement with emigrants from the north following the *reconquista*, and the subsequent long centuries spent as the front line bulwark of Christian Spain against Moorish Granada. At the centre of an area impoverished by lack of economic development and chronic unemployment, you would hardly want to go out of your way to get here, but it makes an easy place to stopover and has a handful of interesting sights.

Some history

Although the area around the city is liberally dotted with Iberian settlements, it was probably as the Roman settlement of Auringis, that the town was born. A centre noted for its **silver mines**, Jaén was settled by the Moors shortly after the conquest of 711

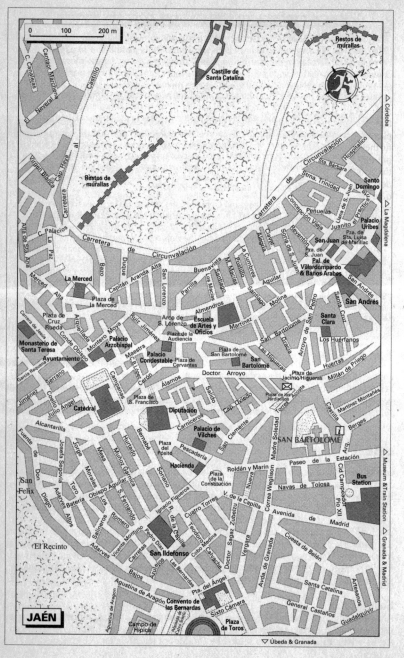

JAÉN

△ Córdoba
△ La Magdalena
△ Museum & Train Station
△ Granada & Madrid

▽ Úbeda & Granada

and to judge by the number of mosques, it must have been a thriving place. The Moors also made use of the **hot springs** that had been known to the Romans and utilized them in the construction of several baths. Fernando III's Christian forces captured the city – then part of the newly-founded Nasrid kingdom of Granada – in 1246 and made its ruler Ibn al-Ahmar (aka Muhammad ibn Yusuf ibn Nasr) into a vassal, obliged to pay annual tribute. It was from Jaén, two and a half centuries later, that the final assault on Boabdil's Granada was launched. The city then entered into a slow decline which gathered pace in the seventeenth and eighteenth centuries and led many of its citizens to emigrate to the imperial colonies, evidenced by towns with the same name in countries as far apart as Peru and the Philippines. Although Jaén's strategic importance played a part in the War of Independence, the economic disruption caused brought further decline in its wake, from which the city never really recovered. The situation is not much improved today and in a recent survey carried out by the Junta de Andalucía, the city and province registered the largest percentage of Andalucía's population describing themselves as living in poverty (61 percent). The survey also showed that a quarter of all the province's citizens live on an income of less than 17,000 pesetas a month.

Arrival and accommodation

Jaén's **bus station** is on Plaza Coca de la Pinera, just off the Paseo de la Estación. There are frequent daily services to and from Úbeda and Baeza and, less often, Cazorla. The **train station** is a bit further out, at the end of the same street and has connections to Córdoba and Madrid. The helpful **Turismo**, c/Arquitecto Bergés 1 (Mon–Fri 9am–1.30pm & 5–7pm, Sat 10am–12.30pm; ☎953/222737) is located just off the Paseo de la Estación, on the opposite side to the bus station.

Accommodation

Places to stay in town are limited, basic and relatively expensive. The few budget-priced places in the centre are sited around the cathedral and Plaza de la Constitución. Just a short way north of the cathedral, you could try *Hostal La Española*, c/Bernardo Lopez 9 (☎953/230254; ③) which is friendly and clean; it may be worth noting that mosquitos can be a real problem both here and elsewhere in the town during the high summer season and if they bother you, come prepared. Off the south side of Plaza de la Constitución, *Hostal Martín*, c/Cuatro Torres 5 (☎953/220633; ②) is a less expensive, but more Spartan alternative. A couple of streets down from here, *Hostal Europa*, Plaza de Belén 1 (☎953/222704; ④) has air-conditioning and a garage. Nearby the *Hostal Carlos V*, Avda. de Madrid 4 (☎953/222091; ②) is comfortable and worth a look, but has been known to close without notice. For a truly memorable experience you could stay in the *Castillo de Santa Catalina Parador* (☎953/264411; ⑤) one of the most spectacularly sited, and best value, hotels in Spain. The rooms all have fine balcony views with a sheer drop to the valley below, and there's an excellent pool as well.

The Town

Most of Jaén's sights lie within a few minutes walk of the rather characterless main thoroughfare, the **Paseo de la Estación**. This cuts through the heart of the city from north to south linking the train station with the Plaza de la Constitución, the major hub of activity. The *paseo* is interrupted only by the Plaza de las Batalles, a square dominated by a grotesque sculpture commemorating the battles of Nava de Tolosa (against the Moors) and Bailen (against the French).

The Cathedral and around

Jaén's massive **Catedral** (daily 8.30am–1pm & 4.30–7pm), lying to the west of the Plaza de la Constitución, dwarfs the city. Begun in 1492 after the demolition of the great mosque which had previously occupied the site; it took a long time to get the work seriously under way and it was not completed until 1802. A number of architects turned their hand to the project during this period, including the great Andrés de Vandelvira whose imprint is on most of the building as it looks today. The Baroque west façade flanked by the twin towers is a wonderful work with Corinthian pillars and statuary by the seventeenth-century master, Pedro Roldán. Inside, the overall mood of the building is more sombre, with bundles of great Corinthian columns surging towards the roof of the nave. Fine sixteenth-century **choir stalls** have richly carved images from the Old Testament as well as a number of grisly martyrdoms. The dim side chapels also have some interesting art works, among them an eighteenth-century *Virgen de las Angustias* (Our Lady of the Sorrows) by José de Mora in the fifth side chapel to the right. The church fills up on Friday afternoons when the *Santa Faz* is ritually removed from its coffer behind the high altar. This Byzantine icon is believed locally to be a likeness of Christ taken from the napkin with which St Veronica wiped his face en route to Calvary. Long queues form on Friday afternoons to kiss the icon (preserved behind glass) while the attending priest wipes it with a handkerchief after each devotee.

The **sacristy museum** (Sat & Sun 11am–1pm) displays works by artists of the region as well as the **Tenebrario**, a fifteen-armed candlestick by Master Bartolomé de Jaén who also made the magnificent *reja* in the Capilla Real at Granada. Two fine seventeenth-century sculptures by Montañes, *San Lorenzo* and *Christ Nazareno*, are also on display.

Near the cathedral are a number of **palaces** that are a feature of most of the larger Andalucian towns. The fifteenth-century **Palacio del Condestable**, c/Martínez Molina 24, has a beautiful patio and interior decoration by Moorish craftsmen from the kingdom of Granada. The elegant portico of the **Palacio de los Vilches**, c/Pescadería, once fronted Jaén's central Plaza Mayor before the present, featureless Plaza de la Constitución replaced it. Off the Plaza de San Francisco behind the cathedral, the **Palacio de los Velez** dates from the seventeenth century and has a fine façade with a portico and coats-of-arms decoration. Slightly to the south, the **Palacio de los Nicuesa** of the same period has another fine monumental façade and a Baroque oratory inside.

The Baños Arabes

The main cluster of the city's other sights lies to the north of here, along c/Martínez Molina in what was formerly the old Moorish town. The most interesting of these is the **Baños Arabes** (Tues–Fri 10am–2pm & 5–8pm, Sat & Sun 10am–2pm; 100ptas, free with EC passport) a remarkable Moorish *hamam* or baths, and the largest to survive in Spain. Originally part of an eleventh-century Moorish palace, the baths fell into disuse after the *reconquista* and were used as a tannery. In the sixteenth century the Palacio de Villadompardo (now a museum of popular arts and crafts) was built over them. They were rediscovered early this century and in the 1980s were impressively and painstakingly restored. The various rooms (cold, tepid and hot) have wonderful brickwork ceilings with typical star-shaped windows, and pillars supporting elegant horseshoe arches. An underground passage (now closed) connected the baths with the centre of the Moorish palace, on top of which was built the Monastery of Santo Domingo (see below). The **museum of arts and crafts** (same hours as the baths) contains artefacts, clothing, toys, ceramics and photos documenting the folk history of the province.

The baths are flanked by the **Palacio de los Uribes**, a sixteenth-century mansion, on the northern side, whilst the church of **San Andrés**, which contains a fabulous **reja** (altarscreen) depicting the *Holy Family* and the *Tree of Jesse* by Maestro Bartolomé of Jaén, here working on his home patch, lies just to the south. Slightly west of here, the church of **San Juan** in the Plaza de San Juan, has a Romanesque tower and inside, two sculptures by Martínez Montañes. A couple of streets north, the c/Santisima Trinidad leads to a **path** which climbs, ruggedly in parts, to the castle of Santa Catalina (see below), a much shorter route than the 4km-plus road. The path starts from the *Bar Sobrino Bigotes*.

Santo Domingo, La Magdalena and other churches

North of San Juan, the **Monastery of Santo Domingo** on c/Santo Domingo erected over a Moorish palace, was originally a fourteenth-century Dominican monastery and later became Jaén's university; later still it was a seat of the Inquisition, before being transformed in more recent times into a school. From its earlier incarnations a fine sixteenth-century **portal** by Vandelvira and a beautiful **patio** with elegant twinned Tuscan columns, survive. The monastery is closed to visitors, but you can usually gain access to the patio.

A little further north still from Santo Domingo, the church of **La Magdalena**, the oldest in Jaén, was built over a mosque, the minaret of which is now its bell tower, and a patio at the rear preserves a pool used in Moorish times for ritual ablutions. In the cloister you can still see a few Roman tombstones used in the construction of the original Moorish building; this quarter was also the centre of the ancient Roman town. Inside, the church has a superb **retablo** by Jacobo Florentino depicting scenes from the Passion.

Two more churches nearby are the sixteenth-century **San Bartolomé**, with a fine Mudéjar *artesonado* ceiling, Gothic ceramic font and an outstanding *Expiration of Christ* by José de Medina, and the **Convento de Santa Clara** with a fine choir and sixteenth-century Ecuadorian sculpture of *Cristo de bambú*.

The Museo Provincial

The **Museo Provincial** at Paseo de la Estación 27 (Tues–Fri 10am–2pm & 4–7pm; Sat & Sun 10am–2pm; free with EC passport, otherwise 100ptas) is worth a visit if only for the remarkable collection of **Iberian stone sculptures**, among the most important in Spain. Located in Room 2 they were found near Porcuna, close to the province's western border and date from the fifth century BC. One is of a magnificent bull, whilst another is a strange fragment – titled *grifomaqia* – depicting a struggle between a man and a griffon. All the works betray the artistic influence of the classical Greek world on the fertile Iberian imagination. The strange fact revealed by the archeological excavations when these works came to light is that they had been deliberately broken a short time after their execution and then laid in a long trench. No satisfactory explanation for this has yet been put forward.

Other items here include Phoenician jewellery and ointment phials, Greek vases (demonstrating how widepread trading links were in the Mediterranean world), as well as Roman mosaics and sculpture. Room 3 deals with Jaén's significant **Moorish period** and has lamps and stoneware as well as a whole jugful of money – dhirams and califalas – that someone buried and never got back to collect. This room also has some fine **ceramics** which verify the Moorish origin of the green glazed plates and vases, still the hallmark of the pottery of Jaén province.

Upstairs, the **Museo de Bellas Artes** is a hotchpotch of fairly awful stuff from the nineteenth and twentieth centuries, although there are a few laughs, not to mention a large number of steamy nudes.

Castillo de Santa Catalina

The **Castillo de Santa Catalina**, dominating the crag which rises behind the city, was in origin a Moorish fortress constructed in the thirteenth century by Ibn al–Ahmar. After the Reconquest, the castle was much altered. Part of it has been stylishly converted into a modern *parador*, and little of the Moorish edifice now survives. A number of secret passageways connected the Moorish fortress with the town below and a few of these have been discovered. A path from the *parador* car park leads to the older and ruined part of the edifice at the castle's southern end where a *mirador* beneath a huge, whitewashed cross gives a **spectacular view** of the city laid out below your feet and dominated by the massive cathedral. Beyond, Jaén's wealth and misery, the endless lines of olive groves, disappear over the hills into the haze. Non-residents are welcome to use the *parador's* bar and restaurant.

Eating, drinking and nightlife

It has to be said that Jaén tends to die after dark and in the absence of much nightlife you'll probably compensate by **eating and drinking**. In the centre, the best place to find food is around the east side of the Plaza de la Constitución. Here, the tiny c/Nueva has a whole crowd of *tapas* bars and places to eat; *Mesón Río Chico*, *La Gamba de Oro* and *Bodegón de Pepe* are all good. Across the Paseo de la Estación from here, *Restaurante Montemar*, despite annoyingly twee decor, serves well-cooked food at mid-range prices. Nearby, the more expensive *Restaurante Nelson*, Paseo de la Estación 33, is a pub-style place serving surprisingly good local dishes. Jaén's best

---

JAÉN'S OLIVES OF WRATH

There are rumoured to be over 150 million **olive trees** in the province of Jaén. They dominate the landscape as infinite rows of green against the orange-red earth, occasionally interspersed with stark white farm buildings. It is beautiful on a grand, sweeping scale, though concealing a bitter and entrenched economic reality. The majority of the olive groves, despite numerous government attempts at reform, are still owned by a mere handful of families, and *señoritismo* – the near-feudal domination of these powerful landowners over the peasants that work their vast *latifundia* or estates – still hold sway here.

Nearly five hundred thousand hectares of the province are planted with olives, which adds up to more than 42 percent of the olives planted in the whole of Andalucía. When compared with Málaga's 9 percent it's easy to understand the fundamental social problems which this monocultural domination has brought in its wake. The misery of the *jornaleros* who work the olives for a mere two months a year and then attempt to survive for the rest of it on their earnings, supplemented by odd jobs, is the most obvious outcome. But the *economía sumergida*, or black economy, is also rife in this environment and the women of most families are forced to keep house for the better-off or do piece-work tailoring in their homes for companies who often exploit them.

Many families find that even this is not enough to live on and the men are forced into internal emigration, moving from one area to another – Ciudad Real for the grape harvest, Murcia to pick tomatoes, Lerida to pick fruit – in order to survive. Others try to find work as far away as Madrid labouring in the construction industry, and on Sunday nights, buses tour the province's villages picking up men who are ferried to the capital to start work early the next day. The resistance to change by the landowners and the European recession of recent years has made it difficult to diversify the economy by attracting new domestic and foreign investment to provide much needed jobs. The current condition of the poorest province of the country with the European Community's highest level of unemployment seems only to confirm Ford's description of Jaén in the middle of the last century as "a poor place in the midst of plenty".

restaurant is *Casa Vicente*, c/Maestra 8, just north of the cathedral, housed in an old mansion; specialities include *pastel de carne de caza* (game pie) and *cordero mozárabe* (spiced lamb) and there's also a medium-priced *menú*. To feast in baronial splendour you'll need to climb – or take a taxi – to the *Castillo de Santa Catalina parador* whose recreated medieval dining room with stone vaulted roofs, tapestries and suits of armour can't help but feed your fantasies, although the service can be a bit fussy. A good value *menú*, around 3500ptas, usually includes several local specialities such as *morcilla* and *pipirrana* (cucumber and tomato salad).

Bars around the centre include *Manila*, c/Maestra 4, north of the cathedral or, a couple of streets away the cosy neighbourhood bar, *Tasca los Amigos*, c/Bernardo Lopez, where there's good *jamón* and *tapas* – try their *morcilla* (black pudding). Nearby, *El Gorrión* with good cheese *tapas* and *La Catedral*, popular with a younger crowd, are other possibilities. What **nightlife** there is takes place along the lower end of the Paseo de la Estación towards the train station, where a couple of tame discos and some music bars cater for the city's teenage set.

Around Jaén

Two good **daytrips** from Jaén are to La Guardia de Jaén, 10km southeast, and Martos, 24km to the west, both with impressive hilltop forts. La Guardia is a difficult journey without your own transport, if you don't fancy the walk, but Martos is served by three buses a day.

La Guardia

Reached along a minor road which branches off the main N323 to Granada, **LA GUARDIA** is a charming white-walled village gathered beneath its ruined eighth-century **castillo** which contains elements of previous Iberian, Roman and Visigothic fortifications. The village also has the ruined church of **Santo Domingo**, originally part of a Dominican monastery founded in 1530, and a major work by Andrés de Vandelvera, who was also responsible for the cathedral at Jaén. The arcades around the patio (or cloister) and a central fountain are all that remains of the monastery, whilst the sanctuary, nave and transept crossing give some idea of what a fine construction the church must once have been. At the edge of the village on Monte Salido, a small hill, are some rock-cut **Visigothic graves** where numerous artefacts were found, now on display in the museum at Jaén.

Martos

Along the N321 to the west of Jaén, and surrounded by an ocean of olive groves, it doesn't take long to realize why **MARTOS** is Spain's number one producer of **olives**. The ruins of a Moorish fortress *La Peña*, on a great rock outcrop that towers over the small town, are a vivid reminder of the great struggles of the *reconquista* when the Moorish forts of Jaén became the frontline against hostile Christian incursions, and the scene of bitter battles and sieges. This one fell to Fernando III on St Marta's day in 1225, thus giving the town its present name. In the old quarter with its narrow, winding streets the church of **Santa María de la Villa** is thirteenth-century, built soon after the victory, although it underwent substantial rebuilding in the fifteenth and later centuries. The interior has an outstanding Baroque **retablo** as well as a fine **early Christian sarcophagus** dating from the fourth century. The fifteenth-century church of **Santa Marta** with its Isabelline entrance and the former sixteenth-century prison, now the **Ayuntamiento**, graced by another fine portal, are also worth a look.

If you want **to stay**, *Hostal Fernando IV*, c/Lope de Vega 19 (☎953/551575; ②) is central, pleasant and good value.

Baeza

Fifty kilometres from Jaén along the winding N321, **BAEZA** is tiny, compact and provincial, with a perpetual Sunday air about it. Sited on the escarpment of the Loma de Úbeda, both Baeza, and the neighbouring town of Úbeda (see p.294), have an extraordinary density of exuberant Renaissance palaces and richly endowed churches, plus fine public squares.

The nearest **train station** to Baeza is **Linares-Baeza**, 13km from Baeza (connecting bus for most trains, except Sun). Otherwise, you're dependent on buses, for which Úbeda, 9km away, is the main centre. Between seven and twelve buses a day link the

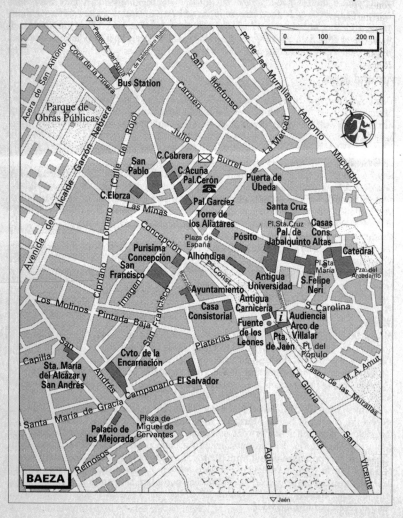

two towns. If you're coming from Granada, there's a 1pm departure, stopping at Jaén for half an hour, and arriving in Baeza at 4.15pm. The **bus station** is officially at Paseo de Elorza Garat 1, which appears on a few maps, but is actually at the end of c/San Pablo and along the Paseo Arca del Agua.

Some history

Important in Roman times as *Beatia*, Baeza was later a Visigothic bishopric and then a prosperous commercial and agricultural centre under the Moors. After a prolonged and bitter struggle the town fell to the Christian forces in 1227, and *hidalgos* or nobles were granted estates in the surrounding countryside with orders to defend this frontier zone. The power of these noble houses was so untrammelled that they were soon warring among themselves for control of the town (a favoured place of battle being Baeza's Alcázar – until Isabel had it demolished). It was later, in the sixteenth century, however, that Baeza embarked on its most prosperous period. The nobility, made rich by farming and textile production, endowed the town with numerous striking Renaissance buildings as the population expanded.

The Town

Most of the main things to see lie within a few minutes walk of the pleasant and central joined squares of **Plaza de España** and the larger **Paseo de la Constitución**. These are flanked by cafés and are very much the hub of the town's limited animation. The sixteenth-century former **Audiencia**, or appeal court, on the *paseo* houses the **Turismo** (Mon–Fri 9.30am–1.30pm & 4.30–7pm; Sat 10am–12.30pm; ☎953/740444) where you can pick up an English-language walking-tour brochure of the town.

Paseo de la Constitución

On the eastern side of the bar-lined *paseo* is **La Alhóndiga**, an elegant porticoed sixteenth-century corn-exchange and, almost opposite, the arcaded eighteenth-century **Casa Consistorial**, or old town hall, which fronted the old market square. At the southern end of the *paseo*, you'll find the **Plaza de los Leones** (also called the Plaza del Populo), an appealing cobbled square enclosed by Renaissance buildings. A central **fountain** incorporates Roman lions and a statue – which locals believe is Imilce, the Iberian wife of the Carthaginian general, Hannibal. The fountain is overlooked by some remarkable buildings including the old **slaughterhouse**, bearing the arms of Carlos V, and beside the arch at the far end, the *Audiencia* (see above). Also here, on a rounded balcony flanking the **double arch** of the Arco de Villalar and the Puerta de Jaén the first Mass of the Reconquest is reputed to have been celebrated. The **Puerta de Jaén** was a memento (or rebuke) left by Carlos V to the town which had opposed him, and commemorated the Germanic ruler's procession through here en route to marry Isabel of Portugal.

Palacio de Jabalquinto and the Antigua Universidad

The stepped street behind the Plaza de los Leones ascends (via c/Romanones and c/Juan de Avila) to another cluster of monuments including the finest of Baeza's palaces, the **Palacio de Jabalquinto** (patio open daily 9am–1pm & 3–6pm), now a seminary, with an elaborate "Isabelline" front (showing marked Moorish influence in its stalactite decoration). Built in the fifteenth century by the Benavides family, the beautifully tranquil interior patio has a double tier of arcades around a central fountain and a superb **Baroque staircase** with fine carving. Next to this palace, the **Antigua Universidad** or old university (patio open daily 9am–2pm) was founded in 1538 and, after functioning for nearly three centuries as a centre of study and debate, its charter was revoked in 1824 during the tyrannical reign of Fernando VII. Since 1875, the buildings have been used as a school. The interior has an elegant patio and, next to a sixteenth-century lecture hall, the preserved classroom used by the noted *sevillano* poet and writer Antonio Machado when he served as a teacher here from 1912 to 1919. This experience must have provided much of the material for his most famous prose work *Juan de Mairena*, the observations on life and culture of a fictional schoolmaster.

A little to the north of here in Plaza Santa Cruz, the church of **Santa Cruz** is Baeza's oldest, built shortly after the Reconquest, although later much restored. The austere, white-walled interior has slender stone columns as well as some fifteenth- and sixteenth-century **frescoes**.

The Cathedral

To the east along the Cuesta de San Felipe, the **Plaza de Santa María** is another of Baeza's glorious squares, with a few welcome and shady trees, fronted by a nucleus of fine Renaissance buildings. The rather squat sixteenth-century **Cathedral of Santa María** (daily 10.30am–1pm & 5–7pm) dominates the square and inside has a fine nave by Andrés de Vandelvira which is, in many ways, a scaled-down version of his cathedral at Jaén. Like many of Baeza's and Úbeda's churches, the cathedral also has brilliant painted **rejas** by Maestro Bartolomé, a local craftsman, who was responsible for some of the finest examples of this uniquely Spanish contribution to Renaissance art. His work enclosing the choir, which has depictions of a Virgin and child accompanied by angels and cherubs is stunning. In the Gothic **cloister**, part of the old mosque – which the church replaced – has been uncovered, but the cathedral's real novelty is a huge silver *custodia* cunningly hidden behind a painting of Saint Peter which whirls aside for a 100-ptas coin. To the east of the cathedral, and beyond Plaza de Arcediano, a narrow street leads to a *mirador* with a fine **view** over the olive groves in the valley of the Guadalquivir towards the distant Cazorla mountain range.

Adjoining the cathedral on the north side is the old Renaissance **town hall** with Plateresque features, formerly the palace of the Cabrera family who have another mansion in the town. In the centre of the Plaza de Santa María, is a sixteenth-century **fountain** erected by the same family, with pilasters and crude caryatids supporting the arms of Felipe II. Beyond this are the graffiti-covered walls of the sixteenth-century seminary of **San Felipe Neri** where students record their names and dates in bull's blood – a traditional way of celebrating graduation.

The Ayuntamiento and more churches

West of the Paseo de la Constitución, in c/Benavides, the magnificent **Ayuntamiento**, was originally the Palace of Justice and prison. Completed in 1559, its richly ornamented façade is exuberantly Plateresque with balconies, coats of arms and gargoyles decorating the cornice. Inside, the main hall has a fine coffered ceiling.

The nearby c/San Francisco passes the exterior of the **Hospital of the Purisima Concepción** with an elegant Renaissance façade. Adjoining it is the ruined convent of **San Francisco** designed by Vandelvira and badly damaged during the War of Independence. Sections of both buildings have now been converted into a hotel, banqueting hall and restaurant (see p.293). At the end of this street and then right along c/San Andrés is the early sixteenth-century church of **San Andrés** with a Plateresque façade and main chapel by Vandelvira.

Renaissance palaces

Heading north from the Plaza de España, c/San Pablo has a number of interesting Renaissance palaces, many with impressive façades. Dating from the sixteenth century, you'll pass the Gothic **Palacio Garcíez**, with a fine patio, the **Palacio Cerón** and the **Casa Acuña**. The best of all is the **Casa Cabrera**, with an elegant Plateresque façade

There are some nice **wandering routes** in town: up through the Puerta de Jaén on the Plaza de los Leones and along the Paseo Murallas/Paseo de Don Antonio Machado takes you round the edge of Baeza and gives good views over the surrounding plains. **El Abuelo**, a house on the Paseo de Don Antonio Machado, is noteworthy for its garden sculpture and towering wrought-iron work. It's the first house past the bronze bust of the poet Antonio Machado looking out over the olive groves. You can cut back to the Plaza Mayor via the network of narrow stone-walled alleys – with the occasional arch – that lies behind the cathedral.

Going further afield, near El Abuelo, some tracks lead down to the plain. Take the right-hand fork and after about 45 minutes you'll come to the right of way of a former rail line, now used as a road for farm vehicles. This offers scope for easy walks across country.

incorporating a double window and frieze over the entrance. In a street to the west of here, the fifteenth-century Gothic church of **San Pablo** has an image of **Christ** by Roldán, and in c/Biedma, behind the church you'll find the **Casa de los Elorza** which is also worth a look.

Practicalities

Baeza is an elegant and relaxing place to stop over and has a good range of accommodation and places to eat. The highlight is the fabulous *Hotel Baeza* and its adjoining *Restaurante Andres de Vandelvira* located in two of the town's historic buildings.

Accommodation

The *Fonda Adriano*, c/Conde Romanones 13, behind the Plaza de los Leones (☎953/740200; ②), is a gem of a building, an old Renaissance mansion set around a courtyard (now enclosed), decorated with mangy mounted bulls heads and a central fountain. The other budget alternative is the equally charming *Hostal Comercio* at c/San Pablo 21, a main road at the end of the central square (☎953/740100; ②). The latter also serves excellent evening meals – handy as the town has few economical restaurants. More upmarket, *Hostal Juanito*, Paseo Arca del Agua s/n, on the Úbeda road out of town (☎953/742324; ④), is good value with air-conditioning and a garden as well as an outstanding restaurant. A more recent upmarket addition to Baeza's accommodation is *Hotel Baeza*, c/Concepción 3, near the Plaza de España (☎953/744361; ⑤) housed in the stylishly restored former Hospital de la Concepción, a fine Renaissance building with a glassed-in patio.

Eating and drinking

Baeza isn't overloaded with **places to eat**, but it's not too difficult to find somewhere with reasonable prices, and there are some quality places here, as well. For *tapas* and *raciones* you're best sticking to the main Paseo de la Constitución and the bars surrounding it; *Bar la Paz* at no. 6 also does inexpensive *platos combinados*. You'll find low-priced *tapas*, *raciones* and *platos combinados* at *Bar Puerta de Úbeda* facing the Úbeda gate at the junction of c/Narvaez and c/Julio Burell. For a good value evening meal, try the restaurant of *Hostal Comercio*. The *Asador Juan Lopez*, c/Benavides 4, behind the main square serves good **take-away** roast chicken, and *Pastelleria Martínez*, on c/San Pablo next to the Palacio Cabrera, is a pleasant **café** serving cakes made on the premises.

Opposite the Renaissance *Ayuntamiento* in c/Benavides, *Restaurante Sali* has a medium-priced *menú* and tables outside so you can feast your eyes on this beautiful building. Not far away on c/San Francisco, *Restaurante Andres de Vandelvira* at no. 14, is installed in the restored ruin of Vandelvira's once-magnificent sixteenth-century convent. The patio has been fitted with a temporary roof to create a banqueting hall whilst the medium-priced restaurant lies beyond this. It's worth a look, even if you don't intend dining and adjoins the *Hotel Baeza* (see above). Baeza's most celebrated restaurant is *Casa Juanito*, Paseo Arca del Agua s/n, about 300m beyond the bus station, which cooks dishes of the region with style and uses local top-quality olive oil; the various pork dishes as well as *alcochafas* (stuffed artichokes), *cordero con habas* (lamb with broad beans) and the delectable house desserts are all memorable.

Nightlife

There's occasional **flamenco** at the *Peña Flamenca*, Conde Romanones 6, just behind the Plaza de los Leones; ask the Turismo for details of imminent performances. Baeza's solitary **disco** is *Al-Bacara* with a pleasant terrace, on the Jaén road out of town.

Úbeda

Little is known of **ÚBEDA**'s previous incarnation as the Roman town of *Betula*, and it's only in the Moorish period that *Obdah*, as it became, grew into a prosperous and important centre endowed with walls and a castle. Following the Christian victory over the Moors at Navas de Tolosa in 1212, the Moors from Baeza moved into the city, feeling it provided a more secure refuge against the Christian forces. Despite this, Úbeda was taken a week later and although an interlude of further freedom for the Muslim occupants was purchased from the Christian armies with massive donations, the town fell conclusively to Fernando el Santo in 1234. As happened in Baeza, numerous noble families were then established by the king and built their mansions in the town. These haughty "lions of Úbeda" as they styled themselves, were soon warring amongst each other, the Arandas fighting the Traperas, and the Molinas against the Cuevas. The fighting got so bad at one point that in 1503 Fernando and Isabel ordered the destruction of the town's walls and towers, to enable the unruly aristocrats to be kept in check. Twelve of these noble families are represented by the twelve lions on the town's coat of arms.

In common with Baeza, it was in the sixteenth century, as a producer of textiles traded across Europe, that Úbeda's fortunes reached their zenith and members of the same noble families came to hold prominent positions in the imperial Spanish court. This was the age of the houses of **Cobos** and **Molinos**, two families who, linked by marriage, dominated the town's affairs. They were also responsible for employing **Andrés de Vandelvira** as their principal architect, whose buildings are the glory of Úbeda today. This prosperity, however, was shortlived and the town declined in the seventeenth century as sharply as it had flourished in the sixteenth, which explains its architectural unity and lack of any significant Baroque edifices. A moderately prosperous provincial town today, Úbeda's main source of income comes from the manufacture of farm machinery and sodium sulphates, as well as the more traditional olives and ceramics, and carpets and baskets made from esparto grass.

The Town

Nine kilometres east of Baeza and built on the same escarpment overlooking the valley of the Guadalquivir, Úbeda looks less promising when you reach it. It's a larger town, and arrival at the bus station locates you in the midst of an uninspiring modern suburb.

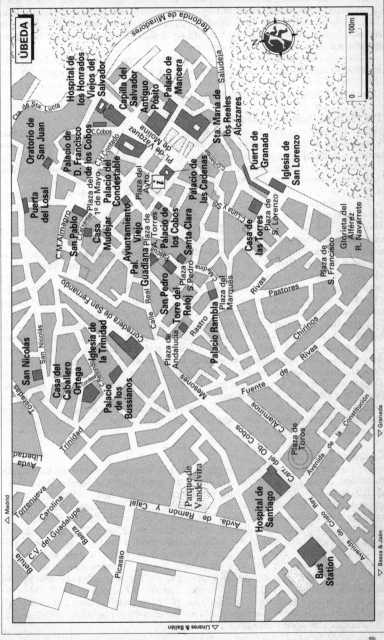

ÚBEDA

100m

Redonda de Miradores

Hospital de los Honrados Viejos del Salvador

Capilla del Salvador

Palacio de Mancera

Antiguo Pósito

Cta. de Sta. Lucía

Oratorio de San Juan

Palacio de D. Francisco

C.Cobos

Casa del Contado

Pl. de Vázquez de Molina

Sta. María de los Reales Alcázares

Puerta del Losal

Palacio del Condestable

Plaza 1º de Mayo

Plaza del Ayto.

i

Palacio de las Cadenas

Puerta de Granada

Iglesia de San Lorenzo

C.M.Almagro

San Pablo

Cervantes

Plaza desde de los Cobos

Casa Mudéjar

Ayuntamiento Viejo

Plaza del Pascual

Palacio de los Cobos

Santa Clara

Cuna y Sol

Medina

Plaza de S. Lorenzo

Casa de las Torres

Calle Real Guadiana

A.Torres

Plaza de

San Pedro

Torre del Reloj

Plaza S.Pedro

Plaza del Marqués

Plaza de S. Francisco

Glorieta del Alférez R. Navarrete

San Nicolás

San Nicolás

Corredera de San Fernando

Plaza de Andalucía

Palacio Rambla

Rivas

Pastores

Casa del Caballero Ortega

Condesa

Cristo

Iglesia de la Trinidad

Rastro

Mesones

Chirinos

Tostadas

Palacio de los Bussianos

Fuente

Rivas

de

Trinidad

Avda Libertad

Carretera

Parque de Vandelvira

Avda. de Ramón y Cajal

C.Alaminos

Plaza de Toros

Torrenueva

Carolina

Baeza

Carr. del Ob. Cobos

Avenida de la Constitución

▷ Granada

C.V. del Guadalupe

Betula

Picasso

Hospital de Santiago

Avenida de Cristo Rey

Bus Station

▷ Baeza & Jaén

◁ Madrid

△ Linares & Bailén

Don't be put off though, for hidden away in the old quarter is one of the finest Renaissance architectural jewels in the whole of Spain, and perhaps even in Europe. The **Turismo** (Mon–Fri 10am–2pm; ☎953/750897) is located on the Plaza del Ayuntamiento behind the Plaza de Vasquez de Molina. When this is closed the nearby *parador* will often provide basic information.

The main **bus station**, c/San José s/n, is to the west of the centre beyond the Hospital de Santiago; there are eight buses a day from Jaén, twelve from Baeza, and three from Córdoba and Sevilla. **Linares-Baeza** is the nearest **train station**, about 15km from Úbeda (connecting bus for most trains, except Sun).

The Plaza de Vazquez de Molina

Follow the signs to the *Zona Monumental* and you'll eventually reach the **Plaza Vázquez de Molina**, a magnificent Renaissance square at the heart of the old town which immediately overshadows anything in Baeza.

Most of the buildings round this square were the late sixteenth-century work of Andrés de Vandelvira, the architect of Baeza's cathedral, and numerous churches in both towns. At the western end he built the **Palacio de las Cadenas** (or "chains", which once decorated the façade), for the secretary of Felipe II, Juan Vázquez de Molina, whose family arms crown the doorway of a beautiful classical façade. The interior, these days occupied by the *Ayuntamiento*, features a superb double-tier arcaded patio. Opposite, and between the lions marking the edge of the mansion's domain, lies the church of **Santa María de los Reales Alcázares**, built on the site of a former mosque. Behind the façade topped by a double belfry, an elegant Gothic cloister encloses what was once the patio of the mosque. The church contains another fine **reja** by Maestro Bartolomé of Jaén depicting the tree of Jesse. At the side of the church, as you move east, is the entrance to the sixteenth-century **Cárcel del Obispo** or bishop's prison, which was formerly a convent and is now used as the court house. Opposite this is the **Palacio de Marqués de Mancera**, another stately Renaissance edifice with an elegant tower. Next to this and fronting the plaza is the **Antiguo Pósito** or old granary, which later served as a prison and now houses the police station. Across the square again, the **Condestable Dávalos**, which Vandelvira had a hand in designing, is the former dwelling of the chaplain of the church of El Salvador. This elegant building now houses what must be the most impressive *parador* in Andalucía. Above the door two angels support the arms of the first chaplain Déan (dean) Fernando Ortega Salido, who was also responsible for its construction. A stunning **arcaded interior patio** now serves as the hotel's bar, and is perhaps best contemplated over a cool drink.

Chapel of El Salvador

At the eastern end of the Plaza Vasquez de Molina, Vandelvira erected the **Capilla del Salvador**, Úbeda's finest church and one of the masterpieces of Spanish Renaissance architecture. Although executed by Vandelvira, he was in fact working to a design created in 1536 by Diego de Siloé (architect of the Málaga and Granada cathedrals) but typically added his own flourishes. The church was originally the chapel of the mansion – which later burned down – of Francisco de Cobos y Molina, secretary of state to Carlos V and one of the most powerful men of his time. This remarkable building is almost unique in Spain for being built within a very short period (1540–1556) with hardly any later alterations. It also preserves most of its interior furnishings. The exterior **façade** has a carving of the Transfiguration of Christ flanked by statues of San Pedro and San Andrés with a wealth of Plateresque detail. Above the north door around the corner, Vandelvira has placed an image in the tympanum which is almost his trade mark – Santiago the Moor slayer, used in Baeza and on the hospital of Santiago in the north of the town.

To enter the church you have to go through the sacristy at the north side – ring for the caretaker at the fine doorway in the white wall on c/Francisco de Cobos. The single nave interior with a beautiful cupola, has a brilliantly animated **retablo** on the high altar representing the Transfiguration with a sensitively rendered image of Christ by Alonso de Berruguete who studied under Michelangelo; this is the only part of the altarpiece to completely survive damage during the Civil War. The **reja** fronting the altar is yet another fine work by Maestro Bartolemé de Jaén. In the **sacristy** (all Vandelvira's work) there's a photograph of a statue by Michelangelo given to Francisco de Cobos by the state of Venice, which alas was another Civil War casualty.

Behind El Salvador, and beyond the sixteenth-century **Hospital de los Honorados Viejos del Salvador** (another Vandelvira work) Úbeda comes to a sudden halt at a **mirador** with fine views over a sea of olive groves backed by the Sierra de Cazorla.

The Casa de las Torres and Palacio Vela de los Cobos

To the west of the Plaza Vasquez y Molina along calles Orbaneja and Luna y Sol lies the **Casa de las Torres**, a sombre building with two enormous keeps, framing an ornate Plateresque facade. Now an art school, when open you can view the building's elegant double-tiered patio.

Just to the north of Plaza Vasquez de Molina, the Plaza del Ayuntamiento has **Palacio Vela de los Cobos**, another impressive building by Vandelvira dating from the middle of the sixteenth century with an interesting corner balcony and an elegant façade topped off by a delightful arcaded gallery. This is one of the few palaces that can be visited but prior application must be made to the Turismo which is in same square, opposite.

Oratorio de San Juan de la Cruz and the Church of San Pablo

To the north of Plaza Vasquez de Molina (easily reached along c/Francisco de los Cobos) the **Oratorio de San Juan de La Cruz** is where San Juan (Saint John of the Cross) an accomplished poet and mystic died of gangrene in 1591. The original monastery was damaged in the Civil War and little of it survives, although a small **museum** (Tues–Sun 11am–1pm & 5–7pm) preserves memorabilia from the saint's lifetime as well as his writing desk and the cell in which he died. At the end of c/San Juan de la Cruz facing the monastery, the **Plaza del Primero de Mayo** (formerly the Plaza del Mercado) is a charming acacia-lined square with a bandstand at its centre marking the site of the fires of the *autos da fé* which were once carried out here on the orders of the Inquisition. The Town Council presided over these grisly events from the superb arcaded sixteenth-century **ayuntamiento viejo** on the square's western side. Dominating its northern flank is the idiosyncratic **Iglesia de San Pablo**, incorporating various Romanesque, Gothic and Renaissance additions and crowned by a Plateresque tower. It boasts a thirteenth-century balcony (a popular feature in Úbeda), and a superb **portal**. The interior has a fine **capilla** by Vandelvira (chapel of Camarero Vago) as well some intricate carving in the Capilla de la Mercedes and more superb *rejas*.

Around the Plaza del Primero de Mayo

Calle Horno Contado which leaves Plaza del Primero de Mayo at the southeast corner has two more palaces you might want to see: a short way down on the right, the **Casa de los Manueles** has a fine façade and a little further down on the left, the fifteenth-century **Casa de los Salvajes** (savages) is named after the two figures clothed in animal skins supporting the arms of its founder, Francisco de Vago. In reality they are probably natives of the imperial colonies, from whose exploitation much of this conspicuous wealth was derived. Off the north side of the square in c/Cervantes the **Casa Mudéjar** at no. 6 is a fine fourteenth-century building whose elegant Mudéjar **patio** has pointed horseshoe arches. It houses a small **archeological museum** (Tues–Sat 10am–2pm & 4–7pm; Sun 10am–12.30pm).

Calle Melchor Almagro, leaving the square on the north side of San Pablo, has another mansion, the wonderful Plateresque **Casa Montiel** and further along, a sixteenth-century Carmelite convent.

The Potters' Quarter

Leaving the Plaza del Primero de Mayo by the c/Losal in its northeast corner leads to the **Puerta de Losal**, a thirteenth-century Mudéjar gate with a double horseshoe arch which was formerly one of the main entrances to the old walled town. At the end of c/de la Merced, facing the arch and beyond the Plaza Olleros, c/Valencia is the old **potters' street** where the workshops of Úbeda's main ceramic craftsmen are located. *Alfarería Tito*, c/Valencia 44, is one of the friendliest and they will not only show you around the workshop but also allow you downstairs to see one of the two brothers – Paco or Francisco – at work on the potter's wheel. Nearby is the kiln, where the system used to fire the pots – most glazed and tinted with Úbeda's traditional deep green – is one inherited from the Moors; once the wood is burning, olive stones are introduced into the fire which builds up a more intense heat giving superior results in both colour and strength.

Plaza San Pedro and Calle Real

Starting out from Plaza San Pedro (to the west of the Plaza del Ayuntamiento) there are a number of other important sights to see in the north of the town. On the Plaza San Pedro itself, the thirteenth-century **Convento de Santa Clara** contains a patio with a fine Gothic–Mudéjar multi-lobed portal. The convent also sells its home-made *dulces* – tasty cakes, biscuits and pastries. Another mansion, the **Palacio de la Rambla**, lies at the end of c/Medina off the west side of the square. The façade is another graceful work by Vandelvira, and the interior is now an upmarket hotel. Otherwise, across the square, the church of **San Pedro** with a noteworthy portal leads into c/Pascua where, on the junction with c/Real stands the impressive tower of the **Palacio del Conde de Guadiana** one of the most striking of all Úbeda's palaces. The impressive tower is, in fact, a seventeenth-century work and the richly ornamented balconies are a delight.

Turning into **Calle Real** brings you to the heart of the old town and its former main shopping street. Many establishments are now deserting this for new premises in the modern town but a few of the more traditional traders are still here. Pedro Blanco at no. 47 is still making and selling goods made from traditional esparto grass, a versatile material used in the area since ancient times. Although much of the business is devoted to supplying the olive oil industry with collecting and extracting baskets, the firm also makes carpets, bags and all kinds of accessories. Heading north along here brings you eventually to the **Plaza de Andalucía**, an unremarkable square with a monument to General Saro, a Civil War general with Fascist affiliations. The general's bullet-hole riddled metal skull shows how local disapproval of his ideas was expressed. Just off the plaza, the **Torre del Reloj** is a remnant of the thirteenth-century ramparts with a later sixteenth-century temple crowning it.

San Nicolas and the Hospital de Santiago

Just to the north of the Plaza de Andalucía at the start of c/Trinidad is the **Iglesia de la Trinidad**, an eighteenth-century – and unusual for Úbeda – Baroque building. Further along c/Trinidad, it's back to the Renaissance with the **Palacio de los Bussianos**, attributed to Vandelvira. Taking the next right after this, c/Redondo, and then first left into c/Condesa you pass the **Casa de Caballerizo Ortega** a sixteenth-century Plateresque mansion. Calle Condesa continues to the church of **San Nicolás**, which although a fourteenth-century building has a fine Renaissance west portal by Vandelvira. The sober interior is relieved by a profusely decorated but incredibly sinister, "sculpted" **chapel of Déan Ortega** by Vandelvira whose effect is only partially offset by a life-size, plastic choirboy. The **reja** (iron screen) fronting it by Álvarez de Molina is another fine example of the art.

Five minutes west of here along c/Cobos, and worth every bead of sweat getting there, is Vandelvira's huge **Hospital de Santiago**. Perhaps the scale put him off, for the exterior decoration is untypically restrained, and its austere dignity as a result has led to the building being described as "Andalucía's Escorial". Commissioned by Bishop Cobos y Molina and begun in 1562, the flight of steps at the entrance is flanked by more "lions of Úbeda", beyond which Vandelvira has inserted his trade mark – Santiago the Moor slayer – above the arch. The equally restrained interior has a patio with columns of Genoa marble and a staircase with stunning vaulting, in addition to a superb chapel – all further evidence of Vandelvira's mastery.

Practicalities

Accommodation and restuarants in the old quarter are expensive, and if you're on a tight budget you'll be forced to base yourself in the modern town where there are plenty of lower-priced choices.

Accommodation

If you want to stay, most of the lower-priced **accommodation** options are within walking distance of the bus station, in the modern part of town. The *Hostal Castillo*, Avda Ramon y Cajal 16 (☎953/750430; ③) is friendly, clean and comfortable and has a good restaurant. Nearby, *Hostal Sevilla*, Avda. Ramon y Cajal 9 (☎953/750612; ③) is also reasonable and slightly less expensive. Close to the Hospital de Santiago and just east of the bullring, the recently refurbished *Hostal Victoria*, c/Alaminos 5 (☎953/752952; ③) is another good value place. The only budget possibility is *Hostal Miguel*, Avda. Libertad 69 (☎953/752049; ②), some distance away in the north of town. In the *casco antiguo* or old quarter, the only options are both upmarket. The Renaissance *Palacio de la Rambla*, Plaza del Marqués 1 (☎953/750196; ⑥) is owned by the Marquesa (marchioness) de la Rambla who has decided to raise a little extra cash by letting out a few rooms. The lavish interior with all its furnishings and rare artworks remains intact, which is why you have to use an entryphone to get in. The *Parador Condestable Dávalos*, Plaza de Vázquez de Molina 1 (☎953/750345; ⑥) though, perhaps shades it for location and style and is housed in a fabulous sixteenth-century Renaissance mansion on arguably the most beautiful square in Andalucía; look in for a drink.

Eating, drinking and nightlife

For **food** it's much the same again, with most of the restaurants sited along the Avda. Ramon y Cajal. The restaurant of the *Hostal Sevilla* is good and reasonably priced. Further along, *Restaurante El Olivo*, Avda. Ramon y Cajal 6, does economical *platos combinados*. At the end of this street and close to the junction with the Avda. de la Libertad, *El Gallo Rojo*, c/Torrenueva 3, set back from the road, is the town's best restaurant which isn't saying a lot; serving local specialities, it has a medium-priced *menú* and puts out tables in the evening. Just north from here along c/Virgen de Guadalupe, *Pintor Orbaneja* at no. 5 does *platos combinados* and excellent *tapas* and *raciones*. In the old part of town *Mesón Navarro*, Plaza del Ayuntamiento, behind the Palacio de las Cadenas, is one of only two restaurants, but most people stick to *tapas* here – especially as one comes free with every *fino*. Otherwise, if you want to dine in the old quarter and in style it has to be the *Parador Condestable Dávalos* who offer superbly-prepared regional dishes many of which are available on a set *menú* (about 3000ptas); unfortunately they don't put tables out on that magnificent square.

Nightlife is limited but does exist. There's a **disco**, *El Califa*, Avda. Cristo Rey s/n, near the bus station and sometimes **flamenco** takes place at the *Peña Flamenca El*

Quejío, Alfareros 5, in the northern suburbs – but enquire first at the Turismo to save a wasted journey. Úbeda's big **fiesta** is the *Día de San Miguel* on September 29, when carnival giants, fireworks and a *flamenco* festival honour the town's patron saint.

Towards Cazorla

From Úbeda, the next destination for most travellers is the spectacular **Cazorla Natural Park**, a wilderness area filled with deep ravines, wooded valleys and which, in its mountains, gives birth to the mighty Río Guadalquivir. The park's towering rock cliffs are the preserve of the acrobatic ibex, whilst the valleys and gorges swarm with birdlife and are home to unique pre-Ice Age plants. From Úbeda there are **two routes into the park**. The more conventional one, taken by the bus, is via the village of Cazorla located on the park's southern edge and the main gateway to it. Another route however, skirts the park's western flank and allows visits to a number of interesting sights – including the picturesque hill villages of **Sabiote**, with a castle and Renaissance mansions, and **Iznatoraf**, with its distinctive Moorish feel – before turning into the park close to the village of Villanueva.

Into the Park via Sabiote, Villacarillo and Iznatoraf

Leaving Úbeda by the N322 brings you first to Torreperogil, 8km east and – unusually for Jaén – a centre of wine rather then olive production. A turning here leads to the pretty hill village of **SABIOTE**, 4km distant, with a pedigree dating back to Roman times. A cobble-streeted hamlet still girdled by much of its medieval walls, the church of **San Pedro Apostól** at its heart has a fine, if worn, Plateresque façade. At the foot of c/Castillo which has a couple of striking Renaissance mansions, the ruined **castillo** dates back to Roman times, although the Moors made subsequent alterations. More modifications were added during the Renaissance period by Francisco Cobos of the noble house based at Úbeda, and it's thought that he drafted in his architect Andrés de Vandelvira to carry them out. The elegant **cloister** of the sixteenth-century Carmelite convent is also worth a look.

Villacarillo and Iznatoraf

VILLACARILLO, 20km further along the N322, is a fairly featureless town surrounded by olive groves but it has an impressive Renaissance **Church of the Asunción** attributed to Vandelvira, whose major interior features are some finely painted domes. Six kilometres after this, a road on the left snakes dizzily upwards to the spectacularly-sited hilltop village of **IZNATORAF**. At the end of the climb, the village is clustered around a pleasant Plaza Mayor with a Renaissance arch and the great stone church of **Santo Cristo** dominating its eastern end. When you've wandered around the narrow Moorish streets, many decorated with colourful geraniums in summer, and had a look over the ruins of its walls and castle, don't miss the spectacular **views** over the valley of the Río Guadalimar towards the bordering province of Albacete from a *mirador* perched above the cliff at the village's northern edge.

Not quite 2km beyond the turn off for Iznatoraf and before Villanueva del Arzobispo, a road leaves the N322 on the right for Tranco and the Cazorla Natural Park. Take note of the signs warning you that there is **no petrol to be had in the park**, and a full tank would be a wise precaution. Seven kilometres from the turn-off the road joins the densely wooded valley of the newly born Guadalquivir, a mere stream compared to the mighty torrent which flows through Sevilla over 200km downstream. After 14km the road arrives at Tranco on the banks of the Embalse del Tranco (reservoir) which is described in the main account on the park below.

Into the Park via Peal de Becerro and Cazorla

The bus route to Cazorla heads south from Úbeda, passing through olive country and crossing the Guadalquivir before turning off the main road to the village of **PEAL DE BECERRO**. The village spreads over a low hill beneath the crumbling towers of its medieval fort. With your own transport, you can take a minor road out of the village 4km southeast to **Toya**, where there's an important Iberian underground tomb.

Toya Iberian necropolis

In 1909 a large rectangular underground stone tomb was discovered by a farmer near to the hamlet of **Toya**, the former Iberian settlement of *Tugia*. Unfortunately, the family cleared the tomb – used from the fifth to the second centuries BC – of a whole treasure house of artefacts which they then sold. Some fine Greek vases were later recovered and testified to this remote tribe's sophistication and trading contacts with the Mediterranean world. The stone-built **necropolis** is impressive and the largest of its kind in Spain. The tomb is located a few kilometres outside Toya, but you'll need to visit the *Ayuntamiento* there first to get the key; they will also provide directions.

Cazorla

The village of **CAZORLA**, 15km beyond Peal at an elevation of 900m, huddles towards the top of a valley which runs from the rugged limestone cliffs of the *Peña de los Halcones*. This rocky bluff, with its wheeling buzzards and occasional eagle, marks the southwestern edge of a vast, protected area, the **Cazorla Natural Park**, containing the sierras of Cazorla and Segura and the headwaters of the Río Guadalquivir.

Little about the town today would lead you to believe that Cazorla had been around for over two thousand years, but not only were there significant Iberian and Roman settlements here, this was also the see of one of the first bishoprics of early Christian Spain. Under the Moors it was a strategic stronghold and one of dozens of fortresses and watchtowers guarding the Sierra. Taken after a bitter struggle in 1235, during the Reconquest of Andalucía, the town then acted as an outpost for Christian troops. Nowadays, the two castles which dominate the village testify to its turbulent past, both were originally Moorish but later altered and restored by their Christian conquerors.

Arrival and information

Arrival is somewhat inauspicious as the main road climbs between concrete blocks of flats, disgorging you into the busy, commercial Plaza de la Constitución, but look up and there are staggering vistas to the backdrop of mountains. Three buses a day (10am, 1.30pm & 6.15pm) go from Úbeda to Cazorla. There are also buses from Jaén, and a daily bus from Granada (currently leaves at 2.30pm, arriving 7.30pm).

In the Plaza de la Constitución, you'll find a privately run **Turismo**, *Quercus* (☎953/ 720115). There is also a **Turismo** (summer only) based in the *Ayuntamiento* on Plaza de la Corredera. The official Junta de Andalucía **Natural Park Information Centre** (11am–2pm & 4–7pm; closed Thurs; ☎953/720125) is at c/Martinez Falero 11, off the Plaza de la Constitución. They can provide details on all aspects of the park and dole out lots of free literature.

The Town

A few minutes' walk along the main c/de Muñoz leads to a second square, the Plaza de la Corredera (or *del Huevo*, "of the Egg", because of its shape). This is the traditional meeting place for the *señoritos*, the class of landowners and their descendants who, through influence and privilege, still lay claim to the most important jobs and mould local destiny. The seat of the administration, the *Ayuntamiento*, is here too – a fine Moorish-style palace at the far end of the plaza.

Beyond, you reach a labyrinth of narrow, twisting streets, and Cazorla's liveliest square, the **Plaza Santa María**. This takes its name from the sixteenth-century cathedral church of **Santa María** designed by Andrés de Vandelvira which, although damaged by floods in the seventeenth century, was later torched by Napoleonic troops. Its impressive ruins, now preserved, and the fine open square with a Renaissance fountain form a natural amphitheatre for concerts and local events as well as being a popular meeting place. The square is dominated by **La Yedra**, the austere, reconstructed tower of the lower of two Moorish castles. It also houses the **Museo de Artes y Costumbres** (Tues–Sat 10am–3pm; closed September), a notable folklore museum. There's a fine **view** from just above the plaza of the castle perched on its rock.

Two kilometres up the road heading into the park from Cazorla, the village of **LA IRUELA** has a ruined Moorish **fortress** perched on a daunting but picturesque rock peak which must have been a wretched struggle for the Christian troops to subdue. It was later rebuilt by the Templars. There's also another ruined church, Santo Domingo, here attributed to Vandelvira. The village has a fair number of more expensive hotels (see below).

Practicalities

Cazorla has plenty of accommodation in all price ranges and, whilst the same can't be said for finding food, you're unlikely to starve. The daily **market** in Plaza del Mercado is a good place to gather ingredients for picnics in the park.

Accommodation

Finding **accommodation** is usually no problem as most visitors are either en route to, or are leaving, the park. The least expensive place to stay is the *Pensión Taxi* (①), up the steps opposite the bus and taxi stop; as a resident, you can also eat in their *comedor*. More pleasant accommodation is available at the *Hostal Guadalquivir*, c/Nueva 6 (☎953/720268; ③), down the steps to the right just as you enter the middle plaza, Corredera – it's spotlessly clean and very friendly, though disconcertingly close to the municipal slaughterhouse for those with sensitive ears. Perhaps a better bet would be the friendly and good value *Hostal Betis*, Plaza Corredera 19 (☎953/720540; ②) nearby, with many rooms overlooking the square. Another budget possibility is *Hostal La Estrella*, c/Tercia 1 (☎953/720208; ②) close to the Plaza de la Constitución. There are also a surprising number of more upmarket hotels, of which the *Andalucía*, c/Martínez Falero 42 (☎953/721268; ④) is typical.

If you have a car there are some very attractive alternatives out in the Sierra, including the *Sierra de Cazorla* (☎953/720015; ④), just 2km outside the village in La Iruela, with a pool, and the *Parador El Adelantado* (☎953/721075; ⑤; also with pool), a featureless modern building made up for by a wonderful setting, 25km away in the park. In extremis, Cazorla also has a **youth hostel** on Mauricio Martínez 2 (☎953/720329; open July–Sept) – ring to check that it's open.

Eating, drinking and nightlife

Several spit-and-sawdust **bars** with good *tapas* cluster round the Plaza Santa María, along with the rustic *Mesón la Cueva* (☎953/721225) which offers authentic local food cooked on a wood-fired range but reheated, discreetly, in a microwave. The proprietor here also rents out apartments for longer stays. Other places where you can **eat** well and cheaply are the two *mesones* on Plaza de la Corredera; the one next to the church is excellent value and the other prepares exquisite fish – both serve *tapas* and *raciones* rather than full meals. *La Montería* on Plaza de la Constitución is also a good place for *tapas*. The only other restaurant in town – avoid the one attached to the *Hotel Cazorla* – is the expensive *La Sarga*, opposite the market.

There are two **discos** (weekends only) and several "pubs" with loud music. On May 14 Cazorla honours its its patron, San Isicio, with a vibrant **romería** and in mid-September there's the **fiesta de Cristo del Consuelo**, with fairgrounds, fireworks and religious processions.

Day trips from Cazorla

Wild and relatively unspoiled country, with grand panoramas west over the olive plain of Jaén, begins at the edge of Cazorla, and if you choose to base yourself here, you can make a number of good **day trips**.

Just over an hour's walk away (head up behind the fountain on Plaza Santa María, then pick up the mule track which skirts the hill topped by the ruined upper castle of *Cinco Esquinas*) is the intriguing sixteenth-century **Monasterio de Monte Sion**. Two of the brothers who worked on its reconstruction remain there, and they will proudly show you round their home. Be prepared to step back into the Middle Ages – as exemplified by the scourges hanging over the beds in the cells used for retreat. Another hour's walk beyond the cloister will bring you to the base of **Gilillo**, highest point in the southwest of the park, with a yawning gorge to the right.

You can follow the main path over a pass from here to a dilapidated *casa forestal* and then down to **Cañada de las Fuente**s, source of the Guadalquivir, within another two hours. Alternatively – and a more feasible day walk – you might bear left at the saddle on to a trail descending towards Cazorla town through the **canyon of Riogazas**. This path ends in a jumble of tractor tracks after an hour, and then you must pick your way down through the various water courses for another hour and a half. This five-hour walking day allows ample time for dawdling, but unfortunately many of the pools in the stream on the descent are either difficult to get to or on private property.

The Cazorla Natural Park

The Cazorla Natural Park is not as lofty as the Sierra Nevada (the highest peaks are 2000m), but outdoes it for beauty, slashed as it is by river gorges and largely covered in forest. The **best times to visit** are late spring and early autumn. The winters can be uncomfortably wet and cold, and roads are often closed due to snow. During summer, although walking is pleasant before noon, the climate tends to be hot and dry.

Judging from the number of *cabra hispanica* (Spanish mountain goat), deer, wild pig, birds and butterflies that even the casual visitor is likely to spot, the Cazorla reserve is fulfilling its role handsomely. Ironically, though, much of the best wildlife viewing will be at the periphery, or even outside the park, since the wildlife is most successfully stalked on foot and walking opportunities within the park itself are somewhat limited.

There's practically no **public transport** in the park and distances between points are enormous, so to explore it well you'll need a car or be prepared for long hikes; otherwise day trips to the outskirts of the park are possible. However a number of **campsites** – both *camping libre* (free camping) and official sites – dotted around the park make walking tours possible.

There are in fact only three **signposted tracks**, all pitifully short. One leads from the Empalme de Vadillo to the Puente de la Herrera via the Fuente del Oso (2km one way), another of about 1700m curls round the Cerrada (Narrows) de Utrero near Vadillo-Castril village; the best marked segment, through the lower Barrossa gorge (see below), is also a mere 1700m long.

Information

Before heading into the park, its worth stopping at the private cooperative Turismo *Quercus* (☎953/720115) in Cazorla (see p.301) to buy either the 1:100,000 map entitled *Parque Natural de las Sierras de Cazorla y Segura*, or the 1:50,000 version called "Cazorla". The staff are friendly but their information, especially that pertaining to independent ramblings, is none too reliable; the office exists to promote nature tours, Land Rover excursions (which some readers have found worthwhile), photo safaris and the like, so they have an interest in getting visitors to sign on for their services. However, their **horse riding** treks into the park are popular and horses can be rented hourly, or by the day or half day.

The official Natural Park Information Centre at Cazorla (see p.301) will provide a complete list and map of campsites within the park. Inside the park, there is a visitors' centre at Torre del Vinagre (see below).

Torre del Vinagre and Coto Ríos

Two daily **buses** link Cazorla town with **Coto Ríos** in the middle of the park via Torre del Vinagre: one at 6.30am, the other at 2pm, returning from Coto at 5.30pm. Taking the early departure allows you to do the classic **walk along the Río Barrosa** as a day trek. The road into the park climbs over the Puerto de las Palomas with spectacular views before descending into the valley of the Guadalquivir. A little further on there's a turning for the scenically sited **parador** (see p.302) which, with your own transport, would allow you to stop off for a drink; they also offer a good value set menu for lunch and dinner which sometimes includes the excellent local river trout served *a la cazuleña* (with *jamón serrano* and almonds).

The Río Barrosa walk begins at **TORRE DEL VINAGRE**, where there is a visitors' centre, the **Centro de Interpretación Torre del Vinagre** (Tues–Sun 11am–2pm &

THE RÍO BARROSSA WALK

From the visitors' centre at Torre del Vinagre, cross the Guadalquivir on a low causeway which is a bridge or a ford, depending on the season; 2km later you pass a trout hatchery, and just beyond this is a car park where all private vehicles must be left.

From here follow the rough track along the northwest (right) bank of the Barrosa, swift and cold even in summer. Within a few minutes a signposted footpath diverges to the right; this also marks the beginning of the **gorge**. Two or three wooden bridges now take the path back and forth across the river, which is increasingly confined by sheer rock walls. At the narrowest points the path is routed along planked catwalks secured to the limestone cliff. The walk from Torre del Vinagre to the end of the narrows takes about two hours.

Here the footpath rejoins the track; after another half-hour's walk you'll see a turbine and a long metal pipe bringing water from **two lakes** – one natural, one a small dam – up the mountain. The road crosses one last bridge over the Barrosa and stops at the turbine house. When you get to the gate, beyond which there's a steeply rising gully, count on another full hour up to the lakes. Cross a footbridge and start the steep climb up a narrow track over the rocks below the cliff (at one point the path passes close to the base of the palisade – beware falling stones). At the top of the path is a cavernous amphitheatre, with a waterfall in winter. The path ends about halfway up the cliff, where an artificial tunnel has been bored through the rock; walk through it to get to the lake.

Allow three and a half hours' walking time from Torre del Vinagre for the whole route, slightly less going down. It's a very full day's excursion but you should have plenty of time to catch the afternoon bus back, which passes the visitors' centre at 5pm.

5–8pm; ☎953/720102). This has informative displays explaining the park's ecology as well as a disturbing number of stuffed animals and mounted ibex and deer heads, including one bagged by General Franco who used to do his hunting here. Next to the centre a botanical garden has living specimens of the park's flora. The centre also offers tours of the park by Land Rover, as well as horse and mountain bike excursions.

Coto Ríos

COTO RÍOS, 4km on from Torre del Vinagre, is a pleasant village with a river beach on the Guadalquivir. There's also a **campsite** here, *Camping Chopera de Coto-Ríos* (☎953/721905). Four kilometres further on, keeping to the river's west bank, at the southern end of the Embalse del Tranco reservoir, is the *Parque Cinegético*, a **wildlife park** which eventually hopes to include specimens of all the park's fauna, although at present you'll be lucky to see some rather bewildered deer from the viewing balcony.

Tranco and the north of the Park

The road continues along the banks of the reservoir passing more official **campsites** en route to **TRANCO**, which dams the Guadalquivir, 18km north. The island in the centre of the lake contains the ruined castle of **Bujaraiza**, all that remains of the village of the same name which disappeared beneath the waters when the dam was created. Apart from a few holiday villas and a lakeside bar, Tranco has little of interest. There are two **camping libre** sites on each side of Tranco village, *Fuente Negra* to the south and *Montillana* to the north.

Hornos

From Tranco, the road circles around the northern end of the reservoir before turning into the valley of the Río Hornos from where you can glimpse the village of **HORNOS**, perched on a daunting rock pinnacle beneath the tower of its Moorish castle. When you reach it, the village has an isolated air with plenty of Moorish atmosphere. It's narrow white-walled streets are perfect for wandering around, and the castle is worth a look, although once you've scrambled up, there isn't much to it apart from the tower. The pleasant Plaza Mayor is overlooked by a solid fifteenth-century church, the interior of which is pretty bare of features but a *mirador* through a door at the back has wonderful views over the reservoir, flanked by mountains of the Sierra de la Segura. The waters, which lapped the foot of the outcrop below, have receded dramatically in recent years – a symptom of Andalucía's chronic and continuing draught. A stretch of the village's ancient walls are still intact, complete with a horseshoe-arched Moorish gateway.

If you want **to stay**, try *Hostal El Cruce* (☎953/495035; ③) whose gable mural is hard to miss as you enter the village. They also do **meals** here, served on a terrace in summer, although the well-meaning service can sometimes be haphazard. There are other less appealing places serving food in the village.

A pleasant **walk** can be made from here along the reservoir's eastern banks to the hamlet of La Platera and the hill of Montero, with views along the reservoir, 4km beyond. The rock faces above the pine covered slopes are home to a variety of plants including yellow-flowered flax and throatwart. Common bird species in this area include azure-winged magpies, kestrels and sparrowhawks, but you will be extremely lucky to see the **Lammergeier** or bearded vulture in this, its only breeding habitat in Spain outside the Pyrenees, and now down to a mere handful of breeding pairs as the carrion these scavengers rely on has diminished. Known as the *quebrantahuesos* (bone-breaker) in Spanish, this nickname comes from its habit of hoisting the leg bones of victims high into the air and dropping them on to a rock below (nearly always the same one) from which, once broken, it extracts the marrow with its specially suited tongue.

Orcera

Pressing on from Hornos brings you to **ORCERA**, another hill village and logging centre, 15km to the north. There's a fine sixteenth-century church here plus a couple of inexpensive *hostales;* try *La Montería*; Avda de Andalucía 43 (☎953/480768; ②). In August the village hosts a wild *encierro* when bulls are turned loose in the streets to chase the nimble-footed local youths.

Segura de la Sierra

The village of Orcera is overshadowed in every sense by the Cazorla park's most spectacularly-sited town, **SEGURA DE LA SIERRA**, 5km to the south. With a romantic castle crowning an almost conical 1100m-high hilltop, beneath which the tiered village streets seem in danger of collapsing into the olive groves far below, it's a landmark for miles around.

Once you've managed to climb the road which snakes up to it and passed through the medieval gate, the town is a warren of narrow streets left behind by its former Moorish occupants. But its history goes back much further, perhaps and improbably, as far as the Phoenicians who, local historians claim, called it *Tavara*. Greeks, Carthaginians, Romans and Visigoths came in their wake until the latter were prised out of this mountain eyrie by the invading Moors who constructed the castle they called *Saqura*. When it fell to the Christian forces under Alfonso VIII during the thirteenth century *reconquista*, the fort became a vital strategic outpost on the frontiers of the kingdom of Granada, whose borders were framed by the Guadalquivir and Segura river valleys.

The **castle** – now somewhat over-restored after being torched by French troops during the War of Independence – can be visited between 10am–2pm and 5–7.30pm. First, however, you'll need to call at the **Turismo**, to the right before the arch at the top of the street leading into the village (☎953/480280), to collect an impressive key (you'll need to deposit your passport). If the office is likely to be closed before you return, they have an informal arrangement with *Bar Snack Bar* just down the hill and you can collect your documents there. Once you've climbed up to the castle and enjoyed the views over the country for miles around – including an amusingly primitive rectangular **bullring** below – you'll feel extremely proprietorial as you insert the sizeable key and swing open the castle's heavy doors. Inside, you can climb the tower from which there are more magnificent **views**.

The Turismo also has the key to the **Baños Arabes**, a Moorish bathhouse off the central Plaza Mayor in the basement of a house below a bakery. Nearby is a Renaissance **fountain** which bears the arms of Carlos V.

Practicalities

Since the closure of a delightful *hostal* close to the Plaza Mayor, there is **no overnight accommodation** in Segura. However, this situation may well change and it's worth enquiring at the Turismo. Otherwise there's a cluster of *hostales* 15km southwest at **Cortijos Nuevos**, or you could try **Orcera** (see above). If you want to **camp**, the nearest site is *Camping Garrote Gordo*, 8km away and close to the junction with the Siles road.

There are a number of places to **eat** including the friendly *Bar Snack Bar*, on the way in to town. They not only serve excellent *tapas* and *raciones* here but will also sell you bottles of the famed local olive oil (including an organic variety) for which Segura has a coveted *Denominación de Origen* label (one of only four in the whole of Spain). Should you want to cool down there's a pleasant **swimming pool** on the road leading to the castle.

WALKS AROUND SEGURA

Seven kilometres east of Segura there's a pleasant **walk** along the banks of the densely wooded **Río Madera** which you can follow as far as La Toba, a good 20km away. Alternatively, with a map, you could leave the river and cut across country to **Monte Yelmo** from where a track leads north and back towards Segura.

To pick up the Río Madera follow the road east out of Segura to the junction with the Siles road. Turn right and a little way down you pass a fountain by the roadside beyond which is a *casa forestal* in a pinewood. To the right of the fountain a track descends towards the *Río Madera Campamento Juvenil* (kids' summer camp) a short way beyond which lies the river, noted for its trout. Turn right along it to follow the west bank south.

Leaving the park

With your own transport, you can avoid backtracking to Cazorla and take an alternative and attractive route out of the park heading south from Hornos along the C321 through the **Sierra de Segura** to **Pontones** and **Santiago de Espada**, on the border with Granada. There are plenty more campsites signed along this route and Santiago has *hostales*. The same road continues to Puebla de Don Fadrique where you have a choice between the routes to Granada and Almería. The Granada route via Huéscar takes in the interesting towns of Baza (see p.359) and Guadix (see p.358); otherwise the C321 heads across the deserted but picturesque wheatfields of Granada province's eastern panhandle towards Velez Blanco (see p.380) with its prehistoric caves, and eventually hits the coast near the Almerian resort of Mojácar (see p.376).

travel details

Trains

Córdoba to: Algeciras (3 daily; 5hr 30min); Granada (3 daily; 2hr); Jaén (2 daily; 2hr); Madrid (5 daily; 4hr 30min–8hr); Málaga (8 daily; 2–3hr); Ronda (3 daily; 3hr); Sevilla (16 daily; 1hr 30min–2hr).

Jaén to: Córdoba (1 daily; 2hr); Madrid (2 daily; 4hr 30min–6hr); Sevilla (1 daily; 3hr).

Buses

Baeza to: Granada (8 daily; 2hr 30min), Jaén (9 daily; 1hr), Úbeda (12 daily; 15min).

Córdoba to: Badajoz (1 daily; 6hr 30min), Cádiz (1 daily; 4hr), Écija (4 daily; 1hr 15min), Granada (5 daily; 4hr), Jaén (5 daily; 2hr), Madrid (1 daily; 5hr 30min), Málaga (4 daily; 3hr 30min), and Sevilla (5 daily; 2hr 30min).

From Jaén to: Baeza/Úbeda (8 daily; 1hr/1hr 30min), Cazorla (2 daily; 2hr), Córdoba (4 daily; 4hr 30min), Granada (10 daily; 2hr), Madrid (3 daily; 6hr), Málaga (4 daily; 4hr) and Sevilla (3 daily; 5hr).

From Úbeda to: Baeza (7 daily; 15min), Córdoba (3 daily; 2hr 30min), Jaén (11 daily; 1hr 30min), Sevilla (3 daily; 5hr).

CHAPTER FOUR

GRANADA AND ALMERÍA

T here is no more convincing proof of the diversity of Andalucía than its eastern provinces: **Granada**, dominated by Spain's highest mountains, the snow-capped Mulhacén and Veleta peaks of the Sierra Nevada; and **Almería**, a waterless, and in part, semi-desert landscape.

For most visitors, **Granada** city is not only the highlight of its province but one of the great destinations of Spain, as the home of Andalucía's most precious monument, the exquisite Moorish **Alhambra** palace and gardens. The city preserves, too, the old Moorish quarter of Albaicín and gypsy *barrio* of Sacromonte – places filled with the lingering atmosphere of this last outpost of Muslim Spain – as well as a host of Christian monuments, including the beautiful Capilla Real, with the tombs of Fernando and Isabel, *Los Reyes Católicos*, who finally wrested the kingdom from Moorish rule. Granada is also a good place to be during **Semana Santa** (the Easter week of floats and processions), and a place of literary pilgrimage through its associations with Spain's greatest modern poet, Federico García Lorca.

South from Granada rear the peaks of the **Sierra Nevada** and its lower slopes, **Las Alpujarras**, a series of wooded valleys sprinkled with whitewashed villages. This is wonderful country for walks and wildlife, with ancient cobbled paths connecting many of the villages, among them **Yegen**, one-time base of author Gerald Brenan, and **Trevelez**, Spain's highest village, famed for its snow-cured *jamón serrano*. The province makes the boast that you can ski in the Sierra Nevada's snowcapped peaks in the morning and swim on the coast in the afternoon. And so you could, if you really wanted to: the resorts of **Almuñecar**, **Salobreña** and **Castell de Ferro**, along the so-called **Costa Tropical**, all have fine beaches and less development than the Costa del Sol.

There's less of interest west and east of Granada. To the west, **Alhama de Granada** is a delightful spa on a scenic backroad to Málaga. To the east, amid a landscape of dusty hills covered with clumps of esparto grass lies **Guadix**, famous for its cave dwellings hacked out of the soft tufa rock, and the redstone Renaissance castle of **La Calahorra**. Beyond here, Granada's panhandle extends past the ancient country town of **Baza** to a lonely landscape of rolling *sierras* where small farms and isolated villages watch over fields of wheat, fruit orchards and pasture.

The **province of Almería** is a strange corner of Spain. Inland it has an almost lunar landscape of desert, sandstone cones and dried-up riverbeds; on the coast with a few exceptions, it is relatively unspoilt, with developments thwarted by sparse water supplies. As Spain's hottest province, the beach resorts are worth considering during what would be "off-season" elsewhere, since Almería's summers start well before Easter and last into November. In midsummer it's incredibly hot, frequently touching 35°C in the shade – while all year round there's an intense, almost luminous, sunlight.

The provincial capital and port, **Almería**, enjoyed a brief period of prosperity under the Moors and has been a bit of a backwater ever since – a workaday place with a life very much its own. It is overlooked by the largest castle the Moors built in Andalucía, the Alcazaba, below whose walls is a cave quarter, still populated by gypsies.

Almería's best **beaches and resorts**, the least developed of the Spanish Mediterranean, lie to the east of the capital. One of the nicest, the small resort of **San José**, lies inside the **Cabo de Gata Natural Park**, a wildlife and wetland area that is home to some interesting desert plants as well as a breeding ground for enormous flocks of **flamingos** in summer. Further north, **Las Negras**, **Agua Amarga** and **Carboneras** are all attractively low-key places fronting a crystal-clear blue sea where, if it's isolation you're after, there are strands within walking distance that scarcely see visitors. North again, things liven up at **Mojácar**, Almería's most fashionable resort, an ancient hilltop village that has spawned an enjoyable seafront quarter. To the west of Almería city a dismal sea of plastic tents – *invernaderos* – covers the **plain of Dalías** from the hills to the coast: a bonanza of drip-irrigation agriculture where exotic vegetables are force-grown to supply northern European markets all year round.

Inland, to the northeast of Almería city, begins the most remarkable **desert landscape** in Europe: badlands of twisted gulches, dry river beds and eroded hills that have long attracted film producers. Much of *Lawrence of Arabia* was shot here, along with scores of spaghetti westerns, whose sets have been preserved at **Mini Hollywood**, near Tabernas: a fun visit, especially if you have kids to entertain. This wierd scenery also shelters some interesting hamlets such as **Nijar**, a long established ceramics centre, and the clifftop **Sorbas**.

Almería province also maintains relics of a rich prehistoric past, when the rains were regular and the landscape verdant. In the northeast, near the village of **Velez Rubio**, is the **Cueva de los Letreros**, whose prehistoric cave paintings are among the most important in Spain and where the famous *Indalo* symbol was found. Over to the west, in the Almerian reaches of Las Alpujarras, is the exceptional archeological site of **Los Millares** where nearly five thousand years ago men hunted, mined and farmed.

Granada

> *Los dos ríos de Granada*
> *bajan de la nieve al trigo . . .*

> Granada's twin rivers tumble
> down from the snow to the wheat . . .

Federico García Lorca

The city of **GRANADA** has one of the most dramatic locations in Spain, poised below a magnificent backdrop of the snowcapped peaks of the Sierra Nevada. It is the perfect setting for a near-perfect monument, the extraordinary **Alhambra palace** – the most exciting, sensual and romantic of all European monuments. It was the palace-fortress of the Nasrid Sultans, rulers of the last Spanish Muslim kingdom, and in its construction Moorish art reached a spectacular and serene climax. The building, however, seems to go further than this, revealing something of the whole brilliance and spirit of Moorish life and culture. It should on no account be missed – and neither should the city, with its network of Moorish streets, panoply of Christian monuments and gypsy quarter.

Some history

Before the arrival of the Moors, Granada's mark on history was slight. An early Iberian settlement here, *Elibyrge*, was adapted by the **Romans**, as *Illiberis*, but although its fertility was prized, it was greatly overshadowed by the empire's provincial capital at Córdoba. Later, after the region had come under **Visigothic** control in the sixth century, the old Roman town, centred on the modern-day Albaicín, grew a **Jewish suburb**, *Garnatha,* on the south slope of the Alhambra hill. Popular tradition has it that friction between this Jewish settlement and the Christian town led to the Jews assisting the **Moors** to take the city shortly after the invasion of 711.

The Moors adapted the name to *Karnattah*, and for three centuries it was an important city under the control of the Cordoban Caliphate, and when this fell in 1031, under the Almoravid and Almohad Berber dynasties of Sevilla. When, however, Almohad

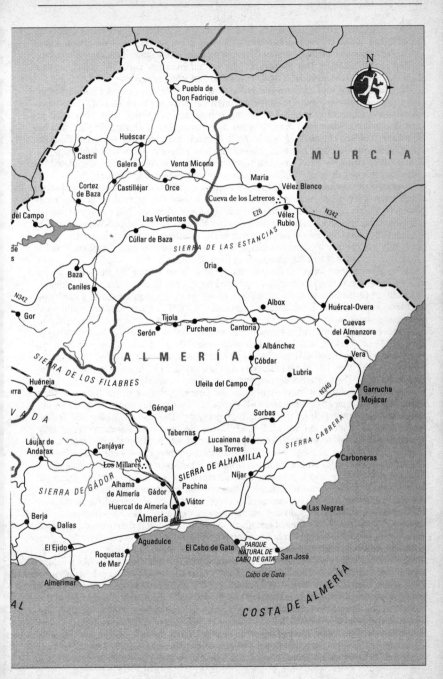

power crumbled in the thirteenth century, as the Christian *reconquista* gathered momentum, an astute Arab prince of the **Nasrid** tribe, which had been driven south from Zaragoza, saw his opportunity to create an indepedent state. The kingdom, established in the 1240s by **Ibn al-Ahmar** (aka Muhammad ibn Yusuf ibn Nasr), was to outlast the vanished *al-Andalus* by a further two and a half centuries.

Nasrid Granada was always a precarious state. Ibn al-Ahmar proved a just and capable ruler but all over Spain the Christian kingdoms were in the ascendant. The Moors of Granada survived only through paying tribute and allegiance to Fernando III of Castile – whom they were forced to assist in the conquest of Muslim Sevilla – and by the time of Ibn al-Ahmar's death in 1273 Granada was the only surviving Spanish Muslim kingdom. It had, however, consolidated its territory, which stretched from just north of the city down to a coastal strip between Tarifa and Almería, and, stimulated by Muslim refugees, developed a flourishing commerce, industry and culture.

Over the next two centuries, Granada maintained its autonomy by a series of shrewd manoeuvres, its rulers turning for protection, as it suited them, to the Christian kingdoms of Aragón and Castile and the Merinid sultans of Morocco. The city-state enjoyed its most confident and prosperous period under **Yusuf I** (1334–54) and **Muhammad V** (1354–91), the rulers responsible for much of the existing Alhambra palace. But by the mid-fifteenth century a pattern of coups and internal strife became established and a rapid succession of rulers did little to stem Christian inroads.

In 1479 the kingdoms of Aragón and Castile were united by the marriage of Fernando and Isabel and within ten years had conquered Ronda, Málaga and Almería. The city of Granada now stood completely alone, tragically preoccupied in a **civil war** between supporters of the sultan's two favourite wives. The *Reyes Católicos* made escalating and finally untenable demands upon it, and in 1490 war broke out. **Boabdil**, the last Moorish king, appealed in vain for help from his fellow Muslims in Morocco, Egypt and Ottoman Turkey, and in the following year Fernando and Isabel marched on Granada with an army said to total 150,000 troops. For seven months, through the winter of 1491, they laid siege to the city. On January 2, 1492, Boabdil formally surrendered its keys. The Christian Reconquest of Spain was complete.

There followed a century of repression for Granada, during which Jews and then Muslims were treated harshly and finally expelled by the Christian state and church, both of which grew rich on the confiscated property. The loss of Muslim and Jewish artesans and traders led to gradual economic decline, which was reversed only temporarily in the seventeenth century, the period when the city's Baroque monuments – La Cartuja monastery and San Juan de Dios hospital – were built. The city suffered heavily under **Napoleonic occupation**, when even the Alhambra was used as a barracks, causing much damage, and, although the nineteenth-century Romantic movement saw to it that the Alhambra suffered few more such violations, the sober *granadino* middle-class have been accused repeatedly since of caring little for the rest of their city's artistic legacy. In the last and present centuries, they have covered in the river Darro – which now flows beneath the town centre – and demolished an untold number of historic buildings to build avenues through the centre of the city.

Lorca described the *granadino*s as "the worst bourgeoisie in Spain", and they are regarded by many other Andalucians as conservative, arrogant and cool – like a colony somehow transplanted from northern Spain. A strong small-shopkeeper economy – which discouraged industrial development – and a society where military and clerics were dominant discouraged innovation and liberal ideas through the early part of the century. This introverted outlook perhaps contributed also to the events of the Civil War – one of the greatest stains on the city's name. In 1936, following Franco's coup, a fascist bloodbath was unleashed during which an estimated four thousand of the city's liberals were assassinated, among them poet and playwright, Federico García Lorca. The poet deserved better from his native city, of which he had written, "the hours are longer and sweeter here than in any other Spanish town . . . Granada has any amount of good ideas but is incapable of acting on them. Only in such a town, with its inertia and tranquility can there exist those exquisite contemplators of water, temperatures and sunsets."

Orientation and arrival

Virtually everything of interest in Granada, including the hills of **Alhambra** (to the east) and **Sacromonte** (to the north), is within easy walking distance of the centre. The only times you really need a local bus or taxi are if arriving or leaving on public transport, since bus and train stations are both some way out.

Gran Vía is the city's main street, cutting its way through the centre. It forms a "T" at its end with **c/Reyes Católicos**, which runs east to the **Plaza Nueva** and west to the **Puerta Real**, the city's two main squares.

The city **Turismo** is located in the Corral del Carbón on c/Mariana Pineda, just east of the cathedral (Mon–Fri 10am–1pm & 4–7pm Sat 10am–1pm; ☎225990). There's also a municipal Turismo at Plaza Mariana Pineda 10 (☎226688; same hours), east of Puerta Real.

Points of arrival

The **train station** is a kilometre or so out on the Avda. de Andaluces, off Avda. de la Constitución; to get in or out of town take bus #11 which runs a circular route: inbound on the Gran Vía de Colón and back out via the Puerta Real and Camino de Ronda; a convenient stop is by the cathedral on the Gran Vía (leaving, take the bus from across the road). Bus #4 also runs between the station and Gran Vía.

For the **main bus station** – the *Alsina Graells* terminal on the Camino de Ronda – the #11 bus is also your best bet, though you'll be coming round in the other direction so get off or pick it up at the Puerta Real. It stops on the same side of the road as the station whether it's coming from, or going to, the centre of Granada.

Alsina Graells runs the **bus services** to Jaén, Úbeda, Córdoba, Sevilla, Málaga, Alpujarras (high and low), Motril, Almería and the coast. The three most obvious destinations which require other terminals are: north side of Sierra Nevada (*Empresa Bonal*, Avda. de la Constitución 19), Guadix (*Empresa Autedia*, c/Rector Martín Ocete 10, off Avda. de la Constitución) and Valencia/Alicante (*Empresa Bacoma* near the railway station); all on the #11 bus route.

If you **fly** in, there's a bus connecting the airport with Plaza Isabel la Católica, by the cathedral.

Accommodation

Finding **accommodation** in Granada is pretty easy except at the very height of season and, especially, during *Semana Santa* (Easter week). There are a lot of *pensiones* and *hostales*, a frequent turnaround of visitors, and prices are no higher than elsewhere in Andalucía.

Most visitors want to put up as close to the Alhambra's doorstep as they can – and there are a couple of pricey (one very pricey) options up inside the walls. Unless you book ahead, however, you will have to content yourself with streets such as the Cuesta de Gomérez, which leads up towards the Alhambra from the Plaza Nueva; it is noisy but then so is much of the city centre. Quieter options are to be found in the streets between the picturesque Plaza de Bib-Rambla and Plaza de la Trinidad in the university area. Don't bother trying to find "interesting" accommodation in the Albaicín area – there isn't any.

If you plan a longer stay, check the noticeboards in the university, especially the translation faculty at c/Puentezuelas 55.

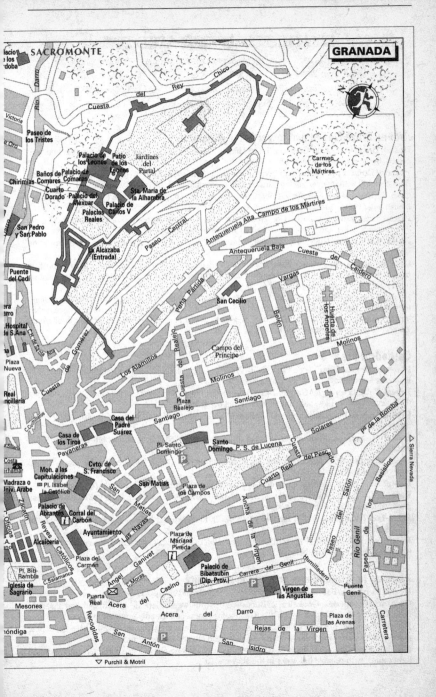

GRANADA

SACROMONTE

Río Darro

del Rey Chico

Cuesta

Victoria

de Oro

Paseo de
los Tristes

Palacio de
los Leones

Patio
de los
Leones

Jardines
del
Partal

Baños de
Chirimías

Palacio de
Comares

Cuarto
Dorado

Palacio del
Mexuar

Sta. María de
la Alhambra

San Pedro
y San Pablo

Palacio de
Carlos V

Palacios
Reales

Carmen
de los
Mártires

La Alcazaba
(Entrada)

Campo de los Mártires

Antequeruela Alta

Antequeruela Baja

Cuesta del Caldero

Puente
del Cadí

Vargas

San Cecilio

Belén

Huerta de
los Ángeles

Hospital
de S. Ana

Molinos

Plaza
Nueva

Cuesta de Gomérez

Los Álamillos

Peña Partida

Campo del
Príncipe

Molinos

Real
ncillería

Cuesta del Realejo

Santiago

Solares

Cuchilleros

Plaza
Realejo

Plaza de la Bomba

Santiago

Cuesta del Pesca..o

Casa del
Padre Suárez

Casa de
los Tiros

Pevaneras

Pl. Santo
Domingo

Santo
Domingo

P. S. de Lucena

Costa
erhamar

Mon. a las
Capitulaciones

Cvto. de
S. Francisco

Cuarto Real

Sierra Nevada

Paseo del Salón

Basisti...

Madraza o
Univ. Árabe

Pl. Isabel
la Católica

San
Matías

San Matías

Plaza de
los Campos

Palacio de
Abrantes

Corral del
Carbón

Ayuntamiento

Reyes Católicos

Las Navas

Ancha de la Virgen

Río Genil

Paseo de

Alcaicería

Plaza de
Mariana Pineda

Oficios

Pl. Bib-
Rambla

Salamanca

Plaza del
Carmen

Ángel

Ganivet

C. Moras

Palacio de
Bibataubín
(Dip. Prov.)

Carrera del Genil

Humilladero

Puente
Genil

Iglesia de
Sagrario

Puerta
Real

Acera

del

Casino

Virgen de
las Angustias

Plaza de
las Arenas

Mesones

Acera

del

Darro

Recogidas

ondiga

San

Antón

San

Isidro

Rejas de la Virgen

Carretera

▽ Purchil & Motril

ACCOMMODATION PRICE SYMBOLS

The symbols used in our hotel listings denote the following price ranges:

① Under 2000ptas   ③ 3000–4500ptas   ⑤ 7500–12,500ptas

② 2000–3000ptas   ④ 4500–7500ptas   ⑥ Over 12,500ptas

See p.28 for more details.

Around Plaza Nueva and towards the Alhambra

Hostal Britz, Cuesta de Gomérez 1 (☎223652). Noisy, but otherwise very comfortable and well placed. Some rooms with bath. ③.

Posada Doña Lupe, Alhambra/Avda. Generalife s/n (☎221473). A fine little pensión on the Alhambra hill with its own *cafetería* and a small swimming pool. All rooms with bath. ②.

Casa de Huéspedes Gomérez, Cuesta de Gomérez 2–3º (☎226398). Simple but convenient guesthouse; basic rooms and charges extra for showers. ②.

Hostal Landázuri, Cuesta de Gomérez 24 (☎221406). Pleasant rooms, some with bath, plus its own restaurant, bar and a roof terrace with a view of the Alhambra. ③.

Hotel Macía, Plaza Nueva 4 (☎227536). Central position and comfortable rooms overlooking the square. ④.

Casa de Huéspedes Santa Ana, c/Puente de Espinosa – over the Río Darro across the first bridge after the church at the east end of Plaza Nueva and at the top of the steps. Brilliant location but a rather unwelcoming management. ②.

Hostal Viena, c/Hospital de Sta. Ana 2, first left off Cuesta de Gomérez (☎221859). Excellent, friendly Austrian-run *hostal* in a quiet street. Some rooms with bath. The same owners have a cluster of places here and if this is full should be able to fit you in at the nearby *Hostal Austria* or *Hostal Venecia* (same phone number). ③.

Cathedral area

Pensión Atenas, Gran Vía de Colón 38 (☎278750). Large place, so worth a try, though rooms vary in quality – some have baths. Parking spaces. ③.

Hostal Fabiola, c/Angel Gavinet 5–5º, close to the Puerta Real (☎223572). Very good value: not too noisy, all rooms have bath and many have sit-out balconies. ③.

Hostal Lisboa, Plaza del Carmen 27 (☎221413). Modern, clean and comfortable place bang in the centre. Some rooms with bath. ③.

Hostal Mesones, c/Mesones 44, west of the cathedral (☎263244). A simple but cosy, family-run place. ③.

Hotel Montecarlo, c/Acera de Darro 44, off the Puerta Real (☎257900). Comfortable modern hotel with video and air-conditioning. ⑤.

Hostal Niza, c/Navas 16, off Plaza del Carmen (☎225430). Small friendly *hostal*. ③.

Pensión Olympia, c/Alvaro de Bazán 6 – off Gran Vía opposite *Banco de Jeréz*. (☎278238). Central, good value pensión run by nice people. ②.

Hotel Los Tilos, Plaza de Bib-Rambla 4 (☎266712). Plain two-star hotel in a good position near the cathedral. ④.

Hostal Verónica, c/Angel 17, south of the above off c/Recogidas (☎258145). Friendly hostal with pleasant rooms, most with bath. ③.

Plaza de la Trinidad and around the university

Hostal Europa, c/Fábrica Vieja 16 (☎278744). Friendly and cheap. ②.

Casa de Huéspedes González, c/Buensuceso 52, between Plaza de la Trinidad and Plaza de Gracia west of the cathedral (☎260351). Good value rooms and friendly proprietors. ②.

Hostal Marquez, c/Fábrica Vieja 8, off north side of Plaza Trinidad (☎275013). Friendly, simple place with lobby dominated by a snarling boar's head bagged by the *patrón*. ③.

Pensión Meridiano, c/Angulo 9, one street west of the one above (☎262981). Cheap, clean and light rooms, with reliable hot water in the showers. ②.

Pensiones La Milagrosa y Matilde, c/Puentezuelas 46, slightly west of Plaza de la Trinidad (☎263429). Two serviceable *pensiones* under the same ownership; their cheaper rooms (which you need to ask for) are good value. ③.

Hotel Reina Cristina, c/Tablas 4, close to Plaza de la Trinidad (☎253211). Modern hotel inside an old building where Lorca spent his last days before being seized by the fascists. ⑤.

Pensión Romero, c/Sillería 1, on corner of Plaza Trinidad (☎266079). Charming family-run place with spotless if basic rooms, many with balconies onto this delightful square. ②.

Hostal San Joaquin, c/Mano de Hierro 14 – near the the church of San Juan (☎282879). A great, rambling old place with simple rooms and charming patios; probably the best deal in this area. ③.

Around the train station

Hostal La Luz, c/Cruz de Arqueros 3 – two blocks northeast of Plaza del Triunfo (☎201368). This is a beautiful little *hostal*, on the edge of the Albaicín, run by an English-speaking Belgian and decorated with old Belgian furniture. It also has a fine restaurant. ②.

Hostal Terminus, Avda. de Andaluces 10 (☎201424). Absolutely no frills, but cheap and right beside the station. ②.

Hostal Turin, Ancha de Capuchinos 16 (☎200311). Another *hostal* near the train station, off the Jardines del Triunfo; cheap and well run. ②.

Inside and around the Alhambra

Hotel América, Real de la Alhambra 53 (☎227471). This charming one-star hotel is in the Alhambra grounds, bang opposite the *parador*, so you can get an early march on the queues and take a siesta midday. You pay for the location but it's worth it. ⑤.

Hotel Kenia, c/Molinos 65 (☎227506). Well-converted old mansion with a garden on the slopes below the Alhambra, south-east of the centre. Easy parking. ⑤.

Parador de San Francisco, Real de la Alhambra (☎221441). Without doubt the best hotel in Granada – a converted monastery in the Alhambra grounds. Alas, it's also the most expensive in the city, as a top-of-the-range *parador*. Rooms to go for are those in the 200s, with views of the Alhambra and Generalife, and booking is advised at least three months ahead in summer or over Easter. ⑥.

Hostal Suecia, Huerta de los Angeles 8, a cul-de-sac off c/Molinos near *Hotel Kenia* (☎225044). Charming small hotel in a quiet, leafy area below the Alhambra with a garden and a terrace to eat breakfast. ④.

Hotel Washington Irving, Paseo del Generalife 2, in the woods just below the Alhambra (☎227550). Described in the nineteenth century as "the most comfortable hotel in Spain", this offers faded grandeur today, and is one of the city's institutions with loads of historical associations. ⑤.

Youth hostels

Albergue de Juventud, Camino de Ronda 171, near the *Alsina Graells* bus station (☎958/272638). If you arrive late, this has some virtue, being handy for the train or bus stations (from the train station, turn left onto Avda. de la Constitución, left again onto Camino de Ronda – it's the large white building by the stadium). Lots of facilities including a pool (in summer) and good beds, but in the past has been institutional and unfriendly – maybe things will have changed for the better after its recent refit. There is also an excellent new hostel at Viznar, in the hills above the city (see p.333). ①.

Women-only hostel, c/San Juan de Dios 14–4º (press 4th floor buzzer). Nameless private hostel for women only in the student area. Clean, friendly and helpful. ①.

Campsites

Camping Sierra Nevada Avda. de Madrid 107 – easiest reached from the centre on #3 bus (☎958/150062). The closest site to the centre (March–Oct only), and – with a pleasant pool – probably the best too.

El Último Camino Huetor Vega 22 (☎958/123069). A second choice, not much further out, via Avda. de Cervantes, and again equipped with a pool.

The phone code for Granada is ☎958

The Alhambra and Generalife

The Sabika hill sits like a garland on Granada's brow,
In which the stars would be entwined
And the Alhambra (Allah preserve it)
Is the ruby set above that garland

Ibn Zamrak, vizier to Muhammad V (1362–1391)

There are three distinct groups of buildings on the Alhambra hill (known as Sabika to the Moors): the **Casa Real** (Royal Palace), the palace gardens of the **Generalife**, and the **Alcazaba**. This latter, the fortress of the eleventh-century Ziridian rulers, was all that existed when the Nasrids made Granada their capital but from its reddish walls the hilltop had already taken its name; *Al Qal'a al-Hamra* in Arabic means literally "the red fort".

The first Nasrid king, Ibn al-Ahmar, rebuilt the Alcazaba and added to it the huge circuit of walls and towers which forms one's first view of the castle. Within the walls he began a palace, which was supplied with running water by diverting the Río Darro nearly 8km to the foot of the hill; water is an integral part of the Alhambra and this engineering feat was Ibn al-Ahmar's greatest contribution. The Casa Real was essentially the product of his fourteenth-century successors, particularly **Muhammad V**, who built and decorated many of its rooms in celebration of his accession to the throne (in 1354) and conquest of Algeciras (in 1369).

After their conquest of the city, **Fernando and Isabel** lived for a while in the Alhambra. They restored some rooms and converted the mosque but left the palace structure unaltered. As at Córdoba and Sevilla, it was their grandson **Emperor Carlos V** who wreaked the most insensitive destruction. He demolished a whole wing of rooms in order to build yet another grandiose Renaissance palace. This and the Alhambra itself were simply ignored by his successors and by the eighteenth century the Royal Palace was in use as a prison. In 1812 it was taken and occupied by **Napoleon's forces**, who looted and damaged whole sections of the palace, and on their retreat from the city tried to blow up the entire complex. Their attempt was thwarted only by the action of a crippled soldier who remained behind and removed the fuses.

Two decades later the Alhambra's "rediscovery" began, given impetus by the American writer **Washington Irving**, who set up his study in the empty palace rooms and began to write his marvellously romantic *Tales of the Alhambra* (on sale all over Granada – and good reading amid the gardens and courts). Shortly after its publication the Spaniards made the Alhambra a **national monument** and set aside funds for its restoration. This continues to the present and is now a highly sophisticated project, scientifically removing the accretions of later ages in order to expose and meticulously restore the Moorish creations.

Approaches to the Alhambra

The standard **approach** to the Alhambra is along the Cuesta de Gomérez, the road which climbs uphill from Plaza Nueva. After a few hundred metres you reach the **Puerta de las Granadas**, a massive Renaissance gateway erected by Carlos V and topped by three open pomegranates (*granada* is the fruit's Spanish name) which became the city's symbol. Here two paths diverge to either side of the road: the one on the right climbs up towards a group of fortified towers, the **Torres Bermejas**, parts of which may date from as early as the eighth century. Take the left-hand path through the woods, past a huge terrace-fountain (again courtesy of Carlos V), and you reach the main gateway of the Alhambra.

This gate is the **Puerta de la Justicia**, a magnificent tower which forced three changes of direction, making intruders hopelessly vulnerable. It was built by Yusuf I in

1348 and preserves above its inner arch the Koranic symbol of a key (for Allah, the opener of the gates of Paradise) and, over the outer arch, an outstretched hand whose five fingers represent the five Islamic precepts: prayer, fasting, alms-giving, pilgrimage to Mecca and the oneness of God. A Moorish legend stated that the gate would never be breached by the Christians until the hand reached down to grasp the key.

Within the citadel stood a complete "government city" of mansions, smaller houses, baths, schools, mosques, barracks and gardens. Of this only the **Alcazaba fortress** and the **Royal Palace** remain; they face each other across a broad terrace (constructed in the sixteenth century over a dividing gully), flanked by the majestic though incongruous **Palace of Carlos V**.

Within the walls of the citadel, too, are a handful of overpriced **restaurants** and the beautiful **Parador de San Francisco**, whose terrace-bar (and restaurant) are open to allcomers. There are a handful of **drinks stalls**, too, including one, very welcome, in the Plaza de Los Aljibes just beyond the Puerta del Vino, near the ticket office, and another in the Portal gardens (towards the Carlos V Palace after you leave the Casa Real). No one, however, seems to mind if you take a bottle of wine into the Generalife and cool it in one of the fountains – and this is perhaps the best way to enjoy and appreciate the luxuriance.

Leaving the Alhambra, a lovely route down to the city is the **Cuesta de los Chinos**, which winds past the walls, just below the entrance to the Generalife, towards the Río Darro and the old Arab quarter of the Albaicín.

The Alcazaba

Passing from the ticket office through the **Puerta del Vino** – named from its use in the sixteenth century as a wine cellar – across the Plaza de los Aljibes you are confronted by the walls of the **Alcazaba**, the earliest, though most ruined, part of the fortress. Quite apart from filling in time before your ticket admits you to the Royal Palace, this is an interesting part of the complex and one where you can get a grip on the whole site.

Once inside, thread your way to the left, through remnants of the barracks, to take a look at the **Jardín de los Ardaves**, a delightful seventeenth-century garden laid out

---

ADMISSION TO THE ALHAMBRA

The Alhambra complex is open daily: in summer from 9am to 7.45pm; in winter from 9am to 5.45pm. **Tickets** cost 625ptas (student discounts only for those studying in Spain) for the complex, or 250ptas for the Generalife only. On Sunday afternoons there is free admission after 3pm, though you will still need to obtain an admission ticket – and before 5pm. The tickets have tear-off slips for each part of the complex (Alcazaba, Casa Real, Portal and Torres, Generalife) and these must be used on the same day. The two Museums in the Palace of Carlos V have separate admission fees (free entry with an EC passport).

In an attempt to cope with the drastic overcrowding of recent years tickets are stamped with a half-hour **time slot**, during which period you must enter the Casa Real part of the complex; you will not be allowed to enter before or after this time but once inside you can stay as long as you like. Arriving early is usually the best tactic to beat the queues and once you've got your ticket, any waiting time – usually up to an hour – can be spent in the Alcazaba or at one of the cafés. Another good time to avoid the crowds is the period from 4pm until closing time when most of the coach tours have gone. A reservation system (☎220912) allows you to book a time for your visit prior to arrival.

The Alhambra palaces and gardens are also open for floodlit **night-time visits** from 10pm until 11.45pm on Tuesday, Thursday and Saturday nights in season (out of season Sat 8–10pm). Admission is a further 600ptas. In the summer months, there are also occasional evening **concerts** held in the courtyards.

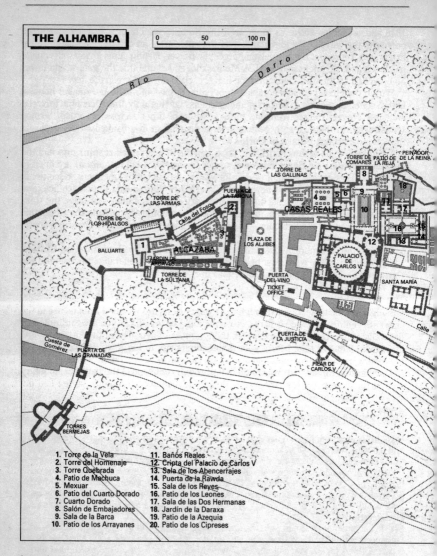

THE ALHAMBRA

0   50   100 m

1. Torre de la Vela
2. Torre del Homenaje
3. Torre Quebrada
4. Patio de Machuca
5. Mexuar
6. Patio del Cuarto Dorado
7. Cuarto Dorado
8. Salón de Embajadores
9. Sala de la Barca
10. Patio de los Arrayanes
11. Baños Reales
12. Cripta del Palacio de Carlos V
13. Sala de los Abencerrajes
14. Puerta de la Rawda
15. Sala de los Reyes
16. Patio de los Leones
17. Sala de las Dos Hermanas
18. Jardín de la Daraxa
19. Patio de la Azequia
20. Patio de los Cipreses

along the fort's southern parapets with creepers, fountains and sweet-scented bushes.
There is access from here to the Alcazaba's summit, the **Torre de la Vela**, named after
a huge bell on its turret which until recent years was rung to mark the irrigation hours
for workers on the *vega*, Granada's vast and fertile plain. The views from here are spectacular: west over the plunging ravine of the Darro with the city and the *vega* beyond,
and north towards the Albaicín and Sacromonte hills, with the Alhambra itself behind
and the snowcapped peaks of the Sierra Nevada forming a backdrop. It was on this
same parapet at 3pm on January 2, 1492, that the Cross was first displayed above the

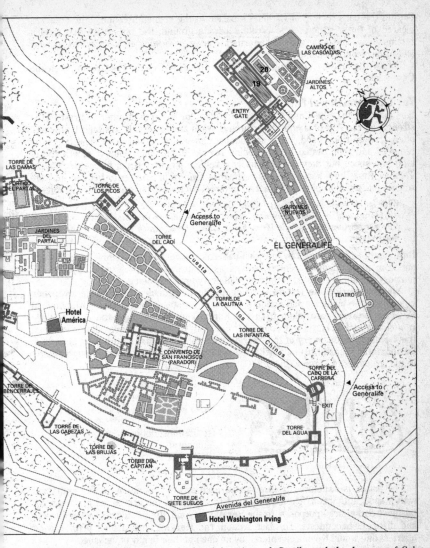

city, alongside the royal standards of Aragón and Castile and the banner of Saint James. Boabdil, leaving Granada for exile in the Alpujarras, turned and wept at the sight, earning from his mother Aisha the famous rebuke: "Do not weep like a woman for what you could not defend like a man."

To gain access to the palace you need to recross the **Plaza de los Aljibes**. In Nasrid times this area was a ravine dividing the hill between the royal palace on one side, and the Alcazaba on the other. Following the *reconquista* the ravine was filled in to hold two rainwater cisterns (*aljibes*) and the surface above laid out with fortifications.

During the construction of Carlos V's palace in the sixteenth century, the area was cleared of these structures to create a parade ground, the rather desolate form it retains today. The underground **cisterns** are open for viewing on Monday, Wednesday and Friday from 9.30am to 1.30pm.

Follow the arrows indicating the Palacios Nazaries (Nasrid Palaces) to reach the Casa Real.

The Casa Real (Royal Palace)

It is amazing that the **Casa Real** has survived, for it stands in utter contrast to the strength of the Alcazaba and the encircling walls and towers. It was built lightly and often crudely from wood, brick and adobe, and was designed not to last but to be renewed and redecorated by succeeding rulers. Its buildings show a superb use of light and space but they are principally a vehicle for ornamental stucco decoration. This, as Titus Burckhardt explains in *Moorish Culture in Spain*, was both an intricate science and a philosophy of abstract art in direct contrast to pictorial representation:

> With its rhythmic repetition, [it] does not seek to capture the eye to lead it into an imagined world, but, on the contrary, liberates it from all pre-occupations of the mind. It does not transmit any specific ideas, but a state of being, which is at once repose and inner rhythm.

Burckhardt adds that the way in which patterns are woven from a single band, or radiate from many identical centres, served as a pure simile for Islamic belief in the oneness of God, manifested at the centre of every form and being.

Arabic inscriptions feature prominently in the ornamentation. Some are poetic eulogies of the buildings and builders, others of various sultans – notably Muhammad V. Most, however, are taken from the Koran, and among them the phrase *Wa-la ghaliba illa-Llah* (There is no Conqueror but God) is tirelessly repeated. It is said that this became the battle cry of the Nasrids upon Ibn al-Ahmar's return from aiding the Castilian war against Muslim Sevilla; it was his reply to the customary, though bitterly ironic, greetings of *Mansur* (Victor).

Wa-la ghaliba illa-Llah

(stylized inscription from the Alhambra).

The palace is structured in three parts, each arrayed round an interior court and with a specific function. The sultans used the **Mexuar**, the first series of rooms, for business and judicial purposes. In the **Serallo**, beyond, they would receive embassies and distinguished guests. The last section, the **Harem**, formed their private living quarters and would have been entered by no one but their family or servants.

THE MEXUAR

The council chamber, the main reception hall of the **Mexuar**, is the first room you enter. It was completed in 1365 and hailed (perhaps formulaically) by the court poet Ibn Zamrak as a "haven of counsel, mercy and favour". Here the sultan heard the pleas and petitions of the people and held meetings with his ministers. At the room's far end is a small **oratory**, one of a number of prayer niches scattered round the palace and immediately identifiable by their angular alignment to face Mecca.

This "public" section of the palace, beyond which few would have penetrated, is completed by the Mudéjar **Cuarto Dorado** (Golden Room), redecorated under Carlos V, whose *Plus Ultra* motif appears throughout the palace, and the **Patio del Cuarto Dorado**. This latter has perhaps the grandest facade of the whole palace, for it admits you to the formal splendour of the Serallo.

THE SERALLO

The **Serallo** was built largely to the design of Yusuf I, a romantic and enlightened sultan who was stabbed to death by a madman while worshipping in the Alhambra mosque. Its rooms open out from delicate marble-columned arcades at each end of the long **Patio de los Arrayanes** (Myrtles) with its serene fountain and pool flanked by clipped myrtle bushes. At the court's northern end is the **Sala de la Barca**, with a fine copy of its original cedar ceiling (destroyed by fire in the last century), and the fortified **Torre de Comares**, two floors of which are occupied by the royal throne room.

This, the **Salón de Embajadores** (Hall of the Ambassadors), is the palace's largest and most majestic chamber. It was where the delicate diplomacy with the Christian emissaries would have been transacted – the means by which the Nasrid dynasty preserved itself – and as the sultan could only be approached indirectly it stands at an angle to the entrance from the Mexuar. It is perfectly square, with a stunning wooden dome, a superb example of *lacería*, the rigidly geometric "carpentry of knots" domed roof, and with a complex symbolism representing the seven heavens. The walls are completely covered in tile and stucco decoration and inscriptions, one of which states simply "I am the Heart of the Palace". It was here, symbolically, that Boabdil signed the terms of his city's surrender to the *Reyes Católicos*, whose motifs (the arms of Aragón and Castile) were later worked into the dome. Here too, so it is said, Fernando met with Columbus to discuss his planned voyage to find a new sea route to India – the trip which led to the discovery of the Americas.

Carlos V tore down the rooms at the southern end of the Patio de los Arrayanes. From the arcade there is access to the gloomy **chapel crypt** (*cripta*) of his palace; it has a curious "whispering gallery" effect.

THE HAREM

The **Patio de los Leones** (Court of the Lions), which has become the archetypal image of Granada, constitutes the heart of the harem section of the palace. It was this area that moved Washington Irving to write in his *Tales of the Alhambra*:

> *It is impossible to contemplate this scene, so perfectly Oriental, without feeling the early associations of Arabian romance, and almost expecting to see the white arm of some mysterious princess beckoning from the gallery, or some dark eye sparkling through the lattice. The abode of beauty is here as if had been inhabited but yesterday.*

The court was designed as an interior garden and planted with shrubs and aromatic herbs; it opens on to three of the finest rooms in the palace, each of which looks directly on to the fountain. The stylized and archaic-looking lions beneath this probably date, like the court itself, from the reign of Muhammad V, Yusuf's successor; a poem inscribed on the bowl tells how much fiercer the beasts would look if they weren't so restrained by respect for the sultan.

At the far end of the court is the **Sala de los Reyes** (Hall of the Kings), whose dormitory alcoves preserve a series of unique paintings on leather. These, in defiance of Koranic law, represent human scenes. They were probably painted by a Christian artist in the last decades of Moorish rule and were once thought to portray images of the Nasrid rulers – hence the room's name.

The most sophisticated rooms in this part of the complex, apparently designed to give a sense of the rotary movement of the stars, are the two facing each other across the court. The largest of these, the **Sala de los Abencerrajes**, has the most fabulous ceiling in the whole Alhambra complex: sixteen-sided, supported by niches of stalactite vaulting, lit by windows in the dome and reflected in a fountain on the floor. Its light and airy quality stands at odds with its name and history, for here Abu al-Hassan, Boabdil's father, murdered sixteen princes of the Abencerraj family, whose chief had fallen in love with his favourite, Zoraya. The stains in the fountain – popularly supposed to be indelible traces of blood from the severed heads thrown into it – are more likely to be from rust.

The second of these two chambers, the **Sala de las dos Hermanas** (Hall of the Two Sisters), is more mundanely named – from two huge slabs of white marble in its floor – but just as spectacularly decorated, with a dome of over 5000 "honeycomb cells". It was the principal room of the sultan's favourite, opening on to an inner apartment and balcony, the **Mirador de la Daraxa** ("Eyes of the Sultana"); the romantic garden patio below was added after the Reconquest.

Beyond, you are directed along a circuitous route through **apartments** redecorated by Carlos V (as at Sevilla, the northern-reared emperor installed fireplaces) and later used by Washington Irving. Eventually you emerge at the **Peinador de la Reina** (Queen's pavilion), which served as an oratory for the sultanas and as a dressing room for the wife of Carlos V; perfumes were burned beneath its floor and wafted up through a marble slab in one corner.

From there, passing the **Patio de la Reja** (Patio of the Grille) added in the seventeenth century, you pass the **Baños Reales** (Royal Baths). These are tremendous, decorated in rich tile mosaics and lit by pierced stars and rosettes once covered by coloured glass. The central chamber was used for reclining and retains the balconies where singers and musicians – reputedly blind to keep the royal women from being seen – would entertain the bathers. At present, entry is not permitted to the baths, though you can make out most of the features through the doorways.

Towers and the palacio de Carlos V

Before leaving the palace compound a number of the **towers** are worth a look. Most are richly decorated – particularly the first, the **Torre de las Damas**, which stands in front of its own patio, well restored to the original design.

The usual exit from the Casa Real is through the courtyard of the **Palacio de Carlos V**, where bullfights were once held. The palace itself was begun in 1526 but never finished. It seems totally out of place here but is a distinguished piece of Renaissance design in its own right – the only surviving work of Pedro Machuca, a former pupil of Michelangelo.

The palace's lower floor houses a **Museum of Hispano-Muslim Art** (open Tues–Fri 10am–2pm; Sat 10am–1pm; free entry with EC passport), a wonderful collection of artefacts which visitors are often too jaded to take in after the marvels of the Moorish palace outside. As well as fragments of sculptured plaster arabesques saved from the Alhambra, and a splendid ceramic collection, the fourteenth and fifteenth century Nasrid paintings in Room 3 are outstanding, as are various carved wood panels and screens. The rare and beautiful fifteenth-century **Alhambra Vase** in Room 8 is the Museum's centrepiece. Almost a metre and a half in height, and made for the Nasrid palace from local red clay enamelled in blue and gold with leaping gazelles, it is the ceramic equal of the artistic splendours in the palace.

On the upper floors of the palace is a **Museo de Bellas Artes** (same hours and entry conditions as above), a cavernous gallery whose paintings and sculpture might command more attention elsewhere. In Room 1 there's a fine bas-relief of the *Virgin and Child* by Diego de Siloé. Room 5 contains a number of works by Alonso Cano, the seventeenth-century *granadino* painter and sculptor; his *Virgin and Child* and *San Bernardino de Siena* panels are outstanding, as are the sculptures of *San Antonio* and a head of *San Juan de Dios*, the latter executed with some assistance from Granada's other great sculptor, Pedro de Mena. Room 6 has more examples of the Andalucian sculptural tradition with a brace of *Dolorosas* matched by a pair of *Ecce Homos*, a fervent theme of the region's artists reflected in the *pasos* carried during the *Semana Santa* processions; the *Ecce Homo* by Diego de Mora is the better of the two, whilst his more famous brother José de Mora has the finer *Dolorosa*. The later rooms, devoted to paintings from the nineteenth and twentieth centuries, are fairly forgettable.

The Convento de San Francisco

Behind Carlos V's palace are the remnants of the town (with a population of 40,000 during the Nasrid period) which once existed within the Alhambra's walls. On the main street are a cluster of overpriced restaurants and tatty tourist shops, which you'd do well to pass by.

However, before proceeding to the Generalife, it is worth looking into the fifteenth-century **Convento de San Francisco**. Built by Fernando and Isabel on the site of another Moorish palace, this is now a *parador* whose superb plant-filled patio preserves part of the chapel where the Catholic monarchs were buried – commemorated by a marble slab – before being removed to the Cathedral. At the back, there is a restaurant and a very pleasant terrace bar.

The Generalife

Paradise is described in the Koran as a shaded, leafy garden refreshed by running water where the "fortunate ones" may take their rest under tall canopies. It is an image which perfectly describes the **Generalife**, the gardens and summer palace of the sultans. Its name means literally "garden of the architect" and the grounds consist of a luxuriantly imaginative series of patios, enclosed gardens and walkways.

By chance an account of the gardens during Moorish times, written rather poetically by a Moorish historian called Ibn Zamrak, survives. The descriptions that he gives aren't all entirely believable but they are a wonderful basis for musing as you lie around by the patios and fountains. There were, he wrote, celebrations with horses darting about in the dusk at speeds that made the spectators rub their eyes (a form of festival still indulged in at Moroccan *fantasías*); rockets shot into the air to be attacked by the stars for their audacity; tightrope walkers flying through the air like birds; men bowled along in a great wooden hoop, shaped like an astronomical sphere . . .

Today, even devoid of such amusements, the gardens remain deeply evocative, above all, perhaps, the **Patio de los Cipreses**, a dark and secretive walled garden of sculpted junipers where the Sultana Zoraya was suspected of meeting her lover Hamet, chief of the unfortunate Abencerrajes. The trunk of the seven-hundred year old **cypress tree** (marked by a plaque) is where legend says their trysts took place and where the grisly fate of the Abencerraj clan was sealed.

Nearby is the inspired flight of fantasy of the **Camino de las Cascadas**, a staircase with water flowing down its stone balustrades. At its base is a wonderful little **Summer Palace**, with various decorated belvederes.

Granada's other sights

If you're spending just a couple of days in Granada it's hard to resist spending both of them in the Alhambra. It takes a distinct readjustment and effort of will to appreciate the city's later Christian monuments – although the **Capilla Real**, at least, demands a visit, and Baroque fans are in for a treat at the Cartuja. There are, too, a handful of minor Moorish sites in and around the run-down medieval streets of the **Albaicín**, the largest and most characteristic Moorish quarter that survives in Spain, and the quarter also has an excellent **archeology museum**.

The Albaicín

The **Albaicín** stretches across a fist-shaped area bordered by the Río Darro, Sacromonte hill, the old town walls and the winding Calle de Elvira (which runs parallel to the Gran Vía). From the centre, the best approach is from the Plaza Nueva and along the Corredera del Darro, beside the river. Coming from the Alhambra or Generalife, you can make your way down the Cuesta de los Chinos – a beautiful path and shortcut.

PLAZA NUEVA AND CUESTA DE GOMEREZ

Before starting out from the **Plaza Nueva**, take a look at the square itself. It was constructed just after the *reconquista* as a new focus for the city, and soon served as the site of an act of stunning Christian barbarity: a bonfire of 80,000 books from the former Muslim university.

Flanking the square's north side is the austerely impressive **Real Chancillería** (Royal Chancery), built at the same time as the square, and now the law courts. Beyond its monumental entrance lies an elegant two-storied **patio** designed by Diego de Siloé with marble Doric columns and a staircase with stalactite ceiling.

On the opposite side of the square, the **Cuesta de Gomerez** leads up to the Alhambra. Ironically, it is here – on the noisiest street in town – that most of Granada's renowned guitar manufacturers are gathered. Behind the windows of these places you may catch sight of a major concert or *flamenco* musician trying out a new instrument. On a recent visit I encountered the noted *granadino* classical guitarist José-Carlo Gutierrez purchasing a new guitar from *Casa Morales* at number 9; he treated the shop to a virtuoso display whilst the jovial Señor Morales beamed approvingly.

SANTA ANA AND THE ARAB BATHS

Perched over the Darro at the Plaza Nueva's eastern end is the sixteenth century church of **Santa Ana**, whose bell-tower is the converted minaret of the mosque it replaced. Following the river's northern bank along the **Corredera del Darro**, glance back to where the river disappears from sight under the city and "moans as it loses itself in the absurd tunnel" as the young Lorca put it.

A little way up at no. 31 are the remains of the **Baños Árabes** (Tues–Sat 10am–2pm), a marvellous and very little-visited Moorish public bath complex. Built in the eleventh-century, the sensitively-restored building consists of a series of brick-vaulted rooms with typical star-shaped skylights (originally glazed) and columns incorporating Roman and Visigothic capitals. When Richard Ford was here in the 1830s he found it being used as a wash-house by the local women because "one of the first laws after the conquest of the Catholic sovereigns was to prohibit bathing by fine and punishment."

CASA DE CASTRIL: THE ARCHEOLOGICAL MUSEUM

At Corredera del Darro no. 43 is the **Casa de Castril**, a Renaissance mansion with a fine Plateresque facade and doorway, which houses the city's interesting **Museo Arqueológico** (Tues–Sun 10am–2pm; 200ptas).

This exhibits finds from throughout the province. Rooms 1 and 2 cover the Palaeolithic and Neolithic periods among which are some remarkable artefacts from the **Cueva de los Murciliegos** near to Albuñol. In this fourth millennium BC Neolithic cave, alongside a dozen cadavers arranged in a semi-circle around that of a woman, were found some modern-looking esparto grass sandals and baskets, as well as a golden diadem. Room 4 contains the Iberian and pre-Roman collection with some fine examples of early lapidary work, including a hefty carved stone bull, stone vases and outstanding alabaster vessels. The finds from the necropolis at **Punté Noye** near Almuñecar (the Phoenician *Sexi*) suggest a large colony here trading as far afield as Egypt and Greece from where the vases (some bearing pharaonic titles) were imported. The Roman section in Room 5 has a striking third-century bronze statue as well as some interesting **early Christian lamps** from the fourth-century; exhibit 4420 bears the Chi-Rho symbol, the first two letters of Christ's name in Greek. Among some Visigothic artefacts in Room 6 is a carved stone plaque with another Chi-Rho symbol.

Pride of place in the **Moorish section** (Room 7) is a fourteenth-century **bronze astrolabe**, demonstrating the superior scientific competence of the Arabic world at this time. The instrument was adopted by the Arabs from ancient Greece and used for charting the position of the stars in astrology, precisely orienting the *mihrab* of the mosques towards Mecca, determining geographical coordinates as well as trigonometry and converting Muslim dates into Christian ones. Its transmission from the Arab to the Christian world made possible the voyages of discovery to both east and west. More Moorish symmetry is evident in the designs on the vases, wooden chests and amphoras also displayed here.

FURTHER ALONG THE DARRO AND THE CASA DEL CHAPIZ

Alongside the Casa de Castril, c/Zafra has a Moorish house, the **Casa Zafra**, with a pleasant patio and pool, whilst close by again is the convent of **Santa Catalina de Zafra**, housed in a sixteenth-century Moorish palace. The nuns here are renowned for their convent *dulces* and will gladly supply you (through a *torno*) with their speciality, *glorias* (almond cakes); they're open daily except in August. At the top of the same street, **San Juan de los Reyes** is another church – the first established in Granada after the *reconquista* – built around the courtyard of a former mosque whose minaret, with characteristically Moorish *sebka* decoration, now serves as a belfry.

Continuing along the Darro you'll eventually come to **Paseo de los Tristes** (aka Paseo del Padre Manjón) a delightful esplanade beside the river overlooked by the battlements of the Alhambra high on the hill above, a great spot for a drink and especially so at night when the Alhambra is floodlit. There are several attractive bars backing onto the river.

Two streets off here also contain **Moorish houses**: c/del Horno de Oro (no. 14) and, two streets further along, Cuesta de la Victoria (no. 9). The street after this, the **Cuesta del Chapiz**, climbs left into the heart of the Albaicín, passing first, on the right, the **Casa del Chapiz**, in origin a sixteenth-century Moorish mansion – with a charming patio – and today reclaimed as a school of Arabic studies. The **Camino del Sacromonte**, just beyond it, heads east towards the *gitano* caves where, after sundown, the gypsies will attempt to entice you in for some raucous but often dubious *flamenco*.

SACROMONTE: GRANADA'S GYPSY QUARTER

Granada has an ancient and still considerable gypsy population, from whose clans many of Spain's best *flamenco* guitarists, dancers and singers have emerged. Traditionally the gypsies inhabited cave homes on the **Sacromonte hill**, and many still do, giving lively displays of dancing and music in their *zambras* (shindigs).

These were once spontaneous but are now blatantly contrived for tourists, and are often shameless rip-offs: you're hauled into a cave, leered at if you're female, and systematically extorted of all the money you've brought along (for dance, the music, the castanets, the watered-down sherry . . .). Which is not to say that you shouldn't visit – just to take only as much money as you want to part with. Turn up mid-evening; the lines of caves begin off the Camino de Sacromonte, just above the Casa del Chapiz (centre top on our map). When the university is in session, the cave dwellings are turned into **discos** and are packed with students at weekends.

For revelations of a different kind wander up to Sacromonte a little earlier in the day and take a look at the old **caves** – most of them deserted after severe floods in 1962 – on the far side of the old Moorish wall. There are fantastic views from the top.

The Cuesta de Chapiz eventually loops around to the Plaza del Salvador where the church of **San Salvador** is built on the site of a mosque of which the **courtyard** with whitewashed arches and Moorish cisterns is beautifully preserved. Diego de Siloé, the architect of the sixteenth-century church, converted the Mosque's original **minaret** into its tower.

PLAZA LARGA AND THE MIRADOR DE SAN NICOLÁS

From San Salvador, the Caniceros Panaderos leads into **Plaza Larga**, the busy heart of the Albaicín, with a concentration of restaurants and bars. Just behind here, too, at c/ Pardo 5, is a splendid Moorish house, now converted into a bar named the **Casa Arabe**. It's a clip joint but worth the one drink to look over this exquisite Moorish dwelling with its marvellous patio (with original pebbled floor) and arches with fine arabesque plaster work. Slightly west, the c/del Agua has more **Moorish dwellings**: try numbers 1, 37, 28, and 19.

From here the obvious route is to the **Mirador de San Nicolás** with its justly famous panoramic **view** of the Sierra Nevada, the Alhambra and Granada spread out below. To get there from Plaza Larga, take c/Moral followed by c/Charca. On the square, the fifteenth-century church is of little note but the nearby **fountain** is a Moorish original, one of many in the Albaicín to survive from the time when every mosque – there were more than thirty of them – had its own.

Below the mirador, c/Nuevo de San Nicolás descends into c/Santa Isabel la Real, passing, on the right, the early sixteenth-century convent of **Santa Isabel**, partly constructed within a Nasrid palace – La Daralhorra – of which only the patios and some arches survive. The convent church (open 10am–6pm) has a superb Plateresque doorway and, inside, a Mudéjar ceiling. You could detour north from here – climbing uphill beyond the walls – to the church of **San Cristobal**, which has another fine **view** of the Alhambra from its *mirador*.

PLAZA DE SAN MIGUEL AND SAN JOSÉ

Alternatively, c/Santa Isabel drops into one of the Albaicín's most delightful squares, **Plaza de San Miguel Bajo**, lined with acacia and chestnut trees. The church of **San Miguel** on its eastern side is another sixteenth-century work by Diego de Siloé, built over yet another mosque, and preserves its original **thirteenth-century fountain** where the ritual ablutions would have been performed before entering. The square also has a couple of good bars, whose terraces are extremely popular at night; *Bar Lara* serves the potent barrelled *costa* wine brewed in the Alpujarras. The opposite end of the plaza leads to the **Mirador del Carril de la Lona** with its views over the western side of the city.

One final church worth taking in on the way back to the centre is **San José**, reached along c/Cauchiles from Plaza San Miguel. This is another sixteenth-century conversion from a ninth-century mosque, whose minaret forms its belfry, and its interior has a superb gilded Mudéjar coffered ceiling and octagonal dome.

C/Cauchiles winds into Cuesta de San Gregorio where you could take a look at the **Casa de Porras** with its Plateresque façade and, opposite, the **carmen de Cipreses**, one of the most picturesque garden-villas in the Albaicín. At the bottom of here, Plaza San Gregorio gives access to Plaza Nueva.

Other Moorish remains

A further group of Moorish buildings are located just outside the Albaicín. The most interesting of them, and oddly one of the least well known, is the so-called **Palacio Madraza**, a strangely painted building opposite the Capilla Real. Built in the early fourteenth century at the behest of Yusuf I, though much altered since, this is a former

Islamic college (*medressa* in Arabic) and retains part of its old prayer hall, including a magnificently decorated *mihrab*. It is open somewhat sporadically for exhibitions; you may have to knock for admission.

More reliably open, as it houses the city's tourist office, is the **Corral del Carbón**, a fourteenth-century *caravanserai* (an inn where merchants would lodge and, on the upper floors, store their goods) which is unique in Spain. A wonderful horseshoe arch leads into a courtyard with a marble water trough. Remarkably, it survived intact through a stint as a sixteenth-century theatre – with the spectators watching from the upper galleries – and later as a charcoal burners' factory, the origin of its present name. The building is little tricky to find: it lies down an alleyway off the c/de los Reyes Católicos, opposite the **Alcaicería**, the old Arab silk bazaar, burned down in the nineteenth century and poorly restored as an arcade of souvenir shops.

Another impressive Moorish mansion, the **Casa de los Tiros** (currently closed) stands on c/Pavaneras, just behind Plaza de Isabel Católica. This was actually built just after the *reconquista* and has a curious façade adorned with various Greek deities and heroes as well as a number of *tiros* (muskets) projecting from the upper windows. Above the door is a representation of the sword of Boabdil which the family who lived here claimed they held in custody. The interior, should entry ever again become possible, has a couple of elaborately decorated rooms and a fine Moorish courtyard.

Capilla Real

The **Capilla Real** (Royal Chapel; daily March–Sept 10.30am–1pm & 4–7pm; Oct–Feb 11am–1pm & 3.30–6pm; 200ptas) is Granada's most impressive Christian building, flamboyant late Gothic in style and built ad hoc in the first decades of Christian rule as a mausoleum for *Los Reyes Católicos*, the city's "liberators". Isabel, in accordance with her will, was originally buried on the Alhambra hill (in the church of the San Francisco convent, now part of the *parador*) but her wealth and power proved no safeguard of her wishes; both her remains and those of her spouse Fernando, who died eleven years later in 1516, were removed here in 1522. Isabel's final indignity occurred in the 1980s, when the candle that she asked should perpetually illuminate her tomb was replaced by an electric bulb. But, as with Columbus's tomb in Sevilla, there is considerable doubt as to whether any of the remains in these lead coffins – so reverentially regarded by visiting Spaniards – are those of the monarchs at all. The chapel and tombs were desecrated by Napoleon's troops in 1812 and the coffins opened and defiled.

The monarchs' **tombs** are as simple as could be imagined: Fernando and Isabel, flanked by their daughter Joana ("the Mad") and her husband Felipe ("the Handsome"), rest in lead coffins placed in a plain crypt (the 'F' marking that of the king). Above them, however, is an elaborate Renaissance monument, with sculpted effigies of all four monarchs: the response of their grandson Carlos V to what he found "too small a room for so great a glory". The figures of Fernando and Isabel are easily identified by the rather puny-looking lion and lioness at their feet. Popular legend has it that Isabel's head sinks deeper into the pillow due to the weight of her intelligence compared with that of her husband; this is not without some truth as Fernando was never much more than a consort. Carved in Carrera marble by the Florentine Domenico Fancelli in 1517, the **side panels** depicting the Apostles and scenes from the life of Christ are especially fine. The Latin inscription at the monarchs' feet is brutally triumphalist in tone: "Overthrowers of the Mahometan sect and repressors of heretical stubborness." The tomb of Joana and Felipe is by Ordóñez, a much inferior work.

In front, dating from the same period, is an equally magnificent **reja**, or gilded grille, the work of Maestro Bartolomé of Jaén, and considered one of the finest in Spain. Its outstanding upper tier has scenes from the life of Christ and a crucifixion. The altar's striking **retablo** is by Felipe Vigarny dated 1522, depicting in one scene San Juan being boiled in oil; beneath the kneeling figures of Fernando and Isabel – possibly sculptures by Diego de Siloé – are images depicting events close to both their hearts, Boabdil surrendering the keys of Granada for him, the enforced baptism of the defeated Moors for her.

In the capilla's **Sacristy** are displayed the sword of Fernando, the crown of Isabel, and the banners used at the conquest of Granada. Also here is Isabella's outstanding personal collection of **medieval Flemish paintings** – including important works by Memling, Bouts and van der Weyden – and various Italian paintings, including panels by Botticelli and Pedro Berruguete.

The Cathedral

For all its stark Renaissance bulk, Granada's **Catedral**, adjoining the Capilla Real and entered from the door beside it (same hours and another 200ptas), is a disappointment. It was begun in 1521, just as the chapel was finished, but was then left uncompleted – like Málaga's *La Manquita* (the one armed lady) it still lacks a tower – until well into the eighteenth century. The main west façade by Diego de Siloé and Alonso Cano is worth a look, however. It has a provocative inscription glorifying Primo de Rivera, founder of the fascist Falange Party, added in the Franco period, and significantly for Granada today, never removed.

Inside, the church is pleasantly light and airy due to its painted stonework and twenty giant pillars which push the central dome to a height of over thirty metres. The Capilla Mayor has figures by Pedro de Mena of Fernando and Isabel at prayer, with, above them, oversize busts of Adam and Eve by Alonso Cano, who also left quite a bit of work in the other chapels.

In the eighteenth-century **Sagrario** there are more works by Cano as well as a fine *Crucifixion* by Montañes. If you have a fistful of coins, you can light up some of the chapels, too, revealing a triumphant sculpture of Santiago (St. James) in the saddle, by Pedro de Mena (Capilla de Santiago) and an El Greco *Saint Francis* (Capilla de Jesús Nazareno).

The University quarter: San Juan and San Jerónimo

Other of Granada's churches have, perhaps, rather more to offer than the cathedral and with sufficient interest you could easily fill a day of visits. The university quarter contains a couple of outstanding ones.

North of the cathedral, ten minutes' walk along c/San Jerónimo, the Renaissance **Hospital de San Juan de Dios** is well worth a visit. It was founded in 1552 by Juan de Robles (Juan de Dios) as a hospital for the sick and a refuge for foundlings, and its elaborate façade has a statue by Mora depicting the saint on his knees and holding a cross, which popular legend says is how he died. The hospital itself is still a going concern and you'll have to get by a sometimes grumpy porter who will allow you "cinco minutos" to view two marvellous **patios**. The outer and larger one is a beautiful double-tiered Renaissance work with a palm at each of its four corners and a fountain in the centre; the inner patio – with orange trees in the corners here – has delightful, but deteriorating, frescoes depicting the saint's miracles. Next door, the church, a Baroque addition, has a Churrigueresque *retablo* – a glittering, gold extravaganza by Guerrero.

Close by lies a little known jewel: the sixteenth-century **Convento de San Jerónimo** (open, not always on time, 10am–1.30pm & 4–7.30pm; 200ptas), founded by the Catholic monarchs, though built after their death. This has a further exquisite pair of Renaissance **patios** (or cloisters in this context), the largest an elegant work by Diego de Siloé with two tiers of thirty-six arches. The **church**, also by Siloé, has been wonderfully restored after use as cavalry barracks. It has fabulous eighteenth–century frescoes, another monumental carved and painted *retablo*, and, on either side of the altar monuments to "El Gran Capitán" Gonzalo de Córdoba and his wife Doña María. The remains of this general, responsible for many of the Catholic monarchs' victories, may lie in the vault beneath but the Napoleonic French were here too and, as Ford noted not much later, had "insulted the dead lion's ashes before whom, when alive, their ancestors had always fled." The church is little visited and on most days you'll probably have the place to yourself. In late afternoon you may hear the nuns singing their offices in the railed off choir loft above, and, if it's a feast day the altar will be filled with lilies, their fragrant perfume wafting through the church. A small shop at the entrance sells the convent's marmalade and *dulces*.

A short walk away along c/de la Duquesa and left into Plaza Universidad lies the **old University building** – now the Law faculty – founded by Carlos V with a Baroque portal flanked by twin barley-sugar pillars; no one minds if you step inside to view the patio. In the same square the eighteenth-century **Iglesia de Santos Justo y Pastor** has an impressive facade and, inside, an elaborately decorated cupola and retablo.

Just behind this church, with its entrance on c/San Jerónimo, the **Colegio de San Bartolomé y Santiago**, is a sixteenth-century university college with an elegant patio, off which is a students' cafetería which they don't mind sharing with visitors. Slightly further out, to the north along the Ancha de Capuchinos, the **Hospital Real** (open Mon–Fri 9am–2pm), a magnificent Renaissance building and formerly known as the Hospital de los Locos, was founded by the Catholic monarchs and finished by Carlos V. As its name implies, it was one of the first lunatic asylums in Europe, though it now houses the main library of the University of Granada. Its beautiful, arcaded patio is worth a look.

La Cartuja

Granada's **Cartuja** (Mon–Sat 10am–1pm & 4–7pm; Sun 10am–12noon & 4–7pm; 150ptas), on the north outskirts of town, is the grandest and most outrageously decorated of all the country's lavish Carthusian monasteries. On foot, it is a further ten to fifteen-minute walk beyond San Juan de Dios; alternatively, bus #8 going north along Gran Vía passes by.

The monastery was founded in 1516 on land provided by "El Gran Capitán", Gonzalo de Córdoba (see above), though the building is noted today for its heights of Churrigueresque-inspired Baroque extravagance – added, some say, to rival the Alhambra. The **church** is of staggering wealth, surmounted by an altar of twisted and coloured marble described by one Spanish writer as "a motionless architectural earthquake". There are Bocanegra paintings and a seventeenth-century sculpture of the *Assumption* by José de Mora.

The **sagrario** drips with more marble, jasper and porphyry and has a beautiful frescoed cupola by Antonio Palomino, while the **sacristía** pulls out yet more stops with another stunning painted cupola and features influenced by the art of the Aztec and Maya civilizations encountered in the New World. Here also are fine sculptures of *San Bruno* by José de Mora in a side niche, and an *Immaculada* by Alonso Cano.

Eating, drinking and nightlife

Granada is quite a sedate place, at least compared to Sevilla or Málaga, and if it weren't for the university, you sense the city would go unnaturally early to bed. However, on a brief stay, there's more than enough to entertain you, with some decent restaurants and plenty of animated bars, especially in the **Albaicín** quarter, whose streets make for enjoyable (if confusing) evening wanderings, around the **Campo del Principe**, a spacious square with outdoor eating and drinking, at the foot of the west slopes of the Alhambra hill, and along the Carrera del Darro.

LORCA'S GRANADA

One of the ghosts that walks Granada's streets and plazas is that of Andalucía's greatest poet and dramatist **Federico García Lorca**. He was born in 1898 at Fuente Vaqueros, a village in the *Vega,* the fertile plain to the west of the city, and moved to Granada eleven years later; this childhood spent growing up on the family farm, where he soaked up both the countryside and the folklore of its people, was to have an enduring influence on his work.

Lorca published his first book of essays and poems while still at university in Granada, in 1918. It was in 1928, however, aged thirty, that he came to national prominence with *El Romancero Gitano*, an anthology of gypsy ballads. This success led to a trip to New York in 1929 where he spent a year ostensibly at Columbia University learning English, but actually gathering material for the collection of poems, *Poeta in Nueva York*, published after his death.

He returned to Spain in 1931 at the advent of the Spanish Republic. It was a time of great optimism and Lorca was given a government grant to run a travelling theatre group, *La Barraca* (the cabin), taking drama to the people. From this period the poet's major works for the stage – *Bodas de Sangre* (Blood Wedding) and *Yerma* – emerged.

In July 1936, on the eve of the Civil War, Lorca went back to Granada for the summer. It was the eve of Franco's coup and control of the city was wrested by the Falangists, who initiated a reign of terror. Lorca, as a Republican sympathizer and declared homosexual was hunted down by fascist thugs at the house of a friend, now the *Hotel Reina Cristina*. Two days later he was brutally murdered in an olive grove near to the village of Viznar, in the hills to the east of the city. His body has never been found.

It has taken the city a long time to accord Lorca the recognition he deserves, partly because of his sexual inclinations, and mainly through guilt concerning the way he died. Should you have an interest in tracing the locations of his life, both in Granada and around, the most important are detailed below. More avid followers will want to get hold of the excellent *Lorca's Granada* by Ian Gibson, his biographer.

Huerta de San Vicente

West of the centre is the **Huerta de San Vicente**, an orchard where the poet's family used to spend the summer months. It spreads back from c/de la Virgen Blanca, behind the *Los Jardines Neptuno flamenco* night club; to get there it's easiest to take a taxi.

The **house** – now completely restored – has been set in the centre of what is set to become the largest rose garden in Europe, the **Parque Federico García Lorca**, the city's belated tribute. When the Lorcas had it, the five-acre holding was planted with vegetables and fruit trees. Then a tranquil rural plot on the city's edge, it has since been enveloped by ugly urban sprawl and it's hard to square the scene today with the poet's description of a "paradise of trees and water and so much jasmine and nightshade in the garden that we all wake up with lyrical headaches." The house is presently closed to visitors but plans are in progress to open it as a museum. Rooms contain some of their original furniture including, in Lorca's bedroom, his work table, a poster of the *Barraca* theatre company and the balcony looking towards the Sierra Nevada, which inspired one of his best-known poems, *Despedida* (Farewell):

Si muero, dejad el balcón abierto.
El niño come naranjas. (Desde mi balcón lo veo.)
El segador siega el trigo. (Desde mi balcón lo siento.)
Si muero, dejad el balcon abierto!

If I die, leave the balcony open.
The child eats oranges. (From my balcony I see him.)
The harvester scythes the corn. (From my balcony I hear him.)
If I die leave the balcony open!

If you don't get admitted to the house, you can see the balcony – the centre one of three – on the east wall.

Fuente Vaqueros

> *In this village I dreamt my first ambitious dreams. In this village one day I will merge*
> *with the earth and flowers...*

Lorca's birthplace in the solid farming village of **FUENTE VAQUEROS**, 17km west of Granada is the site of the **Lorca Museum** (Tue–Sun 10am–1pm & 5–7pm; guided visits on the hour; 200ptas; ☎958/516453). The house lies just off the village's main square on c/ Poeta Garcia Lorca. Now a charming shrine to Lorca's memory and watched over by the amiable director Juan De Loxa (a poet himself), the museum is stuffed with Lorca memorabilia, manuscripts and personal effects. It also has a fleeting video fragment of Lorca on tour with the *Teatro Barraca* – the only piece of cinema film to capture the poet and his engaging smile.

After you have seen the house, pay a visit to the parish church at the end of the street opposite, where Lorca's mother took him regularly as a child. Although the church has been heavily reconstructed since, the old stone font where Lorca – or "Federico" as he is known to all the world here – was baptized, can still be seen.

From Granada, **buses** operated by *Ureña* run to the village from the Avda. de Andaluces fronting the train station; the weekday outward service leaves on the hour (except 10am) from eight in the morning, with the return also hourly from Fuente Vaqueros; it's a twenty-minute trip. If you want **to stay** there's a friendly *hostal* at c/Ancha Escualas 11, (☎958/516348; ③) next to the church, and a decent place **to eat**, *Restaurante Genil*, on the outskirts of the village on the Chauchina road.

Viznar and Lorca's death

The village of Viznar, 10km northeast of Granada, in the foothills of the Sierra Nevada, will always be linked to the assassination of Lorca in August, 1936. After his arrest in Granada by the Fascist insurgents, Lorca was taken to Viznar – along with hundreds of others during the reign of terror – and held for two days at a farmhouse called La Colonia before being taken to a *barranco*, a bleak gully nearby, where he was shot. A poem of Lorca's seemed eerily prescient about his own end:

> *... I realized I had been murdered.*
> *They searched cafés and cemeteries and churches,*
> *they opened barrels and cupboards,*
> *they plundered three skeletons to remove their gold teeth.*
> *They did not find me.*
> *They never found me?*
> *No. They never found me.*

From the centre of the village – the Falangist headquarters were in the eighteenth-century archbishop's palace behind the fountain – take the road out towards La Fuente Grande. You will pass the site of **La Colonia** (later demolished), which stood on a bend, near to a whitewalled cottage. From here, the road curves around the valley to the **Parque Federico García Lorca**, an ugly monumental garden marking the *barranco* and honouring all the Civil War dead. Climb the steps to the garden and veer left: the site of Lorca's murder was here, beneath a solitary olive tree. After the killing – he was shot with three others – a young gravedigger threw the bodies into a narrow trench. The supposed site is marked by a granite memorial.

Viznar is served by **bus** from Granada's Arco de Elvira terminal (near Plaza Nueva) at 7.30am, 2.15pm and 8pm, with the return buses at 7am, 8am, 4pm and 7.30pm. The village also has a superb new **youth hostel** (☎958/543307), complete with swimming pool which is open to all.

Restaurants

Good value restaurants and *comedores* are to be found all over Granada, and there are a number of places worth paying a bit more for, too. Beware, of course, the inevitable tourist traps, particularly around the Plaza Nueva.

ALBAICÍN

El Ladrillo II, Placeta de Fatima – close to El Salvador church. This specializes in *barcos* (boats) of fried fish, served at economical prices on tables beneath the stars. All of which make the climb worthwhile.

Restaurante "La Luz es como el Agua", c/Cruz de Asqueros 3 – two blocks northeast of Plaza del Triunfo. A gorgeous little Belgian-run restaurant, with lavishly prepared food. It is right on the edge of the Albaicín, down towards the train station. **Bar La Mancha Chica**, c/Nueva de San Nicolas 1 – a little way down from the *mirador*. A cheap and simple place with an outdoor terrace serving *platos combinados*.

Mirador de Morayma, c/Pianista García Carrillo 2 – east of El Salvador. To experience a true Albaicín *carmen* (villa and garden), with a fine view of the Alhambra, you could not do better than dine at this *granadino* kitchen. House specialities include (naturally) *tortilla de Sacromonte*, whilst the desserts are made by the sisters at the Convento de Santa Catalina de Zafra below. Cheap it isn't, but for what you're getting here the *menú* is fine value.

Cafetin La Porrona, Plaza Larga. A welcoming neighbourhood restaurant with a *menú economico*, and pleasant dining room decorated with *corrida* and *flamenco* posters, plus photos of regulars, including author Ian Gibson.

CATHEDRAL AREA

Restaurante Abenhamar, c/Abenhamar 6 – off c/Reyes Católicos. A pleasant mid-priced restaurant offering *granadino* cooking with a good value *menú*; the *sopa ajo granadino* (garlic soup) and *lenguado de la casa* (sole) are specialities.

Al-Faquara, c/Calder ía Nueva – just off c/Elvira. Juices, teas and crêpes to the accompaniment of classical music.

Al Jaima, c/Caldería Nueva 15. A great little place serving take-away *cous-cous* on the door or in their cosy diner upstairs.

Mesón Andaluz, c/Elvira 10. A pleasant, slightly pricey restaurant with a renowned *fritura mixta* (fried fish platter).

Cafetería-Restaurante La Riviera, c/Cettimeriem 5. Features a decent *menú económico*, including a vegetarian option.

Naturi Albaicin, c/Caldería Nueva 10. Imaginative veggie cooking – fine salads, spinach-stuffed mushrooms and the like – served up with New Age music and green magazines. Take tea or coffee after at the hippie-kitsch teahouse opposite.

Nueva Bodega, c/Cettimeriem 3 – off Gran Vía. Good value local *bodega*.

Patio Andaluz, Escudo del Carmen 10 – off Plaza del Carmen. Not much to shout about on the gastronomic front but one of the cheapest *menús* in town.

Bar-Restaurante Sevilla, c/Oficios 12 – opposite the entrance to the Capilla Real. One of the few surviving pre-war restaurants from the old Granada. It's steeped in literary history and Lorca spent many happy hours here. There's also a great *tapas* bar and, in the evenings, tables outside with a view of the Capilla. The famous *tortilla del Sacromonte* is a house speciality and their 2,500 ptas *menú* is recommended.

PLAZAS BIB-RAMBLA AND TRINIDAD

Casa Cepillo, Plaza Pescadería 8. Cheap *comedor* with an excellent *menú*; the soups are especially good here.

Restaurante-Marisquería Cunini, Plaza Pescadería 14 – a marketplace linking the two squares. This gleaming, marble-topped bar serves standing customers with superb fish *tapas* and *raciones* and has a pricier small restaurant behind.

Bar Ferroviaria, c/Lavadero Tablas 1 – off c/Tablas (open 2–4.30pm & 8–10pm). This is in fact a Railway Pensioners' club but don't let that put you off, for behind the anonymous exterior you'll find an amazingly cheap *menú* which attracts workers and students for miles around; if the *paella* is on, it's your lucky day.

PICNIC SNACKS

It's hard to beat a picnic in the Generalife gardens, and putting one together is not a problem.

Plaza Pescadería has a daily fruit and vegetable market, while the main covered **Mercado** is along c/San Agustín, north of the Cathedral. For natural/Moroccan/traditional Spanish groceries try **c/Caldería Nueva**, just off c/Elvira: the street's entire length is a bonanza for such goods, and there's an excellent health food store, *La Tienda*, at no. 8.

If you want ready-made **snacks**, pizza by weight, croissants and pies are sold at *Croissanterie la Petite*, opposite Plaza del Carmen (corner of c/Salamanca), and for the homesick there's a *Cookie Man* stall on Puerta Real. For **cakes and pastries**, *Pastelería Flor y Nata*, c/Mesones 15 (north of the Puerta Real) will lead you drooling into temptation; they have another branch at Avda. de la Constitución 15.

Restaurante Los Reyes, c/Buensuceso 9 – west side of Plaza Trinidad. A wonderful neighbourhood restaurant serving *granadino* specialities; excellent value with an economical *menú* and great seafood *tapas* at the bar.

Café-Bar El Rocío, c/Sillería 4 – off Plaza Trinidad. A bustling, friendly and inexpensive place specializing in *pollo asado con patatas* (chicken and chips).

PLAZA DEL CARMEN AREA

El Amir, c/General Narváez 3 – west along c/Recogidas from Puerta Real and off to the right. A fairly pricey Arab restaurant with delicious *hummus* and *falafel*, and dishes made of rice and ground meat with pine nuts and cinnamon.

El Mesón, Plaza Campos 2 – just behind the *Ayuntamiento*. A classy medium-priced restaurant good for *granadino* specialities such as *habas y jamón* (beans and ham).

Restaurante Nuevo, c/Navas 25. Good budget restaurant.

ALHAMBRA

Parador de San Francisco, Alhambra. The *parador's* restaurant has incredible views and offers a varied and not-too-bank-breaking *menú*; *a la carte*, though, is another story.

Tapas and drinking bars

Granada's proximity to the Sierra Nevada brings a coolness to the city which carries over into its imbibing and its nightlife. In the bars here you're just as likely to find locals ordering a glass of *Rioja* as soon as the beloved *fino* of the rest of Andalucía. One local wine which the *granadinos* do cherish, though (and which you shouldn't miss), is *vino de la costa* (coast wine – ironically made in the mountains of the Alpujarras); amber in colour, fairly potent, but relatively easy on hangovers, it's the ideal partner for a *tapa*.

The **bars** recommended below are mainly for drinking, though most serve *tapas* and you could happily fill up and forget about restaurant fare. The city has quite a reputation for its *tapas*, which are more elaborate than is usual in Andalucía.

PLAZA NUEVA AND CATHEDRAL AREA

Bodegas Castañeda, corner of c/Elvira and c/Almireceros – across Gran Vía from the cathedral. This is one of the city's oldest bars, though, alas, refurbished and prettified. Still, it makes an attractive first stop of an evening.

Bodegas La Mancha, c/Joaquin Costa – around the corner from *Bodegas Castañeda*. A monumental spit-and-sawdust establishment hung with hams, and with great wine vats stationed behind the bar like rockets on a launch pad. The ruddy-featured (and often boisterous) clientele here are kept in check by the taciturn bar staff; when there's football on TV it's something to behold. A stand-up place, it also has great *tapas* including *jamón serrano*.

Casa Enrique, Acera de Darro 8 – Puerta Real end. A good daytime or early evening haunt with a wide *tapas* selection.

Casa Julio, c/Hermosa – off Plaza Nueva. A boozers' bar that nonetheless turns out some excellent seafood *tapas*.

Café-Bar Oliver, Plaza Pescadería 12. A fine *tapas* bar.

Bar Reca, Plaza de la Trinidad – corner with c/Infantes. A good *tapas* bar on a leafy square which fairly hums at lunchtime and in the early evening.

El Rincon de Guijuelo, c/Rosario 12 – on Plaza Campos. A lunchtime and early evening stop for fans of *jamón serrano* and *fino*, both served up with style; the *bocadillo iberico* filled with the best *pata negra jamón* is recommended.

Bar Sabanilla, c/San Sebastian 14 – not easy to find, just east of the Plaza Bib-Rambla, down a passage way behind an unmarked door. This bar claims to be the oldest in Granada (it certainly looks it) and it is one of the few in the central area that stays open really late. It's a basic, poky place, run by two women who offer a free *tapa* with every drink. The barrelled *costa* wine here (from the Alpujarra village of Albondón) is recommended.

La Trastienda, c/Cuchilleros 11 – on a small plaza just off c/Reyes Católicos. A plush little drinking den hidden behind a shop selling wine, cheese and *jamón serrano*. Once you've negotiated your way around the counter it's surprisingly cosy in the back. Up the steps behind, *Café Alhaljibe* has minimalist decor, loud music and a younger crowd.

CAMPO DEL PRINCIPE, CARRERA DEL DARRO AND ALBAICÍN

Bar Amparo, Campo del Principe 18. One of the best bars on this ever-popular square, with fine *tapas* to wash down with *manzanilla* and *fino*.

En un lugar del Alhambra, Carrera del Darro 51. One of the most attractive bars on this street, which follows the river gorge dividing the Alhambra hill from the Albaicín. *Puerta del Vino*, further along, is another good stopover, catering for a trendier crowd, while further along still is *Pie de la Vela*, a women-only bar.

Bar Lara, Plaza San Miguel Bajo. A fine bar which puts out tables on this picturesque Albaicín square, serving *platos combinados* and an excellent *costa* wine.

Café-Bar Ocaña, Plaza del Realejo 1 – north of Campo del Principe. A bustling neighbourhood bar serving great *bocadillos* with a very spicey *tomate* relish.

Paseo de los Tristes (aka Paseo del Padre Manjon). This is a plaza – at the far end of Carrera del Darro – and a wonderful place to sit out at night with a drink and look up at the illuminated battlements. There are several bars and the city council often puts on concerts here during the summer.

Calle Panederos. This Albaicín street, near the church of El Salvador, has a number of drinking places.

UNIVERSITY AREA

C/Gran Capitán, c/San Juan de Dios and c/Pedro Antonio de Alarcón. If you want to go on drinking through the early hours, head out to these streets in the student area round the university. A promising place to start is *Los Girasoles* at c/San Juan de Dios 2538.

La Sal, c/Marqués de Falces – off Gran Vía. Women only bar.

Breakfast and ice cream

Granada's **breakfast bars** set the city up for work in the mornings and to watch the best of them dishing up *pan tostada, chocolate* and *cafés exprés* with production-line efficiency is an entertainment in itself. The show begins all over town around 8am and lasts around an hour. You'll soon spot the best places – they're packed – but a personal favourite is *Café Bib-Rambla* on the plaza of the same name. Late or early travellers might appreciate *Café Bar Ochando*, by the train station on Avda. de los Andaluces, open 24 hours and serving a good breakfast.

One of the best places in town for **ice-cream** is *La Perla* (Plaza Nueva 16) where all of Granada seems to get their nocturnal ice cream scoops. The *Café Football Heladería*, Plaza Maria Pineda (near Puerta Real), is another pleasant place with tables on the square; they also do good breakfast *churros* here.

Discobares and discotecas

Conventional **discotecas** aren't too popular with the restrained *granadinos* though the university guarantees a bit of action during term time, and there are, as everywhere in Spain, a fair scattering of **discobares** – drinking bars with loud sound systems, trendy decor and clientele.

Berlín and **Espacio Abierto**, c/Obispo Hurtado – west of Plaza Trinidad. Two *discobares* with *moda* sounds and decor.

Camborio, Sacromonte. A newly fashionable *discobar*.

Entresuelo, c/Azacayas – off Gran Vía. Popular *discobar* frequented by English-language teachers.

La Estrella, c/Cuchilleros – near Plaza Nueva. A central *discobar*.

Granada 10, c/Carcel Baja 10 – off Gran Vía near the cathedral. A small but central disco.

Oh! Granada, c/Dr Guirao (no number – it's at the near end of this street leading to the Plaza de Toros). The city's largest disco has three dance floors and plenty of strobes.

Patapalo, c/Naranjos 2 – behind Plaza del Carmen. Stylish *discobar*.

Planta Baja, Carril del Picón – north off c/Obispo Hurtado. A long-established *discobar* now in a new home.

Sacromonte caves. When the university is in session, the line of caves just above the Casa del Chapiz are turned into discos. They're always packed out at weekends and generally fun.

Live music, theatre and dance

Like many cities of Andalucía, Granada lays claim to the roots of **flamenco**, though you'd hardly believe it from the travesties dished up these days in the gypsy quarter of Sacromonte (see box on p.327). The *"flamenco* shows" on offer in the city aren't much better, either, being geared firmly to tourism. However, up in the Albaicín there is one genuine club (see below), with consistently good artists and an audience of aficionados.

Generally more rewarding are the **festivals** held throughout the year, such as the city's Theatre Festival at the end of May or the International Music and Dance Festival at the end of June, during which you may just be lucky enough to see a performance under the stars in the Alhambra. Other **concerts** by folk, rock and *flamenco* artistes are staged throughout the year in locations such as the **Corral del Carbón** or Moorish patios in the Albaicín. Check listings in the local daily paper *Ideal* or the weekly *El Faro*, or ask the Turismo what's on.

FLAMENCO

Los Jardines Neptuno, junction of c/Arabial and c/Virgen Blanca – 2km southeast of the centre. Long-established *flamenco* theatre which in summer is a tourist trap; in the winter months it is more like the Real McCoy.

Peña Platería, Patio de los Aljives 13, Albaicín (closed August). This is a private club devoted to the celebration of Andalucía's great folk art. *Flamenco* is performed most nights, and visitors are generally welcomed, so long as they show a genuine interest and aren't in too large a group. You'll need to speak some Spanish and use a bit of charm.

JAZZ

Club de Musica, c/de las Moras 2, just above the Puerta Real (☎224126). Live jazz is often performed here but ring ahead before turning up.

Listings

Airport Handles domestic flights to Madrid and Barcelona; details from *Iberia* (☎227592).

Banks Numerous banks and cash points are available along c/Reyes Católicos and Gran Vía.

Bicycle rental Try *Pedal Moto*, c/Albhaca 1 – at the eastern end of the Camino de Ronda, across the Genil (☎132154), or *Taller Manolo* c/Manuel de Falla 12, south of Puerta Real.

Books/Newspapers *Librería Continental*, Puerta Real, and *Librería Atlantida*, Gran Vía 9, both have wide selections of books, including a good array on aspects of Granada.

Bullfights are held in season at the Plaza de Toros, Avda del Doctor Olóriz.

Buses/trains See "Arrival" for details and addresses of the various bus terminals. For train times and tickets the RENFE office at c/Reyes Católicos 63 (☎227170) will save you a trek out to the station.

Camping equipment *Armeria*, c/Mesones 53 (near Plaza Trinidad), stocks a range of camping and hiking gear.

Car removals If your car disappears it's probably been hauled away from an illegal parking spot by the *Grúa* (tow-truck). Phone (☎816051) and prepare to pay.

Car rental *Atesa*, Plaza Cuchilleros 1, off Plaza Nueva (☎224004), have reasonable deals with national back-up.

Hiking maps for the Sierra Nevada and Las Alpujarras can be obtained from the Turismo, though for a wider selection try the *Librería Dauro* at c/Zacatín 3 (a pedestrian street between the cathedral and c/Reyes Católicos). The *CNIG* (National Geographic Institute), c/Divina Pastora 7, near the eastern end of Gran Vía, also sells 1:50,000 and 1:25,000 maps.

Hospital Cruz Roja, c/Escoriaza 8, (☎222222) or Hospital Clinico San Cecilio, Avda. Dr. Olóriz, near the Plaza de Toros; (☎270200). For advice on emergency treatment ☎282000.

Police For emergencies ☎091. The Policía Nacional station is in Plaza Campos, close to Plaza Mariana Pineda. Lost and found section ☎248103.

Post Office Puerta Real; open daily until 9pm, Sat 9am–2pm.

Sierra Nevada If you plan to drive in the mountains outside the safe period of July and August, information on road conditions is available in English on ☎480153.

Ski information General information for the Sierra Nevada is available on ☎249100.

Swimming Pool The Jardines Neptuno, junction c/Arabial and c/Virgen Blanca (west of the centre), has an Olympic-size pool, kids' pool and restaurant.

Telephones The main *telefónica* is at c/Reyes Católicos 55 (Mon–Sat 9am–2pm & 5–10pm).

West towards Málaga: Alhama de Granada

Travelling from Granada to Málaga by bus will take you along the fast but dull N342, which crosses the *Vega* to the west of the city. With your own transport and time to spare, a more interesting and scenic route passes through the delightful but little visited town of **Alhama de Granada** and traverses the spectacular **Zafarraya Pass**, descending into Málaga by way of the ruggedly beautiful **Axarquia** region.

Leave Granada by the route for the airport, the N323 – but avoid the *autovía*. The road branches right at Armilla, 4km southwest of the city, where you should take the C340, past the village of **Malá** (which has a fine roadside inn), and, 10km beyond, **Ventas de Huelma**. From here the road twists and climbs into the Sierra de Pera and, after descending to the lakeside village of **Poblado del Embalse**, continues through a rich landscape of bubbling streams and rocky gulches overlooked by hills planted with olives, to Alhama de Granada, 14km further.

Alhama de Granada

Scenically sited along along a ledge overlooking a broad gorge or *tajo* created by the Río Alhama, the spa town of **ALHAMA DE GRANADA** is one of the unsung gems of Granada province and makes a wonderful overnight stop. It has a number of striking churches in a well preserved old quarter, and its baths, dating back to Roman and Moorish times (*Al Hamma* in Arabic means "hot springs") still draw in numerous visitors during the season to take the waters. They were greatly treasured during Moorish times, and the Spanish expression of regret – "¡Ay di mi Alhama!" – was the cry of sorrow attributed to Abu al-Hacen (the Mulhacen after whom the Sierra Nevada peak is named) when he lost the town in a crucial battle here against the Christian forces in 1482. It was this loss that severed the vital link between Granada and Málaga (and hence North Africa), foreshadowing the end of eight centuries of Moorish rule.

RICHARD FORD AND THE *HANDBOOK FOR SPAIN*

Very few books have been written about Spain that do not draw on **Richard Ford** and his 1845 *Murray's Handbook for Spain* – arguably the best, the funniest and the most encyclopaedic guidebook ever written on any country.

Born in 1796 into a family of means, Ford studied law but never practised and in 1824 married Harriet Capel, the attractive daughter of the Earl of Essex. When she received medical advice to seek a warmer climate for her health, Ford – inspired by Irving's recent publication of the *Conquest of Granada* – took his family off to Spain where they lived for three years, wintering in Sevilla and spending the summers living in part of the Alhambra in Granada.

Ford spent most of his time traversing the length and breadth of the country – but particularly Andalucía – on horseback, making notes and sketches (his mother had been a skilled amateur artist). It's hard to believe that all this was not meant for some literary purpose, but it was only back in England – and six years after his return – when publisher John Murray asked him to recommend someone to write a Spanish travel guide, that Ford suggested himself.

His marriage now broken, he settled down in a Devon village in a house to which he added many Spanish features (including some souvenirs from the Alhambra) to work solidly for nearly five years on what became the *Handbook for Spain*. When Murray and others took exception to the final manuscript's often caustic invective, he was advised to tone it down and a revised – but still gloriously outspoken – edition finally appeared in 1845 to great acclaim. Curiously, although he became *the* resident expert on Spain he never returned to the country which had put him on the literary map.

Ford's blind spots, such as British prejudice against Baroque architecture (the more extravagant styles of which he dismissed as "vile Churrigueresque") are often irritating, and High Tory attitudes sometimes verging on jingoism, added to a splenetic Francophobia, often threaten to tip over into the worst kind of churlishness. However, the author's enduring fascination with Spain and all things Spanish – he personally introduced *amontillado* sherry and Extremaduran *jamón serrano* into England – allied to a crisp writing style and a dry wit, invariably save him, and some of his passages are still hilariously funny and related with a wry irony.

His description of the hostelry at Alhama is typical:

"The *Posada* at Alhama, albeit called *La Grande*, is truly iniquitous; diminutive indeed are the accommodations, colossal the inconveniences; but this is a common misnomer, *en las cosas de España*. Thus Philip IV was called El Grande, under whose fatal rule Spain crumbled into nothing; like a ditch he became greater in proportion as more land was taken away. All who are wise will bring from Málaga a good hamper of eatables, a bota of wine, and some cigars, for however devoid of creature comforts this grand hotel, there is a grand supply of creeping creatures, and the traveller runs risk of bidding adieu to sleep, and passing the night exclaiming, *Ay! de mi Alhama*."

Settlement started here much earlier, however, and the ancient Iberian town on the site was referred to by the Romans as *Artigi*.

The Town

Most of Alhama's sights are within a short walk of Plaza de la Constitución, the main square fronted by bars and restaurants. At the square's southern end there's a ruined and now privately owned **Moorish castle** with the unfortunate addition of nineteenth-century crenellated battlements. To the right of this, the sixteenth– to eighteenth–century **Iglesia del Carmen** is Alhama's prettiest church, overlooking the **Tajo** and fronted by an old fountain where the farmers water their donkeys on sultry summer evenings. A little further down on the right, on Paseo de Montes Jovellar, is a friendly local library which doubles up as the **Turismo**, and can provide maps and information.

To reach the other monuments you'll need to backtrack slightly to c/Baja Iglesia which leads up to Plaza los Presos, passing en route (up a ramp to the left) the **Casa de la Inquisición**, which may have nothing to do with the Inquisition at all, but is noted for a fine Plateresque façade. The town's main church, **La Encarnación**, dominates the pleasant little square with a central fountain. Donated by Fernando and Isabel after the conquest of the town from the Moors, it was completed in the first half of the sixteenth century by some of the major architects of the time – among them Enrique Egas and Diego de Siloé, the designers of the Capilla Real and cathedral at Granada. Siloé was responsible for the striking and massive Renaissance belfry which towers above the town. The restrained interior has an impressive *artesonado* ceiling and the sacristia has fifteenth-century vestments with embroidery attributed to Isabel herself.

Opposite the church, on the same square, there's an ancient **posito** (granary) dating from the thirteenth century but incorporating parts of an earlier synagogue. Leaving the square to the right of the church along c/Alta Iglesia takes you past the misleadingly named **Casa Romana** on the right, an eighteenth-century mansion believed to have been constructed on the site of a Roman villa. The same street returns to the Plaza Mayor.

The only other sites of note are some Neolithic caves and a **Roman bridge** at the edge of the town, close to the C340 to Granada. A few hundred metres beyond this are the **baths** which give the town its name. Although little remains of the Roman baths seen by Ford in the last century, elements of the Moorish *hammam* survive and can be seen by enquiring at the *Hotel Balneario* whose staff will conduct you into the depths to see some astonishing Moorish arches and the odd stone inscribed in Latin.

Practicalities

On the **accommodation** front things have improved immeasurably since Ford was here (see p.339) and the dreaded *La Grande* is no more. If you want to stay, outside August there's usually no problem fixing up a room at one of Alhama's two *hostales*. The best one, *Hostal San José*, Plaza de la Constitución 27 (☎958/350156; ③), is right on the main square whilst the cheaper *Pensión Ana* (☎953/350382; ①) is at Carretera de Granada 4 in the less attractive lower town behind the petrol station. A more upmarket option is the spa hotel *Balneario de Granada* (☎958/350011; ④), at the baths on the road into town from Granada.

Meals are available from a couple of restaurants on the main square, the *Pensión Ana* and the *Hotel Balneario*. There's also a **swimming pool** with shade just out of town along the Málaga road.

Towards the Zafarraya Pass

South of Alhama, the C335 climbs out towards Ventas de Zafarraya, cutting through a rich agricultural area where tomatoes, cereals and other vegetables are planted in deep brown soil. The spectacular **Zaffaraya Pass** which slips through a cleft in the Sierra de Tejeda and was part of the old coach route provides a dramatic entrance into the Axarquia region of Málaga province, with superb views to the distant Mediterranean.

Around 6km beyond the pass lies the deserted medieval village of **Zalía** (see p.83), after which the road continues to **Velez-Málaga** (see p.80) and the coast.

The Sierra Nevada

South from Granada rise the mountains of the **SIERRA NEVADA**, a startling backdrop to the city, snowcapped for most of the year and offering skiing from November until late May. The ski slopes are at **Solynieve**, an unimaginative, developed resort just

---

SIERRA NEVADA FLORA AND FAUNA

The Sierra Nevada is particularly rich in **wild flowers**. Some fifty varieties are unique to these mountains, among them five gentians, including *Gentiana bory*, the pansy *Viola nevadensis*, a shrubby mallow *Lavatera oblongifolia*, and a spectacular honeysuckle, the seven to ten metre high *Lonicera arborea*.

Wildlife, too, abounds away from the roads. One of the most exciting sights is the *Cabra hispanica*, a wild horned goat which you'll see standing on pinnacles, silhouetted against the sky. They roam the mountains in flocks and jump up the steepest slopes with amazing agility when they catch the scent of the walker on the wind. The higher slopes are also home to a rich assortment of **butterflies**, among them the rare Nevada Blue as well as varieties of Fritillary. **Bird-watching** is also superb, with the colourful hoopoe – a bird with a stark, haunting cry – a common sight.

30km away (40min by bus). Here, except in July and August, the direct car route across the range stops, but from this point walkers can make the three-hour trek up to **Veleta** (3470m), the second highest peak of the range (see overpage).

Before the road was constructed in the 1920s few *granadinos* ever came up to the sierra, but one group who had worn out a trail since the times of the Moors were the *neveros* or icemen, who used mules to bring down blocks of ice from the mountains, which they then sold in the streets. Their route to Veleta can still be followed beyond the village of **Monachil**, to the south-east of the city, which has, incidentally, a good little restaurant, the *Venta Bienvenido*. The GR420 road, though, has been a mixed blessing for the delicate ecosystem of the Sierra and the expanding horrors of the Solynieve ski centre threaten even more ecological damage as it prepares to host the 1995 World Ski Championships.

The best **map** of the Sierra Nevada and of the lower slopes of the Alpujarras is the one co-produced by the *Instituto Geográfico Nacional* and the *Federación Española de Montañismo* (1:50,000), generally available in Granada.

Solynieve and the Capileria road

Throughout the year *Autocares Bonal* runs a **daily bus** from Granada to the Solynieve resort and, just above this, to the *Parador de Sierra Nevada*. The bus leaves from the Palacio de Congresos (Paseo del Violon) across the Río Genil, east of the centre, at 9am, returning from the *parador* at 5pm (and passing Solynieve 10 minutes later). Bus #3 going east along Gran Vía will drop you near the Palacio stop if you don't want to walk from the centre, and tickets can be bought in advance from *Bar El Ventorrillo* next door.

The route leaves Granada via the Paseo del Salon where two wagons stand as a memory to the tram-service which, from the 1920s until 1970, used to ascend as far as Güejar Sierra. Beyond Pinos de Genil the road begins to climb seriously and – with your own transport – you could make a stop at the **Balcón de Canales** with fine views over the Río Genil and its dam. After 30km the ski resort of **Solynieve** appears.

Solynieve

SOLYNIEVE is a hideous-looking ski resort – worse than usual – and regarded by serious Alpine skiers as something of a joke. But with snow lingering so late in the year (Granada's Turismo should be able to advise on the state of this, and on accommodation, or you could contact the *Federación Andaluz de Esquí*, Paseo de Ronda 78, ☎958/250706), it has obvious attractions. At least you can have fun. From the middle of the resort a lift takes you straight up to the main ski lift, which provides access to most of the higher **slopes**, and when the snow is right you can ski a few kilometres back down to the *zona hotelera* (the lifts run only when there's skiing). There are plenty of places to rent gear.

The cheapest **place to stay** is the *Albergue Universitario* (☎958/480122; ③ half board) at Peñones de San Francisco, just off the main road, towards the *parador*. The bus turns around at the *Parador Sierra Nevada* (☎958/480200; ⑤), which is modern and less elaborate and expensive than most.

The Capileira road, Veleta and Mulhacen

In summer the bleak, cluttered landscape of the ski resort is good to leave behind. From the *parador* the **Capileira-bound road** runs past the **peak of Veleta**; the dirt surface is perfectly walkable even when it's closed to cars and in summer an enterprising roadside vendor dispenses gin and tonic midway from a bucket of snow.

The bus normally turns around at the *parador* but if enough people are interested the drivers will continue closer to the trailhead for Veleta (200ptas supplement). The **ascent of Veleta** is a scramble rather than a climb but should only be attempted in July or August unless you're properly geared up; allow a good three hours for the trek up from where the bus drops you, two hours down.

In **July and August**, when the unsurfaced road is open to traffic (it is snowbound the rest of the year), you can drive on to **Capileira** (see "Las Alpujarras" following). This is practicable in an ordinary car but be warned that it's an arduous and occasionally spine-tingling drive on a shocking road. With a great deal of energy you could conceivably walk the same route, though it's a good 30km, there's nothing along the way, and this being the highest motorable pass in Europe, temperatures drop pretty low by late afternoon.

En route, an hour beyond Veleta, you pass just under **Mulhacén** – the tallest peak on the Iberian peninsula at 3481m. The climb is two hours of exposed and windy ridge-crawling from the road, and with a sudden, sheer drop on its northwest face. There is a gentler slope down to the Siete Lagunas valley to the east.

Ruta de los Tres Mil (High Peaks Traverse)

The classic *Ruta Integral de los Tres Mil*, a complete traverse of all the Sierra's peaks over 3000m high, starts in Jeres del Marquesado on the north side of the Sierra Nevada (due south of Guadix) and finishes in Lanjarón, in the Alpujarras. It's an exhausting **three to four day itinerary** – four unless you're an active and experienced climber. Taking four days, entails overnight stays near Puntal de Vacares, in the Siete Lagunas valley noted above, at the *Refugio Félix Méndez* and at the Cerro de Caballo hut. Slightly shorter, and more practicable, variations involve a start from the Vadillo refuge in the Estrella valley (northwest of Vacares), or from Trevélez in the Alpujarras, and a first overnight at Siete Lagunas.

Whichever way you choose, be aware that the section between Veleta and Elorrieta calls for rope, an ice axe (and crampons before June) and good scrambling skills. (There is another difficult section between Peñón Colorado and Cerro de Caballo.) If you're not up to this, it is possible to **detour** round the Veleta–Elorrieta section, but you will end up on the ridge flanking the Lanjarón river valley on the east rather than on the west; here there is a single cement hut, the *Refugio Forestal*, well-placed for the final day's walk to Lanjarón.

For **any exploration of the Sierra Nevada**, it is essential to take a tent, proper gear and ample food. It's a serious mountain and you should be prepared for the eventuality of not being able to reach or find the huts (which are marked correctly on the 1:50,000 map), or the weather turning nasty.

An approach from Trevélez

The full *Ruta de los Tres Mil* is probably more than most walkers – even hardy trekkers – would want to attempt. A modified version, starting in Trevélez (see "Las Alpujarras" section) and ending in Lanjarón, with the detour noted above, is a bit easier – though still strenuous.

Ascending Mulhacén from Trevélez is going to take a full six hours up one way, four hours down – assuming that you do not get lost or rest (both unlikely) and that there is no snowpack on Mulhacén's east face (equally unlikely until July). If you decide to try, be prepared for an overnight stop. Heading out of Trevélez, make sure that you begin on the higher track over the Crestón de Posteros, to link up with *acequias* (irrigation channels) coming down from the top of the Río Culo Perro (Dog's Arse River) valley; if you take the main, tempting trail which goes toward Jeres del Marquesado, and then turn into the mouth of the Río Culo Perro, you face quagmires and thorn patches that beggar belief. The standard place to camp is in the Siete Lagunas valley below the peak, allowing an early-morning ascent to the summit before the mists come up.

Continuing the traverse, you can drop down the west side of Mulhacén (take care on this awkward descent) to the dirt road coming from Veleta. Follow this toward Veleta, and you can turn off the road to spend a second night at the *Refugio Félix Méndez* (main area not open until after spring snow melt, meal service thereafter; the hut's annexe with four bunks should always be open). Moving on, to the west, plan on a third night spent at either Cerro de Caballo or the *Refugio Forestal*, depending on your capabilities.

Las Alpujarras

The road south from Granada to Motril crosses the fertile *Vega* after leaving the city and then climbs steeply until at 850m above sea level it reaches the **Puerto del Suspiro del Moro** – the Pass of the Sigh of the Moor. Boabdil, last Moorish king of Granada, came this way, having just handed over the keys of his city to the *Reyes Católicos* in exchange for a fiefdom over the Alpujarras. From the pass you catch your last glimpse of the city and the Alhambra. The road then descends and beyond Padul crosses the valley of Lecrín planted with groves of orange, lemon and almond trees, the latter a riot of pink and white blossom in late winter. To the east through a narrow defile close to Béznar, lie the great **valleys of the Alpujarras** – "the Switzerland of Spain" as Ford described them – first settled in the twelfth century by Berber refugees from Sevilla, and later the Moors' last stronghold in Spain.

Some Alpujarran history – and developments

The valleys are bounded to the north by the Sierra Nevada, and to the south by the lesser *sierras* of Lujar, La Contraviesa and Gador. The eternal snows of the high *sierras* keep the valleys and their seventy or so villages well watered all summer long. Rivers have cut deep gorges in the soft mica and shale of the upper mountains, and over the centuries have deposited silt and fertile soil on the lower hills and in the valleys; here the villages have grown, for the soil is rich and easily worked. The intricate terracing that today preserves these deposits was begun perhaps as long as 2000 years ago by Visigoths or Ibero-Celts, whose remains have been found at Capileira.

The Moors carried on the tradition, and modified the terracing and irrigation in their inimitable way. They transformed the Alpujarras into an earthly paradise, and there they retired to bewail the loss of their beloved lands in *al-Andalus*. After the fall of Granada, many of the city's Muslim population settled in the villages, and there

resisted a series of royal edicts demanding their forced conversion to Christianity. In 1568 they rose up in a final, short-lived revolt, which led to the expulsion of all Spanish Moors. Even then, however, two Moorish families were required to stay in each village to show the new Christian peasants, who had been marched down from Galicia and Asturias to repopulate the valleys, how to operate the intricate irrigation systems.

Through the following centuries, the villages fell into impoverished existence, with the land owned by a few wealthy families, and worked by peasants. It was one of the most remote parts of Spain in the 1920s, when the author Gerald Brenan settled in one of the eastern villages, Yegen, and described the life in his book *South from Granada*, and things changed little over the next forty-odd years. During the Civil War, the occasional truckload of Nationalist youth trundled in from Granada, rounded up a few bewildered locals, and shot them for "crimes" of which they were wholly ignorant;

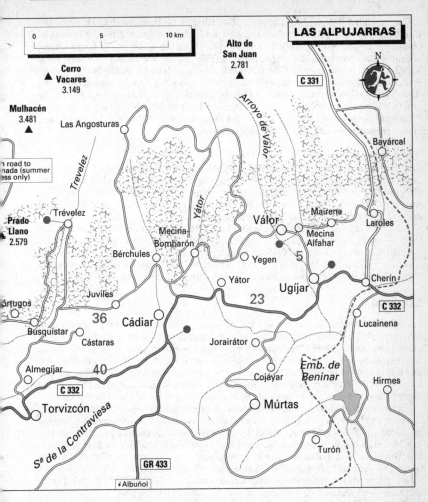

Republican youths came up in their trucks from Almería and did the same thing; towards the end, there was a front here of sorts, though it remained out of the mainstream. In the aftermath, under Franco, there was real hardship and suffering, and in the 1980s the region had one of the lowest per capita incomes in Spain, with – as an official report put it – "a level of literacy bordering on that of the Third World, alarming problems of desertification, poor communications and high under-employment".

Ironically, the land itself is still very fertile – oranges, chestnuts, bananas, apples and avocados grow here, while the southern villages produce a well known dry rosé wine, *costa*. However, it is largely the recent influx of **tourism** and **foreign purchase of houses and farms** that has turned the area's fortunes around, bringing pockets of wealth and a bit of new life to the region.

The so-called **"High Alpujarras"** – the villages of **Pampaneira**, **Bubión** and **Capileira** – have all been scrubbed and whitewashed and are now firmly on the tourist circuit, as popular with Spanish as foreign visitors. Lower down, in the **Órgiva area**, are the main concentration of expatriates – mainly British, Dutch and Germans, seeking new Mediterranean lives. Most seem to have moved here permanently, rather than establishing second homes (though there are houses for rent in abundance), and there's a vaguely alternative aspect to the new community, which sets it apart from the coastal expats. In addition to property owners, the area has also attracted groups of British "new age travellers" – the youthful hippies of the 1990s. The locals, to their credit, seem remarkably tolerant of the whole scene.

Approaches and buses

From Granada, the most straightforward **approach to the Alpujarras** is to take the Lanjarón turning off the Motril road. Coming from the south, you can bear right from the road at Velez Benaudalla and continue straight to Órgiva, the market town of the western Alpujarras. There are several **buses** a day from both Granada and Motril, and one a day from Almería, to **Lanjarón** and **Órgiva**.

A bus direct to the **"High Alpujarras"**, via Trevélez as far as Bérchules, leaves the main Granada bus station at noon and 5.15pm daily: in the other direction it passes Berchules at 6am, Trevélez at 6.45am, arriving in Granada around eleven. There's also a bus from Granada to Ugíjar in the "Low Alpujarras", via Lanjarón, Órgiva, Torvizcón, Cadiar, Yegen and Valor; this takes about four hours to the end of the line.

Lanjarón

LANJARÓN has known tourism and the influence of the outside world for longer than anywhere else in the Alpujarras due to the curative powers of its **spa waters**. These gush from seven natural springs and are sold in bottled form throughout Spain. Between June and October, when the spa baths are open, the town fills with the aged and infirm and the streets are lined with racks of herbal remedies, all of which imparts a rather melancholy air. This might seem good reason for passing straight on to the higher villages, though to do so would be to miss out on some beautiful local walks.

Like so many spa towns Lanjarón is Roman in origin, though today the place is largely modern, with a ribbon of buildings on its pleasant tree-lined thoroughfare, the Avenida de Andalucía. Below, marking Lanjarón's medieval status as gateway to the Alpujarras, is a **Moorish castle**, now dilapidated and barely visible. It was here on March 8, 1500 that the Moorish population made its final heroic stand against the Christian troops under the command of Fernando. Pounded by artillery, hundreds died as the town was taken. A ten-minute stroll reveals its dramatic setting – follow the signs downhill from the main street and out onto the terraces and meadows below the town.

Lanjarón's **Turismo** has recently closed down but *Viajes Simbel* (occupying the old site on the main street) can provide basic information. Midway along the main street is the *Alsina Graells* **bus terminal**.

Walks from Lanjarón

The countryside and mountains around Lanjarón are beyond compare. Wander up through the backstreets behind the town and you'll come across a track that takes you steeply up to the vast spaces of the **Reserva Nacional de la Sierra Nevada**.

For a somewhat easier **day's walk**, go to the bridge over the river just east of town and take the sharply climbing, cobbled track which parallels the river. After two to two-and-a-half hours' walk through small farms, with magnificent views and scenery, a downturn to a small stone bridge lets you return to Lanjarón on the opposite bank. Allow a minimum of six hours for a leisurely day's expedition.

Accommodation

There's no shortage of **hotels** in the town, though in summer it is almost essential to book ahead – as indeed it is worth doing throughout the Alpujarras. Good choices include:

Hostal El Dólar, Avda. de Andalucía 5 (☎958/770183). Pleasant and inexpensive with mountain-view rooms. ②.

Hotel España, Avda. de Andalucía 44 (☎958/770187). A grand-looking hotel which is very friendly and excellent value. ③.

Bar Galvez, Avda. de Andalucía. Cheapest rooms in town and excellent meals. ②.

Pensión El Mirador (☎958/770181). A quiet spot, 1km east of town. ②.

Hotel Miramar, Avda. de Andalucía 10 (☎958/770161). For a step up in price you can enjoy the relative luxury of this hotel with pool, garden and garage. ④.

Hostal Nacional, Avda. de Andalucía 2 (☎958/770011). Another decent, inexpensive option. ②.

Hostal El Sol, Avda. de Andalucía 22 (☎958/770130). A good choice if you're here in winter as there is reliable heating in the rooms. ③.

Eating and drinking

Bars and restaurants line the Avenida de Andalucía and many of the *hostales* have good value meals and *tapas*, too – especially the *Bar Galvez* and the *Hotel Mirador*. *Manolete*, c/Queipo de Lano 107, is another good tapas bar, while *El Club* at Avda. de Andalucía 18 specializes in Alpujarran dishes and is reckoned to serve the best food in town. For seafood, try *Los Mariscos* in the square off Avda. Andalucía, just west of the kink in the centre. On the corner of the same square is *Noche Azul*, a popular nightclub for late night dancing and drinking. Opposite are a couple of good ice-cream parlours and, nearby, Lanjarón's celebrated *churrería*, claimed by some to sell the best home-made potato crisps in Andalucía.

Las Barreras

Heading east from Lanjarón towards Órgiva or the High Alpujarras, you pass through the village of **LAS BARRERAS**. If you're not in a hurry, stop for a **meal** at the *Venta María* on the roadside – a somewhat quirky establishment that can, with luck, come up with a magnificent meal. Next door is a tiny **tile factory**, started recently by local women, using traditional techniques and designs.

Órgiva (Órjiva)

ÓRGIVA, 11km east of Lanjarón, is the market centre of the western Alpujarras. It is a lively little town, with a number of good bars and hotels, and an amazing **Thursday market**, when everyone from miles around – Spanish and foreign –turns up with something to sell or buy, a drum to beat, a pipe to finger, a guitar to strum and a bowl to fill with *duros*. The contrast between the timeworn *campesinos* and their pack-mules, and some of the foreign "new age travellers" who seek their indulgence and charity is as bizarre as anything this side of Madrid.

The everyday covered **mercado**, just north of the Plaza Mayor, is quite a sight, too. With its juggling and health food stalls, and its posters for the local yoga centre, *Cortijo Romero*, with its programmes of shiatsu and other activities – it could as easily be in Amsterdam or Bristol. The foreign input, however, is probably crucial to the market's survival. The *mercado* was once the most important institution in most Spanish villages, but most struggle these days to keep their head above water in competition with the local supermarkets.

Órgiva's other sights line the main street: a sixteenth-century **Baroque church**, whose towers add a touch of fancy to the townscape, and a crumbling **Moorish palacio** which today houses various shops.

Practicalities

Órgiva has a fair choice of **accommodation**. Cheap options include: the basic *Fonda Alma Alpujarra* (with a restaurant) and the *Pensión Nemesis*, facing each other across the main road; a *fonda* above the *Bar Ortega*; and a *comidas/camas* next to the *Alsina Graells* office (all ①/②). More luxurious, and not a lot pricier, is the *Hostal Mirasol* at c/González Robles 3 (☎958/785159; ③), which also does good *tapas* and reasonable *menús* inside or on their terrace.

The best **tapas and raciones** in town, however, are the *calamares* at *Bar Semaforo*, by the traffic lights. Other good *tapas* places include *Retumba* and *Agustín*, opposite one another at the top of the town near the health centre, and *Nemesis* and *Paraiso* in the church plaza. For coffee and cakes there's *Galindo Plaza* on the square, and the town *churreria* is just round the corner.

Órgiva comes to life with its **fiesta** on September 24 and 25 when the population doubles as prodigal sons and daughters all return to join in the fun. A more eccentric festival is the **Dia del Señor** – two weeks before Maundy Thursday. This fiesta opens with a terrifying salvo of rockets – two years ago it all went disastrously wrong when the bank's windows were blown in – then on the Friday morning all the old women attack the church until they are able to make off with the effigy of *El Señor* (Christ), which is then paraded around town accompanied by great displays of emotion – not to mention more rocketry.

Buses from Órgiva run east across the Alpujarras to Ugijar, and up to all the High Alpujarran villages; the latter service is the Granada bus, which passes through Lanjarón at 1pm and Órgiva around 1.20pm. If you're **driving**, note that Órgiva is the last stop for petrol before Cadiar or Ugíjar.

The High Alpujarras: Órgiva to Capileira

From Órgiva, you can reach the High Alpujarran villages by car or bus, or you could walk – the best way to experience the region. There is a network of paths in the region, though to avoid getting lost it's wise to equip yourself with a compass and the *Instituto Geográfico Nacional/Federación Española de Montañismo* 1:50,000 map, which covers all the territory from Órgiva up to Berja.

At their best, **Alpujarran footpaths** are remnants of the old Camino Real, the mule-routes which crossed Spain, and are engineered with cobblestones, and beautifully contoured, alongside mountain streams, through woods of oak, chestnut and poplar, or across flower-spangled meadows. In their bad moments they deteriorate to incredibly dusty firebreaks, forestry roads or tractor tracks, or (worse) dead-end in impenetrable thickets of bramble and nettle. Progress is slow, gradients are sharp and the heat (between mid-June and Sept) is taxing. A reasonable knowledge of Spanish is a big help, as is a compass.

HIGH ALPUJARRAS HIKES: THE HIGHLIGHTS

Rewarding **hikes** in the High Alpujarras include:

Pitres to Mecina Fondales: Twenty minutes' hike, and then a good hour-plus from neighbouring Ferreirola to Busquistar.

Busquistar toward Trevélez: One hour's hike, and then two-plus hours of road walking.

Pórtugos toward Trevélez: Two hours' hike, meeting the tarmac a little beyond the end of the Busquistar route.

Trevélez to Berchules: Four hours' hike, but the middle two hours is dirt track.

Trevélez to Juviles: Three hours' hike, including some sections of firebreak.

Cañar, Soportújar and Carataunas

Following the high road from Órgiva, the first settlements you reach, almost directly above the town, are **CAÑAR** and **SOPORTÚJAR**. Like many of the High Alpujarran villages, they congregate on the neatly terraced mountainside, planted with poplars and laced with irrigation channels. Both have **bars** where you can get a meal and a **room** (②) for the night; both are perched precariously on the steep hillside with a rather sombre view of Órgiva in the valley below, and on a clear day the mountains of Africa over the ranges to the south. Cañar also has a sixteenth-century church in a terrible state of disrepair.

Just below the two villages, the tiny hamlet of **CARATAUNAS** is particularly pretty. Above the village, on the main road is the small *Motel El Montañero* (☎958/784328; ③); a reasonably priced and pleasant place to stay, owned by a polyglot German and serving a hearty *menú*. The owner is an expert on walking in the Alpujarras and occasionally leads hikes as well.

Continuing up the road from Carataunas to the High Alpujarras, you pass *Los Llanos*, another foreign-owned **bar-restaurant** which despite some hideous decor (mind the stalactites don't drop in your soup) provides gastronomic treats and real German beer. Two more bends along and you come to another **restaurant**, *Sol y Nieve*, which seems to go through an annual change of name and ownership. The curse may be broken this time, however, as the latest occupants are serving up an excellent range of Basque, French and Alpujarran dishes.

The Poqueira Gorge and up to Capileira

Shortly after Carataunas the road swings to the north, and you have your first view of the **Gorge of the Poqueira**, a huge gash into the heights of the Sierra Nevada. Trickling deep in the cleft is the Río Poqueira, which has its source near the peak of Mulhacén. The steep walls of the gorge are terraced and wooded from top to bottom, and dotted with little stone farmhouses. Much of the surrounding country looks barren from a distance, but close up you'll find that it's rich with flowers, woods, springs and streams. A trio of spectacular villages – Pampaneira, Bubión and Capileira – teeters on the steep edge of the gorge among their terraces. They are, justifiably, the most touristy villages in the region and a bit over-prettified, with craftshops and the like, but nonetheless well worth a visit and, even if you have a car, some walking on the local mulepaths.

Pampaneira and the Tibetan monastery

PAMPANEIRA, the first of the Poqueira villages, is a neat, prosperous place, and a bit less developed and spoilt than its neighbours. Around its main square are a number of bars, restaurants and *hostales* and, just down the hill, a weaving workshop that specializes in traditional *Alpujarreño* designs. The cheapest **rooms** are at *Casa Diego* (②), by the fountain, followed by the homely *Hostal Pampaneira* (☎958/763002; ②), at c/José Antonio 1. For a bit more comfort try the *Hostal Ruta del Mulhacén* at c/José Antonio 6 (☎958/763010; ③) which has balcony rooms and central heating,

In Pampaneira's plaza you'll also find **Nevadensis** (☎958/763127; English spoken), a locally-run initiative that coordinates the services and facilities of the **Natural Park of the Sierra Nevada**. As well as providing information they organize guided walks (botanical, ornithological, speleological) and rent out bikes, horses, donkeys, hangliders, balloons and cross-country skis. They also offer hostels, village houses, and farmhouses for rent throughout the Alpujarras.

Above Pampaneira, on the very peak of the western flank of the Poqueira gorge, is the **Tibetan Buddhist Monastery of Al Atalaya**. The Spanish reincarnation of the former head lama – one Yeshé – is currently undergoing training under the Dalai Lama in the Himalayas. Lectures and courses on Buddhism are held regularly and facilities exist for those who want to visit the monastery for periods of retreat.

Bubión

BUBIÓN is next up the hill, backed for much of the year by snowcapped peaks. The tranquility here may not last long if the property developers – whose multilingual signs litter the village – have their way. There is already plenty of **accommodation**, including a fancy hotel, the *Villa Turística del Poqueira* (☎958/763111; ⑤), a comfortable *pensión*, *Las Terrazas* (☎958/763034; ③), and cheaper rooms in private houses.

The village also has a ranch for **horseback riding** in the Alpujarras; trips of from one to five days are offered in groups with a guide (☎958/763135 or 763034). A new private **tourist office**, named – we kid you not – *Global Spirit* (☎958/763054) can also book horse-riding tours and help with accommodation.

Capileira

CAPILEIRA is the highest of the three villages and the terminus of the seasonal road – Europe's highest – across the heart of the Sierra Nevada to Granada. It's a fine walking base and, like its neighbours, is increasingly full of craft and art shops. It actually has a house, the *Residencia de Artistas*, reserved for the use of visiting artists, and a part of this is set aside as a **museum** containing various bits and pieces belonging to, or produced by, Pedro Alarcón, the nineteenth-century Spanish writer, born in Guadix, who visited the Alpujarras and wrote a book about it.

Among several **bars**, **hostales and restaurants**, the *Casa Ibero* (aka the *Mesón Alpujarreña*) serves excellent food; the *Mesón-Hostal Poqueira* (☎958/763048; ③) has good value heated rooms plus one of the best set *menús* in the province; and the *Fonda Restaurante El Tilo* (②), on Plaza Calvario, has quiet rooms, away from the main road.

There are daily midday and afternoon **buses** to Capileira from Granada, via Órgiva, which continue to Murtas and Bérchules (see "travel details"). Buses out to Órgiva and Granada leave at 6.30am, 3.30pm and 6.30pm.

The Poqueira gorge

Capileira is a handy base for easy day walks in the **Poqueira gorge**. For a not too strenuous ramble, take the northernmost of the three paths below the village, each of which span bridges across the river. This one sets off from alongside the *Pueblo Alpujarreño* villa complex and winds through the huts and terraced fields of the river valley above Capileira, ending after about an hour and a half at a dirt track within sight of a power plant at the head of the valley. From here, you can either retrace your steps or cross the stream over a bridge to follow a dirt track back to the village. In May and June, the fields are tended laboriously and by hand, as the steep slopes dictate.

A number of reasonably clear paths or tracks also lead to **Pampaneira** (2–3hr, follow the lower path to the bridge below Capileira), continuing to **Carataunas** (a further 1hr, mostly road) and **Órgiva** (another 45min on an easy path) from where you can get a bus back.

In the other direction, taking the Sierra Nevada road and then the first major track to the right, by a ruined stone house, you can reach **Pitres** (2hr), **Pórtugos** (30min more) and **Busquístar** (45min more). Going in the same direction but taking the second decent-sized track (by a sign encouraging you to "conserve and respect nature"), **Trevélez** is some five hours away.

Further along the High Route to Trevélez and Cadiar

The "High Route" continues east from Pampaneira through **Pitres** and **Pórtugos** before making a great loop to Trevélez, Spain's highest permanent settlement. From there, the road drops down to a junction, with a crossing to **Torvizcón**, on the south side of the Alpujarras, and east to the valley and village of **Cadiar**.

Pitres
PITRES is less picturesque and less developed than the trio of high villages to its west and, like its neighbour, Pórtugos, has more chance of rooms during high season. All around, too, spreads some of the best Alpujarran walking country.

Accommodation includes the *Fonda Sierra Nevada* (②), on the main square, which is flanked by a couple of bar/restaurants and, on the village's eastern edge, the *Refugio Los Albergues* (①), an old Civil War hostel refurbished to provide dormitory beds and cooking facilities. The latter is signposted on the main road but if you get lost ask for *Casa Barbara* (Hauch), the name of the friendly German who runs it. She's also knowledgable about local walking routes and has one standard double room (②) as well.

Alternatively, there's a **campsite**, the *Balcón de Pitres* (☎958/766111), in a stunning position just out of town, with a swimming pool; it also has a charming little **restaurant** serving Alpujarran specialities such as *solomillo de cerdo* (sirloin of pork) and *cordero rellena* (stuffed shoulder of lamb). You may also be lucky enough on Saturday or Sunday nights here to stumble on an authentic mountain *flamenco* session.

Pórtugos and its neighbours
PÓRTUGOS is equally rustic, though its centre has a couple of ugly smarter hotels, including the upmarket *Hostal Mirador* (☎958/766014; ④), on the main square. A kilometre east, at Los Castaños, there's a delightful *fonda* (②), with excellent food.

Down below the main road are a trio of villages – **MECINA FONDALES**, **FERREIROLA** and **BUSQUÍSTAR** – which along with Pitres and Pórtugos formed a league of villages known as the *Taha* (from the Arabic "Tá" meaning obedience) under the Moors. Ferreirola and Busquistar – the latter a huddle of grey *launa* roofs – are especially attractive, as is the path between the two, clinging to the north side of the valley of the Río Trevélez. You're out of tourist country here and the villages display their genuine characteristics to better effect; there's an unmarked **inn** – the basic *Hostal Mirador de la Alpujarra* (☎958/857470; ②) – just uphill from the church in Busquistar. It has one of the best views in the Alpujarras and is well sited for a hike up to Trevélez and beyond.

A circuit of the three villages starting out from either Pitres or Pórtugos need take no more than two hours walking, though you'll probably want to linger along the way.

Trevélez

The cut into the mountain made by the Río Trevélez – sadly, rather polluted on its lower reaches – is similar to the Poqueira, but grander and more austere. **TREVÉLEZ** village stands on a flank at the end of the ravine and its altitude makes it a cool place even in summer. It is built in traditional Alpujarran style with upper and lower *barrios*, overlooking a grassy, poplar-lined valley where the river starts its long descent. There are fine walks in the valley and you can swim, too, in a makeshift pool by the bridge.

The village is well provided with **hostales**, in both the lower and upper squares, and with *camas* advertised over a few bars. Try the pleasant *Hostal Fernando* (c/Pista s/n; ☎958/858565; ②), on the road into town, with great views, or the *Pensión Regina* (Plaza Francisco Abellán; ☎958/858564; ③ with heating). The *Hostal Mulhacén* (Ctra. Ugíjar s/n; ☎958/858587; ④ with heating) in the lower *barrio* is another slightly more expensive option with more great views down the valley. There's also a **campsite**, *Camping Trevélez* (☎958/858575), 1km out on the Órgiva road; it's officially open all year, though who would wish to brave the arctic conditions at this altitude in midwinter is a mystery.

Among **restaurants**, the *Río Grande*, down near the bridge, has good, solid food and is often the only place open in the evening. *Jamón serrano* is justifiably a local speciality and can be tried along with many other specialities at *Mesón del Jamón*, which has an attractive terrace above the Plaza de la Iglesia. Another *jamón* specialist is *Mesón Joaquín*, at the entrance to the village, where beneath a ceiling hung with hams, regional specialities are served including *habas con jamón* (beans with ham), *plato alpujarreño* (mixed fry with black pudding, *jamón* and egg) and river trout (*trucha*) with *jamón*. These famous *jamónes dulces* sent Ford into raptures when he passed through Trevélez on horseback in the 1830s: "No gastronome should neglect these sweet hams. Very little salt is used; the ham is placed eight days in a weak pickle, and then hung up in the snow."

Trevélez is traditionally the jump-off point for the **high Sierra Nevada peaks** (to which there is a bona fide path) and for treks across the range (on a lower, more conspicuous track). The latter begins down by the bridge on the eastern side of the village. After skirting the bleak Horcajo de Trevélez (3182m), and negotiating the Puerto de Trevélez (2800m), up to which it's a very distinct route, it drops down along the north flank of the Sierra Nevada to Jeres del Marquesado. (For more details, see the section on the *Ruta de los Tres Mil*, p.342).

South to Torvizcón

South from Trevélez, you can head by road – or by footpath – to **Almegijar and Torvizcón**. On foot, it is around 15km: a very pleasant walk, lined with masses of wild-flowers and fragrant herbs in spring and early summer.

Start by following the road down the valley from Trevélez in the direction of Juviles. At the junction after 7km, ignore the road going east to Juviles and take the turn on the right signed to Castaras. Two kilometres along this you'll meet another junction; ignore the route east to Castaras and veer right towards Almegijar, then down another left turning after 2km. You could call in at Almegijar which you'll pass on the left or carry on descending through olive groves and orchards to Torvizcón.

TORVIZCÓN is another sturdy Alpujarran village with cobbled streets and white-washed houses stacked up the northern slopes of the Sierra de Contraviesa. **Rooms** are available at *Pensión Moreno* (②), a friendly, family-run place on the main square which also serves the local *costa* wine.

East to Juviles, Bérchules and Cadiar

Heading east from Trevélez, either by vehicle or on foot, you come to **JUVILES**, once a great centre of silk production in Moorish times, and today an attractive village straddling the road. At its centre is an unwhitewashed, peanut-brittle-finish church with a clock that's slightly slow (like most things round here). In the evening people promenade in the road, knowing that there will be no traffic. A single all-in-one *fonda-restaurante*-bar-store, *Bar Fernandez* (☎958/753030; ②) has rooms with great views east over the valley from the second floor, and will cook meals on demand.

BÉRCHULES, a high village of grassy streams and chestnut woods, lies just 6km beyond Juviles, but a greater contrast can hardly be imagined. It is a large, abruptly demarcated settlement, three streets wide, on a sharp slope overlooking yet another canyon. The *Fonda-Restaurante Carvol* has decent **rooms** (②), and next door there's an excellent grocery – a godsend if you're planning on doing any walking out of here, since most village shops in the Alpujarras are primitive.

CADIAR, just below Bérchules and the central town – or "navel" as Gerald Brenan termed it – of the Alpujarras, is more attractive than it seems from a distance. Most of the life is around its main square fronted by a sixteenth-century stone church. There are a few *hostales* and *camas* if you're **staying**, among them the inexpensive *Hostal Montoro* (c/San Isidro 20; ☎958/750068; ②), near the central plaza, with heated rooms. Various events are worth keeping in mind, too. There's a colourful **produce market** on the 3rd and 18th of every month, sometimes including livestock. And from October 5–9 a **Wine Fair** takes place, turning the waters of the fountain literally to wine.

The eastern and southern Alpujarras

Cadiar and Bérchules mark the end of the western Alpujarras, and a striking change in the landscape; the dramatic, severe, but relatively green terrain of the Guadalfeo and Cadiar valleys gives way to open, rolling and much more arid land. The villages of the **eastern Alpujarras** display many of the characteristics of those to the west but as a rule they are poorer and less visited by tourists. There are attractive places nonetheless, among them **Yegen**, which Brenan wrote about, the market centre of **Ugijar**, and, down on the southern slopes, the *costa* wine-producing villages of **Albuñol** and **Albondón**.

Yegen and Mecina Bombarón

YEGEN, some 7km northeast of Cadiar, is where **Gerald Brenan** lived during his ten or so years of Alpujarran residence. His autobiography of these times, *South from Granada*, is the best account of rural life in Spain between the wars, and describes the visits made here by Virginia Woolf, Bertrand Russell and the arch-complainer Lytton Strachey. Disillusioned with the strictures of middle-class life in England after World War I, Brenan rented a house in Yegen and shipped out a library of 2000 books, from which he was to spend the next eight years educating himself. He later moved to the hills behind Torremolinos, where he died in 1987, a writer better known and respected in Spain (he made an important study of Saint John of the Cross) than in his native England. The contribution he made to informing the world about the Alpujarras, its history and culture is recorded on a plaque fixed to the **Casa de Brenan**, just along from the fountain in the main square.

Brenan connections aside, Yegen is one of the most characteristic Alpujarran villages, with its two distinct quarters, cobbled paths and cold-water springs. It has a **fonda**, the *Bar La Fuente* (①), opposite the fountain in the square.

From Yegen there's an easy 4km walk up to the hamlet of **Mecina Bombarón**, along one of the old cobbled mulepaths. This starts out from the old bridge across the gorge and is easy to follow from there, with Mecina clearly visible on the hill above.

Valor and Ugíjar

VALOR, 6km beyond Yegen, and sited between deep ravines is a charming and sleepy hamlet which belies its history as a centre of stubborn resistance in the sixteenth-century revolt by the Moors against the "insults and outrages" of the Christian ascendancy. These events are "celebrated" in the annual *Fiestas Patronales* in mid-September when the whole story – including battles between Moors and Christians – are colourfully re-enacted in the main square. Should you wish to stay, **rooms** are to be had at the comfortable *Hostal Las Perdices* on c/Torrecilla (☎958/851821; ②).

UGÍJAR, 6km from Valor, is the largest community of this eastern part, and a quietly attractive market town. There are easy and enjoyable walks to the nearest villages – up the valley to Mecina-al-Fahar, for example – and plenty of **places to stay**. Try the comfortable *Pensión Pedro* (☎958/767149; ②), which has heating and serves midday meals; the slightly cheaper *Hostal Vidaña* (☎958/767010; ②) on the Almería road; or the very cheap *camas* opposite the bus stop in the central plaza. *Seis Estrellas*, on the corner of the plaza by the church, serves excellent food. Buses run onward to Almería (3hr).

The southern ranges

The tiny hamlets of the **southern Alpujarras** have an unrivalled view of the Mediterranean, the convexity of the hills obscuring the developments and acres of growers' plastic that mar the coast. There are few villages of any size, as there is little water, but the hills host the principal **wine-growing district** of the Alpujarras. For a taste of the best of this *costa* wine, try the *venta* at **HAZA DEL LINO** (Plain of Linen) on the western edge of the Sierra de la Contraviesa; the house brew is a full-bodied rosé. Also worth a look on the village's northern edge is an enormous **chestnut tree**, reputedly the oldest in Andalucía.

ALBUÑOL and **ALBONDÓN** to the east are other scenic places to try the local wines and various *bodegas* can be located along the main street in both places. Much of the *costa* wine drunk in Granada comes from Albondón and excellent stuff it is, too. If you want to buy, take your own container, or be prepared to have it served to you in a rinsed *Pepsi* bottle. Just outside Albondón (and signposted) is the Neolithic **Cueva d Los Murciélagos** which produced the remarkable esparto baskets, sandals and jewellery now exhibited in the museum at Granada. The cave can be visited but there's not an awful lot to see.

The Almerian Alpujarras

From Ugíjar the C332 toils eastwards and, once across the Río de Alcolea enters the province of Almería where the starker – but no less impressive terrain – gradually takes on the harsh and dessicated character of the deserts that lie ahead. There are still the odd oases to be found, however, in **Laujar de Andarax** and the spa of **Alhama de Almería**, and a remarkable prehistoric site, **Los Millares**.

Laujar de Andarax

It was at **LAUJAR DE ANDARAX**, 16km east of Ugíjar, at the source of the Río Andarax, that Boabdil, the deposed Moorish king of Granada, settled in 1492 and from where he intended to rule the Alpujarras fiefdom granted to him by the Catholic monarchs. But Christian paranoia about a Moorish resurgence led them to tear up the treaty and within a year Boabdil had been shipped off to Africa, an event which set in train a series of uprisings by the Alpujarran Moors, ending in their suppression and eventual deportation, to be replaced by Christian settlers from the north.

The **Río Andarax's source** is at the town's eastern edge; it is signposted (*nacimiento*) and a pleasant and shady spot, with a café, serving hearty *platos combinados* at lunchtime, beside the falls. In the centre of town, the **Plaza Mayor** has a seventeenth-century four-spouted fountain and an elegant late eighteenth-century **Ayuntamiento**, where you can pick up a street map. This will enable you to find four seventeenth-century **palacios** as well as an impressive Mudéjar-style seventeenth-century church of **La Encarnación**, which contains a sculpture of the Virgin by Alonso Cano.

Should you decide **to stay**, *Hostal Fernandez* (c/General Mola 4; ☎951/113128; ③) is a good bet and lowers the prices of its rooms in slack periods; it has a superb restaurant with an excellent value *menú*. Nearby, the cheaper *Hostal Pon y Pongo* (c/General Mola 10; ☎951/113354; ②) is another possibility.

For a good **walk** in this area, follow the road forking right on the western edge of the town which climbs into the wooded slopes of the Sierra Nevada, where there are forest tracks east towards the abandoned lead mines, and west to the mountain villages of **Paterna del Río**, a spa with a sulphur spring, and **Bayarcal**, higher still. On these lower slopes of the Sierra Nevada covered with ilex and pine, you may be lucky enough to spot the *cabra hispanica*, or wild Spanish goat, as well as eagles and a variety of other birdlife, plus the odd wild boar.

East to Alhama de Almería

The road east of Laujar de Andarax passes a series of unremarkable villages, surrounded by slopes covered with vine-trellises, little changed since Moorish times and little visited today. Among them is **FONDÓN**, whose church tower was the minaret of the former mosque, and **PADULES**, 11km beyond Laujar, whose municipal swimming pool might prove a greater lure in the baking heat of high summer. The prettier village of **CANJÁYAR**, 4km further on, also has a swimming pool, and becomes a centre of frenetic activity during the autumn *vendimia*, when the grapes are gathered in. At other times it reverts to a sleepy hamlet beneath its small church.

The road then trails the course of the Andarax river valley through an arid and eroded landscape, skirting the Sierra de Gádor before climbing slightly to **ALHAMA DE ALMERÍA**, 16km further on. This is a pleasant spa town, dating back to Moorish times, and most of its visitors are here to take the waters – hence the rather incongruous three-star *Hotel San Nicolas* (☎951/100101; ④), sited on the location of the original baths. If you want a cheaper **place to stay** – and Los Millares (see below) is a reason why you might – there is an unnamed *camas* and *comidas* establishment on the main street. Alhama also has a delightful municipal **swimming pool** with plenty of shade, at the western end of the town.

Los Millares: the Chalcolithic settlement

Leaving Alhama by the Almería road, after 4km the road passes the remarkable pre-Bronze Age settlement of **LOS MILLARES**, one of the most important of its kind in Europe. Situated on a low triangular spur between two dried-up river beds, this was exposed in 1891 during the construction of the Almería to Linares railway line that passes below the site today. Two Belgian mining engineers, Henri and Louis Siret, who were also enthusiastic amateur archeologists, took on the excavations at the turn of the century, funding them from their modest salaries. What they revealed is a Chalcolithic or Copper Age (the period between the Neolithic and the Bronze Age) **fortified settlement**. It dates from c2700 BC and was occupied until c1800 BC, when both stone and copper but not bronze was used for weapons and tools. Whilst it is not entirely clear who the occupants were – possibly emigrants from the eastern Mediterranean or perhaps an indigenous group – the settlement they left behind is exceptional. Spread over five hectares (12 acres) it consists of four sets of defensive walls, with a number of advanced fortlets beyond these, as well as an extraordinary cemetery with over one hundred **tombs** which are without equal in Europe.

Looking over the barren landscape that surrounds the site today, it is hard to believe that five thousand years ago this was a fertile area of pine and ilex forests, inhabited by deer and wild boar. The nearby Río Andarax was then navigable and the inhabitants used it to bring copper down from mines in the Sierra de Gádor to the west. The population – perhaps as many as two thousand – not only hunted for their food but bred sheep, goats and pigs, grew vegetables and cereals, made cheese and were highly

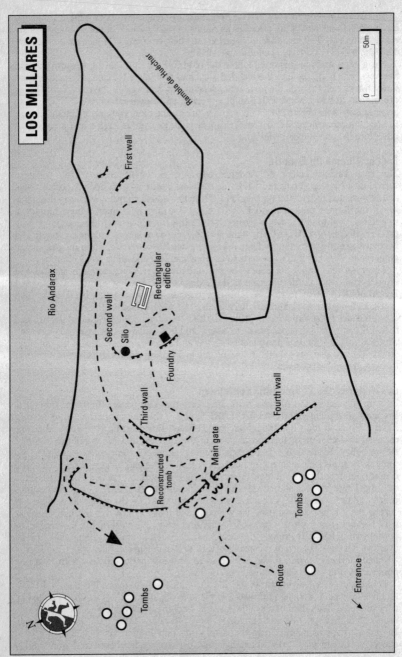

LOS MILLARES

First wall

Rambla de Huechar

Rio Andarax

Second wall

Rectangular edifice

Silo

Foundry

Third wall

Fourth wall

Main gate

Reconstructed tomb

Tombs

Route

Tombs

Entrance

Tombs

N

0   50m

skilled in the manufacture of pottery, basketwork and jewellery, as is evidenced by the finds now in museums at Almería and Madrid.

THE SITE

A tour of the **site** (Tues–Sat 9.30am–1.30pm & 5–7.30pm; Sun 9.30am–2.30pm; 200ptas; free with EC passport) begins with the outermost of **four exterior walls** which were built successively further west as the settlement expanded across the escarpment in the latter part of the third millenium BC. An impressive structure four metres high when built, the **fourth** (and last) **wall** was lined with outward-facing bastions or towers, and at 310m is the longest wall known in Europe from this period. Its layout bears a striking similarity to a wall of the same epoch at the early Cycladic site of Halandriani on the island of Síros in Greece, suggesting a possible link with the Aegean. The **main gate**, towards the centre, is flanked by barbicans or watchtowers, beyond which a walled passage gave access to the settlement.

A little way north of here are the remains of a primitive **aqueduct** which cut through the wall to carry water from a spring near to the village of Alhama into the populated area. Fifty metres east of the main gate remains can be seen from the **third wall**. Close to here also are the remains of a number of **circular huts** – one of which has been partially reconstructed – in which the inhabitants of the site lived. Six to seven metres in diameter with pounded earth floors, they consisted of cavity stone walls filled with mud and pebbles, with a roof probably made from straw. Inside the huts the excavators found remains of hearths as well as grindstones, pottery and a variety of utensils.

Moving east again, beyond the **second wall** lies a **primitive foundry** where the copper ore was crudely smelted by means of fire and bellows before being hammered into the required form. Moulds only arrived in the later Bronze Age. Further north, on the line of the wall, lies a **silo** used for storing grain. Behind this wall are the foundations of a **rectangular edifice**, 32m in length, whose function is as yet unknown. The settlement at first appeared to lack a hierarchical social structure due to the overall similarity of the huts, but after the discovery of this building – much larger than the rest – some have speculated that it could have served as a form of council chamber or even a royal palace.

The remains of the **first wall**, enclosing what may have been the citadel, lie further back still and excavations here recovered many of the patterned, bellshaped vases to be seen in the museum at Almería.

THE NECROPOLIS

Retracing your steps to the outer (or fourth) wall will bring you to one of the reconstructed tombs, part of the **ancient necropolis**. This "bee-hive" **tomb**, originally sited outside the third wall, was encompassed by the later fourth wall. One of more than a hundred tombs (the rest lie west of this wall), the typical structure of a low corridor punctuated by perforated slate slabs leading to a domed burial chamber bears a striking resemblance to tholos tombs of a similar date from the Aegean, particularly southern Crete. It has been suggested that early Cretans (for whom the bull was religiously significant) may have found their way here and that the traditional importance of bulls and bull-fighting on the Iberian peninsula may owe something to this link. Present academic thinking, however, tends towards the idea that the civilization here was of local origin.

More tombs, most in a collapsed state, in which clan members were buried together with their possessions such as arms, tools and what appear to be ceramic idols (suggesting the existence of a cult) lie beyond the outer wall. Originally, and again as in the Aegean, the tombs were covered with an earth mound or tumulus. Try to resist climbing over them as many are in a fragile condition and the importance of this site for posterity is hard to overstate.

Inland towards Almería: Guadix and Baza

An alternative **route from Granada to Almería** – covered by the *Empresa Autodia* buses from c/Rector Marín – runs via **Viznar** (where Lorca was assassinated – see p.332) and **Purullena**, whose pottery output is on show at colourful roadside stalls, to **Guadix**, a crumbling old Moorish town with a vast and extraordinary cave district. For those with transport, the route also offers the opportunity for a detour to the impressive Renaissance castle of **La Calahorra**.

To the north, on the road from Guadix to Lorca and Murcia, there is a last possible *Andaluz* stop at the pleasant market town of **Baza**.

Guadix

Sited on the banks of the Río Guadix, in the midst of a fertile plain, **GUADIX** is a ramshackle, windblown sort of town, coated in red dust blown in from the surrounding hills. It is not a particularly attractive place and if it were not for its remarkable cave district there would be little reason to stop.

It is in fact an ancient settlement, established by the Romans as a base for exploiting seams of silver in the surrounding hills, and later a a substantial Moorish town. The Moors named it *Wadi-ash* (River of Life), from which the modern Guadix derives, and developed an important silk industry, whose mulberry trees can still be seen along the river. More recently, its industry was based upon the production of esparto products and cutlery. It endured terrifying atrocities during the Civil War, which Gerald Brenan described in *South from Granada*.

The Town

Guadix's old quarter is still largely walled, and the circuit includes an imposing Moorish gateway, the Puerta San Turcuato. Within, it is dominated by the red sandstone towers of its sixteenth-century **Catedral** (Mon–Sat 10.30am–1pm & 4.30–6pm; Sun 10.30am–2pm), built on the site of a former mosque. This has been much hacked around and embellished over the years and the exterior is eighteenth-century Corinthian, the work of Vincente Acero; it still bears a commemorative plaque to Primo de Rivera, founder of the Falangist party. The sombre late-Gothic interior was designed by Diego de Siloé, based on that of the cathedral at Málaga. Its best feature is the superb Churrigueresque choirstalls by Ruiz del Peral.

Just across from the cathedral entrance, beneath an arch, stands the **Plaza Mayor**, an arcaded Renaissance square which was reconstructed after severe damage in the Civil War. A right-turn in the stepped street (c/Ancha) at the far end of the square leads up to to the Renaissance **Palacio de Peñaflor**. Nearby in the Placeta de Santiago the whitewashed church of **Santiago** has a fine Plateresque entrance.

Next to the Peñaflor mansion a theological seminary gives access to the conclusively ruined ninth-century Moorish **Alcazaba** (9am–1pm & 4–6pm; 100ptas). From the restored battlements there are **views** over the cave district of Santiago (see below) and beyond towards the Sierra Nevada.

The cave district

Close to the alcazaba and sited in a weird landscape of pyramidal red hills, the cave district of the **Barrio Santiago**, still houses some 10,000 people (most of whom, incidentally, are not gypsies), and to take a look round it is the main reason for most visitors stopping off.

The quarter extends over a square mile or so in area, and the lower caves, on the outskirts, are really proper cottages sprouting television aerials, with upper storeys, electricity, and running water. But as you walk deeper into the suburb, the design quickly becomes simpler – just a whitewashed front, a door, a tiny window and a chimney – and the experience increasingly voyeuristic. Penetrating right to the back you'll come on a few caves which are no longer used: too squalid, too unhealthy, their long-unrepainted whitewash a dull brown. Yet right next door there may be a similar, occupied hovel, with a family sitting outside and other figures following dirt tracks still deeper into the hills.

Beware that offers to show you around the interior of a cave are all too often accompanied by a demand for substantial sums of money when you emerge.

Practicalities

Guadix is not a large place and, if you arrive at the **bus station**, it's easy enough to set your sights on the walls and cathedral – around five minutes' walk.

If you want to **stay** overnight, try the *Fonda García* (☎958/660596; ②), just inside the walls by the Puerta San Turcuato, or either of the *hostales* on the main Carretera de Murcia at the edge of town: *Hostal Río Verde* (☎958/660729; ③) or *Pensión Mulhacén*; ☎958/660750; ③). For **meals**, *Restaurante Accitano* at c/Jardín 3, opposite the Puerta de San Turcuato, has a good value *menú*, as does *Mesón Cato* at Pasaje la Purisima 6, off the end of the Plaza Mayor. *Restaurante El Albergue* at Avda. Medina Olmos 48, next to the bus station, is reasonable, too.

Baza

BAZA, 44km northeast of Guadix along the N342, is another old Moorish town, well worth a detour if you have time and transport. Approached through an ochre landscape dotted with weird conical hillocks covered with esparto grass, the town is slightly larger than Guadix, with a web of streets encircling its ancient central plaza. As with many towns in these parts, it has a history dating back well into prehistoric times. A prosperous Iberian settlement here produced the remarkable *Dama de Baza* sculpture (see below) and the town remained a considerable centre under the Romans and later, like Guadix, a centre of silk production under the Moors; it was especially renowned for its silk prayer mats. Taken by Christian forces in 1489 after a long siege, the town has had a less than glorious past few centuries, in part due to trouble from earthquakes, which have crumbled away most of the old Moorish alcazaba.

Like Guadix Baza also has a **cave quarter**, on the eastern side of town, beyond the railway tracks and close to the bullring.

The Town

The impressive Renaissance collegiate church of Santa María – and its eighteenth-century brick tower – leads you to the Plaza Mayor. The church's Plateresque main door is worth a look and inside there's an interesting marble pulpit and *retablo*. Along a narrow street to the north, c/Arco de la Magdalena, is a **Turismo** which will provide you with a good map for further explorations.

On the opposite side of the Plaza Mayor a small **Museo Arqueológico** (open summer only 7–10pm) preserves finds from the town's ancient past, including a copy of the *Dama de Baza*, a magnificent life-size fourth-century BC Iberian painted sculpture unearthed in 1971 in a necropolis on the outskirts of the town. The original is now in Madrid, where it is exhibited alongside the century later *Dama de Elche*, another iconic work of Spain's early artistic tradition.

A few minutes walk to the east of Plaza Mayor, following c/Cabeza then turning left along c/del Agua, are the **Baños Arabes**, a tenth-century Moorish bath complex – one of the oldest surviving in Spain. The building is still privately owned (the local council are negotiating to take it over) you'll need to visit the owners' home at c/Caniles 19, close by, to get someone to show you around.

FIESTA DE LOS CASCAMORROS

Guadix and Baza are linked by old rivalries which are kept alive in the annual **Fiesta de los Cascamorros** from September 6–9. At the outset of this festival a man dressed as a buffoon and carrying a sceptre walks from Guadix to Baza in an attempt to retrieve an ancient image of the Virgin, over which the two towns have disputed ownership since the sixteenth century. However, to retrieve the sacred image from the church he must remain unblemished and so, as he nears the town, a huge reception committee awaits him armed with drums of used engine oil at the ready.

Needless to say, the poor devil is coated from head to toe in the stuff within seconds of crossing the city limits – as are a whole crowd of the Virgin's protectors – and the oily mass then squelches its way to the Plaza Mayor where, amidst the tolling of church bells, the mayor (from the safety of a balcony) proclaims that Guadix has blown it yet again, after which the town lets rip on a three day binge of celebration.

The other sight of note is the **Palacio de los Enriquez**, an early sixteenth-century Mudéjar mansion. Built by Don Enrique Enriquez, uncle of king Fernando, it served as a country residence and has many Moorish features including stunning *artesonado* ceilings and ornamentation. It is on the Carrera de Palacio, to the south of the Plaza Mayor, and has erratic opening hours: enquire at the Turismo for help, if you want to visit.

Practicalities

Accommodation is easy to find. *Hostal Mariquita* (☎958/701037; ③), c/Caños Dorados 4, to the south of the Plaza Mayor, is excellent value and all rooms have TV and bath. Other possibilities are the nearby *Hostal Eusabio*, c/Serrano 15 (☎958/700614; ②), and, a bit further south on c/María de Luna, the pricier *Hostal Anabel* (☎958/860998; ④).

The *Mariquita* and *Anabel* have decent **restaurants**. Other food and drink options include **tapas** at *Bar El Yoyo* in c/Serrano, or at a nice bar with outdoor tables in Plaza Santo Domingo, just to the north of Plaza Mayor. **Flamenco** accompanies the meals and *tapas* at *Taberna Al Andalus*, c/Sor Florencia, southwest of the Plaza Mayor and close to the train station.

The **bus station** (Avda de los Reyes Católicos) with frequent connections to Guadix, is a couple of blocks to the north of the Plaza Mayor. **Heading on**, possible destinations include the Cazorla Natural Park (see p.303), to the north, or the Almería coast via Vélez Rubio (see p.379).

Guadix to Almería: La Calahorra

Continuing southeast of Guadix along the N324 to Almería, the spectacular domed **Renaissance castle** of **LA CALAHORRA** heaves into view at the 16km point. A turn off to the right takes you the 4km to the village of the same name, where, brooding on its hill above, this red stone monster was constructed in 1510. Its architect was Italian and its owner, one Rodrigo de Mendoza, the bastard son of the powerful Cardinal Mendoza, who did much to establish Isabel on the throne. Rodrigo was created Marquis of Zenete by Isabel and, after acquiring a taste for the Renaissance during an Italian sojourn, he ordered the castle as a wedding gift for his wife María de Fonseca. The bleak situation proved unattractive both to them and their descendants, however, and it was rarely used.

The castle is normally open to the public but it was recently closed for renovation. If access is possible (keys from c/de los Claveles 2 in the village, if it's closed), you'll be able to view a magnificent interior **patio** – the last thing you'd expect behind such a dour exterior. The doorways, arches and stairway of this two-storey courtyard are beautifully carved from Carrara marble.

From La Calahorra a lonely but scenic road – the C331 – toils north to Valor and Ugijar in the Alpujarras.

Towards Almería

Beyond La Calahorra, the N324 crosses the border into Almería and passes by **FIÑANA**, with another castle, this time Moorish and in a more ruinous state. Some 26km further on there's a turn off for **GERGAL**, with another well-preserved fortress and, on the highest summit of the Sierra de los Filabres behind, an observatory housing one of the largest telescopes in Europe, sited here by a German-Spanish venture to take advantage of the almost constantly clear skys. The N324 gradually descends into the valley of the Río Andarax which it follows to Almería.

Almería

Cuando Almería era Almería, Granada era su alquería.
(When Almería was Almería, Granada was but its farm).

A traditional Almerian couplet.

ALMERÍA is a pleasant and largely modern city, spread at the foot of a stark grey hill dominated by a magnificent Moorish fort. It was founded by the Phoenicians and developed by the Romans but it was as a Moorish city – renamed al-Mariyat ("the mirror of the sea") – that Almería grew to prominence. The sultan Abd ar-Rahman I began the building programme soon after the conquest, in 713, with an arsenal beside the port, and the great **Alcazaba**, still the town's dominant feature, was added, in the tenth century by Abd ar-Rahman III, when the city formed part of the Cordoban Caliphate.

The splendours created here by the Moors – most of which have been lost – inspired the popular rhyme at the beginning of this section, contrasting this early prosperity with the much later glories of Nasrid Granada. After the collapse of Moorish Córdoba, Almería's prosperity was hardly affected and as a principality or *taifa* state, it became the country's most important port, as well as a pirates' nest feared around the adjacent coasts. This period ended when the city fell to the forces of Fernando in 1490 and the Moors were expelled. Their possessions and lands were doled out to the officers of the conquering army, forming the basis for the *señoritismo* which has plagued Almería and Andalucía throughout modern times. Predictably, there followed a prolonged decline over the next three hundred years, reversed only by the introduction of the railway and the building of a new harbour in the last century, as well as the opening up to exploitation of the province's vast mineral wealth, particularly iron, lead and gold.

The Civil War interrupted this progress. The city's communist dockworkers gave staunch backing to the Republic, at one point in 1937 causing Hitler to order that the city be shelled from offshore by the German fleet. It was one of the last cities to fall to Franco's forces in 1939, after which many suicides took place to avoid the fate planned for the most bitter enemies of the new order.

Although still the centre of one of the poorest zones in Europe, Almería today is seeking a more prosperous future based upon intensive vegetable production in the surrounding *vega*, in tandem with gaining a greater share of Spain's tourist economy. Whilst even its most devoted admirers wouldn't describe it as a beautiful place, it deserves more visitors than it gets. There are pockets of the town with considerable charm; a handful of fascinating sights; and a friendly welcome in some great bars and restaurants, which may well may make you want to give it a bit longer than the customary one-night transit.

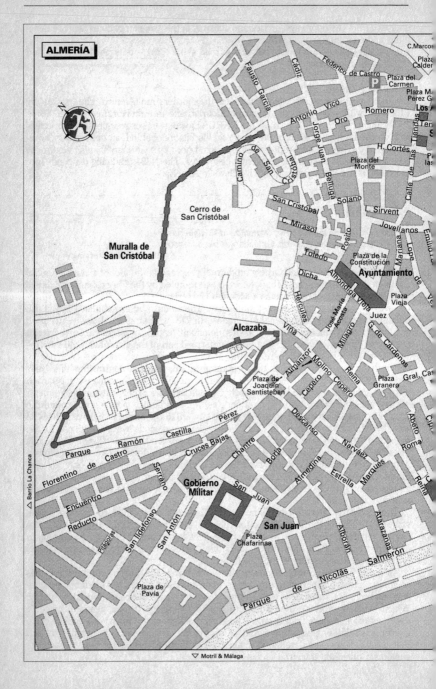

Rambla del Obispo Orbera

Puerta de rchena

Circunvalación

Market Mércado **Diputación**

Rodrigo

C.A. de Campo

Zaragoza

Navarro

Minero

Javier

Eguilior

Av. de la Estación

Picos

Paseo de Almeria

San

Concepción

Arenal

Castelar

Francisco

Sanz

Núñez

Méndez

Padre Santaella

Avenida de Federico García Lorca

C. Hermanos Machado

San Pedro

Plaza de San Pedro

C.P. Alfonso

La Unión

Plaza del Ecuador

Paseo

Rueda López

Marqués de Comilla

Belén

Padre Luque

San Pedro

Conde

C. Guzmán

Sócrates

Trajano

Ofalia

Tamayo

de

Segura

Almeria

C.C. Molina Alonso

Plaza Campomanes

Calle Infanta

Real

Villaespesa

P

Teatro Cervantes

E. Pérez

Plaza Masnou

Basílica de Nuestra Señora del Mar

Plaza Virgen del Mar

General

Arapiles

Plaza de Emilio Pérez

Plaza de Catedral

Plaza Bendicho

Olmos

Real

Álvarez de Castro

Martínez

Gerona

Campos

Gobierno Civil

Av. Reina Regente

Catedral

Duende

Calle Alicante

P. Díaz

Liceo

Molina

Pintor M. Vega

Stma. Trinidad

López

Falcón

Arapiles

Palacio de Justicia

Hospital Real

Parque de Nicolás Salmerón

Andén de Costa

Muelle de Levante

Mar Mediterráneo

▷ Bus & Train Stations

i

◁ Cabo de Gata & Mojácar ▷

▷ Paseo Marítimo

0 100 200 m

Orientation and accommodation

The **Rambla de Belén**, an unsightly dry river bed (due to be landscaped) which sees water only for a week in March with the snowmelt, divides the city from north to south. Most of the action takes place to the west of this boundary, where you will find the **old town** and, to the north, the **Puerta de Purchena**, a busy traffic junction, where six thoroughfares meet, and which effectively marks the centre of the modern city.

Arriving and leaving

The **bus station** is on Plaza Barcelona, in the east of the city, just a few minutes' walk north from the splendid neo-Moorish **train station**, with direct services to Guadix, Granada and Baeza as well as longer-haul destinations such as Madrid (via Linares). There's a train to Granada very early in the morning, and another in the afternoon.

Train tickets and schedules are also available from the *RENFE* office at c/Alcalde Muñoz 7, behind the church of San Sebastián near the Puerta de Purchena. For bus schedules, it's easiest to consult the **Turismo** (Mon–Fri 9am–2pm & 3–7.30pm; Sat 9am–1pm; ☎950/230858) at c/Hermanos Machado 3, just east of the Rambla de Belén.

Almería's **airport** (☎950/221954) is 8km out from the city. Local buses make the journey from the centre every half-hour between 7am and 9pm; they are labelled "El Alquián" and in the city centre there are stops along c/Obispo Oberá to the east of the Puerta de Purchena. The airport bus stop is by a lone *hostal* on the main road 200m from the terminal. Taxis also lurk outside the departure lounge.

There is a **daily boat to Melilla** on the Moroccan coast throughout the summer (less often out of season), an eight-hour journey, but one which cuts out the haul to Málaga or the usual port for Morocco, Algeciras. For information and tickets contact the *Compañia Aucona-Transmediterránea* (☎950/236356), Parque Nicolás Salmerón 28, near the port.

Accommodation

Rooms are generally easy to come by at any time of the year and there are concentrations of *hostales* particularly around the Puerta de Purchena. Decent options include:

Hostal Americano, Avda. de la Estación 6 – near the bus and train stations (☎950/258011). Nothing special but convenient if you arrive late or plan to leave early. ②.

Hostal Andalucía, c/Granada 9 – near Puerta de Purchena (☎950/237733). A charming old hotel which has seen better days but maintains clean, good value rooms. ②.

Hostal Bristol, Plaza San Sebastián 8 – near Puerta de Purchena (☎950/231595) is another possibility in the same category with similar facilities. ②.

Casa Francesca, c/Narvaez 18 (☎950/237554). A cheap and characterful *fonda* a couple of blocks west of the cathedral. ②.

Hotel Costasol, Paseo de Almería 58 – near the Rambla end (☎950/234011). The best of the more upmarket hotels. Comfortable and central. ⑤.

Hostal Maribel, Avda. García Lorca 153 (☎950/235173). A friendly place fronting the Rambla de Belén; it has rooms at various prices – some very cheap. ②.

Hostal Nixar, c/Antonio Vico 24 – uphill from Puerta de Purchena (☎950/237255). Good value; ask for the higher rooms, which are airier. ③.

Hostal Sevilla, c/Granada 23 – near Puerta de Purchena (☎950/230799). A good value modern *hostal* with air-conditioning and TV in each room. ④.

Fonda Universal, Puerta de Purchena 3 (☎950/235557). A basic place but the cleanest of a number of *fondas* in this zone. ②.

CAMPING

Camping a Garrofa (☎950/235770). This is the nearest campsite – 5km west, on the coast at La Garrofa. It is easily reached by the buses to Aguadulce and Roquetas de Mar (where there's another, giant site).

At the time of writing, the city's **youth hostel** is closed.

The Town

Almería's most impressive monument, the formidable **Alcazaba**, is probably the best surviving example of a Moorish military fortification. It can be reached by following any of the narrow streets which climb the hill west of the cathedral, aiming for the entrance below the walls in the Plaza Joaquin Santisteban, at the end of c/Almanzor. The city's other sights pale by comparison, though it is worth taking time to look over the **cathedral** and the **Puerta de Purchena** area.

The Alcazaba

The **Alcazaba** (daily 10am–2pm & 5.30–8pm; free with EC passport, otherwise 250ptas) was begun by Abd ar-Rahman III of Córdoba in 955 and was just one part of a massive building programme which included a great mosque and city walls. During the eleventh-century when the city enjoyed a period of prosperous independence, between the fall of the Cordoban Caliphate and its capture by the Almoravids, the medina (walled city) here contained immense gardens and palaces and housed some 20,000 people. It was adapted after the *reconquista* by the Catholic monarchs but severely damaged during a great earthquake in 1522. A programme of restoration in recent years has begun to reverse the centuries of crumbling decay.

Through the **Puerta Exterior**, a zig-zagged entrance ramp – a traditional Moorish architectural feature to make attack precarious – leads to the **Puerta de la Justicia**, the gateway to the first of the Alcazaba's three great compounds. Halfway up the ramp to the right is the **Tower of Mirrors**, a fifteenth century addition, where mirrors were employed to communicate with ships approaching the port below.

THE FIRST COMPOUND

The first compound is the largest of the three. It is laid out today as a garden but was designed as a military camp and an area in which the populace could seek protection when under siege. A **well** in the centre of this area raised water from a depth of 70m to supply the site. At the eastern end of the enclosure, the **Saliente Bastion** was a look-out point over the town below, and the sea beyond.

Below the north side of the compound, the **eleventh-century wall** descends the hill; it originally formed part of a great complex of walls, not only surrounding the city but dividing it internally also. Above the wall, which divides the first and second compounds, is the **Campana de Vela**, a bell erected during the eighteenth century to announce ships sighted nearing the port, or to summon soldiers to their battle stations.

THE SECOND COMPOUND

The second compound accommodated the Moorish kings, when resident in the city, and at other times served as the governor's quarters. In the eleventh century, when Almería was the wealthiest, most commercially active city of Spain, the buildings here were of unparalleled brilliance. Their grandeur was even reputed to rival the later court of Granada, but the ruins that remain today make a valid comparison impossible.

What you can see, however, are the remains of **cisterns**, the old **mosque** – converted into a chapel by the *Reyes Católicos* – and once palatial dwellings, but sadly no sign of the magnificent stuccowork said to equal that of the Alhambra, the last remnants of which were sold off by the locals in the eighteenth century. The **Ventana de Odalisca**, a *mirador* window in the compound's northern wall, is a poignant reminder of lost glory. A legend attached to this concerns an eleventh-century Moorish slave-girl, Galiana, the king's favourite, who fell in love with a prisoner and arranged to help him to escape. But the guards discovered them in the attempt and the prisoner threw himself from this window into the valley below, whilst Galiana died of a broken heart a few days later.

THE THIRD COMPOUND

The third and highest compound demonstrates the starkly contrasting style of the conquering Christians. When they took the city, the Catholic monarchs found the fortress substantially damaged due to an earthquake a couple of years before. They thererefore built walls much stronger than the original Moorish structure, to cope both with potential future earthquakes and the recent innovation of artillery. Triangular in form, this upper fort is guarded by three semi-circular towers built of ashlar masonry, both features at odds with the earlier Moorish design.

To the right, the **Torre del Homenaje** (tower of homage) bears the crumbling escutcheon of the Catholic monarchs. An open hole nearby, in the centre of the **Patio de Armas** (courtyard of arms), could lead to a nasty fall into a deep **silo**, which was probably used for the storage of grain. An iron ladder allows a more dignified descent, although once you get a whiff of the urine-soaked depths you may change your mind. From the **Torre de Pólvora** (gunpowder tower) and the battlements (take care as there are few handrails) fine views are to be had of the coast and of Almería's *gitano* cave quarter – the Barrio La Chanca – on a low hill to the west.

The Mirador de San Cristóbal and Wildlife Centre

The hilltop **Mirador de San Cristóbal**, which can be seen from the Alcazaba, has more fine views over the town and the coast, and can be visited by following c/Antonio Vico west from the Puerta de Purchena. Adjoining the *mirador* is a chapel with a huge figure of Christ, erected in 1928 over the site of an earlier chapel founded by the Templars after the Christians, under Alfonso VI, took the city, briefly, in 1147. The open-air chapel's altar at the rear of Christ's statue has been completely hacked apart and the walls covered with graffiti – a telling comment on Spain's rapid transition to a secular state. The **sunsets** to be seen both from here and the alcazaba are legendary.

North of the *mirador* and alcazaba – and visible from both – is a curious-looking farm, where you can often see gazelles sprinting around. This is the **Sahara Wildlife Rescue Centre** (☎951/236500), a research organisation studying animals in danger of disappearing from their natural habitat. The centre can be visited only by prior application.

The Cathedral

Located in the heart of the old quarter, the **Catedral** (daily 10.30am–12.00pm & 5.30–6.30pm and service hours) is another building with a fortress look about it. Begun in 1524 on the site of the great mosque – conveniently destroyed by the 1522 earthquake – it was designed in the late Gothic style by Diego de Siloé, the architect of the cathedral at Granada. Because of the danger of attack in this period from Barbarossa and other Turkish and North African pirate forces the corner towers once held cannons. The threat was real and not long after its construction the cathedral chapter is recorded purchasing guns, muskets and gunpowder.

Like many of Andalucía's cathedrals, it was never completely finished and it may be that the city's inhabitants had no great affection for this austere giant, preferring instead their more intimate parish churches. The exterior is of little interest apart from a curious pagan-looking relief of a garlanded **radiant sun** on the eastern wall – that is, facing the rising sun. Echoing the Roman *Sol Invictus*, or unconquerable sun, its appearance on the church has been put down to a sixteenth century bishop with masonic leanings, but its true significance will probably never be known.

The cathedral is entered through the Puerta Principal, an elegant Renaissance doorway flanked by buttresses. Within, the sober Gothic **interior** is distinguished by some superb sixteenth-century **choirstalls** carved in walnut by Juan de Orea. Just behind this, the **retrochoir** is a stunning eighteenth-century altar in contrasting red and black jasper. Behind the Capilla Mayor (or high altar), the Capilla de la Piedad has a painting of the *Annunciation* by Alonso Cano and the Capilla de Santo Cristo – next door to the right – contains the sixteenth-century tomb of Bishop Villalán, the cathedral's founder, complete with faithful hound at his feet. Further along again, a door (often closed) leads to the sacristy and a rather uninspiring Renaissance cloister. The church also contains a number of fine **pasos** of the Passion carried in the *Semana Santa* processions at Easter; among these, *El Prendimiento* (the Arrest of Christ) is outstanding.

Around the old town

To the west of the cathedral stands the seventeenth-century church of **San Juan** (open service times only), built over a tenth-century mosque. Inside, the church's southern wall preserves the *mihrab* (or prayer niche) of the original building. Next to this, there's another niche that would have contained the wooden pulpit used for readings from the Koran.

West of here lies the **Barrio de Chanca**, an area of grinding poverty which has hardly changed since Brenan vividly described it in his *South from Granada*; it's not a place to visit alone at night. Nearby, on c/Hospital, the eighteenth-century **Hospital Real** has an elegant neo-classical façade and, inside, a beautiful marble tiled patio usually containing a few prostrate patients on hospital trolleys. Like many others in Spain, this is still a fully-functioning infirmary two and a half centuries after it was built.

To the north of the cathedral the **Plaza Vieja** (officially Plaza de la Constitución) is a wonderful pedestrian square which – because of its restricted entrance – you would hardly know was there. It contains the **Ayuntamiento**, a flamboyant turn-of-the-century building with a pink and cream façade. This square has bags of potential and elsewhere would be full of restaurants and nightlife; presently though, it's a rather melancholy place after dark.

Around the Puerta de Purchena

A few further sights are located within a couple of minutes walk of the **Puerta de Purchena**, which takes its name from a Moorish gate – long gone – where al-Zagal, the city's last Moorish ruler, surrendered to the Catholic monarchs in 1490.

On the west side of the junction, just off c/de las Tiendas at c/de los Aljibes 20, are ancient Moorish water cisterns – known as **Los Aljibes**. As the premises are now occupied by a *peña de flamenco*, you can usually get access to see them during late afternoon and evening. The **Calle de las Tiendas** itself – the oldest street in the city – was formerly called Calle Lencerías (drapers' street) and in the last century was Almería's most fashionable shopping thoroughfare. Some of the street lamps survive from this period, although the place has now become seedy.

A little further down you'll arrive at the church of **Santiago**, dating from the same period as the cathedral, and built with stone from the same quarry. A fine Plateresque portal incorporates a statue of Santiago slaying the Moors as well as the coat of arms of the all-powerful Bishop Villalán, the cathedral's founder.

Finally, across the Paseo de Almería, the main street which leaves the Puerta de Purchena from its southern side, a **daily market** at the end of c/Aguilar de Campo is also worth a look.

The Archeological Museum

Almería's **Museo Arqueológico** has been closed since the building developed dangerous structural faults. When it reopens (almost certainly on a new site) its important collection of **artefacts from the prehistoric site of Los Millares** (see p.355) will be on view again. The museum also has interesting Roman and Moorish sections. The Turismo should be able to advise on developments.

Eating, drinking and entertainment

Almería has a surprising number of interesting and good value places to **eat and drink**. Most of the best eating options are to be found around the Puerta de Purchena and in the web of narrow streets lying between the Paseo de Almería and the cathedral. For seafood there are a number of places in the Barrio de los Pescadores, the old fishing quarter, at the western end of the commercial port. On the **nightlife** front, the city's music bars can be lively and in summer there are late-night marquees on the beach.

In August the city holds its annual **music and arts festival**, the *Fiesta de los Pueblos Ibéricos y del Mediterraneo*, with concerts and dance events, many of them free, taking place in the squares and various other locations throughout the city. During the last week of the month, the city's main **annual fiesta**, the *Romaría de Augusto*, also takes place.

Restaurants and tapas bars

The best place for early evening *tapas* is around the Puerta de Purchena, where the whole town turns out during the evening *paseo* to see and be seen. Places around the cathedral and old town are more lively at lunchtime.

AROUND PUERTA DE PURCHENA

Bar El Alcázar, Paseo de Almería 4. A popular *marisquería* and *freiduría* with plenty of *tapas* possibilities and tables to sit out at to watch the early evening *paseo*.

Restaurante Alfareros, c/Marcos 6 – behind the *Hotel Andalucía*. A wonderful and cheap place to eat, packed at lunchtime with people in town for the market. There is an excellent value *menú* served up by an ebullient proprietor.

Bodega Las Botas, c/Fructuoso Perez 3. A great *tapas* place. Legs of *jamón serrano* hang from pillars and the tables are upturned sherry butts; to accompany the excellent *fino* and *manzanilla* (served with a traditional "free" *tapa*) you may want to try the tasty house speciality, *merluza en escabeche* (marinated hake) or the more expensive *jamón*.

Bar-Restaurante Imperial, Puerta de Purchena. This is a lively *tapas* bar with a cheap bar *menú*, which you can eat at the tables outside – best in the evening when there are less traffic fumes. The restaurant is good, too, but avoid the room upstairs, with non-existent service.

Rincon de Juan Pedro, Plaza del Carmen. One of the town's pricier restaurants, serving top quality Almerian specialities. On a budget, stick to the medium-priced *menú*.

Restaurante Valentin, c/Tenor Iribarne 7. Owned by the same people as *Bodega Las Botas*, this lacks a terrace and can be bit oppressive in the summer heat but the food is equally good. This whole street is full of good *tapas* bars.

TOWARDS THE CATHEDRAL

Bar Bahia de la Palma, Plaza de la Constitución. A good lunchtime *tapas* stop.

Casa Joaquín, c/Real 2. A fine *tapas* bar where all business is done verbally – with no assistance from menus or bills.

Bodega Montenegro, Plaza Granero – just west of the cathedral. This delightful neighbourhood bar is stacked with barrels. Once they've got over the initial novelty of seeing a foreigner walk through the door, they will serve up great local wines and seafood *tapas*.

Bodega del Patio, c/Real 84. Another wonderful old Almerian *bodega*, little changed for decades.

Casa Puga, corner of c/ Lope de Vega and c/Jovellanos. With marble-topped tables and walls covered with *azulejos*, this is another *tapas* bar with a great atmosphere; however, the *raciones* can work out pricey if you let yourself go.

Bodega Ramon and **Bodega El Ajoli**, c/Padre Alfonso. Two good *tapas* bars on a pleasant street, both with tables to sit out at. *El Ajoli* specializes in pork products – try their *surtido*, which gets you a bit of everything.

BARRIO DE LOS PESCADORES
Pavía, Plaza Pavía 10. Fine fish and seafood served on tables in the square in summer.
Los Sobrinos, Cuesta de Muelle 32. A cheaper place, further west.

Breakfast

For breakfast, there are plenty of bars and *pastelerias* along the Paseo de Almería, but a good and cheap personal favourite is *El Oasis*, a self-service kiosk bar on the western side of the Puerta de Purchena. There are tables to sit out at and – because it's self service – you avoid the normal terrace surcharge.

Nightlife and flamenco

Most of the **nightlife** takes place in the beach resorts to the west of the town. However, if you're determined the bars in the streets around the Plaza Masnou attract big night-time crowds and further east across the Rambla de Belén the *Lord Nelson* **disco**, c/ Canónigo Molina Alonso), is sometimes lively. Another disco off the west side of the Alameda is *Garage*, c/Guzman s/n).

To move the nightime *marcha*, or scene, away from the residential area in summer, the city council erects a line of **disco marquees** at the start of the Paseo Marítimo, near the beach. Around three in the morning these places start to get quite wild. At other times of the year the focus moves back into town and the streets around c/Trajano off the Alameda where Indie bars *Vértice* and *Vhada* are popular. The *Port of Spain* bar along the Avenida Parque fronting the port, sometimes has **live jazz**.

For **flamenco** the only genuine establishment is *Peña El Taranto*, c/Los Aljibes 20. This holds concerts (except in August) in the old Arab cisterns, behind the Puerta de Purchena. It also runs an all-year, friendly, rooftop terrace bar with grilled *tapas*.

Listings

Banks The major banks, most with cash dispensers, are located along the Alameda (Paseo de Almería) and close at 2pm. Some of the *Cajas de Ahorro* (savings banks), which also have exchange facilities, re-open in the afternoon from 4pm to 6.30pm.
Beaches The city beach, southeast of the centre beyond the rail lines, is long but crammed with daytrippers for most of the summer. For a daytrip, the best options are Cabo de Gata or San José, both easily accessible by bus.
Car removal If you park illegally, your car stands a fair chance of being hauled off by the *Grua* (crane). Phone ☎950/234966 and prepare to pay for your sins.
Car rental Try *Europcar*, c/Rueda López 23, on the east side of the Alameda (☎950/234966).
Emergency health treatment *Cruz Roj* , Parque de Nicolás Salmerón 28, facing the port (☎950/ 222222).
Phone calls International calls can be made from most phone boxes in the centre, or the *Telefonica* office at c/Navarro Rodrigo 9, near the market.
Post office The main *Correos* is at Plaza Cassinello 1, near Plaza del Ecuador, off Paseo de Almería.

West of Almería: the Costa Tropical

Almería's best beach resorts lie on its eastern coast, the Costa de Almería, between the city and Mojácar. On the so-called **Costa Tropical**, west of the city, the nearest beaches such as **Aguadulce**, **Roquetas de Mar** and **Almerimar** are overdeveloped and the landscape is dismal, backed by an ever-expanding plastic sea of *invernaderos*, hothouses for cultivation of fruit and vegetables for the export market (see box over the page). Beyond Adra things improve, and smaller resorts such as **La Rábita**, **Castell de Ferro** and **Calahonda** make tolerable places to stop.

Almería to Adra

This section of coast is described here for little other reason than completeness – it's certainly not an unspoilt paradise; indeed no one comes here for the beaches. The one half-decent reason for a stop in these parts is if you're a birdwatcher, in which case the inland salt lakes may well appeal.

Aguadulce, Roquetas de Mar – and some birdwatching

AGUADULCE, 13km west of Almería, is the oldest of the city's local resorts, with a palm-lined promenade that does its best to offset the miserable concrete boxes flanking it. There's a reasonable beach, the usual *costa* nightlife, and some fairly expensive accommodation, full all summer.

The next place along, **ROQUETAS DE MAR** used to be another old fishing port, though its remaining whitewashed core is now submerged by an ugly conglomeration of hotels and and beach emporia. On the plain behind the resort, plastic greenhouses compete fiercely with developers for land and this must be the only place in Spain where agricultural land – a single hectare sells for millions of pesetas – is more profitable than tourist development. The centre of the cultivation is the boom town of **EL EJIDO** (see box), 30km inland from Roquetas de Mar along the arrow-straight N340.

PLASTICULTURA: EL EJIDO'S ELDORADO

West of Almería, and stretching from beneath the hills of the Sierra de Gador to the sea, lies the **Campo de Dalías**, a vast plain of salt flats and sand dunes which has become a shining sea of *plasticultura* – the forced production of millions of tons of tomatoes, peppers, cucumbers, strawberries and exotic flowers. This industry has wrought quite a revolution in impoverished Almería, covering a once barren wilderness with a shimmering sea of 15,000 hectares of polythene canopies propped up by eucalyptus supports.

The boom is all due to the invention of drip feed irrigation and it has led to phenomenal increases in the year-round production of crops, allowing cheap tropical fruit and flowers to fill the supermarket shelves of northern Europe throughout the year. The appliance of biological engineering now means that El Ejido's farmers can produce vegetables to almost any specification – tomatoes made to measure to any desired size and weight, red peppers with thick skins and large cavities for stuffing or lettuces without coarse outer leaves which look green even under fluorescent supermarket lights. The miracle, however, may be precarious. Scientists have serious worries about the draining of the province's meagre water resources through the tapping of countless artesian wells – many as deep as 100m.

The centre of this area is **El Ejido**, which appears on most maps as an inconspicuous dot and on others not at all, despite a conurbation getting on for city status. Indeed, it has grown from a modest population of two thousand, twenty years ago, to some fifty thousand, which makes it second in the province only to the capital itself. Like some Wild West town, El Ejido has grown up for a dozen kilometres along the main highway with little or no planning restraints and with the free market in almost total control. The bonanza has lured in peasants from all over Spain and beyond, and many *Andaluzes* who formerly worked in the the factories of Barcelona and Germany have come home with their savings and bought plots.

The lack of facilities for this enormous population growth has led to serious problems and the social cost of this boom has been high: the suicide rate has risen sharply as those who don't make the easy money anticipated get deep into debt, and the twelve to fifteen hour days worked in jungle humidity all year long inside the *invernaderos* (plastic tents) often leads to breakdowns. Besides illness, alcoholism, gambling and drug addiction are also taking their toll.

Some relief from the tedium can be found 5km to the south of Roquetas, where **Las Marinas** is a good place for spotting birdlife. A saline marsh fringed by tamarisks, it attracts greater flamingos, little egrets and avocets, and, in winter, the white wagtail. The lake is reached by turning left beyond the *Urbanización Roquetas de Mar*. A road joins this to a second area at **Punta Sabinar** 1km south consisting of beach, sand dunes and salt-marsh with possible sightings of crested larks, great grey shrikes and fantailed warblers.

Almerimar and Adra

ALMERIMAR is a long 18km from Roquetas, past the plastic-covered desert – and not much relief when you eventually arrive. A tasteless collection of *urbanizaciones* – with more being assembled by cranes dominating the skyline – crowd around a dismal yacht harbour tarted up with a few newly planted trees. Less interested in attracting foreign package tours, this is the "glitz" resort for the nouveau riche of El Ejido, and the place where these peseta multi-millionaires can indulge in conspicuous consumption. Tacky shopping arcades with neo-Moorish façades, overpriced restaurants and a golf course designed by Gary Player, complete the picture.

It's a relief to join the main N340 heading west, although not for long because you soon arrive in **ADRA**, another place with non-existent charms. "The last king of the Moors, the unfortunate Boabdil, stayed in Adra immediately before leaving Spain for good. If he sighed when leaving Granada, he would have sighed even more had Adra in the fifteenth century been anything like it is today." Few would argue with Michael Jacobs' comments on this seedy industrial port in his book *Andalusia*. The best that can be said for it is that the planners have considerately sited the **bus station** on the seafront near the harbour, thus allowing for a speedy and relatively painless getaway.

Some 16km inland from Adra is the solid farming town of **BERJA**, the capital of *Alpujarra Baja*, surrounded by vineyards and fruit orchards, with a considerable Roman and Moorish past (there's a ruined alcazaba) and a lively daily market. Its eastern suburb, Alcaudique, has the remains of a Moorish bath. Nearby **DALÍAS**, another pleasant farming village, is founded upon the ruins of Roman *Murgis*.

Adra to Motril

Things start to look up along the coast to the west of Adra, and there are attractions inland, too. From La Rábita a scenic secondary road, the C333, heads up into Las Alpujarras, passing by the *costa* wine villages of **Albuñol** and, along the GR433, **Albondón** (see p.354).

Güainos Bajos and Castillo de Baños

Around 5km west of Adra, **GÜAINOS BAJOS** fronts a pleasant and small beach. A further 10km – and over the provincial border in Granada – you reach **LA RÁBITA**, another place that might invite a stop. Enclosed in a rocky creek, it has a reasonable beach (though it is often litter-strewn after the weekend onslaught), as well as a clutch of bars and restaurants. The central *Hostal Las Olas*, Avda. Generalisimo s/n (☎958/839089; ②), has decent and inexpensive **rooms**.

CASTILLO DE BAÑOS, 13km east of La Rábita, takes its name from a nearby *atalaya* or watchtower and is another possibility for a stopover with a decent beach and a good **campsite**, *Camping Castillo de Baños*; (☎958/829528).

Castell de Ferro and beyond

CASTELL DE FERRO, 6km on from Castillo de Baños, is by far the best of the resorts along the Costa Tropical and even preserves remnants of its former existence as a fishing village. Dominated by another hill-top *atalaya*, it's quite sheltered and has a couple of wide, if pebbly, beaches to the west and especially east, although the town beach fronting the small assemblage of bars, restaurants, and *hostales* is a filthy disgrace. Among the **places to stay** (all on the seafront Plaza de España), the friendly *Pensión Bahia* (☎958/656060; ③) is the best value and has seaview rooms with terrace, with the *Costa del Sol* (☎958/656054; ③) a second choice. Of Castell's four **campsites**, *Camping Las Palmeras* (☎958/646130) to the east is the best, with shade, plenty of space and access to the beach. For **meals**, *Restaurante La Brisa* does a good and inexpensive *menú*, as do most of the places along the seafront.

The coast road east again from here skirts the foothills of the Sierra de Carchuna where **CALAHONDA** is another small resort with a good beach, often full to the gunnels in summer. Next comes the unremarkable **TORRENUEVA**, where there's a reasonable beach but little else to stop for, then the road crosses a dreary plain planted with sugar-cane, to the north of which lies the large and ugly chemical and industrial town of **MOTRIL**, and to the south its equally unappealing port-resort. The beaches to the west of Motril are described in the *Málaga and Cádiz* chapter.

The Costa de Almería

The **Costa de Almería**, east of Almería, has a somewhat wild air, with developments constrained by lack of water and roads and by the confines of the **Parque Natural de Cabo de Gata** – a protected zone since 1987. If you have transport, it's still possible to find deserted beaches without too much difficulty, while small inlets shelter relatively low-key resorts such as **San José**, **Los Escullos**, **Las Negras** and **Agua Amarga**.

Further north is **Mojácar**, a picturesque hill village, which has grown a beach resort of quite some size over the past decade. It is easiest approached on the inland routes through Nijar or the "desert" road through Tabernas (see p.380).

Almería to Mojácar

The coast between Almería and Mojácar is backed by the **Sierra del Cabo de Gata**, which gives it a bit of character and wilderness. **Buses** run from Almería to all the main resorts, though to do much exploring, or seek out deserted strands, transport of your own is invaluable; the heat is blistering here throughout the summer.

El Cabo de Gata and Las Salinas

Heading east along the main N344, a turn-off to the right, 4km beyond the airport, heads south to **EL CABO DE GATA**. This is the closest resort to the city with any appeal: a lovely expanse of coarse sand, best in the mornings before the sun and wind get up. Seven buses a day (four on Sundays) run between Almería and El Cabo, making an intermediate stop at Retamar, a retirement/holiday development.

Arriving at El Cabo, you pass a lake, the **Laguna de Rosa**, a protected locale that is home to flamingos and other waders. Nearby there's a summer **campsite**, *Camping Cabo de Gata*. In the village itself there are plentiful bars, cafés and shops, plus a fish market. The two *fondas* above the bars on the beach are both a little overpriced (③); **rooms** at the *Pizzería Pedro* are cheaper (②) and self-contained.

Just south of the village is another area known as **Las Salinas** – The Salt Pans – and it is exactly that, with a commercial slat-drying enterprise at its southern end. In summer **flamingos** and other migrants are a common sight here (see box, p.374), so take binoculars if you have them. The hills of salt are a striking sight in the bright sun, too, and the industry here has quite a pedigree for it was the Phoenicians way back in the first millennium BC who first controlled the seawater which entered through the

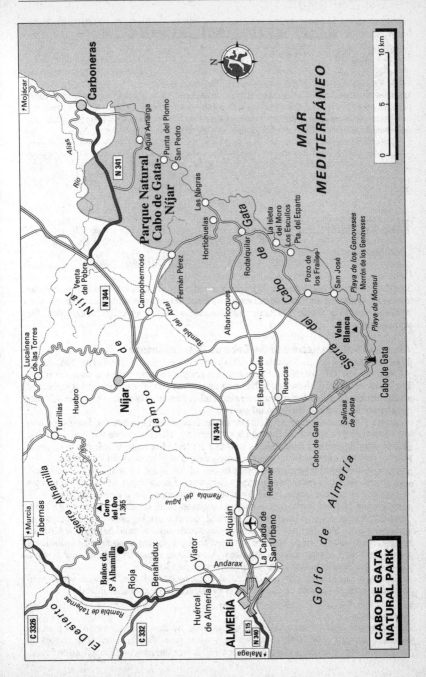

PARQUE NATURAL DE CABO DE GATA

Protected since 1987, the 29,000 hectares of the **Parque Natural de Cabo de Gata** stretch from Retamar to the east of Almería across the cape to the Barranco del Honda, just north of Agua Amarga. The Sierra de Gata is volcanic in origin and its adjacent dunes and saltings are some of the most important wetland areas in Spain for **breeding birds and migrants**. At the Las Salinas saltings alone (see text) more than eighty species can be sighted throughout the year, including the magnificent pink flamingos as well as avocet, storks and egrets during their migrations. And there have been rarer sightings of Andouin's gull, as well as Bonelli's eagle and eagle owls around the crags.

Other **fauna** include the rare Italian wall lizard (its only habitat in Spain), with its distinctive green back with three rows of black spots, as well as the more common fox (sporting its Iberian white tail tip), hare and grass snake. Among the **flora**, the stunted dwarf fan palm is Europe's only native palm and the salt marshes are home to a strange parasitic plant – the striking yellow-flowering *Cistanche phelypaea* – which feeds on goosefoot.

The best time for sightings of much of the fauna is at **dawn and dusk** for, with temperatures among the highest in Europe, and rainfall at 10cm a year the lowest, energy has to be conserved. Cabo de Gata village has the park's main **Oficina de Información** at Avda. Miramar 88 (☎950/380299); there's also a sub-office on c/Correos in at San José.

---

marshes to create pools for the extraction of salt. The park authorities like to cite the modern industry as an example of resource extraction and environmental conservation working hand in hand. Certainly the flamingos seem perfectly happy with the arrangement.

Almadraba de Montelva and the Cabo de Gata lighthouse

Four kilometres to the south of El Cabo village, just beyond Las Salinas, is **ALMADRABA DE MONTELVA**, more a continuation rather than a separate place, but altogether more pleasant for hanging around. It has a few bars and a couple of **restaurants**: *La Almadraba* has a terrace and prices to reflect it, whilst the *Morales* nearby is friendlier and serves good seafood.

Another 4km south, past a hill known as the Pico de San Miguel, the **Faro de Cabo de Gata** (lighthouse) marks the cape's southern tip. There's a *tapas* bar here, *Bar José María*, serving up tasty fried fish, as well as a *mirador* from where you can get a great view of the rock cliffs and – on clearer days – a sight of Morocco's Rif mountains.

Beyond the lighthouse a track leads to two of the finest **beaches** in the province, and to the resort of San José beyond. This track has recently been closed to cars because of its perilous state, which is all to your advantage for it makes for a fine walk through the Natural Park. It starts out as a paved road, climbing up from the lighthouse, but soon degenerates into a dirt track, passing prickly pear cactus plantations grown for their fruit, and access tracks to the wonderful fine sand beaches of **Monsul** – with fresh water springs and a track west to the even more secluded Media Luna cove – and further east, **Los Genoveses**. A couple of kilometres ahead, and beyond another spur, you'll sight the sea and the resort of San José.

To reach San José **by car**, assuming this coast road/track is still closed, you'll need to double back to El Cabo de Gata and follow the signed road further inland.

San José

The attractive little resort of **SAN JOSÉ** (served by bus from Almería) has a sandy beach in a small cove, with shallow water, while more fine beaches (see above) lie within walking distance. Only a few years ago it was almost completely undeveloped, though things are changing, with a rash of apartments and a new yacht harbour. Hopefully, it won't go the way of the resorts west of Almería.

Rooms can be hard to come by in high season, and prices and standards vary greatly – you'll have to hunt around; oddly, the *fondas* tend to be pricier than the *hostales*. *Casa de Huéspedes Costa Rica* (②), on the main road a little way out, is one of the cheapest and also serves a reasonable *menú*. Of the hostales, *Pensión El Paraiso*, Bda. San José s/n (☎950/380025; ③) is the only budget hope; don't confuse it with the more expensive *El Paraiso II* nearby. *Hostal Bahia* (c/Correos 5; ☎950/380114; ④) is the best of the pricier places, especially if you get a balcony/sea view room. There's also a good **campsite**, *Camping Tau* (☎950/380166; April–Oct), on the beach.

For **food and drink** there are numerous excellent bars – a good one up the hill to the west of the main square – and a good fish restaurant, *La Cueva*, on c/del Puerto Deportivo – try their *salmonetes* (red mullet fried with garlic). There's also a well-stocked supermarket for picnic supplies.

If you've followed the walk from the lighthouse to San José (described above) and want to continue along the coast there's another **track** (risky for non-four wheel drive vehicles) running 12km north to Los Escullos and La Isleta. To start the walk take the road north out of San José, shortly along which you'll come to a turn-off along a dirt track on the right that heads around a hill – Cerro del Enmedio – towards the coast. The track branches at various points and you'll have to decide whether to follow the coastal tracks (which can be impassable) or the surer inland route. The first track off to the coast provides access to a beautiful and secluded cove.

Further on, the route skirts the 500m high Cerro de los Frailes, beyond which lie the inlets of Los Escullos and La Isleta.

Los Escullos, La Isleta and Las Negras

Next along this rugged coastline is **LOS ESCULLOS**, 8km north by road, with a good if rather pebbly beach, a ruined castle and a pleasant if overpriced beachfront hotel-restaurant, *Casa Emilio* (☎950/389761; ④). There's also a **campsite**, *Camping Los Escullos* (☎950/389810), set back from the sea and with very limited shade. **LA ISLETA**, 2km beyond, is another fishing village, with a sleepy atmosphere, a rather scruffy pebble beach and a **hostal**, *Isleta de Moro* (☎950/389713; ③), overlooking the harbour; this is reasonably priced and has a good bar for *tapas*, but you'll need to book well ahead in season.

If you don't use Juanito's boat, you'll have to walk to the deserted coastal village of **SAN PEDRO** with its caves and a ruined castle; it is 4km north on a poor track. The place used to be inhabited until a few years ago when the mainly elderly residents upped sticks to Las Negras, which had acquired a road, leaving their houses to crumble. Unfortunately, the village has been infested of late with a particularly odious band of German hippies, which somewhat takes the shine off an otherwise beautiful location. If you are feeling really energetic you could walk 7km on from here along the coast to Agua Amarga, via another German hippy colony at **Cala del Plomo**.

Agua Amarga

Officially there's no road from **Las Negras to Agua Amarga** (10km north as the crow flies) but if you are willing to take a few risks with your car's suspension, a hellish, dusty and boulder-strewn track – not on the maps – heads east from the inland village of **Fernan Perez** through a no-man's-land. Eventually you'll come to a white farm-house fronted by an old sail-less windmill. Veer right here and the track will bring you into Agua Amarga. By this point you will undoubtedly be in need of a drink and wishing you'd taken the longer – and paved – route back to the N344, heading east and turning off at Venta del Pobre. This more rational detour would also allow a visit to Níjar (see p.381), 4km beyond the main road. There is no public transport on either route.

AGUA AMARGA, when you reach it, is a delightful little fishing hamlet cut off from the surrounding world by a long road and a lack of cheap accommodation. Most of the summer visitors here are Italians who rent a tasteful crop of villas. The fine EC blue flagged sand beach is excellent, and there are a number of bars and restaurants backing it. Should you have the urge **to stay** there's a solitary French-run **hostal**, the *Pensión Family* on c/La Lomilla (☎951/138014; ④ including breakfast), with a small pool, garden, and restaurant. It doesn't come cheap and needs to be booked well ahead in season.

Carboneras

Leaving the Natural Park behind, **CARBONERAS**, 11km north of Agua Amarga, is a larger but easy-going fishing port with an average beach, somewhat marred by the shadow of a massive cement factory around the bay. The seafront has a few *tapas* bars and there are a couple of **hostales**: *San Antonio* on c/Pescadores (☎951/130019; ③) is reasonable or there's the slightly cheaper *Hostal Café-Bar Trebol* (☎951/454225; ③) on the north side of town, 50m back from the beach, on Avda. Garrucha. Cheaper still is the central *La Marina* at c/Gen. Mola 1 (☎951/454070; ②).

Towards Mojácar

North of Carboneras lies a succession of small, isolated coves, backed by a characteristically arid Almerian landscape of scrub-covered hills and dried up *arroyos*, or watercourses. The **Carboneras–Mojácar road** itself winds perilously – and scenically – through the hills and offers access to some deserted grey-sand beaches before ascending to the Punta del Santo with fine views along the coast. The descent from here brings you to the **Playa de Macenas**, another pleasant beach with wild-camping possibilities. There are a couple more beaches – **Costa del Pirulico** is a good one with a beach *chiringuito* – before the urban sprawl of Mojácar takes over.

Mojácar

MOJÁCAR, Almería's main and growing resort, is split between the ancient hilltop village – **Mojácar Pueblo** – that lies a couple of kilometres back from the sea, a striking town of white cubist houses wrapped round a harsh outcrop of rock, and the resort area of **Mojácar Playa** which ribbons for a couple of miles along the seafront.

In the 1960s, when the main Spanish *costas* were being developed, this was virtually a ghost town, its inhabitants – among them the infant Walt Disney – having long since taken the only logical step, and emigrated. The town's fortunes revived, however, when the local mayor, using the popularity of other equally barren spots on the Spanish islands and mainland as an example, offered free land to anyone willing to build within a year. The bid was a modest success, attracting one of the decade's multifarious "artist colonies", now long supplanted by package holiday companies and second-homers. A plush new 280-room hotel has opened in the village as well as a *parador* on the beach, and there's a burgeoning foreign jet-set which lives here for half the year and migrates in summer, all of which has rapidly downgraded Mojácar's obvious charms.

Mojácar Pueblo

Mojácar's hilltop settlement goes back to prehistoric Iberian times, and probably earlier, and became prominent during the Roman period when Pliny described it as one of the most important towns of *Baetica*, as the Roman province was called. Coins found from this era give the Roman name as *Murgis*, which the later Moors adapted to *Muxacra*. Near the village's central fountain, where thirty years ago veiled women used to do the family washing, a plaque relates how keen the Moors were to hang on to their hilltop eyrie by first declaring their loyalty to the *Reyes Católicos* and then stating – in the words of the Moorish mayor, Alvarez – that if the Catholic monarchs wouldn't accede to their request to be left in peace, "rather than live like a coward I shall die like a Spaniard. May Allah protect you!" The monarchs were impressed and, for a time at least, prudently granted Alvarez's wish.

An ancient custom, no longer practised but parodied on every bangle and trinket sold in the tourist shops, was to paint an **indalo** on the doorways of the village to ward off evil. This symbol – a match-stick figure with arms outstretched, holding an arc – comes from the six-thousand year old Neolithic drawings in the caves at Vélez Blanco (see below) to the north, and anthropologists believe that it is a unique case of a prehistoric symbol being passed down in one location for numerous millennia.

Indalos apart, sights in the upper village are limited and when you've strolled around the narrow whitewalled streets, looked over the heavily restored fifteenth–century church of **Santa María**, and savoured the view over the strangely-formed surrounding hills and coast to the north from the **mirador** in the main square, it's either a tour of the boutiques and souvenir shops, or a seat on the terraces of drinking dens with names like *Time and Place* and *Gordon's Bar*.

There's a **Turismo** just below the main square and a bank **cash machine** next door to it. If you wanted to stay in the village, there are a handful of small **hostales**, the most reasonable of which is *Casa Justa* at c/Morote 5 (☎950/478372; ③) behind the church. Alternatives include *La Esquinica* on nearby c/Cano (☎950/475009; ③), or, on the way into town, the more upmarket *Mamabel's* at c/Embajadores 3 (☎950/475126; ④), which has a restaurant and fine views.

Places to **eat and drink** are a bit pretentious and most of the overpriced restaurants are best avoided. To dodge the rip-offs stick with the *tapas* bars on the square: *Bar Indalo* and *Bar Elizabeth* are decent value. If you must have a three-course meal the medium-priced *menú* at *Mamabel's* (see above) is worth it, if only for the spectacular view from their terrace. One curiosity definitely worth a look though, is *Delfos,* an eccentric, rambling place which is beer garden, pizza restaurant, art gallery and antiques emporium rolled into one. Sited 3km inland along the road to Turre it's the creation of Italian artist Salvatore Brancaccio. The walls are covered both with his own and other artists' work and you dine and drink on the antique tables and chairs which are up for sale. The pizzas, too, are authentic and cooked in a wood-burning oven.

Mojácar Playa

Down below on the seafront, **Mojácar Playa** is refreshingly brash: an excellent beach with warm and brilliantly clear waters, flanked by lots of fine beach bars (currently a little overwhelmed by Spanish heavy metal and techno *bacalao*), **rooms for rent**, several **hostales**, and a good cheap **campsite**, *El Cantal de Mojácar* (☎950/478204).

Among the *hostales*, try *Hostal El Puntazo* on the Paseo del Mediterráneo (☎950/478229; ③) with a pool, or next door, *Hostal Nuevo Puntazo* (☎951/478265; ④), a swish ultra-modern expansion where rooms have TV, wall-safe, sea-view terrace and there's also a restaurant. Nearby, the simpler *Hostal Africano* (☎951/478010; ③) has rooms around a charming patio and a good seafood restaurant. Next door, *Pizzería Pepa* (☎951/478436; ③) rents out apartments with kitchen and TV. Mojácar's nondescript *parador*, the modern *Reyes Católicos* (☎950/478250; ⑤), with a pleasant garden and pool, also fronts the beach.

Nightlife happens all along the beach strip. The most unusual disco is *Tuareg*, 5km south of the town towards Carboneras, set in expansive gardens beneath palm and eucalyptus trees.

Buses from the beach up to Mojácar Pueblo run from a stop outside the ugly *Centro Comercial* at the main intersection. The long-haul bus services reflect Mojácar's popularity with Catalans: you can arrange a ticket to Barcelona, from the beach, at the *Viajes Solar* travel agent at the La Gaviota complex.

Turre and its Bronze Age site

The village of TURRE, 5km inland of Mojácar, is a superb little spot, refreshingly off the tourist trail and with a fair chance of rooms, even in high season. It is distinguished by a beautiful church with a Mudéjar tower, and has a pleasant rustic air as the sun goes down and the farmers head in from the fields with their tractors. Rooms are available at the friendly *Fonda Los Angeles* at Avda. Almería 62 (☎950/479079; ②), the ground floor of which is a pretty good restaurant. Further along the main street are a couple of bars, another restaurant, and a *heladería*.

Four kilometres back along the road to Mojácar, and just before the football ground on the right, the recently discovered early Bronze Age site of Loma del Belmonte is believed to be an offshoot settlement of the remarkable Los Millares culture to the east of Almería. There's not much to see apart from some caved-in graves from which numerous artefacts – stone axes, arrow-heads and pottery – were removed to the museum in Almería. The site dates from around 2000 BC.

North from Mojácar

North from Mojácar, there are a few further resorts – none of them much to write home about – and a few last sights of interest, before you cross the border into Murcia. At Vélez Rubio, there is a cave with prehistoric paintings depicting the *indalo*; at Vélez Blanco, a Renaissance castle; and at Villaricos, a Punic necropolis. Transport of your own will make these detours more rewarding.

La Garrucha and Vera

North from Mojácar, and served by occasional buses, LA GARRUCHA is a lively, if unattractive, town and fishing harbour with a sizeable fleet. In the process of development, with villas now thick on the ground and many more in the offing, the harbour sees that it does have a life of its own besides tourism. The fleet lands a good supply of the seafood served at the numerous fish restaurants lining the seafront harbour. Watch the prices here, though, as even the ordinary-looking places can be expensive. *Los Porrones* is one of the better value possibilities at the southern end of the palm-lined promenade. You probably won't want to stay – there are several expensive hostales and a summer-only youth hostel if you do – but with a reasonable beach it makes a good afternoon's break from Mojácar.

From La Garrucha, the road heads 9km inland, skirting the estaury of the Río Almanzora, to VERA, a large farming village with a sixteenth-century church with four huge towers, and a Renaissance Ayuntamiento, as well as a couple of economical hostales of which *Hostal Regio* on c/Batallón de Cádiz (☎950/390725; ③) is okay. The vilage is noted for its Phoenician and Moorish influenced pottery, which is available from *Bernardino* at c/Alfarería 11, one of its best practitioners.

North along the coast

The town of CUEVAS DE ALMANZORA, 6km north of Vera, has a well preserved sixteenth-century Gothic castle built to defend the settlement from piracy, and a handful of Guadix-style cave dwellings, but not a lot more. Slightly back from here, there's a road which returns you to the coast and the village of PALOMARES – of nuclear notoriety (see Box). The rather curious feature of this otherwise dull hamlet is a church tower which resembles – with its rounded cone – an atom bomb . . .

Three kilometres on from Palomares, VILLARICOS is a hum-drum resort with an uncomfortable black pebble beach. It does, however, retain remains of a Punic (or Phoenician) necropolis. This is now part-buried beneath a modern *urbanización* of holiday villas but the rock-cut graves and burial niches, built into a hillside, can be viewed

PALOMARES AND SOME BOMBS

Just for the record – and as a chilling reminder of nuclear madness – it should be recorded that the village of **Palomares**, by the mouth of the Río Almanzora, was once at the centre of one of the world's biggest nuclear scares. Here, on January 17, 1966, an American B-52 bomber collided with a tanker aircraft during a mid-air refuelling operation. Following the collision, three ten-megaton **H-bombs** fell on land and a fourth into the sea, just off the village.

Those that fell in the fields were recovered quickly, though one had been damaged, causing radioactive contamination nearby. Fifteen US warships and two submarines searched for many weeks before the fourth bomb was recovered. On March 19, thousands of barrels of plutonium-contaminated soil were transported by the USAF for disposal in South Carolina. Nobody has ever convincingly explained how the incident happened, nor is it known why the bombs didn't explode, for the damaged bomb had actually lost its safety catch.

behind the barred entrances. On approaching the village from the Almanzora/Palomares direction the site lies immediately before the *urbanización*, on the left, and near to where the village's nameboard stands.

North again from here, the road cuts between the sea and the **Sierra Almagrera**, riddled with mine workings. The mining settlements beyond these hills, in a landscape of scrub and desert cactuses, are eerie, godforsaken places where any strangers are regarded with suspicion. Back on the coast, **POZO DEL ESPARTO**, 12km from Villaricos, has a reasonable pebble beach with plenty of shade, and quite a few places where wild-campers can pitch their tents. Another 4km on, **SAN JUAN DE LOS TERREROS** straddles the seafront behind a narrow beach flanked by characterless *hostales* and holiday apartments. Just to the north of here, however, the coast road passes a number of temptingly isolated coves and inlets with small beaches, before the border with Murcia is reached.

Vélez Rubio, the Letreros cave and Vélez Blanco

Inland from Vera, a rambling 60km detour will bring you out at the town of **VÉLEZ RUBIO**, surrounded by *sierras* and fields of cereals. It is no great shakes, with just one monument of note, the magnificent church of **La Encarnación** on the plaza of the same name. Constructed in the eighteenth century, this has an imposing carved façade which includes, above the entrance, the arms of the Marquises of Villafranca y Vélez, who built it. Inside, there's a superb *artesonado* roof and a fine **retablo**.

The reason for this trip, however, is to see the prehistoric **Cueva de los Letreros**, 4km north, signed on the left of the road towards Vélez Blanco. To reach it from this turn-off, you'll need to follow a dirt track – passable by car for some of the way – for about 2km, turning first left and then right. As you approach, you can see a concrete stairway leading half way up a cliff to the cave, or *abrigo* (rock shelter). Although fenced off by a grille, you can just make out the red and brown sketches of human figures, animals, astronomical signs and the *indalo* (see Mojácar) which have been dated to around 4000 BC and are amongst the oldest representations of people and animals together.

Further paintings at **La Cueva del Gabar**, another *abrigo* to the north of Vélez Blanco, are in a much better state of preservation but currently closed to the public. However, if you're interested the **Turismo** (c/San Pedro; ☎950/410148) at Vélez Rubio or the *Ayuntamiento* at Vélez Blanco (c/La Corredera) can advise on a guide who will produce a rope and ladder to get you up the sheer rock face – one of the reasons, of course, why they have survived more or less intact.

Nestling at the foot of a rocky hill, **VÉLEZ BLANCO** is a smaller and more attractive conurbation. Atop the hill is a remarkable **Renaissance castle** – an extension of the original Moorish alcazaba built by the Marquises of Vélez Blanco in the early years of the sixteenth century. It is today something of a trompe l'oeil, with an empty shell behind the crenellated battlements: a gutting that took place as recently as 1903, after the castle was sold off by the impecunious Marquis to an American millionaire, George Blumenthal, who tore out the whole interior – including a fabulous patio carved in marble by Italian craftsmen – and shipped it off to the United States. After service as this plutocrat's Xanadu, it has since been reconstructed inside the Metropolitan Museum of Art in New York. The interior, much of it now supported by steel girders, has fragments of original decoration and fine views from the tower. A local man (and a bit of a character) known as "Tío Perez" is usually about to let you have a look around.

The sixteenth-century **Convento de San Luís**, also built by the Vélez family, has a fine chapel which was damaged during the Civil War.

Should you need a place **to stay** in Vélez Blanco, the *Hostal La Sociedad* on c/ Corredera (☎ 950/415027; ③) is central and friendly.

Inland Almería: Movieland and Níjar

An alternative way of reaching the coast to the east of Almería is to take a trip through the weird lunar landscape of Almería's distinctive **desert scenery**. There are two possible routes: via **Níjar** along the N344 *autovía* to Carboneras, or via the more interesting **Tabernas** and **Sorbas** route to Mojácar. The latter and more northerly route, described below, passes by Almería's old western film set, **"Mini Hollywood"**, and a detour off this road can easily be made to the pottery centre of Níjar. The N344 is the main route for the Costa del Sol-bound holiday traffic and heavy trucks which thunder down from the north.

Mini Hollywood and Tabernas

The main road to Tabernas heads north out of Almería along the valley of the Río Andarax and forks right at Benhadux – along the N340 – passing the village of **Rioja** before it enters a dramatic brown-tinged-with-purple eroded landscape which looks as if it should be the backdrop for a Hollywood Western. Ten kilometres past Rioja, in a particularly gulch-riven landscape, at **Mini Hollywood** you discover that someone else had the same idea first.

Mini Hollywood and Mini Hollywood I
A visit to **MINI HOLLYWOOD** (July–Sept daily 10am–8pm; 500ptas, kids half price) is hard to resist. The pay booth sets the scene straight out with an endless tape-loop of this old film set's most famous production, *A Fistful of Dollars*. Beyond lies a main street overlooked by a water tower, which you may just recognize from the 1960s classic, or from *The Good, the Bad and the Ugly*, both of which were filmed here along with countless spaghetti and paella westerns. You can wander into the Tombstone Gulch saloon for a drink, and on Saturday (in season) the fantasy is carried a step further with a mock bank raid.

Further along the road towards Tabernas, on the left, is **Mini Hollywood I** (aka *Decoradas Cinematograficas*), where a couple of less commercialized film sets have an Indian village complete with wigwams and a Mexican town. To reach these you'll have to put your vehicle's suspension through a hairy ride along a boulder-strewn dry riverbed.

As well as the landscape (and the cheap labour costs), the film-makers were also drawn to the same unpolluted crystalline air which has lured astronomers here, and to the north of Tabernas, in the Sierra de Filabres, they have installed a series of high powered telescopes to study the heavens.

Tabernas

Surrounded by torrid scrubland, **TABERNAS** lies at the foot of a hill dominated by an impressive-looking **Moorish castle** where Fernando and Isabel esconced themselves during the siege of Almería. Unfortunately, closer inspection reveals it to be mainly ruined and there's little to hang around for, except a drink, in the searing summer heat.

Just beyond the village a road on the left – followed after 1km by a right turn towards the hamlet of Senes – leads to the **Centro Solar**, one of Europe's biggest solar energy fields, where row upon row of mirrors reflect the powerful sunlight and generate heat energy. Still at the development stage, it's hoped that when the system is commercially viable it could power massive desalination plants to regenerate the desert.

A detour to Níjar and Sorbas

Beyond Tabernas there are more dramatic landscapes – badlands with naked ridges of pitted sandstone, cut through by twisted and dried-up river beds, all of which vary in colour from yellow to red and from green to lavender-blue depending on the time of day and the nature of the stone. After 9km a road on the right opens up the possibility of a wonderfully scenic trip south to Níjar across the **Sierra Alhamilla**.

This road climbs through more Arizona-type landscape, first to the hamlet of **Turrillas** and then turns east to **LUCAINENA DE LAS TORRES**, a cluster of white boxes surrounding its red-roofed church. Here, a narrow main street leads up to the church, fronted by a tiny square where old men sit around staring at nothing in particular as the sun beats down remorselessly. The road beyond snakes over the rugged Sierra Alhamilla to descend into Níjar, 16km to the south.

Níjar

NÍJAR is a neat, white and typically Almerian little town, with narrow streets designed to give maximum shade. Now firmly on the tourist trail due to the inexpensive **hand-made pottery** manufactured in workshops around the town and sold in the shops along the broad main street, it still retains a relaxed and tranquil air. Little remains of the Moorish fort here but the pottery tradition – dating back to when the Moors held sway and including attractive traditional patterns created with mineral dyes – lives on, as exhibits in the Museum at Almería clearly demonstrate. The town is also known for its *jarapas*: bedcovers, curtains and rugs made from rags.

There are a couple of small **hostales** of which the best is *Montes* (☎950/360157; ②) at Avda. García Lorca 26 – the main street – with a *comedor* serving an excellent value *menú*. There's also a *pizzeria* on the way in from the south, the only other place to eat.

In the hills just above Níjar, the village of **HUEBRO** also has Moorish roots and is known locally for its staging of a Moors-against-Christians mock battle duing the first week in October.

Sorbas

This corner of Almería has one last dramatic sight in **SORBAS**, an extraordinary place, surrounded by more moonscapes, whose houses overhang an ashen gorge, best seen from the main road. Like Níjar, it is reputed for its pottery – although the designs are less original – which is sold at a trio of inconspicuous *alfarerías* (workshops) in the lower part of the village, near a white-walled church. In the central plaza of this tidy little

LORCA'S "BLOOD WEDDING"

An event that happened at Níjar in 1928 inspired one of Lorca's most powerful plays, *Bodas de Sangre* (Blood Wedding). A young woman named Francisca was about to marry a man named Casimiro at a farmhouse near to Níjar. She was an heiress with a modest dowry and a reluctant bride, he a labourer pressured by his scheming brother and sister-in-law to make this match and thus bring money into the family. A few hours prior to the wedding taking place, Francisca eloped with her cousin, with whom she had been in love since childhood, but who had only realized his feelings when confronted with the reality of losing her. They were swiftly intercepted by Casimiro's brother, who shot her cousin dead. His brother was convicted of the murder, whilst Casimiro, the groom, was unable to overcome his humiliation and, it is said, never looked upon Francisca or even her photograph again. Francisca never married and lived as a recluse until her death in 1978.

Lorca avidly followed the story in the newspapers and had a knowledge of the area from time spent in Almería as a child. An interesting afterword is told by the writer Nina Epton, who, on a visit to San José in the 1960s, was dining at the house of a wealthy Spanish *señoron*, or landowner, while a group of farm labourers waited outside on a long bench, no doubt for payment. In her book *Andalusia* she describes what happened when eventually she accompanied Don José, her host, to speak to the men:

> *Among them was a wizened old man called Casimiro whom I would not have looked at twice before I was told that a dramatic incident in his youth had inspired Federico García Lorca to take Casimiro for his model of the novio in "The Blood Wedding".*

village, there is a *Casa de Huespedes* (②) with clean and economical **rooms** and a bar. On the main road to the east of town – where you'll get the best view of the clifftop houses – the *Cafe-Bar Chacho* does *platos combinados*.

To reach Sorbas from Níjar you could retrace your path back over the **Sierra Alhamilla** (there's a 4km short cut to the N340 from Lucainena) or, for a bit of variety, follow the N344 east for about 18km, turning off along a minor road (the AL140) for the final 10km to Sorbas.

If you find this surreal landscape to your taste – and it's surprising how it begins to grow on you – you might like to try a trip starting 10km east of Sorbas, where a turn-off on the left heads into relatively uncharted territory, north along the C3325 to **COBDAR** in the **Sierra de los Filabres**. A surprisingly neat little village in an area which possesses some woodland, the inhabitants will be bemused, but pleased, to see you. Alternatively, you can continue east along the N340, turning off along the minor AL150 to Turre (p.378) and, slightly further, Mojácar.

travel details

Trains

Almería to: Granada (3 daily; 4hr); (Guadix 3 daily; 3hr); Madrid (2 daily; 10hr); Sevilla (1 daily; 1hr).

Granada to: Algeciras (2 daily; 6hr); Almería (3 daily; 3hr 45min–4hr 15min); Córdoba (3 daily; 4hr); Guadix (3 daily; 2hr); Madrid (2 daily; 6–8hr, via Linares-Baeza (6hr 30min); Málaga (3 daily; 4hr); Ronda (1 daily; 5hr); Sevilla (3 daily; 4hr).

Buses

Granada to: Almería (4 daily; 4hr); Almuñecar (6 daily; 1hr 30min); Baza (8 daily; 2hr 15min); Córdoba (7 daily; 3hr 30min); Guadix (11 daily; 1hr 15min), Jaén (8 daily; 2hr), Madrid (1 daily; 8hr); Málaga (15 daily; 2hr 30min); Motril (7 daily; 2hr); Nerja (2 daily; 2hr); Salobreña (7 daily; 1hr 15min); Sevilla (8 daily; 4–5hr); Sierra Nevada/ Alpujarras: the following all pass Lanjarón and Órgiva, a 1hr trip from the city; current departure times from Granada to other villages are: 8am & 5.45pm Ugíjar; 10.30am Pitres; noon & 5.15pm Berchules; 1pm Berja; 1.30pm Órgiva; 4pm Albondón (weekdays only); 8pm Órgiva (weekdays only).

Almería to: Carboneras (3 daily; 1hr 15min); Granada (2 daily; 4hr); Guadix (2 daily; 2hr 30min); Laujar de Andarax (2 daily; 1hr); Málaga (5 daily; 4hr 30min); Mojácar (4 daily; 2hr); Las Negras (2 daily; 1hr 15min); Níjar (2 daily; 45min); San José (2 daily; 1hr); Santa Fe de Mondújar/ Los Millares (2 daily; 30min); Tabernas (7 daily; 1hr).

Ferries
Almería to: Melilla, seasonal boat (daily, except Sun; 8hr).

CONTEXTS

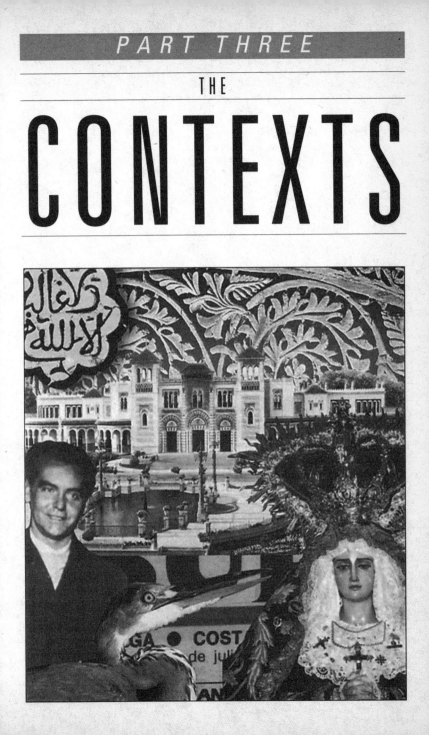

THE HISTORICAL FRAMEWORK

As the southernmost region of the Iberian peninsula, Andalucía has manifested throughout its history a character essentially different from the rest of Spain. Due to the variety of peoples who settled here, the region has always had an enriching influence on the territories further north. This meeting place of seas and cultures, with Africa only nine miles off the coast of its southern tip, brought Andalucía into early contact with the sophisticated civilizations of the eastern Mediterranean and a long period as part of the north African Moorish empire. The situation was later reversed when Andalucía sent out explorers to the New World and became the gateway to the Spanish American Empire.

PREHISTORY

Andalucía has evidence of occuption by Stone Age man stretching back some 400,000 years and at **Venta Micena** in the province of Granada – believed to be the oldest such site in Europe – these early inhabitants hunted elephant and rhino and left behind tools and camp fires. Some of the earliest **human fossils** found on the Iberian Peninsula were unearthed inside the **Gibraltar** caves with evidence of **Neanderthal man** dating from around 100,000 BC. In the Paleolithic period, the first **homo sapiens** arrived on the Iberian peninsula from southern France settling around the Bay of Biscay as well as in the south. They were cave dwellers and hunter-gatherers and at the Pileta and Nerja caves in Málaga have left behind remarkable **cave paintings** depicting the animals that they hunted. During the later Neolithic phase, a sophisticated material culture developed in southern Spain attested to by the finds of esparto sandals and baskets as well as jewellery in the **Cueva de los Murciliegos** in Granada.

Subsequent prehistory is more complex and confused. There does not appear to have been any great development in the cave cultures of the north. Instead the focus shifts south – where **Neolithic colonists** had arrived from North Africa – to Valencia and **Almería**. Cave paintings have been found in rock shelters such as those at **Velez Blanco** dating from around 4000 BC. Here also, not long afterwards, **metalworking** began and the debate continues as to the cause of this dramatic leap forward: a development by the indigenous inhabitants or the arrival of "technicians" – evidenced by many trading artefacts such as ivory and turquoise – from the eastern Mediterranean. The fortified site of **Los Millares** (c.3000 BC) in the centre of a rich mining area in Almería, with its Aegean-style "bee-hive" tombs is one of the most important remains from this period. In the same period, **dolmens** were being built such as those at **Antequera**, a building style which spread from here throughout the peninsula and into Europe. This dolmenic culture also influenced a ceramic style, typified by bell-shaped artefacts and giving rise to the name **Beaker folk**. More developments occurred in the same area of Almería about 1700 BC when the **El Argar** civilization started to produce bronze and worked silver and gold, trading across the Mediterranean. This culture fanned out across the south between 1700 and 1000 BC, and during the first millennium BC, the **Iberian civilization** fully established itself.

TARTESSUS AND THE IBERIANS

The **kingdom of Tartessus** appeared early in the first millennium BC and typifies the great strides forward being made by the Iberians of the south. Both the Bible (which names it Tarshish) and Greek and Latin texts refer to this important kingdom and trading centre. Probably sited on the estuary of Río Guadalquivir on the border of Huelva and Sevilla provinces its precise location has yet to be identified, although its prowess as a producer and exporter of bronze, gold and silver as well as a creator of sophisticated **jewellery** is apparent from the finds displayed in the museum at Sevilla. The Tartessians were also a literate people but nothing of their literature survives apart from scattered inscriptions which have yet to be translated. In the mid-sixth century BC Tartessus incurred the wrath of the rising power of Carthage through its friendship with the Greeks and not long after this appears to have been destroyed by them.

The Iberians at other centres in the south also developed sophisticated cultures based upon agriculture, stock breeding, fishing, mining and iron production. When the Romans came into contact with them in the third century BC they found a literate people with written laws, and a vibrant culture which included music and dance. Their skills in the plastic arts – an enduring flair throughout the peninsula's history – are displayed in artefacts such as the splendid **Dama de Baza** a dramatic fourth-century BC painted terracotta statue of a woman, discovered at Baza in Granada. The Iberian skill with masonry and stone sculpture can be seen at the necropolis at **Toya** in Jaén province, and the remarkable works from the fifth century BC are in the museum at Jaén itself.

THE FIRST COLONISTS

The southern coast attracted colonists from different regions of the Mediterranean. The **Phoenicians** – founders of a powerful trading empire based on modern Lebanon – established the port of Gadir (Cádiz) about 1100 BC. This was obviously connected with their intensive **trading operations** in the metals of the Guadalquivir valley carried from Tartessus where they may even have had a factory. Their wealth and success gave rise to a Spanish "Atlantis" myth, based around Huelva. Besides metals, the Phoenicians also came for the rich fishing along the southern coast which stimulated industries for salting and preserving the catch. The salt itself was gained from beds such as those at the **Cabo de Gata** – still in

commercial operation – in Almería. Other operations, such as the **purple dyeing industry**, for which the Phoenicians were famous, exploited the large stocks of murex shellfish in coastal waters. The coastline of Andalucía is dotted with Phoenician **settlements** from this time such as those at Malaka (Málaga), Sexi (Almuñecar) and Abdera (Adra). Market rivalry also brought the **Greeks**, who established their trading colonies along the northeastern coast – the modern Costa Brava – before penetrating southwards into the Phoenician zone. They were encouraged by the Tartessians, no doubt in an attempt to break the Phoenician economic stranglehold on the region.

When the Phoenicians were incorporated into the Persian empire in the sixth century BC, however, a former colony, **Carthage**, moved into the power vacuum, destroyed Tartessus and ejected the Greeks from the south. Carthage then turned the western Mediterranean into a jealously guarded trading monopoly, sinking ships of other states who attempted to trade there. This she tenaciously held onto, as the rising power of Rome forced her out of the central Mediterranean. In the course of the third century BC, Carthage built up Spain into a new base for her empire, from which to regain strength and strike back at her great rival. Although making little impact inland, the Carthaginians occupied most of Andalucía and expanded along the Mediterranean seaboard to establish a new capital at Cartagena ("New Carthage") in Murcia. The mineral wealth of Andalucía, particularly **silver**, was to used to finance the military build up as well as to recruit an enormous army of Iberian mercenaries. Under Hannibal they prepared to invade Italy and in 214 BC attacked Saguntum (modern Sagunto), a strategic ally of the growing Roman Empire. This precipitated the **Second Punic War** bringing Roman legions to the Spanish peninsula for the first time. Heading south from modern Catalunya, the coastal towns were successively conquered and the **end of Carthaginian domination** of Spain was sealed in 207 BC at the battle of Ilipa (Alcalá del Río), just north of Sevilla. When Cádiz fell the following year, Rome became master of the southern peninsula and **Italica (**near Sevilla) was founded as the first Roman city in Spain. A new and very different age had begun.

ROMANS AND VISIGOTHS

The **Roman colonization** of the peninsula was far more intense than anything previously experienced and met with great resistance from the Celtiberian tribes of the north and centre, much less so in Andalucía where the Turditanian people, tired of Carthaginian oppression, welcomed the invaders. In the final years of the Roman republic many of the crucial battles for control of the Roman state were fought out in Spain ending with Julius Caesar's victory at Munda, south of Córdoba, in 45 BC. After Caesar's assassination, his successor Augustus reorganized Spain into three provinces, the southernmost of which became **Hispania Baetica**, roughly modern Andalucía, with **Corduba** (Córdoba) as its capital.

In this period Spain became one of the most important and wealthiest centres of the Roman Empire and Andalucía was its most urbane heartland. Unlike the rugged and fractious Celtiberians further north, the sophisticated Iberians of the south had their own municipal traditions and took easily to Roman ideas of government. Indeed, their native languages and dialects had disappeared early in the first century AD as Latinization became complete. For four centuries Andalucía enjoyed a **"Golden Age"** with unprecedented prosperity based on the production of olive oil, wool, grain, wine and the highly prized *garum* fish sauce made at centres such as **Baelo Claudia** near Tarifa. Another important development was a massive expansion of mining at **Río Tinto** in Huelva. During this period, Baetica supplied no less than **three Roman emperors**, Trajan (one of the greatest), Hadrian and Theodosius, along with the outstanding writers Seneca and Lucan. The finest monuments of the period were built in the provincial capital at Córdoba, and cities such as Cádiz, Italica, Málaga and Carmona, linked by a network of superb roads and adorned with temples, baths, amphitheatres and aqueducts, were the equal of any in the empire.

In the fourth and fifth centuries, however, the Roman political framework began to show signs of **decadence and corruption**. Although the actual structure didn't totally collapse until the Muslim invasions of the early eighth century, it became increasingly vulnerable to **barbarian invasions** from northern Europe. Early in the fourth century AD, the Suevi (Swabians), Alans and Vandals swept across the Pyrenees leaving much devastation in their wake. The Romans, preoccupied with attempts to stave off Gothic attacks on Italy bought off the invaders by allowing them to settle within the imperial borders. The Suevi settled in Galicia, the Alans in Portugal and Murcia, whilst the **Vandals** put down roots in Baetica providing the origin of Andalucía's name. The resulting wars between the invaders only served to weaken further Rome's grip on the peninsula as a burgeoning Christian Church gained more influence over the population.

Internal strife was heightened by the arrival of the **Visigoths** from Gaul, allies of Rome and already Romanized to a large degree. The triumph of Visigothic strength in the fifth century resulted in a period of spurious unity, based upon an exclusive military rule from their capital at Toledo, but their numbers were never great and their order was often fragmentary and nominal, with the bulk of the subject people kept in a state of disconsolate servility and held ransom for their services in times of war. Above them in the ranks of the military elite there were constant plots and factions – exacerbated by the Visigothic system of elected monarchy and by their adherence to the heretical Arian philosophy. When **King Leovigild** attempted ito impose this creed on Andalucía in the mid-sixth century the region revolted with the king's son Hermenegild at its head, but the insurrection was brutally crushed. In 589 **King Recared** converted to Catholicism which for a time stiffened Visigothic control, but religious strife was only multiplied: forced conversions, especially within the Jewish enclaves, maintained a constant simmering of discontent. The Visigoths precariously held on to their domain for a further century as plots and counterplots surrounded the throne. This infighting led indirectly to the Moorish invasions of Andalucía when **King Witiza**, who died in 710, was thwarted by a usurper, Roderic, Duke of Baetica, from handing over the throne over to his son, Achila. Once **King Roderic** had installed himself on the throne the embittered family of Witiza appealed to the Muslims in North Africa for assistance to overthrow him. The North Africans, who had long eyed the riches of Andalucía with envy, now saw their opportunity.

THE MOORISH CONQUEST

In contrast to the long-drawn-out Roman campaigns, **Moorish conquest** of the peninsula was effected with extraordinary speed. This was a characteristic phenomenon of the spread of Islam – Muhammad left Mecca in 622 and by 705 his followers had established control over all of North Africa. Spain, with its political instability, its wealth and fertile climate, was an inevitable extension of their aims. In 711 **Tariq**, governor of Tangier, led a force of 7000 Berbers across the straits and routed the Visigoth army of King Roderic on the banks of the Río Guadalete close to Jerez. Two years later the Visigoths made a last desperate stand at Mérida and within a decade the Moors had conquered all but the wild mountains of Asturias. The land under their authority was dubbed "**al-Andalus**", a fluid term which expanded and shrunk with the intermittent gains and losses of the Reconquest. It was Andalucía, however, which was destined to become the heartland of the Moorish ascendancy and where the Moors were to remain in control for most of the next eight centuries.

The Moorish incursion was not simply a military conquest. The Moors (a collective term for the numerous waves of Arab, Syrian and Berber settlers from North Africa) were often content to grant a limited autonomy in exchange for payment of tribute; their administrative system was tolerant and easily absorbed by both Spanish Jews and Christians, those who retained their religion being known as "Mozarabs". This **tolerant attitude** was illustrated when the Moorish army reached Córdoba where they found the large Visigothic church of St. Vincent, now the fabulous Mezquita. Unlike previous invaders, they did not sack or burn the heathen temple but purchased half of it to use as a mosque whilst the Christians continued to use the other half for their own services.

Al-Andalus was a distinctly Spanish state of Islam. Though at first politically subject to the Eastern Caliphate (or empire) of Baghdad, it was soon virtually independent. In the tenth century, at the peak of its power and expansion, Abd ar-Rahman III asserted total independence, proclaiming himself Caliph of a new **Western Islamic Empire**. Its capital was **Córdoba** – the largest, most prosperous and most civilized city in Europe. This was the great age of Muslim Spain: its scholarship, philosophy, architecture and craftsmanship were without rival and there was an unparalleled growth in urban life, trade, and agriculture aided by magnificent irrigation projects. These and other engineering feats were not, on the whole, instigated by the Moors who instead took the basic Roman models and adapted them to a new level of sophistication. In **architecture** and the **decorative arts**, however, their contribution was original and unique – as may be seen in the astonishingly beautiful monuments of Sevilla, Córdoba and Granada.

The Cordoban Caliphate created a remarkable degree of unity, despite a serious challenge to its authority by the rebel leader **Ibn Hafsun** from his Bobastro fortress (north of Málaga) in the latter years of the ninth century. But its rulers were to become decadent and out of touch, prompting the brilliant but dictatorial **al-Mansur** to usurp control. Under this extraordinary ruler Moorish power reached new heights, using a professional Berber army to push the Christian kingdom of Asturias-León back into the Cantabrian mountains and sacking its most holy shrine, Santiago de Compostela in 997. However, after al-Mansur's death the Caliphate quickly lost its authority and in 1031 disintegrated into a series of small independent kingdoms or "*taifas*", the strongest of which was Sevilla.

Internal divisions amongst the *taifas* offered less resistance to the Christian kingdoms which were rallying in the north, and twice North Africa had to be called upon for reinforcement. This resulted in two distinct new waves of Moorish invasion – first by the fanatically Islamic **Almoravids** (1086) and later by the **Almohads** (1147), who restored effective Muslim authority and left behind one of Moorish Spain's most elegant monuments, the **Giralda** tower in Sevilla. However, their crushing defeat by the Christian forces under Alfonso VIII in 1212 at the battle of **Las Navas de Tolosa** in Jaén, marked the beginning of the end for Moorish Spain.

THE CHRISTIAN RECONQUEST

The **reconquest** of land and influence from the Moors was a slow and intermittent process. It began with a symbolic victory by a small force of Christians at Covadonga in the region of Asturias (727) in northern Spain and was not completed until 1492 with the conquest of Granada by Fernando and Isabel.

Covadonga resulted in the formation of the tiny Christian **Kingdom of the Asturias**. Initially just 40 by 30 miles in area, it had by 914 reclaimed León and most of Galicia and northern Portugal. At this point, progress was temporarily halted by the devastating campaigns of al-Mansur. However, with the fall of the Cordoban Caliphate and the divine aid of Spain's Moor-slaying patron saint, the avenging Santiago (Saint James the Apostle), the Reconquest moved into a new and powerful phase.

The frontier castles built against Arab attack gave name to **Castile**, founded in the tenth century as a county of León-Asturias. Under Fernando I (1037–65) it achieved the status of a kingdom and became the main thrust and focus of the Reconquest. In 1085 this period of confident Christian expansion reached its zenith with the capture of the great Moorish city of Toledo. The following year, however, the Almoravids arrived on invitation from Sevilla, and military activity was effectively frozen – except, that is, for the exploits of the legendary **El Cid**, a Castilian nobleman who won considerable lands around Valencia in 1095, thus checking Muslim expansion up the eastern coast.

The next concerted phase of the Reconquest began as a response to the threat imposed by the Almohads. The Kings of León, Castile, Aragón and Navarra united in a crusade which resulted in the great victory at Las Navas de Tolosa. Thereafter Muslim power was paralyzed and the **Christian armies** moved on to take most of al-Andalus. Fernando III ("el Santo", the saint) led Castilian soldiers into Córdoba in 1236 and twelve years later into Sevilla. By the end of the thirteenth century only the Nasrid **Kingdom of Granada** remained under Muslim authority and this was to provide a brilliant sunset to Moorish rule in Andalucía. Its survival for a further two centuries whilst surrounded by its Christian enemies was due as much to skilful diplomacy as to payment of tribute to the monarchs of Castile.

Two factors should be stressed regarding the Reconquest. First, its unifying religious nature – the **spirit of crusade**, intensified by the religious zeal of the Almoravids and

Almohads, and by the wider European climate (which in 1085 gave rise to the First Crusade). At the same time the Reconquest was a movement of **recolonization**. The fact that the country had been under arms for so long meant that the nobility had a major and clearly visible social role, a trend perpetuated by the redistribution of captured land in huge packages, or "**latifundia**". Heirs to this tradition still remain as landlords of the great estates, most conspicuously in Andalucía where it has produced wretched conditions for the workers on the land ever since. Men from the ranks were also awarded land, forming a lower, larger stratum of nobility, the **hidalgos**. It was their particular social code that provided the material for Cervantes in *Don Quijote*.

Any spirit of mutual cooperation that had temporarily united the Christian kingdoms disintegrated during the fourteenth century, and independent lines of development were once again pursued. **Castile** emerged as the strongest over this period: self-sufficiency in agriculture and a flourishing wool trade with the Netherlands enabled the state to build upon the prominent military role under Fernando III.

LOS REYES CATÓLICOS

Los Reyes Católicos – **the Catholic Monarchs** – was the joint title given to **Fernando V of Aragón** and **Isabel I of Castile**, whose marriage in 1479 united the two largest kingdoms in Spain. Unity was in practice more symbolic than real: Castile had underlined its rights in the marriage vows and Aragón retained its old administrative structure. So, in the beginning at least, the growth of any national unity or Spanish – as opposed to local – sentiment was very much dependent on the head of state. Nevertheless, from this time on it begins to be realistic to consider Spain as a single political entity.

At the heart of Fernando and Isabel's popular appeal lay a **religious bigotry** that they shared with most of their Christian subjects. The **Inquisition** was instituted in Castile in 1480 and in Aragón seven years later. Aiming to establish the purity of the Catholic faith by rooting out heresy, it was directed mainly at Jews (despite Fernando's half-Jewish parentage) – resented for their enterprise in commerce and influence in high places, as well as for their faith. Expression had already been given to these feelings in a pogrom in 1391; it was reinforced by an edict issued in 1492 which forced up to 400,000 Jews to flee the country. A similar spirit was embodied in the reconquest of the Nasrid **Kingdom of Granada**, also in 1492. During this long campaign Gonzalo Fernández de Córdoba, "El Gran Capitán," developed the Spanish army into a formidable force that was set to dominate the battlefelds of Europe for tne next century and a half. As the last stronghold of Muslim authority, the religious rights of Granada's citizens were guaranteed under the treaty of surrender. Then the policy was reversed and forced mass conversions were introduced. The subsequent and predictable rebellions – particularly violent in **Las Alpujarras** – were brutally put down and within a decade those Muslims under Christian rule had been given the choice between conversion or expulsion.

The year 1492 was symbolic of a fresh start in another way: it was in this year that **Columbus** sailed from Huelva to make the **discovery of America**, and the Papal Bull that followed, entrusting Spain with the conversion of the American Indians, further entrenched Spain's sense of a mission to bring the world to the "True Faith". The next ten years saw the systematic conquest, colonization and exploitation of the **New World**, with new territory stretching from Labrador to Brazil, and new-found wealth pouring into the royal coffers. The control of trade with the New World was carried on through **Sevilla** where the Casa de Contración (House of Trade) was established in 1503. The city rapidly grew into one of the great cities of Europe during which it enjoyed two centuries of commercial monopoly. Paradoxically, Andalucía as a whole benefitted little from this wealth which was appropriated by the crown for its foreign campaigns and by absentee landlords. Over the succeeding two centuries the region languished as a backwater and the poverty of the peasants led many to emigrate to the New World in order to better themseves, at the same time turning much of the region into a vast, unpopulated desert.

THE HABSBURG AGE

Carlos I, a Habsburg, came to the throne in 1516 as a beneficiary of the marriage alliances of the Catholic monarchs. Five years later, he was elected Emperor of the Holy Roman Empire as Carlos V (**Charles V**), inheriting not only Castile and Aragón, but Flanders, the Netherlands, Artois, the Franche-Comté and all the American colonies to boot. With such responsibilities it was inevitable that attention would be diverted from Spain, whose chief function became to sustain the Holy Roman Empire with gold and silver from the Americas. It was only with the accession of **Felipe II** in 1556 that Spanish politics became more centralized and that the notion of an absentee king was reversed.

This was a period of unusual religious intensity: the **Inquisition** was enforced with renewed vigour, and a "final solution" to the problem of the Moriscos (subject Moors) who continued to adhere to their ancient traditions and practised Muslim worship in secret, resulted in a decree banning Arabic dress, books and speech. The result was another rising of Moriscos in Las Alpujarras which was fiercely suppressed with Muslims being forcibly deported to other parts of the country. Felipe III later ordered the expulsion of half the total number of Moriscos in Spain – allowing only two families to remain in each village in order to maintain irrigation techniques. The **exodus** of both Muslim and Jew created a large gulf in the labour force and in the higher echelons of commercial life – and in trying to uphold the Catholic cause, an enormous strain was put upon resources without any clearcut victory. Despite being a golden literary and artistic age, politically and economically the seventeenth century was a disaster for Spain. Lurching progressively deeper into debt, she suffered heavy defeats on the battlefield as her possessions in the Netherlands and France were lost, and recurring financial crises and economic stagnation engendered a deepening mood of disillusionment. **Andalucía** shared in this decline, exacerbated by the tendency of the mercantile classes to involve themselves only in entrepot trade which left most of the profits in the hands of other countries. There was also no stimulus given to industrial production by the custom of merchants retiring from commerce and investing their profits in land, which created a landed gentry weighed down by honours and titles whose lifestyle came to be looked upon as being incompatible with commerce.

THE BOURBONS

The **Bourbon dynasty** succeeded to the Spanish throne in the person of Felipe V (1700); with him began the **War of Spanish Succession** against the rival claim of Archduke Charles of Austria, assisted by British forces. As a result of the Treaty of Utrecht which ended the war (1713), Spain was stripped of all territory in Belgium, Luxembourg, Italy and Sardinia, but Felipe V was recognized as king. **Gibralta**r was seized by the British in the course of the war. For the rest of the century Spain fell very much under the French sphere of influence, an influence that was given political definition by an alliance with the French Bourbons in 1762.

This Gallic connection brought the ideas of Enlightenment Europe into the peninsula and during the reign of Carlos III (1759-88) a number of radically-minded ministers attempted to deal with the nation's chronic problems. Along with a more tolerant attitude towards the **gypsies** who had become victims of racial abuse and hostility, the king's minister, Pablo de Olavide, began an imaginative, if ultimately unsuccessful, scheme to **repopulate the Sierra Morena** in Andalucía with foreign immigrants.

Contact with France also made involvement in the **Napoleonic Wars** inevitable and led eventually to the defeat of the Spanish fleet at the **Battle of Trafalgar** off the coast of Cádiz in 1805. Popular outrage was such that the powerful prime minister, Godoy, was overthrown and King Carlos IV forced to abdicate (1808). Napoleon seized the opportunity to install his brother, Joseph, on the throne, whilst French armies and generals ransacked and stole much of the country's artistic heritage.

Fierce local resistance in the form of guerrilla warfare was accompanied by armies raised by the various local administrations. Thus it was that a militia put in the field by the *junta* of Sevilla inflicted a resounding defeat on a French army at **Bailen** in Jaén in 1808, which forced Joseph, the "intruder king" to flee back across the border. This resistance was eventually backed by the muscle of a British army, first under Sir John Moore, later under the Duke of Wellington, and the French were at last driven out in the course of the **War of Independence** (Peninsular War). Meanwhile,

the **American colonies** had been successfully asserting their independence from a preoccupied centre and with them went Spain's last real claim of significance on the world stage. The entire nineteenth century was dominated by the struggle between an often reactionary monarchy and the aspirations of liberal constitutional reformers.

SEEDS OF CIVIL WAR

Between 1810 and 1813, whilst the war raged on across the peninsula, an *ad hoc* Cortes (parliament) meeting in **Cádiz** had set up a **liberal constitution** which stipulated a strict curtailment of the powers of the crown with ministers responsible to a democratically elected chamber. The first act of the despotic Fernando VII on being returned to the throne was to abolish this, and until his death in 1833 he continued to stamp out the least hint of liberalism. But the Constitution of 1812 was to remain a "sacred text" for a future democratic Spain, besides introducing the word "liberal" to Europe's political vocabulary. On Fernando's death, the right of succession was contested between his brother, Don Carlos, backed by the Church, conservatives and Basques, and his infant daughter, Isabel, who looked to the Liberals and the army for support.

So began the **First Carlist War**, a civil war that divided Spanish emotions for six years. Isabel II was eventually declared of age in 1843, her reign a long record of scandal, political crisis and constitutional compromise. Liberal army generals under the leadership of General Prim effected a coup in 1868 and the queen was forced to abdicate, but attempts to maintain a Republican government foundered. The Cortes was again dissolved and the throne returned to Isabel's son, Alfonso XII. The military began increasingly to move into the power vacuum left by the weakened monarchy. The **pronunciamiento** – whereby an officer backed by military force "pronounced" what was in the best interests of a city or region – was born in this period and was to plague the country into modern times.

The **nineteenth century in Andalucía** mirrored Spain's national decline. The loss of the American colonies had badly hit the region's trade, and this was compounded by the phylloxera plague in the 1870s onwards which wiped out most of the vineyards, brought the sherry industry to its knees, and fuelled the growth of strikes in the cities and popular uprisings on the land as the economy deteriorated. Parodoxically, this century also did more than any other to bestow on Andalucía the image it has held ever since. Writers, artists and travellers of the **Romantic Age** saw in its bullfights, *flamenco*, bandits and beguiling women a world of gaiety and colour epitomized in the operas *Carmen* and the *Barber of Seville*, both works from this period.

The years preceding World War I merely heightened the discontent, which found expression in the growing **political movements** of the working class. The Socialist Workers' Party was founded in Madrid after the restoration of Alfonso XII, and spawned its own trade union, the UGT (1888). Its anarchist counterpart, the CNT (Confederación Nacional de Trabajo), was founded in 1911, gaining substantial support among the oppressed peasantry of Andalucía.

The loss of **Cuba** in 1898 emphasized the growing isolation of Spain in international affairs and added to economic problems with the return of soldiers seeking employment where there was none. In Andalucía a regionalist movement known as *Andalucismo* was born demanding land reform and greater Andalucian autonomy. A call-up for army reserves to fight in **Morocco** in 1909 provoked a general strike and the "Tragic Week" of rioting in Barcelona. Between 1914 and 1918, Spain was outwardly neutral but inwardly turbulent; inflated prices made the postwar recession harder to bear.

The general disillusionment with parliamentary government, together with the fears of employers and businessmen for their own security, gave **General Primo de Rivera** sufficient support for a military coup in 1923. Coming himself from Jerez de la Frontera, the paternalistic general backed the great **Ibero-American Exhibition of 1929** at Sevilla which was hoped would calm the agitation for radical change by promoting a "rose-coloured" image for the troubled region; its most immediate effect was to bankrupt the city. Dictatorship did result in an increase in material prosperity, heavily asssisted by a massive public works policy, but serious political misjudgments and the collapse of the peseta in 1929 made Rivera's voluntary resignation and departure into exile inevitable. The legacy of this dictatorship was to reinforce a belief on the Right that only a firm military hand would be capable of holding the society together, and many of those who served in Primo de Rivera's administration were to back the Franco regime in the next decade. The victory of anti-monarchist parties in the 1931 municipal elections forced the abdication of the hopelessly out of touch King Alfonso XIII, and the **Second Republic** was declared.

THE SECOND REPUBLIC

The Second Republic which lasted from 1931-6 was ushered in on a wave of optimism that finally some of the nation's fundamental ills and injustices would be rectified. But the government – a coalition of radicals, socialists and leftist republicans – struggling to curb the dominance of powerful vested interests such as the army, the church and the landowning class, was soon failing to satisfy even the least of the expectations which it had raised. Moreover it lost support when it got involved in activities identified with earlier repressive regimes when, as happened at the village of **Casa Viejas** in Cádiz, it ordered the troops to open fire on a group of starving workers who had been the victims of a lockout by the local landowner and who were attempting to raise the area in an Anarchist revolt.

Anarchism was gaining strength among the frustrated middle classes as well as among workers and peasantry. The **Communist Party** and left-wing **Socialists**, driven into alliance by their mutual distrust of the "moderate" Socialists in government, were also forming a growing bloc. There was little real unity of purpose on either left or right, but their fear of each other and their own exaggerated boasts made each seem an imminent threat. On the right the **Falangists**, basically a youth party founded in 1923 by **José Antonio Primo de Rivera** (son of the dictator), made uneasy bedfellows with conservative traditionalists and dissident elements in the army upset by modernizing reforms.

In an atmosphere of growing confusion, with mobs fighting on the streets and churches and monasteries being torched whilst landed estates were taken over by those impatient for agrarian reform, the left-wing Popular Front alliance won the general election of **February 1936** by a narrow margin. Normal life, though, became increasingly impossible: the economy was crippled by strikes, the universities became hotbeds for battles between Marxists and Falangists, and the government failed to exert its authority over anyone. Finally, on July 17, 1936, the military garrison in Morocco rebelled under **General Franco**'s leadership, to be followed by risings at military garrisons throughout the country. It was the culmination of years of scheming in the army, but in the event far from the overnight success its leaders almost certainly expected. Airlifting his troops into Sevilla by means of German transport planes, Franco ensured that the south and west quickly fell into Nationalist hands, but Madrid and the industrialized north and east remained loyal to the Republican government.

THE CIVIL WAR

The ensuing **Civil War** was undoubtedly one of the most bitter and bloody the world has seen. Violent reprisals were taken on their enemies by both sides – the Republicans shooting priests and local landowners wholesale, the Nationalists carrying out mass slaughter on the population of almost every town they took. Contradictions were legion in the way the Spanish populations found themselves divided from each other. Perhaps the greatest irony was that Franco's troops, on their "holy" mission against a godless "anti-Spain", comprised a core of Moroccan troops from Spain's North African colony.

It was, too, the first modern war – Franco's German allies demonstrated their ability to wipe out entire civilian populations with their bombing raids on Gernika and Durango in the Basque country, and radio proved an important weapon, as Nationalist propagandists offered the starving Republicans "the white bread of Franco".

Despite sporadic help from Russia and thousands of volunteers in the International Brigades, the Republic could never compete with the professional armies and the massive assistance from Fascist Italy and Nazi Germany enjoyed by the Nationalists. As hundreds of thousands of refugees flooded into France, General Francisco Franco, who had long before proclaimed himself Head of State, took up the reins of power.

FRANCO'S SPAIN

The early reprisals taken by the victors were on a massive and terrifying scale. Executions were commonplace in town and village and upwards of two million people were put in concentration camps until "order" had been established by authoritarian means. Only one party was permitted and censorship was rigidly enforced. By the end of World War II, during which Spain was too weak to be anything but neutral, **Franco** was the only fascist head of state left in Europe, one responsible for sanctioning more deaths than any other in Spanish history. Spain was economically and politically isolated and, bereft of markets, suffered – almost half the population were still tilling the soil for little or no return. The misery of the peasantry was particularly acute in Andalucía and forced mass emigrations to Madrid and Barcelona and Europe beyond.

When General Eisenhower visited Madrid in 1953 with the offer of huge loans, it came as water to the desert, and the price, the **establishment of American nuclear bases** such as that at Rota near Cádiz, was one Franco was more than willing to pay. However belated, economic development was incredibly rapid, with Spain enjoying a growth rate second only to that of Japan for much of the 1960s, a boom fuelled by the tourist industry, the remittances of Spanish workers abroad and the illegality of strikes and industrial action at home.

Increased **prosperity**, however, only underlined the bankruptcy of Franco's regime and its inability to cope with popular demands. Higher incomes, the need for better education, and a creeping invasion of western culture made the anachronism of Franco ever clearer. His only reaction was to attempt to withdraw what few signs of increased liberalism had crept through, and his last years mirrored the repression of the postwar period. Franco finally died in November 1975, nominating **King Juan Carlos** as his successor.

THE NEW SPAIN

On October 28, 1982, *sevillano* Felipe González's Socialist Workers' Party – the *PSOE* – was elected with massive support to rule a country that had been firmly in the hands of the right for forty-three years. The **Socialists** captured the imagination and the votes of nearly ten million Spaniards with the simplest of appeals: "for change". It was a telling comment on just how far Spain had moved since Franco's death, for in the intervening years change seemed the one factor that could still threaten the new-found democracy.

Certainly, in the Spain of 1976 the thought of a freely elected left-wing government would have been incredible. **King Juan Carlos** was the hand-picked successor of Franco, groomed for the job and very much in with the army – of which he remains official Commander-in-Chief. His initial moves were cautious in the extreme, appointing a government dominated by loyal Francoists who had little sympathy for the growing opposition demands for "democracy without adjectives".

To his credit, however, Juan Carlos recognized that some real break with the past was now urgent and inevitable, and set in motion the process of **democratization**. He legitimized the Socialist Party and, controversially, the Communists. When elections were held in June 1977, the centre-right **UCD** party gained a 34 percent share of the vote, the Socialists coming in second with 28 percent, and the Communists and Francoist *Alianza Popular* both marginalized at 9 percent and 8 percent.

It was almost certainly a vote for democratic stability rather than for ideology. The king, perhaps recognizing that his own future depended on the maintenance of the new democracy, lent it his support – most notably in February 1981 when Civil Guard Colonel Tejero stormed the Cortes and, with other officers loyal to Franco's memory, attempted to institute an **army coup**. The crisis, for a while, was real. Tanks were brought out on to the streets of Valencia, and only three of the army's ten regional commanders remained unreservedly loyal to the government. But as it became clear that the king would not support the plotters, most of the rest affirmed their support.

Tejero's continued role as a figurehead for the extreme right is evidenced by the graffiti proclaiming his name everywhere. But for most Spaniards his attempted coup is now an irrelevant and increasingly distant concern. Spanish democracy – even in army circles – has become institutionalized. And in **Felipe González** (known always as "Felipe") and the PSOE it has found a party of enduring **stability** and (to the left) of exasperating **moderation**.

MODERN ANDALUCÍA

Andalucía shared in the progressive decentralization of power in Spain throughout the post-Franco period and in 1980 became an **Autonomous Region** with a regional government based in Sevilla exercising a large amount of control over its own destiny for the first time. Largely because of its enduring social problems, Andalucía remained a socialist bulwark for the PSOE throughout the eighties – the so-called *sartenilla* (frying pan) of the south which traditionally "fries" the right-wing votes further north. However, whilst the government's reluctance to grasp the nettle of fundamental change, especially in the area of land reform, lost it some support in the 1993 elections, the region's enduring, if increasingly sceptical, committment to "Felipe" ensured the PSOE's narrow election victory over the emergent *Partido Popular* conservatives.

Despite the sunny image presented to most of its visitors, the chronic economic and social problems remain, and not for nothing is Andalucía known as the "workhouse of Spain". The **unemployment** level is among the European Community's highest at 28 percent (compared with 18 percent for Spain as a whole), and earnings per head are a third lower here. Recently, efforts have been made to remove some of the serious obstacles to progress with radical improvements in the infrastructure and above all communications with the rest of the country and Europe. **Expo 92** brought new road and rail links aimed at providing faster connections with Madrid and Barcelona and a start was made on upgrading the internal links between the provinces of Andalucía as well.

The position of the 200,000 **agricultural workers** on the land who face nine months unemployment each year and depend on patronage from the great landowners for work during the other three remains unresolved, despite the government having introduced a minimal unemployment benefit scheme in the 1980s. Vastly increased land improvement grants from the European Community have further enriched the landowners, enabling them to mechanize their farms, whilst the *braceros* or landless day-labourers get nothing and have fewer job opportunities as a result.

All this has compelled a greater dependance on **tourism** at a time when the the European recession has reduced the number of tourists coming to the beaches. The regional government is trying to attract tourists inland but some feel the great days are already over. And whilst the Junta de Andalucía is striving to provide a basis for future prosperity by a dramatic expansion and improvement of the region's education system, it seems that the land which produced Picasso, Manuel de Falla, Federico García Lorca and Juan Ramón Jiminez will have to wait sometime yet for all its people to enjoy, as well as to endure, their place in the sun.

CHRONOLOGY OF MONUMENTS

c.25,000 BC	Cave dwellers occupying caves in Málaga province.	**Cave paintings** at La Pileta and Nerja.
c.4000 BC	Neolithic colonists arrive from North Africa.	Esparto baskets, sandals and jewellery found in the Cueva de Murciliégos near Albuñol in Granada.
c.2500 BC	Los Millares Chalcolithic site flourishes in Almería.	Dolmens constructed at Antequera.
c.1100 BC	**Phoenicians** found Cádiz.	Remains of later Phoenician settlements at Málaga, Almuñecar and Adra.
C9th–4th BC	Celts settle in the north of Spain. Kingdom of **Tartessus** flourishes around Guadalquivir estuary. **Greeks** establish trading posts along east coast.	
C5th BC	**Carthage** colonizes southern Spain.	Celto-Iberian culture develops, with Greek influence: statue of La Dama de Baza, necropolis at Toya (Jaén), Iberian stone sculptures made at Porcuna (Jaén museum).
214 BC	Second Punic War with Rome.	
210 BC	**Roman colonization** begins.	Important Roman cities at Italica, Córdoba, Cádiz, Carmona, Málaga.
27 BC	Octavian-Augustus becomes first Roman emperor and divides Spain into three parts: Andalucía is named **Baetica**.	**Golden Age** and Latinization of Baetica. Mining expanded at Río Tinto.
c.409	**Vandals** invade southern Spain.	
C5th–7th	**Visigoths** arrive and take control of most of Spain including Andalucía.	Visigothic cities founded at Mérida and Córdoba.
711	**Moors** under Tariq invade and defeat Visigothic King Roderic at Río Guadalete, near Jerez. Peninsula conquered in seven years.	
718	Pelayo defeats Moors in a battle at Covadonga in Asturias in northern Spain marking the start of the **Reconquest**.	
756	Abd ar-Rahman I proclaims **Emirate of Córdoba**.	Great Mosque (**Mezquita**) begun at Córdoba, climax of early Moorish architecture.
928	Abd ar-Rahman II establishes Cordoban Caliphate.	**Mozarabic churches** built by Arabized Christians. Construction of palace at **Medina Azahara** and extensions to Mezquita in **caliphal style**.

967	**Al-Mansur** usurps caliphal powers and forces Christians back into Asturias.	Final enlargement of the Mezquita at Córdoba.
1013	Caliphate disintegrates into **taifas**, petty kingdoms.	Medina Azahara palace destroyed by Berber mercenaries. Alcazabas built at Málaga, Sevilla, Carmona, Ronda, etc.
1086	**Almoravids** invade from North Africa.	Philosopher Averroës born at Córdoba (1126). Sevilla becomes new Moorish capital in Spain. Almohad minarets include La Giralda and Torre del Oro.
1146	Invasion by **Almohads** from Morocco; Muslim authority re-established.	
1212	Almohad advance halted by **Christian victory** at La Navas de Tolosa (Jaén).	**Mudéjar** style emerges through Moorish craftsmen working on Christian buildings: good examples in Sevilla (Alcázar, Casa de Pilatos) and in Córdoba (Capilla Real inside Mezquita).
1236-48	Fernando III conquers Córdoba and then Sevilla.	
1238	Ibn al-Ahmar (aka Muhammad ibn-Yusuf ibn-Nasr) takes Granada and founds the Nasrid dynasty.	Granada's **Alhambra** palace constructed under Ibn Ahmar (1238–73) and his successors.
1262–92	Cádiz falls to Alfonso X, Sancho IV takes Tarifa.	
1479	Castile and Aragón united under **Fernando and Isabel**. Spanish Inquisition set up in Sevilla.	**Sevilla Cathedral** built (1402–1506).
1492	**Fall of Granada**, the last Moorish kingdom. Discovery of America by Columbus. Expulsion of Jews from Spain.	
1516	**Carlos V** succeeds to the throne and in 1520 becomes Holy Roman Emperor inaugurating the **Golden Age**.	**Renaissance** reaches Spain. Elaborate early style known as Plateresque, best represented by the *Ayuntamiento* at Sevilla and the Colegiata at Osuna. Later key figures include Diego de Siloé (1495–1563; Granada, etc) and Andres de Vandelvira (d. 1575; Jaén, Úbeda, Baeza).
1519	**Magellan** starts global voyage from Sanlúcar de Barrameda; Córtes lands in Mexico.	
1556	**Felipe II** (d. 1598).	Painters include: El Greco (1540–1614), Ribera (1591–1652), Zurbarán (1598–1664), Alonso Cano (1601–1667), Velázquez (1599–1660), Murillo (1618–1682). All are represented in Museo de Bellas Artes, Sevilla.
1587	Drake carries out raid on Cádiz.	
1588	Sinking of the Armada.	
1609	Expulsion of Moriscos, last remaining Spanish Muslims.	
1649	Great plague in Sevilla wipes out one third of the population.	

1700	War of the Spanish Succession brings Felipe V (1713–1745), a Bourbon, to the throne. British seize Gibraltar.	**Baroque** develops in reaction to the severity of the High Renaissance and reaches a flamboyant peak in the Churrigueresque style of the C18th: La Cartuja (Granada), Caridad (Sevilla), Écija, Lucena, Priego de Córdoba, etc.
1759–88	Reign of Carlos III.	**Enlightenment** ideas enter Spain. Colonies of Germans, French and Swiss settled in the Sierra Morena.
1808	French occupy Spain. Liberal constitution declared in Cádiz (1812). Andalucía divided into eight provinces (1834).	Romantic era brings travellers to Spain. English cemetery set up at Málaga (1830). Washington Irving publishes *Tales of the Alhambra* (1832).
1835	**First Carlist War**. Peasant risings begin throughout Andalucía (1855).	**Dissolution of monasteries** and confiscation of church lands.
1874	**Second Carlist War**.	Many of Andalucía's greatest creative artists born in last part of C19th: Manuel de Falla (Cádiz) 1876; Picasso (Málaga), Juan Ramón Jiminez (Moguer) both 1881; guitarist Segovia (Andújar) 1893; Federico García Lorca (Granada) 1898.
1898	Loss of Cuba, Spain's last American colony.	
1923	Primo de Rivera dictatorship	Ibero-American Exhibition flops in Sevilla (1929). Site now Plaza de España.
1931	Second Republic.	
1936–9	**Spanish Civil War**. Franco dictatorship begins.	
1953	Franco secures economic aid from US in return for military bases	
		Costa del Sol opened up to tourist development (1962).
1975	Death of Franco; restoration of democracy.	
1980	Andalucía votes to become an **Autonomous Region**.	
1982	*Sevillano* **Felipe González** elected prime minister. Elections for first Andalucian parliament.	
1985	Frontier between Spain and Gibraltar opens (1985). Spain joins European Community (1986).	
1992		Expo '92 in Sevilla celebrates the 500th anniversary of Columbus's discovery of America.

FLAMENCO

Scratch a hot night in Andalucía, even on the much maligned Costa del Sol, and you'll find *flamenco*. "You carry it inside you", said a man in his sixties sitting next to me in the local municipal stadium in downtown Marbella. There was not a tourist in sight, it was 2am, the sky was deep blue-black, patterned with stars, the stadium cluttered with families enjoying the most pleasant hours of the andaluz summer, flapping their fans until dawn, children asleep on laps.

Flamenco is undoubtedly the most important musical-cultural phenomenon in Spain, and over the past decade or so it has experienced a huge resurgence in popularity, and a profile that has reached out far beyond its Andalucian homeland. It owes its new-found influence in part, perhaps, to the southern-dominated socialist governments – Prime Minister Felipe González is from Sevilla, as are many of his associates. In part perhaps, it is down to Spain's unconscious desire, now it is part of the EC, to establish a **national identity** that challenges European stereotypes. The sanitized kitsch *flamenco*, all frills and castanets, exploited as an image of tourist Spain during the Franco period, has been left far behind by a new age expressing the vitality and attitudes of a younger generation of *flamenco* clans.

In the 1980s, the Spanish press hailed **Ketama** (named after a Moroccan village famed for its hashish) as creators of the music

of the "New Spain", after their first album which fused *flamenco* with rock and Latin salsa. Since then they have pushed the frontiers of *flamenco* still further by recording *Songhai*, an album collaborating with Malian kora player Toumani Diabate and British bassist Danny Thompson. *Blues de la Frontera* (Frontier Blues) the first disc of **Pata Negra** ("black leg" – the succulent tasty bit of an Andalucian leg of smoked ham – and an everyday term used for anything good), caused an equal sensation.

This *flamenco* revival of the '80s and '90s is no longer confined to the purists who kept old-time *flamenco* alive in their *peñas* or clubs. On radio and on cassettes blaring from market stalls right across the country you hear the typical high-pitched treble tones of commercial *flamenco* singers like **Tijeritas**. The European success of the *flamenco*-rumba of the **Gipsy Kings**, a high profile gypsy group from southern France, has further opened and prepared the ear of European popular audiences for something more powerful. Rumba, a Latin form, has come back to Spain from Latin America, and so is known as a music of *ida y vuelta* ("go and return"), one of the many fusions of the Spanish music taken to the New World with the Conquistadores and their descendents, where it has mixed with African and other elements, before making its way back again .

The impetus began at the end of the 1970s, with the innovations of guitarist **Paco de Lucia** and, especially, the great, late singer, **El Camaron de la Isla**. These were musicians who had grown up learning from their *flamenco* families but whose own musical tastes have embraced international rock, jazz and blues. Paco de Lucia blended jazz and salsa onto the *flamenco* sound. Camarón, simply, was an inspiration – and one whose own idols (and fans) included Chick Corea and Miles Davis, as well as *flamenco* artists.

ORIGINS

The **roots of *flamenco*** evolved in southern Spain from many sources: Morocco, Egypt, India, Pakistan, Greece and other parts of the Near and Far East. How exactly they came together as *flamenco* is a source of great debate and obscurity, though most authorities believe the roots of the music were brought by **gypsies** arriving in the fifteenth century. In the following century, it fused with elements of

Arab and Jewish music in the Andalucian mountains, where Jews, Muslims and "pagan" gypsies had taken refuge from the forced conversions and clearances effected by the Catholic kings and church. The main *flamenco* centres and families are to be found today in quarters and towns of gypsy and refugee origin, such as Alcalá del Río, Utrera, Jerez, and Cádiz, and the Triana *barrio* of Sevilla.

There are two theories about the origins of the name *flamenco*. One contends that Spanish Jews migrated through trade to Flanders, where they were allowed to sing their religious chants unmolested, and that these chants became referred to as *flamenco* by the Jews who stayed in Spain. The other is that the word is a mispronunciation of the Arabic words *felag* (fugitive) and *mengu* (peasant), a plausible idea, as Arabic was a common language in Spain at the time.

Flamenco aficionados enjoy heated debate about the purity of their art and whether it is more validly performed by a **gitano** (gypsy) or a **payo** (non-gypsy). Certainly, *flamenco* seems to have thrived, enclosed, preserved and protected by the oral tradition of the gypsy clans. Its power, and the despair which its creation overcomes, has emerged from the precarious and vulnerable lives of a people surviving for centuries at the margins of society. *Flamenco* reflects a passionate need to preserve their self-esteem.

These days, there are as many acclaimed *payo* as *gitano flamenco* artists. However, the concept of an **active inheritance** is crucial. The veteran singer **Fernanda de Utrera**, one of the great voices of "pure *flamenco*", was born in 1923 into a gypsy family in Utrera, one of the *cantaora* centres. She was the granddaughter of the legendary singer "Pinini", who had created her own individual *flamenco* forms, and with her younger sister Bernarda, also a notable singer, inherited their *flamenco* with their genes. Even the members of Ketama, the Madrid-based *flamenco*-rock group, come from two gypsy clans – the Sotos and Carmonas.

Although *flamenco's* exact origins are obscure, it is generally agreed that its "laws" were established in the nineteenth century. Indeed, from the mid-nineteenth into the early-twentieth centuries *flamenco* enjoyed a legendary **"Golden Age"**, the tail-end of which is preserved on some of the earliest 1930's recordings. The original musicians found a home in the *café cantantes*, traditional taverns which had their own group of performers (*cuadros*). One of the most famous was the *Café de Chinitas* in Málaga, immortalized by the Granada-born poet García Lorca. In his poem *A las cinco de la tarde* (At five in the afternoon), Lorca claimed that *flamenco* is deeply related to bullfighting, not only sharing root emotions and passions, flashes of erratic genius, but because both are possible ways to break out of social and economic marginality.

Just such a transformation happened in 1922 when the composer Manuel de Falla, the guitarist Andrés Segovia and the poet García Lorca were present for a legendary *Concurso de Cante Jondo*. A gypsy boy singer, **Manolo Caracol**, reportedly walked all the way from Jerez and won the competition with the voice and the flamboyant personality that was to make him a legend throughout Spain and South America. The other key figure of this period, who can be heard on a few recently re-mastered recordings, was **Pastora Pavon**, known as *La Nina de Los Peines*, and popularly acclaimed as the greatest woman *flamenco* voice of twentieth century.

In addition to *café cantantes*, *flamenco* surfaced – as it does today – at fiestas, in bars or *tablaos*, and at *juergas*, informal, private parties. The fact that the Andalucian public are so knowledgeable and demanding about *flamenco* means that musicians, singers and dancers found even at the most humble local club or festival are usually very good indeed.

THE ART OF FLAMENCO

It is essential for an artist to invoke a response, to know they are reaching deep into the emotional psyche of their audience. They may achieve the rare quality of **duende** – total emotional communication with their audience, and the mark of great *flamenco* of whatever style or generation. *Duende* is an ethereal quality: moving, profound even when expressing happiness, mysterious but neverthless felt, a quality that stops a listener in their tracks. And many of those listeners are intensely involved, for *flamenco* is not just a music, for many it is a way of life, a **philosophy** that influences daily activities. A *flamenco* is not only a performer but anyone who is actively and emotionally involved in the unique philosophy.

For the musicians, this fullness of expression is integral to their art, which is why for as many famous names as one can list, there are many, many other lesser known musicians whose work is startlingly good. Not every superb *flamenco* musician gets to be famous, or to record, for *flamenco* thrives most in **live performance**. Exhilarating, challenging and physically stimulating, it is an art form which allows its exponents huge scope to improvize while obeying certain rules. *Flamenco* guitarist Juan Martin has remarked that "in microcosm it imitates Spanish society – traditional on the outside but within, incredible anarchy".

There is a **classical repertoire** of more than sixty *flamenco* songs (*cantes*) and dances (*danzas*) – some solos, some group numbers, some with instrumental accompaniment, others a capella. These different forms of *flamenco* are grouped in "families" according to more or less common melodic themes. The most common beat cycle is twelve – like the blues. Each piece is executed by juxtaposing a number of complete musical units called *coplas*. Their number varies depending on the atmosphere the *cantaor* wishes to establish and the emotional tone they wish to convey. A song such as a *cante por solea* may take a familiar 3/4 rhythm, divide phrases into 4/8 measures, and then fragmentally sub-divide again with voice ornamentation on top of that. The resulting complexity and the variations between similar phrases constantly undermines repetition, contributing greatly to the climactic and cathartic structure of each song.

SONGS AND SINGERS

Flamenco **songs** often express pain, and with a fierceness that turns that emotion inside out. Generally, the voice closely interacts with improvizing guitar, the two inspiring each other, aided by the **jaleo**: the hand-clapping *palmas*, finger-snapping *palillos* and shouts from participants at certain points in the song. This *jaleo* sets the tone by creating the right atmosphere for the singer or dancer to begin, and bolsters and appreciates the talent of the artist as they develop the piece.

Aficionados will shout encouragement, most commonly "¡olé!" – when an artist is getting deep into a song – but also a variety of stranger-sounding phrases. A stunning piece of dancing may, for example, may be greeted with "¡Viva la maquina escribir!" (long live the typewriter), as the heels of the dancer move so fast they sound like a machine; or the cry may be "¡agua!" (water), for the scarcity of water in Andalucía has given the word a kind of glory.

It is an essential characteristic of *flamenco* that a singer or dancer takes certain risks, by putting into their performance feelings and emotions which arise directly from their own life experience, exposing their own **vulnerabilities**. Aficionados tend to acclaim a voice that gains effect from surprise and startling moves than one governed by recognized musical logic. Vocal prowess or virtuosity can be deepened by sobs, gesticulation and an intensity of expression that can have a shattering effect on an audience. Thus pauses, breaths, body and facial gestures of anger and pain transform performance into **cathartic events**. *Siguiriyas* which date from the Golden Age, and whose theme is usually death, have been described as cries of despair in the form of a funeral psalm. In contrast there are many songs and dances such as *tangos*, *sevillanas* and *fandangos* which capture great **joy** for fiestas.

The **sevillana** originated in medieval Sevilla as a spring country dance, with verses improvized and sung to the accompaniment of guitar and castanets (which are rarely used in other forms of *flamenco*). **El Pali** (Francisco Palacios), who died in 1988, was the most well-known and prolific *sevillana* musician, his unusually gentle voice and accompanying strummed guitar combining an enviable musical pace with a talent for composing popular poetic lyrics. In the last few years dancing *sevillanas* has become popular in bars and clubs throughout Spain, but their great natural habitats are **Sevilla's April Feria** and the annual pilgrimage to **El Rocio**. It is during the Sevilla *feria* that most new recordings of *sevillanas* emerge.

Among the best contemporary singers are the aforementioned **Fernanda and Bernarda de Utrera**, **Enrique Morente**, **El Cabrero**, **Juan Peña El Lebrijano**, the **Sorderas**, **Fosforito**, **José Menese** and **Carmen Linares**. However, one of the most popular and commercially successful singers of modern *flamenco* was the extraordinary **El Camarón de la Isla**, (the "shrimp" of the "isle" de Leon near his Cádiz home), who died in 1992.

Collaborating with the guitarists Paco and Pepe de Lucia, and latterly, Tomatito, Camarón raised *cante jondo*, the virtuoso "deep song", to a new art. His high-toned voice had a corrosive, rough-timbred edge, cracking at certain points to release a ravaged core sound. His incisive sense of rhythm coupled with almost violent emotional intensity, made him the quintessential singer of the times.

FLAMENCO GUITAR

The *flamenco* performance is filled with pauses. The singer is free to insert phrases seemingly on the spur of the moment. The **guitar accompaniment**, while spontaneous, is precise and serves one single purpose – to mark the *compas* (measures) of a song and organize rhythmical lines. Instrumental interludes which are arranged to meet the needs of the *cantaor* (as the creative singer is called) not only catch the mood and intention of the song and mirror it, but allow the guitarist to extemporize what are called *falsetas* (short variations) at will. When singer and guitarist are in true rapport the intensity of a song develops rapidly, the one charging the other, until the effect can be overwhelming.

The *flamenco* **guitar** is of lighter weight than most acoustic guitars and often has a pine table and pegs made of wood rather than machine heads. This is to produce the preferred bright responsive sound which does not sustain too long (as opposed to the mellow and longer sustaining sound of classical guitar). If the sound did sustain, particularly in fast pieces, chords would carry over into each other.

The guitar used to be simply an accompanying instrument – originally the singers themselves played – but in the early decades of this century it began developing as a **solo** form, absorbing influences from classical and Latin American traditions. The greatest of these early guitarists was **Ramón Montoya**, who revolutionized *flamenco* guitar with his harmonizations and introduced tremolo and a whole variety of arpeggios – techniques of right-hand playing. The classical guitarist, **Andrés Segovia**, was another influential figure; he began his career playing *flamenco* in Granada. Then in the 1960s came the two major guitarists of modern times, **Paco de Lucia**, of whom more later, and **Manolo Sanlucar**.

Solo guitarists, these days, have immediately identifiable sounds and rhythms: the highly emotive **Pepe Habichuela** and **Tomatito**, for example, or the unusual rhythms of younger players like **Ramón el Portugues**, **Enrique de Melchor** and **Rafael Riqueni**.

NUEVO FLAMENCO

One of *flamenco's* great achievements has been to sustain itself while providing much of the foundation and inspiration for **new music** emerging in Spain today. In the 1950s and 60s, rock'n'roll displaced traditional Spanish music, as it did indigenous musics in many parts of the world. In the 1980s, however, *flamenco* re-invented itself, gaining new meaning and a new public through the music of Paco de Lucia, who mixed in jazz, blues and salsa, and, later, groups like Pata Negra and Ketama, who brought in more rock influences. Purists hated these innovations but, as José "El Sordo" (Deaf One) Soto, Ketama's main singer, explained, they were based on "the classic *flamenco* that we'd been singing and listening to since birth. We just found new forms in jazz and salsa: there are basic similarities in the rhythms, the constantly changing harmonies and improvisations. Blacks and gypsies have suffered similar segregation so our music has a lot in common."

Paco de Lucia, who made the first moves, is the best known of all contemporary *flamenco* guitarists, and reached new audiences through his performance in Carlos Saura's films, *Blood Wedding* and *Carmen*, along with the great *flamenco* dancers, Cristina Hoyos and Antonio Gades. Paco, who is a non-gypsy, won his first *flamenco* prize at the age of 14, and went on to accompany many of the great traditional singers, including a long partnership with Camarón de la Isla. He started forging new sounds and rhythms for *flamenco* following a trip to Brazil, where he fell in love with bossa nova, and in the 1970s he established a sextet with electric bass, Latin percussion, and, perhaps most shocking, flute and saxophone from Jorge Pardo. Over the past twenty years he has worked with jazz-rock guitarists like John McLaughlin and Chick Corea, while his own regular band, featuring singer Ramón de Algeciras, remains one of the most original and distinctive sounds on the *flamenco* scene.

FLAMENCO DANCE

Most popular images of *flamenco* dance – twirling bodies in frilled dresses, rounded arms complete with castanets – are **Sevillanas**, the folk dances performed at fiestas, and, in recent years, on the disco and nightclub floor. "Real" *flamenco* dance is something rather different and, like the music, can reduce the onlooker to tears in an unexpected flash, a cathartic point after which the dance dissolves. What is so visually devastating about *flamenco* dance is the physical and emotional control the dancer has over the body: the way the head is held, the tension of the torso and the way it allows the shoulders to move, the shapes and angles of seemingly elongated arms, and the feet, which move from toe to heel, heel to toe, creating rhythms. These rhythms have a basic set of moves and timings but they are improvised as the piece develops and through interaction with the guitarist.

Flamenco dance dates back to about 1750 and, along with the music, moved from the streets and private parties into the *café cantantes* at the end of the nineteenth century. This was a great boost for the dancers' art, providing a home for professional performers, where they could inspire each other. It was here that legendary dancers like **El Raspao** and **El Estampio** began to develop the spellbinding footwork and extraordinary moves that charcterizes modern *flamenco* dance, while women adopted for the first time the flamboyant *hata de cola* – the glorious long-trained dresses, cut high at the front to expose their fast moving ankles and feet.

Around 1910, *flamenco* dance had moved into Spanish theatres, and dancers like **La Nina de los Peines** and **La Argentina** were major stars. They mixed *flamenco* into programmes with other dances and also made dramatic appearances at the end of comic plays and silent movie programmes. *Flamenco* opera was soon established, interlinking singing, dancing and guitar solos in comedies with a local *flamenco* flavour.

In 1915 the composer Manuel de Falla composed the first *flamenco* ballet, *El Amor Brujo* (Love the Magician), for the dancer Pastora Imperio. **La Argentina**, who had established the

first Spanish dance company, took her version of the ballet abroad in the 1920s, and with her choreographic innovations *flamenco* dance came of age, working as a narrative in its own right. Another key figure in *flamenco* history was **Carmen Amaya**, who from the 1930s to the 60s took *flamenco* dance on tour around the world, and into the movies.

In the 1950s, dance found a new home in the *tablaos*, the aficionado's bars, which became enormously important as places to serve out a public apprenticeship. More recently the demanding audiences at local and national fiestas have played a part. Artistic developments were forged in the 1960s by **Matilde Coral**, who updated the classic dance style, and in the 1970s by **Manuela Carrasco**, who had such impact with her fiery feet movement, continuing a rhythm for an intense and seemingly imposible period, that this new style was named after her (*manuelas*).

Manuela Carrasco set the tone for the highly individual dancers of the 1980s and 90s, such as **Mario Maya** and **Antonio Gades**. These two dancers and choreographers have provided a theatrically inspired staging for the dance, most significantly by extending the role of a dance dialogue and story – often reflecting on the potency of love and passion, their dangers and destructiveness.

Gades has led his own company on world tours but it is his influence on film which has been most important. He had appeared with Carmen Amaya in "Los Araños" in 1963 but in the 1980s began his own trilogy with film-maker Carlos Saura: "Boda de Sangre" (Lorca's play, *Blood Wedding*), "Carmen" (a re-interpretation of the opera), and "El Amor Brujo". The films featured Paco de Lucia and his band, and the dancers **Laura del Sol** and **Christina Hoyos** – one of the great contemporary dancers, who has herself created a superb ballet, "Sueños Flamencos" (Flamenco Dreams).

Aside from the great companies and personalities of *flamenco* dance, there are an enormous number of local dancers all over Andalucía, whose dancing brings *flamenco* to life, and whose moves can be sheer poetry.

Other artists experimented, too, throughout the 1980s. **Lolé y Manuel** updated the *flamenco* sound with original songs and huge success; **Jorge Pardo** followed Paco's jazz

direction; **Salvador Tavora** and **Mario Maya** staged *flamenco*-based spectacles; and **Enrique Morente** and **Juan Peña El Lebrijano** both worked with Andalucian

DISCOGRAPHY

All recommendations below are available on CD.

CLASSIC FLAMENCO ANTHOLOGIES

Early Cante Flamenco – Classic Recordings from the 1930s (Arhoolie, USA).

Cante Flamenco live in Andalucía (Nimbus, UK).

Magna Antología del Cante Flamenco (Hispavox, Spain; 10 volumes).

Noches Gitanas (EPM, Spain; 4CDs).

Sevillanas: the soundtrack of Carlos Saura's film (Polydor, UK).

INDIVIDUAL ARTISTS

Agustín Carbonell Bola *Carmen* (Messidor, Spain).

Camarón de la Isla *Una leyends flamenca, Vivire* and *Autorretrato* (Philips, Spain).

Carmen Linares *La luna en el río* (Auvidis, Spain).

Duquende (Nuevos Medios, Spain).

El Indio Gitano *Nací gitano por la gracia de Dios* (Nuevos Medios, Spain).

Enrique de Melchor *Cuchichi* (Fonodisc, Spain).

Paco de Lucía y Paco Peña *Paco Doble* (Philips, Spain).

José Menese *El viente solano* (Nuevos Medios, Spain).

Moraíto *Morao y oro* (Auvidis, Spain).

Enrique Morente *Negra, si tú supieras* (Nuevos Medios, Spain).

Ramón el Portugués *Gitanos de la Plaza* (Nuevos Medios, Spain).

Tomatito *Barrio Negro* (Nuevos Medios, Spain).

Fernanda et Bernarda de Utrera *Cante Flamenco* (OCORA, France).

NUEVO FLAMENCO AND CROSSOVERS

Los Jóvenes Flamencos Vol I & II (Nuevos Medios, Spain/Rykodisc, UK).

Amalgama y Karnataka College of Percussion (Nuba, Spain).

La Barbería del Sue (Nuevos Medios, Spain).

Chano Dominguez *Chano* (Nuba, Spain).

Ray Heredia *Quien no corre, vuela* (Nuevos Medios, Spain).

Jazzpaña (Nuevos Medios, Spain).

Ketama *Canciones hondas* (Nuevos Medios, Spain) and *Ketama* (Hannibal, UK).

Lole . . . y Manuel (Gong Fonomusic, Spain).

Martirio *Estoy Mala* (Nuevos Medios, Spain).

Paco de Lucía Sextet *Solo Quiero Caminar* (Philips, Spain) and *Live . . . . One Summer Night* (Phonogram, UK).

Juan Peña Lebrijano y Orquestra Andalusi de Tanger *Encuentros* (Ariola/Globestyle).

Paco Peña *Misa Flamenca* (Nimbus, UK).

Pata Negra *Blues de la Frontera* (Nuevos Medios, Spain/Hannibal, UK).

Radio Tarifa *Rumba argelina* (Música Sin Fin, Spain).

Songhai: Ketama/Toumani Diabate/Danny Thompson (Nuevos Medios, Spain/Hannibal, UK).

---

orchestras from Morocco, while **Amalgama** worked with southern Indian percussionists, revealing surprising stylistic unities. Another interesting crossover came with **Paco Peña**'s 1991 *Misa Flamenca* recording, a setting of the Catholic Mass to *flamenco* forms with the participation of established singers like Rafael Montilla "El Chaparro" from Pena's native Córdoba, and a classical academy chorus.

The more commercially successful crossover with rock and blues, pioneered by **Ketama** and **Pata Negra**, has become known, in the 1990s, as *nuevo flamenco*. This "movement" is associated particularly with the label Nuevos Medios and in Andalucía, and also Madrid,

where many of the bands are based, is a challenging, versatile and musically incestuous new scene, with musicians guesting at each others' gigs and on each others' records.

The music is now a regular sound at nightclubs, too, through the appeal of young singers like **Aurora**, whose salsa-rumba song "Besos de Caramelo", written by Antonio Carmona of Ketama, was the first 1980s number to crack the pop charts, and **Martirio** (Isabel Quinones Gutierrez), one of the most flamboyant personalities on the scene, who appears dressed in lace mantilla and shades, like a cameo from a Pedro Almodóvar film, and sings songs with ironical, contemporary lyrics about life in the cities. In general, the new songs are more sensual and erotic than the traditional material, expressing a pain, suffering and love worth dying for.

Martirio's producer, **Kiko Veneno**, who wrote Camarón's most popular song, "Volando voy", is another artist who has brought a *flamenco* sensitivity to Spanish rock music.

Other contemporary bands and singers to look out for on the scene include **La Barbería del Sur** (who add a dash of salsa), **Wili Gimenez** and **Raimundo Amador**, and **Radio Tarifa**, who mix Arabic and pop sounds onto a *flamenco* base.

Jan Fairley

WILDLIFE

The incredible diversity of natural habitats, flora and fauna to be found in Andalucía makes it one of the most attractive destinations for wildlife enthusiasts in western Europe. With 82 protected areas, together accounting for almost 15,000 square kilometres – more than 17 percent of the region – the Junta de Andalucía has shown a dedication to environmental preservation unrivalled in Spain. It also produces a series of leaflets describing the wildlife of Andalucía's protected areas, which can be obtained from park offices and Turismos.

HABITATS

Andalucía lies at two major **geographical crossroads**: the meeting point of Africa and Europe, and the convergence of the Atlantic Ocean with the Mediterranean Sea at the Straits of Gibraltar. Andalucía also harbours a wide range of topographical and climatic conditions, with altitudes ranging from sea level to over 3,700m, and precipitation from 170mm to over 2,000mm (both the driest and the wettest places in Spain are found here).

In terms of habitats, Andalucía can be divided broadly speaking into coasts, arid lands, inland wetlands and mountains. West of Tarifa, the **Atlantic coast** is characterized by long sandy beaches and extensive dune systems, while the relatively flat landscape means that the rivers have so little gradient in

their lower reaches that they are tidal for many kilometres upstream and generally form great marshes where they meet the sea. The mountains lying behind the **Mediterranean coast**, in contrast, give rise to long stretches of sea cliffs, while rivers here have steeper inclines, are faster-flowing and are thus less likely to form great estuarine marshes. The **arid lands** of Almería and eastern Granada, with as little as 170mm of precipitation per year and almost constant sunshine, are one of the driest regions in western Europe, with semi-desert landscapes more appropriate to Morocco.

Throughout Andalucía, a network of **inland wetlands** – permanent or seasonal, freshwater or saline, still or fast-flowing – provides oases for wildlife in a land where there is a pronounced summer drought. Many lie close to the **Straits of Gibraltar**, the primary bird migration route in the western Mediterranean, thus providing refuge for the millions of birds needing to rest and feed en route between Africa and Europe in spring and autumn.

Almost one-fifth of Andalucía is mountain; that is, lies above 1000m. Two great ranges dominate the landscape: the **Sierra Morena**, which separates Andalucía from the rest of Spain, and the **Cordillera Bética**, which runs in a northeasterly direction from Tarifa, continuing out under the Mediterranean to emerge later as the Balearic Islands. The **Sierra Nevada**, at the heart of the Cordillera Bética, possesses the Iberian peninsula's highest mountain: **Mulhacén**, at 3,482m.

PLANTS

More than half of the **8,000 species** of vascular plant known to occur in peninsular Spain and the Balearic Islands are found in Andalucía, including 152 species which are found nowhere else in the world; more than any European country except for Greece. Particular centres of endemism in Andalucía are the arid lands of Almería, the Sierras de Cazorla y Segura, the Serranía de Ronda and the Sierra Nevada.

Perhaps the most important botanical feature of Andalucía, however, is the **pinsapo forests** of the Serranía de Ronda. This tree, *Abies pinsapo*, is a species of fir which is thought to have arrived in Andalucía during the Quaternary, pushed south by the ice sheets, becoming isolated in a few mountain areas when the glaciers retreated. Although only six square kilometres of *pinsapo* forest remained in 1950, an intensive conservation programme has more than quadrupled this area today.

MAMMALS

Andalucía is home to 54 species of mammal, the most outstanding of which is the **pardel lynx**, unique to the Iberian peninsula. It is one of Europe's most endangered vertebrates, with a world population estimated at only 700–1,100 individuals, 60 per cent of which live in Andalucía. The primary enclaves for this magnificent feline are the Doñana National Park and the Sierra Morena. **Genets** and **Egyptian mongooses** are also widespread and abundant in Andalucía, although both are thought to have been introduced from North Africa in ancient times, with other common carnivores including wildcats, otters, polecats, beech martens, badgers and weasels. The main stronghold for the **wolf** in Andalucía is the Sierra Morena, which houses up to 75 individuals in small family groups. The **Algerian hedgehog**, distinguished from its western European relative by its paler colouring, longer legs and larger ears, is another species of northwest African origin; it has tentatively established itself in a few places on the Iberian coast, particularly in eastern Andalucía. The most noteworthy large herbivore of Andalucía is the **Spanish ibex**, the most significant populations inhabiting the Sierras de Cazorla y Segura, the Sierra Nevada and the Serraní de Ronda, with satellite populations recently establishing themselves in some of the nearby ranges. **Mouflon**, originally from Corsica and Sardinia, have been introduced to several areas notably the Sierras de Cazorla y Segura, as a game species.

BIRDS

Outstanding among the **wildfowl** of Andalucía is the **white-headed duck**, the western subspecies of which is confined to southern Spain and a small enclave in the Maghreb. Fifteen years ago the Spanish population was on the verge of extinction, but a phenomenal conservation effort has resulted in a population of 545 birds today. Andalucía is also the European stronghold of the secretive **purple gallinule**, distinguished by its long red legs

and metallic blue-purple plumage, while the Iberian population of the **collared pratincole** is practically the last one in Europe, a major breeding site being the Guadalquivir marshes.

Crested coots, marbled teal and ferruginous ducks are also virtually unknown as European breeding birds outside Andalucía, while the European stronghold of the greater **flamingo** is the salt-lake of Fuente de Piedra, in Málaga, where more than 14,000 pairs have gathered to breed in recent years, relegating the French Camargue to second place. The Spanish **imperial eagle**, Europe's most endangered raptor, is endemic to the Iberian peninsula. The world population of this bird is only 126 pairs, about a quarter of which are found in Andalucía, primarily in the Doñana National Park and the Sierra Morena. The Sierra Morena also contains the largest European enclave of **black vultures**, numbering over 70 breeding pairs.

REPTILES AND AMPHIBIANS

Some 25 species of **reptile** occur in Andalucía, with noteworthy species including the **chameleon**, confined to the coastal areas of Huelva, Cádiz and Málaga, and only found elsewhere in Iberia in the Portuguese Algarve. **Spur-thighed tortoises**, which are globally at risk from habitat loss and collecting, are found in northeastern Almería and Doñana; the only localities in the Iberian peninsula. **Spiny-footed lizards**, endemic to southern and central Iberia and northwest Africa, are extremely common in dry, sandy habitats, the young animals resplendent with bright-red tails. By contrast, two much rarer Andalucian lizards are the Spanish algyroides, known only in a small area in the Sierras de Cazorla y Segura, and the Italian wall lizard, surprisingly present at Cabo de Gata, despite having a main area of distribution in Italy and the Balkans.

The peculiar **amphisbaenian**, like a fat pinkish earthworm, occupies an intermediate position between snakes and lizards. Although found throughout Andalucía, this subterranean creature is rarely seen, although it sometimes comes to the surface at night or after heavy rain. Confined to Iberia and northern Africa are the **false smooth snake**, identified by its dark hood, and **Lataste's viper**, distinguished from all other Iberian vipers by its distinct nose-horn, while the beautifully-patterned **horseshoe**

whipsnake has a similar distribution, but is also found in Sardinia.

Of the 15 species of **amphibian** which occur in Andalucía, the most noteworthy are the sharp-ribbed salamander, a large warty creature up to 30cm long, which is found only in southern Iberia and Morocco; the tiny, orange-bellied Bosca's newt, confined to western Iberia and thus occurring only in Huelva and northern Sevilla in Andalucía; and the Iberian midwife toad, a southwest Iberian endemic, the males of which carry the egg-strings wound around their hind legs until they hatch.

BUTTERFLIES

Andalucía is also home to many **butterflies** which occur only in the southern Iberian peninsula and North Africa, including the desert orange tip, Lorquin's and false baton blues, the Spanish fritillary and the Spanish marbled white. Yet others are true Spanish endemics, such as the Panoptes, Nevada and mother-of-pearl blues and the Nevada grayling. Several interesting butterflies are particularly associated with the Andalucian coast, including the extremely rare **Zeller's skipper**, recorded near Algeciras, as well as the more widespread pygmy and Mediterranean skippers. Several large and attractive vagrant species turn up sporadically from across the Atlantic, including the American painted lady, the milkweed, or monarch and the plain tiger.

WHEN AND WHERE TO GO

The Mediterranean habitats of Andalucía have a climate so mild that a visit at any time of year - even Christmas – will be rewarding for **wild flowers**. The arid lands of Almería are best seen in early spring, however, while the alpine flora of Sierra Nevada and other high mountain regions is not at its peak until summer.

Wetland birds are generally a spring and autumn proposition, although some of the rarer breeding species – purple gallinules, white-headed ducks, crested coots and spoonbills – are perhaps more obvious during the summer. Winter concentrations of wildfowl and waders sometimes number hundreds of thousands, especially in the larger wetlands, such as Doñana. **Raptors** are best seen in late spring and early summer, when the adults must venture out continuously in search of food for

their young. By this time too, the short-toed and booted eagles, Egyptian vultures and Montagu's harriers have arrived from Africa. Many of the smaller, colourful birds typically associated with Mediterranean scrub and forest are also summer visitors.

The **carnivores** are virtually impossible to see at any time of year, as most of them are secretive and nocturnal creatures, although the Egyptian mongoose is sometimes encountered trotting through the scrub in broad daylight. Ibex and mouflon are a different proposition altogether, being easily spotted at all times of year and often approached with relative ease.

Summer is best for the **snakes** and **lizards** of the region, although even in the depths of winter they will emerge on sunny days. Alpine **butterflies** generally only appear in late summer, but many species of the milder Mediterranean habitats have two broods a year and can be seen from early spring onwards.

MARISMAS DEL ODIEL

The **Marismas del Odiel** is an extensive wetland area consisting of a maze of islands, creeks, saltmarshes and salinas lying to the west of the Río Odiel where it flows into the Atlantic. Although immediately adjacent to the industrial port of Huelva, this *paraje natural* supports a rich and varied fauna.

More than 200 species of bird have been recorded here, with pride of place going to the 300-odd pairs of **spoonbills**, about 30 percent of the European population, which nest in the grassy marshes of the Isla del Enmedio; one of only three breeding sites in Europe. The Odiel marshes also support large colonies of purple and grey herons and little egrets, as well as hundreds of pairs of little terns and black-winged stilts. Concentrations of up to 2,000 **flamingos** are commonplace, particularly during the winter and on migration, when they are often accompanied by large numbers of common cranes, sanderling, avocets and curlews. To the west of the Odiel marshes, the coastal juniper forests of Punta Umbría are an important refuge for chameleons.

DOÑANA

One of the greatest of all European wetlands, **Doñana** truly merits its reputation as a superb destination for wildlife enthusiasts. Spain's premier national park covers 500 square kilometres and is centred on the extensive marshes on the west bank of the Río Guadalquivir. It is almost completely surrounded by a *parque natural* known as the Entorno de Doñana, which acts primarily as a protective buffer zone, but is also important for wildlife in its own right. At first sight a flat, monotonous landscape, the Doñana marshes are in fact highly diverse, consisting of *vetas*, raised areas which are rarely covered with water, *lucios*, great depressions, sometimes several kilometres long, which retain water until early summer, and *caños*, the reed-fringed channels which wind through the marshes, carrying water in all but the most extreme periods of drought. The coast of Doñana consists of a wide, sandy beach, backed by four parallel fronts of mobile **dunes** which are gradually advancing inland.

The park also contains large areas of *monte*: dense **Mediterranean scrublands**, dominated by species of Cistus, Halimium, thyme and rosemary. Spring-flowering bulbs include *Dipcadi serotinum*, looking rather like a dull brown bluebell, wild gladioli, irises and trident-shaped asphodels over a metre tall. The *monte* and dune chains also conceal numerous **lagoons**, whilst between the *monte* and the marshlands lies a unique transitional habitat known as the **vera**, its cork-oak studded pastures undoubtedly one of the most diverse ecosystems of the park.

The vertebrate populations of Doñana are almost without parallel in Spain, including eight species of fish, 31 reptiles and amphibians, 29 mammals and 125 breeding birds, with a further 125 species of bird utilizing the park during the winter and on migration. Among the **reptiles**, the most noteworthy species are the chameleon, spur-thighed tortoise, Montpellier and ladder snakes, Lataste's viper, ocellated and spiny-footed lizards, both European pond and stripe-necked terrapins and three-toed skinks, as well as the bizarre, wormlike amphisbaenian, while unusual **amphibians** include stripeless tree-frogs, western spadefoots and sharp-ribbed salamanders.

The list of **mammals** is impressive indeed, topped by the pardel lynx, one of Europe's most endangered mammals, as well as other hunters such as badgers, otters, weasels, mongooses and genets. Wild boar, red deer and the introduced fallow deer are present in considerable numbers, particularly in the *monte*, but the most abundant herbivore is the rabbit, the main prey of the lynx.

Doñana harbours one of the largest populations of Spanish **imperial eagles** in the world (a recent census revealed a minimum of 16 pairs), as well as breeding populations of red and black kites, booted and short-toed eagles and hobbies. Azure-winged magpies, great grey and woodchat shrikes, nightingales, great spotted cuckoos and Scops owls breed in the *monte*, while the venerable cork oaks of the vera support mixed colonies of spoonbills, white storks, little and cattle egrets, and purple, grey, squacco and night herons.

The dunes, open grasslands and stunted halophytic vegetation of the dried-out marshes provide suitable nesting areas for lesser short-toed and Thekla larks, red-necked nightjars, stone curlews and pin-tailed sandgrouse, while the marshes support breeding black-winged stilts, avocets, slender-billed gulls, gull-billed, little and whiskered terns, purple gallinules and collared pratincoles, as well as many species of wildfowl, the most significant being large numbers of red-crested pochard, crested coot and marbled teal, with the rare ferruginous and white-headed ducks putting in a sporadic breeding appearance. Many other birds flock to the marshes in winter and on migration, including tens of thousands of greylag geese, pintails, teal, shovellers and black-tailed godwits, as well as lesser numbers of shelduck, wigeon, red-crested pochard, gadwall, common cranes, flamingos and waders.

BAHÍA DE CÁDIZ

The 100 square kilometre *parque natural* of the **Bahía de Cádiz** encompasses a wide range of coastal habitats, including sand dunes, stone pine forests, sandy beaches, extensive intertidal saltmarshes, abandoned saltpans and small lagoons. Despite the proximity of the 400,000-plus inhabitants of Cádiz itself, the bay is a veritable paradise for **birds**, supporting one of the largest breeding colonies of little terns in Spain, as well as several hundred breeding pairs of black-winged stilts, avocets and Kentish plovers. Its proximity to the European-North African migration route is responsible for a number of more unexpected guests, including arctic skuas, red-breasted mergansers, razorbills and scoters.

The extensive stone pine forests, best preserved at La Algaida, close to Puerto Real, are renowned for their **chameleons**, many of which unfortunately meet their maker on the plethora of busy roads which ring the bay.

ACANTILADO Y PINAR DE BARBATE

With the exception of Gibraltar, the *parque natural* of the **Acantilado y Pinar de Barbate** is the only cliffed section on the Atlantic coast of Andalucía. The sheer walls of **Los Caños de Meca**, plunging over 80m into the sea, are topped by one of the most diverse and best conserved coastal plateau forests on the Andalucian shore, **El Pinar de la Breña**. Stone pines and junipers are interspersed with Mediterranean scrub, hosting barn owls, kestrels and buzzards, as well as a thriving population of chameleons. The isolation of the cliffs themselves has encouraged the establishment of a great colony of **cattle egrets**, numbering over 2,500 pairs and unique on the Andalucian coast, as well as breeding peregrines, blue rock thrushes and rock doves.

SIERRAS DE LA PLATA Y RETÍN

These small sierras lie close to the coast between Barbate and Tarifa, close to the town of Zahara de los Atunes, where, in the 1960s, the first **white-rumped swifts** to breed in Europe were observed; curiously, this bird will only rear its young in the abandoned nests of red-rumped swallows.

The **vegetation** is primarily Mediterranean scrub, dominated by Kermes and cork oaks, lentisc, wild olives and dwarf fan palms, forming a mosaic with limestone grasslands that are a riot of colour in spring; some of the more eye-catching species are Spanish iris, Peruvian squill, wild tulip, palmate anemone and star of Bethlehem. Commonly seen **butterflies** include cleopatras, Moroccan orange tips, Spanish festoons and long-tailed blues plus the occasional monarch, a vagrant from North America.

The skies above the sierras are rarely without the profile of **griffon vultures** riding the thermals – the precipitous cliffs, known locally as *lajas*, support dozens of pairs of nesting griffon vultures – but you can also expect to see Egyptian vultures, Montagu's harriers and peregrines. The Mediterranean scrub is home to a colourful array of smaller birds, including woodchat shrikes, hoopoes, Orphean warblers, roll-

ers and golden orioles, while the drier areas support both great and little bustards, Calandra and crested larks, black-eared and black wheatears and Spanish sparrows.

PLAYA DE LOS LANCES

Close to Tarifa, on the Atlantic coast of Cádiz, lies the *paraje natural* of **Playa de los Lances**, a classic coastal site, comprising a long beach of fine white sands, a ridge of dunes and the marshlands of the Ríos Jara and Valle, both of which run parallel to the coast here for several kilometres.

The **beach flora** includes such gems as sea daffodil, cotton-weed, southern birdsfoot-trefoil and sea medick, while further inland, a mosaic of stone pine forests, dense Mediterranean scrub dominated by lentisc and dwarf-fan palms and dry grasslands covers the plains and hills of the Santuario valley.

Great flocks of **waders** visit the reserve in winter and on migration, the most commonplace being sanderling, dunlin, grey, ringed and Kentish plovers, turnstones, bar-tailed godwits and oystercatchers, as well as hundreds of the rare Audouin's gull. It is a particularly important migration stopover for thousands of white storks and black kites, particularly when bad weather prevents them from crossing the Straits, while ospreys too put in an occasional appearance. Little terns and Kentish plovers both breed in fair numbers on the beach and dunes, while the wealth of piscine life in the rivers and marshes attracts otters, the most characteristic mammal of the reserve.

PUNTA ENTINAS-SABINAR

The *paraje natural* of **Punta Entinas-Sabinar**, which extends along 15km of coast, contains a wide range of habitats, including a sandy beach, littoral dunes clothed with Mediterranean scrub, the saltpan complex of Salinas Viejas and Salinas de Cerillos, and the lagoons of Punta Entinas, all of which are backed by the scarp of Los Alcores, itself a superb example of a raised beach.

Mammals recorded here include the garden dormouse and Mediterranean pine vole, the latter confined to the southern Iberian peninsula, while Lataste's viper is a noteworthy member of the reptilian fauna. But it is the birdlife of the reserve that is truly outstanding, the tally to date numbering almost 200 species.

Among the **breeding birds**, hundreds of pairs of stone curlews and lesser short-toed larks make use of the drier habitats, while the *salinas* attract post-nuptial concentrations of flamingos of up to 1,000 birds, as well as red-crested pochard, cormorants, grey herons and avocets. May is a particularly good time to visit the reserve, affording the chance to see Montagu's harriers, collared pratincoles, Mediterranean and Audouin's gulls, sandwich and whiskered terns, fan-tailed and spectacled warblers and black-eared wheatears. Look out also for woodchat and great grey shrikes, red-necked nightjars, Thekla larks and Marmora's and Dartford warblers in the Mediterranean scrublands.

CABO DE GATA-NÍJAR

This *parque natural* in southern Almería extends over some 260 square kilometres of the volcanic headland known as **Cabo de Gata** and the steppes of the **Campo de Níjar**. Essentially an arid area with large expanses of semi-desert vegetation, it also includes a wide variety of coastal habitats, ranging from precipitous cliffs over 100m high to dunes, saltmarshes and salinas, as well as encompassing the marine ecosystem to a depth of 100m.

The sierra itself boasts important formations of **dwarf fan-palm**, Europe's only native species of palm, growing amid lentisc, holly oak, Mediterranean mezereon and wild olive, as well as extensive steppes dominated by drought-adapted shrubby thymes or the spiny, deciduous shrub Zizyphus lotus. Cabo de Gata-Níjar is home to many plants which occur nowhere else in the world, including the **snapdragon** *Antirrhinum charidemi*, known locally as *flor del dragon*, which grows only on volcanic pinnacles in the sierra, as well as the **pink** *Dianthus charidemi* and the **toadflax** *Linaria benitoi*, which flowers only at the onset of the spring rains. Look out too for the short-stalked clusters of mauve-striped white flowers of the endangered lily *Androcymbium europaeum*, also endemic to this part of Spain.

No less than 16 species of **reptiles** and **amphibian**, including Lataste's viper, Iberian wall lizards, confined to Iberia, NW Africa and the western Mediterranean coast of France, and Italian wall lizards, a more easterly species which is found in only a handful of places in Spain. **Butterflies** of interest include desert orange tip and common tiger blue, both essentially African species whose only European populations are found in southern Spain.

Breeding **birds** of the saltmarshes include little terns, Kentish plovers, black-winged stilts and avocets, with Cetti's and great reed warblers in the reedbeds. Between June and September, 2000–3000 **flamingos** descend on the coastal areas to feed, particularly when other Andalucian sites have dried out, while wintering and passage birds on the coast include spoonbills, Audouin's gulls, shelduck and red-breasted mergansers. The sierra itself is renowned for its breeding **eagle owls**, **Bonelli's eagles** and **Montagu's harriers**, as well as rufous bushchats and red-necked nightjars, but it is the dry steppes of Níjar which are of supreme ornithological significance, supporting important nesting concentrations of little bustards, stone curlews, black-bellied sandgrouse, lesser short-toed larks and trumpeter finches. Perhaps the most noteworthy bird of Cabo de Gata-Níjar, however, is **Dupont's lark**, an essentially North African species which was only recently discovered as a breeding bird in Europe.

DESIERTO DE LAS TABERNAS

Immediately inland from Cabo de Gata, sandwiched between the Sierras Alhamilla and de los Filabres, lies one of the most spectacular landscapes in the Iberian peninsula: the arid lands of the **Desierto de las Tabernas**.

The vegetation of Tabernas consists mainly of **steppes**, dominated either by false esparto grass and *Stipa tenacissima*, or by stunted spiny bushes of Ziziphus lotus, the endemic crucifer *Euzomodendron bourgaeanum*, and aromatic thymes, or by salt-tolerant, often succulent, members of the goosefoot family, particularly *Salsola genistoides* and *S. papillosa*, both of which are endemic to southern Spain.

These arid lands are home to many plants which are found nowhere else in the world, including the **toadflax** *Linaria nigricans*, the **rockrose** *Helianthemum almeriense*, and the **sea lavender** *Limonium insignis*, which flowers promptly in response to the first rains.

Reptiles are in their element here, the commonest species being ocellated and spiny-footed lizards and ladder snakes. Animals requiring greater humidity in order to survive, such as marsh frogs, natterjack toads, stripe-necked terrapins and viperine snakes, are found only in the seasonal creeks, or ramblas, which thread their way between the eroded hills and plateaux. The Desierto de las Tabernas is also one of the few places where both western and Algerian hedgehogs occur, the latter essentially a NW African species, established in only a few places on the Spanish coast.

The **birdlife** of Tabernas is extremely diverse, with the soft, eroding cliffs formed by the meanders of the ramblas supporting breeding jackdaws, blue rock thrushes, crag martins, black wheatears, bee-eaters, rollers and alpine and pallid swifts. The steppes themselves support important populations of stone curlews, black-bellied sandgrouse, Thekla larks and black wheatears, as well as being one of the best places in Europe to see trumpeter finches.

AROUND TABERNAS

To the south of the Desierto de las Tabernas lies the 25km-long range of the **Sierra Alhamilla**, where, amid the dry, rocky outcrops, steep gullies and arid grasslands and scrub, you can hope to see little bustards, black-bellied sandgrouse, trumpeter finches, Thekla and Dupont's larks, the latter distinguished by their long, down-curved bills, as well as stone curlews and black wheatears galore.

To the west of Tabernas, in the eastern part of the province of Granada, two great semi-arid depressions also support important populations of steppe birds. The **Hoya de Baza** is largely dedicated to dry cereal croplands today, but nevertheless supports important breeding populations of little bustards, stone curlews, black-bellied sandgrouse and Dupont's and lesser short-toed larks, while the nearby **Hoya de Guadix** is formed predominantly of soft gypsum, carved by flash floods into steep-sided ravines.

Guadix is one of the best areas for observing dry grassland birds in Andalucía, its extensive steppes, cereal cultivations and patches of holm oak scrub providing the perfect habitat for hundreds of little bustards, stone curlews and black-bellied sandgrouse. Montagu's harriers, peregrines and hobbies hunt here by day, replaced by long-eared and eagle owls at dawn and dusk.

ZONAS HÚMEDAS DEL SUR DE CÓRDOBA

The **Zonas Húmedas del Sur de Córdoba** is a series of widely dispersed wetlands in the southern part of the province of Códoba. The six *reservas naturales* – three permanent and three seasonal **lagoons** – which make up the complex have a total area of over ten square kilometres; the reservoirs of Cordobilla and Malpasillo on the Río Genil, both *parajes naturales*, are also sometimes included.

The permanent lagoons are **Zóñar**, **Amarga** and **Rincón**, of which the largest and deepest is the Laguna de Zóñar, up to 8m deep. All are slightly brackish and contain abundant submerged vegetation as well as being surrounded by thick belts of peripheral vegetation – poplars, tamarisks, reeds and reedmace – up to 15m wide in places.

The abundance of submerged vegetable matter supports a wealth of breeding wildfowl, the most noteworthy of which is undoubtedly the **white-headed duck**; these wetlands are the main breeding area for this diminutive stifftail in Spain, with over 45 nesting pairs and winter concentrations of 100-plus birds. Red-crested pochard, pochard, little grebes, purple gallinules, little bitterns, great reed warblers and kingfishers also breed here. In winter and during migration periods, the resident birdlife of the permanent lagoons is swelled by the arrival of large numbers of tufted duck, shovellers, wigeon, teal and pintail, with greylag geese, scaup, shelduck and the rare ferruginous duck also putting in an occasional appearance.

All three permanent lagoons support interesting **reptiles and amphibians**, notably stripe-necked terrapins, grass and viperine snakes, painted frogs and sharp-ribbed salamanders. By contrast, the shallow seasonal lakes of **El Conde o Salobral**, **Los Jarales** and **Tíscar** contain notably saline waters and are surrounded by halophytic vegetation. During the summer these lagoons often dry out completely, such that their ornithological significance is largely concerned with wintering and passage birds. A visit after the autumn rains should turn up black-winged stilts, avocets, grey herons, red-crested pochard, shoveller and wigeon, as well as an occasional greylag goose, flamingo or shelduck. Great bustards are sometimes seen in the dry cereal croplands surrounding the Laguna del Conde o Salobral, while the Laguna de los Jarales, rather surprisingly, supports populations of apparently salt-tolerant natterjack toads, western spadefoots and painted and marsh frogs.

FUENTE DE PIEDRA

A little further south, in the north of Málaga, lies the reserva natural of **Fuente de Piedra**, a shallow saline **lagoon** of endorreic origin; that is, it is the result of the accumulation of ground and surface water from the surrounding area and has no outlet. Some 6km long and 2.5km wide, Fuente de Piedra is the largest natural lake in Andalucía.

Salt-tolerant herbs and shrubs surround the lagoon and also thrive on the long banks which traverse the lake. It is these raised areas that support Fuente de Piedra's pride and joy: the largest breeding colony of **flamingos** in Europe, and the only regular nesting site on the continent, apart from the French Camargue. In 1991, more than 14,000 pairs of flamingos raised some 12,000 young at Fuente de Piedra. During the winter, when full, the lake covers an area of some 14 square kilometres, but during the summer it becomes little more than a glistening sheet of dried salts, although pumps installed in recent years ensure that sufficient water remains in the centre of the lake for the young flamingos to fledge. During times of low water, the adult flamingos disperse all over Andalucía in search of food, turning up hundreds of kilometres away at Doñana, the Odiel marshes and Cabo de Gata.

A freshwater channel surrounds the main lagoon, supporting a rich marsh vegetation and attracting **other wetland birds**: at least 20 pairs of marsh harriers, up to 200 pairs of the rare gull-billed tern, a few pairs of the equally rare slender-billed gull, black-winged stilts, avocets, red-crested pochard, gadwall, garganey and great crested and black-necked grebes all breed here. In the winter, look out for common cranes, as well as greylag geese and shelduck among the 50,000 wildfowl present, while in spring the lake becomes a focal point for thousands of black terns on migration.

The cereal fields and Mediterranean scrublands surrounding Fuente de Piedra are worth a look for crested larks, stone curlews bee-eaters, great grey shrikes, hoopoes and pallid and alpine swifts in the summer.

LAGUNAS DE CÁDIZ

The **Lagunas de Cádiz**, which are scattered across the hinterland of the Bahía de Cádiz, are renowned for their important breeding populations of white-headed duck, crested coot and purple gallinules, all virtually unknown as European breeding birds outside Andaluíca.

The most important lake in the complex is the **Laguna de Medina**, the largest in Cádiz. Like most of the lagoons it is surrounded by a thick belt of emergent vegetation, dominated by reeds, reedmace, rushes and stands of tamarisk, which grades into cereal cultivations interspersed with dense patches of Mediterranean scrub away from the shore. Here spring brings a flush of orchids into bloom, including the exotic sawfly, mirror, yellow bee and bumblebee orchids.

Other **breeding birds** of the Lagunas de Cádiz include black-necked grebes, red-crested pochard, black-winged stilts and Kentish plover, with the reedbeds attracting little bitterns, great reed and Cetti's warblers, marsh harriers and possibly spotted crakes.

The lagoons come into their own in the winter months and during migration periods, when thousands of ducks, coots and geese arrive, including greylag geese, wigeon, garganey, gadwall, pintail and such rarities as marbled teal and ferruginous duck. White storks, purple squacco and night herons, bitterns and little bitterns, spoonbills, flamingos and common cranes can be seen feeding here when the lagoons are full, as well as black and whiskered terns, collared pratincoles and an occasional osprey on migration.

SIERRA MORENA

The 500km-long ridge of the **Sierra Morena**, which virtually cuts Andalucía off from the rest of Spain, reaches a maximum altitude of only 1,323m, comprising for the most part low, rounded hills, clothed with dense forests that are favoured by many animals not found elsewhere in the region.

Within Andalucía much of the Sierra Morena is protected by a series of *parques naturales*. At the western end, bordering Portugal and Extremadura, lie the **Sierra de Aracena y Picos de Aroche**, the **Sierra Norte** and the **Sierra de Hornachuelos**, while the eastern Sierra Morena holds the

Sierra de Cardeña-Montoro and the adjacent **Sierra de Andúar**. In northern Jaén, the kilometre-deep river gorge of Despeñaperros – the only crossing point between Andalucía and the *meseta* in ancient times – is also a *parque natural*.

The vegetation of the Sierra Morena was originally composed of **Mediterranean forests** dominated by holm, Lusitanian and cork oaks, interspersed with wild olives, cistuses, lentisc, strawberry tree and myrtle; the best preserved examples are found today in the Sierra de Andújar. Other woodland types are also present, however, such as the magnificent enclave of Spanish chestnuts which thrives around Galaroza and Fuenteheridos, in the Sierra de Aracena, and the rich gallery forests of alders, elms, ashes and willows which line many of the rivers of the sierra. In the western Sierra Morena, extensive areas of the original Mediterranean forest have been converted to *dehesa* – the evergreen oak "parkland-and-pastures" which dominates much of southwestern Iberia – dedicated largely to cork and charcoal production and the rearing of black pigs, whose succulent, acorn-fed hams are famous worldwide. The dehesa grasslands are a riot of colour in spring, some of the more attractive species including Spanish bluebell, wild tulip, star-of-Bethlehem, tassel hyacinth, asphodels, Spanish iris, Barbary nut, peonies and palmate anemone.

The mammalian fauna of the Sierra Morena comprises good populations of **wild boar** and red and fallow **deer**, as well as all the Andalucian small carnivores: weasels, beech martens, polecats, badgers, mongooses, genets and wildcats, with otters particularly abundant along the Río de las Yeguas, which separates the Sierra de Cardeña-Montoro from Andújar. The Andalucian stronghold for the **wolf** is the eastern Sierra Morena, although it also strays westwards into the Sierra Norte, while the endangered **pardel lynx** is known to occur in the Sierras de Hornachuelos, Cardeña-Montoro and Andújar.

The Sierra Morena is also a superb locality for **birds of prey**, housing important populations of golden, Bonelli's, short-toed and booted eagles, griffon and Egyptian vultures and eagle owls, as well as a few pairs of Spanish imperial eagles. Here, too, you will find the most important population of **black vultures** in Andalucía, nesting in the tops of the ancient cork and holm oaks, with more than 30 pairs in the Sierra de Aracena and 20-plus pairs in the Sierra de Hornachuelos. The Sierra Morena is also the only place in Andalucía with breeding **black storks**.

SIERRA NEVADA

Almost 80km long and 15–30km wide, the **Sierra Nevada** is one of the best-known mountain ranges in Spain, not least for its highest peak, **Mulhacén**, which at 3,482m is known colloquially as the "roof" of the peninsula. The southern foothills of the Sierra Nevada, the **Alpujarras**, have an almost tropical climate owing to their proximity to Africa, while the highest peaks – twelve of which are over 3,000m – are snow-clad for up to nine months of the year. Composed mainly of mica schist, the Sierra Nevada is very different geologically from the nearby limestone ranges, which may account partly for the large number of endemic species found here.

A botanical enclave of supreme importance, the Sierra Nevada houses almost **2,000 species of vascular plant**, more than 70 of which are found nowhere else in the world. Most of the endemic species occur in the highest peaks, forming part of a unique snow-tolerant community whose members include the endangered daffodil *Narcissus nevadensis*, one of the first plants to flower in the spring, the white-flowered Nevada saxifrage (*Saxifraga nevadensis*), the wormwood *Artemisia granatensis*, found only above 3,000m, glacier toadflax (*Linaria glacialis*), another endangered species which occurs at similar altitudes, the white-flowered buttercup *Ranunculus acetosellifolius*, distinguished by its arrow-shaped leaves and mauve sepals, and the cushion-forming, pinkish-flowered violet *Viola crassiuscula*.

The Sierra Nevada is also famed for its large number of endemic **butterflies**, including the subspecies of the Spanish brassy ringlet, found only above 2000m; *ssp. nevadensis* of the apollo, which can be seen in late summer at altitudes ranging from 700 to a phenomenal 3000m; and the Nevada blue, which flies between 2100 and 2400m, while the zullichi subspecies of the Glandon blue, perhaps **Iberia's rarest butterfly**, has only been found by a handful of specialists near Pico Veleta.

The lower slopes of the Sierra Nevada have Lorquin's and zephyr blues, which also occur in the Sierra Morena.

Even among the larger animals, the diversity is incredible. Within the boundaries of the *parque natural* alone, you could find 35 mammals, 125 breeding birds and 29 reptiles and amphibians. The **Spanish ibex**, which almost became extinct here in the 1930s, now numbers more than 3000 individuals, but the largely treeless terrain is less favourable for other mammals; the pine plantations of the lower slopes support a few badgers, beech martens and wildcats. Breeding raptors include golden, Bonelli's, short-toed and booted eagles, goshawks and peregrines. Several hundred pairs of choughs nest around the high level cliffs, while the alpine grasslands are the only place where alpine accentors – undoubtedly the tamest high mountain birds – breed in the southern half of Spain. The approach into the Sierra Nevada via the Alpujarras will add some of the smaller and more colourful birds to your list, including hoopoes, bee-eaters, woodchat shrikes, black redstarts, black-eared wheatears and blue rock thrushes.

SIERRA MARÍA

At the eastern end of the **Cordillera Subbética** in Andalucía lies the *parque natural* of **Sierra María**, centred on the almost naked limestone outcrop of María (2045m). The lower slopes support extensive shady forests of aleppo and laricio pine, interspersed with relict Scots pines and small patches of junipers, maples and holm oak: home to wildcats, badgers and red squirrels, as well as eagle owls. Above the tree-line you should be able to spot golden, booted and short-toed **eagles** soaring on the thermals, as well as wallcreepers, peregrine falcons and alpine swifts. An interesting botanical locality, Sierra María contains several endangered species, including the knapweeds Centaurea mariana and C. macrorrhiza, both of which are found only here and in the adjacent Sierra del Gigante in Murcia, and Sideritis stachydioides, a member of the mint family which is unique to María.

Sierra Maria is also renowned for its **butterfly** fauna, particularly at high altitudes, including the Spanish argus, unique to Iberia, an endemic subspecies of apollo (s*sp. mariae*), and the Nevada grayling (also in the Sierra Nevada),

represented in Spain by the subspecies *williamsi*; this species is otherwise only found in southern Russia, some 5000km distant.

SIERRAS DE CAZORLA, SEGURA Y LAS VILLAS

In the extreme northeast of Andalucía, in the province of Jaén, lies a series of deep valleys separated by parallel limestone ridges running in a northeast-southwesterly direction: the *parque natural* of the **Sierras de Cazorla, Segura y las Villas** (over 2000 square kilometres), the largest protected area in Andalucía. With average annual precipitation exceeding 2000mm, this is one of the rainiest places in Spain, and it is here that the headwaters of the great Guadalquivir river rise. Originally one of Spain's foremost hunting reserves, the park has lost much of its native vegetation owing to extensive planting with aleppo, maritime and laricio pines, although the latter is a very ancient species which also occurs here naturally. Above the tree-line the vegetation is more or less still in a natural state, the predominant plants being stunted laricio pines and junipers and cushion-forming members of the pea family: purple-flowered hedgehog broom, yellow-flowered Echinospartium boissieri and white- or pink-flowered mountain tragacanth, as well as the spiny crucifer Ptilotrichum spinosum.

The **flora** of the Sierras de Cazorla, Segura y las Villas numbers some 1300 species, including more than 30 endemics, such as the pale blue columbine Aquilegia cazorlensis and the cranesbill Geranium cazorlense, neither of which was discovered until the 1950s. The stronghold for both species is the peak of Cabañas (2036m).

Other endemics are the insectivorous butterwort Pinguicula vallisneriifolia, an endangered species whose bluish-white flowers are only found on damp, shady limestone cliffs, and the smallest Iberian narcissus – a tiny hooppetticoat daffodil which goes under the name of *Narcissus hedreanthus* – as well as the largest, the 1.5m *N. longispathus*. The carmine-flowered Cazorla violet (*Viola cazorlensis*), a rare species of limestone rock gardens which flowers towards the end of May, also occurs in the nearby Sierra Mágina.

The park is also home to more than 140 species of bird and is an important refuge for

raptors. Griffon vultures and booted eagles nest in large numbers (the lammergeier, or bearded vulture is now extinct here as a breeding bird), as well as a few pairs of Egyptian vultures, golden, Bonelli's and short-toed eagles, peregrine falcons, hobbies and goshawks. At dusk look (or listen) out for eagle, Scops and tawny owls in the forests.

Red and fallow **deer** and **mouflon** were introduced as game species during the park's time as a game reserve, but the outstanding large herbivore is undoubtedly the **Spanish ibex**, which inhabits the rocky pastures above the tree-line. Unfortunately, in 1987 the Cazorla ibex became infected with mange, which wiped out almost 90 per cent of the population, but it is on the increase again today.

Mammalian **predators** include wildcats, genets, beech martens and polecats, with pardel lynx reputed to frequent the Segura forests, while otters occur on all the major rivers. Greater white-toothed shrews, an endemic subspecies of red squirrel (s.*sp. segurae*) and garden dormice provide the main diet for the forest carnivores, since rabbits and hares are both uncommon here. The tiny Spanish algyroides, sometimes called Valverde's lizard, is endemic to the Sierras de Cazorla y Segura, where it inhabits damp rock-strewn habitats; it was only discovered in 1957 and can be distinguished by its coffee-coloured back, usually with a narrow black vertebral stripe, and distinct collar. Other **reptiles** of interest include Lataste's viper, horseshoe whipsnake, ladder snake, amphisbaenian, Bedriaga's skink, Iberian wall lizard and stripe-necked terrapin. The more notable **butterflies** of the park include the mother-of-pearl blue and Spanish argus, both of which are unique to Spain, but they are outshone by an endemic subspecies of the Spanish moon moth (*ssp. ceballosi*), a pale green and bronze beauty, a hand's span across, which occurs only in pine forests in Spain and parts of the French Alps.

SIERRA MÁGINA

At the heart of the Cordillera Subbética lies the *parque natural* of the **Sierra Mágina** , centred on the 2167m peak of Mágina itself. Above the tree-line is a landscape dominated by cushion-forming species such as hedgehog broom, junipers and the prickly crucifer *Ptilotrichum spinosum*, domain of Spanish ibex,

blue rock thrush, choughs and alpine swifts, while golden and Bonelli's eagles soar overhead.

The middle zone is occupied by fairly humid deciduous **Mediterranean forest**, with Montpellier maple and Lusitanian oak, Spanish barberry and St Lucie's cherry, haunt of wild boar and small predators such as wildcats, beech martens and weasels, although you're more likely to see one of the recently introduced red deer. Short-toed treecreepers, crested tits and goshawks are the most typical birds to look for at this level.

The lowest levels are clothed with the typical **evergreen forests** and scrub of the region, characterized by holly and holm oaks, prickly juniper and Mediterranean mezereon. Although rarely seen, polecats, genets and badgers favour the dense vegetation, with Moorish geckoes, ocellated and Iberian wall lizards, and ladder and Montpellier snakes frequenting the more open areas. Some of the more interesting vascular plants of the Sierra Mágina limestone include the Iberian endemic *Lonicera arborea*, an unusual honeysuckle in that it takes the form of a small tree rather than a climber, the red-berried mistletoe *Viscum cruciatum*, and several southern Iberian endemics: the Cazorla violet *Viola cazorlensis*, the dwarf daffodil *Narcissus cuatrecasasii* and the yellow-flowered, shrubby kidney vetch *Anthyllis ramburii*. The gromwell *Lithodora nitida*, which grows between the cushions of hedgehog broom and *Echinospartium boissieri*, is an endangered species unique to Mágina.

EL TORCAL DE ANTEQUERA

In the centre of the province of Málaga, just a few kilometres south of Fuente de Piedra, lies **El Torcal de Antequera**, a remarkable landscape resembling a petrified city, and considered to be one of the best karstic phenomena in southern Europe.

The fluted and scalloped limestone turrets are dotted with **rock-plants** such as the endemic saxifrage *Saxifraga biternata*, Antequera toadflax, which is also found in the Serranía de Ronda, the yellow violet *Viola demetria*, with flowers often only millimetres across, and the glaucous-leaved *Rupicapnos africana*, a bizarre member of the poppy family. Grassy areas between the pillars are a paradise for spring-flowering **orchids**, including many members of the genus Ophrys: yellow bee, bumblebee, brown bee, mirror, sawfly and woodcock orchids, to mention but a few.

From the top of El Torcal, at 1369m, the view over the surrounding countryside is spectacular, as well as offering the possibility of spotting a passing griffon or Egyptian vulture, or short-toed or Bonelli's eagle.

SERRANÍA DE RONDA

The westernmost massif of the Cordillera Subbética is the **Serranía de Ronda**, which straddles the borders of Cádiz and Málaga. The eastern part of this huge limestone range coincides with the *parque natural* of the **Sierra de las Nieves**, a formidable landscape riddled with deep gorges and vertiginous cliffs, while the western massifs lie within the *parque natural* of the **Sierra de Grazalema** one of southern Spain's prime wildlife sites, also renowned for being the rainiest place in Iberia. The vegetation is predominantly Mediterranean evergreen and deciduous woodlands and low scrub, interspersed with extensive dry pastures, nibbled to the roots by wild and domestic herbivores alike, but studded with rocky outcrops where huge flowering clumps of saxifrages, catchflies and stonecrops thrive by virtue of their inaccessibility. More than **1300 species of vascular plant** have been recorded in the Serranía de Ronda, among the more eye-catching being six daffodils, including the endangered *Narcissus baeticus*, seven irises and 27 orchids. Several species are found nowhere else in the world, such as the delicate orange-red poppy *Papaver rupifragum*, the toadflax *Linaria platycalyx* and the endangered *Merendera androcymbioides*, a member of the lily family. The outstanding botanical feature of the Serranía de Ronda, however, is the **pinsapo**; a species of fir which is found nowhere else in the world. Although the largest forests lie in the Sierra de las Nieves, the more accessible examples occupy the northern slopes of Grazalema's Sierra del Pinar.

Over 200 species of vertebrates are known to occur in the Serranía de Ronda, 40 of which are mammals, including several thriving populations of Spanish ibex, roe and red deer and small carnivores such as genets, mongooses, wildcats, badgers and otters. The cave system of Hundidero-Gata houses more than 100,000 **Schreiber's bats** in winter: one of the largest concentrations of hibernating bats in Europe.

The birds of prey are outstanding here, the Serranía being one of the primary breeding areas for **griffon vultures** in Europe. Bonelli's, golden, short-toed and booted eagles are all common here, as well as Egyptian vultures, goshawks, peregrines and eagle owls. The rock-bird community includes choughs, alpine swifts, black wheatears and blue rock thrushes, as well as a colony of the rare white-rumped swift.

LOS ALCORNOCALES

Immediately south of the Sierra de Grazalema lies a range of low, forested sandstone hills that extends almost to Tarifa. Known as **Los Alcornocales**, it houses **one of the largest cork-oak forests** in the world. The vegetation here is a superb example of the original Iberian forests, comprising jungle-like, thick forests of massive Lusitanian and cork oaks and wild olives, some of which are thought to be over 1000 years old. Laurels and rhododendrons also thrive here, relics of the Tertiary semitropical flora that was once widespread in Europe but has virtually disappeared today as a result of climatic change. These forests are the haunt of the southern-most population of roe deer in Europe, as well as of red deer, genets, mongooses and wildcats. Golden eagles, griffon vultures and eagle owls are the commonest birds of prey, while a handful of black vultures nest in the ancient cork oaks and olives.

Teresa Farino

BOOKS

Listings below represent a highly selective reading list on Andalucía and matters Spanish, especially in the sections on history. Most titles are in print, although we've included a few older classics, many of them easy enough to find in second hand bookshops and libraries. For all books in print, publishing details are in the form (UK publisher/US publisher), where both exist; if books are published in one country only, this follows the publisher's name (eg Serpent's Tail, UK). University Press is abbreviated as UP.

IMPRESSIONS, TRAVEL AND GENERAL ACCOUNTS

THE BEST INTRODUCTIONS

David Baird *Inside Andalusia* (Lookout, Málaga). A book that grew out of the author's series of articles published in *Lookout* magazine. Anecdotal yet perceptive overview of the region with plenty of interesting and offbeat observations and glossy illustrations.

Ian Gibson *Fire in the Blood: the New Spain* (Faber/BBC, UK). Gibson is a Madrid-based writer, resident since 1978, and a Spanish national since 1984. He is a passionate enthusiast and critic of Spain and the Spanish, both of which he gets across brilliantly in this 1993 book – the accompaniment to a gripping TV series – in all their mass of contradictions, attitudes, obsessions, quirks and everything else. Hugely recommended with strong pieces on Andalucía, but did receive flack from outraged Spanish reviewers.

John Hooper *Spaniards: A Portrait of the New Spain* (Penguin, UK/US). Excellent, insightful portrait of post-Franco Spain and the new generation by *The Guardian*'s correspondent there for the last decade; written in 1986 with a new edition due in 1994. Although it has only passing references to Andalucía, along with Ian Gibson's book (above), this is the best possible introduction to contemporary Spain.

Michael Jacobs *Andalusia* (Viking, UK/US) Well crafted, opinionated and wide ranging introduction to Andalucía. Covers everything from prehistory to the Civil War and manages to cram in perceptive pieces on *flamenco*, gypsies and food and drink. A gazeteer at the back details major sights. The best single volume introduction to the region.

Allen Josephs *White Wall of Spain* (Iowa State UP, US) An insightful series of essays on the mysteries of Andalucian folk culture from the origins of flamenco to the significance of *Semana Santa* and bullfights.

RECENT TRAVELS

Alaistair Boyd *Travels in the Mountains of Andalusia* (Collins, UK). Another volume in one Englishman's continuing love affair with the region. His earlier *The Road from Ronda* (Collins, UK) is a Sixties view of the same landscape – the peasants are still struggling.

Sarah Jane Evans *Seville* (Sinclair-Stevenson, UK). One of a number of books released to coincide with Sevilla's new-found popularity in the wake of Expo '92 exposure, this is more thorough than most and provides a useful, if sometimes rather jejune, introduction to the city.

David Gilmour *Cities of Spain* (Pimlico/Ivan R Dee). A modern cultural portrait of Spain which attempts to describe the country's history through portraits of selected cities. Very much in the old tradition, it is a little fogeyish at times but excellent, nonetheless, in its evocation of history, especially on the Moorish cities – though not Granada – of Andalucía.

Adam Hopkins *Spanish Journeys: A Portrait of Spain* (Penguin, UK). Published in 1993, this is an enjoyable and highly stimulating exploration of Spanish history and culture, weaving its (considerable) scholarship in an accessible and unforced travelogue form, and full of illuminating anecdotes.

Ted Walker *In Spain* (out of print). The poet Ted Walker has lived and travelled in Spain on and off since the 1950s. This is a lyrical and absorbing account of the country and people, structured around his various sorties, a couple of them in Andalucía.

James Woodall *In Search of the Firedance: Spain through Flamenco* (Sinclair Stevenson, UK). This is a terrific history and exploration of flamenco, and as the subtitle suggests it is never satisfied with "just the music" in getting to the heart of the culture.

EARLIER 20TH CENTURY WRITERS

Gerald Brenan *South From Granada* (Penguin/CUP) and *Face of Spain* (Penguin, UK). *South From Granada* is an enduring classic. Brenan lived in a small village in Las Alpujarras in the 1920s, and records this and the visits of his Bloomsbury contemporaries Virginia Woolf, Lytton Strachey and Bertrand Russell. *The Face of Spain* is a later collection of highly readable travel writings gathered on a trip through Franco's Spain in 1949 with a substantial chunk devoted to Andalucía.

Penelope Chetwood *Two Ladies in Andalucía* (Century, UK). Poet John Betjeman's wife took to the roads of Andalucía with another middle-aged lady – her horse. Southern Spain seen from a quaintly English perspective.

Nina Epton *Andalusia* (Wiedenfeld & Nicolson, UK). Sixties portrait of the region by a friend of Gerald Brenan. Contains interesting vignettes on people and places prior to the arrival of mass tourism.

Laurie Lee *As I Walked Out One Midsummer Morning* (Penguin, UK/US), *A Rose For Winter* (Penguin, UK), *A Moment of War* (Penguin/New Press). *Midsummer Morning* is the irresistibly romantic account of Lee's walk through Spain – from Vigo to Málaga – and his gradual awareness of the forces moving the country towards Civil War. As an autobiographical novel, of living rough and busking his way from the Cotswolds with a violin, it's a delight; as a piece of social observation, painfully sharp. In *A Rose For Winter* Lee describes his return, twenty years later, to Andalucía, while in *A Moment of War* he looks back again to describe a winter fighting with the International Brigade in the Civil War – an account by turns moving, comic and tragic.

Rose Macaulay *Fabled Shore* (out of print). The Spanish coast as it was in 1949 (read it and weep), travelled and described from Catalunya to the Portuguese Algarve. More focussed on culture rather than people.

James A. Michener *Iberia* (Corgi/Crest). A bestselling, idiosyncratic and encyclopedic compendium of interviews and impressions of Spain on the brink – in 1968 – looking forward to the post-Franco years. Fascinating, still.

Jan Morris *Spain* (Penguin/Prentice-Hall). Morris wrote this in six months in 1960, on her (or, at the time, his) first visit to the country. It is an impressionistic account – good in its sweeping control of place and history, though prone to see everything as symbolic. The updated edition is plain bizarre in its ideas on Franco and dictatorship – a condition for which Morris seems to believe Spaniards were naturally inclined.

Walter Starkie *Don Gypsy* (out of print). The tales of a Dublin professor who set out to walk the roads of Spain and Andalucía in the 1930s with a only a fiddle for company. The pre-Civil War world – good and bad – is astutely observed and his adventures are frequently amusing. Like Borrow earlier he fell for the gypsies and became an expert on their culture.

OLDER CLASSICS

George Borrow *The Bible in Spain* and *The Zincali* (both out of print). On first publication in 1842, Borrow subtitled *The Bible in Spain* "Journeys, Adventures and Imprisonments of an English-man"; it is one of the most famous books on Spain – slow in places but with some very amusing stories. *Zincali* is an account of the Spanish gypsies, whom Borrow got to know pretty well and for whom he translated the Bible into *gitano*.

Richard Ford *A Handbook for Travellers in Spain and Readers at Home* (Centaur Press/Gordon Press); *Gatherings from Spain* (out of print). The *Handbook* must be the best guide ever written to any country and stayed in print as a *Murray's Handbook* (one of the earliest series of guides) well into this century. Massively opinionated, it is an extremely witty book and in its British, nineteenth-century manner, incredibly knowledgeable and worth flicking through for the proverbs alone. Copies of *Murray's* may be available in second-hand bookstores – the earlier the edition the purer the Ford. The *Gatherings* is a rather timid abridgement of the general pieces.

Washington Irving *Tales of the Alhambra* (originally published 1832; abridged editions are on sale in Granada). Half of Irving's book consists of oriental stories, set in the Alhambra; the rest of accounts of his own residence there and the local characters of his time. A perfect read in situ. Irving also wrote *The Conquest of Granada* (1829; out of print), a description of the fall of the Nasrids.

ANTHOLOGIES

Jimmy Burns (ed) *Spain: A Literary Companion* (John Murray, UK). A good anthology, including worthwhile nuggets of most authors recommended here, amid a whole host of others.

David Mitchell *Travellers in Spain: An Illustrated Anthology* (Cassell, UK). A well-told story of how four centuries of travellers – and most often travel-writers – saw Spain. It's interesting to see Ford, Brenan, Laurie Lee and the rest set in context.

HISTORY

EARLY, MEDIEVAL AND BEYOND

Manuel Fernández Álvarez *Charles V* (out of print); **Peter Pierson** *Philip II of Spain* (Thames & Hudson, UK). Good studies in an illustrated biography series.

James M. Anderson *Spain: 1001 Archaeological Sites* (Hale/Calgary UP). A good guide and gazeteer to 95 percent of Spain's archeological sites with detailed instructions of how to get there.

Henri Breuil *Rock Paintings of Southern Andalucía* (Oxford UP, UK). Published in 1929, this is still the definitive guide to the subject.

J. M. Cohen *The Four Voyages of Christopher Columbus* (Cresset Library, UK) The man behind the myth; one of the best books on Columbus in English.

John A. Crow *Spain: The Root and the Flower* (California UP, US/UK). Cultural/social history from Roman Spain to the present.

J.H. Elliott *Imperial Spain 1469–1716* (Penguin, US/UK). Best introduction to "the Golden Age" – academically respected and a gripping tale.

Richard Fletcher *Moorish Spain* (Weidenfeld & Nicolson/California UP). A fascinating, provocative and highly readable narrative with a suitably iconoclastic conclusion to the history of Moorish Spain.

L.P. Harvey *Islamic Spain 1250–1500* (Chicago UP, US/UK). Comprehensive account of its period – both the Islamic kingdoms and the Muslims living beyond their protection.

S.J. Keay *Roman Spain* (British Musuem Publications/California UP). Relatively new and definitive survey of a neglected subject, well illustrated and highly readable.

Elie Kedourie *Spain and the Jews: The Sephardi Experience, 1492 and After* (Thames & Hudson, UK/US). A collection of essays on the three-million-strong Spanish Jews of the Middle Ages and their expulsion by the Catholic Kings.

Henry Kamen *The Spanish Inquisition* (Mentor, US) Highly respected examination of the causes and effects of this grisly institution and the long shadow it cast across Spanish history and development.

THE 20TH CENTURY AND THE CIVIL WAR

Gerald Brenan *The Spanish Labyrinth* (CUP, US/UK). First published in 1943, Brenan's study of the social and political background to the Civil War is tinged by personal experience, yet still an impressively rounded account.

Raymond Carr *Modern Spain 1875–1980* (OUP, US/UK) and *The Spanish Tragedy: the Civil War in Perspective* (Weidenfeld, UK). Two of the best books available on modern Spanish history – concise and well-told narratives.

Ronald Fraser *Blood of Spain* (Pantheon, US). Subtitled "The Experience of Civil War, 1936–39", this is an impressive piece of research, constructed entirely of oral accounts. *In Hiding* (Penguin, UK), by the same author, is a fascinating individual account of a Republican mayor of Mijas (in Málaga) hidden by his family for thirty years until the Civil War amnesty of 1969. *The Pueblo* (Allen Lane, UK) is a penetrating and compelling study of the trials and struggles of one Costa del Sol mountain village seen through the eyes of its inhabitants which speaks for much of Andalucía today.

Ian Gibson *Federico García Lorca* (Faber & Faber/Pantheon), *The Assassination of Federico García Lorca* (Penguin, UK) and *Lorca's Granada*

(Faber & Faber, US/UK). The biography is a gripping book and *The Assassination* a brilliant reconstruction of the events at the end of his life, with an examination of fascist corruption and of the shaping influences on Lorca, twentieth-century Spain and the Civil War. *Granada* explores Lorca's city by way of a collection of fascinating walks around the town.

Joe Monk *With the Reds in Andalucía* (out of print). One Irishman's account of the optimism, hell, and finally despair, of fighting with the Irish Brigade of the international volunteers during the Civil War.

Paul Preston *The Spanish Civil War* (Weidenfeld, UK), *Franco* (Harper Collins, UK/US). A formidable expert on the period, Preston has succeeded in his attempt to provide a manageable guide to the Civil War labyrinth – with powerful illustrations. *Franco* is a penetrating – and monumental – biography of the dictator and his regime, which provides as clear a picture as any yet published of how he won the Civil War, survived in power so long, and what, twenty years on from his death, was his significance.

Hugh Thomas *The Spanish Civil War* (Penguin/Touchstone). This exhaustive 1000-page study is regarded (both in Spain and abroad) as the definitive history of the Civil War, but is not as accessible for the general reader as Preston's account (above).

ART AND ARCHITECTURE

Marianne Barrucand and Achim Bednoz *Moorish Architecture* (Taschen, Germany). A beautifully illustrated guide to the major Moorish monuments.

Titus Burckhardt *Moorish Culture in Spain* (out of print). An outstanding book which opens up ways of looking at Spain's Islamic monuments, explaining their patterns and significance and the social environment in which, and for which, they were produced.

Jerrilyn D. Dodds *Al-Andalus* (Abrams, UK/US). An in-depth study of the arts and monuments of Moorish Andalucía, put together as a catalogue for a major exhibition at the Alhambra.

Godfrey Goodwin *Islamic Spain* (Chronicle Books, US). Architectural guide with descriptions of virtually every significant Islamic building in Spain, and a fair amount of background. Portable enough to take along.

José Gudiol *The Arts of Spain* (Thames and Hudson, UK). Good general introduction to Spanish art covering prehistory to Picasso.

David Talbot Rice *Islamic Art* (Thames & Hudson, UK). A classic introduction to the whole subject.

Meyer Schapiro *Romanesque Art* (Thames & Hudson/Braziller). An excellent, illustrated survey of Romanesque art and architecture – and its Visigothic and Mozarabic precursors.

Sacheverell Sitwell *Spanish Baroque* (Ayer, US). First published in 1931, this is interesting mainly for the absence of anything better on the subject.

George Kubler and Martin Soria *Art and Architecture in Spain and Portugal 1500-1800* (Pelican, UK). Provides an alternative to, if not a vast improvement on, the work above.

Anatzu Zabalbeascoa *The New Spanish Architecture* (Rizzoli, UK/US). A superb, highly illustrated study of the new Spanish architecture of the 1980s and 90s in Barcelona, Madrid, Sevilla, and elsewhere.

FICTION AND POETRY

SPANISH FICTION

Pedro de Alarcón *The Three-Cornered Hat and Other Stories* (out of print). Ironic nineteenth-century tales of the previous century's corruption, bureaucracy and absolutism by a writer born in Guadix. He also wrote *Alpujarra* (out of print), a not very well observed tour through the Sierra Nevada.

Miguel de Cervantes *Don Quixote* (Penguin/Signet). *Quixote* (or *Quijote*) is of course the classic of Spanish literature and remains an excellent and witty read especially in J. M. Cohen's fine translation.

Juan Ramón Jiminez *Platero and I* (out of print). Andalucía's Nobel prizewinning poet and writer from Moguer in Huelva paints a lyrically evocative picture of Andalucía and its people in conversations with his donkey, Platero.

Antonio Machado *Eighty Poems* and *Juan de Mairena* (out of print). The best-known works in English of this eminent *Sevillano* poet and writer. The latter novel draws on his experience as a schoolteacher in Baeza.

MODERN FICTION

Arturo Barea The Forging of a Rebel (out of print). Superb autobiographical trilogy, taking in the Spanish war in Morocco in the 1920s, and Barea's own part in the Civil War in Andalucía and elsewhere. The books were published under the individual titles The Forge, The Track and The Clash.

PLAYS AND POETRY

A J Arberry (trans.) Moorish Poetry (CUP, UK) Excellent collection of Hispano-Arab verse.

Cola Franzen (trans.) Poems of Arab Andalusia (City Lights, US) Sensitively rendered collection of verse by some of the best poets of Moorish al–Andalus.

Federico García Lorca Five Plays: Comedies and Tragicomedies (Penguin/New Directions); Selected Poems (Bloodaxe Books, UK); Poem of the Deep Song (City Lights, US) Andalucía's great pre-Civil War playwright and poet. The first two volumes have his major theatrical works and poems, whilst the latter is a moving poetic paean to cante jondo, flamenco's blues, inspired by his contact with gitano culture. Arturo Barea's Lorca: the Poet and His People is also of interest.

San Juan de la Cruz The Poetry of Saint John of the Cross (Penguin, UK). Excellent translation by South African Roy Campbell of the poems of this mystical confessor to Teresa of Ávila who died at Úbeda.

FOREIGN FICTION

Tariq Ali Shadows of the Pomegranate Tree (Chatto & Windus, UK). Pakistani/British author digs into his Muslim roots to come up with a story about the end of Nasrid Granada seen through the eyes of a well-to-do family.

Douglas Day Journey of the Wolf (Penguin, UK). Outstanding first novel by an American writer, given the seal of approval by Graham Greene ("gripping and poignant"). The subject is a Civil War fighter, "El Lobo", who returns as a fugitive to Poqueira, his village in the Alpujarras, forty years on.

Ernest Hemingway Fiesta/The Sun Also Rises (Cape/ Scribner) and For Whom the Bell Tolls (Cape/ Scribner). Hemingway remains a big part of the American myth of Spain – Fiesta contains some lyrically beautiful writing while

the latter – set in Civil War Andalucía – is a good deal more laboured. He also published an enthusiastic and not very good account of bull-fighting, Death in the Afternoon (Cape/ Scribner).

Amin Malouf Leo the African (Quarter, UK). A wonderful historical novel, recreating the life of Leo Africanus, the fifteenth-century Moorish geographer, in the last years of the kingdom of Granada, and on his subsequent exile in Morocco and world travels.

SPECIALIST GUIDEBOOKS

M.J. Gómez Lara & J. Jiménez Barrientos Guía de la Semana Santa en Sevilla (Taba Press, Spain). The best guide available to Semana Santa – and a book for which you don't need very much Spanish; all the processions and routes are detailed along with superb illustrations.

Charles Teetor Strolling through Seville (Iberica, UK/US) More anecdotal version of the above with rather wobbly references to the Civil War.

Christopher Turner The Penguin Guide to Seville (Penguin, UK/US). A set of guided walks around Andalucía's capital city.

HIKING AND CYCLING

Robin Collomb Sierra Nevada (West Col, UK). A detailed guide aimed primarily at serious hikers and climbers.

Chris Craggs Andalusian Rock Climbs (Cicerone Press, UK). Introductory guide to one of Andalucía's fastest-growing sports. Has descriptions of all the major climbs plus details of how to get there.

Marc S. Dubin Trekking in Spain (Lonely Planet, UK/US). A detailed and practical trekking guide (with maps) by a Rough Guide author moonlighting for the opposition. It has a section on Andalucía's Sierra Nevada.

J.L. Barrenetxea & K. Munoz La Alpujarra en Bici (Sua Edizioak, Spain). An excellent guide to getting your bike around the villages and landscape of this stunningly picturesque corner of Andalucía. It forms part of a superb range of regional guides for cyclists, functionally ring-bound, with detailed maps and route contours.

Guias Penthalon (Penthalon, Spain). A detailed and reliable series of walking guides to various regions of Andalucía.

WILDLIFE

Ernest García and Andrew Paterson *Where to Watch Birds in Southern Spain* (A&C Black, UK). A well planned guide to birdwatching sites throughout Andalucía with location maps and reports detailing species to be seen according to season.

Frederic Grunfeld and Teresa Farino *Wild Spain* (Sheldrake Press/Sierra Club). A knowledgable and practical guide to Spain's national parks, ecology and wildlife with a section on Andalucía. Highly recommended.

John Measures *The Wildlife Travelling Companion:Spain* (Crowood Press, UK). Clearly laid-out field guide to specific wildlife areas complete with an illustrated index of the most common flora and fauna.

Peterson, Mountfort and Hollom *Collins Field Guide to the Birds of Britain and Europe* (Collins Reference/Houghton Mifflin). Standard reference book – covers most birds in Spain though you may find yourself confused by the bird-song descriptions.

Heinzel, Fitter and Parslow *Collins Guide to the Birds of Britain and Europe* (Collins, UK). Alternative to the above. Also includes North Africa and the Middle East.

Oleg Polunin and Anthony Huxley *Flowers of the Mediterranean* (Chatto, UK). Useful if by no means exhaustive field guide.

FOOD AND WINE

Nicholas Butcher *The Spanish Kitchen* (Macmillan, UK). A practical unstuffy guide to creating Spanish food when you get back. Lots of informative detail on *tapas*, olive oil, *jamón serrano* and herbs.

Penelope Casas *The Foods and Wines of Spain* (Penguin/Knopf) and *Tapas – the little dishes of Spain* (Pavilion). An excellent overview of classic Spanish and Andalucian cuisine, plus the same author's guide to the *tapas* labyrinth.

Alan Davidson *The Tio Pepe Guide to the Seafood of Spain and Portugal* (Anness, UK). An indispensible pocket book that details and illustrates every fish and crustacean you're likely to meet in Andalucía.

Julian Jeffs *Sherry* (Faber, UK). The story of sherry – history, production, blending and brands. Rightly a classic and the best introduction to Andalucía's great wine.

Elisabeth Luard *The La Ina Book of Tapas* (Martin/Simon & Schuster). Once you're hooked on *tapas*, this is the bible for all classic recipes.

Maite Manjon *Gastronomy of Spain and Portugal* (Garamond) Useful alphabetical guide to food and drink on the peninsula.

Mark and Kim Millon *Wine Roads of Spain* (HarperCollins, UK/US). Everything you ever wanted to know about Spanish wine and sherry: when it's made, how it's made and where to find it, with lots of useful maps.

LANGUAGE

Once you get into it, Spanish is one of the easiest languages to learn – and you'll be helped everywhere by people who are eager to try and understand even the most faltering attempt. English is spoken, but only in the main tourist areas to any extent, and wherever you are you'll get a far better reception if you at least try communicating with Spaniards in their own tongue. Being understood, of course, is only half the problem – getting the gist of the reply, often rattled out at a furious pace, may prove far more difficult.

The rules of **pronunciation** are pretty straightforward and, once you get to know them, strictly observed. Unless there's an **accent**, words ending in d, l, r, and z are stressed on the last syllable, all others on the second last. All **vowels** are pure and short; combinations have predictable results.

A somewhere between the "A" sound of back and that of father

E as in get

I as in police

O as in hot

U as in rule

C in castellano (standard Spanish) is lisped before E and I, hard otherwise: cerca is pronounced "thairka". However, many parts of Andalucía pronounce this case as an "s" – "sairka" or even "Andalusia".

G works the same way, a guttural "H" sound (like the ch in loch) before E or I, a hard G elsewhere – gigante becomes "higante".

H is always silent

J the same sound as a guttural G: jamón is pronounced "hamon".

LL sounds like an English Y or LY: tortilla is pronounced torteeya/torteelya.

N is as in English unless it has a tilde (accent) over it, when it becomes NY: mañana sounds like "manyana".

QU is pronounced like an English K.

R is rolled, RR doubly so.

V sounds more like B, vino becoming "beano".

X has an S sound before consonants, normal X before vowels.

Z (in castellano) is the same as a soft C, so cerveza becomes "thairvaitha", but again much of Andalucía prefers the "s" sound - "sairvaisa".

A list of a few essential words and phrases follows which should be enough to get you started, though if you're travelling for any length of time a dictionary or phrasebook is obviously a worthwhile investment. If you're using a dictionary, bear in mind that in Spanish CH, LL, and Ñ count as separate letters and are listed after the Cs, Ls, and Ns respectively.

SPANISH WORDS AND PHRASES

BASICS

Yes, No, OK	*Sí, No, Vale*	With, Without	*Con, Sin*
Please, Thank you	*Por favor, Gracias*	Good, Bad	*Buen(o)/a, Mal(o)/a*
Where, When	*Dónde, Cuando*	Big, Small	*Gran(de), Pequeño/a*
What, How much	*Qué, Cuánto*	Cheap, Expensive	*Barato, Caro*
Here, There	*Aqui, Alli*	Hot, Cold	*Caliente, Frío*
This, That	*Esto, Eso*	More, Less	*Más, Menos*
Now, Later	*Ahora, Más tarde*	Today, Tomorrow	*Hoy, Mañana*
Open, Closed	*Abierto/a, Cerrado/a*	Yesterday	*Ayer*

GREETINGS AND RESPONSES

Hello, Goodbye	*Hola, Adiós*	Not at all/You're welcome	*De nada*
Good morning	*Buenos días*		
Good afternoon/night	*Buenas tardes/noches*	Do you speak English?	*¿Habla (usted) inglés?*
See you later	*Hasta luego*	I don't speak Spanish	*(No) Hablo español*
Sorry	*Lo siento/disculpéme*	My name is . . .	*Me llamo . . .*
Excuse me	*Con permiso/perdón*	What's your name?	*¿Como se llama usted?*
How are you?	*¿Como está (usted)?*	I am English/	*Soy inglés(a)/*
I (don't) understand	*(No) Entiendo*	Australian/Canadian/ American/ Irish/	*australiano(a)/canadiense(a)/ americano(a)/irlandes(a)*

NEEDS – HOTELS AND TRANSPORT

I want	*Quiero*	How do I get to . . . ?	*¿Por donde se va a . . . ?*
I'd like	*Quisiera*	Left, right, straight on	*Izquierda, derecha, todo recto*
Do you know . . . ?	*¿Sabe . . . ?*		
I don't know	*No sé*	Where is . . . ?	*¿Dónde está . . . ?*
There is (is there)?	*(¿)Hay(?)*	. . . the bus station	*. . . la estación de autobuses*
Give me . . .	*Deme . . .*		
(one like that)	*(uno así)*	. . . the railway station	*. . . la estación de ferrocarril*
Do you have . . . ?	*¿Tiene . . . ?*		
. . . the time	*. . . la hora*	. . . the nearest bank	*. . . el banco mas cercano*
. . . a room	*. . . una habitación*		
. . . with two beds/ double bed	*. . . con dos camas/ cama matrimonial*	. . . the post office	*. . . el correos/la oficina de correos*
. . . with shower/bath	*. . . con ducha/baño*	. . . the toilet	*. . . el baño/aseo/ servicio*
It's for one person (two people)	*Es para una persona (dos personas)*	Where does the bus to . . . leave from?	*¿De dónde sale el autobús para . . . ?*
. . . for one night (one week)	*. . . para una noche (una semana)*	Is this the train for Sevilla?	*¿Es este el tren para Sevilla?*
It's fine, how much is it?	*¿Está bien, cuánto es?*	I'd like a (return) ticket to . . .	*Quisiera un billete (de ida y vuelta) para . . .*
It's too expensive	*Es demasiado caro*		
Don't you have anything cheaper?	*¿No tiene algo más barato?*	What time does it leave (arrive in . . .)?	*¿A qué hora sale (llega a . . .)?*
Can one . . . ?	*¿Se puede . . . ?*	What is there to eat?	*¿Qué hay para comer?*
. . . camp (near) here?	*¿ . . . acampar aqui (cerca)?*	What's that?	*¿Qué es eso?*
Is there a hostel nearby?	*¿Hay un hostal aquí cerca?*	What's this called in Spanish?	*¿Como se llama este en español?*

NUMBERS AND DAYS

1	*un/uno/una*	16	*diez y seis*	1000	*mil*
2	*dos*	20	*veinte*	2000	*dos mil*
3	*tres*	21	*veintiuno*	first	*primero/a*
4	*cuatro*	30	*treinta*	second	*segundo/a*
5	*cinco*	40	*cuarenta*	third	*tercero/a*
6	*seis*	50	*cincuenta*	fifth	*quinto/a*
7	*siete*	60	*sesenta*	tenth	*décimo/a*
8	*ocho*	70	*setenta*		
9	*nueve*	80	*ochenta*	Monday	*lunes*
10	*diez*	90	*noventa*	Tuesday	*martes*
11	*once*	100	*cien(to)*	Wednesday	*miércoles*
12	*doce*	101	*ciento uno*	Thursday	*jueves*
13	*trece*	200	*doscientos*	Friday	*viernes*
14	*catorce*	201	*doscientos uno*	Saturday	*sábado*
15	*quince*	500	*quinientos*	Sunday	*domingo*

SPANISH TERMS: A GLOSSARY

ALAMEDA park or grassy promenade.

ALCAZABA Moorish castle.

ALCÁZAR Moorish fortified palace.

ALMOHADS Muslims originally of Berber stock, who toppled the Almoravids and ruled Spain in the late twelfth and early thirteenth centuries.

ALMORAVIDS fanatical Berber dynasty from the Sahara who ruled much of Spain in the eleventh and twelfth centuries.

ARTESONADO inlaid wooden ceiling of Moorish origin or inspiration.

ATALAYA watch tower.

AYUNTAMIENTO town hall (also CASA CONSISTORIAL).

AZULEJO glazed ceramic tilework.

BARRIO suburb or quarter.

BODEGA cellar, wine bar, or warehouse.

BRACERO landless agricultural worker.

CALLE street.

CAMARÍN shrine (inside a church) of a venerated image.

CANTE JONDO deeply-felt *flamenco* song.

CAPILLA MAYOR chapel containing the high altar.

CAPILLA REAL royal chapel.

CARMEN Granadan villa with garden.

CARRETERA main road

CARTUJA Carthusian monastery.

CASINO social and gaming club.

CASTILLO castle.

CHIRINGUITO beachfront restaurant.

CHURRIGUERESQUE extreme form of Baroque art named after José Churriguera (1650–1723) and his extended family, its main exponents.

CIUDAD town or city.

CIUDADELA citadel.

COLEGIATA collegiate (large parish) church.

COMUNIDAD AUTÓNOMIA autonomous region.

CONVENTO monastery or convent.

CONVERSO Jew who converted to Christianity.

CORO central part of church built for the choir.

CORO ALTO raised choir, often above west door of a church.

CORREOS post office.

CORRIDA DE TOROS bullfight.

CORTIJO rural farmhouse in Andalucía.

COTO hunting reserve.

CUESTA slope/hill.

CUEVA cave.

CUSTODIA large receptacle for Eucharist wafers.

DESAMORTIZACIÓN (disentailment) nineteenth-century expropriation of church buildings and lands.

DUENDE to have soul (in *flamenco*).

EMBALSE artificial lake, reservoir or dam.

ERMITA hermitage.

FERIA annual fair.

GITANO gypsy.

IGLESIA church.

ISABELLINE ornamental form of late Gothic developed during the reign of Isabel and Fernando.

JORNALERO landless agricultural day labourer.

JUDERÍA Jewish quarter.

JUERGA (gypsy) shindig.

JUNTA DE ANDALUCÍA government of the Autonomous Region of Andalucía.

LATIFUNDIO large estate.

LONJA stock exchange building.

MARISMAS marshes.

MEDINA Moorish town.

MERCADO market.

MIHRAB prayer niche of Moorish mosque.

MIRADOR viewing point (literally balcony).

MONASTERIO monastery or convent.

MORISCO Muslim Spaniard subject to medieval Christian rule – and nominally baptized.

MOZARABE Christian subject to medieval Moorish rule; normally allowed freedom of worship.

MUDÉJAR Muslim Spaniard subject to

medieval Christian rule, but retaining Islamic worship; most commonly a term applied to architecture which includes buildings built by Moorish craftsmen for the Christian rulers and later designs influenced by the Moors. The 1890s–1930s saw a Mudéjar revival, blended with Art Nouveau and Art Deco forms.

PALACIO aristocratic mansion.

PANTANO reservoir held by a dam.

PARADOR luxury state-run hotel, often converted from minor monument.

PASEO promenade; also the evening stroll thereon.

PASO float bearing tableau carried in *Semana Santa* processions.

PATIO inner courtyard.

PISCINA swimming pool

PLATERESQUE elaborately decorative Renaissance style, the sixteenth-century successor of Isabelline forms. Named for its resemblance to silversmiths' work (platería).

PLAZA square.

PLAZA DE TOROS bullring.

PLAZA MAYOR a town or city's main square regardless of its name.

POSADA old name for an inn.

PUEBLO village or town.

PUERTA gateway, also mountain pass.

PUERTO port.

RAMBLA dry river bed.

RECONQUISTA the Christian reconquest of Moorish Spain between 718 and 1492.

REJA iron screen or grille, often fronting a window or guarding a chapel.

RETABLO carved or painted altarpiece.

RÍO river.

ROMERÍA religious procession to a rural shrine.

SACRISTÍA, **SAGRARIO** sacristy or sanctuary of a church.

SAETA passionate *flamenco* song in praise of the Virgin and Christ.

SEBKA decorative brickwork devloped by the Almohads (eg, Giralda).

SEO, **SEU**, **LA SE** ancient/regional names for cathedrals.

SEVILLANA rythmic *flamenco* dance.

SIERRA mountain range.

SILLERÍA choir stall.

SOLAR aristocratic town mansion.

SOLERA blending system for sherry and brandy.

TABLAO *flamenco* show.

TAIFA small Moorish kingdom, many of which emerged after the disintegration of the Córdoba caliphate.

TRASCORO end-wall of the choir.

VEGA cultivated fertile plain.

VENTA roadside inn.

POLITICAL PARTIES AND ACRONYMS

CNT anarchist trade union.

ETA Basque terrorist organization. Its political wing is *Herri Batasuna*.

FALANGE Franco's old fascist party; now officially defunct.

FUERZA NUEVA descendants of the above, also on the way out.

IR *Izquierda Republicana*, left-wing republican party.

IU *Izquierda Unida*, broad-left alliance of communists and others.

MC *Movimiento Comunista* (Communist Movement), small radical offshoot of the PCE.

MOC *Movimiento de Objectores de Conciencia*, peace group, concerned with NATO and conscription.

OTAN NATO.

PA *Partido Andalucista*, the Andalucian Nationalist Party

PASOC *Partido de Acción Socialista*, "traditional" socialist group to the left of the PSOE.

PCE *Partido Comunista de España* (Spanish Communist Party).

PP *Partido Popular*, the new right-wing alliance formed by Alianza Popular and the Christian Democrats led by José María Aznar.

PSOE *Partido Socialista Obrero Español*, the Spanish Socialist Workers' Party – currently in power under Prime Minister Felipe González.

UGT *Unión General de Trabajadores*, the Spanish TUC.